THE MAKING OF THE WEST

PEOPLES AND CULTURES

THE MAKING OF THE WEST

PEOPLES AND CULTURES

Volume B: 1320–1830

LYNN HUNT
University of California at Los Angeles

THOMAS R. MARTIN
College of the Holy Cross

BARBARA H. ROSENWEIN
Loyola University Chicago

R. PO-CHIA HSIA
New York University

BONNIE G. SMITH
Rutgers University

BEDFORD/ST. MARTIN'S   Boston ◆ New York

FOR BEDFORD/ST. MARTIN'S

Executive Editor: Katherine E. Kurzman
Senior Development Editor: Elizabeth M. Welch
Project Manager: Tina Samaha
Production Supervisor: Catherine Hetmansky
Map Development Editors: Heidi Hood, Laura Arcari
Editorial Assistants: Sarah Barrash, Molly E. Kalkstein
Marketing Manager: Jenna Bookin Barry
Assistant Production Editor: Coleen O'Hanley
Copyeditor: Barbara G. Flanagan
Text Designer: Wanda Kossak
Page Layout: DeNee Reiton Skipper
Cover Designer: Donna Lee Dennison
Photo Researchers: Carole Frohlich and Martha Shethar, The Visual Connection
Proofreaders: Mary Lou Wilshaw-Watts, Jan Cocker
Indexer: Maro Riofrancos
Composition: York Graphic Services, Inc.
Cartography: Mapping Specialists Limited
Printing and Binding: R.R. Donnelley & Sons Company

President: Charles H. Christensen
Editorial Director: Joan E. Feinberg
Director of Marketing: Karen Melton
Director of Editing, Design, and Production: Marcia Cohen
Managing Editor: Elizabeth Schaaf

Library of Congress Control Number: 00–133169
Copyright © 2001 by Bedford/St. Martin's

Manufactured in the United States of America.

5   4   3   2   1
f   e   d   c   b

For information, contact: Bedford/St. Martin's, 75 Arlington Street, Boston, MA 02116
617-399-4000
www.bedfordstmartins.com

ISBN: 0–312–18370–4 (hardcover complete edition)
ISBN: 0–312–18369–0 (paperback Volume I)
ISBN: 0–312–18368–2 (paperback Volume II)
ISBN: 0–312–18365–8 (paperback Volume A)
ISBN: 0–312–18364–X (paperback Volume B)
ISBN: 0–312–18363–1 (paperback Volume C)

Cover Art: Top left; title page spread: *La Primavera* (Details of Mercury and the Three Graces). Sandro Botticelli (1444–1510). Uffizi, Florence. Courtesy of Art Resource. Bottom left: *Lieden Baker Arent Oostwaert and His Wife* (1658). Jan Havicksz Steen (1625–1679). © Rijksmuseum, Amsterdam. Right: *Le Premier Consul franchissant les Alpes au col du Grand-Saint-Bernard.* Jacques Louis David (1748–1825). Châteaux de Malmaison et Bois-Préau. © Photo RMN–Daniel Arnaudet.

A Conversation with Lynn Hunt

A RENOWNED SCHOLAR OF THE FRENCH REVOLUTION who has trained a generation of graduate students at the University of California at Berkeley, the University of Pennsylvania, and now as Eugen Weber Professor of Modern European History at the University of California at Los Angeles, Lynn Hunt has long been committed to the centrality of the Western civilization survey course to undergraduate education. In this conversation she explains why she and her coauthors Thomas R. Martin, Barbara H. Rosenwein, R. Po-chia Hsia, and Bonnie G. Smith wrote *The Making of the West: Peoples and Cultures*.

Q You taught the Western civilization survey for many years before deciding to write a textbook for the course. What inspired you to undertake such a time-consuming project at this point in your career?

A When I started teaching Western civ in the 1970s, I found the prospect daunting. How can any one person make sense of such a long time span—in my case, the West from the sixteenth century to the present? In addition, historical research was undergoing major changes: social history produced much new information about the lower classes, women, and minorities; then cultural historians began to draw attention to the importance of religious festivals, political rituals, and a variety of cultural expressions. How could these new subjects, new findings, and new methods be incorporated into the narrative of Western historical development?

Every generation needs new textbooks that synthesize the most recent findings. But after 1989 the need for a new vision became especially acute. Not only did new information need to be integrated in a course that was already jam-packed with important material about political personalities, events, and movements, but the very notion of the West was beginning to change. Just as immigration was creating a United States that was much more multiethnic and multicultural than ever before, so too historians had become much more interested in the interactions between the West and the rest of the world. Textbooks conceived and written during the era of the cold war had been oriented toward explaining the conflict between the West and their eastern-bloc opponents, eastern Europe and the Soviet Union. In the post-1989 world,

"Every generation needs new textbooks that synthesize the most recent findings."

political conflicts no longer fit into that neat mold: conflict takes place on a global stage at a time when many important social, economic, and cultural trends have became global. The new histories had to reflect these momentous changes. Since my coauthors and I have all been personally involved in the new approaches to historical research and in the effort to understand the West in a world setting, we felt we would make an effective team for integrating these perspectives and showing how they offer a more coherent and convincing view of the important issues in Western civ.

Q **Textbooks for the course typically contain "Western Civilization" in the title. Why is your book named** *The Making of the West: Peoples and Cultures?* **What are its themes and objectives, and how are they realized?**

A Our title makes two important points about our approach: (1) that the history of the West is the story of a process that is still ongoing, not a finished result with only one fixed meaning; and (2) that "the West" includes many different peoples and cultures, that is, that there is no one Western people or culture that has existed from the beginning until now. Although our book emphasizes the best of recent social and cultural history—hence our subtitle, *Peoples and Cultures*—it integrates that new material into a solid chronological framework that does full justice to political, military, and diplomatic history. We try to suggest the richness of themes available for discussion and challenge students to think critically without limiting instructors to just one or two points of view. My coauthors and I have learned from our own teaching that students need a compelling chronological narrative, one with enough familiar benchmarks to make the material readily assimilable, but also one with enough flexibility to incorporate the new varieties of historical research. We aimed for a strong central story line that could integrate the findings of social and cultural history into the more familiar accounts of wars, diplomacy, and high politics, yet we also endeavored to include the experiences of many individual women and men. Nothing makes sense in history if it cannot be related back to the actual experiences of real people. For this reason we begin each chapter with an anecdote about an individual and his or her particular experience and then incorporate that information into the discussion of

> *"Although our book emphasizes the best of recent social and cultural history—hence our subtitle,* Peoples and Cultures—*it integrates that new material into a solid chronological framework that does full justice to political, military, and diplomatic history."*

> *"Nothing makes sense in history if it cannot be related back to the actual experiences of real people."*

general themes and trends. It is, after all, the interaction between public events and private experiences that makes history of enduring interest to students. Among the ordinary people we chose for special attention, we focused in particular on those who had contacts with the world outside the West, from missionaries and soldiers to naturalists and painters.

Q Four other well-known historians join you on the author team: Thomas Martin, Barbara Rosenwein, R. Po-chia Hsia, and Bonnie Smith. How did the author team come into being? Knowing the potential dangers of a multiauthored textbook, how did you all work together to ensure a single, cohesive work?

A No one scholar can hope to offer a truly authoritative and balanced synthesis of the rich materials available on the whole course of Western history. It is hard enough for one person to teach a semester of Western civ! This

> *"This kind of undertaking requires collaboration among colleagues of great expertise who can bring to their writing the experience that comes from years of teaching different kinds of students."*

kind of undertaking requires collaboration among colleagues of great expertise who can bring to their writing the experience that comes from years of teaching different kinds of students. Our team is made up of just these kinds of scholars and teachers. Each author has an international reputation for research that has helped to shape the agenda for history in the new century. Each one has taught a wide range of students with different levels of skills. We have worked intensively together over the years— meeting often, reading one another's chapters—to develop a clearly focused, integrated narrative that combines the best of new social and cultural approaches with the traditional political narrative and seeks to put Western history in a worldwide context. We have benefited as well from an exceptionally intensive review process that has provided us with helpful input from scores of scholars and teachers with expertise different from our own. They and our editors at Bedford/St. Martin's have helped ensure that the text offers a coherent, continuous narrative. Reading the book, even I can't detect a change in authorship from chapter to chapter!

Q   The authors—you in particular—are known for cutting-edge scholarship. In what ways does *The Making of the West* reflect your research and interpretations?

A   From long experience in teaching, we know that students can grasp the most recent advances in scholarship only if those advances can be put in a clear framework that builds on what the students already find familiar. And we also know, like all of our fellow Western civ instructors, that new materials have to be carefully calibrated so as not to overwhelm students who might not be familiar at all with Western history or the methods of historical criticism. For this reason, we have confined much of the explicit discussion of methods and interpretations to the features, which instructors can use or not as they see fit. The narrative itself reflects the authors' most recent research, but it never neglects to explain the relevance of social, cultural, gender, or minority history to the central political problems of an age. Our team has a distinct advantage in this regard because each of us works on topics that have clear relevance for the most "traditional" kinds of political or economic history. In my work on the cultural aspects of the French Revolution, for example, I have always tried to use those approaches to illuminate the most traditional questions: How is a new form of power created? What makes people change their minds and endorse new ideas? Tom Martin, our specialist on ancient history, has considered equally fundamental issues in his study of ancient Greek coinage. How did coins originate in Western civilization? What is the function of money in a society? How are money and power related? As a consequence of these kinds of linkages, we as a team are particularly well placed to show how social and cultural developments can illuminate the most enduring questions of history.

"As a consequence of these kinds of linkages, we as a team are particularly well placed to show how social and cultural developments can illuminate the most enduring questions of history."

Q   *The Making of the West: Peoples and Cultures* represents a major revision of *The Challenge of the West* (Heath, 1995). From the narrative itself to features, pedagogy, maps, and artwork, the book has changed dramatically. Can you describe these revisions and explain why the authors made them? Let's start with the narrative.

A   There is no better way to find out what works and what doesn't than by trying out an approach. Since *Challenge* was published in 1995, we have had the opportunity to teach the book and to get feedback from scores of colleagues around the country who have used it. We now have a much surer sense of how to make our case. *The Making of the West* offers much clearer signposts of the development of the argument along the way. For example, we added a third level of chapter heading to signal supporting as well as main ideas and developments, and we worked hard to provide clear and compelling chapter and section introductions

"Much of our excitement in this project arose from its very nature: textbook writing, unlike the scholarly books to which we were accustomed, offers historians the rare chance to revise the original work, to keep it fresh, and to make it better."

and summaries. Although we maintained our strong chronological organization, we loosened it here and there—the scientific revolution provides one example, the World Wars of the twentieth century another—to allow the completion of a story in progress, to streamline discussion, and to underline the main themes in our narrative. While offering a clearer sense of our overall direction, we also incorporated even more material on the West's interactions with the rest of the world. And of course we brought in the new research published since 1995. Much of our excitement in this project arose from its very nature: textbook writing, unlike the scholarly books to which we were accustomed, offers historians the rare chance to revise the original work, to keep it fresh, and to make it better.

Q   **New to the book are extensive pedagogical support, recurring special features, and large map and art programs. Knowing the time pressures that teachers and students face, why did you decide to devote many pages to these elements?**

A   More and more is required of students these days (and not just in Western civ), and we know from our own teaching that students need all the help they can get in assimilating information, acquiring skills, learning about historical debate, and sampling the very newest approaches. It is a truism now, but an important one, that education must foster the ability to keep on learning how to adapt to new requirements in the future. Frankly, in *Challenge* we stuck too much to the traditional approach, expecting students to comprehend by simply reading straight through. In *The Making of the West*, we try to teach both traditional skills and new perspectives with the aim of preparing students to grasp the past and understand the history that is yet to come. For example, mastery of chronology is perhaps the most fundamental task for history students: to help them accomplish it, each chapter in our text opens with a comparative timeline that allows students to see at a glance how politics and diplomacy, economic and social trends, and intellectual, religious and cultural developments interact. A list of important dates near the close of each chapter provides a view of key events, while topic-specific timelines outline particular themes and processes. Even the running heads at the top of pages support our effort to help students keep track of chronology and stay focused on their reading by linking subject matter to time frame.

> *"We try to teach both traditional skills and new perspectives with the aim of preparing students to grasp the past and understand the history that is yet to come."*

But like a clear narrative synthesis, strong pedagogical support is not enough on its own to encourage active learning. Setting out to revise *Challenge*, we paid special care to the boxed feature program, eager to hold to our goal of maximum flexibility for teachers while offering student readers the best introduction to historical thinking available in a survey text. We are very proud of the result: an integrated set of features that genuinely extend the narrative by revealing the process of interpretation, providing a solid introduction to the principles of historical argument, and capturing the excitement of historical investigation. The **Contrasting Views** feature, for example, provides three or four often conflicting eyewitness accounts of a central event, person, or development, such as the English civil war, Martin Luther, late-nineteenth-century migration. But it does not just present these views inertly. Introductory paragraphs provide needed context for the primary sources, and questions for debate help students focus on the big questions and alert them at the same time to the ways that history is susceptible to ongoing reinterpretation.

The **New Sources, New Perspectives** feature shows students how historians continue to develop new kinds of evidence about the past—from tree rings to Holocaust museums. This feature will fascinate students with unexpected information and also prompt them to consider how new evidence leads to new interpretations. Curious students will find suggested references for further study of these issues. Questions for Debate that appear at the end of the feature might spark a class discussion about the relationship between evidence and interpretation in our understanding of history.

Too often, textbooks seem to assume that students already know the meaning of some of the most important and contested terms in the history of the West: feudalism, the Renaissance, progress, and revolution, not to mention civilization itself. We do not make this assumption. Instead we offer a **Terms of History** feature in which we explain the meaning of these terms and show how those meanings have developed—and changed—over time. Thus, for example, the discussion of *progress* shows how the term took root in the eighteenth century and has been contested in the twentieth. For the student who is struggling to make sense of Western history, this feature explains the meaning of key terms. For a more sophisticated student, this feature can shed yet more light on the question of historical interpretation.

Since we want to emphasize the interactions between the West and the broader world, a short illustrated feature, **Did You Know?**, offers unexpected and sometimes even startling examples of cultural interchange ranging from the invention of "smoking" (derived from the New World) to the creation of polo (adapted from South Asia). History can be fun as well as provocative, after all! From our many years of teaching, we know that students learn best when they are engaged by the material.

Now, more than ever, quantitative or statistical literacy is vitally important. The **Taking Measure** feature, which appears in every chapter, highlights a chart, table, graph, or map of historical statistics that illuminates an important political, social, or cultural development. Learning how to read such information is crucial preparation for students, no matter what their eventual field of study.

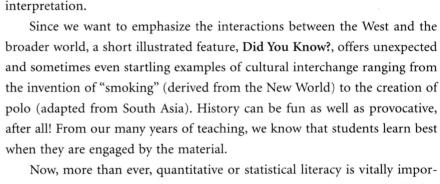

"We learned from our experience with Challenge that the look of the textbook plays a vital role in capturing students' interest."

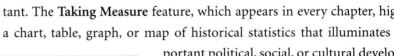

Q   **Your rationale for extensive pedagogy and features is clear; what about the space devoted to art and maps?**

A   We learned from our experience with *Challenge* that the look of the textbook plays a vital role in capturing students' interest, and we were pleased to work with a publisher who similarly understood the importance of a striking, full-color design and rich art and map programs. Students have become much more attuned to visual sources of information, yet they do not always receive systematic instruction in how to "read" such visual sources. Our captions aim to help them learn how to make the most of these visually attractive and informative materials. Over 480 illustrations not only reinforce the text but show the varieties of primary sources from which historians build their narratives and interpretations. We are proud as well of our map program: fundamental to any good history book, maps take on special importance in a text intended to stress interactions between the West and the wider world, and we worked intensively with our publisher to provide the most comprehensive map program available in a survey text. Thus we offer in each chapter 4–5 full-size maps, 2–4 "spot maps"—that is, small maps on single but crucial issues that are exactly located in related discussion—and, another first for our map program, "summary maps" at the end of each chapter, which individually provide a snapshot of the West at the close of a transformative period and collectively help students visualize the West's changing contours over time.

Q You and your coauthors have written many well-received and influential scholarly works. What response to *The Making of the West: Peoples and Cultures* would please you most?

A We aim to communicate the vitality and excitement as well as the fundamental importance of history. The highest compliment we could receive would be to hear that reading this textbook has encouraged students to take more history courses, major in history, perhaps even want to become historians themselves. We also hope that our text helps instructors overcome the obstacles in teaching this course and perhaps even revives their own interest in the materials covered here. History is never an entirely settled matter; it is always in process. If we have succeeded in conveying some of the vibrancy of the past and the thrill of historical investigation, we will be encouraged to start rethinking and revising—as historians always must—once again.

"History is never an entirely settled matter; it is always in process."

❖ Supplements

The authors of *The Making of the West: Peoples and Cultures* oversaw development of the well-integrated ancillary program that supports their text. A comprehensive collection of print and electronic resources for students and instructors provides a host of practical learning and teaching aids.

For Students

Study Guide to Accompany The Making of the West: Peoples and Cultures—Volumes I (to 1740) and II (since 1560)—by Victoria Thompson, Arizona State University. This carefully developed study guide offers overview and review materials to help students master content and learn to analyze it. For each chapter in the textbook, the study guide offers a summary; an expanded outline with matching exercises; a glossary of important terms with related questions; multiple-choice and short-answer questions; and map, illustration, and documents exercises that help students synthesize the material they have learned as well as appreciate the skills historians use to understand the past. Answers for all questions and exercises, with references to relevant pages in the textbook, are provided.

The ***Online Study Guide for* The Making of the West: Peoples and Cultures** is like none other: thoroughly integrated with the text and based on the print study guide, the online study guide takes advantage of the Internet to offer structured and easily accessed help for each chapter and innovative multimedia exercises designed to reinforce themes and content. For each chapter, an initial multiple-choice test assesses student comprehension of the material and a Recommended Study Plan suggests specific exercises that cover the subject areas they still need to master. Three multiple-choice tests per chapter help students improve their command of the material. Additional exercises encourage students to think about chapter themes as well as to develop skills of analysis.

Using the highly acclaimed course-tools software developed by QuestionMark, the online study guide for *The Making of the West* allows students to keep track of their performance chapter by chapter.

Sources of The Making of the West: Peoples and Cultures—Volumes I (to 1740) and II (since 1560)—by Katharine Lualdi, Colby College. For each chapter in *The Making of the West*, this companion sourcebook features four important political, social, or cultural documents that either reinforce or extend text discussion. Short chapter summaries, headnotes, and discussion questions highlight chapter themes and encourage students to think critically about these primary sources.

The Bedford Series in History and Culture—Advisory Editors Natalie Z. Davis, Princeton University; Ernest R. May, Harvard University; David W. Blight, Amherst College. Any of the volumes from this highly acclaimed series of brief, inexpensive, document-based supplements can be packaged with *The Making of the West* at a reduced price. The fourteen European history titles include *Spartacus and the Slave Wars, Utopia, Candide, The French Revolution and Human Rights,* and *The Communist Manifesto.*

For Instructors

Instructor's Resource Manual for The Making of the West: Peoples and Cultures—Volumes I (to 1740) and II (since 1560)—by Michael Richards, Sweet Briar College. This comprehensive collection of tools offers both the first-time and the experienced instructor extensive teaching information for each chapter in the textbook: outlines of chapter themes, chapter summaries, lecture and discussion topics, ideas for in-class work with maps and illustrations, writing and classroom presentation assignments, and research topic suggestions. The manual also includes seven essays for instructors with titles such as "What Is Western Civilization?," "Teaching Western Civilization with Computers and Web Sites," and "Literature and the Western Civilization Classroom," as well as over a dozen reprints of frequently assigned primary sources for easy access and distribution.

Test Items to Accompany The Making of the West: Peoples and Cultures—Volumes I (to 1740) and II (since 1560)—by Tamara Hunt, Loyola Marymount University. In addition to twenty fill-in-the-blank,

fifteen multiple-choice, ten short-answer, and four essay questions, this test bank includes for each chapter in the text a relationship-causation exercise, which asks students to place five events in chronological order and to explain a common theme that runs through them, and four map and documents exercises that test students' comprehension of chapter material and their ability to use sources. Answers for identification, multiple-choice, and short-answer questions, with references to relevant pages in the textbook, are provided. So that instructors may customize their tests to suit their classes, the answer key labels multiple-choice questions by difficulty.

The test bank is available in book format, with perforated pages for easy removal, or in Macintosh and Windows formats on disk. Easy-to-use software allows instructors to create and administer tests on paper or over a network. Instructors can generate exams and quizzes from the print test bank or write their own. A grade management function helps keep track of student progress.

Map Transparencies. A set of approximately 145 full-color acetate transparencies, free to adopters, includes all the full-size maps in the text.

CD-ROM with Presentation Manager Pro. For instructors who wish to use electronic media in the classroom, this new CD includes images, maps, and graphs from *The Making of the West: Peoples and Cultures* in an easy-to-use format that allows instructors to customize their presentations. The CD-ROM may be used with Presentation Manager Pro or with PowerPoint for instructors who wish to add their own slides to a presentation.

Using the Bedford Series in the Western Civilization Survey by Maura O'Connor. Recognizing that many instructors use a survey text in conjunction with supplements, Bedford/St. Martin's has made the fourteen Bedford Series volumes available at a discount to adopters of *The Making of the West: Peoples and Cultures.* This short guide gives practical suggestions for using volumes from the Bedford Series in History and Culture with *The Making of the West.* The guide not only supplies links between the text and the supplements but also provides ideas for starting discussions focused on a single primary-source volume.

The *Web Site for* **The Making of the West: Peoples and Cultures.** At http://www.bedfordstmartins .com/makingwest, instructors will find our useful Syllabus Manager as well as annotated pedagogical links with teaching suggestions tied to *The Making of the West.* A print guide is available for instructors looking for guidance in setting up their own Web sites.

❖ Acknowledgments

From the first draft to the last, the authors have benefited from repeated critical readings by many talented scholars and teachers. Our thanks to the following instructors, whose comments often challenged us to rethink or justify our interpretations and always provided a check on accuracy down to the smallest detail.

Dorothy Abrahamse, *California State University at Long Beach*

F. E. Beeman, *Middle Tennessee State University*

Martin Berger, *Youngstown State University*

Raymond Birn, *University of Oregon*

Charmarie J. Blaisdell, *Northeastern University*

Keith Bradley, *University of Victoria*

Paul Breines, *Boston College*

Caroline Castiglione, *University of Texas at Austin*

Carolyn A. Conley, *University of Alabama*

William Connell, *Seton Hall University*

Jo Ann H. Moran Cruz, *Georgetown University*

John P. Daly, *Louisiana Tech University*

Suzanne Desan, *University of Wisconsin at Madison*

Michael F. Doyle, *Ocean County College*

Jean C. England, *Northeastern Louisiana University*

Steven Epstein, *University of Colorado at Boulder*

Steven Fanning, *University of Illinois at Chicago*

Laura Frader, *Northeastern University*

Alison Futrell, *University of Arizona*

Gretchen Galbraith, *Grand Valley State University*

Timothy E. Gregory, *Ohio State University*

Katherine Haldane Grenier, *The Citadel*

Martha Hanna, *University of Colorado at Boulder*

Julie Hardwick, *Texas Christian University*

Kenneth W. Harl, *Tulane University*

Charles Hedrick, *University of California at Santa Cruz*

Robert L. Hohlfelder, *University of Colorado at Boulder*

Maryanne Horowitz, *Occidental College*

Gary Kates, *Trinity University*

Ellis L. Knox, *Boise State University*

Lawrence Langer, *University of Connecticut*

Keith P. Luria, *North Carolina State University*

Judith P. Meyer, *University of Connecticut*

Maureen C. Miller, *Hamilton College*

Stuart S. Miller, *University of Connecticut*

Dr. Frederick Murphy, *Western Kentucky University*

James Murray, *University of Cincinnati*

Phillip C. Naylor, *Marquette University*

Carolyn Nelson, *University of Kansas*

Richard C. Nelson, *Augsburg College*

John Nichols, *University of Oregon*

Byron J. Nordstrom, *Gustavus Adolphus College*

Maura O'Connor, *University of Cincinnati*

Lawrence Okamura, *University of Missouri at Columbia*

Dolores Davison Peterson, *Foothill College*

Carl F. Petry, *Northwestern University*

Carole A. Putko, *San Diego State University*

Michael Richards, *Sweet Briar College*

Barbara Saylor Rodgers, *University of Vermont*

Sally Scully, *San Francisco State University*

Jane Slaughter, *University of New Mexico*

Donald Sullivan, *University of New Mexico*

Victoria Thompson, *Arizona State University*

Sue Sheridan Walker, *Northeastern Illinois University*

John E. Weakland, *Ball State University*

Theodore R. Weeks, *Southern Illinois University at Carbondale*

Merry Wiesner-Hanks, *University of Wisconsin at Milwaukee*

Each of us has also benefited from the close readings and valuable criticisms of our coauthors, though we all assume responsibility for our own chapters. Thomas Martin has written Chapters 1–7; Barbara Rosenwein, Chapters 8–12; Ronnie Hsia, Chapters 13–15; Lynn Hunt, Chapters 16–22; and Bonnie Smith, Chapters 23–30.

Many colleagues, friends, and family members have helped us develop this work as well. Lynn Hunt wishes to thank in particular Anne Engel, Margaret Jacob, Rick Weiche, and Melissa Verlet for their help with various aspects of this project. Tom Martin and Ronnie Hsia express warm thanks to their families for their forbearance and support. Barbara Rosenwein extends special gratitude to Steven Epstein, Naomi Honeth, Maureen Miller, and Frank, Jess, and Tom Rosenwein. Bonnie Smith thanks Julie Taddeo, Cathy Mason, Scott Glotzer,

Tamara Matheson, and Todd Shepard for research assistance.

We also wish to acknowledge and thank the publishing team who did so much to bring this book into being. Katherine E. Kurzman, executive editor for history, introduced us to Bedford/St. Martin's and guided our efforts throughout the project. Charles H. Christensen, president, and Joan E. Feinberg, editorial director, shared generous resources, mutual vision, and, best, confidence in the project and in us. Special thanks are due to many other individuals: Tina Samaha, our project manager, who with great skill and professionalism pulled all the pieces together with the help of Coleen O'Hanley, assistant production editor; photo researchers Carole Frohlich and Martha Shethar and map editors Heidi Hood and Laura Arcari, who did so much to help us realize our goals for the book's art and map programs; our original development editor, Ellen Kuhl, and the fine editors she brought to the project, Louise Townsend, Barbara Muller, and Jane Tufts; editorial assistants Sarah Barrash and Molly Kalkstein, who helped in myriad ways on many essential tasks; and our superb copyeditor, Barbara Flanagan. Last and above all, we thank Elizabeth M. Welch, senior development editor, who provided just the right doses of encouragement, prodding, and concrete suggestions for improvement. Her intelligence, skill, and determination proved to be crucial at every step of the process.

Our students' questions and concerns have shaped much of this work, and we welcome all our readers' suggestions, queries, and criticisms. Please contact us at our respective institutions or through our Web site: www.bedfordstmartins.com/makingwest.

L.H.   T.R.M.   B.H.R.   R.P.H.   B.G.S.

Brief Contents

Contents

CHAPTER 13

The Crisis of Late Medieval Society, 1320–1430   *451*

Maps and Figures

MAPS

Chapter 18

Chapter 19

Chapter 20

Chapter 21

FIGURES

Special Features

TAKING MEASURE

About the Authors

LYNN HUNT, Eugen Weber Professor of Modern European History at the University of California at Los Angeles, received her B.A. from Carleton College and her M.A. and Ph.D. from Stanford University. She is the author of *Revolution and Urban Politics in Provincial France* (1978); *Politics, Culture, and Class in the French Revolution* (1984); and *The Family Romance of the French Revolution* (1992). She is also the coauthor of *Telling the Truth about History* (1994); editor of *The New Cultural History* (1989); editor and translator of *The French Revolution and Human Rights* (1996); and co-editor of *Histories: French Constructions of the Past* (1995) and *Beyond the Cultural Turn* (1999). She has been awarded fellowships by the Guggenheim Foundation and the National Endowment for the Humanities and is a fellow of the American Academy of Arts and Sciences. She is currently preparing a CD-ROM of documents, images, and songs from the French Revolution and a book on the origins of human rights.

THOMAS R. MARTIN, Jeremiah O'Connor Professor in Classics at the College of the Holy Cross, earned his B.A. at Princeton University and his M.A. and Ph.D. at Harvard University. He is the author of *Sovereignty and Coinage in Classical Greece* (1985) and *Ancient Greece* (1996, 2000) and one of the originators of *Perseus 1.0: Interactive Sources and Studies on Ancient Greece* (1992, 1996) and www.perseus.tufts .edu, which, among other awards, was named the EDUCOM Best Software in Social Sciences (History) in 1992. He also wrote the lead article on ancient Greece for the revised edition of the Encarta electronic encyclopedia. He serves on the editorial board of STOA (www.stoa.org) and as codirector of its DEMOS

project (online resources on ancient Athenian democracy). A recipient of fellowships from the National Endowment for the Humanities and the American Council of Learned Societies, he is currently conducting research on the history and significance of freedom of speech in Athenian democracy.

BARBARA H. ROSENWEIN, professor of history at Loyola University Chicago, earned her B.A., M.A., and Ph.D. at the University of Chicago. She is the author of *Rhinoceros Bound: Cluny in the Tenth Century* (1982); *To Be the Neighbor of Saint Peter: The Social Meaning of Cluny's Property, 909 – 1049* (1989); and *Negotiating Space: Power, Restraint, and Privileges of Immunity in Early Medieval Europe* (1999). She is the editor of *Anger's Past: The Social Uses of an Emotion in the Middle Ages* (1998) and coeditor of *Debating the Middle Ages: Issues and Readings* (1998) and *Monks and Nuns, Saints and Outcasts: Religion in Medieval Society* (2000). A recipient of Guggenheim and National Endowment for the Humanities fellowships, she is currently working on a history of emotions in the early Middle Ages.

R. PO-CHIA HSIA, professor of history at New York University, received his B.A. from Swarthmore College and his M.A. and Ph.D. from Yale University. He is the author of *Society and Religion in Münster, 1535 – 1618* (1984); *The Myth of Ritual Murder: Jews and Magic in Reformation Germany* (1988); *The German People and the Reformation* (1998); *Social Discipline in the Reformation: Central Europe, 1550 – 1750* (1989); *Trent 1475: Stories of a Ritual Murder Trial* (1992); and *The World of the Catholic Re-*

newal (1997). He has been awarded fellowships by the Woodrow Wilson International Society of Scholars, the National Endowment for the Humanities, the Guggenheim Foundation, the Davis Center of Princeton University, and the Mellon Foundation. Currently he is working on sixteenth-to-eighteenth-century cultural contacts between Europe and Asia.

BONNIE G. SMITH, professor of history at Rutgers University, earned her B.A. at Smith College and her Ph.D. at the University of Rochester. She is the author of *Ladies of the Leisure Class* (1981); *Confessions of a Concierge: Madame Lucie's History of Twentieth-Century France* (1985); *Changing Lives: Women in European History since 1700* (1989); *The Gender of History: Men, Women, and Historical Practice* (1998); and *Imperialism* (2000). She is also the coauthor and translator of *What Is Property?* (1994); editor of *Global Feminisms since 1945* (2000); and coeditor of *History and the Texture of Modern Life: Selected Writings of Lucy Maynard Salmon.* She has received fellowships from the Guggenheim Foundation, the National Endowment for the Humanities, the National Humanities Center, the Davis Center of Princeton University, and the American Council of Learned Societies. Currently she is studying the globalization of European culture and society after World War II.

Tandē p̄ stragem loim maximã luct͛ ieiunia et
pīnas graues ꝑp processionalr eunti p romã cum
uniūsa plebe et clero apparet angelus languino
tenti ense magna reponens sup palacii magr͛

The Crisis of Late Medieval Society

1320–1430

The Last Days of the Plague
In this scene from the Book of Hours *of the Duke de Berry, the burial of Roman victims of the plague takes place. The angel in heaven heralds God's mercy after his chastisement of sins. Books of Hours were prayer books for individual use. This scene is a reminder of the imminence of death for all Christians and the need to lead a pious life: sudden death does not spare even those in the holy city of Rome. The Book of Hours of the Duke de Berry, located in the Chateau de Chantilly, north of Paris, is the best-known text of its kind.* The Metropolitan Museum of Art, The Cloisters Collection, 1954. (54.1.1) Photograph © 1987 The Metropolitan Museum of Art (detail).

"I N THE YEAR OF OUR LORD 1349," so began the chronicle kept by the Nuremberg citizen Ulman Stromer, "the Jews resided in the middle of the square, and their houses lined its sides as well as a street behind where Our Lady's now stands. And the Jews were burned on the evening of St. Nicholas's as it has been described." These terse words belie the horror experienced by the Jewish community. Robbed of their belongings in an uprising, the Jews of Nuremberg were later rounded up by the city magistrates, and those who refused to convert to Christianity were burned at the stake. A new church dedicated to Our Lady went up on the site where their synagogue was razed.

Nuremberg in central Germany was but one of numerous sites of anti-Jewish furor in 1349. After decades of increasing control through religious and political institutions, the violence of 1349 represented the breakdown of authority in the face of widespread warfare, catastrophic losses of population, and unprecedented challenges to religious authority. The coming together of these political, demographic, and religious developments resulted in a general crisis of late medieval society.

The first crisis was a political one, centering on the conflict between the English and the French that came to be called the Hundred Years' War (1337–1453). The war not only laid waste to large areas of France but also pushed neighboring countries into the maelstrom of violence. High taxes and widespread devastation also led to popular revolts that shook political society.

In society at large, order gave way to chaos and violence. Groups of flagellants, who whipped themselves as a form of penance, roamed centra'

1320	1342	1364	1386	1408	1430

Politics and War

Beginning of the Hundred Years' War

Polish-Lithuanian federation founded

Battle of Kosovo

Battle of Agincourt

Society and Economy

The Great Famine

The Black Death

English peasants revolt

Anti-Jewish pogroms in Central Europe

Anti-Jewish pogroms in Castille and Aragon

Economic stagnation, population decline, rise in real wages

Culture, Religion, and Intellectual Life

Marsilius of Padua,
The Defender of the Peace

The Great Schism

Christine de Pisan,
The Book of the City of Ladies

Chaucer, *The Canterbury Tales*

Beginning of the Hussite revolution

Froissart, *Chronicles*

Europe. Jews were persecuted on a scale not surpassed until the twentieth century. Anti-Jewish persecutions, or pogroms, broke out in the Holy Roman Empire, southern France, Aragon, and Castile, ravaging the once-flourishing Jewish culture of the Middle Ages.

Both the flagellant movement and the anti-Semitic violence were manifestations of the general crisis. In the mid-fourteenth century a series of disasters—famine, climatic changes, and disease—scourged a society already weakened by overpopulation, economic stagnation, social conflicts, and war. The plague, or Black Death, wiped out at least a third of Europe's population. With recurring plagues and continuous warfare through the second half of the fourteenth century, population density would not reach thirteenth-century levels again until the sixteenth, and in many areas not until the eighteenth, century.

Dynastic conflicts, popular uprisings, and an external menace to the Christian nobility as the Muslim Ottoman Turks advanced steadily in southeastern Europe. All undermined political authority and threat-

ened the social order. During the later Middle Ages, the idea of universal Christendom that had fueled and sustained the Crusades receded, while loyalties to state, community, and social groups deepened. The papacy, the very symbol of Christian unity and authority, remained divided by the claims of rival popes and challenged by heretical movements.

The word *crisis* implies a turning point, a decisive moment, and during the hundred-plus years between 1320 and 1430, European civilization faced such a time. Departing from the path of expansion, it entered a period of uncertainty, disunity, and contraction.

✦ Political Crises across Europe

The crises of the fourteenth century affected political allegiances as well as social and religious tensions. Just as many people no longer accepted the church's dictates, so did citizens refuse to trust rulers to serve the ordinary person's best interests. The idea of Christian solidarity, always stronger in theory than in practice, dissolved in the face of national rivalries, urban and rural revolts, and the military resurgence of the Muslims. The conflict between the English and the French known as the Hundred Years' War destroyed the lives of countless thousands of noncombatants as well as soldiers. Commoners—town residents and peasants—challenged the political status quo, wanting a share of the power their rulers wielded over them or at least a voice in how they were governed. The Ottoman Turks battled Christian Europe in a bloody war to reclaim the land westerners had conquered in the Crusades. The political crises of the later Middle Ages shaped the pattern of conflicts for the next two hundred years.

The Changing Nature of Warfare

The nobility continued to dominate European society in the later Middle Ages, but their social and political roles were gradually but fundamentally transformed. Although the ranks of the nobility encompassed a wide range of people—from powerful magnates whose wealth rivaled that of kings to humble knights who lived much like peasants—two developments in the later Middle Ages affected all of them: an agrarian crisis and the changing nature of warfare.

Traditionally the nobles had been the warrior class and had lived on the profits from the land they owned. In the wake of the Black Death, their income from their land dwindled as food prices declined because of the dramatic drop in population. Forced to seek additional revenues, knights turned enthusiastically to war. Noblemen from many nations served willingly in foreign campaigns, forming units at their own expense, motivated solely by material gain. The English knight John Hawkwood put it best: "Do you not know that I live by war, and peace would be my undoing?" Captain of an army that sold its services to various Italian states vying for power, Hawkwood represented the new soldier: the mercenary who lived a life of violence and whose loyalty was given to the side that paid the most.

As if to compensate for the cynical reality of mercenary warfare, the European nobility emphasized the traditional knightly codes of behavior in an effort to bolster their authority. Romances associated with King Arthur and his round table of

chivalrous knights became a vogue, not only in reading but also in life. Edward III of England, for example, created the Order of the Garter in 1344 to revive the idea of chivalry. During truces in the Hundred Years' War, English and French knights jousted, glorifying mock combat according to the rules of chivalry. The French chronicler Jean Froissart noted that English and French knights scorned their German counterparts for ignoring the rules and rituals of war that masked the exercise of violence and power.

Yet chivalric combat waged by knights on horseback was quickly yielding to new military realities. By the last decades of the fourteenth century, cannons were becoming common in European warfare. New military technologies—firearms, siege equipment,

Siege Warfare

Siege warfare during the Hundred Years' War pitted cannons against fortifications. As cannons grew in caliber, walls became thicker, and protruding battlements and gun emplacements were added to provide counter-firepower. Late-medieval sieges were time-consuming affairs that often lasted for years. Bibliothèque Nationale de France.

and fortification, for example—undermined the nobility's preeminence as a fighting force. Well-equipped fighting forces counted more than valor and often determined the outcome of battles. Commoners, criminals, and adventurers often joined the ranks. To maintain their social eminence, the nobles were forced to become entrepreneurs as either military captains or estate managers. Many turned to state service to reinforce their social stations. Kings and princes welcomed such service. By appointing nobles to the royal household, as military commanders and councilors, kings and princes could further consolidate the power of emerging states.

The Hundred Years' War, 1337–1453

The Hundred Years' War was a protracted struggle in western Europe that involved the nobility of almost every nation. It was sparked by conflicting French and English interests in southwestern France. As part of the French royal policy of centralizing jurisdiction, Philip VI in 1337 confiscated the southwestern province of Aquitaine, which had been held by the English monarchs as a fief of the French crown. To recover his lands, Edward III of England in turn laid claim to the French throne.

The Combatants. To rally Englishmen to their cause, English kings spread anti-French propaganda throughout their realm. Yeomen (freemen farmers) as well as the nobility rallied to serve their king, fired by patriotism and the lust for plunder. The spectacular victories won by various English kings at Crécy, Poitiers, and Agincourt further fueled popular fervor for war, as knights, yeomen, and adventurers returned home with booty, hostages, and tales of bloody slaughter and amorous conquests. War became its own engine. Mercenary companies came to replace levies of freemen archers in the English army. These companies remained in France during the long intervals of armistice between short, destructive campaigns punctuated by a few spectacular battles. For the English soldier, in time the lush, green, and fertile French countryside, with its wealthy towns and fabulous chateaux and its riches and beautiful women, represented the rewards of war far more promising than peaceful poverty.

Elaborate chivalric behavior, savage brutality, and unabashed profiteering permeated the fighting in the Hundred Years' War. Warfare in this era involved definite rules whose application depended on social status. English and French knights took one another prisoner and showed all the formal courtesy required by chivalry—but they slaughtered captured common soldiers like cattle. Overall the pattern of war was not pitched battles but a series of raids in which English fighters plundered cities and villages, causing terrible destruction. English knights financed their own campaigns, and war was expected to turn a profit, either in captured booty or in ransom paid to free noble prisoners of war.

Ruling over a more populous realm and commanding far larger armies, the French kings were, nevertheless, hindered in the war by the independent actions of their powerful barons. Against the accurate and deadly English freemen archers, the French knights met repeated defeats. Yet the French nobility despised their own peasants, fearing them and the urban middle classes more perhaps than they did their noble English adversaries. Their fears were not unfounded, for a deep chasm separated the warrior class from their social inferiors in medieval Europe.

The Course of the War. Historians divide the Hundred Years' War into three periods: the first marked by English triumphs, the second in which France slowly gained the upper hand, and the third ending in the English expulsion from France (Map 13.1). In the first period (1338–1360), the English won several famous victories such as Crécy, in which the vastly outnumbered English knights and longbowmen routed the French cavalry. In another victory at Poitiers (1356), Edward the Black Prince (heir to the English throne, named for his black armor) defeated a superior French army and captured the French king John and a host of important noblemen, whom they ransomed for hefty sums. Divided and demoralized, the French signed the peace treaty of Brétigny in 1360, ceding vast territories in the southwest to England.

The second phase of the war lasted from 1361 to 1413. In Charles V (r. 1364–1380) and his brother Philip the Bold (the duke of Burgundy), the French finally found energetic leaders who could resist the English. In 1372, aided by a Castilian fleet, a French force took La Rochelle, long an English stronghold in Gascony. In 1386, in the aftermath of a peasant revolt in England, the French even assembled a fleet to conquer England. Although unsuccessful in landing an

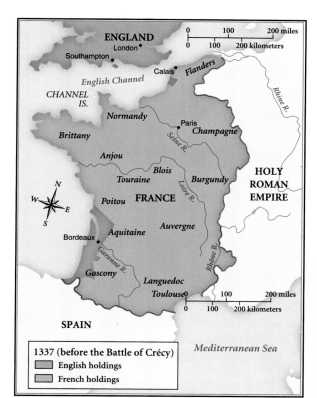

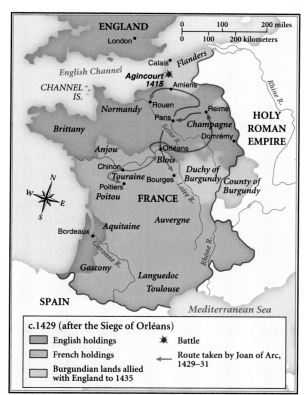

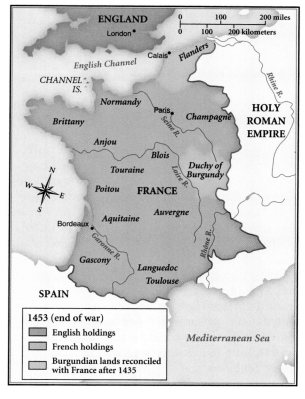

MAP 13.1 The Hundred Years' War, 1337–1453

*As rulers of Aquitaine, English kings contested the French monarchy for the domination of France.
Squeezed between England and Burgundy, the effective possession of the French kings was vastly
reduced after the battle of Poitiers.*

The Spoils of War
This illustration from Jean Froissart's Chronicles *depicts soldiers pillaging a conquered city. Looting in the Hundred Years' War became the main income for mercenary troops and contributed to the general misery of late medieval society. Food, furniture, even everyday household items were looted. War had come to feed on itself.*
Bibliothèque Nationale de France.

army, the French raided English ports into the early fifteenth century.

At the turn of the century a new set of players entered the political stage. In 1399, the English noble Henry Bolingbroke forced Richard II (grandson of Edward III) to abdicate. The coup made Bolingbroke Henry IV of England (r. 1399–1413), whose story was later made famous (and much distorted) by Shakespeare's plays. Factional strife poisoned French political unity. The struggle for power began in 1392 after Charles VI (r. 1380–1422), called the Mad King of France, suffered his first bout of insanity. Two factions then began to coalesce—one around John of Burgundy (the son of Philip the Bold) and the other around the duke of Orléans. In 1407, Burgundian agents assassinated the duke, whose followers, called the Armagnacs, sought vengeance and plunged France into civil war. When both parties appealed for English support in 1413, the young King Henry V (r. 1413–1422), who had just succeeded his father, Henry IV, launched a full-scale invasion of France.

The third phase of the war (1413–1453) began when Henry V crushed the French at Agincourt (1415). Unlike the earlier battles of Crécy and Poitiers, however, this isolated victory achieved little in the long run. Three parties now struggled for domination. Henry occupied Normandy and claimed the French throne; the dauphin (son of Charles VI and heir apparent to the French throne), later Charles VII of France (r. 1422–1461),* ruled central France with the support of the Armagnacs; and the duke of Burgundy held a vast territory in the northeast that included the Low Countries. Burgundy was thus able to broker war or peace by shifting support first to the English and then to the French. But even with Burgundian support the English could not establish firm control. In Normandy, a savage guerrilla war harassed the English army. Driven from their villages by pillaging and murdering soldiers, the Norman peasants retreated

---

*Although the dauphin was not crowned until 1429, he assumed the title Charles VII in 1422, following the death of his father.

into forests, formed armed bands, and attacked the English. The miseries of war inspired prophecies of miraculous salvation; among the predictions was the belief that a virgin would deliver France from the English invaders.

Joan of Arc.   At the court of the dauphin, in 1429, a sixteen-year-old peasant girl presented herself and her vision to save France. Born in a village in Lorraine, Joan of Arc, La Pucelle ("the Maid"), as she always referred to herself, grew up in a war-ravaged country that longed for divine deliverance. (See "Contrasting Views," page 458.) The young maid had first presented herself as God's messenger to the local noble, who was sufficiently impressed to equip Joan with horse, armor, and a retinue to send her to the dauphin's court. (According to her later testimony, Joan ran away from home when her father threatened to drown her because she refused an arranged marriage.) Joan of Arc's extraordinary appearance inspired the beleaguered French to trust in divine providence. In 1429, she accompanied the French army that laid a prolonged but successful siege on Orléans, was wounded, and showed great courage in battle. Upon her urging, the dauphin traveled deep into hostile Burgundian territory to be anointed King Charles VII of France at Reims cathedral, thus strengthening his legitimacy by following the traditional ritual of coronation.

Joan's fortunes declined after Reims. She promised to capture Paris, then in Anglo-Burgundian hands, and in 1430 attacked the city on the feast of the Virgin Mary, thus violating one of the holiest religious feast days. After the Anglo-Burgundian defenders drove back her troops, the French began to lose faith in the Maid. When the Burgundians captured her in 1430 during a minor skirmish, Charles and his forces did little to save her. Still, Joan was a powerful symbol, and the English were determined to undermine her claim to divine guidance. In a trial conducted by French theologians in Anglo-Burgundian service, Joan was accused of false prophecy, suspected of witchcraft because she wore male clothes and led armies, and tricked into recanting her prophetic mission. Almost immediately, however, she retracted her confessions, returned the female attire given her after an English soldier had raped her in prison, and reaffirmed her divine mission. The English then burned her at the stake as a relapsed heretic in 1431.

Joan the Warrior
Joan of Arc's career as a charismatic military leader was an extraordinary occurrence in fifteenth-century France. In this manuscript illumination, Joan, in full armor, directs French soldiers as they besiege the English at Orléans. The victory she gained here stunned the French people.
Erich Lessing/Art Resource, NY.

After Joan's death, the English position slowly crumbled when their alliance with the Burgundians fell apart in 1435. The duke of Burgundy recognized Charles VII as king of France, and Charles entered Paris in 1437. Skirmish by skirmish, the English were driven from French soil, retaining only the port of Calais when hostilities ceased in 1453. Two years later, the French church rescinded the 1431 verdict that had condemned Joan of Arc as a heretic. Some five centuries later, she was canonized and declared the patron saint of France.

Consequences of the War.   The Hundred Years' War profoundly altered the economic and political landscape of western Europe. It had three major impacts. First, the long years of warfare aggravated the demographic and economic crises of the fourteenth century. In addition to recurrent plagues, the population was further ravaged by pillage and warfare. Constant insecurity caused by marauding bands of soldiers prevented the cultivation of fields even in times of truce. In a region such as Normandy in France, perhaps up to half the population had perished by the end of the war, victims of disease, famine, and warfare.

Joan of Arc: Who Was "the Maid"?

Looming above the confused events and personalities of the Hundred Years' War, the figure of Joan of Arc gained eternal fame when she was canonized in 1921 and remembered as the heroine who saved France. But who was this slender young woman from the Lorraine? Calling herself "the Maid," Joan left home after she was instructed in a vision to present herself as God's messenger at the court of Charles, the dauphin of France (Document 1). Initial skepticism turned to adulation when in 1430 Joan led the French army that lifted the siege of Orléans and dealt the English a crushing blow. Either captivated by her piety and bravery or threatened by her power and actions, contemporaries labeled Joan everything from a divine symbol to a relapsed heretic (Documents 2–4). Her capture by the Burgundians, her year-long imprisonment, torture, interrogation, and subsequent execution generated documentation and ensured her immortality (Document 5).

1. Joan's Vision

Joan first spoke of her visions at length after her capture by her enemies, who were eager to prove that she was inspired by the devil. This document is the only information we have from Joan herself about her childhood. Notice three things about the document: first, the description of the vision refers to light and voice, a standard representation by medieval visionaries; second, Joan was instructed not to tell her father about her mission, which implied that she actually left home without his consent; and third, the reference to the siege of Orléans might have been an addition to her memory after the momentous events of her career. It was likely that she thought of her mission in a more general way of saving France.

When I was thirteen years old, I had a voice from God to help me govern my conduct. And the first time I was very fearful. And came this voice, about the hour of noon, in the summer-time, in my father's garden; I had not fasted on the eve preceding that day. I heard the voice on the right-hand side, towards the church; and rarely do I hear it without a brightness. This brightness comes from the same side as the voice is heard. It is usually a great light. When I came to France, often I heard this voice. . . . The voice was sent to me by God and, after I had thrice heard this voice, I knew that it was the voice of an angel. This voice has always guarded me well and I have always understood it clearly. . . .

It has taught me to conduct myself well, to go habitually to church. It told me that I, Joan, should come into France. . . . This voice told me, twice or thrice a week, that I, Joan, must go away and that I must come to France and that my father must know nothing of my leaving. The voice told me that I should go to France and I could not bear to stay where I was. The voice told me that I should raise the siege laid to the city of Orléans. . . . And me, I answered it that I was a poor girl who knew not how to ride nor lead in war.

Source: Régine Pernoud, ed., *Joan of Arc: By Herself and Her Witnesses* (Lanham, Md.: Scarborough House, 1994), 30.

2. Messenger of God?

When Joan appeared at the court of the dauphin, her reputation as the messenger of God had preceded her. The French court received her with a mixture of wonder, curiosity, and outright skepticism. The political and military situation looked so desperate that many had been hoping for a divine deliverance when Joan made her arrival in history. There was debate among the dauphin's counselors whether Joan should be taken seriously, however, and the dauphin referred the case to a panel of theologians to determine whether Joan's mission was divine in origin. The following account of Joan's first visit to the dauphin was recorded by Simon Charles, president of the Chamber of Accounts.

I know that, when Joan arrived in [the castle and town of] Chinon, there was deliberation in counsel to decide whether the King should hear her or not. To start with they sent to ask her why she was come and what she was asking for. She was unwilling to say anything without having spoken to the King, yet was she constrained by the King to say the reasons for her mission. She said that she had two [reasons] for which she had a mandate from the King of Heaven; one, to raise the siege of Orléans, the other to lead the King to Rheims for his [coronation]. Which being heard, some of the King's counsellors said that the King should on no account have faith in Joan, and the others that since she said that she was sent by God, and that she had something to say to the King, the King should at least hear her.

Source: Pernoud, 48–49.

3. Normal Girl?

This memoir, written by Marguerite la Touroulde, one of the women who lived with Joan and took care of her after the dauphin had accepted Joan's services to save France, testifies to Joan's ordinariness. The messenger of God appears in these words as a normal, devout young girl, whose only remarkable quality seems to be her physical and martial prowess.

"I did not see Joan until the time when the King returned from Rheims where he had been crowned. He came to the town of Bourges where the Queen was and me with her. . . . Joan was then brought to Bourges and, by command of the lord d'Albret, she was lodged in my house. . . . She was in my house for a period of three weeks, sleeping, drinking and eating, and almost every day I slept with Joan and I neither saw in her nor perceived anything of any kind of unquietness, but she behaved herself as an honest and Catholic woman, for she went very often to confession, willingly heard mass and often asked me to go to Matins. And at her instance I went, and took her with me several times.

"Sometimes we talked together and some said to Joan that doubtless she was not afraid to go into battle because she knew well that she would not

be killed. She answered that she was no safer than any other combatant. And sometimes Joan told how she had been examined by the clerks and that she had answered them: 'In Our Lord's books there is more than in yours. . . .' Joan was very simple and ignorant and knew absolutely nothing, it seems to me, excepting in the matter of war. I remember that several women came to my house while Joan was staying there, and brought paternosters [rosary beads] and other objects of piety that she might touch them, which made her laugh and say to me, 'Touch them yourself, they will be as good from your touch as from mine.' She was open-handed in almsgiving and most willingly gave to the indigent and to the poor, saying that she had been sent for the consolation of the poor and the indigent.

"And several times I saw her at the bath and in the bath-houses, and so far as I was able to see, she was a virgin, and from all that I know she was all innocence, excepting in arms, for I saw her riding on horseback and bearing a lance as the best of soldiers would have done it, and at that the men-at-arms marvelled."

Source: Pernoud, 64–65.

4. Relapsed Heretic?

After her capture, Joan was interrogated for more than a year by a panel of theologians, who were determined to destroy her reputation. Headed by Pierre Cauchon, the judges cast doubt on the divine origins of Joan's visions, suggesting that they had come instead from the devil. They also accused her of disobedience to the church and of violating social and religious norms by dressing in man's clothing. Worn down by her long imprisonment and abandoned to her enemies, Joan recanted and admitted that the voices had not come from God. But after Joan was raped in jail by English soldiers, she retracted her confession, reverted to dressing in man's clothing, and reasserted her divine mission. This occasion provided the legal pretext for condemning Joan as a lapsed heretic. The following document recounts the long judgment condemning Joan.

Cauchon wasted no time in bringing Joan to trial for her "relapse." After the interrogation . . . , on May 28th, he summoned the principal assessors to meet on the 29th, and gave them a brief *exposé* of the state of her case: after the solemn preaching and admonitions addressed to her, Joan had renounced the error of her ways and signed an abjuration [retraction] with her own hand. . . . However, at the suggestion of the devil she had started saying again that her voices and spirits had come to her, and having rejected woman's clothes, had resumed the wearing of male attire. Which was why he was now asking the assessors to give their opinion on what should now be done.

The first asked to speak happened to be Master Nicolas de Venderès. . . . As may well be imagined, his opinion was clear: Joan must be held to be a heretic and without further delay handed over to the secular arm, "with a recommendation to be gentle with her." This was a conventional formula [employed by Inquisition courts] and everyone knew what it implied.

But Giles de Duremort, abbot of Fécamp, asked next to give his opinion, introduced a request which must have made Cauchon uneasy. "It seems to me," he said, "that she is a relapsed heretic and that the word of God should be preached to her; that the abjuration which was read to her shall be read to her again and explained; that done, the judges will have to declare her a heretic and abandon her to secular justice." . . .

Whereupon—we are still quoting the official proceedings—"Having heard the opinion of each one, we, the judges, thanked them and thereafter concluded that the said Joan be proceeded against as a relapsed heretic according to law and reason."

Source: Pernoud, 223–24.

5. Sacred Martyr?

Condemned to burn at the stake, Joan went to her death in 1431 clutching a crucifix and uttering the name of Christ. Her actions and demeanor moved many to remember the event. Their testimonies ten years later provided the evidence for judges to overturn her conviction. Her good name restored, Joan would live on in the memory of France as its greatest heroine. Pierre Cusquel, a stonemason from Orléans, offered this testimony.

"I heard say that Master Jean Tressard, secretary to the King of England, returning from Joan's execution afflicted and groaning, wept lamentably over what he had seen in that place and said indeed: 'We are all lost, for we have burnt a good and holy person,' and that he believed that her soul was in God's hands and that, when she was in the midst of the flames, she had still declaimed the name of the Lord Jesus. That was common repute and more or less all the people murmured that a great wrong and injustice had been done to Joan. . . . After Joan's death the English had the ashes gathered up and thrown into the Seine because they feared lest she escape or lest some say she had escaped."

Source: Pernoud, 233.

QUESTIONS FOR DEBATE

1. What was Joan's vision? Was her vision understood differently by the French king, by her inquisitors, and by herself during her trial?

2. How did her judges try to frame a charge against her during her captivity? Why?

3. What was the source of Joan's charisma? Why did she inspire such a wide range of responses?

Second, the war prevented a quick resolution of the crisis in spiritual authority. As we will see, the collapse of papal authority known as the Great Schism owed much to the fact that rival popes could call on the respective belligerents to support their own claim. Locked in combat, the French, English, and Burgundian rulers could not put aside their political differences to restore papal authority.

The third long-term consequence of the war was the changing political landscape of western Europe.

The necessity of mobilization strengthened the hand of the French monarchy. Under Charles VII a standing army was established to supplement the feudal noble levies, an army financed by increased taxation and expanded royal judicial claims. By 1500, the French monarchy would emerge as one of the leading powers of Europe, ready to battle Burgundy and the empire for the domination of Europe.

Burgundy also emerged as a strong power from the Hundred Years' War. By absorbing the Low

Countries, this French duchy was evolving into an independent state, a rich power situated between France and Germany and commanding the fabulous wealth of Flemish cities. The Burgundian dukes became rivals of French kings after about 1450 and established a brilliant court and civilization.

Defeated in war, the English monarchy suffered through decades of disunity and strife. Defeat abroad spread discontent at home. From the 1460s to 1485, England was torn by civil war—the War of the Roses between the red rose of Lancaster and the rival white rose of York. A deposed king (Henry VI), a short reign (Edward IV), and the murder of two princes by their uncle (Richard III) followed in quick succession in a series of conflicts that decimated the leading noble families of England. When Henry Tudor succeeded to the throne in 1485, England was exhausted from years of confusion. Henry managed to end the civil war and unite the houses of Lancaster and York, but only slowly did England begin to recover strength.

The heavy financial burden of warfare also destabilized the banking system. Default on war loans by the English king, Edward III, precipitated the collapse of several of the largest banks in Europe, all based in Italy. The political crisis of the Hundred Years' War thus had a direct impact on the economic crisis of the fourteenth century.

Popular Uprisings

English and French knights waged war at the expense of the common people. While French peasants and townsfolk were taxed, robbed, raped, and murdered by marauding bands of mercenaries, their English counterparts had to pay ever higher taxes to support their kings' wars. Widespread resentment fueled popular uprisings, which contributed to the general disintegration of political and social order. In 1358, a short but savage rebellion erupted in the area around Paris, shocking the nobility. And in 1381, a more widespread and broadly based revolt broke out in England.

Jacquerie Uprising in Paris, 1358. Historians have traditionally described the 1358 Jacquerie—named after the jacket (*jacque*) worn by serfs—as a "peasant fury," implying that it represented simply a spontaneous outburst of aimless violence. More recent research, however, reveals the complex social origins

of the movement. The revolt broke out after the English captured King John at the battle of Poitiers, when the estates of France (the representatives of the clergy, nobility, and the cities) met in Paris to discuss monarchical reform and national defense. Unhappy with the heavy war taxes and the incompetence of the warrior nobility, the townspeople, led by Étienne Marcel, the provost of the merchants of Paris, sought greater political influence. Through merchants' and artisans' guilds, the citizens and government of Paris now assumed a new political importance. In the absence of royal authority, the common people vied with the nobles for control of government, and a clash between peasants and nobles near Paris led to a massive uprising.

The rebels began to destroy manor houses and castles near Paris, massacring entire noble families in a savage class war. Contemporaries were astonished at the intensity and violence of the Jacquerie. The chronicler Jean Froissart, sympathetic to the nobility, reflected the views of the ruling class in

The English Peasant Uprising, 1381
In this manuscript illumination, depicting a much more orderly scene than ever must have been the reality, a host of rebellious peasants led by John Ball (on horseback) confronts troops gathered under the royal banners of England and St. George. Such confrontations, frequent in late-medieval and early modern Europe, always ended with the same result, as well-armed soldiers mowed down desperate village folk.
British Library, London/The Bridgeman Art Library.

describing the rebels as "small, dark, and very poorly armed." As for the violence, Froissart continued, "They thought that by such means they could destroy all the nobles and gentry in the world." Repression by nobles was even more savage, as thousands of rebels died in battles or were executed. In Paris the rebel leader Marcel was killed in factional strife, but urban rebellions continued until the fifteenth century.

English Peasant Revolt of 1381. In England, rural and urban discontent intensified as landlords, peasants, and workers pursued increasingly opposing interests. The trigger for outright rebellion was the imposition of a poll tax passed by Parliament in 1377 to raise money for the war against France, a war that peasants believed benefitted only the king and the nobility. Unlike traditional subsidies to the king, the poll tax was levied on everyone. In May 1381, a revolt broke out to protest the taxes. Rebels in Essex and Kent joined bands in London to confront the king. The famous couplet of the radical preacher John Ball, who was executed after the revolt, expresses the rebels' egalitarian, antinoble sentiment:

> *When Adam delved* [dug] *and Eve span*
> *Who was then a gentleman?*

Forced to address the rebels, young King Richard II agreed to abolish serfdom and impose a ceiling on land rent, concessions immediately rescinded after the rebels' defeat.

Unrest in Flanders. Popular uprisings also took place in the Low Countries, especially in the cities of Flanders, the most densely populated and urbanized region of Europe. For over a century, Flanders had been Europe's industrial and financial heartland, importing raw wool from England, manufacturing fine cloth in cities, and exporting woolen goods to all parts of Europe.

Because the region depended on trade for food and goods, Flanders was especially sensitive to the larger political and economic changes. Between 1323 and 1328, unrest spread from rural Flanders to Bruges and Ypres, as citizens refused to pay the tithe to the church or taxes to the count of Flanders. Later, the Hundred Years' War undermined the woolen industry as Edward III of England declared a trade embargo, thus halting shipments of raw ma-

terials to Flemish industries. Although Flanders was a French fief, weavers and other artisans opposed their count's pro-French policy as they depended on English wool. From 1338 to 1345, the citizens of the large industrial city of Ghent rebelled against their prince. In the tumultuous years 1377–1383, the townspeople of Ghent sought an alliance with the citizens of Paris, fielded an army to battle the count, and held out into the fifteenth century despite their disastrous defeat by the French army in 1382. Thus the urban insurrections in Flanders became part of the economic and political struggles of the Hundred Years' War.

Urban Insurrections in Italy. Revolts in Rome and Florence resulted in part from the long absence of the popes during the Avignon papacy. Factional violence between powerful noble clans in Rome fueled popular hatred of local magnates and provided the background for the dramatic episode of the Roman commune. The Florentine chronicler Giovanni Villani narrates that "on May 20, 1347 . . . a certain Cola di Rienzo had just returned to Rome from a mission on behalf of the Roman people to the court of the Pope, to beg him to come and live, with his court, in the see of St. Peter, as he should do." Although unsuccessful in his mission to Avignon, Rienzo so impressed the Romans with his speech that they proclaimed him "tribune of the people," a title harking back to the plebeians' representatives in the ancient Roman republic. "Certain of the Orsini and the Colonna," continues Villani, "as well as other nobles, fled from the city to their lands and castles to escape the fury of the tribune and the people." Inspired by his reading of ancient Roman history, Rienzo and his followers took advantage of the nobles' flight and tried to remake their city in the image of classical Roman republicanism. But like the revolts in Paris and Ghent, the Roman uprising (1347–1354) was suppressed by the nobility.

The pattern of social conflict behind these three failed urban revolts is best exemplified by the Ciompi uprising in Florence. Florence was one of the largest European cities in the fourteenth century and a center of banking and the woolen industry in southern Europe. There the large populations of woolworkers depended on the wool merchants, who controlled both the supply of raw material and the marketing of finished cloth. Unlike artisans in other trades, woolworkers were prohibited from forming their own guild and thus constituted a politically unrepresented wage-earning working class. As the wool industry declined because of falling demand, unemployment became an explosive social problem. During the summer of 1378, the lower classes, many of them woolworkers, rose against the regime, demanding a more egalitarian social order. A coalition of artisans and merchants, supported by woolworkers, demanded more equitable power sharing with the bankers and wealthy merchants who controlled city government. By midsummer, crowds thronged the streets, and woolworkers set fire to the palaces of the rich and demanded the right to form their own guild. The insurrection was subsequently called the Ciompi uprising, meaning "uprising by the little people." Alarmed by the radical turn of events, the guild artisans turned against their worker allies and defeated them in fierce street battles. The revolt ended with a restoration of the patrician regime, although Ciompi exiles continued to plot worker revolts into the 1380s.

The Ciompi rebellion, like the uprisings in Paris, Ghent, and Rome, signaled a pattern of change in late medieval Europe. Although they represented a continuation of the communal uprisings of the eleventh and twelfth centuries, which helped establish town governments in some parts of Europe, the primary causes in the fourteenth century were the disruptions of the Black Death and the subsequent economic depression. But as significant as their motivations was their failure. Urban revolts did not redraw the political map of Europe, nor did they significantly alter the distribution of power. Instead they were subsumed by larger political transformations from which the territorial states would emerge as the major political forces.

Fragmentation and Power in Central and Eastern Europe

While England and France struggled for domination in western Europe, the Holy Roman Empire, unified in name only, became an arena where princes and cities assumed more power in their own hands. This political fragmentation, together with a stronger orientation toward the Slavic lands of eastern Europe, signified a growing separation between central and western Europe (Map 13.2). Within the empire the four most significant developments were the shift of political focus from the south and west to the east, the changing balance of power between the emperor and the princes, the development of cities, and the rise of self-governing communes in the Alps.

Three of the five emperors in this period belonged to the House of Luxembourg: Charles IV (r. 1347–1378), Wenceslas (r. 1378–1400), and Sigismund (r. 1410–1437). Having obtained Bohemia by marriage, the Luxembourg dynasty based its power in the east, and Prague became the imperial capital. This move initiated a shift of power within the Holy Roman Empire, away from the Rhineland and Swabia toward east central Europe.

The Seven Electors
This miniature from a German manuscript in Koblenz shows the seven electors of the Holy Roman Empire in 1308. They were the archbishops of Cologne, Mainz, and Trier; the electors of the Palatinate, Saxony, and Brandenburg; and the king of Bohemia, identifiable through their coat of arms on the shields hanging above them. Hence the electors were composed of three clergymen and four secular princes.
Mary Evans Picture Library.

MAP 13.2 Central and Eastern Europe, c. 1400

Through the Holy Roman Empire and the Teutonic Knights, Germanic influence extended far into eastern Europe including Bohemia, Moravia, and the Baltic coast. The Polish-Lithuanian Commonwealth, united in 1386, and the Kingdom of Hungary were the other great powers in eastern Europe.

Except for a continuous involvement with northern Italy, theoretically a part of the Holy Roman Empire, German institutions became more closely allied with eastern rather than western Europe. For example, the Holy Roman Empire's first university, Charles University (named after its royal founder, Charles IV), was established in 1348 in Prague. Bohemians and Hungarians also began to exert more influence in imperial politics.

Another development that separated central from western Europe was the fragmentation of political authority in the empire at a time when French, English, and Castilian monarchs were consolidating their power. Charles IV's coronation as emperor in 1355 did not translate into more power at home. The Bohemian nobility refused to recognize his supreme authority, and the German princes secured from him

a constitutional guarantee for their own sovereignty. In 1356, Charles was forced to agree to the Golden Bull, a document that required the German king to be chosen by seven electors: the archbishops of Mainz, Cologne, and Trier and four princes, namely, the king of Bohemia, the elector of Saxony, the count of the Palatinate, and the margrave of Brandenburg. The imperial electoral college also guaranteed the existence of numerous local and regional power centers, a distinctive feature in German history that continued into the modern age.

Although no single German city rivaled Paris, London, Florence, or Ghent in population, its large number of cities made Germany the economic equal of northern Italy and the Low Countries. But rivalry among powerful princes prevented the urban communes from evolving into city republics like those in Italy. In 1388, for example, the count of Württemberg defeated the Swabian League of cities, formed in 1376. Nevertheless, the cities were at the forefront of economic growth. Nuremberg and Augsburg became centers of the north-south trade, linking Poland, Bohemia, and the German lands with the Mediterranean. In northern Germany the Hanseatic League, under the leadership of Lübeck, united the many towns trading between the Baltic and the North Sea. At its zenith in the fifteenth century, the Hanseatic fleet controlled the Baltic, and the league was a power to be reckoned with by kings and princes.

Another sign of political fragmentation was the growth of self-governing peasant and town communes in the high Alpine valleys that united in the Swiss Confederation. In 1291, the peasants of Uri, Schwyz, and Unterwalden had sworn a perpetual alliance against their oppressive Habsburg overlord. After defeating a Habsburg army in 1315, these free peasants took the name "Confederates" and developed a new alliance that would become Switzerland. In the process, the Swiss enshrined their freedom in the legend of William Tell, their national hero who was forced by a Habsburg official to prove his archery skills by shooting an apple placed on the head of his own son. This act so outraged the citizens that they rose up in arms against the Habsburg rule. By 1353, Lucerne, Zurich, and Bern had joined the confederation. The Swiss Confederation continued to acquire new members into the sixteenth century, defeating armies sent by different princes to undermine its liberties.

Growth of the Swiss Confederation to 1353

Also in the mid-fourteenth century, two large monarchies took shape in northeastern Europe—Poland and Lithuania. In the early twelfth century, Poland had splintered into petty duchies, and the Mongol invasion of the 1240s had caused frightful devastation. But recovery was under way by 1300, and unlike almost every other part of Europe, Poland experienced an era of demographic and economic expansion in the fourteenth century. Both Jewish and German settlers, for example, helped build thriving towns like Cracow. Monarchical consolidation followed. King Casimir III (r. 1333–1370) won recognition in most of the country's regions for his royal authority, embodied in comprehensive law codes. A problem that persisted throughout his reign, however, was conflict with the neighboring princes of Lithuania, Europe's last pagan rulers, who for centuries fiercely resisted Christianization by the German crusading order, the Teutonic Knights. After the Mongols overran Russia, Lithuania extended its rule southward, offering western Russian princes protection against Mongol and Muscovite rule. By the late fourteenth century, a vast Lithuanian principality had arisen, embracing modern Lithuania, Belarus, and Ukraine.

Casimir III died in 1370 without a son; the failure of a new dynasty to take hold opened the way for the unification of Poland and Lithuania. In 1386, the Lithuanian prince Jogailo accepted Roman Catholic baptism, married the young queen of Poland, and later assumed the Polish crown. Under the Jagiellonian dynasty, Poland and Lithuania kept separate legal systems. Catholicism and Polish culture prevailed among the principality's upper class, while most native Lithuanian village folk remained pagan for several centuries. With only a few interruptions, the Polish-Lithuanian federation would last for five centuries.

Multiethnic States on the Frontiers

While some Christian princes were battling one another within Christendom, others fought Muslim foes at the frontiers of Christian Europe. Two regions at opposite ends of the Mediterranean—Spain and the Ottoman Empire—were unusual in medieval Europe for their religious and ethnic diversity. As a result of the Spanish reconquista of the twelfth and thirteenth centuries, the Iberian Christian kingdoms contained large religious and ethnic minorities. In Castile, where historians estimate the population before the outbreak of the plague in 1348 at four to

Christian Territory in Iberia, c. 1350

five million, 7 percent of the inhabitants were Muslims or Jews. In Aragon, of the approximately 1 million people at midcentury, perhaps 3 to 4 percent belonged to these two religious minorities. In the Iberian peninsula, the Christian kingdoms consolidated their gains against Muslim Granada through internal colonization, bringing sizable minority populations into newly Christian regions. At the same time, the orthodox Byzantine Empire, hardly recovered from the Fourth Crusade, fought for survival against the Ottoman Turks. In the Balkans and Anatolia, the Ottomans created a multiethnic state, but one different from the model of the Hispanic kingdoms.

The Iberian Peninsula. In the mid-fourteenth century, the Iberian peninsula encompassed six areas: Portugal, Castile, Navarre, Aragon, and Catalonia—all Christian—and Muslim Granada. Among these territories, Castile and Aragon were the most important, both politically and economically. The Muslim population was concentrated in the south: from the Algarve in Portugal eastward across Andalusia to Murcia and Valencia. Initially, the Iberian Muslims (called Moors) could own property, practice their religion, and elect their own judges, but conditions worsened for them in the fifteenth century as fears of rebellions and religious prejudices intensified among Christians. As Christian conquerors and settlers advanced, most Muslims were driven out of the cities or confined to specific quarters. Many Muslims were captured and enslaved by Christian armies. These slaves worked in Christian households or on large estates called *latifundia*, which were granted by the Castilian kings to the crusading orders, the church, and powerful noble families. Slavery existed on a fairly large scale at both ends of the Mediterranean, where Christian and Muslim civilizations confronted one another: in Iberia, North Africa, Anatolia, and the Balkans.

Unlike the Muslims, Jews congregated exclusively in cities, where they practiced many urban professions. Prior to 1391, they encountered few social obstacles to advancement. Jewish physicians and tax collectors made up part of the administration of Castile, but the Christian populace resented their social prominence and wealth. Moreover, the religious fervor and sense of crisis in the later fourteenth century intensified the ever-present intolerance toward Jews. In June 1391, incited by the

sermons of the priest Fernandon Martínez, a mob attacked the Jewish community in Seville, plundering, burning, and killing all who refused baptism. The anti-Semitic violence spread to other cities in Andalusia, Castile, Valencia, Aragon, and Catalonia. Sometimes the authorities tried to protect the Jews, who were legally the king's property. In Barcelona the city government tried to suppress the mob, but the riot became a popular revolt that threatened the rich and the clergy. About half of the two hundred thousand Castilian Jews converted to Christianity to save themselves; another twenty-five thousand were murdered or fled to Portugal and Granada. The survivors were to face even more discrimination and violence in the fifteenth century.

The Ottoman and Byzantine Empires. The fourteenth century also saw a great power rise at the other end of the Mediterranean. Under Osman I (r. 1280–1324) and his son Orhan Gazi (r. 1324–1359), the Ottoman dynasty became a formidable force in Anatolia and the Balkans, where political disunity opened the door for Ottoman advances (Map 13.3). The Ottomans were one of several Turkish

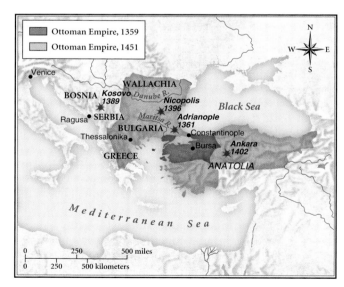

MAP 13.3 Ottoman Expansion in the Fourteenth and Fifteenth Centuries
The Balkans were the major theater of expansion for the Ottoman Empire, whose conquests also included Egypt and the North African coast. The Byzantine Empire was long reduced to the city of Constantinople and surrounded by the Ottomans before its final fall in 1453.

Janissaries in the Ottoman Army

Literally "new infantry," Janissaries were recruited from among Christian boys raised by the sultan.
They were distinguished by their ornamental, high headgear and their use of firearms, which made
them a particularly effective component of the Ottoman forces. Here a squad of Janissaries is shown
on parade, with a model of a Turkish war galley.
Österreichische Nationalbibliothek.

tribal confederations in central Asia. As converts to Islam and as warriors, the Ottoman cavalry raided Byzantine territory in an Islamic *jihad,* or holy war.

Under Murat I (r. 1360–1389), the Ottomans reduced the Byzantine Empire to the city of Constantinople and the status of a vassal state. In 1364, Murat defeated a joint Hungarian-Serbian army at the Maritsa River, alerting Europe for the first time to the threat of an Islamic invasion. Pope Urban V called for a crusade, but the Christian kingdoms in the west were already fighting in the Hundred Years' War. In the Balkans the Ottomans skillfully exploited Christian disunity, playing Serbian, Albanian, Wallachian, Bulgarian, and Byzantine interests against one another. Moreover, Venice, Genoa, and Ragusa each pursued separate commercial interests. Thus an Ottoman army allied not only with the Bulgarians but even with some Serbian princes won the battle of Kosovo (1389), destroying the last organized Christian resistance south of the Danube. The Ottomans secured control of southeastern Europe after 1396, when at Nicopolis they crushed a crusading army summoned by Pope Boniface IX.

The Ottoman invasion was more than a continuation of the struggle between Christendom and Islam. The battle for territory transcended the boundaries of faith. Christian princes also served the Ottoman Empire as vassals to the sultan. The Janissaries, Christian slave children raised by the sultan as Muslims, constituted the fundamental backbone of the Ottoman army. They formed a service class, the *devshirme*, which was both dependent on and loyal to the ruler.

At the sultan's court, Christian women were prominent in the harem; thus many Ottoman princes had Greek or Serbian mothers. In addition to the Janissaries, Christian princes and converts to Islam served in the emerging Ottoman administration. In areas conquered, existing religious and social structures remained intact when local people accepted Ottoman overlordship and paid taxes. Only in areas of persistent resistance did the Ottomans drive out or massacre the inhabitants, settling Turkish tribes in their place. A distinctive pattern of Balkan history was thus established at the beginning of the Ottoman conquest: the extreme diversity of ethnic and religious communities were woven together into the fabric of an efficient central state.

By the mid-fourteenth century, the territory of the Byzantine Empire consisted of only Constantinople, Thessalonika, and a narrow strip of land in modern-day Greece. During the fourteenth century, the Black Death, three civil wars between rivals to the throne, and numerous Ottoman incursions devastated Byzantine land and population. Constantinople was saved in 1402 from a five-year Ottoman siege only when Mongol invaders crushed another Ottoman army near Ankara in Anatolia. Although the empire's fortunes declined, Byzantium experienced a religious and cultural ferment, as the elites compensated for their loss of power in a search for past glory. The majority asserted the superiority of the Greek orthodox faith and opposed the reunion of the Roman and Greek churches, the political price for western European military aid. Many adhered to tradition, attacking any departures from ancient literary models and Byzantine institutions. A handful, such as the scholar George Gemistos (1353–1452), abandoned Christianity and embraced Platonic philosophy. Gemistos even changed his name (meaning "full" in Greek) to Plethon, its classical equivalent. The scholar Manuel Chrysoloras became professor of Greek in Florence in 1397, thus establishing the study of ancient Greece in western Europe. This revival of interest in Greek antiquity would eventually blossom into the broad cultural movement known as the Renaissance.

❖ The Plague and Society

Confronted with the rise of the Muslim Ottoman Empire to the east, Latin Christendom faced internally a series of crises that wrought havoc on its population and economy. In the fifty years after 1348, Europe lost one-third of its population to repeated outbreaks of the bubonic plague, which originated in central Asia and inflicted epidemic outbreaks in

China and the Middle East before it reached Europe. A healthy population could have resisted the plague. But Europeans were far from healthy: because food production failed to keep up with the great population increase of the thirteenth century, they had been suffering from famines and hunger for two generations before the first outbreak of the plague. In the face of massive deaths, a new climate of fear settled on the landscape. Some people tried to avert the "scourge of God" in rituals of religious fanaticism; others searched out scapegoats, killing Jews and burning synagogues.

Beyond these immediate reactions of fear, the demographic crisis also had important consequences for the economy. The catastrophic reduction in population caused falling demands for food and goods, leading to economic contraction, as farms and settlements were abandoned. Further symptoms of this social and economic crisis were social unrest, labor strife, rising wages, and falling investments. A mood of uncertainty prevailed in business, and women were excluded more and more from the urban economy.

Rise and Spread of the Plague

Well before the plague struck, European economic growth had slowed and then stopped. By 1300, the economy could no longer support Europe's swollen population. Having cleared forests and drained swamps, the peasant masses now divided their plots into ever smaller parcels and farmed marginal lands; their income and the quality of their diet eroded. In the great urban centers, where thousands depended on steady employment and cheap bread, a bad harvest, always followed by sharply rising food prices, meant hunger and eventual famine. A cooling of the European climate also contributed to the crisis in the food supply. Modern studies of tree rings indicate that fourteenth-century Europe entered a colder period, with a succession of severe winters beginning in 1315. The extreme cold upset an ecological system already overtaxed by human civilization. Crop failures were widespread. In many cities of northwestern Europe, the price of bread tripled in a month, and thousands starved to death. Some Flemish cities, for example, lost 10 percent of their population. But the Great Famine of 1315–1317 was only the first in a series of catastrophes confronting the overpopulated and undernourished society of fourteenth-century Europe. In midcentury death, in the form of an epidemic, mowed down masses of weakened bodies.

From its breeding ground in central Asia, the bubonic plague passed eastward into China, where it decimated the population and wiped out the remnants of the tiny Italian merchant community in Yangzhou. Bacteria-carrying fleas, living on black rats, transmitted the disease. They traveled back to Europe alongside valuable cargoes of silk, porcelain, and spices. In 1347, the Genoese colony in Caffa in the Crimea contracted the plague from the Mongols.

Fleeing by ship in a desperate but futile attempt to escape the disease, the Genoese in turn communicated the plague to other Mediterranean seaports. By January 1348, the plague had infected Sicily, Sardinia, Corsica, and Marseilles. Six months later the plague had spread to Aragon, all of Italy, the Balkans, and most of France. The disease then crept northward to Germany, England, and Scandinavia, reaching the Russian city of Novgorod in 1350 (Map 13.4).

Nothing like the Black Death, as this epidemic came to be called, had struck Europe since the great plague of the sixth century. The Italian writer

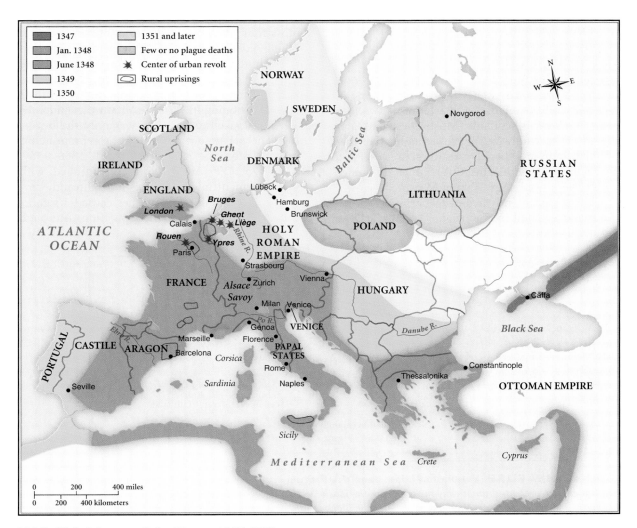

MAP 13.4 Advance of the Plague, 1347–1350
The gradual but deadly spread of the plague followed the roads and rivers of Europe. Note the earlier transmission by sea from the Crimea to the ports of the Mediterranean before the general spread to northern Europe.

Giovanni Boccaccio (1313–1375) reported the plague

first betrayed itself by the emergence of certain tumors in the groin or the armpits, some of which grew as large as a common apple, others as an egg . . . . From the two said parts of the body this . . . began to propagate and spread itself in all directions indifferently; after which the form of the malady began to change, black spots or livid making their appearance in many cases on the arm or the thigh or elsewhere, now few and large, now minute and numerous.

Inhabitants of cities, where crowding and filth increased the chances of contagion, died in massive numbers. Florence lost almost two-thirds of its population of ninety thousand; Siena lost half its people. Paris, the largest city of western Europe, came off relatively well, losing only a quarter of its two hundred thousand inhabitants. Most cities the plague visited on its deadly journey lost roughly half their population in less than a year. Rural areas seem to have suffered fewer deaths, but regional differences were pronounced. (See "Taking Measure," below.)

Helplessness and incomprehension worsened the terror wrought by the plague. The Black Death was not particular: old and young, poor and rich were equally affected, although the wealthy had a better chance of avoiding the disease if they escaped to their country estates before the epidemic hit their city. Medical knowledge of the time could not explain the plague's causes. The physicians at the University of Paris blamed the calamity on the stars. In a report prepared for King Philip VI of France in 1348, the professors of medicine described a conjunction of Saturn, Mars, and Jupiter in the house of Aquarius in 1345, resulting in widespread death and pestilence on earth. Various treatments were used in an attempt to combat the plague, ranging from bloodletting, a traditional cure to balance the body's four humors, to the commonsense remedy of lying quietly in bed and the desperate suggestion of breathing in the vapors of latrines. Many people believed that poisoned air caused the disease, and upon hearing of an outbreak, they walled in their neighbors, hoping in vain to contain the epidemic.

The devastation of 1348 was only the beginning. The plague cut down Europeans repeatedly. Further outbreaks occurred in 1361, 1368–1369, 1371, 1375, 1390, and 1405; they continued, with longer dormant intervals, into the eighteenth century. Together with wars, plagues caused a significant long-term decrease in population. Although

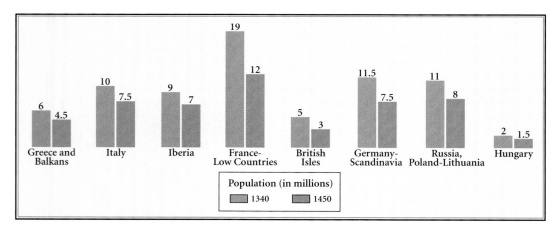

TAKING MEASURE Population Losses and the Plague

The bar chart represents dramatically the impact of the Black Death and the recurrent plagues between 1340 and 1450. More than a century after the Black Death, none of the regions of Europe had made up for the losses of population. The population of 1450 stood at about 75–80 percent of the pre-plague population. The hardest hit areas were France and the Low Countries, which also suffered from the devastations of the Hundred Years' War.

From Carlo M. Cipolla, ed., *Fontana Economic History of Europe: The Middle Ages.* (Great Britain: Collins/Fontana Books, 1974), 36.

general figures are unavailable, detailed local studies convey the magnitude of the destruction wreaked by the Black Death and war. In eastern Normandy, for example, the population in 1368 was only 42 percent of its height in 1314; and it declined still further in the fifteenth century.

Responses to the Plague: Flagellants, Preachers, and Jews

Some believed the plague was God's way of chastising a sinful world and sought to save themselves by repenting their sins. In 1349, bands of men and women wearing tattered clothes, marching in pairs, carrying flags, and following their own leaders appeared in southern Germany. When they reached a town or village, they visited the local church and, to the great astonishment of the congregation and the alarm of the clergy, sang hymns while publicly whipping themselves, according to strict rituals, until blood flowed. The flagellants, as they soon came to be called, cried out to God for mercy and called upon the congregation to repent their sins.

From southern Germany the flagellants moved throughout the Holy Roman Empire. In groups of several dozen to many hundred, they traveled and attracted great excitement. The flagellants' flamboyant piety moved many laypeople, but most of the clergy distrusted a lay movement that did not originate within the church hierarchy. At the inception of the movement, the flagellants recruited only from respectable social groups, such as artisans and merchants. Converts who joined the wandering bands, however, often came from the margins of society, and discipline began to break down. In 1350, the church declared the flagellants heretical and suppressed them.

In some communities the religious fervor aroused by the flagellants spawned violence against Jews. From 1348 to 1350, anti-Semitic persecutions, beginning in southern France and spreading through Savoy to the Holy Roman Empire, destroyed many Jewish communities in central and western Europe. Sometimes the clergy incited the attacks against the Jews, calling them Christ-killers, accusing them of poisoning wells and kidnapping and ritually slaughtering Christian children, and charging them with stealing and desecrating the host (the communion wafer that Catholics believed became the body of Christ during Mass). In towns throughout Europe,

Flagellant Procession
Flagellants hoping to stave off the Black Death are depicted in this German manuscript from Munich. The text describes their ritual of self-inflicted tortures during processions of penance, when they would call out loudly for the forgiveness of sins.
Bayerische Staatsbibliothek, Munich.

economic resentment fueled anti-Semitism as those in debt turned on creditors, often Jews who became rich from the commercial revolution of the thirteenth century. Perhaps most cynical were the nobility of Alsace, heavily indebted to Jewish bankers, who sanctioned the murder of Jews to avoid repaying money they had borrowed.

Many anti-Semitic incidents were spontaneous, with mobs plundering Jewish quarters and killing anyone who refused baptism. Authorities seeking a focus for the widespread anger and fear orchestrated some of the violence. Relying on chronicles, historians have long linked the arrival of the Black Death with anti-Jewish violence. More recent historical research shows that in some cities the anti-Semitic violence actually preceded the epidemic. This revised chronology of events demonstrates official

The Burning of Jews
While knights and noblewomen watch, an executioner carries more firewood to the pyre of Jews. There were many incidents of anti-Jewish violence in the fourteen century because Christians suspected Jews of desecrating the Eucharist and of kidnapping and murdering Christian children. This religious violence, arising out of the confrontation between Christianity and Judaism, had the opposite effect to that intended by Christians. Instead of converting, most Jews honored their martyrs and felt less incentive to accept the faith of their oppressors.
Bibliothèque Royale Albert 1er, Brussels.

complicity and even careful premeditation in the destruction of some Jewish communities. For example, the magistrates of Nuremberg obtained approval from Emperor Charles IV before organizing the 1349 persecution directed by the city government. Thousands of German Jews were slaughtered. Many fled to Poland, where the incidence of plague was low and where the authorities welcomed Jews as productive taxpayers. In western and central Europe, however, the persecutions destroyed the financial power of the Jews.

Consequences of the Plague

Although the Black Death took a horrible human toll, the disaster actually profited some people. In an overpopulated society with limited resources, massive death opened the ranks for advancement. For example, after 1350, landlords had difficulty acquiring new tenant farmers without making concessions in land contracts; fewer priests now competed for

the same number of benefices (ecclesiastical offices funded by an endowment), and workers received much higher wages because the supply of laborers had plummeted. The Black Death and the resulting decline in urban population meant a lower demand for grain relative to the supply and thus a drop in cereal prices. All across Europe noble landlords, whose revenues dropped as prices dropped, had to adjust to these new circumstances. Some revived seigneurial demands for labor services; others looked to their central government for legislation to regulate wages; and still others granted favorable terms to peasant proprietors, often after bloody peasant revolts. Many noblemen lost a portion of their wealth and a measure of their autonomy and political influence. Consequently, European nobles became more dependent on their monarchs and on war to supplement their incomes and enhance their power.

For the peasantry and the urban working population, the higher wages generally meant an improvement in living standards. To compensate for the lower demand and price for grain, many peasants and landlords turned to stock breeding and grape and barley cultivation. As European agriculture diversified, peasants and artisans consumed more beer, wine, meat, cheese, and vegetables, a better and more varied diet than their thirteenth-century forebears had eaten. The reduced cereal prices also stimulated sheep raising in place of farming, so that a portion of the settled population, especially in the English Midlands and in Castile, became migratory.

Because of the shrinking population and decreased demand for food, cultivating marginal fields was no longer profitable, and many settlements were simply abandoned. By 1450, for example, some 450 large English villages and many smaller hamlets had disappeared. In central Europe east of the Elbe River, where German peasants had migrated, large tracts of cultivated land reverted to forest. Estimates suggest that some 80 percent of all villages in parts of Thuringia (Germany) vanished.

Also as a result of the plague, production shifted from manufacturing for a mass market to a highly lucrative, if small, luxury market. The drastic loss in urban population had reduced the demand for such mass-manufactured goods as cloth. Fewer people now possessed proportionately greater concentrations of wealth. In the southern French city of Albi, for example, the proportion of citizens possessing more than 100 livres in per capita income doubled between 1343 and 1357, while the number of poor people, those with less than 10 livres, declined by half.

Faced with the possibility of imminent and untimely death, some of the urban populace sought immediate gratification. The Florentine Matteo Villani described the newfound desire for luxury in his native city in 1351. "The common people . . . wanted the dearest and most delicate foods . . . while children and common women clad themselves in all the fair and costly garments of the illustrious who had died." Those with means increased their consumption of luxuries: silk clothing, hats, doublets (snug-fitting men's jackets), and boots from Italy; expensive jewelry and spices from Asia became fashionable in northwestern Europe. Whereas agricultural prices continued to decline, prices of manufactured goods, particularly luxury items, remained constant and even rose as demand for them outstripped supply.

The long-term consequences of this new consumption pattern spelled the end for the traditional

Deserted Fields
Aerial photography has revealed the outlines of cultivated fields and old settlements in many areas of northern Europe invisible from the ground. These are the signs marking the expansion and contraction of human settlement and cultivation in fourteenth-century Europe before and after the Black Death. As the plague swept through the land, and as whole populations of smaller settlements died off, villages were deserted and cultivated fields reverted back to nature. In England, for example, of about 900 medieval churches, more than 225 were abandoned and nearly 250 were in ruins in the later half of the fourteenth century. This photograph shows the former cultivated fields of the village of Tusmore, Oxfordshire, whose inhabitants all died of the plague.
Copyright reserved Cambridge University, Collection of Air Photographs.

woolen industry that had produced for a mass market. Diminishing demand for wool caused hardships for woolworkers, and social and political unrest shook many older industrial centers dependent on the cloth industry. In the Flemish clothing center of Ypres, for example, production figures fell from a high of ninety thousand pieces of cloth in 1320 to fewer than twenty-five thousand by 1390. In Ghent, where 44 percent of all households were woolworkers and where some 60 percent of the working population depended on the textile industry, the woolen market's slump meant constant labor unrest.

Much more difficult to measure was the sense of economic insecurity. One trend, however, seemed clear: the increasingly restrictive labor market for women in the urban economy in this age of crisis. In the German city of Cologne, for example, more and more artisan guilds excluded women from their ranks. By the late fifteenth century the independent women's guilds had become a relic of the past. Everywhere, fathers favored sons and sons-in-law to succeed them in their crafts. Daughters and widows resisted this patriarchal regime in the urban economy. They were most successful in industries with the least regulations, such as in beer-brewing—where in Munich, for example, women held productive positions in this climate of economic recession.

❖ Challenges to Spiritual Authority

The crises of confidence and control that swept late medieval Europe extended to the papacy, the very symbol of Christian unity and authority. The popes' claim to supremacy in Christendom had never been unchallenged. Kings and princes contested the popes' dual authority as spiritual and temporal rulers; friars and preachers questioned their wealth and power; theologians doubted the monarchical pretensions of popes over general church councils; heretics and dissenters denied outright their claims of apostolic succession. While some voices opposed papal authority within the church, other movements offered alternative visions and institutions for the faithful's guidance and salvation.

Papal Monarchy and Its Critics

Papal government continued to grow even after the papal residence moved to Avignon in 1309. In the fourteenth century, the papacy's government and institutions were more sophisticated than those of secular states. A succession of popes, all lawyers by training, concentrated on consolidating the financial and legal powers of the church, mainly through appointments and taxes. Claiming the right to assign all benefices, the popes gradually secured authority over the clergy throughout western and central Europe. Under the skillful guidance of John XXII (r. 1316–1334), papal rights increased incrementally without causing much protest. By 1350, the popes had secured the right to appoint all ma-

jor benefices and many minor ones. To gain these lucrative positions, potential candidates often made gifts to the papal court. The imposition of papal taxes on all benefice holders developed from taxation to finance the Crusades. Out of these precedents the papacy instituted a regular system of papal taxation that produced the money it needed to consolidate papal government.

Papal government, the curia, consisted of the pope's personal household, the College of Cardinals, and the church's financial and judicial apparatus. Combining elements of monarchy and oligarchy, the curia developed a bureaucracy that paralleled the organization of secular government. The pope's relatives often played a major role in his household; many popes came from extended noble lineages, and they often gave their family members preferential treatment.

After the pope, the cardinals, as a collective body, were the most elevated entity in the church. Like great nobles in royal courts, the cardinals, many of them nobles themselves, advised and aided the pope. They maintained their own households, employing scores of scribes, servants, and retainers. Most posts in the papal bureaucracy went to clerics with legal training, thus accentuating the juristic and administrative character of the highest spiritual authority in Christendom. During the fourteenth and fifteenth centuries, the papal army also grew, as the popes sought to restore and control the Papal States in Italy.

This growing papal monarchy was sharply criticized by members of the mendicant orders, who denounced the papal pretension to worldly power and wealth. William of Ockham (c. 1285–1349), an English Franciscan who was one of the most eminent theologians of his age, believed that church power derived from the congregation of the faithful, both laity and clergy, not from the pope or the church council. Rejecting the confident synthesis of Christian doctrine and Aristotelian philosophy by Thomas Aquinas, Ockham believed that universal concepts had no reality in nature but instead existed only as mere representations, names in the mind— a philosophy that came to be called *nominalism*. Perceiving and analyzing such concepts as "man" or "papal infallibility" offered no assurance that the concepts expressed truth. Observation and human reason were limited as the means to understand the universe and to know God. Consequently, God might be capricious, contradictory, or many rather than one. Denying the possibility of an evil or erratic God, Ockham emphasized the covenant between God and his faithful. God promises to act consistently—for example, to reward virtue and punish vice. Ockham stressed simplicity in his explanations of universal concepts. His insistence that shorter explanations were superior to wordy ones became known as "Ockham's razor." Imprisoned by Pope John XXII for heresy, Ockham escaped in 1328 and found refuge with Emperor Louis of Bavaria.

Another antipapal refugee at the imperial court was Marsilius of Padua, a citizen of an Italian commune, a physician and lawyer by training, and rector of the University of Paris. Marsilius attacked the very basis of papal power in *The Defender of the Peace* (1324). The true church, Marsilius argued, was constituted by the people, who had the right to select the head of the church, either through the body of the faithful or through a "human legislator." Papal power, Marsilius asserted, was the result of historical usurpation, and its exercise represented tyranny. In 1327, John XXII, the living target of the treatise, decreed the work heretical.

The Great Schism, 1378–1417

By the second half of the fourteenth century, the Avignon papacy had taken on a definitive French character. All five popes elected between 1305 and 1378 were natives of southern France, as were many of the cardinals and most of the curia. Moreover, French parishes provided half of the papacy's income. Subjected to pressure from the French monarchy and turning increasingly secular in its opulence and splendor, the papacy was lambasted by the Italian poet Francesco Petrarch as being "in Babylonian Captivity," like the Jews of ancient Israel who were exiled by their Babylonian conquerors. Nonetheless, Gregory XI, elected pope in 1371, was determined to return to Rome, where he expected to exert greater moral force to organize a crusade against the Muslim Ottomans. Before he could carry out his plans, however, Florence declared war against the Papal States in 1375, and Gregory hastened to Rome to prevent the collapse of his territorial power in Italy.

When Gregory died in 1378, sixteen cardinals—one Spanish, four Italian, and eleven French—met in Rome to elect the new pope. Although many in the curia were homesick for Avignon, the Roman people, determined to keep the papacy and its revenues in Rome, clamored for the election of a Roman. An unruly crowd rioted outside the conclave, drowning out the cardinals' discussions. Fearing for their lives, the cardinals elected the archbishop of Bari, an Italian, who took the title Urban VI. If the cardinals thought they had elected a weak man who would both do their bidding and satisfy the Romans, they were wrong: Urban immediately tried to curb the cardinals' power. In response, thirteen cardinals elected another pope, Clement VII, and returned to Avignon.

Thus began the Great Schism, which was perpetuated by political divisions in Europe (Map 13.5). Charles V of France, who did not want the papacy to return to Rome, immediately recognized Clement, his cousin, as did the rulers of Sicily, Scotland, Castile, Aragon, Navarre, Portugal, Ireland, and Savoy. An enemy of Charles V, Richard II of England, professed allegiance to Urban and was followed by the rulers of Flanders, Poland, Hungary, most of the empire, and central and northern Italy. Faithful Christians were equally divided in their loyalties. Even the greatest mystic of the age—Catherine of Siena (1347–1380), who told of her mystical unions with God and spiritual ecstasies in more than 350 letters and was later canonized a saint—found herself forced to take sides. Catherine supported Urban. But another holy man, Vincent Ferrer (1350–1419), a popular Dominican preacher, supported Clement. All Christians theoretically found themselves deprived of the means of salvation, as bans from Rome and Avignon each placed a part of Christian Europe under interdict, or censure from participation in most sacraments and from Christian burial. Because neither pope would step down willingly, the leading intellectuals in the church tried to end the schism. Success would elude them for nearly forty years.

The Conciliar Movement

According to canon law, only a pope could summon a general council of the church, a sort of parliament of all Christians. But given the state of confusion in Christendom, many intellectuals argued that the crisis justified calling a general council to represent the body of the faithful, over and against the head of the church. Jean Gerson, chancellor of the

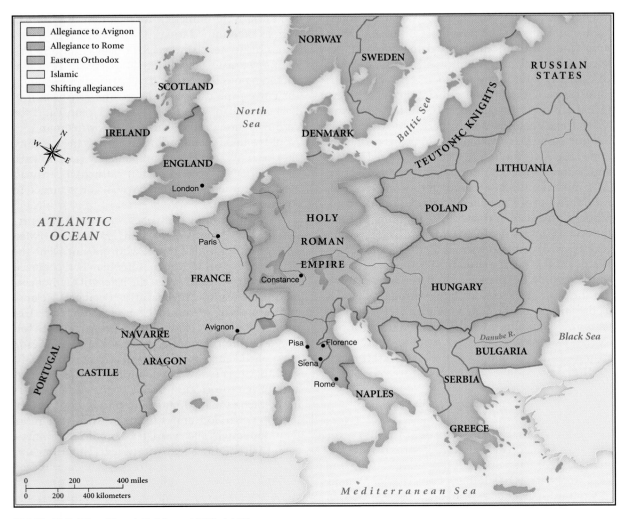

MAP 13.5 The Great Schism, 1378–1417
The allegiances to Roman and Avignon popes followed the political divisions between the European monarchs. The Great Schism weakened the Latin West during a period of Islamic expansion through the Ottoman Empire.

University of Paris, asserted that "the pope can be removed by a general council celebrated without his consent and against his will." He justified his claim by reasoning that "normally a council is not legally . . . celebrated without papal calling. . . . But, as in grammar and in morals, general rules have exceptions. . . . Because of these exceptions a superior law has been ordained to interpret the law."

The first attempt to resolve the question of church authority came in 1409, at the Council of Pisa, attended by cardinals who had defected from the two popes. The council asserted its supremacy by declaring both popes deposed and electing a new pontiff, Alexander V. When the popes at Rome and Avignon refused to yield to the authority of the council, Christian Europe found itself in the embarrassing position of choosing among three popes. Pressure to hold another council then came from central Europe, where a new heretical movement, ultimately known as Hussitism, undermined orthodoxy from Bohemia to central Germany. Threatened politically by challenges to church authority, Emperor Sigismund pressed Pope John XXIII, the successor to Alexander (who had died ten months after being elected), to convene a church council at Constance in 1414.

The cardinals, bishops, and theologians assembled in Constance felt compelled to combat heresy, heal the schism, and reform the church. They ordered Jan Hus, the Prague professor and inspiration behind the Hussite movement, burned at the stake in spite of an imperial safe conduct he had been promised, but this act failed to suppress dissent. They deposed John XXIII, the "Pisan pope," because of tyrannical behavior, condemning him as an antipope. The Roman pope, Gregory XII, accepted the council's authority and resigned in 1415 (having been elected in 1406). At its closing in 1417, the council also deposed Benedict XIII (Clement's successor), the "Spanish mule," who refused to abdicate the Avignon papacy and lived out his life in a fortress in Spain, still regarding himself as pope and surrounded by his own curia. The rest of Christendom, however, hailed Martin V, the council's appointment, as the new pope, thus ending the Great Schism. The council had taken a stand against heresy and had achieved unity under one pope.

Dissenters and Heretics

Religious conflict in the later Middle Ages took a variety of forms. The papacy struggled with its critics within the church but found religious dissension outside the church even more threatening.

Free Spirits, Beguines, and Beghards.   One movement of dissent, the Free Spirits, did not oppose the pope, yet the church still labeled them heretics. The Free Spirits, found mostly in northern Europe, practiced an extreme form of mysticism. They asserted that humans and God were of the same essence and that individual believers could attain salvation, even sanctity, without the church and its sacraments. In the fourteenth century, the Free Spirits found converts among the Beguines, pious laywomen who lived together, and the Beghards, men who did not belong to a particular religious order but who led pious lives and begged for their sustenance. Living in community houses (*beguinages*), the Beguines imitated the convent lives of nuns but did not submit to clerical control. First prevalent in northern Europe, beguinages sprang up rapidly in the Low Countries and the Rhineland, regions of heavy urbanization. This essentially urban development represented the desire by many urban women to achieve salvation through piety and good works, as

many began to feel that the clergy did not adequately address their spiritual needs.

For the church, the existence of Free Spirits among the Beghards and Beguines raised the larger question of ecclesiastical control, for this development threatened to eliminate the boundary between the laity and the clergy. In the 1360s, Emperor Charles IV and Pope Urban V extended the Inquisition to Germany in a move to crush this heresy. In the cities of the Rhineland, fifteen mass trials took place, most around the turn of the fifteenth century. By condemning the "heretics" and requiring beguinages to be under the control of the mendicant orders, the church contained potential dissent. Throughout the fifteenth century the number of beguinages continued to drop.

Lollards.   In England, intellectual dissent, social unrest, and nationalist sentiment combined to create a powerful anticlerical movement that the church hierarchy labeled Lollardy (from *lollar*, meaning "idler"). John Wycliffe (c. 1330–1384), who inspired the movement, was an Oxford professor. Initially employed as a royal apologist in the struggle between state and church, Wycliffe gradually developed ideas that challenged the very foundations of the Roman church. His treatise *On the Church*, composed in 1378, advanced the view that the true church was a community of believers rather than a clerical hierarchy. In other writings, Wycliffe repudiated monasticism, excommunication, the Mass, and the priesthood, substituting reliance on Bible reading and individual conscience in place of the official church as the path to salvation. Responsibility for church reform, Wycliffe believed, rested with the king, whose authority he claimed exceeded that of the pope.

At Oxford, Wycliffe gathered around him like-minded intellectuals, and together they influenced and reflected a widespread anticlericalism in late medieval England. Wycliffe actively promoted the use of English in religious writing. He and his disciples attempted to translate the Bible into English and to popularize its reading throughout all ranks of society, although he died before completing the project. His supporters included members of the gentry, but most were artisans and other humbler people who had some literacy. Religious dissent was key in motivating the 1381 peasant uprising in England, and the radical preacher John Ball was only

Burning of a Heretic
Execution by fire was the usual method of killing heretics. This illustration shows the burning of a Lollard, a follower of the teachings of Wycliffe, who opposed the established church. While heretics were condemned by the Church, their executions were at the hands of secular authorities, who are present here.
Hulton Getty/Liaison Agency.

one of the many common priests who supported the revolt. Real income for parish priests had fallen steadily after the Black Death, and as a result the sympathy of the impoverished clergy lay with the common folk against the great bishops, abbots, and lords of the realm.

After Wycliffe's death, the English bishops suppressed intellectual dissent at Oxford. In 1401, Parliament passed a statute to prosecute heretics. The only Lollard revolt occurred when John Oldcastle, a knight inspired by Wycliffe's ideas, plotted an assault on London. It was crushed in 1414. But in spite of persistent persecutions, Lollardy survived underground during the fifteenth century, to resurface during the convulsive religious conflict of the early sixteenth century known as the Reformation.

The Hussite Revolution

The most profound challenge to papal authority in the later Middle Ages came from Bohemia. Here the spiritual, intellectual, political, and economic criticisms of the papacy that sprang up in other countries fused in one explosive spark. Religious dissent quickly became the vehicle for a nationalist uprising and a social revolution.

Under Emperor Charles IV the pace of economic development and social change in the Holy Roman Empire had quickened in the mid-fourteenth century. Prague, the capital, became one of Europe's great cities: the new silver mine at Kutná Hora boosted Prague's economic growth, and the first university in the empire was founded there in 1348. Prague was located in Bohemia, a part of the Holy Roman Empire settled by a Slavic people, the Czechs, since the early Middle Ages. Later, many German merchants and artisans migrated to Bohemian cities, and Czech peasants, uprooted from the land, flocked to the cities in search of employment. This diverse society became a potentially explosive mass when heightened expectations of commercial and intellectual growth collided with the grim realities of the plague and economic problems in the late fourteenth century. Tax protests, urban riots, and ethnic conflicts signaled growing unrest, but it was religious discontent that became the focus for popular revolt.

Critics of the clergy, often clergy themselves, decried the moral conduct of priests and prelates who held multiple benefices, led dissolute lives, and ignored their pastoral duties. How could the clergy, living in a state of mortal sin, legitimately perform the sacraments? critics asked. Advocating greater lay participation in the Mass and in the reading of Scripture, religious dissenters drew some of their ideas from the writings of the English intellectual John Wycliffe. Among those influenced by Wycliffe's ideas were Jan Hus (d. 1415) and his follower Jerome of Prague (d. 1416), both Prague professors, ethnic Czechs, and leaders of a reform party in Bohemia. Although the reform party attracted adherents from all Czech-speaking social groups, the German minority, who dominated the university and urban elites in Prague, opposed it out of ethnic rivalry. The Bohemian nobility protected Hus; the common clergy rebelled against the bishops; and the artisans and workers in Prague were ready to back the reform party by force. These disparate social interests all focused on one symbolic but passionately felt religious demand: the ability to receive the Eucharist as both bread and wine at Mass. In traditional Roman liturgy, the chalice was reserved for the clergy; the Utraquists, as their opponents called them (from *utraque*, Latin for "both"), also wanted to drink wine from the chalice, to achieve a measure of equality between laity and clergy.

Despite a guarantee of safety from Emperor Sigismund, Hus was burned at the stake while attending the Council of Constance in 1415. Hus's death caused a national uproar, and the reform movement, which had thus far focused only on religious issues, burst forth as a national revolution.

Sigismund's initial repression of the revolt in the provinces was brutal, and many dissenters were massacred. To organize their defense, Hussites gathered at a mountain in southern Bohemia, which they called Mount Tabor after the mountain in the New Testament where the transfiguration of Christ took place. Now called Taborites, they began to restructure their community according to biblical injunctions. Like the first Christian church, they initially practiced communal ownership of goods and thought of themselves as the only true Christians awaiting the

The Hussite Revolution, 1415–1436

return of Christ and the end of the world. As their influence spread, the Taborites compromised with the surrounding social order, collecting tithes from peasants and retaining magistrates in towns under their control. Taborite leaders were radical priests who ministered to the community in the Czech language, exercised moral and judicial leadership, and even led the people into battle.

Modeling themselves after the Israelites of the Old Testament and the first Christians of the New Testament, the Taborites impressed even their enemies. Aeneas Sylvius Piccolomini, the future Pope Pius II (r. 1458–1464), observed that "among the Taborites you will hardly find a woman who cannot demonstrate familiarity with the Old and New Testaments." The Taborite army, drawn from many social classes and led by priests, repelled five attacks by the "crusader" armies from neighboring Germany, triumphing over their enemies using a mixture of religious fervor and military technology, such as a wagon train to protect the infantry from cavalry charges. Resisting all attempts to crush them, the Czech revolutionaries eventually gained the right from the papacy to receive the Eucharist as both bread and wine, a practice that continued until the sixteenth century.

❖ The Social Order and Cultural Change

An abundance of written and visual records documenting the lives of all social groups has survived from the fourteenth century. Sources ranging from chronicles of dynastic conflicts and noble chivalry to police records of criminality paint a vivid picture of late medieval society, showing the changed relations between town and country, noble and commoner, and men and women. These sources reveal Europeans' struggles to adjust to uncertainties and changes related to the plague, war, and religious dissent. New material wealth allowed some to enjoy more comfortable lives, but the disruptions and dislocations caused by various crises forced many on the margins of society—the poor, beggars, and prostitutes—into a violent underworld of criminality.

One response to the upheavals of the later Middle Ages was the blossoming of a broad cultural movement. As the Byzantines recovered their appreciation of Greek antiquity, so did Italians revive ancient Roman culture. This movement focused initially on imitating classical Latin rhetoric, but it later extended to other disciplines, such as the study of history. The brilliant achievements in the visual arts and vernacular literature realized at this time were the beginnings of the great movement known as the *Renaissance* (French for "rebirth").

The Household

Family life and the household economy formed the fabric of late medieval society. In contrast to the nobility and great merchants, whose power rested on their lineages, most Europeans lived in a more confined social world, surrounded by smaller families and neighbors. The focus of their lives was the house, where parents and children, and occasionally a grandparent or other relative, lived together. This pattern generally characterized both urban and rural society. In some peasant societies, such as in Languedoc (southern France), brothers and their families shared the same roof; but the nuclear family was by far the norm.

For artisans and peasants of medium wealth, the family dwelling usually consisted of a two-to-three-story building in the city and a single farmhouse in the countryside. For these social groups the household generally served as both work and private space; shopkeepers and craftspeople used their ground floors as workshops and storefronts, reserving the upper stories for family life. By today's standards, late medieval urban life was intolerably crowded, with little privacy. Neighbors could easily spy on each other from adjoining windows or even come to blows, as did two Florentine neighbors who argued over the installation of a second-story latrine that emptied from one's property to the other's. In rural areas the family house served a variety of purposes, not least to shelter the farm animals during the winter.

In a society with an unequal distribution of power between women and men, the worlds of commerce and agriculture were those in which women came closest to partnership with their husbands. As a consequence of the plague and labor shortages, women found themselves in relatively favorable working positions. In cities all over Europe, women worked in retail trade. They sold dairy products,

June
Real farmwork in fourteenth-century France was never as genteel as in this miniature painting, part of a series illustrating the months of the year in the beautiful devotional book, the Book of Hours *of the Duke de Berry. Nevertheless, the scene does faithfully represent haying and suggests the gendered division of village labor, as the men swing their scythes and the women wield rakes.*
Giraudon/Art Resource, NY.

meat, cloth, salt, flour, and fish; brewed beer; spun and wove cloth; and often acted informally as their husbands' business partners. Although excluded from many crafts and professions and barred from all but a few guilds, fourteenth-century women played a crucial role in the urban economy.

The degree to which women participated in public life, however, varied with class and region.

February

As in all the miniatures in the Duke de Berry's prayer book, this cozy scene shows that the late-medieval nobility liked to imagine their peasants and livestock securely housed in warm, separate shelters, while the customary work of rural society goes on peacefully. But in reality, peasants led a hard life, faced with the uncertainties of weather and the depredations of war.

Giraudon/Art Resource, NY.

Women in Mediterranean Europe, especially in upper-class families, lived more circumscribed lives than their counterparts in northern Europe. In the southern regions, for example, women could not dispose of personal property without the consent of males, be they fathers, husbands, or grown sons. In the north, women regularly represented themselves in legal transactions and testified in court.

Partnership in marriage characterized the peasant household. Although men and women performed different tasks, such as plowing and spinning, many chores required mutual effort. During harvests, all family members were mobilized. The men usually reaped with sickles, while the women gleaned the fields. Viticulture (the cultivation of grapes for wine making) called for full cooperation between the sexes: both men and women worked equally in picking grapes and trampling them to make wine.

Because the rural household constituted the basic unit of agricultural production, most men and women remarried quickly after a spouse died. The incidence of households headed by a single person, usually a poor widow, was much lower in villages than in cities. Studies of court records for fourteenth-century English villages show relatively few reports of domestic violence, a result perhaps of the economic dependency between the sexes. Violence against women was more visible in urban societies, where many women worked as servants and prostitutes.

The improved material life of the middle classes was represented in many visual images of the later Middle Ages. Italian and Flemish paintings of the late fourteenth and early fifteenth centuries depict the new comforts of urban life such as fireplaces and private latrines and show an interest in material objects: beds, chests, rooms, curtains, and buildings provide the ubiquitous background of Italian paintings of the period. An illustration in *The Book of Hours* (1416), commissioned by the duke of Berry, brother of the French king, depicts a romanticized view of country life that might have characterized the peasant elite. Surrounded by a low fence, the family compound includes a house, a granary, and a shed. Animals and humans no longer intermingle, as they did in the thirteenth century and still did in poorer peasant households. The picture shows peasants warming themselves and drying their laundry in front of the fire, while the sheep are safe and warm in the shed.

The Underclass

If family life and the household economy formed the fabric of late medieval society, the world of poverty and criminality represented its torn fringes. Indeed, the boundary between poor and criminal was very thin. Fourteenth-century society rested on a broad base of underclass—poor peasants and laborers in the countryside, workers and servants in the cities. Lower still were the marginal elements of society, straddling the line between legality and criminality.

Men populated the violent criminal underworld. Organized gangs prowled the larger cities. In Paris, a city teeming with thieves, thugs, beggars, prostitutes, and vagabonds, the Hundred Years' War led to a sharp rise in crime. Gang members were mostly artisans who vacillated between work and crime. Sometimes disguised as clerics, they robbed, murdered, and extorted from prostitutes. Often they served as soldiers. War was no longer an occupation reserved for knights but had become a vocation that absorbed young men from poor backgrounds. Initiated into a life of plunder and killing, soldiers adjusted poorly to civilian life after discharge; between wars, these men turned to crime.

A central feature of social marginality was mobility. Those on society's fringes were mostly young, lacking stable families; they wandered extensively, begging and stealing. Criminals were even present among the clergy. While some were laymen who assumed clerical disguises to escape the law, others were bona fide clerics who turned to crime to make ends meet during an age of steadily declining clerical income. "Decent society" treated these marginal elements with suspicion and hatred. During the later Middle Ages, attitudes concerning poverty hardened. Townspeople and peasants distrusted travelers and vagabonds. New laws restricted vagabonds and begging clerics, although cities and guilds also began building hospitals and almshouses to deal with these social problems.

Women featured prominently in the underclass, reflecting the unequal distribution of power between the sexes. In Mediterranean Europe, some 90 percent of slaves were women in domestic servitude. Their actual numbers were small—several hundred in fourteenth-century Florence, for example—because only rich households could afford slaves. They came from Muslim or Greek Orthodox countries and usually served in upper-class households in the great commercial city republics of Venice, Florence, and Ragusa. Urban domestic service was also the major employment for girls from the countryside, who worked to save money for their dowries. In addition to the usual household chores, women also worked as wet nurses.

Given their exclusion from many professions and their powerlessness, many poor women found prostitution the only available way to make a living. Male violence also forced some women into prostitution: rape stripped away their social respectability and any prospects for marriage. Condemned by the church, prostitutes were tolerated throughout the Middle Ages, but in the fourteenth and fifteenth centuries the government intensified its attempts to control sexuality by institutionalizing prostitution. Restricted to particular quarters in cities, supervised by officials, sometimes under direct government management, prostitutes found themselves confined to brothels, increasingly controlled by males. In legalizing and controlling prostitution, officials aimed to maintain the public order. In Florence such state sponsorship was intended to check homosexuality and concubinage by offering female sexuality to young men who did not have the means to hire prostitutes on their own. Female sexuality directed by the state in this way also helped define and limit the role of women in society at large.

Hard Times for Business

Compared with the commercial prosperity of the twelfth and thirteenth centuries, the later Middle Ages was an age of retrenchment for business. As the fourteenth-century crises afflicted the business community, a climate of pessimism and caution permeated commerce, especially during the second half of the century.

The first major crisis that undermined Italian banks was caused by the Hundred Years' War, during which the English king Edward III borrowed heavily from the largest Italian banking houses, the Bardi and Peruzzi of Florence. With many of their assets tied up in loans to the English monarchy, the Italian bankers had no choice but to extend new credits, hoping vainly to recover their initial investments. In the early 1340s, however, Edward defaulted. Adding to their problems, the Florentine bankers were forced to make war loans to their own government. These once-illustrious and powerful banks could not rebound from the losses they incurred, and both of them fell.

This breakdown in the most advanced economic sector reflected the general recession in the European economy. Merchants were less likely to take risks and more willing to invest their money in government bonds than in production and commerce. Fewer merchants traveled to Asia, partly

IMPORTANT DATES

1315–1317 Great Famine in Europe

1324 Marsilius of Padua denies the legitimacy of papal supremacy in *The Defender of the Peace*

1328 Pope John XXII imprisons the English theologian William of Ockham for criticizing papal power

1337–1453 Hundred Years' War

1348–1350 First outbreak in Europe of the Black Death

1349–1351 Anti-Jewish persecutions in the empire

1358 Jacquerie uprising in France

1378 Beginning of the Great Schism in the church; Ciompi rebellion in Florence; John Wycliffe's treatise *On the Church* asserts that the true church is a community of believers

1381 English peasant uprising

1389 Ottomans defeat Serbs at Kosovo

1414 Wycliffe's followers, called Lollards, rebel in England

1414–1417 Council of Constance ends the Great Schism

1415 Execution of Jan Hus; Hussite revolution begins

1430 Joan of Arc leads French to victory at siege of Orléans

because of the danger of attack by Ottoman Turks on the overland routes that had once been protected by the Mongols. The Medici of Florence, who would dominate Florentine politics in the next century, stuck close to home, investing part of their banking profits in art and politics and relying mostly on business agents to conduct their affairs in other European cities.

Historians have argued that this fourteenth-century economic depression diverted capital away from manufacturing and into investments in the arts and luxuries for immediate consumption. Instead of plowing their profits back into their businesses, merchants acquired land, built sumptuous townhouses, purchased luxury items, and invested in bonds. During the last decades of the fourteenth century, the maritime insurance rates in the great merchant republics of Venice and Genoa rose, also reflecting the general lack of confidence in business.

The most important trade axis continued to link Italy with the Low Countries. Italian cities produced silk, wool, jewelry, and other luxury goods that northern Europeans desired, and Italian merchants also imported spices, gold, and other coveted products from Asia and Africa. Traveling either by land through Lyons or by sea around Gibraltar, these products reached Bruges, Ghent, and Antwerp, where they were shipped to England, northern Germany, Poland, and Scandinavia. The reverse flow carried raw materials and silver, the latter to help balance the trade between northern Europe and the Mediterranean. Diminished production and trade eventually caused turmoil in northern Europe and a crisis for financiers in the Low Countries. Bruges, the financial center for northwestern Europe, saw its power fade during the fifteenth century when a succession of its money changers went bankrupt. The Burgundian dukes eventually enacted a series of monetary laws that undermined Bruges's financial and banking community and, by extension, the city's political autonomy as well.

The Flourishing of Vernacular Literature and the Birth of Humanism

From the epics and romances of the twelfth and thirteenth centuries, vernacular literature blossomed in the fourteenth. Poetry, stories, and chronicles composed in Italian, French, English, and other national languages helped articulate a new sense of aesthetics. No longer did Latin and church culture dominate the intellectual life of Europe, and no longer were writers principally clerics or aristocrats.

Middle-Class Writers and Noble Patrons. The great writers of late medieval Europe were of urban middle-class origins, from families that had done well in government or church service or commercial enterprises. Unlike the medieval troubadours, with their aristocratic backgrounds, the men and women who wrote vernacular literature in this age typically came from the cities, and their audience was the literate laity. Francesco Petrach (1304–1374), the poet laureate of Italy's vernacular literature, and his younger contemporary and friend Giovanni Boccaccio (1313–1375) were both Florentine. Petrarch was born in Arezzo, where his father, a notary, lived in political exile from Florence. Boccaccio's father worked for the Florentine banking firm of Bardi in Paris, where Boccaccio was born. Geoffrey Chaucer (c. 1342–1400) was the first great vernacular poet of medieval England. His father was a wealthy wine merchant; Chaucer worked as a servant to the king and controller of customs in London. Even writers who celebrated the life of the nobility were children of commoners. Although born in Valenciennes to a family of moneylenders and merchants, Jean Froissart (1333?–c. 1405), whose chronicle vividly describes the events of the Hundred Years' War, was an ardent admirer of chivalry. Christine de Pisan (1364–c. 1430), the official biographer of the French king, was the daughter of a Venetian municipal counselor.

Life in all its facets found expression in the flourishing vernacular literature, as writers told of love, greed, and salvation. Boccaccio's *Decameron* popularized the short story, as the characters in this novella tell sensual and bizarre tales in the shadow of the Black Death. These stories draw on Boccaccio's own experiences in banking and commerce. Members of different social orders parade themselves in Chaucer's *Canterbury Tales,* journeying together on a pilgrimage. He describes a merchant on horseback:

> *A marchant was ther with a forked berd*
> *In mottelee, and hye on horse he sat*
> *up-on his heed a Flaundrish bever hat*
> *his botes clasped faire and fetisly . . .*
> *For sothe he was a worthy man withalle*
> *but sooth to seyn, I noot how men him calle.*

Chaucer also vividly portrayed other social classes—yeomen, London guildsmen, and minor officials.

Noble patronage was crucial to the growth of vernacular literature, a fact reflected in the careers of the most famous writers. Perhaps closest to the model of an independent man of letters, Petrarch nonetheless relied on powerful patrons at various times. His early career began at the papal court in Avignon, where his father worked as a notary; during the 1350s, he enjoyed the protection and patronage of the Visconti duke of Milan. For Boccaccio, who started out in the Neapolitan world of commerce, the court of King Robert of Naples initiated him into the world of letters. Chaucer served in administrative posts and on many diplomatic missions, during which he met his two Italian counterparts. Noble patronage also shaped the literary creations of Froissart and Christine de Pisan. Com-

Poet and Queen
Christine de Pisan, kneeling, presents a manuscript of her poems to Isabelle of Bavaria, the queen of France. Isabelle's royal status is marked by the French coat of arms, the fleur-de-lis that decorates the bedroom walls. The sumptuous interior (chairs, cushions, tapestry, paneled ceiling, glazed and shuttered windows) was typical of aristocratic domestic architecture. Even in the intimacy of her bedroom, Queen Isabelle, like all royal personages, was constantly attended and almost never alone (note her ladies-in-waiting).
The British Library Picture Library, London.

missioned to write the official biography of King Charles V, Christine would have been unable to produce most of her writings without the patronage of women in the royal household. She presented her most famous work, *The Book of the City of Ladies* (1405), a defense of women's reputation and virtue, to Isabella of Bavaria, the queen of France and wife of Charles VI. Christine's last composition was a poem praising Joan of Arc, restorer of French royal fortunes and, like Christine herself, a distinguished woman in a world otherwise dominated by men.

Classical Revival. Vernacular literature blossomed not at the expense of Latin but alongside a classical revival. In spite of the renown of their Italian writings, Petrarch and Boccaccio, for example, took great pride in their Latin works. Latin represented the language of salvation and was also the international language of learning. Professors taught and wrote in Latin; students spoke it as best they could; priests celebrated Mass and dispensed sacraments in Latin; and theologians composed learned

Paradise Lost
This fourteenth-century paint-ing by the Sienese Giovanni di Paolo depicts the expulsion of Adam and Eve from the Garden of Eden. At right, an angel chases away the ancestors of humanity. At left, Paradise is the core around which the seven celestial spheres rotate, propelled by the action of God. By positioning Adam and Eve to the right-hand side of the panel, Paolo dramati-cally represents their expulsion from the Garden of Eden.
The Metropolitan Museum of Art, Robert Lehman Collection, 1975. (1975.1.31) Photograph © 1981 the Metropolitan Museum of Art.

treatises in Latin. Church Latin was very different from the Latin of the ancient Romans, both in syntax and in vocabulary. In the second half of the fourteenth century, writers began to imitate the rather antiquated "classical" Latin of Roman literature. In the forefront of this literary and intellectual movement, Petrarch traveled to many monasteries in search of long-ignored Latin manuscripts. For writers like Petrarch, medieval church Latin was an artificial, awkward language, whereas classical Latin and, after its revival, Greek were the mother tongues of the ancients. Thus the classical writings of Rome and Greece represented true vernacular literature, only more authentic, vivid, and glorious than the poetry and prose written in Italian and other contemporary European languages. Classical allusions and literary influences abound in the works of Boccaccio, Chaucer, Christine de Pisan, and others. The new intellectual fascination with the ancient past also stimulated translations of classical works into the vernacular.

This attempt to emulate the virtues and learning of the ancients gave rise to a new intellectual movement: humanism. For humanists the study of history and literature was the chief means of iden-

tifying with the glories of the ancient world. By the early fifteenth century, the study of classical Latin had become fashionable among a small intellectual elite, first in Italy and gradually throughout Europe. Reacting against the painstaking logic and abstract language of the scholastic philosophy that predominated in the medieval period, the humanists of the Renaissance preferred eloquence and style in their discourse, imitating the writings of Cicero and other great Roman authors.

Italian lawyers and notaries had a long-standing interest in classical rhetoric because eloquence was a skill essential to their professions. Gradually the imitation of ancient Roman rhetoric led to the absorption of ancient ideas. In the writings of Roman historians such as Livy and Tacitus, fifteenth-century Italian civic elites (many of them lawyers) found echoes of their own devout patriotism. Between 1400 and 1430 in Florence, a time of war and crisis, the study of the humanities evolved into a republican ideology that historians call "civic humanism." In the early fifteenth century, the Florentines waged a highly successful propaganda war on behalf of virtuous republican Florence against tyrannical Milan, invoking the memory of the overthrow of Etruscan

MAPPING THE WEST   Europe, c. 1430

Two of the dynamic regions of expansion lie in the southeastern and southwestern sectors of this map: the Ottoman Empire, which continued its attacks into central Europe and the Mediterranean, and the Iberian countries that opposed Muslim advances by their own Crusades and maritime expansions. While England, France, Iberia, and the Balkans were consolidated into large political entities, central Europe and Italy remained fragmented. Yet it was these two fragmented regions that gave Europe the cultural and technological innovations of the age.

tyrants by the first Romans. Thus the study of ancient civilization was not only an antiquarian quest but a call to public service and political action.

Conclusion

Between 1320 and 1430, Europe was a civilization in crisis. The traditional order, achieved during the optimism and growth of the High Middle Ages, was undercut first—and most severely—by the Black Death and the Hundred Years' War, which combined to cause a drastic reduction in population and contraction of the economy. Faced with massive death and destruction, some people sought escape in rituals of religious fanaticism. Others searched out scapegoats, spawning a wave of anti-Jewish persecutions that reached from southern France to the extent of the Holy Roman Empire; the Nuremberg pogrom of 1349 was only one example. Empire and papacy, long symbols of unity, collapsed into political disintegration and spiritual malaise.

The disintegration of European order hastened the consolidation of some states, as countries such as England and France developed political, linguistic, and cultural boundaries that largely coincided. Other areas, such as Spain and the Ottoman Empire, included different linguistic and religious groups under one political authority. Still other regions, principally central Europe and Italy, remained divided into competing city-states characterized more by the sense of local differences than by their linguistic similarity.

In the eastern Mediterranean, European civilization retreated in the face of Ottoman Turk advances. Christian Europe continued to grow, however, in the Iberian peninsula; for the next three centuries the Mediterranean would be the arena for struggles between Christian and Islamic empires. The papacy would clamor for new crusades.

The conciliar movement, although instrumental in ending the Great Schism, failed to limit supreme papal power, identified by its critics as the source of spiritual discontent. Traumatized, perhaps by the crisis of authority, the next generations of popes would concentrate on consolidating their worldly power and wealth. Successful in repressing or compromising with the Lollard, Hussite, and other heretical movements, the church would focus its attention on control and would neglect, to its future regret, the spiritual needs of a laity increasingly estranged from a dominating clerical elite.

Suggested References

Political Crises across Europe

The scholarship on the political conflicts of late medieval Europe has shifted from narrative of military campaigns and diplomacy to focus on peasant uprisings, urban revolts, and their relationship to the larger struggles between dynasties and countries. In addition to the Hundred Years' War, southeastern Europe and Iberia have also come into focus.

Allmand, Christopher. *The Hundred Years' War: England and France at War, c. 1300–1450.* 1988.

Froissart, Jean. *Chronicles.* Trans. Geoffrey Brereton. 1968.

Hilton, R. H., and T. H. Aston, eds. *The English Rising of 1381.* 1984.

Index of Late Medieval Maps–Index of Cartographic Images Illustrating Maps of the Late Medieval Period 1300–1500 A.D. http://www.henry-davis.com/MAPS/LMwebpages/LML .html.

Joan of Arc: By Herself and Her Witnesses. Ed. Régine Pernoud. 1966.

Leuschner, Joachim. *Germany in the Late Middle Ages.* 1980.

Mollat, Michel, and Philippe Wolff. *The Popular Revolutions of the Late Middle Ages.* 1973.

Nichols, David. *The van Arteveldes of Ghent: The Varieties of Vendetta and the Hero in History.* 1988.

O'Callaghan, Joseph F. *A History of Medieval Spain.* 1975.

Shaw, Stanford J. *History of the Ottoman Empire and Modern Turkey.* Vol. 1, *Empire of the Gazia: The Rise and Decline of the Ottoman Empire, 1280–1808.* 1976.

Warner, Marina. *Joan of Arc: The Image of Female Heroism.* 1981.

Plague and Society

Recent scholarship stresses the social, economic, and cultural impact of the plague. One particularly exciting direction of research focuses on the persecution of religious minorities as a result of the Black Death.

Bois, Guy. *The Crisis of Feudalism: Economy and Society in Eastern Normandy, c. 1300–1550.* 1984.

Duby, Georges. *A History of Private Life.* Vol. 2, *Revelations of the Medieval World.* 1988.

Geremek, Bronislaw. *The Margins of Society in Late Medieval Paris.* 1987.

Hanawalt, Barbara A., ed. *Women and Work in Preindustrial Europe.* 1986.

Miskimim, Harry A. *The Economy of Early Renaissance Europe, 1300–1460.* 1975.

Nirenberg, David. *Communities of Violence: Persecution of Minorities in the Middle Ages.* 1996.

Rörig, Fritz. *The Medieval Town.* 1967.

Ziegler, Philip. *The Black Death.* 1970.

Plague and public health in Renaissance Europe: http:// jefferson.village.virginia.edu/osheim/intro.html.

Challenges to Spiritual Authority

While there continues to be a great deal of interest in dissident thinkers who challenged the authority of the medieval church, much recent scholarship is devoted to the popular movements of dissent against papal and ecclesiastical authority.

Kaminsky, Howard. *A History of the Hussite Revolution.* 1967.

Leff, Gordon. *Heresy in the Later Middle Ages: The Relation of Heterodoxy to Dissent, c. 1250–1450.* 1967.

Oakley, Francis. *Council over Pope? Towards a Provisional Ecclesiology.* 1969.

Ozment, Steven. *The Age of Reform, 1250–1550: An Intellectual and Religious History of Late Medieval and Reformation Europe.* 1980.

Renouard, Yves. *The Avignon Papacy, 1305–1403.* 1970.

14

Renaissance Europe

1400–1500

Sacred and Social Body
The fifteenth-century Venetian state used lavish, dignified ceremony to impress citizens and visitors with its grandeur and to symbolize its divine protection. Here the great Venetian Renaissance painter Gentile Bellini depicts one such scene, a procession of the Eucharist across the Piazza San Marco uniting in common purpose the clergy and the Venetian governing elite. Scala/Art Resource, NY.

IN 1461, THE OTTOMAN RULER MEHMED II sent a letter to Sigismondo Malatesta, the Lord of Rimini, asking the Italian prince to lend him the Rimini court painter and architect Matteo de Pasti. The Ottoman sultan was planning to build a new palace in the recently conquered capital, Constantinople (modern Istanbul), as a fitting symbol of his imperial dominion, and he had heard of Matteo de Pasti's reputation. Not only had the Rimini painter produced illuminated manuscripts and portrait medals of Sigismondo's mistress for his patron, he had also designed a monument to the prince's military glory, modeled after the principles described in Vitruvius's treatise *On Architecture* (first century B.C.), a work rediscovered in 1414 in Italy.

Armed with a letter from Sigismondo, with maps and gifts, de Pasti set out for Constantinople, ready to court favors for his patron, who was eager to form an alliance with the Turkish ruler. Venetian authorities, however, intercepted the artist in Crete. Anxious to prevent a political connection between another Italian power and the sultan, the Venetians confiscated the gifts and sent de Pasti back to Rimini. Thus Mehmed's new palace was constructed without de Pasti's help, but with the aid of several Venetian painters instead. The palace came to be called the Topkapi Saray and still stands today looking across the Bosporus, the strait that divides European and Asian Turkey.

The story of Matteo de Pasti's failed mission illustrates the central theme of the Renaissance: the connection among power, culture, and fame in an age that was rediscovering the arts and worldview of

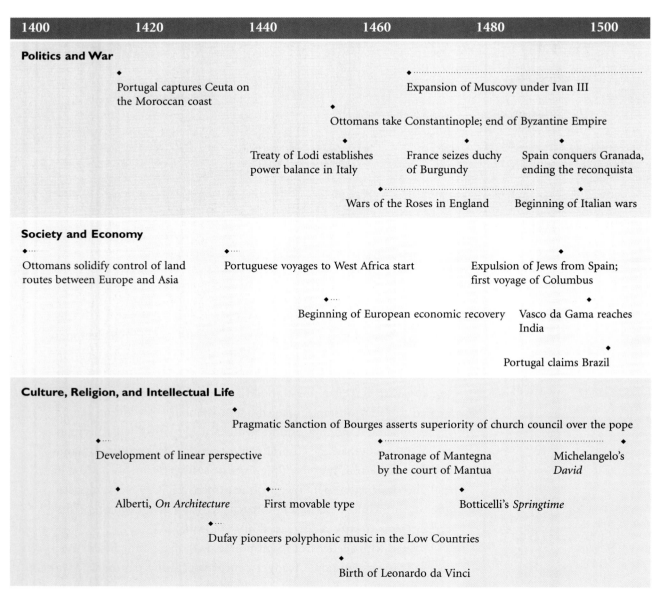

1400	1420	1440	1460	1480	1500

Politics and War

Portugal captures Ceuta on the Moroccan coast

Expansion of Muscovy under Ivan III

Ottomans take Constantinople; end of Byzantine Empire

Treaty of Lodi establishes power balance in Italy

France seizes duchy of Burgundy

Spain conquers Granada, ending the reconquista

Wars of the Roses in England

Beginning of Italian wars

Society and Economy

Ottomans solidify control of land routes between Europe and Asia

Portuguese voyages to West Africa start

Expulsion of Jews from Spain; first voyage of Columbus

Beginning of European economic recovery

Vasco da Gama reaches India

Portugal claims Brazil

Culture, Religion, and Intellectual Life

Pragmatic Sanction of Bourges asserts superiority of church council over the pope

Development of linear perspective

Patronage of Mantegna by the court of Mantua

Michelangelo's *David*

Alberti, *On Architecture*

First movable type

Botticelli's *Springtime*

Dufay pioneers polyphonic music in the Low Countries

Birth of Leonardo da Vinci

classical antiquity. This rediscovery, which scholars in the sixteenth century labeled the *Renaissance* (French for "rebirth"), signified the revival of forms of classical learning and the arts following the long interval they characterized as the Middle Ages. (See "Terms of History," page 492.) After the crisis of the fourteenth century, European civilization seemed to rise in the fifteenth like a phoenix from the ashes of the Black Death. This Renaissance of civilization had two main trajectories: a revolution in culture that originated in Italy and gradually expanded

north to other countries of Europe and, an even more profound and far-reaching development, the expansion of European control to the non-European world.

The story of de Pasti's mission further illustrates three secondary themes. First, it shows how specific Renaissance artistic practices were based on the revival of classical learning. Second, it reflects the competition between Italian city-states set against a larger backdrop of changing relations between Christian Europe and the non-Christian world, in this case the rising Muslim Ottoman Empire. And third, it demonstrates a new and important use of culture by both Christian and non-Christian rulers to justify and glorify power and fame.

The Renaissance of culture took many forms: in learning, in the visual arts, in architecture, and in music. Much new work was created in praise of personal and public lives. Portraits, palaces, and poetry commemorated the glory of the rich and powerful, while a new philosophy called *humanism* advocated classical learning and argued for the active participation of the individual in civic affairs. Family, honor, social status, and individual distinction— these were the goals that fueled the ambitions of Renaissance men and women.

A new feeling of power characterized the spirit of the Renaissance, as Europeans recovered their sense of control of the world after the crisis of the fourteenth century. The quest for power by families and individuals duplicated on a smaller scale the enhanced power of the state. Like individuals, the Renaissance states competed for wealth, glory, and honor. While warfare and diplomacy channeled the restless energy of the Italian states, monarchies and empires outside of Italy also expanded their power through conquests and institutional reforms. The European world changed drastically as new powers such as the Ottoman Empire and Muscovy rose to prominence in the east, while the Iberian kingdoms of Portugal and Spain expanded European domination to Africa, Asia, and the Americas.

❖ Widening Intellectual Horizons

A revolution in the arts and learning was in the making. Europeans' rediscovery of Greek and Roman writers reflected an expanded interest in human achievements and glory. New secular voices celebrating human glory were added to the old prayers for salvation in the afterlife. While the intense study of Latin and Greek writings focused on rhetoric and eloquence in learning, revolutionary techniques in bookmaking, painting, architecture, and music created original forms and expressed a new excitement with the beauty of nature. In the center of this fascinating nature was humanity.

The Humanist Renewal

Europeans' fascination with the ancient past in turn gave rise to a new intellectual movement: *humanism,* so called because its practitioners studied and supported the liberal arts, the humanities. As a group the humanists were far from homogeneous, although they were overwhelmingly wellborn. Some were professional scholars, others high-ranking civil servants, still others rich patricians who had acquired a taste for learning. Many were notaries or government officials. Nonetheless, all humanists focused on classical history and literature in their attempt to emulate the glories of the ancient world.

By the early fifteenth century the study of classical Latin (which had begun in the late fourteenth century) as well as classical and biblical Greek had become fashionable among a small intellectual elite, first in Italy and, gradually, throughout Europe. The fall of Constantinople in 1453 sent Greek scholars to Italy for refuge, giving extra impetus to the revival of Greek learning in the West. Venice and Florence assumed leadership in this new field—the former by virtue of its commercial and political ties to the eastern Mediterranean, the latter thanks to the patronage of Cosimo de' Medici, who sponsored the Platonic Academy, a discussion group dedicated to the study of Plato and his followers under the intellectual leadership of Marsilio Ficino (1433–1499). Thinkers of the second half of the fifteenth century had more curiosity about Platonic and various mystical neo-Platonic ideas—particularly alchemy, numerology, and natural magic—than about the serious study of natural phenomena and universal principles.

Most humanists did not consider the study of ancient cultures a conflict with their Christian faith. In "returning to the sources"—a famous slogan of the time—philosophers attempted to harmonize the disciplines of Christian faith and ancient learning. Ficino, the foremost Platonic scholar of the Renaissance, was deeply attracted to natural magic and was also a priest. He argued that the immortality of the soul, a Platonic idea, was perfectly compatible with Christian doctrine and that much of ancient wisdom actually foreshadowed later Christian teachings.

In Latin learning, the fifteenth century continued in the tradition of Petrarch. Reacting against the

Renaissance

The term *Renaissance* originated with the Italian painter and architect Giorgio Vasari (1511–1574) in his *Lives of the Most Excellent Italian Architects, Painters, and Sculptors* (1550). Vasari argues that Greco-Roman art declined after the dissolution of the Roman Empire, to be followed by a long period of barbaric insensitivity to classical monuments. Only in the past generations had Italian artists begun to restore the perfection of the arts, according to Vasari, a development he called *rinascita,* the Italian for "rebirth." It was the French equivalent—*renaissance*—that stuck.

Referring initially to a rebirth in the arts and literature, the term *Renaissance* came to define a consciousness of modernity. The writings of the Florentines Petrarch and Boccaccio in the fourteenth century showed that they thought of themselves as living in an age distinct from a long preceding period—which they dubbed the "middle age"—with values different from those of the classical civilizations of Greece and Rome. Petrarch, Boccaccio, and other Florentines began to consider their civilization a revival of the classical model in art, architecture, and language, the latter evidenced by an increased interest in classical Latin and Greek. From Florence and Italy, the Renaissance spread to France, Spain, the Low Countries, and central Europe by the fifteenth century. It inspired a golden age of vernacular literature in those countries during the second half of the sixteenth century; scholars speak of a "Northern Renaissance" as late as 1600.

The term *Renaissance* acquired widespread recognition with the publication of Jakob Burckhardt's *The Civilization of the Renaissance in Italy* in 1860. A historian at the University of Basel, Burckhardt considered the Renaissance a watershed in Western civilization. For him, the Renaissance ushered in a spirit of modernity, freeing the individual from the domination of society and creative impulses from the repression of the church; the Renaissance represented the beginning of secular society and the preeminence of individual creative geniuses.

Dominant for a long time, Burckhardt's ideas have been strongly revised by scholars. Some point out the many continuities between the Middle Ages and the Renaissance; others argue that the Renaissance was not a secular but a profoundly religious age; and still others see the Renaissance as only the beginning of a long period of transition from the Middle Ages to modernity. The consensus among scholars is that the Renaissance represents a distinct cultural period lasting from the fourteenth to the sixteenth century, centered on the revival of classical learning and spreading from Italy to northern Europe. Historians disagree about the significance of this cultural rebirth for society at large, but they generally understand it to represent some of the complex changes that characterized the passing of medieval society to modernity.

FURTHER READING

Jakob Burckhardt, *The Civilization of the Renaissance in Italy.* 1860.

Wallace K. Ferguson, *The Renaissance in Historical Thought.* 1948.

Denis Hay, "Idea of Renaissance," in *Dictionary of the History of Ideas.* 1973.

Guido Ruggiero, ed., *The Blackwell Companion to the World of the Renaissance.* 2001.

painstaking logic and abstract language of scholastic philosophy, the humanists of the Renaissance advocated eloquence and style in their discourse, imitating the writings of Cicero and other great Roman authors. The Roman influence manifested itself especially in the transformation of historians' writings, as Italian humanists used the classical genre to explore the role of human agency in political affairs.

Between 1400 and 1430 in Florence, which at the time was at war with the duchy of Milan, the study of the humanities evolved into a republican ideology that historians call *civic humanism*. In the early fifteenth century, the Florentines waged a highly successful propaganda war on behalf of virtuous republican Florence against tyrannical Milan, invoking the memory of the overthrow of Etruscan tyrants by the first Romans. Whereas Florentine humanists modeled their praise of republicanism after the Romans Livy and Cicero, humanists serving the duke of Milan drew their inspiration from the writings of Suetonius's biographies of Roman emperors. Thus the study of ancient civilization was not only an antiquarian quest but a call to public service and political action.

Through their activities as educators and civil servants, professional humanists gave new vigor to the humanist curriculum of grammar, rhetoric, poetry, history, and moral philosophy. By the end of the fifteenth century, European intellectuals considered a good command of classical Latin, with perhaps some knowledge of Greek, as one of the requirements of an educated man. This humanist revolution would influence school curricula up to the middle of the nineteenth century and even beyond.

The Advent of Printing

The invention of mechanical printing aided greatly in making the classical texts widely available. Printing with movable type—a revolutionary departure from the old practice of copying by hand—was invented in the 1440s by Johannes Gutenberg, a German goldsmith (c. 1400–1470). Mass production of identical books and pamphlets made the world of letters more accessible to a literate audience. Two preconditions proved essential for the advent of printing: the industrial production of paper and the commercial production of manuscripts.

Increased paper production in the fourteenth and fifteenth centuries was the first stage in the rapid growth of manuscript books—hand-copied works bound as books—which in turn led to the invention of mechanical printing. Papermaking came to Europe from China via Arab intermediaries. By the fourteenth century, paper mills were operating in Italy, producing paper that was more fragile but much cheaper than parchment or vellum, the animal skins that Europeans had previously used for writing. To produce paper, old rags were soaked in a chemical solution, beaten by mallets into a pulp, washed with water, treated, and dried in sheets—a method that still produces good-quality paper today.

By the fifteenth century, a brisk industry in manuscript books was flourishing in Europe's university towns and major cities. Production was in

Printing Press

This illustration from a French manuscript of 1537 depicts typical printing equipment of the sixteenth century. To the left an artisan is using the screw press to apply the paper to the inked type. Also shown are the composed type secured in a chase, the printed sheet (four pages of text printed on one sheet) held by the seated proofreader, and the bound volume. When two pages of text are printed on one sheet, the bound book is called a folio. *A bound book with four pages of text on one sheet is called* in quarto *("in four"), and a book with eight pages of text on one sheet is called* in octavo *("in eight"). The last is a pocket-size book, smaller than today's paperback.*
Giraudon/Art Resource, NY.

the hands of stationers, who organized workshops known as *scriptoria*, where the manuscripts were copied, and acted as retail booksellers. The largest stationers, in Paris or Florence, were extensive operations by fifteenth-century standards. The Florentine Vespasiano da Bisticci, for example, created a library for Cosimo de' Medici by employing forty-five copyists to complete two hundred volumes in twenty-two months. Nonetheless, bookmaking in *scriptoria* was slow and expensive.

The invention of movable type was an enormous technological breakthrough that took bookmaking out of the hands of human copyists.

Printing—or "mechanically writing," as contemporaries called it—was not new: the Chinese had been printing by woodblock since the tenth century, and woodcut pictures made their appearance in Europe in the early fifteenth century. Movable type, however, allowed entire manuscripts to be printed. The process involved casting durable metal molds to represent the letters of the alphabet. The letters were arranged to represent the text on a page and then pressed in ink against a sheet of paper. The imprint could be repeated numerous times with only a small amount of human labor. In 1467, two German printers established the first press in Rome and produced twelve thousand volumes in five years, a feat that in the past would have required one thousand scribes working full time for the same number of years.

After the 1440s, printing spread rapidly from Germany to other European countries (Map 14.1). Cologne, Strasbourg, Nuremberg, Basel, and Augsburg had major presses; many Italian cities had established their own by 1480. In the 1490s, the German city of Frankfurt-am-Main became an international meeting place for printers and booksellers. The Frankfurt Book Fair, where printers from different nations exhibited their newest titles, represented a major international cultural event and remains an unbroken tradition to this day. Early books from the presses were still rather exclusive and inaccessible, especially to a largely illiterate population. Perhaps the most famous early book, Gutenberg's two-volume edition of the Latin Bible, was unmistakably a luxury item. Altogether 185 copies were printed. First priced at well over what a

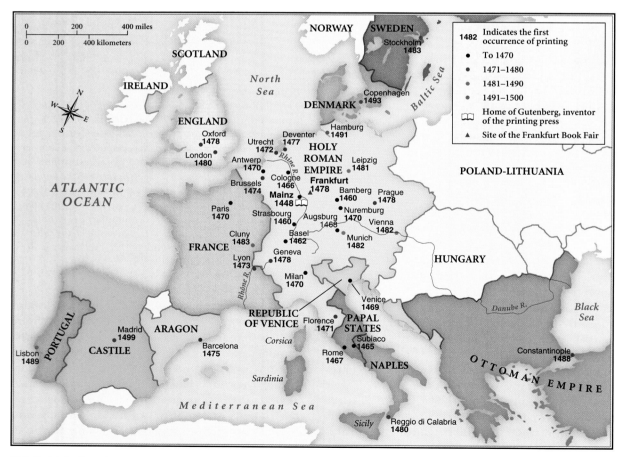

MAP 14.1 The Spread of Printing in the Fifteenth Century
The Holy Roman Empire formed the center of printing. Presses in other countries were often established by migrant German printers, especially in Italy. Printing did not reach Muscovy until the sixteenth century.

fifteenth-century professor could earn in a year, the Gutenberg Bible has always been one of the most expensive books in history, for both its rarity and its exquisite crafting.

Some historians argue that the invention of mechanical printing gave rise to a "communications revolution" as significant as, for example, the widespread use of the personal computer today. The multiplication of standardized texts altered the thinking habits of Europeans by freeing individuals from having to memorize everything they learned; it certainly made possible the relatively speedy and inexpensive dissemination of knowledge, and it created a wider community of scholars, no longer dependent on personal patronage or church sponsorship for texts. Printing facilitated the free expression and exchange of ideas, and its disruptive potential did not go unnoticed by political and ecclesiastical authorities. Emperors and bishops in Germany, the homeland of the printing industry, moved quickly to issue censorship regulations.

❖ Revolution in the Arts

The Renaissance was one of the most creative periods in the European arts. New techniques in painting, architecture, and musical performance fostered original styles and new subjects. Three transformations were particularly significant. First, artists, previously seen as artisans, acquired a more prominent social status, as individual talent and genius were recognized by a society hungry for culture. Second, artists developed a more naturalistic style, especially in representing the human body, in their sculpture and paintings. And finally, the use of perspective in Renaissance art reflected a new mathematical and scientific basis for artistic creation, which was manifest not only in the visual arts but also in architecture and musical composition.

From Artisan to Artist

Like the copyists before them, the printers who operated the new presses saw themselves as artisans practicing a craft. The result might be genuinely artistic, but the producer did not think of himself as an artist, uniquely gifted. The artist was a new social model in the Renaissance. In exalting the status of the artist, Leonardo da Vinci (1452–1519),

painter, architect, and inventor who was himself trained in the artisanal tradition, described his freedom to create, as a gentleman of leisure. "The painter sits at his ease in front of his work, dresses as he pleases, and moves his light brush with the beautiful colors . . . often accompanied by musicians or readers of various beautiful works." If this picture fits with today's image of the creative genius, so do the stories about Renaissance painters and their eccentricities: some were violent, others absentminded; some worked as hermits, others cared little for money. Leonardo was described by his contemporaries as "capricious," and his work habits (or lack of them) irritated at least one employer.

The point of stories about "genius," often told by Renaissance artists themselves, was to convince society that the artists' works were unique and their talents priceless. The artist, as opposed to the artisan, was an individual with innate talents who created works of art according to his imagination, rather than following the blueprints of a patron. During the fifteenth century, as artists began to claim the respect and recognition of society, however, the reality was that most relied on wealthy patrons for support. And although they wished to create as their genius dictated, not all patrons of the arts allowed artists to work without restrictions. While the duke of Milan appreciated Leonardo's genius, the duke of Ferrara paid for his art by the square foot. For every successful artist—such as the painter Andrea Mantegna (1431–1506), who was exalted by Pope Innocent VIII—there were many others who painted marriage chests and look-alike Madonnas for middle-class homes.

A successful artist who did fit the new vision of unfettered genius was the Florentine sculptor Donatello (1386–1466), one of the heroes in Giorgio Vasari's *Lives*. Not only did Donatello's sculptures evoke classical Greek and Roman models, but the grace and movement of his work inspired Cosimo de' Medici, the ruler of Florence, to excavate antique works of art. Moreover, Donatello transcended material preoccupations. According to Vasari:

> Donatello was free, affectionate, and courteous . . . and more so to his friends than to himself. He thought nothing of money, keeping it in a basket suspended by a rope from the ceiling, so that all his workmen and friends took what they wanted without saying anything to him.

A favorite artist of the most powerful man in fifteenth-century Florence, Donatello owed his ability to be generous in large part to Medici patronage.

Renaissance artists worked under any of three conditions: long-term service in princely courts, commissioned piecework, and production for the market. Mantegna, for example, worked from 1460 until his death in 1506 for the Gonzaga princes of Mantua. In return for a monthly salary and other gifts, he promised to paint panels and frescoes (paintings on a wet plaster surface). His masterpieces—fresco scenes of courtly life with vivid and accurate portraits of members of the princely family—decorated the walls of the ducal palace. In practice, however, Mantegna sometimes was treated more as a skilled worker in service to the prince than as an independent artist: he was once asked to adorn his majestic Gonzaga tapestries with life sketches of farm animals.

The workshop—the norm of production in Renaissance Florence and in northern European cities such as Nuremberg and Antwerp—afforded the artist greater autonomy. As heads of workshops, artists trained apprentices and negotiated contracts with clients, with the most famous artists fetching good prices for their work. Famous artists developed followings, and wealthy consumers came to pay a premium for work done by a master instead of apprentices. Studies of art contracts show that in the course of the fifteenth century artists gained greater control over their work. Early in the century clients routinely stipulated detailed conditions for works of art, specifying, for instance, gold paint or "ultramarine blue," which were among the most expensive pigments. Clients might also determine the arrangement of figures in a picture, leaving the artist little more than the execution. After midcentury, however, such specific directions became less common. In 1487, for example, the Florentine painter Filippo Lippi (1457–1504), in his contract to paint frescoes in the Strozzi chapel, specified that the work should be "all from his own hand and particularly the figures." The shift underscores the increasing recognition of the unique skills of individual artists.

A market system for the visual arts emerged in the Renaissance, initially in the Low Countries. In the fifteenth century, most large-scale work was commissioned by specific patrons, but the art market, for which artists produced works without prior arrangement for sale, was to develop into the major force for artistic creativity, a force that prevails in contemporary society. Limited at first to smaller altarpieces, woodcuts, engravings, sculpture, and pottery paintings, the art market began to extend to larger panel paintings. A vigorous trade in religious art sprang up in Antwerp, which was becoming the major market and financial center in Europe. Ready-made altarpieces were sold to churches and consumers from as far as Scandinavia, and merchants could buy small religious statues to take along on their travels. The commercialization of art celebrated the new context of artistic creation itself: artists working in an open, competitive, urban civilization.

The Human Figure

If the individual artist is a man of genius, what greater subject for the expression of beauty is there than the human body itself? From the fourteenth-century Florentine painter Giotto (see Chapter 12), Renaissance artists learned to depict ever more expressive human emotions and movements. The work of the short-lived but brilliant painter Masaccio (1401–1428) exemplifies this development. His painting *The Expulsion from Paradise* shows Adam and Eve grieving in shame and despair; another painting, *Naked Man Trembling*, demonstrates his skill in depicting a man trembling in the cold.

Feminine beauty also found many masterpiece representations in Renaissance art. They range from the graceful movements of classical pagan figures and allegories, as in Sandro Botticelli's (c. 1445–1510) *The Birth of Venus* and *Springtime*, to Raphael's (1483–1520) numerous tender depictions of the Virgin Mary and the infant Jesus. In addition to rendering homage to classical and biblical figures, Renaissance artists painted portraits of their contemporaries.

The increasing number of portraits in Renaissance painting illustrates the new, elevated view of human existence. Initially limited to representations of pontiffs, monarchs, princes, and patricians, portraiture of the middle classes became more widespread as the century advanced. Painters from the Low Countries such as Jan van Eyck (1390?–1441) distinguished themselves in this genre; their portraits achieved a sense of detail and reality unsurpassed until the advent of photography.

The ideal of a universal man was elaborated in the work of Giovanni Pico della Mirandola (1463–1494). Born to a noble family, Pico avidly studied Latin and Greek philosophy. He befriended Ficino, Florence's leading Platonic philosopher, and enjoyed the patronage of Lorenzo de' Medici (1449–1492), who provided him with a villa after the papacy condemned some of his writings. Pico's oration *On the Dignity of Man* embodied the optimism of Renaissance philosophy. To express his marvel at the human species, Pico imagined God's words at his creation of Adam: "In conformity with your free judgment, in whose hands I have placed them, you are confined by no bounds, and you will fix limits of nature for yourself." Pico's construct placed mankind at the center of the universe as the measure of all things and "the molder and maker of himself." In his efforts to reconcile Platonic and Christian philosophy, Pico stressed both the classical emphasis on human responsibility in shaping society and the religious trust in God's divine plan. For the first time after classical antiquity, sculptors again cast the human body in bronze, in life-size or bigger freestanding statues. Donatello's equestrian statue of a Venetian general was one of the finest examples of this new endeavor; consciously based on Roman statues of mounted emperors, it depicted a relatively minor but successful professional commander (ironically nicknamed "Honey Cat" for his failure to inspire awe). Free from fabric and armor, the human body was idealized in the eighteen-foot marble sculpture *David*, the work of the great Michelangelo Buonarroti (1475–1564).

Order through Perspective

Renaissance art was distinguished from its predecessors by its depiction of the world as the eye perceives it. The use of *visual perspective*—an illusory three-dimensional space on a two-dimensional surface and the ordered arrangement of painted objects from one viewpoint—became one of the distinctive features of Western art. Neither Persian, Chinese, Byzantine, nor medieval Western art—all of which had been more concerned with conveying symbolism than reality—expressed this aesthetic for order through the use of perspective. Underlying the idea of perspective was a new Renaissance worldview: humans asserting themselves over nature in painting and design by controlling space. Optics became the organizing principle of the natural world in that it detected the "objective" order in nature. The Italian painters were keenly aware of their new technique, and they criticized the Byzantine and the northern Gothic stylists for "flat" depiction of the human body and the natural world. The highest accolade for a Renaissance artist was to be described as an "imitator of nature": the artist's teacher was nature, not design books or master painters. Leonardo described how "painting . . . compels the mind of the painter to transform itself into the mind of nature itself and to translate between nature and art, setting out, with nature, the causes of nature's phenomena regulated by nature's laws." To imitate nature, Leonardo continued, required the technique of visual perspective.

The perspectival representation that now dominated artistry is illustrated aptly by the work of three artists: Lorenzo Ghiberti (c. 1378–1455), Andrea Mantegna, and Piero della Francesca (1420–1492). In 1401, the sculptor and goldsmith Ghiberti won a contest to design bronze doors for the San Giovanni Baptistry in Florence, a project that would occupy the rest of his life. Choosing stories from the Old and New Testaments as his themes, Ghiberti used linear perspective to create a sense of depth and space in his bronze panels. His representation of the sacrifice of Isaac, for example, created a majestic scene of movement and depth. His doors were so moving that Michelangelo in the sixteenth century described them as "the Gates of Paradise."

Mantegna's most brilliant achievement, his frescoes in the bridal chamber of the Gonzaga Palace, completed between 1465 and 1474, created an illusory extension of reality, a three-dimensional representation of life, as the actual living space in the chamber "opened out" to the painted landscape on the walls. By contrast, the painter Piero della Francesca set his detached and expressionless figures in a geometrical world of columns and tiles, framed by intersecting lines and angles. Human existence, if della Francesca's painting can be taken as a reflection of his times, was shaped by human design, in accordance with the faculties of reason and observation. Thus the artificially constructed urban society of the Renaissance was the ideal context in which to understand the ordered universe.

Masaccio's Trembling Man (above)

Renaissance paintings differ from medieval art in many ways, one of which is naturalism, in which subjects—human and nature—are depicted in a realistic rather than a symbolic way. Here, the important subject is baptism, but Masaccio's representation emphasizes the feeling of cold water, a naturalistic treatment intended to connect the subject of the painting and the viewer.

Erich Lessing/Art Resource, NY.

Madonna and Child (upper right)

Raphael's Madonna and Child *flows with natural grace: Jesus and the Virgin Mary are unfrozen from their static representations in Byzantine and medieval art. This naturalistic portrayal reflects how religious feelings were permeated by the everyday in the Renaissance.*

Scala/Art Resource, NY.

Botticelli's *Spring* (right)

This detail from Botticelli's Spring *depicts the graceful movements of dance and the beauty of the female body through the naturalistic technique of Renaissance art. Note the contrast between the stillness of the formal composition, with the figures anchored by the trees in the background, and the movement conveyed by the gently flowing robes and the swirling motion of the dancing figures.*

Scala/Art Resource, NY.

Michelangelo's *David* (upper left)
Commissioned of the great Florentine artist when he was twenty-six, David (1501–1504) represents a masterpiece of sculpture that equaled the glory of ancient human sculpture. This huge marble figure—the earliest monumental statue of the Renaissance—depicts David larger than life-size in the full beauty and strength of the male body.
Nimatallah/Art Resource, NY.

Equestrian Statue of Gattamelata (upper right)
The artist's largest freestanding work in bronze, Donatello's equestrian monument of a Venetian general (1445–1450) consciously imitates the examples of ancient Rome. Unlike triumphant Caesars and Roman generals, however, Gattamelata, the recently deceased commander depicted, did not enjoy a particularly successful career in terms of victories.
Scala/Art Resource, NY.

The Sacrifice of Isaac (left)
Ghiberti's brilliant work (1401–1402) forms one of the panels on the door of the Baptistery of Florence. Technically difficult to execute, this bronze relief captures the violence of movement as the angel intervenes as Abraham is about to slit the throat of Isaac, a story told in the Hebrew Scriptures.
Scala/Art Resource, NY.

Piero della Francesca, The Flagellation of Christ
Active in Urbino in the mid-fifteenth century, the Tuscan artist Piero della Francesca was a master of dramatic perspective and design, as exemplified in this small panel painting. His use of cool colors and his imaginative manipulation of geometric space have led many art historians to regard Piero as the earliest forebear of the abstract artists of our own time.
Scala/Art Resource, NY.

Frescoes of the Camera degli Sposi
Andrea Mantegna's frescoes in the ducal palace depict members of the Gonzaga family, together with their court and animals, in various festive scenes. In masterly use of the perspective techniques, four painted walls lead to a vaulted ceiling decorated as heaven. The landscape view to the left of the door reflects the Renaissance idea of a painting as a window to the real world.
Scala/Art Resource, NY.

Perhaps even more than the visual artists, fifteenth-century architects embodied the Renaissance ideals of uniting artistic creativity and scientific knowledge. Among the greatest talents of the day was Filippo Brunelleschi (1377–1446), a Florentine architect whose designs included the dome of the city's cathedral, modeled after ancient Roman ruins; the Ospedale degli Innocenti (a hospital for orphans); and the interiors of several Florentine churches. Son of a lawyer and a goldsmith by train-

ing, Brunelleschi also invented machines to help with architectural engineering.

One of the first buildings designed by the Florentine architect Leon Battista Alberti (1404–1472), the Rucellai Palace in Florence, shows a strong classical influence and inaugurated a trend in the construction of urban palaces for the Florentine ruling elite. Although Alberti undertook architectural designs for many princes, his significance lies more in his theoretical works, which strongly influenced his contemporaries. In a book on painting dedicated to Brunelleschi, Alberti analyzed the technique of perspective as the method of imitating nature. In *On Architecture* (1415), modeled after the Roman Vitruvius, Alberti argued for large-scale urban planning, with monumental buildings set on open squares, harmonious and beautiful in their proportions. His ideas were put into action by Pope Sixtus IV (r. 1471–1484) and his successors in the urban renewal of Rome, and they served to transform that unruly medieval town into a geometrically constructed monument to architectural brilliance by recalling the grandeur of its ancient origins.

New Musical Harmonies

Italy set the standards for the visual arts in Europe, but in musical styles it was more influenced by the northern countries. Around 1430, a new style of music appeared in the Low Countries that would dominate composition for the next two centuries. Instead of writing pieces with one major melodic line, composers were writing for three or four instrumental or human voices, each equally important in expressing a melody in harmony with the others.

The leader of this new style, known as *polyphonic* ("many sounds") music, was Guillaume Dufay (1400–1474), whose musical training began in the cathedral choir of his hometown, Cambrai in the Low Countries. His successful career took him to all the cultural centers of the Renaissance, where nobles sponsored new compositions and maintained a corps of musicians for court and religious functions. In 1438, Dufay composed festive music to celebrate the completion of the cathedral dome in Florence designed by Brunelleschi. Dufay expressed the harmonic relationship among four voices in ratios that matched the mathematically precise dimensions of Brunelleschi's architecture. After a period of employment at the papal court, Dufay returned to his native north and composed music for the Burgundian and French courts.

Although his younger counterpart Johannes Ockeghem (c. 1420–1495), whose influence rivaled Dufay's, worked almost exclusively at the French court, Dufay's mobile career was typical. Josquin des Prez (1440–1521), another Netherlander, wrote music in Milan, Ferrara, Florence, and Paris and at the papal court. The new style of music was beloved by the elites: Lorenzo de' Medici sent Dufay a love poem to set to music, and the great composer maintained a lifelong relationship with the Medici family.

Within Renaissance polyphony were three main musical genres: the canon (central texts) of the Catholic Mass; the motet, which used both sacred and secular texts; and the secular *chanson*, often using the tunes of folk dances. Composers often adapted familiar folk melodies for sacred music, expressing religious feeling primarily through human voices instead of instruments. The tambourine and the lute were indispensable for dances, however, and small ensembles of wind and string instruments with contrasting sounds performed with singers in the fashionable courts of Europe. Also in use in the fifteenth century were new keyboard instruments—the harpsichord and clavichord—which could play several harmonic lines at once.

❖ The Intersection of Private and Public Lives

Paid for largely by the patronage of the ruling elites, Renaissance culture served not only for their enjoyment but also to glorify the republics, principalities, and kingdoms and to justify the legitimacy of their rulers. Just as lineage and descent shaped political power in dynastic states in the fourteenth century, the state itself, through its institutions and laws, now attempted to shape private life. Nowhere was this process more evident than at Florence, the leading center of Renaissance culture. Considerations of state power intruded into the most intimate personal concerns: sexual intimacy, marriage, and childbirth could not be separated from the values of the ruling classes. With a society dominated by upper-class, patriarchal households, Renaissance Italy specified rigid roles for men and women, subordinating women and making marriage a vehicle for consolidating social hierarchy.

Renaissance Social Hierarchy

To deal with a mounting fiscal crisis, in 1427 the government of Florence ordered that a comprehensive tax record of households in the city and territory be compiled. Completed in 1430, this survey represented the most detailed population census then taken in European history. From the resulting mass of fiscal and demographic data, historians have been able to reconstruct a picture of the Florentine state, particularly its capital—the most important city of the Renaissance and a city whose records for this period are unparalleled in their detail.

The state of Florence, roughly the size of Massachusetts, had a population of more than 260,000. Tuscany, the area in which the Florentine state was located, was one of the most urbanized regions of Europe. With 38,000 inhabitants, the capital city of Florence claimed 14 percent of the total population and an enormous 67 percent of the state's wealth. Straddling the Arno River, Florence was a beautiful, thriving city with a defined social hierarchy. In describing class divisions, the Florentines themselves referred to the "little people" and the "fat people." Some 60 percent of all households belonged to the "little people"—workers, artisans, small merchants. The "fat people" (roughly our middle class) made up 30 percent of the urban population and included the wealthier merchants, the leading artisans, notaries, doctors, and other professionals. At the very bottom of the hierarchy were slaves and servants, largely women employed in domestic service. Whereas the small number of slaves were of Balkan origin, the much larger population of domestic servants came to the city from the surrounding countryside as contracted wage earners. At the top, a tiny elite of patricians, bankers, and wool merchants controlled the state with their enormous wealth. In fact, the richest 1 percent of urban households (approximately one hundred families) owned more than one-quarter of the city's wealth and one-sixth of Tuscany's total wealth. The patricians in particular owned almost all government bonds, a lucrative investment guaranteed by a state they dominated.

Surprisingly, men seem to have outnumbered women in the 1427 survey. For every 100 women there were 110 men, unlike most past and present populations, in which women are the majority. In addition to female infanticide, which was occasionally practiced, the survey itself reflected the society's bias against women: persistent underreporting on women probably explained the statistical abnormality; and married daughters, young girls, and elderly widows frequently disappeared from the memories of householders. Most people, men and women alike, lived in households with at least six inhabitants, although the form of family unit—nuclear or extended—varied, depending mainly on wealth, with poor people rarely able to support

extended families. Among urban patricians and landowning peasants, the extended family held sway. The number of children in a family, it seems, reflected class differences as well. Wealthier families had more children; childless couples existed almost exclusively among the poor, who were also more likely to abandon the infants they could not feed.

Family Alliances

Wealth and class clearly determined family structure and the pattern of marriage and childbearing. In a letter to her eldest son, Filippo, dated 1447, Alessandra Strozzi announced the marriage of her daughter Caterina to the son of Parente Parenti. She described the young groom, Marco Parenti, as "a worthy and virtuous young man, and . . . the only son, and rich, 25 years old, and keeps a silk workshop; and they have a little political standing." The dowry was set at one thousand florins, a substantial sum—but for four to five hundred florins more, Alessandra admitted to Filippo, Caterina would have fetched a husband from a more prominent family.

The Strozzi belonged to one of Florence's most distinguished traditional families, but at the time of Caterina's betrothal the family had fallen into political disgrace. Alessandra's husband, an enemy of the Medici, was exiled in 1434; Filippo, a rich merchant in Naples, lived under the same political ban. Although Caterina was clearly marrying beneath her social station, the marriage represented an alliance in which money, political status, and family standing all balanced out. More an alliance between families than the consummation of love, an Italian Renaissance marriage was usually orchestrated by the male head of a household. In this case, Alessandra, as a widow, shared the matchmaking responsibility with her eldest son and other male relatives. Eighteen years later, when it came time to find a wife for Filippo, who had by then accumulated enough wealth to start his own household, Marco Parenti, his brother-in-law, would serve as matchmaker.

The upper-class Florentine family was patrilineal, that is, it traced descent and determined inheritance through the male line. Because the distribution of wealth depended on this patriarchal system, women occupied an ambivalent position in the household. A daughter could claim inheritance only through her dowry, and she often disappeared from family records after her marriage. A wife seldom emerged

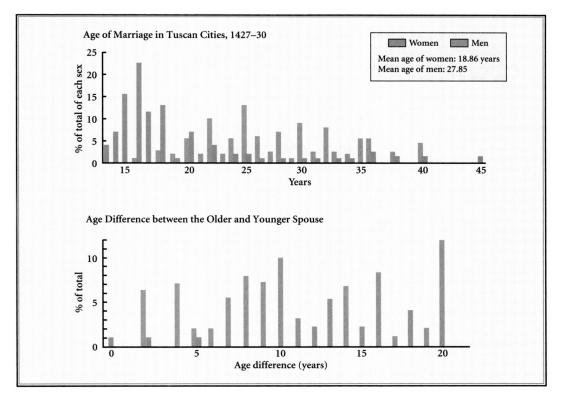

TAKING MEASURE Age of Marriage in Tuscan Cities, 1427–1430

The 1427–1430 Florentine tax and census records indicate two distinctly different marriage patterns for men and women. While the mean marriage age for women was 18.86 years, that for men was 27.85 years. This difference reflected the considerable difficulty for young men to amass enough wealth to start a household. More revealing is the chart showing the differences in age between the spouses. Some 12 percent of all spouses had a difference of twenty years. While the great majority of these marriages involved older, wealthier, established males, often in second marriages after the death of their first spouses, a small number involved younger men marrying up in the social ladder to widows of guild members to acquire a position. Together these charts give important information on gender relations and reflect the underlying class and gender inequalities in Renaissance society.

From David Herlihy and Christiane Klapisch-Zuber, *Tuscans and Their Families: A Study of Florentine Catasto of 1427* (New Haven: Yale University Press, 1985), 205. Reprinted by permission of Yale University Press.

from the shadow of her husband, and consequently the lives of many women have been lost to history.

In the course of a woman's life, her family often pressured her to conform to conventional expectations. At the birth of a daughter, most wealthy Florentine fathers opened an account at the Dowry Fund, a public fund established in 1425 to raise state revenues and a major investment instrument for the upper classes. In 1433, the fund paid annual interest of between 15 and 21 percent, and fathers could hope to raise handsome dowries to marry their daughters to more prominent men when the daughters became marriageable in their late teens. The

Dowry Fund supported the structure of the marriage market, in which the circulation of wealth and women consolidated the social coherence of the ruling classes. (See "Taking Measure," above.)

Women's subordination in marriages often reflected the age differences between spouses. The Italian marriage pattern, in which young women married older men, contrasted sharply with the northern European model, in which partners were much closer in age. Significant age disparity also left many women widowed in their twenties and thirties, and remarriage often proved a hard choice. A widow's father and brothers frequently pressed her to remarry to form a new family alliance. A widow, however, could not bring her children into her new marriage because they belonged to her first husband's family. Faced with the choice between her children and her paternal family, not to mention the question of her own happiness, a widow could hope to gain greater autonomy only in her old age, when, like Alessandra, she might assume matchmaking responsibilities to advance her family's fortunes.

In northern Europe, however, women enjoyed a relatively more secure position. In England, the Low Countries, and Germany, for example, women played a significant role in the economy—not only in the peasant household, in which everyone worked, but especially in the town, serving as peddlers, weavers, seamstresses, shopkeepers, midwives, and brewers. In Cologne, for example, women could join one of several artisans' guilds, and in Munich they ranked among some of the richest brewers. Women in northern Europe shared inheritances with their brothers, retained control of their dowries, and had the right to represent themselves before the law. Italian men who traveled to the north were appalled at the differences in gender relations, criticizing English women as violent and brazen and disapproving of the mixing of the sexes in German public baths.

The Regulation of Sexuality

Along with marriage patterns, child care and attitudes toward sexuality also reflected class differences in Renaissance life. Florentine middle- and upper-class fathers arranged business contracts with wet nurses to breast-feed their infants; babies thus spent prolonged periods of time away from their families. Such elaborate child care was beyond the reach of the poor, who often abandoned their children to strangers or to public charity.

By the beginning of the fifteenth century, Florence's two hospitals were accepting large numbers of abandoned children in addition to the sick and infirm. In 1445, the government opened the Ospedale degli Innocenti to deal with the large number of abandoned children. These unfortunate children came from two sources: poor families who were unable to feed another mouth, especially in times of famine, war, and economic depression; and women who had given birth out of wedlock. A large number of the latter were domestic slaves or servants who had been impregnated by their masters; in

1445, one-third of the first hundred foundlings at the new hospital were children of the unequal liaisons between masters and women slaves. For some women the foundling hospital provided an alternative to infanticide. Over two-thirds of abandoned infants were girls, a clear indicator of the inequality between the sexes. Although Florence's government employed wet nurses to care for the foundlings, the large number of abandoned infants overtaxed the hospital's limited resources. The hospital's death rate for infants was much higher than the already high infant mortality rate of the time.

Illegitimacy in itself did not necessarily carry a social stigma in fifteenth-century Europe. Most upper-class men acknowledged and supported their illegitimate children as a sign of virility, and illegitimate children of noble lineage often rose to social and political prominence. Any social stigma was borne primarily by the woman, whose ability to marry became compromised. Shame and guilt drove some poor single mothers to kill their infants, a crime for which they paid with their own lives.

In addition to prosecuting infanticide, the public regulation of sexuality focused on prostitution and homosexuality. Intended "to eliminate a worse evil by a lesser one," a 1415 statute established government brothels in Florence. Concurrent with its higher tolerance of prostitution, the Renaissance state had a low tolerance of homosexuality. In 1432, the Florentine state appointed magistrates "to discover—whether by means of secret denunciation, accusations, notification, or any other method— those who commit the vice of sodomy, whether actively or passively." The government set fines for homosexual acts and carried out death sentences against pederasts (men who have sex with boys).

Fifteenth-century European magistrates took violence against women less seriously than illegal male sexual behavior, as the different punishments indicate. In Renaissance Venice, for example, the typical jail sentence for rape and attempted rape was only six months. Magistrates often treated noblemen with great leniency and handled rape cases according to class distinctions. For example, Agneta, a young girl living with a government official, was abducted and raped by two millers, who were sentenced to five years in prison; several servants who abducted and raped a slave woman were sentenced to three to four months in jail; and a nobleman who abducted and raped Anna, a slave woman, was freed.

Whether in marriage, inheritance, illicit sex, or sexual crime, the Renaissance state regulated the behavior of men and women according to differing concepts of gender. The brilliant civilization of the Renaissance was experienced very differently by men and women.

❖ The Renaissance State and the Art of Politics

Among the achievements of the Renaissance, the state seemed to represent a work of art. For the Florentine political theorist Niccolò Machiavelli (1469–1527), the state was an artifice of human creation to be conquered, shaped, and administered by princes according to the principles of power politics. Machiavelli laid out these principles in his work, *The Prince*: "It can be observed that men use various methods in pursuing their own personal objectives, that is glory and riches. . . . I believe that . . . fortune is the arbiter of half the things we do, leaving the other half or so to be controlled by ourselves." *The Prince* was the first treatment of the science of politics in which the acquisition and exercise of power were discussed without reference to an ultimate moral or ethical end. Machiavelli's keen observations of power, scandalous to his contemporaries, were based on a careful study of Italian politics during the Renaissance. Though a republican at heart, Machiavelli recognized the necessity of power in founding a state, whose sustenance ultimately rested on republican virtue. Outside of Italy, other European states also furnished many examples to illustrate the ruthless nature of power politics and the artifice of state building. In general, a midcentury period of turmoil gave way to the restructuring of central monarchical power in the last decades of the fifteenth century. Many states developed stronger, institutionally more complex central governments in which middle-class lawyers played an increasingly prominent role. The expanded Renaissance state paved the way for the development of the nation-state in later centuries.

Republics and Principalities in Italy

The Italian states of the Renaissance can be divided into two broad categories: republics, which preserved the traditional institutions of the medieval

MAP 14.2 Italy, c. 1450
The political divisions of Italy reflected powerful city-centered republics and duchies in the north and the larger but economically more backward south. Local and regional identities remained strong into the modern age.

commune by allowing a civic elite to control political and economic life, and principalities, which were ruled by one dynasty. The most powerful and influential states were the republics of Venice and Florence and the principalities of Milan and Naples. In addition to these four, a handful of smaller states, such as Siena, Ferrara, and Mantua stood out as important cultural centers during the Renaissance (Map 14.2).

Venice. Venice, a city built on a lagoon, ruled an extensive colonial empire that extended from the Adriatic to the Aegean Sea. Venetian merchant ships sailed the Mediterranean, the Atlantic coast, and the Black Sea; Christian pilgrims to Palestine booked passage on Venetian ships; in 1430, the Venetian navy numbered more than three thousand ships. Symbolizing their intimacy with and dominion over the sea, the Venetians celebrated an annual

"Wedding of the Sea." Amid throngs of spectators and foreign dignitaries, the Venetian doge (the elected duke) sailed out to the Adriatic, threw a golden ring into its waters to renew the union, and intoned, "Hear us with favor, O Lord. We worthily entreat Thee to grant that this sea be tranquil and quiet for our men and all others who sail upon it."

In the early fifteenth century, however, Venetians faced threats on both sides. From 1425 to 1454, Venice fought the expanding duchy of Milan on land. The second and greater danger came from the eastern Mediterranean, where the Ottoman Turks finally captured Byzantine Constantinople in 1453. Faced by these external threats, Venice drew strength from its internal social cohesion. Under the rule of an oligarchy of aristocratic merchants, Venice enjoyed stability; and its maritime empire benefited citizens of all social classes, who joined efforts to defend the interests of the "Most Serene Republic," a contemporary name that reflected Venice's lack of social strife.

Florence. Compared with serene Venice, the republic of Florence was in constant agitation: responsive to political conflicts, new ideas, and artistic styles. Like Venice, Florence described its government in the humanist language of ancient Roman republicanism. Unlike Venice, Florentine society was turbulent as social classes and political factions engaged in constant civic strife. By 1434, a single family had emerged dominant in this fractious city: the Medici. Cosimo de' Medici (1388–1464), the head of the family, was ruthless. His contemporary Pope Pius II did not mince words in describing Medici power. "Cosimo, having thus disposed of his rivals, proceeded to administer the state at his pleasure and amassed wealth. . . . In Florence he built a palace fit for a king." As head of one of the largest banks of Europe, Cosimo de' Medici used his immense wealth to influence politics. Even though he did not hold any formal political office, he wielded influence in government through business associates and clients who were indebted to him for loans, political appointments, and other favors.

As the largest bank in Europe, the Medici Bank handled papal finances and established branch offices in many Italian cities and the major northern European financial centers. Backed by this immense private wealth, Cosimo became the arbiter of war and peace, the regulator of law, more master than

citizen. Yet the prosperity and security that Florence enjoyed made him popular as well. At his death, Cosimo was lauded as the "father of his country."

Cosimo's grandson Lorenzo (called "the Magnificent"), who assumed power in 1467, bolstered the regime's legitimacy with his lavish patronage of the arts. But opponents were not lacking. In 1478, Lorenzo narrowly escaped an assassination attempt. Two years after Lorenzo's death in 1494, partisans who opposed the Medici drove them from Florence. The Medici returned to power in 1512, only to be driven out again in 1527. In 1530, the republic fell and the Medici once again seized control, declaring Florence a duchy.

Milan. Unlike Florence, with its republican aspirations, the duchy of Milan had been under dynastic rule since the fourteenth century. The most powerful Italian principality, Milan was a military state relatively uninterested in the support of the arts but with a first-class armaments and textile industry in the capital city and rich farmlands of Lombardy. Until 1447, the duchy was ruled by the Visconti dynasty, a group of powerful lords whose plans to unify all of northern and central Italy failed from the combined opposition of Venice, Florence, and other Italian powers. In 1447, the last Visconti duke died without a male heir, and the nobility proclaimed Milan to be the Ambrosian republic (named after the city's patron saint, Ambrose), thus bringing the Visconti rule to a close.

For three years the new republic struggled to maintain Milan's political and military strength. Cities that the Visconti family had subdued rebelled against Milan, and the two great republics of Venice and Florence plotted its downfall. Milan's ruling nobility, seeking further defense, appointed Francesco Sforza, who had married the illegitimate daughter of the last Visconti duke, to the post of general. Sforza promptly turned against his employers, claiming the duchy as his own. A bitter struggle between the nobility and the townspeople in Milan further undermined the republican cause, and in 1450 Sforza entered Milan in triumph.

The power of the Sforza dynasty reached its height during the 1490s. In 1493, Duke Ludovico married his niece Bianca Maria to Maximilian, the newly elected Holy Roman Emperor, promising an immense dowry in exchange for the emperor's legitimization of his rule. But the newfound Milanese glory was soon swept aside by France's invasion of Italy in 1494, and the duchy itself eventually came under Spanish rule.

Naples. After a struggle for succession between Alfonso of Aragon and René d'Anjou, a cousin of the king of France, the kingdoms of Naples and Sicily came under Aragonese rule between 1435 and 1494. Unlike the northern Italian states, Naples was dominated by powerful feudal barons who retained jurisdiction and taxation over their own vast estates. Alfonso I (r. 1435–1458), called "the Magnanimous" for his generous patronage of the arts, promoted the urban middle class to counter baronial rule, using as his base the city of Naples, the only large urban center in a relatively rural kingdom. Alfonso's son Ferante I (r. 1458–1494) continued his father's policies: two of his chief ministers hailed from humble backgrounds. With their private armies and estates intact, however, the barons constantly threatened royal power, and in 1462 many rebelled against Ferante. More ruthless than his father, Ferante handily crushed the opposition. He kept rebellious barons in the dungeons of his Neapolitan castle and confiscated their properties. When his ministers plotted against him, siding with yet other rebel barons, Ferante feigned reconciliation and then arrested the ministers at a banquet and executed them and their families.

Embroiled in Italian politics, Alfonso and Ferante shifted their alliances among the papacy, Milan, and Florence. But the greater threat to Neapolitan security was external. In 1480, Ottoman forces captured the Adriatic port of Otranto, where they massacred the entire male population. And in 1494, a French invasion ended the Aragonese dynasty in Naples, although, as in Milan, France's claim would eventually be superseded by that of Spain.

The Papal States. In the violent arena of Italian politics, the papacy, an uneasy mixture of worldly splendor and religious authority, was a player like the other states. The vicars of Christ negotiated treaties, made war, and built palaces; a few led scandalous lives. Pope Alexander VI (r. 1492–1503), the most notorious pontiff, kept a mistress and fathered children, one of whom, Cesare Borgia, served as the model ruthless ruler for Machiavelli in *The Prince*.

The popes' concern with politics stemmed from their desire to restore papal authority, greatly undermined by the Great Schism and the conciliar movement. To that end, the popes used both politics and culture to enhance their authority. Politically, they curbed local power, expanded papal government, increased taxation, enlarged the papal army and navy, and extended papal diplomacy. Culturally, the popes renovated churches, created the Vatican Library, sponsored artists, and patronized writers to glorify their role and power as St. Peter's successors. In undertaking these measures, the Renaissance papacy merely exemplified the larger trend toward the centralization of power evident in the development of monarchies and empires outside of Italy as well.

Renaissance Diplomacy

Many features of diplomacy characteristic of today's nation-states first appeared in fifteenth-century Europe. By midcentury, competition between states and the extension of warfare raised the practice of diplomacy to nearly an art form. The first diplomatic handbook, composed in 1436 by Frenchman Bernard du Rosier, later archbishop of Toulouse, declared that the business of the diplomat was "to pay honor to religion . . . and the Imperial crown, to protect the rights of kingdoms, to offer obedience . . . to confirm friendships . . . make peace . . . to arrange past disputes and remove the cause for future unpleasantness."

The emphasis on ceremonies, elegance, and eloquence (Italians referred to ambassadors as "orators") masked the complex game of diplomatic intrigue and spying. In the fifteenth century, a resident ambassador was expected to keep a continuous stream of foreign political news flowing to the home government, not just to conduct temporary diplomatic missions, as earlier ambassadors had done. In some cases the presence of semiofficial agents developed into full-fledged ambassadorships: the Venetian embassy to the sultan's court in Constantinople developed out of the merchant-consulate that had represented all Venetian merchants, and Medici Bank branch managers eventually acted as political agents for the Florentine republic.

Foremost in the development of diplomacy was Milan, a state with political ambition and military might. Under the Visconti dukes, Milan sent ambassadors to Aragon, Burgundy, the Holy Roman Empire, and the Ottoman Empire. Under the Sforza dynasty, Milanese diplomacy continued to function as a cherished form of statecraft. For generations Milanese diplomats at the French court sent home an incessant flow of information on the rivalry between France and Burgundy. Francesco Sforza, founder of the dynasty, also used his diplomatic corps to extend his political patronage. In letters of recommendation to the papacy, Francesco commented on the political desirability of potential ecclesiastical candidates by using code words, sometimes supplemented with instructions to his ambassador to indicate his true intent regardless of the coded letter of recommendation. In more sensitive diplomatic reports, ciphers were used to prevent them from being understood by hostile powers.

As the center of Christendom, Rome became the diplomatic hub of Europe. During the 1490s, well over two hundred diplomats were stationed in Rome. The papacy sent out far fewer envoys than it received; only at the end of the fifteenth century were papal nuncios, or envoys, permanently established in the European states.

The most outstanding achievement of Italy's Renaissance diplomacy was the negotiation of a general peace treaty that settled the decades of warfare engendered by Milanese expansion and civil war. The Treaty of Lodi (1454) established a complex balance of power among the major Italian states and maintained relative stability in the peninsula for half a century. Renaissance diplomacy eventually failed, however, when more powerful northern European neighbors invaded in 1494, leading to the collapse of the whole Italian state system.

Monarchies and Empires

Locked in fierce competition among themselves, the Italian states paid little attention to large territorial states emerging in the rest of Europe that would soon overshadow Italy with their military power and economic resources. Whether in Burgundy, England, Spain, France, the Ottoman Empire, or Muscovy, the ruler employed various stratagems to expand or enhance his power. In Burgundy, the dukes staged lavish ceremonies to win the affection of their diverse subjects; in England, a strengthened monarchy emerged from a civil war that weakened the feudal nobility; in Spain, the monarchs repressed religious minorities in their newly unified land; in France, the kings raised taxes and established a permanent standing army; in the Balkans and Russia, autocratic princes enjoyed powers unheard of in western Europe in their expanding empires. In central Europe, by contrast, the rulers failed to centralize power.

Burgundy. The expansion of Burgundy during the fifteenth century was a result of military might and careful statecraft. The spectacular success of the Burgundian dukes—and the equally dramatic demise of Burgundian power—bear testimony to the artful creation of the Renaissance state, paving the way for the development of the European nation-state.

Part of the French royal house, the Burgundian dynasty expanded its power rapidly by acquiring land, primarily in the Netherlands. Between 1384 and 1476, the Burgundian state filled the territorial gap between France and Germany, extending from the Swiss border in the south to Friesland, Germany, in the north. Through purchases, inheritance, and conquests, the dukes ruled over French-, Dutch-, and German-speaking subjects, creating a state that resembled a patchwork of provinces and regions, each jealously guarding its laws and traditions. The Low Countries, with their flourishing cities, constituted the state's economic heartland, and the region of Burgundy itself, which gave the state its name, offered rich farmlands and vineyards. Unlike England, whose island geography made it a natural political unit; or France, whose borders were forged in the national experience of repelling English invaders; or Castile, whose national identity came from centuries of warfare against Islam, Burgundy was an artificial creation whose coherence depended entirely on the skillful exercise of statecraft.

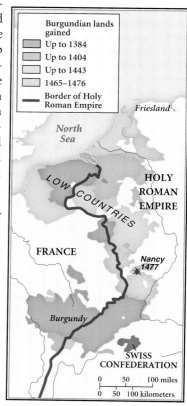

Expansion of Burgundy, 1384–1476

At the heart of Burgundian politics was the personal cult of its dukes. Philip the Good (r. 1418–1467) and his son Charles the Bold (r. 1467–1477) were very different kinds of rulers, but both were devoted to enhancing the prestige of their dynasty and the security of their dominion. A bon vivant who fathered many illegitimate children, Philip was a lavish patron of the arts who commissioned numerous illuminated manuscripts, chronicles, tapestries, paintings, and music in his efforts to glorify Burgundy. Charles, by contrast, spent more time on war than at court, preferring to drill his troops rather than seduce noblewomen. Renowned for his courage (hence his nickname), he died in 1477 when his army was routed by the Swiss at Nancy.

The Burgundians' success depended in large part on their personal relationship with their subjects. Not only did the dukes travel constantly from one part of their dominion to another, they also staged elaborate ceremonies to enhance their power and promote their legitimacy. Their entries into cities and their presence at ducal weddings, births, and funerals became the centerpieces of a "theater" state in which the dynasty provided the only link among very diverse territories. New rituals became propaganda tools. Philip's revival of chivalry in the ducal court transformed the semi-independent nobility into courtiers closely tied to the prince.

In addition to sponsoring political propaganda, the Burgundian rulers controlled their geographically dispersed state by developing a financial bureaucracy and a standing army. But maintaining the army, one of the largest in Europe, left the dukes chronically short of money. They were forced to sell political offices to raise funds, a practice that led to an inefficient and corrupt bureaucracy. The demise of the Burgundian state had two sources: the loss of Charles the Bold, who died without a male heir, and an alliance between France and the Holy Roman Empire. When Charles fell in battle in 1477, France seized the duchy of Burgundy. The Netherlands remained loyal to Mary, Charles's daughter, and through her husband, the future Holy Roman Emperor Maximilian, some of the Burgundian lands and the dynasty's political and artistic legacy passed on to the Habsburgs.

England. In England, defeat in the Hundred Years' War was followed by civil war at home. Henry VI (r. 1422–1461), who ascended to the throne as a

The Burgundian Court
The ideals of late-medieval courtly style found fullest expression in the fifteenth-century Burgundy. This painting of the wedding of Philip the Good and Isabella of Portugal was executed in the workshop of the Flemish master Jan van Eyck. It conveys the atmosphere of chivalric fantasy in which the Burgundian dynasty enveloped itself.
Giraudon/Art Resource, NY.

child, proved in maturity to be a weak and, on occasion, mentally unstable monarch. He was unable to control the great lords of the realm, who wrought anarchy with their numerous private feuds; between 1450 and 1455, six of the thirty-six peers in the House of Lords were imprisoned at some time for violence. Henry was held in contempt by many, particularly his cousin Richard, the duke of York, who resented bitterly that the House of Lancaster had usurped the throne in 1399, depriving the House of York of its legitimate claim. In 1460, Richard rebelled; although he was killed in battle, his son defeated Henry and was then crowned Edward IV (r. 1461–1483). England's intermittent civil wars, later called the Wars of the Roses (after the white and red roses worn by the Yorkists and Lancastrians, respectively), continued until 1485, fueled at home by factions among nobles and regional discontent and abroad by Franco-Burgundian intervention. Edward IV crushed the Lancastrian claim in 1470, but the Yorkist succession ended in 1485 when Richard III (r. 1483–1485), Edward's younger brother, perished at the battle of Bosworth. The ultimate victor was Henry Tudor, who married Elizabeth of York, the daughter of Edward IV, and became Henry VII (r. 1485–1509). The Tudor claim benefited from Richard's notoriety; Richard was widely suspected of obtaining the throne by murdering his young nephews, two of Edward IV's sons—a sinister legend to which William Shakespeare would give even more fantastic proportions one century later in his famous play *Richard III*.

The Wars of the Roses did relatively little damage to England's soil. The battles were generally short, and, in the words of the French chronicler Philippe de Commynes (c. 1447–1511), "England enjoyed this peculiar mercy above all other kingdoms, that neither the country, nor the people nor the houses, were wasted, destroyed or demolished, but the calamities and misfortunes of the war fell only upon the soldiers, and especially on the nobility." As a result, the English economy continued to grow during the fifteenth century. The cloth industry expanded considerably, and the English now used much of the raw wool that they had been exporting to the Low Countries to manufacture goods at home. London merchants, taking a vigorous role in trade, also assumed greater political prominence not only in the governance of London but as bankers to kings and members of Parliament; they constituted a small minority in the House of Commons, which was dominated by the country gentry. In the countryside the landed classes—the nobility, the gentry, and the yeomanry (free farmers)—benefited from rising farm and land-rent income as the population increased slowly but steadily.

Spain. In the Iberian monarchies, decades of civil war over the royal successions began to wane only in 1469, when Isabella of Castile and Ferdinand of Aragon married. Retaining their separate titles, the two monarchs ruled jointly over their dominions, each of which adhered to its traditional laws and privileges. Their union represented the first step toward the creation of a unified Spain out of two medieval kingdoms. Isabella and Ferdinand limited the privileges of the nobility and allied themselves with the cities, relying on the Hermandad (civic militia) to enforce justice and on lawyers to staff the royal council.

The united strength of Castile and Aragon brought the reconquista to a close with a final crusade against the Muslims. After more than a century of peace, war broke out in 1478 between Granada, the last Iberian Muslim state, and the Catholic royal forces. Weakened by internal strife, Granada finally fell in 1492. Two years later, in recognition of the crusade, Pope Alexander VI bestowed the title "Catholic monarchs" on Isabella and Ferdinand, ringing in an era in which

Unification of Spain, Late Fifteenth Century

militant Catholicism became an instrument of state authority and shaped the national consciousness.

The relative religious tolerance of the Middle Ages, in which Iberian Muslims, Jews, and Christians had lived side by side, now yielded to the demand for religious conformity. The practice of Catholicism became a test of one's loyalty to the church and to the Spanish monarchy. In 1478, royal jurisdiction introduced the Inquisition to Spain, primarily as a means to control the *conversos* (Jewish converts to Christianity), whose elevated positions in the economy and the government aroused widespread resentment from the so-called Old Christians. *Conversos* often were suspected of practicing their ancestral religion in secret while pretending to adhere to their new Christian faith. Appointed by the monarchs, the clergy (called "inquisitors") presided over tribunals set up to investigate those suspected of religious deviancy. The accused, who were arrested on charges often based on anonymous denunciations and information gathered by the inquisitors, could defend themselves but not confront their accusers. The wide spectrum of punishments ranged from monetary fines to the *auto de fé* (a ritual of public confession) to

Queen Isabella of Castile

In 1474 Isabella became queen of Castile, and in 1479 her husband Ferdinand took control of the kingdom of Aragon. This union of crowns would lead to the creation of a unified Spain. It would also promulgate a religious hegemony as the "Catholic monarchs" expelled Jews and Muslims from their kingdoms.
Laurie Platt Winfrey, Inc.

Just as with a strong hand and outstretched arm, and much honor and riches, God through Moses had miraculously taken the other people of Israel from Egypt, so in these parts of Spain they had . . . to go out with much honor and riches, without losing any of their goods, to possess the holy promised land, which they confessed to have lost through their great and abominable sins which their ancestors had committed against God.

burning at the stake. After the fall of Granada, many Moors were forced to convert or resettle in Castile, and in 1492 Ferdinand and Isabella ordered all Jews in their kingdoms to choose between exile and conversion.

The single most dramatic event for the Jews of Renaissance Europe was their expulsion from Spain, the country with the largest and most vibrant Jewish communities, and their subsequent dispersion throughout the Mediterranean world. On the eve of the expulsion, approximately 200,000 Jews and 300,000 *conversos* were living in Castile and Aragon. Faced with the choice to convert or leave, well over 100,000 Jews chose exile. The priest Andrés Bernáldez described the expulsion:

France. France, too, was recovering from war. Although France won the Hundred Years' War, it emerged from that conflict in the shadow of the brilliant Burgundian court. Under Charles VII (r. 1422–1461) and Louis XI (r. 1461–1483), the French monarchy began the slow process of expansion and recovery. Abroad, Louis fomented rebellion in England. At home, however, lay the more dangerous enemy, Burgundy. In 1477, with the death of Charles the Bold, Louis seized large tracts of Burgundian territory. France's horizons expanded even more when Louis inherited most of southern France after the Anjou dynasty died out. By the end of the century, France had doubled its territory, assuming close to its modern-day boundaries.

To strengthen royal power at home, Louis promoted industry and commerce, imposed permanent salt and land taxes (called the *gabelle* and the *taille*), maintained the first standing army in western Europe, and dispensed with the meeting of the General Estates, which included the clergy, the nobility, and the major towns of France. The French kings further increased their power with important concessions from the papacy. With the 1438 Pragmatic Sanction of Bourges, Charles asserted the superiority of a general church council over the pope. Harking back to a long tradition of the High Middle Ages, the Sanction of Bourges established what would come to be known as Gallicanism (after Gaul, the ancient Roman name for France), in which the French king would effectively control ecclesiastical revenues and the appointment of French bishops.

Central-Eastern Europe. The rise of strong, new monarchies in western Europe contrasted sharply with the weakness of state authority in central and eastern Europe, where developments in Hungary, Bohemia, and Poland resembled the Burgundian model of personal dynastic authority (Map 14.3). Under Matthias Corvinus (r. 1456–1490), the

MAP 14.3 Eastern Europe in the Fifteenth Century
The rise of Muscovy and the Ottomans shaped the map of eastern Europe. Some Christian monarchies such as Serbia lost their independence. Others, such as Hungary, held off the Ottomans until the early sixteenth century.

Hungarian king who briefly united the Bohemian and Hungarian crowns, a central-eastern European empire seemed to be emerging. A patron of the arts and a humanist, Matthias created a great library in Hungary. He repeatedly defeated the encroaching Austrian Habsburgs and even occupied Vienna in 1485. His empire did not outlast his death in 1490, however. The powerful Hungarian magnates, who enjoyed the constitutional right to elect the king, ended it by refusing to acknowledge his son's claim to the throne.

In Poland, the nobility preserved their power under the monarchy by maintaining their right to elect kings. By selecting weak monarchs and fiercely defending noble liberties, the Polish nobility ruled a land of serfs and frustrated any attempt at the centralization of power and state building. Only in 1506 would Poland and Lithuania again form a loosely united "commonwealth" under a single king.

The Ottoman Empire. In the Balkans, the Ottoman Empire, under Sultan Mehmed II (r. 1451–1481), became a serious threat to all of Christian Europe. After Mehmed ascended the throne, he proclaimed a holy war and laid siege to Constantinople in 1453. A city of 100,000, the Byzantine capital could muster only 6,000 defenders (including a small contingent of Genoese) against an Ottoman force estimated at between 200,000 and 400,000 men. The city's fortifications, many of which dated from Emperor Justinian's rule in the sixth century, were no match for fifteenth-century cannons. The defenders held out for fifty-three days: while the Christians confessed their sins and prayed for divine deliverance, in desperate anticipation of the Second Coming, the Muslim besiegers pressed forward, urged on by the certainty of rich spoils and Allah's promise of a final victory over the infidel Rome. Finally the defenders were overwhelmed, and the last Byzantine emperor, Constantine Palaeologus, died in battle. Some 60,000 residents were carried off in slavery, and the city was sacked. Mehmed entered Constantinople in triumph, rendered thanks to Allah in Justinian's Church of St. Sophia, which had been turned into a mosque, and was remembered as "the Conqueror." In another sign of the times, however, the Muslim ruler would ask Italian court painter Matteo de Pasti to help create the imperial palace intended to communicate Ottoman power.

Muscovy. North of the Black Sea and east of Poland-Lithuania, a very different polity was taking shape. In the second half of the fifteenth century, the princes of Muscovy embarked on a spectacular path of success that would make their state the largest on earth. Subservient to the Mongols in the fourteenth century, the Muscovite princes began to assert their independence with the collapse of Mongol power. Ivan III (r. 1462–1505) was the first Muscovite prince to claim an imperial title, referring to himself as *tsar* (or *czar*, from the name *Caesar*). In

The Medieval Royal Castle of Visegrad
King Matthias Corvinus made Visegrad the political and cultural center of Hungary before it was destroyed in the Ottoman conquests. Situated on top of a hill commanding a strategic position over the road and the Danube River, Visegrad—shown here in a present-day reconstruction— was above all a fortification.
Szabolcs Hámor/MTI/Eastfoto.

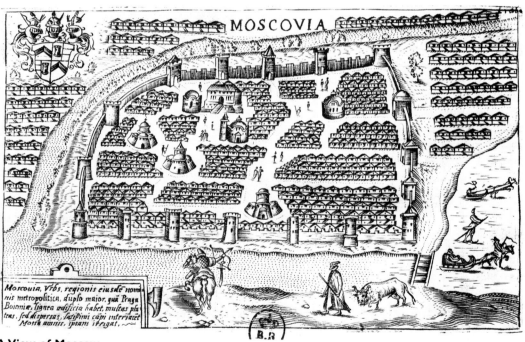

A View of Moscow
This image comes from the travel book of the Habsburg ambassador to Moscow, Sigismund von Herberstein, who engraved it himself in 1547. Note the representation of Muscovite soldiers with bows and arrows, weapons long since outdated in western Europe. Note also the domination of the Kremlin (in the middle of the city) over a city that consisted mostly of modest wooden houses.
Giraudon/Art Resource, NY.

1471, Ivan defeated the city-state of Novgorod, whose territories encompassed a vast region in northern Russia. Six years later he abolished the local civic government of this proudly independent city, which had enjoyed individual trade with economically thriving cities of central Europe. To con- solidate his autocratic rule and wipe out memories of past freedoms, in 1484 and 1489 Ivan forcibly re- located thousands of leading Novgorod families to lands around Moscow. He also expanded his terri- tory to the south and east when his forces pushed back the Mongols to the Volga River.

Unlike monarchies in western and central-eastern Europe, whose powers were bound by collective rights and laws, Ivan's Russian monarchy claimed absolute property rights over all lands and subjects. The expansionist Muscovite state was shaped by two traditions: religion and service. After the fall of the Byzantine Empire, the tsar was the Russian Orthodox church's only defender of the faith against Islam and Catholicism. Orthodox propaganda thus legitimized the tsar's rule by proclaiming Moscow the "Third Rome" (the first two being Rome and Constantinople) and praising the tsar's autocratic power as the best protector of the faith. The Mongol system of service to rulers also deeply informed Muscovite statecraft. Ivan III and his descendants considered themselves heirs to the empire of the Mongols. In their conception of the state as private dominion, their emphasis on autocratic power, and their division of the populace into a landholding elite in service to the tsar and a vast majority of taxpaying subjects, the Muscovite princes created a state more in the despotic political tradition of the central Asian steppes and the Ottoman Empire than of western Europe.

Hence in the intense competition and state building of the fifteenth century, Muscovy joined England, France, and Spain as examples of success, in sharp contrast to Burgundy and Poland. Yet far more significant was the expansion of the boundary of Europe itself, as maritime explorations brought Europeans into contact with indigenous civilizations in Africa, the Americas, and Asia.

❖ On the Threshold of World History: Widening Geographic Horizons

The fifteenth century constituted the first era of world history. The significance of the century lies not so much in the European "discovery" of Africa and the Americas as in the breakdown of cultural frontiers inaugurated by European colonial expansion. Before the maritime explorations of Portugal and Spain, Europe had remained at the periphery of world history. Fourteenth-century Mongols had been more interested in conquering China and Persia—lands with sophisticated cultures—than in invading Europe; Persian historians of the early

fifteenth century dismissed Europeans as "barbaric Franks"; and China's Ming dynasty rulers, who sent maritime expeditions to Southeast Asia and East Africa around 1400, seemed unaware of the Europeans, even though Marco Polo and other Italian merchants had appeared at the court of the preceding Mongol Yuan dynasty. In the fifteenth century, Portuguese and Spanish vessels, followed a century later by English, French, and Dutch ships, sailed across the Atlantic, Indian, and Pacific Oceans, bringing with them people, merchandise, crops, and diseases in a global exchange that would shape the modern world. For the first time the people of the Americas were brought into contact with a larger historical force that threatened to destroy not only their culture but their existence. European exploitation, conquest, and racism defined this historical era of transition from the medieval to the modern world, as Europeans left the Baltic and the Mediterranean for wider oceans.

The Divided Mediterranean

In the second half of the fifteenth century, the Mediterranean Sea, which had dominated medieval maritime trade, began to lose its preeminence to the Atlantic Ocean. To win control over the Mediterranean, the Ottomans embarked upon an ambitious naval program to transform their empire into a major maritime power. War and piracy disrupted the flow of Christian trade: the Venetians mobilized all their resources to fight off Turkish advances, and the Genoese largely abandoned the eastern Mediterranean for trade opportunities presented by the Atlantic voyage.

The Mediterranean states used ships made with relatively backward naval technology, compared with that of Portugal and Spain. The most common ship, the galley—a flat-bottomed vessel propelled by sails and oars—dated from the time of ancient Rome. Most galleys could not withstand open-ocean voyages, although Florentine and Genoese galleys still made long journeys to Flanders and England, hugging the coast for protection. The galley's dependence on human labor was a more serious handicap. Because prisoners of war and convicted criminals toiled as oarsmen in both Christian and Muslim ships, victory in war or the enforcement of criminal penalties was crucial to a state's ability to float large numbers of galleys. Slavery, too, a traditional Mediterranean institution, sometimes provided the necessary labor.

Although the Mediterranean was divided into Muslim and Christian zones, it still offered a significant opportunity for exchange. Sugarcane was transported to the western Mediterranean from western Asia. From the Balearic Islands off Spain (under Aragonese rule), the crop then traveled to the Canary Islands in the Atlantic, where the Spanish enslaved the native population to work the new sugar plantations. In this way, slavery was exported from the western Mediterranean to the Atlantic, and then on to the Americas.

Engraving of Katharina, an African Woman
Like other artists in early-sixteenth-century Europe, Albrecht Dürer would have seen in person Africans who went to Portugal and Spain as students, servants, and slaves. Note Katharina's noble expression and dignified attire. Before the rise of the slave trade in the seventeenth century, most Africans in Europe were household servants of the aristocracy. Considered prestigious symbols, such servants were not employed primarily for economic production.
Foto Marburg/Art Resource, NY.

Different ethnic groups also moved across the maritime frontier. After Granada fell in 1492, many Muslims fled to North Africa and continued to raid the Spanish coast. When Castile expelled the Jews, some of them settled in North Africa, more in Italy, and many in the Ottoman Empire, Greek-speaking Thessalonika, and Palestine. Conversant in two or three languages, Spanish Jews often served as intermediaries between the Christian West and Muslim East. Greeks occupied a similar position. Most Greeks in the homeland adhered to the Greek Orthodox church under Ottoman protection, but some converted to Islam and entered imperial service, making up a large part of the Ottoman navy. The Greeks on Crete, Chios, and other Aegean islands, however, lived under Italian rule, some of them converting to Roman Catholicism and entering Venetian, Genoese, and Spanish service. A region with warring states and competing religions, the Mediterranean remained a divided zone as more and more Europeans turned instead to the unknown oceans.

Portuguese Explorations

The first phase of European overseas expansion began in 1433 with Portugal's systematic exploration of the west African coast and culminated in 1519–1522 with Spain's circumnavigation of the globe (Map 14.4). Looking back, the sixteenth-century Spanish historian Francisco López de Gómora described the Iberian maritime voyages to the East and West Indies as "the greatest event since the creation of the world, apart from the incarnation and death of him who created it." (See "New Sources, New Perspectives," page 518.)

In many ways a continuation of the struggle against Muslims in the Iberian peninsula, Portugal's maritime voyages displayed that country's mixed motives of piety, glory, and greed. The Atlantic explorations depended for their success on several technological breakthroughs, such as the lateen sail adapted from the Arabs (it permitted a ship to tack against headwinds), new types of sailing vessels, and better charts and instruments. But the sailors themselves were barely touched by the expanding intellectual universe of the Renaissance; what motivated these explorers was a combination of crusading zeal against Muslims and medieval adventure stories, such as the tales of the Venetian traveler Marco Polo (1254–1324) and John Mandeville, a fourteenth-

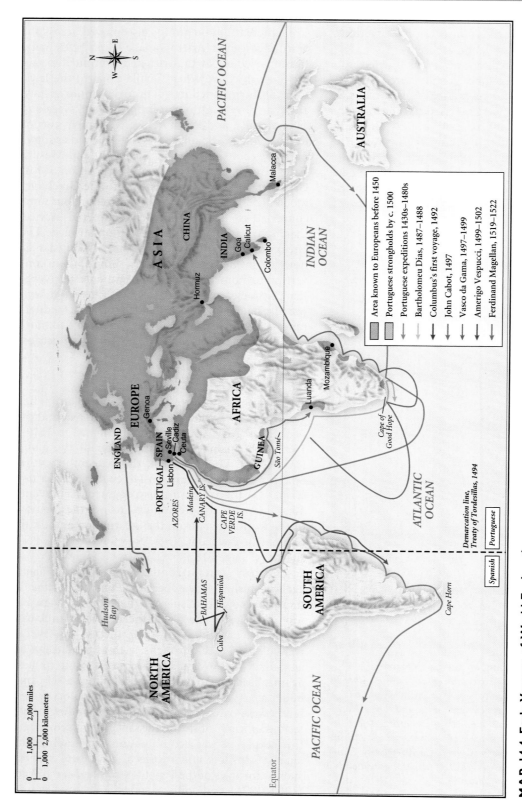

MAP 14.4 Early Voyages of World Exploration

Over the course of the fifteenth and early sixteenth centuries, the Atlantic Ocean was dominated by European shipping following the pioneering voyages of the Portuguese, who also first sailed around the Cape of Good Hope to the Indian Ocean and the Cape Horn to the Pacific. The search for spices and the need to circumnavigate the Ottoman Empire inspired these voyages.

Legend:
- Area known to Europeans before 1450
- Portuguese strongholds by c. 1500
- Portuguese expeditions 1430s–1480s
- Bartholomeu Dias, 1487–1488
- Columbus's first voyage, 1492
- John Cabot, 1497
- Vasco da Gama, 1497–1499
- Amerigo Vespucci, 1499–1502
- Ferdinand Magellan, 1519–1522

Spanish | Portuguese

century English knight who in *Travels of Sir John Mandeville* transfixed readers with his stirring and often fantastic stories. Behind the spirit of the crusade lurked vistas of vast gold mines in West Africa (the trade across the Sahara was controlled by Arabs) and a mysterious Christian kingdom established by Prester John (actually the Coptic Christian kingdom of Abyssinia, or Ethiopia, in East Africa). The Portuguese hoped to reach the spice-producing lands of South and Southeast Asia by sea to bypass the Ottoman Turks, who controlled the traditional land routes between Europe and Asia.

By 1415, the Portuguese had captured Ceuta on the Moroccan coast, thus establishing a foothold in Africa. Thereafter Portuguese voyages sailed farther and farther down the West African coast. By mid-century, the Portuguese chain of forts had reached Guinea and could protect the gold and slave trades. At home the royal house of Portugal financed the fleets, with crucial roles played by Prince Peter, regent of the throne between 1440 and 1448; his more famous younger brother Prince Henry the Navigator; and King John II (r. 1481–1495). As a governor of the Order of Christ, a noble crusading order, Henry financed many voyages out of the order's revenues. Private monies also helped, as leading Lisbon merchants participated in financing the gold and slave trades off the Guinea coast.

In 1455, Pope Nicholas V (r. 1447–1455) sanctioned Portuguese overseas expansion, commending King John II's crusading spirit and granting him and his successors the monopoly on trade with inhabitants of the newly "discovered" regions. By 1478–1488, Bartholomeu Dias could take advantage of the prevailing winds in the South Atlantic to reach the Cape of Good Hope. A mere ten years later (1497–1499), under the captainship of Vasco da Gama, a Portuguese fleet rounded the cape and reached Calicut, India, the center of the spice trade. Twenty-three years later, in 1512, Ferdinand Magellan, a Portuguese sailor in Spanish service, led the first expedition to circumnavigate the globe. By 1517, a chain of Portuguese forts dotted the Indian Ocean: at Mozambique, Hormuz (at the mouth of the Persian Gulf), Goa (in India), Colombo (in modern Sri Lanka), and Malacca (modern Malaysia).

After the voyages of Christopher Columbus, Portugal's interests clashed with Spain's. Mediated by Pope Alexander VI, the 1494 Treaty of Tordesillas settled disputes between Portugal and Spain by dividing the Atlantic world between the two royal houses. A demarcation 370 leagues west of the Cape Verdes Islands divided the Atlantic Ocean, reserving for Portugal the west African coast and the route to India and giving Spain the oceans and lands to the west (see Map 14.4). Unwittingly, this agreement also allowed Portugal to claim Brazil in 1500, which was accidentally "discovered" by Pedro Alvares Cabral (1467–1520) on his voyage to India. The Iberian maritime expansion drew on a mixture of religious zeal and greed that would mark the beginnings of European colonialism in the rest of the world.

The Voyages of Columbus

Historians agree that Christopher Columbus (1451–1506) was born of Genoese parents; beyond that, we have little accurate information about this man who brought together the history of Europe and the Americas. In 1476, he arrived in Portugal, apparently a survivor in a naval battle between a Franco-Portuguese and a Genoese fleet; in 1479, he married a Portuguese noblewoman. He spent the next few years mostly in Portuguese service, gaining valuable experience in regular voyages down the west coast of Africa. In 1485, after the death of his wife, Columbus settled in Spain.

Fifteenth-century Europeans already knew that Asia lay beyond the vast Atlantic Ocean, and *The Travels of Marco Polo*, written more than a century earlier, still exerted a powerful hold on European images of the East. Columbus read it many times, along with other travel books, and proposed to sail west across the Atlantic to reach the lands of the khan, unaware that the Mongol Empire had already collapsed in eastern Asia. Vastly underestimating the distances, he dreamed of finding a new route to the East's gold and spices and partook of the larger European vision that had inspired the Portuguese voyages. (His critics had a much more accurate idea of the globe's size and of the difficulty of the venture.) But after the Portuguese and French monarchs rejected his proposal, Columbus found royal patronage with the recently proclaimed Catholic monarchs Isabella of Castile and Ferdinand of Aragon.

In August 1492, equipped with a modest fleet of three ships and about ninety men, Columbus set sail across the Atlantic. His contract stipulated that he would claim Castilian sovereignty over any new land and inhabitants and share any profits with the

Portuguese Voyages of Discovery

The quincentennial celebration of Vasco da Gama's 1499 voyage to India took place in the same year (1998) that Lisbon staged a World Exposition—thus inspiring the theme of "Discoveries of the Oceans" in Portugal's presentation of its historical past and contributions to civilization. The celebration of Portugal and the oceans strengthened interest in Portuguese maritime history and traditions but it also inspired examination of that country's historical memory and criticism of that history. The result has been a rich mix of new sources and perspectives, presented in publications and exhibitions.

A Nautical Tide Calendar
A high-tide chart, showing at which hour and at which fifth (the hour is divided into twelve minute segments) high tide will recur from the day of the new moon. The left column in black starts with the date of the new moon and day. The red columns indicate first the hour and then the fifth of high tide.

A Nautical Solar Guide
From the codex of Bastiao Lopes (c. 1568), this guide shows the declination angle of the sun for different days in the months of April, May, and June.

The more traditional historical approach emphasizes the technical innovations of Portuguese seamanship. Inventions of new sailing vessels, such as the *caravel,* a high-sided ship capable of carrying a large load and maintaining balance in rough seas, enabled Portuguese sailors to venture ever farther into the oceans. Other nautical instruments reflected a cumulative knowledge of seamanship and geography that reduced the risks of long-distance travel. Sailors compiled nautical guides showing the time of tides (Figure 1) and the position of the sun in the sky at different latitudes at different seasons (Figure 2). Most valuable of all were the pilots' books, or *roteiros* (books of sailing directions), often accompanied by detailed maps of maritime regions and coasts. These books of routes and maritime charts lessened but did not eliminate the dangers of the oceans. The *roteiro* of Diogo Alfonso (1535), for example, gave these directions for the voyage to India:

Setting forth from Lisbon you steer to the southwest until you catch sight of the island of Porto Santo or the island of Madeira. And from thence go southward in search of the Canaries; and as soon as you pass the Canaries set course southwest and south until you reach 15 degrees, that is 50 leagues from Cape Verde.

After passing through the mid-Atlantic, Alfonso advised the pilots to seek the most important landmark of all:

If you come 35 degrees more or less, seeking the Cape of Good Hope, when you come upon cliff-faces, you may know that they are those of the Cape of Good Hope. . . . From hence you should set course northeast by north to $19^{1}/_{4}$ degrees. Then north-northeast, until you reach the latitude of $16^{3}/_{4}$ degrees (59).

Portugal's historical memory, solidified in the centuries since its earliest explorers, has celebrated its national heroes and discoverers as it mourned the numerous ships and men lost at sea. But much of this commemoration developed as a justification for Portuguese colonialism in the late nineteenth and early twentieth centuries, a fact now being examined by scholars in the wake of the Vasco da Gama quincentennial. How did Muslims and Indians see the arrival of the Portuguese, for example? The Indian historian Sanjay Subrahmanyam has argued that Vasco da Gama brought a new level of maritime violence to the Indian Ocean in 1499 by his attacks on Muslim shipping. Still other scholars, such as Antonio Manuel Hespanha, director of the Scientific Committee of the Discoveries, has called upon Portuguese scholars to examine their own past with a critical eye. The many volumes and expositions sponsored by the committee have highlighted the multicultural aspects of the Portuguese encounter with Asia, America, and Africa, one that was too complex and ambivalent to be reduced to a simple heroic mode.

QUESTIONS FOR DEBATE

1. What do the two documents suggest about the dangers faced by Portuguese sailors?

2. What were the motives behind the Portuguese voyages to India?

FURTHER READING

Russell-Wood, A. J. R. *A World on the Move: The Portuguese in Africa, Asia, and America, 1415–1800.* 1992.

Subrahmanyam, S. *The Career and Legend of Vasco da Gama.* 1997.

Portuguese Ships
Maritime voyagers in Portugal were sponsored by the highest authorities in the land, the best known of whom was Prince Henry, nicknamed "the Navigator." This detail from the Altarpiece of Santa Ana depicts monarchs, noblemen, and bishops against a backdrop of different types of sailing vessels. The caravel, the largest ship in the background, was the main type of vessel for Portuguese voyages in the fifteenth and sixteenth centuries.

IMPORTANT DATES

1415   Portugal captures Ceuta, establishing foothold in Africa

1438   Pragmatic Sanction of Bourges

1440s   Gutenberg introduces the printing press

c. 1450–1500   Height of Florentine Renaissance

1453   Fall of Constantinople; end of Byzantine Empire

1454   Treaty of Lodi; power balance in Italy

1460–1485   Wars of the Roses; Tudor dynasty ascendant

1462   Ivan III of Muscovy claims imperial title "tsar"

1471–1484   Reign of Pope Sixtus IV; Renaissance in Rome

1474–1516   Spain unified under Isabella of Castile and Ferdinand of Aragon

1477   Death of Charles the Bold; end of Burgundy

1478   Inquisition established in Spain

1492   Columbus's first voyage; Christians conquer Muslim Granada and expel Jews from Spain

1499   Vasco da Gama reaches India

1500   Portugal claims Brazil

crown. Reaching what is today the Bahamas on October 12, Columbus mistook the islands to be part of the East Indies, not far from Japan and "the lands of the Great Khan." As the Castilians explored the Caribbean islands, they encountered communities of peaceful Indians, the Arawaks, who were awed by the Europeans' military technology, not to mention their appearance. Exchanging gifts of beads and broken glass for Arawak gold—an exchange that convinced Columbus of the trusting nature of the Indians—the crew established peaceful relationships with many communities. Yet in spite of many positive entries in the ship's log referring to Columbus's personal goodwill toward the Indians, the Europeans' objectives were clear: find gold, subjugate the Indians, and propagate Christianity.

Columbus in the Caribbean

Excited by the prospect of easy riches, many flocked to join Columbus's second voyage. When Columbus departed Cádiz in September 1493, he commanded seventeen ships that carried between 1,200 and 1,500 men, many believing all they had to do was "to load the gold into the ships." Failing to find the imaginary gold mines and spices, however, the colonial enterprise quickly switched its focus to finding slaves. Columbus and his crew first enslaved the Caribs, enemies of the Arawaks; in 1494, Columbus proposed a regular slave trade based in Hispaniola. The Spaniards exported enslaved Indians to Spain, and slave traders sold them in Seville. Soon the Spaniards began importing sugarcane from Madeira, forcing large numbers of Indians to work on plantations to produce enough sugar for export to Europe. Columbus himself was edged out of this new enterprise. When the Spanish monarchs realized the vast potential for material gain that lay in their new dominions, they asserted direct royal authority by sending officials and priests to the Americas, which were named after the Italian Amerigo Vespucci, who led a voyage across the Atlantic in 1499–1502.

Columbus's place in history embodies the fundamental transformations of his age. A Genoese in the service of Portuguese and Spanish employers, Columbus had a career illustrating the changing balance between the Mediterranean and the Atlantic. As the fifteenth-century Ottomans drove Genoese merchants out of the eastern Mediterranean, the Genoese turned to the Iberian peninsula. Columbus was one of many such adventurers who served the Spanish and Portuguese crowns. The voyages of 1492–1493 would eventually draw the triangle of exchange among Europe, the Americas, and Africa, an exchange gigantic in its historical impact and its human cost.

A New Era in Slavery

The European voyages of discovery initiated a new era in slavery, both in expanding the economic scale of slave labor and in attaching race and color to servitude. Slavery had existed since antiquity. During the Renaissance, slavery was practiced in many diverse forms. Nearly all slaves arrived as strangers in the Mediterranean ports of Barcelona, Marseille, Venice, and Genoa. Some were captured in war or by piracy; others—Africans—were sold by other Africans and Bedouin traders to Christian buyers; in western Asia, parents sold their children into servitude out of poverty; and many in the Balkans became slaves when their land was devastated by Ottoman invasions. Slaves were Greek, Slav, European, African, and Turk. Many served as domestic slaves in the leading European cities of the Mediterranean. Others sweated as galley slaves in Ottoman and Christian fleets. Still others worked as agricultural laborers on Mediterranean islands. In the Ottoman army, slaves even formed an important elite contingent.

The Portuguese maritime voyages changed this picture. From the fifteenth century, Africans increasingly filled the ranks of slaves. Exploiting warfare in West Africa, the Portuguese traded in gold and "pieces," as African slaves were called, a practice condemned at home by some conscientious clergy. One, Manoel Severim de Faria, observed that "one cannot yet see any good effect resulting from so much butchery; for this is not the way in which commerce can flourish and the preaching of the gospel progress." Critical voices, however, could not deny the enormous profits that the slave trade brought to Portugal. Most slaves toiled in the sugar plantations of the Portuguese Atlantic islands and in Brazil. A fortunate few labored as domestic servants in Portugal, where African freedmen and slaves, some 35,000 in the early sixteenth century, constituted almost 3 percent of the population, a percentage that was much higher than in other European countries. In the Americas, slavery would truly flourish as an institution of exploitation.

Europeans in the New World

In 1500, on the eve of European invasion, the native peoples of the Americas were divided into many sedentary and nomadic societies. Among the settled peoples, the largest political and social organizations centered in the Mexican and Peruvian highlands. The Aztecs and the Incas ruled over subjugated Indian populations in their respective empires. With an elaborate religious culture and a rigid social and political hierarchy, the Aztecs and Incas based their civilizations in large, urban capitals.

The Spanish explorers organized their expeditions to the mainland from a base in the Caribbean (Map 14.5). Two prominent leaders, Hernán Cortés

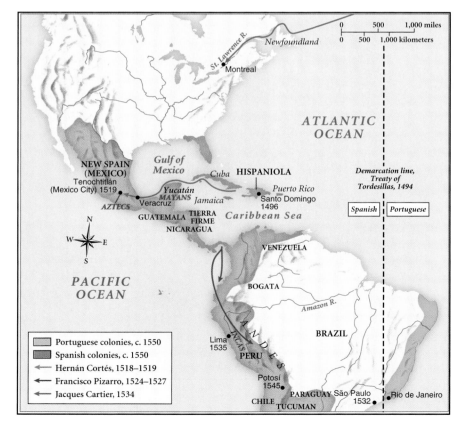

MAP 14.5 European Explorations in the Americas in the Sixteenth Century
While Spanish and Portuguese explorers claimed Central and South America for the Iberian crowns, there were relatively few voyages to North America. The discovery of precious metals fueled the explorations and settlements of Central and South America, establishing the foundations of European colonial empires in the New World.

(1485–1547) and Francisco Pizarro (c. 1475–1541), gathered men and arms and set off in search of gold. Catholic priests accompanied the fortune hunters to bring Christianity to allegedly uncivilized peoples and thus to justify brutal conquests. His small band swelled by peoples who had been subjugated by the Aztecs, Cortés captured the Aztec capital, Tenochtitlán, in 1519. Two years later Mexico, then named New Spain, was added to Charles V's empire. To the south, Pizarro conquered the Andean highlands, exploiting a civil war between rival Incan kings.

By the mid-sixteenth century the Spanish empire, built on greed and justified by its self-proclaimed Catholic mission, stretched unbroken from Mexico to Chile. In addition to the Aztecs and Incas, the Spaniards also subdued the Mayas on the Yucatán peninsula, a people with a sophisticated knowledge of cosmology and arithmetic. The gold and silver mines in Mexico proved a treasure trove for the Spanish crown, but the real prize was the discovery of vast silver deposits in Potosí (today in Bolivia).

Not to be outdone by the Spaniards, other European powers joined the scramble for gold in the New World. In 1500, a Portuguese fleet landed at Brazil, but Portugal did not begin colonizing until 1532, when it established a permanent fort on the coast. In North America, the French went in search of a "northwest passage" to China. By 1504, French fishermen had appeared in Newfoundland. Thirty years later Jacques Cartier led three voyages that explored the St. Lawrence River as far as Montreal. An early attempt in 1541 to settle Canada failed because

MAPPING THE WEST Renaissance Europe, c. 1500

By 1500, the shape of early modern Europe was largely consolidated and would remain stable until the eighteenth century. The only exception was the disappearance of an independent Hungarian kingdom after 1529.

of the harsh winter and Indian hostility, and John Cabot's 1497 voyage to find a northern route to Asia also failed. More permanent settlements in Canada and the present-day United States would succeed only in the seventeenth century.

Conclusion

The Renaissance was a period of expansion: in the intellectual horizons of Europeans through the rediscovery of classical civilization and a renewed appreciation of human potential and achievement; in the greater centralization and institutionalization of expanded power of the state; and, finally, in the widened geographic horizons of an age of maritime exploration. Above all, the Renaissance was one of the most brilliant periods in artistic activity, one that glorified both God and humanity. A new spirit of confidence spurred Renaissance artists to a new appreciation for the human body and a new visual perspective in art and to apply mathematics and science to architecture, music, and artistic composition.

Highlighting the intensity of cultural production was the competition between burgeoning states and between Christian Europe and the Muslim Ottoman Empire. That competition fostered an expansion of the frontiers of Europe first to Africa and then across the Atlantic Ocean to the Americas. While centered in Italy, the Renaissance was also the first period of global history, which would eventually shift the center of European civilization from the Mediterranean to the Atlantic seaboard. But while Europeans of the Renaissance recovered from the deprivations of the later Middle Ages, they would soon enter yet another period of turmoil, one brought about not by demographic and economic collapse but by a profound crisis of conscience that the brilliance of Renaissance civilization had tended to obscure.

Suggested References

Widening Intellectual Horizons

In addition to the study of great artists and writers, recent scholarship has turned its attention to the "consumption" of cultural goods. Its focus has been on issues of education, readership, art markets, and the different habits of reading and seeing in the past.

Baxandall, Michael. *Painting and Experience in Fifteenth Century Italy: A Primer in the Social History of Pictorial Style.* 1972.

Burke, Peter. *The Italian Renaissance: Culture and Society in Italy.* 1986.

Grafton, Anthony, and Lisa Jardine. *From Humanism to the Humanities: Education and the Liberal Arts in Fifteenth and Sixteenth Century Europe.* 1986.

Jardine, Lisa. *Worldly Goods.* 1996.

http://www.lincolnu.edu/~kluebber/euroart.htm. Renaissance art links.

Martin, Henri-Jean, and Lucien Febvre. *The Coming of the Book: The Impact of Printing, 1450–1800.* 1976.

The Intersection of Private and Public Lives

Much scholarship has focused on Italy and the Low Countries, where historical sources from this period are abundant. The investigation of legal records, population censuses, and tax rolls have yielded fascinating insights into the daily life of the period and the relationship between private life and the political process.

Brucker, Gene A., ed. *The Society of Renaissance Florence: A Documentary Study.* 1971.

Herlihy, David, and Christiane Klapisch-Zuber. *Tuscans and Their Families: A Study of the Florentine Catasto of 1427.* 1978.

Martines, Lauro. *Power and Imagination: City-States in Renaissance Italy.* 1979.

Pitkin, Hanna Fenichel. *Fortune Is a Woman: Gender and Politics in the Thought of Niccolò Machiavelli.* 1984.

Po-chia Hsia, R. *Trent 1475: Stories of a Ritual Murder Trial.* 1992.

Prevenier, Walter, and Wim Blockmans. *The Burgundian Netherlands.* 1986.

Ruggiero, Guido. *Boundaries of Eros: Sex Crime and Sexuality in Renaissance Venice.* 1985.

On the Threshold of World History

The recent celebrations of the overseas voyages of Christopher Columbus and Vasco da Gama have inspired studies with new perspectives. The traditional view of "Europe discovers the world" has been replaced by a more nuanced and complex picture that takes in non-European views and uses Asian, African, and Mesoamerican sources.

Boxer, Charles R. *Four Centuries of Portuguese Expansion, 1415–1826.* 1969.

Fuson, Robert H., ed. *The Log of Christopher Columbus.* 1987.

Russell-Wood, A. J. R. *A World on the Move: The Portuguese in Africa, Asia, and America, 1415–1808.* 1992.

Subrahmanyam, Sanjay. *The Career and Legend of Vasco da Gama.* 1997.

15

The Struggle for Reformation Europe

1500–1560

Brueghel the Elder, *Struggle between Carnival and Lent*
In this allegorical painting, Pieter Brueghel the Elder depicts the struggle for Christians between the temptations of Carnival and the observance of Lent, the season of repentance before Easter when the church prescribes fasting and other acts of penitence. At the same time, this picture vividly represents the lively street scenes from the towns of the Low Countries, the most densely urbanized region of sixteenth-century Europe. Carnival revelry still characterizes town festivities in Belgium today.
Erich Lessing/Art Resource, NY.

HILLE FEIKEN LEFT THE CITY of Münster, Germany, on June 16, 1534, elegantly dressed, bedecked with jewels, and determined to kill. Münster, which religious radicals had declared a holy city, lay under siege by armies loyal to its bishop, Franz von Waldeck. Hille was attempting to rescue her city by imitating an ancient Israelite heroine named Judith, who according to the Book of Judith delivered Jerusalem from an invading Assyrian army. The Assyrian commander Holofernes, charmed by Judith's beauty, tried to seduce her; but after he had fallen into a drunken sleep, Judith cut off his head. Terrified, the Assyrian forces fled Jerusalem. Obsessed with this story, Hille crossed enemy lines and tried to persuade the commander of the besieging troops to take her to the bishop, promising to reveal a secret means of capturing the city without further fighting. Unfortunately, a defector recognized Hille and betrayed her. She was beheaded, in her own words, for "going out as Judith and trying to make the Bishop of Münster into a Holofernes."

Hille Feiken and the other radicals in Münster were Anabaptists, part of a sect whose members believed they were a community of saints amid a hopelessly sinful world. The Anabaptists' efforts to form a holy community separate from society tore at the foundations of the medieval European order, and they met merciless persecution from the political and religious authorities. Anabaptism was only one dimension of the Protestant Reformation, which had been set in motion by the German friar Martin Luther in 1517 and had become a sweeping

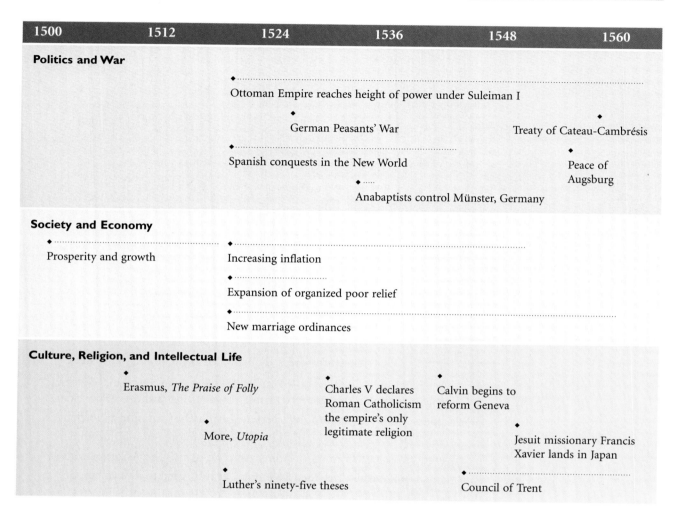

1500	1512	1524	1536	1548	1560

Politics and War

Ottoman Empire reaches height of power under Suleiman I

German Peasants' War

Treaty of Cateau-Cambrésis

Spanish conquests in the New World

Peace of Augsburg

Anabaptists control Münster, Germany

Society and Economy

Prosperity and growth

Increasing inflation

Expansion of organized poor relief

New marriage ordinances

Culture, Religion, and Intellectual Life

Erasmus, *The Praise of Folly*

Charles V declares Roman Catholicism the empire's only legitimate religion

Calvin begins to reform Geneva

More, *Utopia*

Jesuit missionary Francis Xavier lands in Japan

Luther's ninety-five theses

Council of Trent

movement to uproot church abuses and restore early Christian teachings. When Luther first criticized the practices and doctrines of the Catholic church, he had not wished to break away from Rome. As the breach widened, however, Luther and his followers referred to their camp as the "evangelical movement," emphasizing its adherence to the Bible. Supporters of Luther were called "evangelicals" until 1529, when German princes and city delegates lodged a formal protest against imperial authorities who had declared Luther's cause criminal. They were called "protestants," those who protested, and the term quickly stuck to supporters of the Reformation.

Hille Feiken's story was a sign of the times. Inspired by Luther—but often going far beyond what he would condone—ordinary men and women attempted to remake their heaven and earth. Their stories intertwined with bloody struggles among princes for domination in Europe, an age-old conflict now complicated by the clash of rival faiths. In the end the princes would prevail over both a divided Christendom and a restless people. Protestant or Catholic, European monarchs expanded their power at the expense of the church and disciplined their subjects in the name of piety and order.

❖ A New Heaven and a New Earth

The last book of the Bible, Revelation (also known as the Apocalypse), foretells the passing of the old world and the coming of a new heaven and earth presided over by Christ. In 1500, some Europeans expected the Last Judgment to arrive soon. Indeed, the times seemed desperate. Muslim Turks were advancing on Europe while Christian princes fought among themselves. Some critics of the church labeled the pope as none other than the terrifying Antichrist, whose evil reign (according to Revelation) would end with Christ's return to earth.

It was in this frightening atmosphere that many people intensified their search for religious comfort. Popular pilgrimages, devotional acts, and reported miracles multiplied in an atmosphere of fear and hope. Alongside this fervor for religious certainty, important intellectuals within the Catholic church sharply criticized the shortcomings of its leaders and the clergy, who failed to provide the authority sought for by the people. Committed to a gradual reform rather than a drastic break with the Roman church, these intellectuals, known as Christian humanists for their devotion to both Christian and pagan antiquity, envisioned a better world based on education.

The Crisis of Faith

It was the established church, not Christian religion, that proved deficient to believers in Europe. Numerous signs pointed to an intense spiritual anxiety among the laity. People went on pilgrimages; new shrines sprang up, especially ones dedicated to the Virgin Mary and Christ; prayer books printed in vernacular languages as well as Latin sold briskly. Alongside the sacraments and rituals of the official church, laypeople practiced their own rituals for healing and salvation.

The worst excesses in popular piety resulted in a religious intolerance not seen in Christian Europe since the Middle Ages. In the generation before the Reformation, Jews were frequently accused of ritually slaughtering Christian children and defiling the host, the consecrated bread that Catholics believed was the body of Christ. In 1510, a priest in Brandenburg, Germany, accused local Jews of stealing and stabbing the host. When, according to legend, the host bled, the Jews were imprisoned and killed. A shrine dedicated to the bleeding host attracted thousands of pilgrims seeking fortune and health.

Some of the most flagrant abuses occurred within the church itself. Only a thin line separated miracles, which the church accepted, and magic, which it rejected. Clerics who wanted to reform the church denounced superstitions, but other clergy readily exploited gullible laypeople. Perhaps the most notorious scandal prior to the Reformation occurred in the Swiss city of Basel. There, in 1510, several Dominicans claimed that the Virgin Mary had worked "miracles," which they themselves had in fact concocted. For a while their plot brought in crowds of pilgrims, but when the deception was uncovered, the perpetrators were burned at the stake.

Often the church gave external behavior more weight than spiritual intentions. On the eve of the Reformation, numerous regulations defined the gradations of human sinfulness. For example, even married couples could sin by having intercourse on one of the church's many holy days or by making love out of "lust" instead of for procreation. The church similarly regulated other kinds of behavior, such as prohibiting the eating of meat on certain days and censoring blasphemous language.

In receiving the sacrament of penance—one of the central pillars of Christian morality and of the Roman church—sinners were expected to examine their consciences, sincerely confess their sins to a priest, and receive forgiveness. In practice, however, confession proved highly unsatisfactory to many Christians. For those with religious scruples, the demands of confession intensified their anxiety about salvation. Some believers were not sure they had remembered to confess all their sins; others trembled before God's anger and doubted his mercy. Also, some priests abused their authority by demanding sexual or monetary favors in return for forgiveness. They seduced or blackmailed female parishioners and excommunicated debtors who failed to pay church taxes or loans. Such reported incidents, although by no means widespread, seriously compromised the sanctity of the priestly office and the sacrament.

Although a sincere confession saved a sinner from hell, he or she still faced doing penance, either in this life or the next. To alleviate suffering after death in purgatory, a person could earn what is called an *indulgence* by performing certain religious tasks—going on pilgrimage, attending mass, doing holy works. The common church practice of selling indulgences as a substitution for performing good works suggested that the church was more interested in making money than in saving souls.

Another way to diminish time in purgatory was to collect and venerate holy relics. A German prince,

Frederick the Wise of Saxony, amassed the largest collection of relics outside of Italy. By 1518, his castle church contained 17,443 holy relics, including what were thought to be a piece of Moses's burning bush, parts of the holy cradle and swaddling clothes, thirty-five fragments of the True Cross, and the Virgin Mary's milk. A diligent and pious person who rendered appropriate devotion to each of these relics could earn exactly 127,799 years and 116 days of remission from purgatory.

Dissatisfaction with the official church and its inflexible rules prompted several reform efforts by bishops and leading clerics prior to the Reformation; these were, however, limited to certain monastic houses and dioceses. More important, there existed a gulf between clerical privileges and the religious sensibilities of the laypeople. Urban merchants and artisans yearned for a religion more meaningful to their daily lives and for a clergy more responsive to their needs. They wanted priests to preach edifying sermons, to administer the sacraments conscientiously, and to lead moral lives. They criticized the church's rich endowments that provided income for children of the nobility. And they generously donated money to establish new preacherships for university-trained clerics, overwhelmingly from urban backgrounds and often from the same social classes as the donors. Most of these young clerics, who criticized the established church and hoped for reform, were schooled in Christian humanism.

Christian Humanism

Outraged by the abuse of power, a generation of Christian humanists dreamed of ideal societies based on peace and morality. Within their own Christian society, these intellectuals sought to realize the ethical ideals of the classical world. Scholarship and social reform became inseparable goals. Two men, the Dutch scholar Desiderius Erasmus (c. 1466–1536) and the English lawyer Thomas More (1478–1535), stood out as representatives of these Christian humanists, who, unlike Italian humanists, placed their primary emphasis on Christian piety.

Erasmus. Erasmus dominated the humanist world of early-sixteenth-century Europe, just as Cicero had dominated the glory of ancient Roman letters.

He was on intimate terms with kings and popes and his reputation extended across Europe. Following a brief stay in a monastery as a young man, Erasmus dedicated his life to scholarship. After studying in Paris, Erasmus traveled to Venice and served as an editor with Aldus Manutius, the leading printer of Latin and Greek books.

Through his books and letters, disseminated by Manutius's printing press, Erasmus's fame spread. In the *Adages* (1500), a collection of quotations from ancient literature offering his witty and wise commentaries on the human experience, Erasmus established a reputation as a superb humanist dedicated to educational reform. Themes explored in the *Adages* continued in the *Colloquies* (1523), a compilation of Latin dialogues intended as language-learning exercises, in which Erasmus exerted his sharp wit to criticize the morals and customs of his time. Lamenting poor table manners, for example, Erasmus advised his cultivated readers not to pick their noses at meals, not to share half-eaten chicken legs, and not to speak while stuffing their mouths. Turning to political matters, he mocked the clergy's corruption and Christian princes' bloody ambitions.

Only through education, Erasmus believed, could individuals reform themselves and society. His goal was a unified, peaceful Christendom in which charity and good works, not empty ceremonies, would mark true religion and in which learning and piety would dispel the darkness of ignorance. He elaborated many of these ideas in his *Handbook of the Militant Christian* (1503), an eloquent plea for a simple religion devoid of greed and the lust for power. In *The Praise of Folly* (1509), Erasmus satirized values held dear by his contemporaries. Modesty, humility, and poverty represented the true Christian virtues in a world that worshiped pomposity, power, and wealth. The wise appeared foolish, he concluded, for their wisdom and values were not of this world.

Erasmus devoted years to translating a new Latin edition of the New Testament from the original Greek; it was published in 1516 by the Froben Press in Basel. Moved by the pacifism of the apostolic church, Erasmus instructed the young future emperor Charles V to rule as a just Christian prince. He vented his anger by ridiculing the warrior-pope Julius II and expressed deep sorrow for the brutal warfare that had been ravaging Europe for decades.

lated from the Protestant community and his writings condemned by many in the Catholic church, which was divided over the intellectual legacy of its famous son.

Thomas More. If Erasmus found himself abandoned by his times, his good friend Thomas More, to whom *The Praise of Folly* was dedicated,* met with even greater suffering. Having attended Oxford and the Inns of Court, where English lawyers were trained, More had legal talents that served him well in government. As a member of Parliament and then a royal ambassador, he proved a competent and loyal servant to Henry VIII. In 1529, this ideal servant to the king became lord chancellor, the chief official in government, but, tired of court intrigue and in protest against Henry's control of the clergy, More resigned his position in 1532. He would later pay with his life for upholding conscience over political expediency.

Inspired by the recent voyages of discovery, More's best-known work, *Utopia* (1516), describes an imaginary land and was intended as a critique of his own society. A just, equitable, and hard-working community, Utopia (meaning both "no place" and "best place" in Greek) was the opposite of England. In Utopia everyone worked the land for two years; and since Utopians enjoyed public schools, communal kitchens, hospitals, and nurseries, they had no need for money. Greed and private property disappeared in this world. Dedicated to the pursuit of knowledge and natural religion, with equal distribution of goods and few laws, Utopia knew neither crime nor war. But in the real world, unlike More's "Nowhereland," social injustice bred crime and warfare. Desperate men, deprived of their livelihoods, became thieves, and "thieves do make quite efficient soldiers, and soldiers make quite enterprising thieves." More believed that politics, property, and war fueled human misery, whereas for his Utopians, "fighting was a thing they absolutely loathe. They say it's a quite subhuman form of activity, although human beings are more addicted to it than any of the lower animals."

More's tolerant and rational society did have a few oddities—voluntary slavery, for instance, and strictly controlled travel. Although premarital sex

Albrecht Dürer, *The Knight, Death, and the Devil*
Dürer's 1512 engraving of the knight depicts a grim and determined warrior advancing in the face of devils, one of whom holds out an hourglass with a grimace while another wields a menacing pike. An illustration for Erasmus's The Handbook of the Militant Christian, *this scene is often interpreted as portraying a Christian clad in the armor of righteousness on a path through life beset by death and demonic temptations. Yet the knight in early-sixteenth-century Germany had become a mercenary, selling his martial skills to princes. Some waylaid merchants, robbed rich clerics, and held citizens for ransom. The most notorious of these robber-knights, Franz von Sickingen, was declared an outlaw by the emperor and murdered in 1522.*
Giraudon/Art Resource, NY.

A man of peace and moderation, Erasmus found himself challenged by angry younger men and radical ideas once the Reformation took hold; he eventually chose Christian unity over reform and schism. His dream of Christian pacifism shattered, he lived to see dissenters executed—by Catholics and Protestants alike—for speaking their conscience. Erasmus spent his last years in Freiburg and died in Basel, iso-

---

*The Latin title, *Encomium Moriae* ("The Praise of Folly"), was a pun on More's name and the Latin word for *folly.*

brought severe punishment, prospective marriage partners could examine each other naked before making their final decisions. Men headed Utopia's households and exercised authority over women and children. And Utopians did not shy away from declaring war on their neighbors to protect their way of life. Nevertheless, this imaginary society was paradise compared with a Christian Europe battered by division and violence. The Christian humanists dreamed beautiful visions for a better future, but they lived in a time that called for violent and radical changes to solve a profound crisis of faith.

❖ Protestant Reformers

Since the mid-fifteenth century, many clerics had tried to reform the church from within, criticizing clerical abuses and calling for moral renewal, but their efforts came up against the church's inertia and resistance. At the beginning of the sixteenth century, widespread popular piety and anticlericalism existed side by side, fomenting a volatile mixture of need and resentment. A young German friar, tormented by his own religious doubts, was to become the spokesman for a generation. From its origins as a theological dispute in 1517, Martin Luther's reform movement sparked explosive protests. By the time he died in 1546, half of western Europe had renounced allegiance to the Roman Catholic church.

While Luther opened the first act of the Reformation in Germany, Huldrych Zwingli extended the Reformation to Switzerland. The French theologian John Calvin continued the work of religious reform in a later generation. Calvin's challenge to the Catholic church extended far beyond the German-speaking lands of central Europe, eventually shaping Protestantism in England, Scotland, the Low Countries, France, and eastern Europe.

Martin Luther and the German Nation

Son of a miner and entrepreneur, Martin Luther (1483–1546) began his studies in the law, pursuing a career open to ambitious young men from middle-class families and urged on him by his father. His true calling, however, lay with the church. Caught in a storm on a lonely road one midsummer's night, the young student grew terrified by the thunder and lightning. He implored the help of St. Anne, the

mother of the Virgin Mary, and promised he would enter a monastery if she protected him. To the chagrin of his father, Luther abandoned law for a religious life and entered the Augustinian order.

In the monastery the young Luther, finding no spiritual consolation in the sacraments of the church, experienced a religious crisis. Appalled at his own sense of sinfulness and the weakness of human nature, he lived in terror of God's justice in spite of frequent confessions and penance. A pilgrimage to Rome only deepened his unease with the institutional church. A sympathetic superior came to Luther's aid and sent him to study theology, a discipline that gradually led him to experience grace and gain insight into salvation. Luther recalled his monastic days shortly before his death:

> Though I lived as a monk without reproach, I felt that I was a sinner before God with an extremely disturbed conscience. I could not believe that he was placated by my satisfaction [in penance]. I did not love, yes, I hated the righteous God who punishes sinners, and secretly . . . I was angry with God. . . . Nevertheless, I beat importunately upon Paul [in Romans 1:17]. . . . At last, by the mercy of God, meditating day and night, I gave heed to the context of the words, namely, "In [the gospel] the righteousness of God is revealed, as it is written, 'He who through faith is righteous shall live.'" There I began to understand that the righteousness of God is that by which the righteous live by a gift of God, namely by faith.

Luther followed this tortuous and private spiritual journey while serving as a professor of theology at the University of Wittenberg. But subsequent events made Luther a public figure. In 1516, the new archbishop of Mainz, Albrecht of Brandenburg, commissioned a Dominican friar to sell indulgences in his archdiocese (which included Saxony); the proceeds would help cover the cost of constructing St. Peter's Basilica in Rome and also partly defray Archbishop Albrecht's expenses in pursuing his election. Such blatant profiteering outraged many, including Luther. In 1517, Luther composed ninety-five theses—propositions for an academic debate—that questioned indulgence peddling and the purchase of church offices. Once they became public, the theses unleashed a torrent of pent-up resentment and frustration among the laypeople.

What began as a theological debate in a provincial university soon engulfed the Holy Roman Empire. (See "Contrasting Views," page 532.) Two groups predominated among Luther's earliest supporters: younger humanists and those clerics who shared Luther's critical attitude toward the church establishment. They called themselves "evangelicals," after the Gospels.* None of the evangelicals came from the upper echelons of the church; many were from urban middle-class backgrounds, and most were university-trained and well educated. As a group, their profile differed from that of the poorly educated rural clergy or from

Luther's World in the Early Sixteenth Century

their noble clerical superiors, who often owed their ecclesiastical positions to family influence rather than theological learning. The evangelicals also stood apart in that they represented those social groups most ready to challenge clerical authority— merchants, artisans, and literate urban laypeople.

Initially, Luther presented himself as the pope's "loyal opposition." In 1520, he composed three treatises. In *Freedom of a Christian,* which he wrote in Latin for the learned and addressed to Pope Leo X, Luther argued that the Roman church's numerous rules and its stress on "good works" were useless. He insisted that faith, not good works, would save sinners from damnation, and he sharply distinguished between true Gospel teachings and invented church doctrines. Luther argued that Christ, by his suffering on the cross, had freed humanity from the guilt of sin and that only through faith in God's justice and mercy could believers be saved. Thus the church's laws governing behavior had no place in the search for salvation. Luther suggested instead "the priesthood of all believers," arguing that the Bible provided all the teachings necessary for Christian living and that a professional caste of clerics should not hold sway over laypeople. *Freedom of a Christian* was immediately translated into German and was circulated widely. Its principles "by faith

alone," "by Scripture alone," and "the priesthood of all believers" became central features of the reform movement.

In his second treatise, *To the Nobility of the German Nation,* which he wrote in German, Luther appealed to German nationalism. He denounced the corrupt Italians in Rome who were cheating and exploiting his compatriots and called upon the German princes to defend their nation and reform the church. Luther's third major treatise, *On the Babylonian Captivity of the Church,* which he composed in Latin mainly for a clerical audience, condemned the papacy as the embodiment of the Antichrist.

From Rome's perspective, the "Luther Affair," as church officials called it, was essentially a matter of clerical discipline. Rome ordered Luther to obey his superiors and keep quiet. But the church establishment had seriously misjudged the extent of Luther's influence. Luther's ideas, published in numerous German and Latin editions, spread rapidly throughout the Holy Roman Empire, unleashing forces that Luther could not control. Social, nationalist, and religious protests fused into an explosive mass very similar to the Czech revolution that Jan Hus had inspired a century earlier. Like Hus, Luther appeared before an emperor: in 1521, he defended his faith before Charles V (r. 1520–1558), the newly elected Holy Roman Emperor who at the age of nineteen was the ruler of the Low Countries, Spain, Spain's Italian and New World dominions, and the Austrian Habsburg lands. At the Imperial Diet of Worms, the formal assembly presided over by this powerful ruler, Luther shocked Germans by declaring his admiration for the Czech heretic. But unlike Hus, Luther did not suffer martyrdom because he enjoyed the protection of Frederick the Wise, the elector of Saxony (one of the seven German princes entitled to elect the Holy Roman Emperor) and Luther's lord.

Essentially, the early Reformation was an urban movement: during the 1520s, the anti-Roman evangelicals included many German princes, city officials, professors, priests, and ordinary men and women, particularly in the cities. As centers of publishing and commerce, German towns became natural distribution points for Lutheran propaganda. Moreover, urban people proved particularly receptive to Luther's teachings. Many were literate and were eager to read the Scriptures, and merchants and artisans resented the clergy's tax-exempt status and

---

*The word *gospel,* meaning "good tidings," comes from the Old English translation of the Greek word *evangelion.*

Martin Luther: Holy Man or Heretic?

When Martin Luther criticized the papacy and the Catholic church, he was hailed as a godly prophet by some and condemned as a heretic by others. Both Protestants and Catholics used popular propaganda to argue their cause. They spread their message to a largely illiterate or semiliterate society through pamphlets, woodcuts, and broadsheets in which visual images took on increasing importance, to appeal to a wide public. These polemical works were produced in the thousands and distributed to cities and market towns throughout the Holy Roman Empire. A few were even translated into Latin to reach an audience outside of Germany.

The 1521 woodcut by Matthias Gnidias represents Luther standing above his Catholic opponent, the Franciscan friar Thomas Murner, who is depicted here as a crawling dragon, Leviathan, the biblical monster (Document 1). Another positive image of Luther, also published in 1521, depicts him as inspired by the Holy Spirit (Document 2). A few years later, an anti-Luther image represents him as a seven-headed monster (Document 3), signifying that the reformer is the source of discord within Christianity. This image appeared in the 1529 book published by the Dominican friar Johannes Cochlaeus, one of Luther's strongest opponents, in which Cochlaeus also accused Luther of inciting the 1525 peasants' uprising (Document 4). The Catholic attack on Luther stood in sharp contrast with his image among Protestants. For the English Protestant church historian John Foxe (1516–1587), Luther was more than a courageous hero who exposed the corruption of the Roman Catholic church; he was a prophet and a holy man specially blessed by God (Document 5).

◄ *1. Matthias Gnidias's Representation of Luther and Leviathan, 1521*

Dressed in a friar's robes, the Murner-Leviathan monster breathes "ignis, sumus, & sulphur"—fire, smoke, and sulphur. The good friar, Luther, holds the Bible in his hands, and is represented here as a prophet (foretelling the end of the world). The vertical Latin caption declares that the Lord will visit the earth with his sword and kill the Leviathan monster; he will trample underfoot lions and dragons; and the dragon, with a halter around its nostrils, will be dragged away on a hook.

2. Luther as Monk, Doctor, Man of the Bible, and Saint, 1521 ►

This woodcut by an anonymous artist appeared in a volume that the Strasbourg printer Johann Schott published in 1521. In addition to being one of the major centers of printing, Strasbourg was also a stronghold of the reform movement. Note the use of traditional symbols to signify Luther's holiness: the Bible in his hands, the halo, the Holy Spirit in the form of a dove, and his friar's robes.

LVTHERVS.

Leuiathan, de cuⁱ ore procedit ignis fumus, & sulphur.

Luther and Leviathan

Although the cult of saints and monasticism came under severe criticism during the Reformation, the representation of Luther in traditional symbols of sanctity stressed his conservative values instead of his radical challenge to church authorities.

3. The Seven-Headed Martin Luther by Johannes Cochlaeus, 1529

The seven heads are, from left to right: doctor, Martin, Luther, ecclesiast, enthusiast, visitirer, and Barrabas. The term enthusiast *represented a name of abuse, applied usually by the Catholic church to Anabaptists and religious radicals of all sorts.* Visitirer *is a pun in German on the word* Tier, *meaning "animal." Cochlaeus also mocks the new practice of Protestant clergy visiting parishes to enforce Christian discipline. From left to right Luther's many heads gradually reveal him to be a*

rebel, as Barrabas was condemned to die as a rabble-rouser by the Romans but instead was freed and his place taken by Jesus at the crucifixion. The number seven also alludes to the seven deadly sins.

4. Johannes Cochlaeus on Luther and the Peasants' War, 1529

Although Luther eventually condemned the peasants' uprising of 1525, he was at first sympathetic to their cause and blamed the oppression of the princes for the peasants' misery. For Catholics such as Cochlaeus, Luther remained the source of all disorder by challenging established church authority.

There were many peasants slain in the uprising, many fanatics banished, many false prophets hanged, burned, drowned, or beheaded who perhaps

Luther as Monk
The Granger Collection

Seven-Headed Luther
The Granger Collection

would still all live as good obedient Christians had Luther not written. . . . There are still many Anabaptists, assailants of the Sacrament, and other mob-spirits awakened by Luther to rebellion and error. . . . I'd lay you odds, however, that among all the peasants, fanatics, and mob-spirits not one could be found who has written more obscenely, more disdainfully, and more rebellously than Luther has.

Source: Mark U. Edwards, *Printing, Propaganda, and Martin Luther* (1994), 84.

5. John Foxe on Martin Luther as Prospective Saint, 1563

Foxe's work, Actes and Monuments of These Latter and Perillous Days Touching Matters of the Church, *describes the persecutions of Christians in England from the early church to the time of Mary Tudor. A Protestant, Foxe was inspired by the martyrdoms of his fellow believers under Queen Mary (r. 1555–1559), who tried to restore Catholicism to England with widespread persecutions. The compilation of* Actes and Monuments *occupied Foxe during his lifetime and became the most famous work in English church history. In it, Luther occupied a central role, as the founder of the Protestant Reformation. For Foxe, Luther was more than a prophet and hero; he was no less than a man of God, a holy man, a saint, in short, chosen by God for cleansing Christianity.*

Those who write the lives of saints use to describe and extol their holy life and godly virtues, and also to set forth such miracles as be wrought in them by God; whereof there lacketh no plenty in Martin Luther, but rather time lacketh to us, and opportunity to tarry upon them, having such haste to other things. Otherwise what a miracle might this seem to be, for one man, and a poor friar,

creeping out of a blind cloister, to be set up against the pope, the universal bishop, and God's mighty vicar on earth; to withstand all his cardinals, yea, and to sustain the malice and hatred of almost the whole world being set against him; and to work that against the said pope, cardinals, and church of Rome, which no king nor emperor could ever do, yea, durst ever attempt, nor all the learned men before him could ever compass: which miraculous work of God, I account nothing inferior to the miracle of David overthrowing the great Goliath. Wherefore if miracles do make a saint (after the pope's definition), what lacketh in Martin Luther, but age and time only, to make him a saint? who, standing openly against the pope, cardinals, and prelates of the church, in number so many, in power so terrible, in practice so crafty, having emperors and all the kings of the earth against him; who, teaching and preaching Christ the space of nine and twenty years, could, without touch of all his enemies, so quietly in his own country where he was born, die and sleep in peace. In which Martin Luther, first to stand against the pope was a great miracle; to prevail against the pope, a greater; so to die untouched, may seem greatest of all, especially having so many enemies as he had. Again, neither is it any thing less miraculous, to consider what manifold dangers he escaped besides: as when a certain Jew was appointed to come to destroy him by poison, yet was it so the will of God, that Luther had warning thereof before, and the face of the Jew sent to him by picture, whereby he knew him, and avoided the peril.

Source: John Foxe, *Actes and Monuments,* vol. 4 (London, 1837), 818–819.

QUESTIONS FOR DEBATE
1. Why did Johannes Cochlaeus condemn Martin Luther? How did he construct a negative image of Luther?
2. Evaluate the visual and the textual representations of Luther as a godly man: which medium is more effective?

the competition from monasteries and nunneries that produced their own goods. Magistrates began to curtail clerical privileges and subordinate the clergy to municipal authority. Luther's message— that each Christian could appeal directly to God for

salvation—spoke to townspeople's spiritual needs and social vision. Thus inspired, many reform priests led their urban parishioners away from Roman liturgy. From Wittenberg, the reform movement quickly emerged into a torrent of many streams.

Huldrych Zwingli and the Swiss Confederation

While Luther provided the religious leadership for northern Germany, the south came under the strong influence of the Reformation movement that had emerged in the poor, mountainous country of Switzerland. In the late fifteenth and early sixteenth centuries, Switzerland's chief source of income was the export of soldiers; hardy Swiss peasants fought as mercenaries in papal, French, and imperial armies, earning respect as fierce pikemen. Military captains recruited and organized young men from village communes; the women stayed behind to farm and tend animals. Many young Swiss men died on the battlefields of Italy, and many others returned maimed for life. In 1520, the chief preacher of the Swiss city of Zurich, Huldrych Zwingli (1484–1531), criticized his superior, Cardinal Matthew Schinner, for sending the country's young men off to serve in papal armies.

The son of a Swiss village leader, Zwingli became a reformer independent of Martin Luther. After completing his university studies, Zwingli was ordained a priest and served as an army chaplain for several years. Deeply influenced by Erasmus, whom he met in 1515, Zwingli adopted the Dutch humanist's vision of social renewal through education. In 1520, he openly declared himself a reformer and attacked corruption among the ecclesiastical hierarchy as well as the church rituals of fasting and clerical celibacy.

Under Zwingli's leadership, Zurich served as the center for the Swiss reform movement. Guided by his vision of a theocratic (church-directed) society that would unite religion, politics, and morality, Zwingli refused to draw any distinction between the ideal citizen and the perfect Christian—an idea radically different from Luther's—and rooted out internal dissent. Luther and Zwingli also differed in their views of the role of the Eucharist, or holy communion. Luther insisted that Christ was both truly and symbolically present in this central Christian sacrament; Zwingli, influenced by Erasmus, viewed the Eucharist as simply a ceremony symbolizing Christ's union with believers.

In 1529, troubled by these differences and other disagreements, evangelical princes and magistrates assembled the major reformers at Marburg, in central Germany. After several days of intense discus-

The Progress of the Reformation

1517 Martin Luther disseminates ninety-five theses attacking the sale of indulgences and other church practices

1520 Reformer Huldrych Zwingli breaks with Rome

1525 Radical reformer Thomas Müntzer killed in Peasants' War

1529 Lutheran German princes protest the condemnation of religious reform by Charles V; genesis of the term *Protestants*

1529 The English Parliament establishes King Henry VIII as head of the Anglican church, severing ties to Rome

1534–1535 Anabaptists control the city of Münster, Germany, in a failed experiment to create a holy community

1541 John Calvin establishes himself permanently in Geneva, making that city a model of Christian reform and discipline

sions, the north German and Swiss reformers managed to resolve many doctrinal differences, but Luther and Zwingli failed to agree on the meaning of the Eucharist. Thus the German and Swiss reform movements continued on separate paths. The issue of the Eucharist would later divide Lutherans and Calvinists as well.

John Calvin and Christian Discipline

Under the leadership of John Calvin (1509–1564), another wave of reform pounded at the gates of Rome. Born in Picardy, in northern France, to the secretary of the bishop of Noyon, Calvin benefited from his family connections and received a scholarship to study in Paris and Orléans, where he took a law degree. A gifted intellectual who was attracted to humanism, Calvin could have enjoyed a brilliant career in government or church service. Instead, experiencing a crisis of faith, like Luther, he sought eternal salvation through intense theological study.

Influenced by the leading French humanists who sought to reform the church from within, Calvin gradually crossed the line from loyal opposition to questioning fundamental Catholic teachings. His conversion came about after a lengthy and anxious intellectual battle. Unlike Luther, who described his life in vivid detail, Calvin generally revealed nothing about personal matters.

During Calvin's long religious gestation, the Reformation steadily gained adherents in France. On Sunday, October 18, 1534, Parisians found church doors posted with ribald broadsheets denouncing the Catholic Mass. Smuggled into France from the Protestant and French-speaking parts of Switzerland, the broadsheets unleashed a wave of royal repression in the capital. Rumors of a Protestant conspiracy and massacre circulated, and magistrates swiftly promoted a general persecution of reform groups throughout France, including the hitherto unmolested religious dissidents. This so-called Affair of the Placards provoked a national crackdown on church dissenters. Hundreds of French Protestants were arrested, scores were executed, and many more, including Calvin, fled abroad.

On his way to Strasbourg, Germany, a haven for religious dissidents, Calvin detoured to Geneva— the French-speaking city-republic where he would

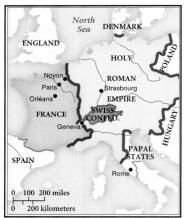

Calvin's World in the Mid-Sixteenth Century

find his life's work. Geneva had renounced allegiance to its bishop, and the local reformer Guillaume Farel threatened Calvin with God's curse if he did not stay and labor in Geneva. This frightening appeal succeeded. Under Calvin and Farel, the reform party became embroiled in a political struggle between two civic factions: their supporters, many of whom were French refugees, and the opposition, represented by the leading old Genevan families, who resented the moralistic regulations of the new, foreign-born clerical regime. A political setback in 1538 drove Calvin and Farel from Geneva, but Calvin returned in 1541, after his supporters triumphed. He remained there until his death in 1564.

Under Calvin's inspiration and moral authority, Geneva became a disciplined Christian republic, modeled after the ideas in Calvin's *The Institutes of the Christian Religion*, first published in 1536. No reformer prior to Calvin had expounded on the doctrines, organization, history, and practices of Chris-

John Calvin
This painting of the reformer (c. 1538) is attributed to the German artist Hans Holbein the Younger, one of the most famous portraitists of the early sixteenth century. Note the serene and learned character conveyed by the painting.
Calvin College and Calvin Theological Seminary/H. Henry Meedon Center.

tianity in such a systematic, logical, and coherent manner. Calvin followed Luther's doctrine of salvation to its ultimate logical conclusion: if God is almighty and humans cannot earn their salvation by good works, then no Christian can be certain of salvation. Developing the doctrine of *predestination*, Calvin argued that God had ordained every man, woman, and child to salvation or damnation—even before the creation of the world. Thus the "elect," in Calvinist theology, were known only to God. In practice, however, Calvinist doctrine demanded rigorous discipline: the knowledge that a small group of "elect" would be saved should guide the actions of the godly in an uncertain world. Fusing church and society into what followers named the "Reformed church," Geneva became a single moral community, a development strongly supported by its very low rate of extramarital births in the sixteenth century. Praised by advocates as a community less troubled by crime and sin than other cities and attacked by critics as despotic, Geneva under Calvin exerted a powerful influence on the course of the Reformation.

Like Zwingli, Calvin did not tolerate dissenters. While passing through Geneva in 1553, the Spanish physician Michael Servetus was arrested because he had published books attacking Calvin and questioning the doctrine of the Trinity, the belief that God exists in three persons—the Father, Son (Christ), and Holy Spirit. Upon Calvin's advice,

Servetus was executed by the authorities. (Calvin did not approve, however, of the method of execution: burning at the stake.) Although Calvin came under criticism for Servetus's death, Geneva became the new center of the Reformation, the place where pastors trained for mission work and from which books propagating Calvinist doctrines were exported. The Calvinist movement spread to France, the Netherlands, England, Scotland, Germany, Poland, Hungary, and eventually New England, becoming the established form of the Reformation in many of these countries (Map 15.1).

MAP 15.1 Spread of Protestantism in the Sixteenth Century

The Protestant Reformation divided northern and southern Europe. From its heartland in the Holy Roman Empire, the Reformation won the allegiance of Scandinavia, England, and Scotland and made considerable inroads in the Low Countries, France, eastern Europe, Switzerland, and even parts of northern Italy. While the Mediterranean countries remained loyal to Rome, a vast zone of confessional divisions and strife characterized the religious landscape of Europe from Britain in the west to Poland in the east.

❖ Reshaping Society through Religion

The religious upheavals of the sixteenth century reshaped European society in two major ways. First, those who challenged the social order were crushed by the political and religious authorities. Such was the fate of the Anabaptists and peasant rebels in the Holy Roman Empire, who tried in vain to establish biblically inspired new social orders in the early years of the Reformation. As a result of these radical movements, both Protestant and Catholic authorities became alarmed by the subversive political potential of religious reforms. They viewed religious reforms, instead, as ways of instilling greater discipline in Christian worship and in social behavior. Hence, the second and most lasting impact of the Reformation was in the realm of church discipline and piety. Through reading the Bible, indoctrinating the young, relieving the poor, revising laws of marriage, and performing sacred music, Protestant reformers and their supporters tried to create a God-fearing, pious, and disciplined Christian society out of corrupt human nature.

Challenging the Social Order

The freedom of the Christian proclaimed by Luther resonated with those who suffered oppression; and the corruption of sin decried by the reformers inspired others to seek Christian perfection. During the early 1520s, two movements emerged in the Holy Roman Empire to challenge the foundations of religious and political order. While peasants and urban artisans staged massive revolts against church and nobility, the Anabaptists attempted to re-create the perfect Christian community on earth.

Pillage of the Abbey of Weissenbau
In the Peasants' War of 1525, monasteries were the first target of rebellious German peasants, who resented them for owning vast tracts of land and ruling over large numbers of serfs. When Luther attacked monks as enemies of Christ, the peasants enthusiastically attacked these institutions of spiritual and material oppression. This engraving from the Chronicle of the Peasants' War *by Abbot Murer reveals the Catholic interpretation of the peasants' revolt.*
© Artephoto/T. Schneiders.

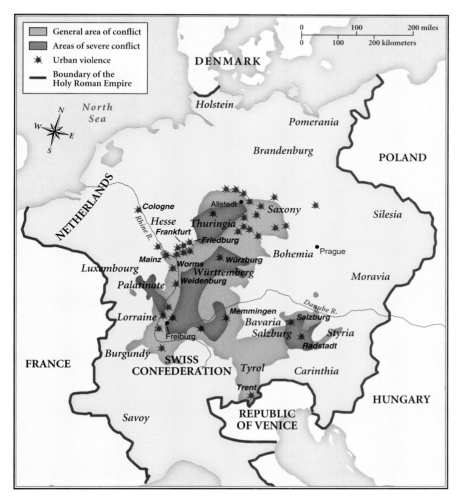

MAP 15.2 The Peasants' War of 1525

The centers of uprisings clustered in southern and central Germany, where the density of cities encouraged the spread of discontent and allowed for alliances between urban masses and rural rebels. The proximity to the Swiss Confederation, a stronghold of the Reformation movement, also inspired anti-establishment uprisings.

The Peasants' War of 1525. Between 1520 and 1525, many city governments, often under intense popular pressure and sometimes in sympathy with the evangelicals, allowed the reform movement to sweep away church authority. Local officials appointed new clerics who were committed to reforming Christian doctrine and ritual. The turning point came in 1525, when the crisis of church authority exploded in a massive rural uprising that threatened the entire social order (Map 15.2).

The church was the largest landowner in the Holy Roman Empire: about one-seventh of the empire's territory consisted of ecclesiastical principalities in which bishops and abbots exercised both secular and churchly power. Luther's anticlerical message struck home with peasants who were paying taxes to both their lord and the church. In the spring of 1525, many peasants in southern and central Germany rose in rebellion, sometimes inspired by wandering preachers. The princes of the church, the rebels charged, were wolves in sheep's clothing, fleecing Christ's flock to satisfy their greed. Some urban workers and artisans joined the peasant bands, plundering monasteries, refusing to pay church taxes, and demanding village autonomy, the abolition of serfdom, and the right to appoint their own pastors. The more radical rebels called for the destruction of the entire ruling class. In Thuringia, the rebels were led by an ex-priest, Thomas Müntzer (1468?–1525), who promised to chastise the wicked and thus clear the way for the Last Judgment.

The revolution of 1525, known as the Peasants' War, split the reform movement. Princes and city authorities turned against the rebels. In Thuringia, Catholic and evangelical princes joined hands to crush Müntzer and his supporters. All over the

Persecution of the Anabaptists
A large number of the more than one thousand martyrs killed for their faith in the Low Countries were Anabaptists. Until persecutions stopped in the 1580s, the authorities executed hundreds of Anabaptist men by beheading and women by drowning. This drawing is from the 1685 Dutch Anabaptist martyrology (a collection of books dedicated to the study and remembrance of martyrs), The Bloody Theater, *compiled by Tilleman van Bracht.*
Beinecke Rare Book and Manuscript Library, Yale University.

empire, princes defeated peasant armies, hunted down their leaders, and uprooted all opposition. By the end of the year, more than 100,000 rebels had been killed and others maimed, imprisoned, or exiled. Luther had tried to mediate the conflict, criticizing the princes for their brutality toward the peasants but also warning the rebels against mixing religion and social protest. Luther believed that rulers were ordained by God and thus must be obeyed even if they were tyrants. The Kingdom of God belonged not to this world but to the next, he insisted, and the body of true Christians remained known only to God. Luther considered Müntzer's mixing of religion and politics the greatest danger to the Reformation, nothing less than "the devil's work." When the rebels ignored Luther's appeal and continued to follow more radical preachers, Luther called on the princes to restore the divinely ordained social order and slaughter the rebels. Fundamentally conservative in its political philosophy, the Lutheran church would henceforth depend on established political authority for its protection.

Emerging as the champions of an orderly religious reform, many German princes eventually confronted Emperor Charles V, who supported Rome. In 1529, Charles declared the Roman Catholic faith the empire's only legitimate religion. Proclaiming their allegiance to the reform cause, the Lutheran German princes protested, and thus came to be called Protestants.

Anabaptists. Common people, however, did not disappear from the Reformation movement. While Zwingli was challenging the Roman church, some laypeople in Zurich were secretly pursuing their own path to reform. Taking their cue from the New Testament's descriptions of the first Christian community, these men and women believed that true faith was based on reason and free will. How could a baby knowingly choose Christ? Only adults could believe and accept baptism; hence the invalidity of Catholic infant baptism and the need for a new rite. These people came to be called Anabaptists—those who were rebaptized. The practice of rebaptism symbolized the Anabaptists' determination to withdraw from a social order corrupted (as they saw it) by power and evil. As pacifists who rejected the authority of courts and magistrates, they considered themselves a community of true Christians unblemished by sin. The Anabaptist movement drew its leadership primarily from the artisan class and its members from the middle and lower classes—men and women attracted by a simple message of peace and salvation.

Zwingli immediately attacked the Anabaptists for their refusal to bear arms and swear oaths of allegiance, sensing accurately that they were repudiating his theocratic order. When persuasion failed to convince the Anabaptists, Zwingli urged Zurich magistrates to impose the death sentence. Thus the Reformation's first martyrs of conscience were victims of its evangelical reformers.

Nevertheless, Anabaptism spread quickly from Zurich to many cities in southern Germany, despite the Holy Roman Empire's general condemnation of the movement in 1529. In 1534, one incendiary Anabaptist group, believing that the end of the world was imminent, seized control of the northwestern German city of Münster. Proclaiming themselves a community of saints and imitating the ancient Israelites, they were initially governed by twelve elders and later by Jan of Leiden, a Dutch Anabaptist tailor who claimed to be the prophesied leader—a second "King David." During this short-lived social experiment, the Münster Anabaptists abolished private property in imitation of the early Christian church and dissolved traditional marriages, allowing men, like Old Testament patriarchs, to have multiple wives, to the chagrin of many women. Besieged by a combined Protestant and Catholic army, messengers like Hille Feiken left Münster in search of relief while the leaders exhorted the faithful to remain steadfast in the hope of the Second Coming of Christ. But with food and hope exhausted, a soldier betrayed the city to the besiegers in June 1535. The leaders of the Münster Anabaptists died in battle or were horribly executed.

The Anabaptist movement in northwestern Europe nonetheless survived under the determined pacifist leadership of the Dutch reformer Menno Simons (1469–1561). Defeated in their bid for a socioreligious revolution, the common people became the subject of religious reforms and discipline. The Reformation strengthened rather than loosened social control in a vast effort to instill religious conformity and moral behavior orchestrated by secular rulers and a new clerical elite.

New Forms of Discipline

The emergence of a new urban, middle-class culture was one result of the religious cataclysms of the sixteenth century. Appearing first in Protestant Europe, it included marriage reforms, an emphasis on literacy, a new educational agenda, and a new work ethic, which came together as a watershed in European civilization. Other changes, although sparked by the Protestant Reformation, represented the culmination of developments that stretched back to the Middle Ages: the advent of public relief for the poor, the condemnation of vagrancy, and a general disciplining of society, from marriage reforms to changes in musical composition.

Reading the Bible. Prior to the Reformation, the Latin Vulgate was the only Bible authorized by the church, although many vernacular translations of parts of the Bible circulated. The Vulgate contains errors of translation from the Greek and Hebrew, as humanists such as Erasmus pointed out. Nevertheless, textual authority was predicated on church authority, and textual revisions were potentially subversive. The challenges to the Roman church from the Hussite and Lollard movements from previous centuries drew their legitimacy from the Scriptures; one of their chief aims was to translate the Bible into the vernacular. Although most sixteenth-century Europeans were illiterate, the Bible assumed for them a new importance because biblical stories were transmitted by pictures and the spoken word as well as through print. The Bible had the potential to subvert the established order.

In 1522, Martin Luther translated Erasmus's Greek New Testament into German, the first full vernacular translation in that language. Illustrated with woodcuts, more than 200,000 copies of Luther's New Testament were printed over twelve years, an immense number for the time. In 1534, Luther completed a translation of the Old Testament. Peppered with witty phrases and colloquial expressions, Luther's Bible was a treasure chest of the German language. Because of a huge appetite for the story of salvation, the popular reception of Luther's Bible was virtually assured. Between 1466 and 1522, more than twenty translations of the Bible had appeared in the various German dialects. Widespread among urban households, the German Bible occupied a central place in a family's history. Generations passed on valuable editions; pious citizens often bound the Scriptures with family papers or other reading material. To counter Protestant success, Catholic German Bibles appeared, thus authorizing and encouraging Bible reading by the Catholic laity, a sharp departure from medieval church practice.

The relationship between Scripture reading and religious reform also highlighted the history of early French and English Bibles. In the same year that Luther's German New Testament appeared in print, the French humanist Jacques Lefèvre d'Étaples (c. 1455–1536) translated the Vulgate New Testament into French. Sponsored by Guillaume Briçonnet, the bishop of Meaux, who wanted to distribute free copies of the New Testament to the poor of the region, the enterprise represented an early attempt to reform the French church without breaking with Rome.

Sensing a potentially dangerous association between the vernacular Bible and heresy, England's church hierarchy reacted swiftly against English-language Bibles. In a country with few printing presses, the first English Protestants could not publish their writings at home. Inspired by Luther's Bible during a visit to Wittenberg, the Englishman William Tyndale (1495–1536) translated the Bible into English. After he had his translation printed in Germany and the Low Countries, Tyndale smuggled copies into England. Later, following Henry VIII's break with Rome and adoption of the Reformation, the government promoted an English Bible based on Tyndale's translation, but Tyndale himself was burned at the stake as a hated heretic.

Although the vernacular Bible occupied a central role in Protestantism, Bible reading did not become widespread until the early seventeenth century. Educational reform and the founding of new schools proceeded slowly throughout the sixteenth century, thus limiting the number of literate people. Furthermore, the complete Bible was a relatively expensive book inaccessible to poorer households. Perhaps most important of all, the Protestant clergy, like their Catholic counterparts, grew suspicious of unsupervised Bible reading. Just as the first reformers cited Scripture against Rome, ordinary men and women drew their own lessons from the vernacular Bible, questioning and challenging the authority of the new Protestant establishment.

Indoctrinating the Young. To realize the Kingdom of God, Luther warned the princes and magistrates of the Holy Roman Empire that they must change hearts and minds. He encouraged them to establish schools, supported by confiscated church property, to educate children in the knowledge and fear of God. The ordinance for a girls' school in Göttingen spelled out that the school's purpose was "to initiate and hold girls in propriety and the fear of God. To fear God, they must learn their catechism, beautiful psalms, sayings, and other fine Christian and holy songs and little prayers."

The Protestant Reformation replaced late medieval church schools with a state school system. Controlled by state officials who examined, appointed, and paid teachers, the new educational system aimed to train obedient, pious, and hardworking Christian citizens. Discipline, not new ideas, informed sixteenth-century pedagogy. Teachers frequently used the rod to enforce discipline while students memorized their catechisms, prayers, and other short Christian texts. In addition to reading and writing, girls' schools included domestic skills in their curriculum.

A two-tier system existed in Protestant education. Every parish had its primary school for children between six and twelve. To train future pastors, scholars, and officials, the Protestant church developed a secondary system of humanist schools. These higher schools for boys, called *gymnasia* (from the Greek *gymnasion*), were intended to prepare students for university study. Greek and Latin classics constituted the core of the curriculum, to which was added religious instruction.

In Catholic Europe, educational reforms at the primary level proceeded unevenly. In northern and central Italian cities, most girls and boys received some education, in a strong pedagogic tradition dating to at least the thirteenth century. Concerning other Catholic territories, such as Spain, France, and southern Germany, our knowledge is fragmentary. But if Catholics lagged behind Protestants in promoting primary education, they did succeed in developing an excellent system of secondary education through the colleges established by the new Society of Jesus (known as the Jesuits), the most important religious order of Catholic Europe in the sixteenth century. Established to compete with the Protestant *gymnasia*, hundreds of Jesuit colleges dotted the landscape of Spain, Portugal, France, Italy, Germany, Hungary, Bohemia, and Poland by the late sixteenth century. Among their alumni would be princes, philosophers, lawyers, churchmen, and officials—the elite of Catholic Europe. The existence of different Christian schools helped to perpetuate the religious divisions of Reformation Europe for many generations.

Public Relief for the Poor. In the early sixteenth century, secular governments began to take over institutions of public charity from the church. This broad development, which took place in both Catholic and Protestant Europe, marked two trends that had become apparent during the later Middle Ages: the rise of a work ethic simultaneous with a growing hostility toward the poor and the widespread poverty brought about by population growth and spiraling inflation. (See "Taking Measure," right.)

Based on an agrarian economy that had severe technological limitations, European society again felt the pressure of population growth on its food resources. By 1500, the cycle of demographic collapse and economic depression triggered by the Black Death of 1348 had passed. Between 1500 and 1560, a new cycle of rapid economic and population growth created prosperity for some and stress —caused or heightened by increased inflation—for many. Wandering and begging in cities were by no means novel, but the reaction to poverty was new.

Sixteenth-century moralists decried the crime and sloth of vagabonds. Rejecting the notion that the poor played a central role in the Christian moral economy and that charity and prayers united rich and poor, these moralists cautioned against charlatans and criminals who brought disease in their wake. Instead, they said, people should distinguish between the genuine poor, or "God's Poor," and vagabonds; the latter, who were able-bodied, should be forced to work.

The Reformation provided an opportunity to restructure relief for the poor. In Nuremberg (1522) and Strasbourg (1523), magistrates centralized poor relief with church funds. Instead of using decentralized, private initiative, magistrates appointed officials to head urban agencies that would certify the genuine poor and distribute welfare funds to them. This development progressed rapidly in urban areas, where poverty was most visible, and transcended religious divisions. During the 1520s, cities in the Low Countries and Spain passed ordinances that prohibited begging and instituted public charity. In 1526, the Spanish humanist Juan Luis Vives wrote *On the Support of the Poor,* a Latin treatise urging authorities to establish public poor relief; the work was soon translated into French, Italian, German, and English. National measures followed urban initiatives. In 1531, Henry VIII asked justices of the peace (unpaid local magistrates) to license the

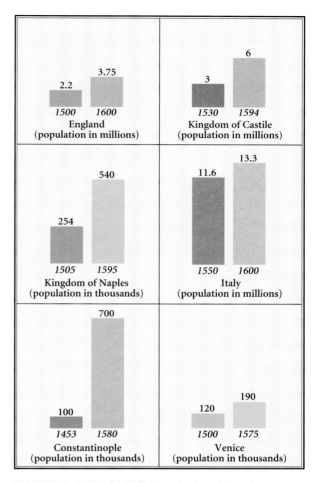

TAKING MEASURE Population Growth in Early Modern Europe
Only in the last quarter of the fifteenth century did Europe experience a sustained population growth, which took on a quick pace during most of the sixteenth century, especially during the first fifty years. The populations of Castile and the Kingdom of Naples doubled, for example. The most spectacular growth occurred in the city of Constantinople, the capital of the far-flung Ottoman Empire.
From Harry K. Miskimin, *The Economy of Later Renaissance Europe, 1460–1600* (Cambridge: Cambridge University Press, 1977) 26. Reprinted by permission of Cambridge University Press.

poor in England and to differentiate between those capable of working and those who could not. In 1540, Charles V (who ruled Spain as Charles I) imposed a welfare tax in Spain to augment that country's inadequate system of private charity.

More prevalent in Protestant areas, public relief for the poor became a permanent feature of Protestant governments once private charity ceased to be

Twelve Characteristics of an Insanely Angry Wife
This 1530 broadsheet depicts with a woodcut and accompanying text "the twelve properties of an insanely angry wife." The negative representation of female anger reflects the values dominant in Reformation society: a harmonious household ruled by a patriarch.
Schlossmuseum, Gotha.

considered a good work necessary to earn salvation. In fact, the number of voluntary donations took a significant drop once poor relief was introduced. The new work ethic acquired a distinctly Protestant aura in that it equated laziness with a lack of moral worth (and frequently associated laziness with Catholics) and linked hard work and prosperity with piety and divine providence. In Catholic lands, by contrast, collective charity persisted, supported by a theology of good works, by societies (in Italy and Spain, for example) more sharply divided between the noble rich and the poor, and by the elites' sense of social responsibility. These new changes in poor relief began to distinguish Protestant social order from traditional Catholic society.

New Marriage Ordinances. In their effort to establish order and discipline in worship and in society, the Protestant reformers decried sexual immorality and glorified the family. The idealized patriarchal family provided a bulwark against the forces of disorder. Protestant magistrates established marital courts, promulgated new marriage laws, closed brothels, and inflicted harsher punishments for sexual deviance.

Prior to the Reformation, marriages had been private affairs between families; some couples never even registered with the church. Under canon law,

the Catholic church recognized any promise made between two consenting adults (with the legal age of twelve for females, fourteen for males) as a valid marriage. In rural areas and among the urban poor, most couples simply lived together as common-law husband and wife. The problem with the old marriage laws had been their complexity and the difficulties of enforcement. Often young men readily promised marriage in a passionate moment only to renege later. The overwhelming number of cases in Catholic church courts involved young women seeking to enforce promises after they had exchanged their personal honor—that is, their virginity—for the greater honor of marriage.

The Reformation proved more effective than the late medieval church in suppressing common-law marriages. Protestant governments asserted greater official control over marriage, and Catholic governments followed suit. A marriage was legitimate only if it had been registered by an official and a pastor. In many Protestant countries, the new marriage ordinances also required parental consent, thus giving householders immense power in regulating marriage and the transmission of family property.

Enjoined to become obedient spouses and affectionate companions in Christ, women approached this new sexual regime with ambivalence. The new laws stipulated that women could seek divorce for desertion, impotence, and flagrant abuse, although in practice the marital courts encouraged reconciliation. These changes from earlier laws came with a price, however: a woman's role took on the more limited definition of obedient wife, helpful companion, and loving mother. Now the path to religious power was closed to women. Unlike Catherine of Siena and Teresa of Ávila (later acknowledged as saints) or other pious Catholic women, Protestant women could not renounce family, marriage, and sexuality to attain recognition and power in the church.

In the fervor of the early Reformation years, the first generation of Protestant women attained greater marital equality than subsequent generations. For example, Katharina Zell, who had married the reformer Matthew Zell, defended her equality by citing Scripture to a critic. The critic had invoked St. Paul to support his argument that women should remain silent in church; Katharina retorted, "I would remind you of the word of this same apostle that in Christ there is no male nor female." Further quoting the Book of Joel, she recited the prophecy that "[God] will pour forth [his] spirit upon all flesh and your sons and daughters will prophesy."

Katharina was much more than the ideal pastor's wife, however. In 1525, she helped feed and clothe the thousands of refugees who flooded Strasbourg after their defeat in the Peasants' War. In 1534, she published a collection of hymns. She encouraged her husband to oppose Protestant persecution of dissenters. After Matthew's death in 1548, Katharina continued to feed the sick, the poor, and the imprisoned. Outraged by the intolerance of a new breed of Protestant clergy, she reprimanded the prominent Lutheran pastor Ludwig Rabus for his persecution of dissenters: "You behave as if you had been brought up by savages in a jungle." Comparing the Anabaptists to beasts pursued by hunters and wild animals, she praised them for bearing witness to their faith "in misery, prison, fire, and water." Rebuking Rabus, she wrote: "You young fellows tread on the graves of the first fathers of this church in Strasbourg and punish all who disagree with you, but faith cannot be forced."

A more typical role model for the average Protestant woman was Katharina von Bora (1499–1550), who married Martin Luther in 1525. Sent to a Catholic nunnery at the age of ten, the adult Katharina responded to the reformers' calls attacking monasticism. With the help of Luther, she and other nuns escaped by hiding in empty barrels that had contained smoked herring. After their marriage, the couple lived in the former Augustinian cloister in Wittenberg, which the elector of Saxony had given to Luther. Katie, as Luther affectionately called her, ran the establishment, feeding their children, relatives, and student boarders. Although she deferred to Luther—she addressed him as "Herr Doktor"—Katherina defended a woman's right as an equal in marriage. When Luther teased her about Old Testament examples of polygamy, Katharina retorted, "Well, if it comes to that, I'll leave you and the children and go back to the cloister." Accepting her prescribed role in a patriarchal household—one of the three estates in the new Christian society of politics, household, and church—Katharina von Bora represented the ideal Protestant woman.

The Sacred and Secular Patronage of Music. Religious reform left its imprint on musical composition as it did on other aspects of social and cultural life. In Catholic Europe the church and, to a lesser extent, the princely courts still employed and commissioned musicians. The two leading composers of the sixteenth century, Orlando de Lassus (1532–1594) and Giovanni Pierluigi da Palestrina (1525–1594), were both in papal service as choirmasters. Lassus, a Fleming by birth, went to Munich in 1556 to enter the service of the court of Bavaria, the most important German Catholic principality in the Holy Roman Empire. A prolific composer, Lassus left 390 secular songs in Italian, French, and German, as well as approximately 500 motets and other substantial sacred vocal works. The Italian Palestrina is remembered for his sacred music, especially for his polyphonies that accompanied the liturgy of the Mass, in which he reaffirmed Catholic tradition by using themes from Gregorian chants.

In Protestant Europe the chorale—or harmonized hymn—emerged as a new musical form. Unlike Catholic services, for which professional musicians sang in Latin, Protestant services enjoined the entire congregation to sing in unison. To encourage participation, Martin Luther, an accomplished lute player, composed many hymns in German. Drawing from Catholic sacred music as well as secular folk tunes, Luther and his collaborators wrote words to accompany familiar melodies.

The best known of Luther's hymns, "Ein' feste Burg," became the beloved English Protestant hymn "A Mighty Fortress" and inspired many subsequent variations.

Protestants sang hymns to signify their new faith. During the Peasants' War of 1525, for example, Thomas Müntzer and the peasant rebels implored God's intercession by singing the hymn "Oh Come, Thou Holy Spirit" before they were mowed down by the knights and mercenaries in a one-sided slaughter. Eyewitnesses also reported Protestant martyrs singing hymns before their executions. In Lutheran Germany, hymnals and prayer books adorned many urban households; the intimate relationship among religious devotion, bourgeois culture, and musical literacy would become a characteristic of Germany in later centuries.

❖ A Struggle for Mastery

In the sixteenth century, new patterns of conflicts generated by the Reformation superimposed themselves on traditional dynastic strife. Two developments came together to create instability: the ambitions of powerful princes and the passions of religious reformers. Almost everywhere in Europe, the conflicts of religious differences accentuated civil and dynastic wars. And almost everywhere, violence failed to settle religious differences. By 1560, an exhausted Europe found itself in a state of compromised peace, but a peace sown fraught with the seeds of future conflict.

The Court

At the center of this politics of dynasty and religion was the court, the focus of princely power and intrigue. European princes used the institution of the royal court to bind their nobility and impress their subjects. Briefly defined, the court was the prince's household. Around the ruling family, however, a small community coalesced, made up of household servants, noble attendants, councilors, officials, artists, and soldiers. During the sixteenth century, this political elite developed a sophisticated culture.

The French court of Francis I (r. 1515–1547) became the largest in Europe after the demise of the Burgundian dukes. In addition to the prince's household, the royal family set up households for other members: the queen and the queen mother each had her own staff of maids and chefs, as did

each of the royal children. The royal household employed officials to handle finances, guard duty, clothing, and food; in addition, physicians, librarians, musicians, dwarfs, animal trainers, and a multitude of hangers-on bloated its size. By 1535, the French court numbered 1,622 members, excluding the nonofficial courtiers.

Although Francis built many palaces (the most magnificent at Fontainebleau), the French court was often on the move. It took no fewer than eighteen thousand horses to transport the people, furniture, and documents—not to mention the dogs and falcons for the royal hunt. Hunting, in fact, was a passion for the men at court; it represented a form of mock combat, essential in the training of a military elite. Francis himself loved war games. He staged a mock battle at court involving twelve hundred "warriors," and he led a party to lay siege to a model town during which several players were accidentally killed. Once Francis almost lost his own life when, storming a house during another mock battle, he was hit on the head by a burning log.

Italy gave Europe the ideological justification for court culture. Two writers in particular were the most eloquent spokesmen for the culture of "courtesy": Ludovico Ariosto (1474–1533), in service at the Este court in Ferrara, and Baldassare Castiglione (1478–1529), a servant of the duke of Urbino and the pope. Considered one of the greatest Renaissance poets, Ariosto composed a long epic poem, *Orlando Furioso* ("The Mad Roland"), which represented court culture as the highest synthesis of Christian and classical values. Set against the historic struggle between Charlemagne and the Arabs, the poem tells the love story of Bradamente and Ruggiero. Before the separated lovers are reunited, the reader meets scores of characters and hundreds of adventures. Modeled after Greek and Roman poetry, especially the works of Virgil and Ovid, *Orlando Furioso* also followed the tradition of the medieval chivalric romance. The tales of combat, valor, love, and magic captivated the court's noble readers, who, through this highly idealized fantasy, enjoyed a glorified view of their own world. In addition, the poem's characters represent the struggle between good and evil and between Christianity and Islam that was so much a part of the crusading spirit of the early sixteenth century.

Equally popular was *The Courtier* by the suave diplomat Castiglione. Like Ariosto, Castiglione tried to represent court culture as a synthesis of military virtues and literary and artistic cultivation. Speaking in eloquent dialogues, Castiglione's characters debate the qualities of an ideal courtier. The true courtier, Castiglione asserts, is a gentleman who speaks in a refined language and carries himself with nobility and dignity in the service of his prince and his lady. Clothing assumes a significant symbolism in *The Courtier;* in the words of one character, "I am not saying that clothes provide the basis for making hard and fast judgments about a man's character. . . . But I do maintain that a man's attire is also no small evidence for what kind of personality he has." The significance of outward appearance in court culture reflected the rigid distinctions between the classes and the sexes in sixteenth-century Europe. In Castiglione's words, the men at court had to display "valor" and the women "feminine sweetness." All the

formalities of court culture, however, could not mask the smoldering religious passions within, and the chivalry of Ariosto's *Mad Roland* had its real-life counterpart in the savage wars between Christianity and Islam in the sixteenth century.

Art and the Christian Knight

Through their patronage of artists, the Habsburg emperors and the Catholic popes created idealized self-images, representations of their era's hopes. The use of art for political glorification was nothing new, but below the surface of sixteenth-century art flowed an undercurrent of idealism. For all his political limitations, Emperor Maximilian I (r. 1493–1519), for example, was a visionary who dreamed of restoring Christian chivalry and even toyed with

Titian, *Charles V at Mühlberg*
The Venetian artist Titian was commissioned by Charles V to paint a series of portraits of the emperor at four stages of his career to show events in his long life for which he wished to be remembered. Titian here captures the emperor's sense of victory at having finally crushed the German Protestant princes in battle in 1547. Charles's triumph was to be short-lived.
Scala/Art Resource, NY.

Titian, *Gloria*
All military glory and earthly power is doomed to fade away, as this detail of Titian's Gloria *vividly depicts. Among the multitude turning to the Trinity in the heavens is the Emperor Charles V, dressed in a white robe. Painted after his abdication in 1556,* Gloria *is a reminder to Charles of the transience of earthly glory, for white is both the color of newborn innocence and that of the burial shroud.*
Institut Amatller d'Art Hispanic.

the idea of ruling as pope and emperor. He appointed the Nuremberg artist Albrecht Dürer (1471–1528) as court painter, to represent the Habsburg vision of universal Christian emperorship. Dürer's design for Maximilian's triumphal carriage in 1518 positioned the figures of Justice, Temperance, Prudence, and Fortitude at a level above the seated emperor, with other important allegorical figures—Reason, Nobility, and Power—also in attendance.

For many artists and humanists, such as Erasmus, Emperor Charles V embodied the ideal Christian knight. The Venetian painter Titian (1477–1576) captured the emperor's life on canvas four times. His 1532 portrait depicts a grand prince in his early thirties. Two portraits from 1548 and 1550 show him victorious over Protestants. Charles's favorite was the final portrait, *Gloria,* one of two Titians he took with him to his monastic retirement: it shows the kneeling emperor wrapped in a white death shroud joining the throng of the saved to worship the Trinity.

The Habsburg dynasty did not monopolize artistic self-glorification, however. The Florentine Michelangelo Buonarroti (1475–1564) matured his multiple talents in the service of the Medici family. After the overthrow of the Medici, he became Pope Julius II's favorite artist, painting with furious energy the Sistine Chapel (including the ceiling) and working on a never-finished tomb and sculpture for that same warrior-pope. Later Michelangelo was commissioned by Pope Paul III to design palaces in Rome; in 1547, he became the chief architect of St. Peter's Basilica. Michelangelo's work signified the transition from the Renaissance to the age of religious conflicts. His artistic talents served to glorify a papacy under siege, just as Titian lent his hand in defending the Habsburg cause against infidels and heretics.

The Field of the Cloth of Gold
This painting by an unknown artist shows the meeting of Henry VIII of England and Francis I of France near Calais for the sealing of an Anglo-French alliance. Note the prominent figure of Henry on horseback among his entourage. The meeting was a scene of ritual display of power and pomp, with carpets laid out over a vast area for the royal receptions, hence the name of the painting, The Field of the Cloth of Gold.
The Queen Royal Collection © 1999 Her Majesty Queen Elizabeth II.

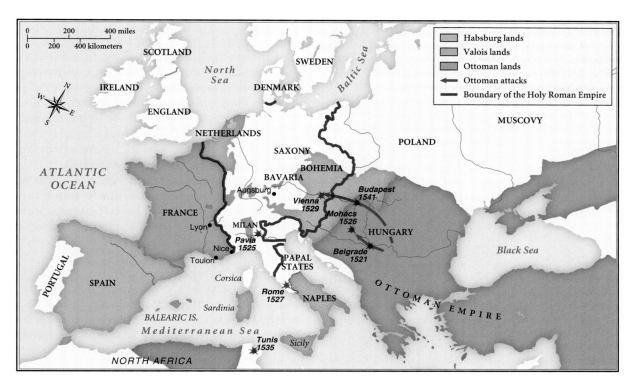

MAP 15.3 Habsburg-Valois-Ottoman Wars, 1494–1559

As the dominant European power, the Habsburg dynasty fought on two fronts: a religious war against the Islamic Ottoman Empire and a political war against the French Valois, who challenged Habsburg hegemony. The Mediterranean, the Balkans, and the Low Countries all became theaters of war.

Wars among Habsburgs, Valois, and Ottomans

While the Reformation was taking hold in Germany, the great powers of Spain and France fought each other for the domination of Europe (Map 15.3). French claims over Italian territories provided the fuse for this conflict. The Italian Wars, started in 1494, escalated into a general conflict that involved most Christian monarchs and the Muslim Ottoman sultan as well. There were two patterns to this struggle. First, from 1494 to 1559 the Valois and Habsburg dynasties remained implacable enemies; only in 1559 did the French king acknowledge defeat and sign the Treaty of Cateau-Cambrésis that established peace. Second, this basic Franco-Spanish (Valois-Habsburg) struggle drew in many other belligerents, who fought on one side or the other for their own benefits. Some acted purely out of power considerations, such as England, first siding with France and then with Spain. Others fought for their indepen-

dence, such as the papacy and the Italian states, who did not want any one power, particularly Spain, to dominate Italy. Still others chose sides for religious reasons, such as the Protestant princes in Germany, who exploited the Valois-Habsburg conflict to extract religious liberties from the emperor in 1555. Finally, the Ottoman Turks considered the religious schism in Christendom an opportunity to further their territorial expanse.

In this arena of struggle, Christian and Muslim armies clashed in Hungary and the Mediterranean. The Ottoman Empire reached its height of power under Sultan Suleiman I "the Magnificent" (r. 1520–1566). In 1526, a Turkish expedition destroyed the Hungarian army at Mohács. Three years later, the Ottoman army laid siege to Vienna; though unsuccesful, the siege sent shock waves throughout Christian Europe. In 1535, Charles V led a campaign to capture Tunis, the lair of North African pirates under Ottoman suzerainty. Desperate to overcome Charles's superior forces, Francis I eagerly forged an

The Battle at Mohács
This Ottoman painting shows the 1529 victory of the sultan's army over the Hungarians at Mohács. The battle resulted in the end of the Hungarian kingdom, which would be divided into three realms under Ottoman, Habsburg, and Transylvanian rule. Note the prominence of artillery and the Janissaries with muskets. The Ottomans commanded a vast army with modern equipment, a key to their military prowess in the sixteenth century.
Topkapi Palace Museum.

alliance with the Turkish sultan. Coming to the aid of the French, the Turkish fleet besieged Nice, on the southern coast of France, which was occupied by imperial troops. Francis even ordered all inhabitants of nearby Toulon to vacate their town so that he could turn it into a Muslim colony for eight months, complete with a mosque and slave market.

Although the Turks eventually evacuated Toulon, many Christians were scandalized that France would ally itself with the Turks to make war on another Christian king. This brief Franco-Turkish alliance, however, reflected the spirit of the times: the age-old idea of the Christian crusade against Islam was in competition with a new political strategy that saw religion as but one factor in power politics.

While the Mediterranean served as the theater of war between Habsburgs and Ottomans, most battles between the Valoises and the Habsburgs were fought in Italy and the Low Countries. There were spectacular and bloody victories, but none led to a speedy and decisive end to the war. During the 1520s, the Habsburgs seemed triumphant. In 1525, the troops of Charles V crushed the French army at Pavia, Italy, counting among their captives the French king, Francis I. Treated with great honor by Charles, Francis was kept in Spain until he agreed to a treaty renouncing all claims to Italy. Furious at this humiliation, Francis repudiated the treaty the moment he reached France, reigniting the conflict. In 1527, Charles's troops captured Rome because the pope had allied with the French. Many of the imperial troops were German Protestant mercenaries, who delighted in tormenting the Catholic clergy. Protestants and Catholics alike interpreted the sack of Rome by imperial forces as a punishment of God; this disaster shocked the Catholic church out of its apathy and turned it toward reform.

The 1530s and 1540s saw more indecisive battles. Constantly distracted by the challenges of the Ottomans and the German Protestants, Charles V could not crush France in one swift blow. Years of conflict drained the treasuries of all monarchs because warfare was becoming more expensive.

The Finance and Technologies of War

The sixteenth century marked the beginning of superior Western military technology. Fueled by warfare, all armies grew in size, and their firepower became ever more deadly. With new weapons and larger armies, the costs of war soared. For example, heavier artillery pieces meant that the rectangular walls of medieval cities had to be transformed into fortresses with jutting forts and gun emplacements.

England had a war expenditure more than double its royal revenues in the 1540s. To pay these bills, the government devalued its coinage (the sixteenth-century equivalent of printing more paper money), causing prices to rise rapidly during those years.

Other European powers fell into similar predicaments. Charles V boasted the largest army in Europe—but he also sank deeper into debt. Between 1520 and 1532, Charles borrowed 5.4 million ducats, primarily to pay his troops; from 1552 to 1556, his war loans soared to 9.6 million ducats. Francis I, his opponent, similarly overspent. On his death in 1547, Francis owed the bankers of Lyon almost 7 million French pounds—approximately the entire royal income for that year.

The European powers literally fought themselves into bankruptcy. France and Spain had to pay 14 to 18 percent interest on their loans. Taxation, the sale of offices, and outright confiscation failed to bring in enough money to satisfy the war machine. Both the Habsburg and the Valois kings looked to their leading bankers to finance their costly wars.

Foremost among the financiers of the warring princes was the Fugger bank, the largest such enterprise in sixteenth-century Europe. Based in the southern German imperial city of Augsburg, the Fugger family and their associates built an international financial empire that helped to make kings. The enterprise began with Jakob Fugger (1459–1525), nicknamed "the Rich," who became personal banker to Charles V's grandfather Maximilian I. Constantly short of cash, Maximilian had granted the Fugger family numerous mining and minting concessions. The Fugger enterprise reaped handsome profits from its Habsburg connections: in addition to collecting interest and collateral, the Fugger banking house, with branches in the Netherlands, Italy, and Spain, transferred funds for the emperor across the scattered Habsburg domains. To pay for the service of providing and accepting bills of exchange, the Fuggers charged substantial fees. By the end of his life, Maximilian was so deeply in debt to Jakob Fugger that he had to pawn the royal jewels.

In 1519, Fugger assembled a consortium of German and Italian bankers to secure the election of Charles V as Holy Roman Emperor. For the next three decades, the alliance between Europe's largest international bank and its largest empire tightened.

Between 1527 and 1547, the Fugger bank's assets grew from 3 million guldens (German currency) to over 7 million; roughly 55 percent of the assets were from loans to the Habsburgs, with the Spanish dynasty taking the lion's share. Nothing revealed the power of international banking more than a letter Jakob Fugger wrote to Charles V in 1523 to recoup his investment in the 1519 election, asking the emperor "[to] graciously recognize my faithful, humble service, dedicated to the greater well-being of Your Imperial Majesty, and that you will order that the money which I have paid out, together with the interest upon it, shall be reckoned up and paid, without further delay."

Charles barely stayed one step ahead of his creditors, and his successor in Spain gradually lost control of the Spanish state finances. To service debts, European monarchs sought revenues in war and tax increases. But paying for troops and crushing rebellions took more money and more loans. The cycle of financial crises and warfare persisted until the late eighteenth century. It forced Spain and France to sign the Treaty of Cateau-Cambrésis in 1559, thus ending more than sixty years of warfare.

The Divided Realm

Throughout Europe, rulers viewed religious divisions as a dangerous challenge to the unity of their realms and the stability of their rule. A subject could very well swear greater allegiance to God than to his lord. Moreover, the Peasants' War of 1525 showed that religious dissent could lead to rebellion. In addition, religious differences intensified the formation of noble factions, which exploited the situation when weak monarchs or children ruled.

France.   In France, Francis I tolerated Protestants until the Affair of the Placards in 1534. Persecutions of Huguenots—as the followers of John Calvin were called in France—were only sporadic, however, and the Reformed church grew steadily in strength. During the 1540s and 1550s, many French noble families converted to Calvinism. Under noble protection, the Reformed church was able to organize openly and hold synods (church meetings), especially in southern and western France. Some of the most powerful noble families, such as the Montmorency and the Bourbon, openly professed Protestantism.

The French monarchy tried to maintain a balance of power between Catholic and Huguenot and between hostile noble factions. Francis and his successor, Henry II (r. 1547–1559), both succeeded to a degree. But after Henry's death the weakened monarchy could no longer hold together the fragile realm. The real drama of the Reformation in France took place after 1560, when the country plunged into decades of religious wars, whose savagery was unparalleled elsewhere in Europe.

England. The English monarchy played the central role in shaping that country's religious reform. During the 1520s, English Protestants were few in number—a handful of clerical dissenters (particularly at Cambridge University) and, more significantly, a small but influential noble faction at court and a mercantile elite in London. King Henry VIII (r. 1509–1547) changed all that.

Until 1527, Henry firmly opposed the Reformation, even receiving the title "Defender of the Faith" from Pope Leo X for a treatise Henry wrote against Luther. A robust, ambitious, and well-educated man, Henry wanted to make his mark on history and, with the aid of his chancellors Cardinal Thomas Wolsey and Thomas More, he vigorously suppressed Protestantism and executed its leaders.

But by 1527, the king wanted to divorce his wife, Catherine of Aragon (d. 1536), the daughter of Ferdinand and Isabella of Spain and the aunt of Charles V. The eighteen-year marriage had produced a daughter, Princess Mary (known as Mary Tudor), but Henry desperately needed a male heir to consolidate the rule of the still new Tudor dynasty, begun by Henry's father, Henry VII. Moreover, he was in love with Anne Boleyn, a lady-in-waiting at court and a strong supporter of the Reformation. Henry claimed that his marriage to Catherine had never been valid because she was the widow of his older brother, Arthur. Arthur and Catherine's marriage, which apparently was never consummated, had been annulled by Pope Julius II so that the marriage between Henry and Catherine could take place to cement the dynastic alliance between England and Spain. Now, in 1527, Henry asked the reigning pope, Clement VII, to declare his marriage to Catherine invalid.

Around "the king's great matter" unfolded a struggle for political and religious control. When

Henry failed to secure a papal dispensation for his divorce, he chose two Protestants as his new loyal servants: Thomas Cromwell (1485–1540) as chancellor and Thomas Cranmer (1489–1556) as archbishop of Canterbury. Under their leadership the English Parliament passed a number of acts between 1529 and 1536 that severed ties between the English church and Rome. The Act of Supremacy of 1529 established Henry as the head of the so-called Anglican church (the Church of England), invalidated the claims of Catherine and Princess Mary to the throne, recognized Henry's marriage to Anne Boleyn, and allowed the English crown to confiscate the properties of the monasteries.

By 1536, Henry had grown tired of Anne Boleyn, who had given birth to the future Queen Elizabeth I but had produced no sons. The king, who would go on to marry four other wives but father only one son, Edward (by his third wife, Jane Seymour), had Anne beheaded on the charge of adultery, an act that he defined as treason (Figure 15.1). Thomas More also had gone to the block in 1535 for treason—in his case, for refusing to recognize Henry as "the only supreme head on earth of the Church of England"—and Cromwell suffered the same fate in 1540 when he lost favor. When Henry died in 1547, the Anglican church, nominally Protestant, still retained much traditional Catholic doctrine and ritual. But the principle of royal supremacy in religious matters would remain a lasting feature of Henry's reforms.

Under Edward VI (r. 1547–1553) and Mary Tudor (r. 1553–1558), official religious policies oscillated between Protestant reforms and Catholic restoration. The boy-king Edward furthered the Reformation by welcoming prominent religious refugees from the continent. With Mary Tudor's accession, however, Catholicism was restored and Protestants persecuted. Close to three hundred Protestants perished at the stake, and more than eight hundred fled to Germany and Switzerland. Finally, after Anne Boleyn's daughter, Elizabeth, succeeded her half-sister Mary to the throne in 1558, the Anglican cause again gained momentum; it eventually defined the character of the English nation.

Scotland. Still another pattern of religious politics unfolded in Scotland, where powerful noble clans directly challenged royal power. Until the 1550s,

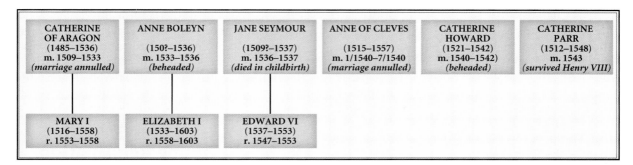

CATHERINE OF ARAGON (1485–1536) m. 1509–1533 (marriage annulled)	ANNE BOLEYN (150?–1536) m. 1533–1536 (beheaded)	JANE SEYMOUR (1509?–1537) m. 1536–1537 (died in childbirth)	ANNE OF CLEVES (1515–1557) m. 1/1540–7/1540 (marriage annulled)	CATHERINE HOWARD (1521–1542) m. 1540–1542 (beheaded)	CATHERINE PARR (1512–1548) m. 1543 (survived Henry VIII)
MARY I (1516–1558) r. 1553–1558	ELIZABETH I (1533–1603) r. 1558–1603	EDWARD VI (1537–1553) r. 1547–1553			

FIGURE 15.1 The Wives of Henry VIII
Henry's increasingly urgent desire for a son to solidify the nascent Tudor dynasty caused him to enter into six marriages. In the process he dissolved all formal English ties to the Roman Catholic church and established the Anglican church.

Protestants had been a small minority in Scotland; they were easy to suppress if they did not enjoy the protection of sympathetic local lords. The most prominent Scottish reformer, John Knox (1514–1572), spent many of his early years in exile in England and on the continent. For Knox, God's cause was obstructed by a woman, who became his greatest enemy.

The queen regent Mary of Guise (d. 1560) stood at the center of Scotland's conflict. After the death of her husband, James V, in 1542, Mary of Guise, a Catholic, cultivated the support of her native France. Her daughter and heir to the throne, Mary Stuart (also a Catholic), had been educated in France and was married to the French dauphin Francis, son of Henry II. The queen regent surrounded herself with French advisers and soldiers. Alienated by this pro-French atmosphere, many Scottish noblemen had joined the pro-English, anti-French Protestant cause.

The era's suspicion of female rulers and regents also played a part in Protestant propaganda. In 1558, John Knox published *The First Blast of the Trumpet against the Monstrous Regiment* [*Rule*] *of Women,* a diatribe against both Mary Tudor of England and Mary of Guise. Knox declared that "to promote a woman to bear rule, superiority, dominion, or empire above any realm, nation, or city is repugnant to nature, contumely to God, a thing most contrary to his revealed will and approved ordinance and, finally, it is the subversion of good order, of all equality and justice." In 1560, the Protestants assumed control of the Scottish Parliament, and Mary of Guise fled to England.

The German States. In the German states, the Protestant princes and cities formed the Schmalkaldic League. Headed by the elector of Saxony and Philip of Hesse (the two leading Protestant princes), the league included most of the imperial cities, the chief source of the empire's wealth. On the other side, allied with Emperor Charles V, were the bishops and the few remaining Catholic princes. Although Charles had to concentrate on fighting the French and the Turks during the 1530s, he had by now temporarily secured the western Mediterranean; thus he turned to central Europe to try to resolve the growing religious differences there.

In 1541, Charles convened an Imperial Diet at Regensburg to patch up the theological differences between Protestants and Catholics, only to see negotiations between the two sides break down rapidly. The schism threatened to be permanent. Vowing to crush the Schmalkaldic League, the emperor secured French neutrality in 1544 and papal support in 1545. Luther died in 1546. In the following year, war broke out. Using seasoned Spanish veterans and German allies, Charles occupied the German imperial cities in the south, restoring Catholic patricians and suppressing the Reformation. In 1547, he defeated the Schmalkaldic League armies at Mühlberg and captured the leading Lutheran princes. Jubilant, Charles proclaimed a decree, the "Interim," which restored Catholics' right to worship in Protestant lands while permitting Lutherans to consecrate holy communion as both bread and wine. Protestant resistance to the Interim was deep and widespread: many pastors went into exile, and riots broke out in many cities.

For Charles V, the reaction of his former allies proved far more alarming than Protestant resistance. His success frightened some Catholic powers. With Spanish troops controlling Milan and Naples, Pope Julius III (r. 1550–1552) feared that papal authority would be subjugated by imperial might. In the Holy Roman Empire, Protestant princes spoke out against "imperial tyranny." Jealously defending their traditional liberties against an over-mighty emperor, the Protestant princes, led by Duke Maurice of Saxony, a former imperial ally, raised arms against Charles. The princes declared war in 1552, chasing a surprised, unprepared, and practically bankrupt emperor back to Italy.

Forced to construct an accord, Charles V agreed to the Peace of Augsburg in 1555. The settlement recognized the Evangelical (Lutheran) church in the empire, accepted the secularization of church lands but "reserved" the existent ecclesiastical territories (mainly the bishoprics) for Catholics, and, most important, established the principle that all princes, whether Catholic or Lutheran, enjoyed the sole right to determine the religion of their lands and subjects. Significantly, Calvinist, Anabaptist, and other dissenting groups were excluded from the settlement. The religious revolt of the common people had culminated in a princes' Reformation. As the constitutional framework for the Holy Roman Empire, the Augsburg settlement preserved a fragile peace in central Europe until 1618, but the exclusion of Calvinists would plant the seed for future conflict.

Exhausted by decades of war and disappointed by the disunity in Christian Europe, Emperor Charles V resigned his many thrones in 1555 and 1556, leaving his Netherlandish-Burgundian and Spanish dominions to his son, Philip II, and his Austrian lands to his brother, Ferdinand (who was also elected Holy Roman Emperor to succeed Charles). Retiring to a monastery in southern Spain, the most powerful of the Christian monarchs spent his last years quietly seeking salvation (Figure 15.2).

❖ A Continuing Reformation

Reacting to the waves of Protestant challenge, the Catholic church mobilized for defense. Drawing upon traditions of fervor prior to the Reformation, Catholicism offered hopes of renewal in the 1540s and 1550s: the Council of Trent defined the beliefs and practices of the Catholic church and condemned Protestant beliefs, while new religious orders, most notably the Society of Jesus, began a vigorous campaign for the reclamation of souls.

Christian Europe was transformed. Not only had the old religious unity passed forever, but new earth emerged under the canopy of a new heaven, as missionaries from Catholic Europe traveled to other parts of the world to win converts who might compensate for the millions lost to the Protestant Reformation.

Catholic Renewal

Many voices for reform had echoed within the Catholic church long before Luther, but the papacy had failed to sponsor any significant change. Nevertheless, a Catholic reform movement gathered

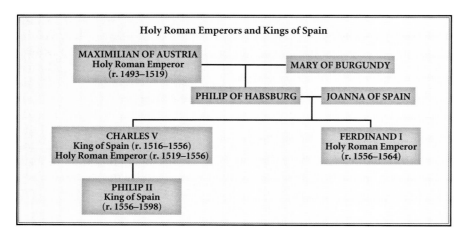

Holy Roman Emperors and Kings of Spain

MAXIMILIAN OF AUSTRIA
Holy Roman Emperor
(r. 1493–1519) — MARY OF BURGUNDY

PHILIP OF HABSBURG — JOANNA OF SPAIN

CHARLES V
King of Spain (r. 1516–1556)
Holy Roman Emperor (r. 1519–1556)

FERDINAND I
Holy Roman Emperor
(r. 1556–1564)

PHILIP II
King of Spain
(r. 1556–1598)

FIGURE 15.2 The Habsburg Succession, 1493–1556
The reign of Charles V ended with the splintering of the largest empire in Europe. Saddled with debts inherited from his grandfather and accrued from perpetual warfare, Charles ceded the Holy Roman Empire to his brother Ferdinand and gave Spain to his son Philip.

momentum in Italy during the 1530s and 1540s. Drawn from the elite, especially the Venetian upper class, the Catholic evangelicals stressed biblical ethics and moral discipline. Gian Matteo Giberti, bishop of Verona from 1524 to 1543, resigned his position in the Roman curia to concentrate on his pastoral duties. Gasparo Contarini (1483–1542), who was descended from a Venetian noble family and had served the republic as ambassador to Charles V, subsequently was elevated to cardinal, in which position he labored to heal the schism within the church.

Under Pope Paul III (r. 1534–1549) and his successors, the papacy finally took the lead in church reform. The Italian nobility also played a leading role, and Spaniards and Italians of all classes provided the backbone for this movement, sometimes called the Counter-Reformation. The Counter-Reformation's crowning achievements were the calling of a general church council and the founding of new religious orders.

The Council of Trent, 1545–1563. In 1545, Pope Paul III and Charles V convened a general church council at Trent, a town on the border between the Holy Roman Empire and Italy. The Council of Trent, which met sporadically over the next seventeen years and finally completed its work in 1563, shaped the essential character of Catholicism until the 1960s. It reasserted the supremacy of clerical authority over the laity and stipulated that bishops reside in their dioceses and that seminaries be established in each diocese to train priests. The council also confirmed and clarified church doctrine and sacraments. On the sacrament of the Eucharist, the council reaffirmed that the bread actually *becomes* Christ's body—a rejection of all Protestant positions on this issue sufficiently emphatic as to preclude compromise. For the sacrament of marriage, the council stipulated that all weddings must henceforth take place in churches and be registered by the parish clergy; it further declared that all marriages remain valid, explicitly rejecting the Protestant allowance for divorce.

The Council of Trent marked a watershed; henceforth, the schism between Protestant and Catholic remained permanent and all hopes of reconciliation faded. The focus of the Catholic church turned now to rolling back the tide of dissent.

The Society of Jesus. The energy of the Counter-Reformation expressed itself most vigorously in the founding of new religious orders. The most important of these, the Society of Jesus, or Jesuits, was established by a Spanish nobleman, Ignatius of Loyola (1491–1556). Imbued with tales of chivalric romances and the national glory of the Reconquista, Ignatius eagerly sought to prove his mettle as a soldier. In 1521, while defending a Spanish border fortress against French attack, he sustained a severe injury. During his convalescence, Ignatius read lives of the saints; once he recovered, he abandoned his quest for military glory in favor of serving the church.

Attracted by his austerity and piety, young men gravitated to this charismatic figure. Thanks to

Death Mask of Ignatius
This death mask of Ignatius of Loyola was executed immediately after his death in 1556 by his close associates in the Society of Jesus. The preservation of the aura of the founder by the early Jesuits was a vigorous effort that ultimately resulted in the canonization of Ignatius.
Leonard von Matt/Photo Research, Inc.

The Portuguese in Japan
In this sixteenth-century Japanese black-lacquer screen painting of Portuguese missionaries, the Jesuits are dressed in black and the Franciscans in brown. At the lower right corner is a Portuguese nobleman depicted with exaggerated "Western" features. The Japanese considered themselves lighter in skin color than the Portuguese, whom they classified as "barbarians." In turn, the Portuguese classified Japanese (and Chinese) as "whites." The perception of ethnic differences in the sixteenth century depended less on skin color than on clothing, eating habits, and other cultural signals. Color classifications were unstable and changed over time: by the late seventeenth century, Europeans no longer regarded Asians as "white."
Laurie Platt Winfrey, Inc.

Ignatius's noble birth and Cardinal Contarini's intercession, Ignatius gained a hearing before the pope, and in 1540 the church recognized his small band. With Ignatius as its first general, the Jesuits became the most vigorous defenders of papal authority. The society quickly expanded; by the time of Ignatius's death in 1556, Europe had one thousand Jesuits. Jesuits established hundreds of colleges throughout the Catholic world, educating future generations of Catholic leaders. Jesuit missionaries played a key role in the global Portuguese maritime empire and brought Roman Catholicism to Africans, Asians, and native Americans. Together with other new religious orders, the Jesuits restored the confidence of the faithful in the dedication and power of the Catholic church.

Missionary Zeal

To win new souls, Catholic missionaries set sail throughout the globe. They saw their effort as proof of the truth of Roman Catholicism and the success of their missions as a sign of divine favor, both particularly important in the face of Protestant challenge. But the missionary zeal of Catholics brought different messages to indigenous peoples: for some the message of a repressive and coercive alien religion, for others a sweet sign of reason and faith. Frustrated in his efforts to convert Brazilian Indians, a Jesuit missionary wrote to his superior in Rome in 1563 that "for this kind of people it is better to be preaching with the sword and rod of iron." This attitude was common among Christian missionaries in the Americas and Africa, despite the isolated missionary voices that condemned Europeans' abuse of native populations.

The Dominican Bartolomé de Las Casas (1474–1566) was perhaps the most severe critic of colonial brutality in Spanish America, yet even he argued that Africans were constitutionally more suitable for labor and should be imported to the plantations in the Americas to relieve the indigenous peoples, who were being worked to death. Under the influence of Las Casas and his followers, the Spanish crown tried to protect the indigenous peoples against exploitation by European settlers, a policy whose success was determined by the struggle among missionaries, *conquistadores* (Spanish conquerors in the Americas), and royal officials for the bodies and souls of native populations.

To ensure rapid Christianization, European missionaries focused initially on winning over local elites. The recommendation of a Spanish royal official in Mexico City was typical. He wrote to the crown in 1525:

> *In order that the sons of caciques [chiefs] and native lords may be instructed in the faith, Your Majesty must command that a college be founded wherein they may be taught . . . to the end that they may be ordained priests. For he who shall become such among them, will be of greater profit in attracting others to the faith than will fifty [European] Christians.*

Nevertheless, this recommendation was not adopted and the Catholic church in Spanish America re-

IMPORTANT DATES

1494	Start of the Italian Wars
1517	Martin Luther criticizes sale of indulgences and other church practices; the Reformation begins
1520	Reformer Huldrych Zwingli breaks with Rome
1520–1558	Reign of Charles V as Holy Roman Emperor
1526	Ottomans defeat Hungarians at Mohács
1529	Imperial Diet of Speyer; genesis of the term *Protestants*
1529	Henry VIII is declared head of the Anglican church
1532–1536	Spanish conquest of Peru
1534–1535	Anabaptists take control of Münster, Germany
1541	John Calvin established permanently in Geneva
1545–1563	Council of Trent
1546–1547	War of Schmalkaldic League
1555	Peace of Augsburg
1559	Treaty of Cateau-Cambrésis

mained overwhelmingly European in its clerical staffing.

The Portuguese were more willing to train indigenous peoples as missionaries. A number of young African nobles went to Portugal to be trained in theology, among them Dom Henry, a son of King Afonso I of Kongo, a Portuguese ally. In East Asia, Christian missionaries under Portuguese protection concentrated their efforts on the elites, preaching the Gospel to Confucian scholar-officials in China and to the samurai (the warrior aristocracy) in Japan. Measured in numbers alone, the missionary enterprise seemed highly successful: by the second half of the sixteenth century, vast multitudes of native Americans had become Christians at least in name, and thirty years after Francis Xavier's 1549 landing in Japan the Jesuits could claim over 100,000 Japanese converts.

After an initial period of relatively little racial discrimination, the Catholic church in the Americas and Africa adopted strict rules based on color. For example, the first Mexican Ecclesiastical Provincial Council in 1555 declared that holy orders were not to be

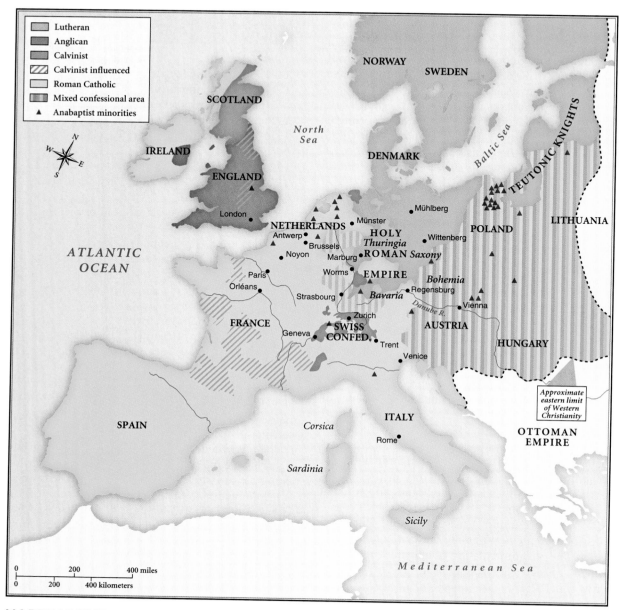

MAPPING THE WEST Reformation Europe, c. 1560
The fortunes of Roman Catholicism were at their lowest point around 1560. Northern Germany and Scandinavia owed allegiance to the Lutheran church, England broke away under a national church headed by its monarchs, and the Calvinist Reformation would extend across large areas of western, central, and eastern Europe. Southern Europe remained solidly Catholic.

conferred on Indians, *mestizos* (people of mixed European-Indian parentage), and *mulattos* (people of mixed European-African heritage); along with descendants of Moors, Jews, and persons who had been sentenced by the Spanish Inquisition, these groups were deemed "inherently unworthy of the sacerdotal [priestly] office." Europeans reinforced their sense of racial superiority with their perception of the "treachery" that native Americans and Africans exhibited whenever they resisted domination.

A different conversion tactic applied to Asia. There, European missionaries, who admired Chinese and Japanese civilization and were not backed by military power, used the sermon rather than the sword to win converts. The Jesuit Francis Xavier preached in India and Japan, his work vastly assisted by a network of Portuguese trading stations. He died in 1552, while awaiting permission to travel to China. A pioneer missionary in Asia, Xavier had prepared the ground for future missionary successes in Japan and China.

Conclusion

Mocking the warlike popes, the Dutch humanist Erasmus compared his times to those of the early Christian church. In *The Praise of Folly*, he satirized Christian prelates and princes, who "continued to shed Christian blood," the same blood as that of the martyrs who had built the foundations of Christianity. Turning from the papacy to the empire, Erasmus and many intellectuals and artists of his generation saw in Emperor Charles V the model Christian prince. As the most powerful ruler in all Europe, Charles was hailed as the harbinger of peace, the protector of justice, and the foe of the infidel Turks. For the generation that came of age before the Reformation, Christian humanism—and its imperial embodiment—represented an ideal for political and moral reform that would save Christendom from corruption and strife.

The Reformation changed this dream of peace and unity. Instead of leading a crusade against Islam—a guiding vision of his life—Charles V wore himself out in ceaseless struggle against Francis I of France and the German Protestants. Instead of the Christian faith of charity and learning that Erasmus had envisioned, Christianity split into a number of hostile camps that battled one another with words and swords. Instead of the intellectual unity of the generation of Erasmus and Thomas More, the mid-sixteenth-century cultural landscape erupted in a burst of conflicting doctrinal statements and left in its wake a climate of censorship, repression, and inflexibility.

After the brutal suppression of popular revolts in the 1520s and 1530s, religious persecution became a Christian institution: Luther called on the princes to kill rebellious peasants in 1525, Zwingli advocated the drowning of Anabaptists, and Calvin supported the death sentence for Michael Servetus. Meanwhile, in Catholic lands persecutions and executions provided Protestants with a steady stream of martyrs. The two peace settlements in the 1550s failed to provide long-term solutions: the Peace of Augsburg gradually disintegrated as the religious struggles in the empire intensified, and the Treaty of Cateau-Cambrésis was but a brief respite in a century of crisis. In the following generations, civil war and national conflicts would set Catholics against Protestants in numerous futile attempts to restore a single faith.

Suggested References

A New Heaven and a New Earth

Recent scholarship on the Reformation era has emphasized the connected nature of religious, political, social, economic, and cultural history. Another new direction is to connect the study of Christian reform movements with Christian-Jewish relations prior to the Reformation.

Brady, Thomas A. *Turning Swiss: Cities and Empire, 1450–1550.* 1985.

Essential Works of Erasmus. Ed. W. T. H. Jackson. 1965.*

Hsia, R. Po-chia. *The Myth of Ritual Murder: Jews and Magic in the Reformation.* 1988.

Protestant Reformers

While continuing to refine our understanding of the leading Protestant reformers, recent scholars have also offered new interpretations that take into consideration the popular impact of the reformers' teachings.

Bouwsma, William J. *John Calvin: A Sixteenth-Century Portrait.* 1988.

Hillerbrand, Hans J., ed. *The Protestant Reformation.* 1969.*

http://www.puritansermons.com/poetry.htm. Puritan and Reformed sermons and other writings.

http://www.wsu.edu/~dee/REFORM/LUTHER.HTM. The life and thought of Martin Luther.

Oberman, Heiko A. *Luther: Man between God and Devil.* 1990.

Scribner, R. W. *For the Sake of Simple Folk: Popular Propaganda for the German Reformation.* 1981.

*Primary sources.

Reshaping Society through Religion

The most important trend in recent scholarship has been the consideration of the impact of the Reformation on society and culture. Many studies have shown the limited influence of the ideas of reformers; others document the persistence of traditional religious habits and practices well past the sixteenth century.

Bainton, Roland. *Women of the Reformation in Germany and Italy.* 1971.

Blickle, Peter. *The Revolution of 1525.* 1981.

Elton, G. R. *Reformation Europe, 1517–1559.* 1963.

Hsia, R. Po-chia. *The German People and the Reformation.* 1988.

Ozment, Steven E. *The Reformation in the Cities.* 1975.

Strauss, Gerald. *Luther's House of Learning: Indoctrination of the Young in the German Reformation.* 1978.

A Struggle for Mastery

Still focused on the struggle between the Habsburg and Valois dynasties, historical scholarship has also moved out in the direction of cultural and military history. Recent works have studied military innovations and artistic representations of the sixteenth-century monarchs.

Elliott, J. H. *The Old World and the New, 1492–1650.* 1970.

Guicciardini, Francesco. *The History of Italy.* Trans. Sidney Alexander. 1969.*

Knecht, R. J. *Francis I.* 1982.

Parker, Geoffrey. *The Military Revolution: Military Innovation and the Rise of the West, 1500–1800.* 1988.

Partridge, Loren, and Randolph Starn. *A Renaissance Likeness: Art and Culture in Raphael's Julius II.* 1980.

Trevor-Roper, Hugh. *Princes and Artists: Patronage and Ideology at Four Habsburg Courts, 1517–1633.* 1976.

A Continuing Reformation

Current scholarship suggests that by comparing the Protestant and Catholic Reformations, we can gain insight into the underlying social and cultural changes that affected all of Christian Europe. Another new direction of research brings the study of Christianity into the non-European realm by focusing on missions.

Crosby, Alfred W. *The Colombian Exchange: Biological and Cultural Consequences of 1492.* 1972.

Evennet, Henry Outram. *The Spirit of the Counter-Reformation.* 1968.

Hsia, R. Po-chia. *The World of the Catholic Renewal.* 1997.

Prodi, Paolo. *The Papal Prince, One Body and Two Souls: The Papal Monarchy in Early Modern Europe.* 1982.

Wars over Beliefs

1560–1648

Grand Duke of Alba
This polychrome wood sculpture from the late 1500s shows the Spanish grand duke of Alba in armor, equipped with a lance. He overshadows three potential sources of trouble: Pope Pius V, who pressed the Spanish to take aggressive action against heretics; Elizabeth I of England, who sent pirates to prey on the Spanish ships carrying gold to the armies; and Elector Augustus I of Saxony, the most influential Lutheran prince. Alba commanded the Spanish armies sent to punish the Netherlands for their rebellion against Philip II. He unleashed a reign of terror to crush the Calvinists and alarmed Protestant rulers all over Europe.
Institut Amatller d'Art Hispanic.

I n May 1618, Protestants in the kingdom of Bohemia furiously protested the Holy Roman Emperor's attempts to curtail their hard-won religious freedoms. Protestants wanted to build new churches; the Catholic emperor wanted to stop them. Tensions boiled over when two Catholic deputy-governors tried to dissolve the meetings of Protestants. On May 23, a crowd of angry Protestants surged up the stairs of the royal castle in Prague, trapped the two Catholic deputies, dragged them screaming for mercy to the windows, and hurled them to the pavement below. One of the rebels jeered: "We will see if your [Virgin] Mary can help you!" But because they landed in a dung heap, the Catholic deputies survived. One of the two limped off on his own; the other was carried away by his servants to safety. Although no one died, this "defenestration" (from the French for "window," *la fenêtre*) of Prague touched off the Thirty Years' War (1618–1648), which eventually involved almost every major power in Europe. Before it ended, the fighting had devastated the lands of central Europe and produced permanent changes in European politics and culture.

The Thirty Years' War grew out of the religious conflicts initiated by the Reformation. When Martin Luther began the Protestant Reformation in 1517, he had no idea that he would be unleashing such dangerous forces, but religious turmoil and warfare followed almost immediately upon his break with the Catholic church. Until the early 1600s, the Peace of Augsburg of 1555 maintained relative calm in the lands of the Holy Roman Empire by granting each ruler the right to

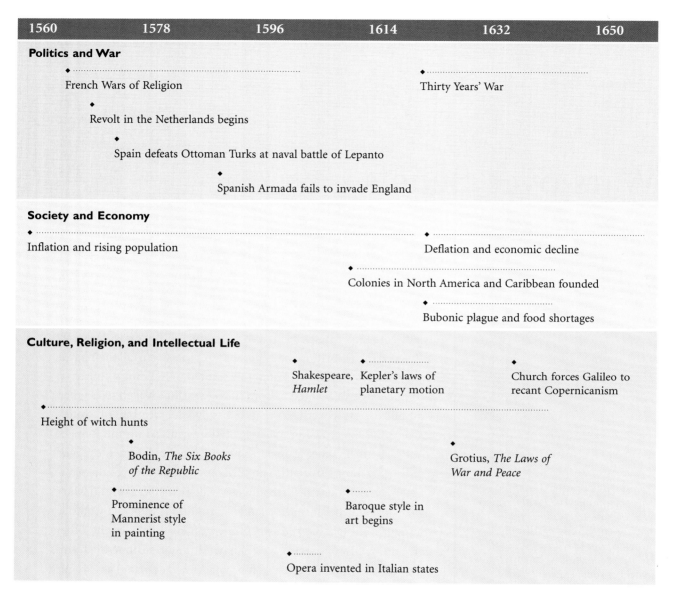

1560	1578	1596	1614	1632	1650

Politics and War

French Wars of Religion

Thirty Years' War

Revolt in the Netherlands begins

Spain defeats Ottoman Turks at naval battle of Lepanto

Spanish Armada fails to invade England

Society and Economy

Inflation and rising population

Deflation and economic decline

Colonies in North America and Caribbean founded

Bubonic plague and food shortages

Culture, Religion, and Intellectual Life

Shakespeare, *Hamlet*   Kepler's laws of planetary motion

Church forces Galileo to recant Copernicanism

Height of witch hunts

Bodin, *The Six Books of the Republic*

Grotius, *The Laws of War and Peace*

Prominence of Mannerist style in painting

Baroque style in art begins

Opera invented in Italian states

determine the religion of his territory. But in western Europe, religious strife increased dramatically after 1560 as Protestants made inroads in France, the Spanish-ruled Netherlands, and England. All in all, nearly constant warfare marked the century between 1560 and 1648. These struggles most often began as religious conflicts, but religion was never the sole motive; political power entered into every equation and raised the stakes of conflict. The Bohemian Protestants, for example, wanted both freedom to practice their religion as Protestants and national independence for the Czechs, the largest ethnic group in Bohemia. Since Bohemia had many Catholics, religious and political aims inevitably came into conflict.

The Thirty Years' War brought the preceding religious conflicts to a head and by its very violence effectively removed religion from future international disputes. Although religion still divided people *within* various states, after 1648 religion no longer provided the rationale for wars *between* European states. The orgy of mutual destruction in the Thirty Years' War left no winners in the religious struggle, and the cynical manipulation of religious issues by both Catholic and Protestant leaders showed that political interests eventually outweighed those of religion. In addition, the violence of religious conflict pushed rulers and political thinkers to seek other, nonreligious grounds for governmental authority. Few would argue for genuine toleration of religious differences, but many began to insist that the interests of states had to take priority over the desire for religious conformity.

Although particularly dramatic and deadly, the church-state crisis was only one of a series of upheavals that shaped this era. In the early seventeenth century, a major economic downturn led to food shortages, famine, and disease in much of Europe. These hit especially hard in the central European lands devastated by the fighting of the Thirty Years' War and helped shift the balance of economic power to northwestern Europe, away from the Mediterranean and central Europe. An upheaval in world-views was also in the making, catalyzed by increasing knowledge of the new worlds discovered overseas and in the heavens. The development of new scientific methods of research would ultimately reshape Western attitudes toward religion and state power, as Europeans desperately sought alternatives to wars over religious beliefs.

❖ Religious Conflicts and State Power, 1560–1618

The Peace of Augsburg of 1555 made Lutheranism a legal religion in the predominantly Catholic Holy Roman Empire, but it did not extend recognition to Calvinists. Although the followers of Martin Luther (Lutherans) and those of John Calvin (Calvinists) similarly refused the authority of the Catholic church, they disagreed with one another about religious doctrine and church organization. Lutheranism flourished in the northern German states and Scandinavia; Calvinism spread from its headquarters in the Swiss city of Geneva. The rapid expansion of Calvinism after 1560 threatened to alter the religious balance of power in much of Europe. Calvinists challenged Catholic dominance in France, the Spanish-ruled Netherlands, Scotland, and Poland-Lithuania. In England they sought to influence the new Protestant monarch, Elizabeth I. Calvinists were not the only source of religious contention, however. While trying to suppress the revolt of Calvinists in the Netherlands, Philip II of Spain also fought the Muslim Ottoman Turks in the Mediterranean and expelled the remnants of the Muslim population in Spain. To the east, the Russian tsar Ivan IV fought to make Muscovy the center of an empire based on Russian Orthodox Christianity. He had to compete with Lutheran Sweden and Poland-Lithuania, itself divided by conflicts among Catholics, Lutherans, and Calvinists.

French Wars of Religion, 1562–1598

Calvinist inroads in France had begun in 1555, when the Genevan Company of Pastors took charge of missionary work. Supplied with false passports and often disguised as merchants, the Calvinist pastors moved rapidly among their growing congregations, which gathered in secret in towns near Paris or in the south. Calvinist nobles provided military protection to local congregations and helped set up a national organization for the French Calvinist—or Huguenot—church. In 1562, rival Huguenot and Catholic armies began fighting a series of wars that threatened to tear the French nation into shreds (Map 16.1).

Religious Division in the Nobility.   Conversion to Calvinism in French noble families often began with the noblewomen, some of whom sought intellectual independence as well as spiritual renewal in the new faith. Charlotte de Bourbon, for example, fled from a Catholic convent and eventually married William of Orange, the leader of the anti-Spanish resistance in the Netherlands. Jeanne d'Albret, mother of the future French king Henry IV, became a Calvinist and convinced many of her clan to convert, though her husband died fighting for the Catholic side. Calvinist noblewomen protected pastors, provided money and advice, and helped found schools and establish relief for the poor.

Religious divisions in France often reflected political disputes among noble families. At least one-third of the nobles—a much larger proportion than in the general population—joined the Huguenots, who usually followed the lead of the Bourbon family. The Bourbons were close relatives of the French king and stood first in line to inherit the throne if the Valois kings failed to produce a male heir. The most militantly Catholic nobles took their cues from

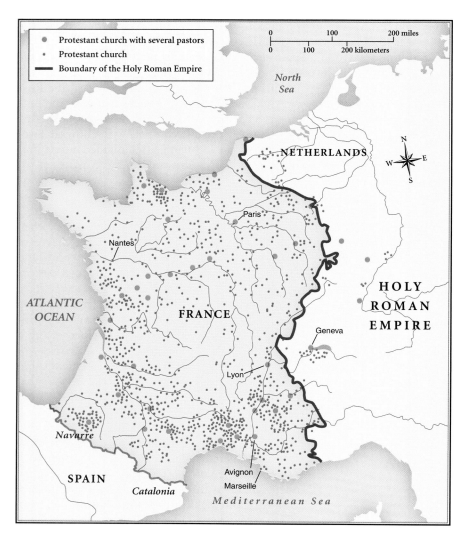

MAP 16.1 Protestant Churches in France, 1562
Calvinist missionaries took their message from their head-quarters in Geneva across the border into France. The strongest concentration of Protestants was in southern France. The Bourbons, leaders of the Protestants in France, had their family lands in southwestern France in Navarre, a region that had been divided between France and Spain.

Map legend:
- Protestant church with several pastors
- Protestant church
- Boundary of the Holy Roman Empire

0 100 200 miles
0 100 200 kilometers

North Sea
NETHERLANDS
Paris
Nantes
ATLANTIC OCEAN
FRANCE
HOLY ROMAN EMPIRE
Geneva
Lyon
Navarre
SPAIN
Catalonia
Avignon
Marseille
Mediterranean Sea

the Guise family, who aimed to block Bourbon ambitions. The Catholic Valois were caught between these two powerful factions, each with its own military organization. The situation grew even more volatile when King Henry II was accidentally killed during a jousting tournament in 1559 and his fifteen-year-old son Francis died soon after. Ten-year-old Charles IX (r. 1560–1574) became king, with his mother, Catherine de Medicis, as regent. Catherine, an Italian and a Catholic, urged limited toleration for the Huguenots in an attempt to maintain political stability, but her influence was severely limited. As one ambassador commented, "It is sufficient to say that she is a woman, a foreigner, and a Florentine to boot, born of a simple house, altogether beneath the dignity of the Kingdom of France." In the vacuum created by the death of Henry II, the Bourbon and Guise factions consolidated their forces, and civil war erupted in 1562. Both sides committed terrible atrocities. Priests and pastors were murdered, and massacres of whole congregations became frighteningly commonplace.

St. Bartholomew's Day Massacre, 1572. Although a Catholic herself, Catherine aimed to preserve the throne for her son by playing the Guise and Bourbon factions off each other. To this end she arranged the marriage of the king's Catholic sister Marguerite de Valois to Henry of Navarre, a Huguenot and Bourbon. Just four days after the wedding in August 1572, assassins tried but failed to kill one of the Huguenot nobles allied with the Bourbons, Gaspard de Coligny. Panicked at the thought of Huguenot revenge and perhaps herself implicated in the botched plot, Catherine convinced her son to order the killing of leading Huguenots. On St. Bartholomew's Day, August 24, a bloodbath began, fueled by years of growing animosity between Catholics and Protestants. The duke of Guise himself killed Coligny. Each side viewed the other as less than human, as a source of moral pollution that had to be eradicated. In three days, Catholic mobs murdered three thousand Huguenots in Paris. Ten thousand died in the provinces over the next six weeks. The pope joyfully ordered the church bells rung throughout Catholic Europe; Spain's Philip II wrote Catherine that it was "the best and most cheerful news which at present could come to me."

The massacre settled nothing. Huguenot pamphleteers now proclaimed their right to resist a tyrant who worshiped idols (a practice that Calvinists equated with Catholicism). This right of resistance was linked to a notion of contract; upholding the true religion was part of the contract imagined as binding the ruler to his subjects. Both the right of resistance and the idea of a contract fed into the larger doctrine of constitutionalism—that a government's legitimacy rested on its upholding a constitution or contract between ruler and ruled. Constitutionalism justified resistance movements from the sixteenth century onward. Protestants and Catholics alike now saw the conflict as an international struggle for survival that required aid to coreligionists in other countries. In this way, the French Wars of Religion paved the way for wider international conflicts over religion in the decades to come.

Henry IV and the Edict of Nantes. The religious division in France grew even more dangerous when, two years after the massacre, Charles IX died and his brother Henry III (r. 1574–1589) became king. Like his brothers before him, Henry III failed to produce an heir. Next in line to the throne was none other than the Protestant Bourbon leader Henry of Navarre. Yet because Henry III and Catherine de

Massacre Motivated by Religion
The Italian artist Giorgio Vasari painted St. Bartholomew's Night: The Massacre of the Huguenots *for a public room in Pope Gregory XIII's residence. The pope and his artist intended to celebrate a Catholic victory over Protestant heresy.* Scala/Art Resource.

Henry IV's Paris
This painting of the Pont Neuf (new bridge) over the Seine River in Paris dates from about 1635 and shows the statue of Henry IV that was erected after his assassination in 1610. Henry IV built the bridge, the first one in Paris to have no houses on it, to link an island in the river with the two banks. This bridge is still one of the most beautiful in Paris.
Giraudon/Art Resource, NY.

Medicis saw an even greater threat to their authority in the Guises and their newly formed Catholic League, which had requested Philip II's help in rooting out Protestantism in France, they cooperated with Henry of Navarre. The Catholic League, believing that Henry III was not taking a strong enough stand against the Protestants, began to encourage disobedience. Henry III responded with a fatal trick: in 1588 he summoned the two Guise leaders to a meeting and had his men kill them. A few months later a fanatical monk stabbed Henry III to death, and Henry of Navarre became Henry IV (r. 1589–1610), despite Philip II's attempt to block his way with military intervention.

The new king soon concluded that to establish control over the war-weary country he had to place the interests of the French state ahead of his Protestant faith. In 1593, Henry IV publicly embraced Catholicism, reputedly explaining his conversion with the phrase "Paris is worth a Mass." Within a few years he defeated the ultra-Catholic opposition and drove out the Spanish. In 1598, he made peace with Spain and issued the Edict of Nantes, in which he granted the Huguenots a large measure of religious toleration. The approximately 1.25 million Huguenots became a legally protected minority within an officially Catholic kingdom of some 20 million people. Protestants were free to worship in specified towns and were allowed their own troops, fortresses, and even courts. The Edict of Nantes pacified a religious minority too large to ignore and impossible to eradicate. Few believed in religious toleration, but Henry IV followed the advice of those neutral Catholics and Calvinists called *politiques* who urged him to give priority to the development of a durable state. Although their opponents hated them for their compromising spirit, the *politiques* believed that religious disputes could be resolved only in the peace provided by strong government. The Edict of Nantes ended the French Wars of Religion.

But the new king needed more than a good theory to strengthen state power. To ensure his own safety and the succession of his heirs, Henry had to reestablish monarchical authority. Shrewdly mixing his famous charm with bravado and cunning, Henry created a splendid image of monarchy and extended his government's control. He used paintings, songs, court festivities, and royal processions to rally subjects and officials around him. Henry also developed a new class of royal officials to counterbalance the fractious nobility. For some time the French crown had earned considerable revenue by selling offices to qualified bidders. Now, in exchange for an annual payment, officeholders could not only own their offices but also pass them to heirs or sell them to someone else. Because these offices carried prestige and often ennobled their holders, rich middle-class merchants and lawyers with aspirations to higher social status found them attractive. By buying offices they could become part of a new social elite known as the "nobility of the robe" (named after the robes that magistrates wore, much like those judges wear today). The monarchy acquired a growing bureaucracy, though at the cost of granting broad autonomy to new officials who could not be dismissed. Nonetheless, new income raised by the increased sale of offices reduced the state debt and helped Henry build the base for a strong monarchy. His efforts did not, however, prevent his own assassination in 1610 after nineteen unsuccessful attempts.

Challenges to Spanish Power

Although he failed to prevent Henry IV from taking the French throne, Philip II of Spain (r. 1556–1598) was the most powerful ruler in Europe (Map 16.2). In addition to the western Habsburg lands in

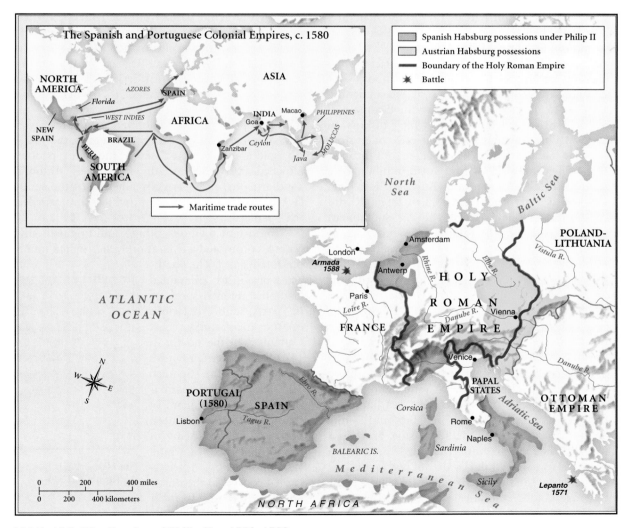

MAP 16.2 The Empire of Philip II, r. 1556–1598
Spanish king Philip II drew revenues from a truly worldwide empire. In 1580 he was the richest European ruler, but the demands of governing such far-flung territories eventually drained many of his resources.

Spain and the Netherlands, he had inherited from his father, Charles V, all the Spanish colonies recently settled in the New World of the Americas. Gold and silver funneled from the colonies supported his campaigns against the Ottoman Turks and French and English Protestants. But all of the money of the New World could not prevent his eventual defeat in the Netherlands, where Calvinist rebels established an independent Dutch Republic that soon vied with Spain, France, and England for commercial supremacy.

Philip II, the Catholic King.   A deeply devout Catholic, Philip II came to the Spanish throne at age twenty-eight. He built a great gray granite structure, half-palace, half-monastery, called the Escorial, in the mountains near Madrid. There he lived in a small room and dressed in somber black, while amassing an impressive collection of books and paintings. His austere personal style hid a burning ambition to restore Catholic unity in Europe and lead the Christian defense against the Muslims. In his quest Philip benefited from a series of misfortunes. He had four wives, who all died, but through them he became part of four royal families: Portuguese, English, French, and Austrian. His brief marriage to Mary Tudor (Mary I of England) did not produce an heir, but it and his subsequent marriage to Elisabeth de Valois, the sister of Charles IX and Henry III of France, gave him reason enough for involvement in English and French affairs. In 1580, when the king of Portugal died without a direct heir, Philip took over this neighboring realm with its rich empire in Africa, India, and the Americas.

Philip insisted on Catholic unity in his own possessions and worked to forge an international Christian coalition against the Ottoman Turks. In 1571, he achieved the single greatest military victory of his reign when he joined with Venice and the papacy to defeat the Turks in a great sea battle off the Greek coast at Lepanto. Fifty thousand sailors and soldiers fought on the allied side, and eight thousand died. Spain now controlled the western Mediterranean. But Philip could not rest on his laurels. Between 1568 and 1570, the Moriscos—Muslim converts to Christianity who remained secretly faithful to Islam—had revolted in the south of Spain, killing 90 priests and 1,500 Christians. The victory at Lepanto destroyed any prospect that the Turks might come to their aid, yet Philip took stern

measures against the Moriscos. He forced 50,000 to leave their villages and resettle in other regions. In 1609, his successor, Philip III, ordered their expulsion, and by 1614 some 300,000 Moriscos had been forced to relocate to North Africa.

The Revolt of the Netherlands.   The Calvinists of the Netherlands were less easily intimidated than the Moriscos: they were far from Spain and accustomed to being left alone. In 1566, Calvinists in the Netherlands attacked Catholic churches, smashing stained-glass windows and statues of the Virgin Mary. Philip sent an army, which executed more than 1,100 people during the next six years. Prince William of Orange (whose name came from the lands he owned in southern France) took the lead of the anti-Spanish resistance. He encouraged adventurers and pirates known as the Sea Beggars to invade the northern ports. The Spanish responded with more force, culminating in November 1576 when Philip's long-unpaid mercenary armies sacked Antwerp, then Europe's wealthiest commercial city. In eleven days of horror known as the Spanish Fury, the Spanish soldiers slaughtered seven thousand people. Shocked into response, the ten largely Catholic southern provinces formally allied with the seven largely Protestant northern provinces and expelled the Spaniards.

Important religious, ethnic, and linguistic differences promoted a federation rather than a union of Dutch states. The southern provinces remained Catholic, French-speaking in parts, and suspicious of the increasingly strict Calvinism in the north. In 1579, the southern provinces returned to the Spanish fold. Despite the assassination in 1584 of William of Orange, after he had been outlawed as "an enemy of the human race" by Philip II, Spanish troops never regained control in the north. Spain would not formally recognize Dutch independence until 1648, but by the end of the sixteenth century the Dutch Republic was a self-governing state sheltering a variety of religious groups.

The Netherlands during the Revolt, c. 1580

Rembrandt's Depiction of Dutch Life
Rembrandt's painting known as The Night Watch *(1642) shows members of a voluntary militia company in action. In fact, it is a group portrait, probably commissioned by the guardsmen themselves. Once responsible for defending the city, the militia companies had become eating and drinking clubs for prosperous businessmen. The painting demonstrates Rembrandt's interest in every aspect of daily life in the Dutch Republic.*
Rijksmuseum, Amsterdam.

The Dutch Republic.   The princes of Orange resembled a ruling family in the Dutch Republic (sometimes incorrectly called "Holland" after the most populous of the seven provinces), but their powers paled next to those of local interests. Urban merchant and professional families known as "regents" controlled the towns and provinces. This was no democracy: governing explicitly included "the handling and keeping quiet of the multitude." In the absence of a national bureaucracy, a single legal system, or a central court, each province governed itself and sent delegates to the one common institution, the States General, which carried out the wishes of the strongest individual provinces and their ruling families.

Well situated for maritime commerce, the Dutch Republic developed a thriving economy based on shipping and shipbuilding. Whereas elites in other countries focused on their landholdings, the Dutch looked for investments in trade. After the

Dutch gained independence, Amsterdam became the main European money market for two centuries. The city was also a primary commodities market and a chief supplier of arms—to allies, neutrals, and even enemies. Dutch entrepreneurs produced goods at lower prices than anyone else and marketed them more efficiently. Dutch merchants favored free trade in Europe because they could compete at an advantage. They controlled many overseas markets thanks to their preeminence in seaborne commerce: by 1670, the Dutch commercial fleet was larger than the English, French, Spanish, Portuguese, and Austrian fleets combined.

Since the Dutch traded with anyone anywhere, it is perhaps not surprising that Dutch society tolerated more religious diversity than the other European states. One-third of the Dutch population remained Catholic, and the secular authorities allowed them to worship as they chose in private. Because Protestant sects could generally count on toleration from local regents, they remained peaceful. The Dutch Republic also had a relatively large Jewish population because many Jews had settled there after being driven out of Spain and Portugal; from 1597, Jews could worship openly in their synagogues. This openness to various religions helped make the Dutch Republic one of Europe's chief intellectual and scientific centers in the seventeenth and eighteenth centuries.

Elizabeth I's Defense of English Protestantism

As the Dutch revolt unfolded, Philip II became increasingly infuriated with Elizabeth I (r. 1558–1603), who had succeeded her half-sister Mary Tudor as queen of England. Philip had been married to Mary and had enthusiastically seconded Mary's efforts to return England to Catholicism. When Mary died in 1558, Elizabeth rejected Philip's proposal of marriage and promptly brought Protestantism back to England. Eventually she provided funds and troops to the Dutch Protestant cause. As Elizabeth moved to solidify her personal power and the authority of the Anglican church (Church of England), she had to squash uprisings by Catholics in the north and at least two serious plots against her life. In the long run, however, her greater challenges came from the Calvinist Puritans and Philip II.

Puritanism and the Church of England. The Puritans were strict Calvinists who opposed all vestiges of Catholic ritual in the Church of England. After Elizabeth became queen, many Puritans returned from exile abroad, but Elizabeth resisted their demands for drastic changes in church ritual and governance. She had assumed control as "supreme governor" of the Church of England, replacing the pope as the ultimate religious authority, and appointed all bishops. The Church of England's Thirty-Nine Articles of Religion, issued in 1563, incorporated elements of Catholic ritual along with Calvinist doctrines. Puritan ministers angrily denounced the Church of England's "popish attire and foolish disguising, . . . tithings, holy days, and a

Glorifying the Ruler
This exquisite miniature (c. 1560) attributed to Levina Teerlinc, a Flemish woman who painted for the English court, shows Queen Elizabeth I dressed in purplish blue, participating in an Easter Week ceremony at which the monarch washed the feet of poor people before presenting them with money, food, and clothing. The ceremony was held to imitate Christ's washing of the feet of his disciples; it showed that the queen could exercise every one of the ruler's customary roles.
Private collection.

thousand more abominations." To accomplish their reforms, Puritans tried to undercut the bishops' authority by placing control of church administration in the hands of a local presbytery made up of the minister and the elders of the congregation. Elizabeth rejected this Calvinist "presbyterianism."

Even though Puritans lost on almost every national issue about church organization, their influence steadily increased in local parishes. Known for their emphasis on strict moral lives, the Puritans opposed traditional forms of merrymaking such as maypole festivals and dances and regarded Sunday fairs as an insult to the Sabbath (observed by Puritans as the day of rest and worship). They abhorred the "hideous obscenities" that took place in theaters and tried to close them down. Every Puritan father—with the help of his wife—was to "make his house a little church" by teaching the children to read the Bible. At Puritan urging, a new translation of the Bible, known as the King James Bible after Elizabeth's successor, James I, was authorized in 1604. Believing themselves God's elect and England an "elect nation," the Puritans also pushed Elizabeth to help Protestants on the continent.

Triumph over Spain. Although enraged by Elizabeth's aid to the Dutch rebels, Philip II bided his time as long as she remained unmarried and her Catholic cousin Mary, Queen of Scots (Mary Stuart), stood next in line to inherit the English throne. In 1568, Scottish Calvinists forced Mary to abdicate the throne of Scotland in favor of her year-old son James (eventually James I of England), who was then raised as a Protestant. Mary spent nearly twenty years under house arrest in England, fomenting plots against Elizabeth. In 1587, when Mary's letter offering her succession rights to Philip was discovered, Elizabeth overcame her reluctance to execute a fellow monarch and ordered Mary's beheading. In response, Pope Sixtus V decided to subsidize a Catholic crusade under Philip's leadership against the heretical queen, "the English Jezebel."

At the end of May 1588, Philip II sent his *armada* (Spanish for "fleet") of 130 ships from Lisbon toward the English Channel. The Spanish king's motives were at least as much political and economic as they were religious; he now had an excuse to strike at the country whose pirates raided his shipping and encouraged Dutch resistance, and he hoped to use his fleet to ferry thousands of troops from the Netherlands across the channel to invade England itself. After several inconclusive engagements, the English scattered the Spanish Armada by sending blazing fire ships into its midst. A gale then forced the Spanish to flee around Scotland. When the Armada limped home in September, half the ships had been lost and thousands of sailors were dead or starving. Protestants throughout Europe rejoiced; Elizabeth struck a medal with the words "God blew, and they were scattered." In his play *King John* a few years later (1596), William Shakespeare wrote, "This England never did, nor never shall, Lie at the proud foot of a conqueror." Philip and Catholic Spain suffered a crushing psychological blow. A Spanish monk lamented, "Almost the whole of Spain went into mourning."

By the time Philip II died in 1598, his great empire had begun to lose its luster. The Dutch revolt ground on, and Henry IV seemed firmly established in France. The costs of fighting the Dutch, the English, and the French mounted, and in the 1590s pervasive crop failures and an outbreak of the plague made hard times even worse. An overburdened peasantry could no longer pay the taxes required to meet rising expenses. In his novel *Don Quixote* (1605), the Spanish writer Miguel de Cervantes captured the sadness of Spain's loss of grandeur. Cervantes himself had been wounded at Lepanto, been held captive in Algiers, and then served as a royal tax collector. His hero, a minor nobleman, wants to understand "this thing they call reason of state," but he reads so many romances and books of chivalry that he loses his wits and wanders the countryside hoping to re-create the heroic deeds of times past. He refuses to believe that these books are only fantasies: "Books which are printed under license from the king . . . can such be lies?" Don Quixote's futile adventures

Retreat of the Spanish Armada, 1588

incarnated the thwarted ambitions of a declining military aristocracy.

England could never have defeated Spain in a head-to-head battle on land, but Elizabeth made the most of her limited means and consolidated the country's position as a Protestant power. In her early years, she held out the prospect of marriage to many political suitors but never married. She cajoled Parliament with references to her female weaknesses, but she knew Latin, French, and Italian and showed steely-eyed determination in protecting the monarchy's interests. Her chosen successor, James I (r. 1603–1625), came to the throne as king of both Scotland and England. Shakespeare's tragedies *Hamlet* (1601), *King Lear* (1605), and *Macbeth* (1606), written about the time of James's succession, might all be read as commentaries on the uncertainties faced by Elizabeth and James. In each play, family relationships are linked to questions about the legitimacy of government, just as they were for Elizabeth and James. But Elizabeth's story, unlike those of Shakespeare's tragedies, had a happy ending; she left James secure in a kingdom of growing weight in world politics.

The Clash of Faiths and Empires in Eastern Europe

State power in eastern Europe was also tied up with religion, but in less predictable ways than in western Europe. In the east, the most contentious border divided Christian Europe from the Islamic realm of the Ottoman Turks. After their defeat at Lepanto in 1571, the Ottomans were down but far from out. Even in the Mediterranean, they continued their attacks, seizing Venetian-held Cyprus in 1573. Ottoman rule went unchallenged in the Balkans, where the Turks allowed their Christian subjects to cling to the Orthodox faith rather than forcibly converting them to Islam. Orthodox Christians thus enjoyed relative toleration and were unlikely to look to western Europe for aid. Even less inclined to turn westward were the numerous and prosperous Jewish communities of the Ottoman Empire, augmented by Jews expelled from Spain.

Orthodox Christians in Russian lands received official protection from the Muscovite tsars, but on occasion some suffered the effects of official displeasure. Building on the base laid by his grandfather Ivan III, Tsar Ivan IV (r. 1533–1584) stopped

at nothing in his endeavor to make Muscovy the center of a mighty Russian empire. Given to unpredictable fits of rage, Ivan tortured priests, killed numerous *boyars* (nobles), and murdered his own son with an iron rod during a quarrel. His epithet "the Terrible" reflects not only the terror he unleashed but also the awesome impression he evoked. Cunning, intelligent, morbidly suspicious, and cruel, Ivan came to embody barbarism in the eyes of westerners. An English visitor wrote that Ivan's actions had bred "a general hatred, distreccion [distraction], fear and discontentment throw [throughout] his kingdom. . . . God has a great plague in store for this people." Such warnings did not keep away the many westerners drawn to Moscow by opportunities to buy furs and sell western cloth and military hardware.

Ivan brought the entire Volga valley under Muscovite control and initiated Russian expansion eastward into Siberia. In 1558, he struck out to the west, vainly attempting to seize the decaying state of the German crusader (Teutonic) knights in present-day Estonia and Latvia to provide Russia direct access to the Baltic Sea. Two formidable foes blocked Ivan's plans for expansion: Sweden (which then included much of present-day Finland) and Poland-Lithuania. Their rulers hoped to annex the eastern Baltic provinces themselves. Poland and the grand duchy of Lithuania

Russia, Poland-Lithuania, and Sweden in the Late 1500s

united into a single commonwealth in 1569 and controlled territory stretching from the Baltic Sea to deep within present-day Ukraine and Belarus. It was the largest state lying wholly within the boundaries of Europe.

Poland-Lithuania, like the Dutch Republic, constituted one of the great exceptions to the general trend in early modern Europe toward greater monarchical authority; the Polish and Lithuanian nobles elected their king and severely circumscribed his authority. Noble converts to Lutheranism or Calvinism feared religious persecution by the Catholic majority, so the Polish-Lithuanian nobility insisted that their kings accept the principle of religious toleration as a prerequisite for election. The numerous Jewish communities prospered under the protection of the king and nobles.

Poland-Lithuania threatened the rule of Ivan's successors in Russia. After Ivan IV died in 1584, a terrible period of chaos known as the Time of Troubles ensued, during which the king of Poland-Lithuania tried to put his son on the Russian throne. In 1613, an army of nobles, townspeople, and peasants finally drove out the intruders and put on the throne a nobleman, Michael Romanov (r. 1613–1645), who established an enduring new dynasty. With the return of peace, Muscovite Russia resumed the process of state building. Reorganizing tax gathering and military recruitment and continuing to create a service nobility to whom the peasantry was increasingly subject, the first Romanovs laid the foundations of the powerful Russian empire that would emerge in the late seventeenth century under Peter the Great.

❖ The Thirty Years' War and the Balance of Power, 1618–1648

Although the eastern states managed to avoid civil wars over religion, the rest of Europe was drawn into the final and most deadly of the wars of religion, the Thirty Years' War. It began in 1618 with conflicts between Catholics and Protestants within the Holy Roman Empire and eventually involved most European states. By its end in 1648, many central European lands lay in ruins and the balance of power had shifted away from the Habsburg powers—Spain and Austria—toward France, England, and the Dutch Republic. Constant warfare created immediate turmoil, but it also fostered the growth of armies and the power of the bureaucracies that fed them with men and money. Out of the carnage would emerge centralized and powerful states that made increasing demands on ordinary people.

The Course of the War

The fighting that devastated central Europe had its origins in a combination of political weakness, ethnic competition, and religious conflict. The Austrian Habsburgs officially ruled over the huge Holy Roman Empire, which comprised eight major ethnic groups, but they could govern only with local cooperation. The emperor and four of the seven electors who chose him were Catholic; the other three electors were Protestants. The Peace of Augsburg of 1555 was supposed to maintain the balance between Catholics and Lutherans, but it had no mechanism for resolving conflicts; tensions rose as the new Catholic religious order, the Jesuits, won many Lutheran cities back to Catholicism and as Calvinism, unrecognized under the Peace, made inroads into Lutheran areas. By 1613, two of the three Protestant electors had become Calvinists. The long and complex war that grew out of these tensions took place in four phases: Bohemian (1618–1625), Danish (1625–1630), Swedish (1630–1635), and French (1635–1648).

Bohemian Phase. War first broke out in Bohemia after the defenestration of Prague in May 1618. The Austrian Habsburgs held not only the imperial crown of the Holy Roman Empire but also a collection of separately administered royal crowns, of which Bohemia was one. When the Catholic Habsburg heir Archduke Ferdinand was crowned king of Bohemia in 1617, he began to curtail the religious freedom previously granted to Protestants and thereby set in motion a fatal chain of events. After the defenestration, the Czechs, the largest ethnic group in Bohemia, established a Protestant assembly to spearhead resistance. A year later, when Ferdinand was elected emperor (as Ferdinand II, r. 1619–1637), the rebellious Bohemians deposed him and chose in his place the young Calvinist Frederick V of the Palatinate (r. 1616–1623). A quick series of clashes ended in 1620 when the imperial armies defeated the outmanned Czechs at the Battle of White Mountain, near Prague. Like the martyrdom of the religious reformer Jan Hus in 1415, White Mountain became an enduring symbol of the Czechs' desire for self-determination. They would not gain their independence until 1918.

White Mountain did not end the war. Private mercenary armies (armies for hire) began to form during the fighting, and the emperor had virtually no control over them. The meteoric rise of one commander, Albrecht von Wallenstein (1583–1634), showed how political ambition could trump religious conviction. A Czech Protestant by birth, Wallenstein offered in 1625 to raise an army for the Catholic emperor and soon had in his employ

125,000 soldiers, who occupied and plundered much of Protestant Germany with the emperor's approval.

Danish and Swedish Phases. The Lutheran king of Denmark Christian IV (r. 1596–1648) responded to Wallenstein's depredations by invading northern Germany to protect the Protestants and to extend his own influence. Despite Dutch and English encouragement, Christian lacked adequate military support, and Wallenstein's forces defeated him. Emboldened by his general's victories, Ferdinand issued the Edict of Restitution in 1629, which outlawed Calvinism in the empire and reclaimed Catholic church properties confiscated by the Lutherans.

With Protestant interests in serious jeopardy, Gustavus Adolphus (r. 1611–1632) of Sweden marched into Germany in 1630. Declaring his support for the Protestant cause, he clearly intended to gain control over trade in northern Europe, where he had already ejected the Poles from present-day Latvia and Estonia. His highly trained army of some 100,000 soldiers made Sweden, with a population of only one million, the supreme power of northern Europe. Now the primacy of political motives became obvious: the Catholic French government under the leadership of Cardinal Richelieu offered to subsidize the Lutheran Gustavus. Richelieu hoped to block Spanish intervention in the war and win influence and perhaps territory in the Holy Roman Empire. The agreement between the Lutheran and Catholic powers to fight the Catholic Habsburgs showed that state interests now outweighed all other considerations.

Gustavus defeated the imperial army and occupied the Catholic parts of southern Germany before he was killed at the battle of Lützen in 1632. Once again the tide turned, but this time it swept Wallenstein with it. Because Wallenstein was rumored to be negotiating with Protestant powers, Ferdinand dismissed his general and had his henchmen assassinate him.

French Phase. France openly joined the fray in 1635 by declaring war on Spain and soon after forged an alliance with the Calvinist Dutch to aid them in their struggle for independence from Spain. The French king Louis XIII (r. 1610–1643) and his chief minister Richelieu (1585–1642) had hoped to profit from the troubles of Spain in the Netherlands and from the conflicts between the Austrian

A Ruler Rides in Majesty
This caparison (ornamental covering) of wool and silk was decorated with the arms of Gustavus Adolphus of Sweden. It was manufactured in 1621 for the king's official entry into Stockholm.
© LSH Fotoavdelningen. Foto Goran Schmidt/Livrustkammaren, Stockholm.

The Horrors of the Thirty Years' War

The French artist Jacques Collot produced this engraving of the Thirty Years' War as part of a series called The Miseries and Misfortunes of War *(1633). The actions depicted resemble those in Hans Grimmelshausen's novel* The Adventures of a Simpleton, *based on Grimmelshausen's personal experience of the Thirty Years' War.*
The Granger Collection.

emperor and his Protestant subjects. Religion took a backseat as the two Catholic powers France and Spain pummeled each other. The Swedes kept up their pressure in Germany, the Dutch attacked the Spanish fleet, and a series of internal revolts shook the cash-strapped Spanish crown. In 1640, peasants in the rich northeastern province of Catalonia rebelled, overrunning Barcelona and killing the viceroy; the Catalans resented government confiscation of their crops and demands that they house and feed soldiers on their way to the French frontier. The Portuguese revolted in 1640 and proclaimed independence like the Dutch. In 1643, the Spanish suffered their first major defeat at French hands. Although the Spanish were forced to concede independence to Portugal (part of Spain only since 1580), they eventually suppressed the Catalan revolt.

France too faced exhaustion after years of rising taxes and recurrent revolts. In 1642 Richelieu died. Louis XIII followed him a few months later and was succeeded by his five-year-old son Louis XIV. With an Austrian queen mother serving as regent and an Italian cardinal, Mazarin, providing advice, French politics once again moved into a period of instability, rumor, and crisis. All sides were ready for peace.

The Effects of Constant Fighting

When peace negotiations began in the 1640s, they did not come a moment too soon for the ordinary people of Europe. Warfare left much of central Europe in shambles and taxed to the limit the resources of people in all the countries involved. The desperate efforts of rulers to build up bigger and bigger armies left their mark on the new soldiers and eventually on state structures as well.

The Experience of Ordinary People. People caught in the paths of rival armies suffered most. Some towns had faced up to ten or eleven prolonged sieges during the fighting. In 1648, as negotiations dragged on, a Swedish army sacked the rich cultural capital Prague, plundered its churches and castles, and effectively eliminated it as a center of culture and learning. Even worse suffering took place in the countryside. Peasants fled their villages, which were often burned down. At times, desperate peasants revolted and attacked nearby castles and monasteries. War and intermittent outbreaks of plague cost some German towns one-third or more of their population. One-third of the inhabitants of Bohemia also perished.

One of the earliest German novels, *The Adventures of a Simpleton* (1669) by Hans Grimmelshausen, recounts the horror of the Thirty Years' War. In one scene, the boy Simplicius looks up from his bagpipe to find himself surrounded by unidentified enemy cavalrymen, who drag him back to his father's farm; ransack the house; rape the maid, his mother, and his sister; force water mixed with dung (called "the Swedish drink" after the Swedish armies) down the hired farmhand's throat; and hold the feet of Simplicius's father to the fire until he tells where he hid his gold and jewels. The invaders then torture neighbors with thumbscrews, throw one alive into the oven, and strangle another with a crude noose. Simplicius hides in the woods but can still hear the cries of the suffering peasants and see his family's house burn down.

The Growth of Armies. Soldiers did not fare all that much better than peasants as rulers sought to expand their armies by any means possible. Governments increasingly short of funds often failed to pay the troops, and frequent mutinies, looting, and pillaging resulted. Armies attracted all sorts of displaced people desperately in need of provisions. In the last year of the Thirty Years' War, the Imperial-Bavarian Army had 40,000 men entitled to draw rations—and more than 100,000 wives, prostitutes, servants, children, maids, and other camp followers forced to scrounge for their own food. The bureaucracies of early-seventeenth-century Europe simply could not cope with such demands: armies and their hangers-on had to live off the countryside. The result was scenes like those witnessed by Simplicius.

The Thirty Years' War accelerated developments in military armament and tactics. To get more firepower, commanders followed the lead of Gustavus Adolphus in spreading out the soldiers firing guns; rather than bunching those firing muskets together, they set up long, thin lines of three to five ranks firing in turn. Tightly packed formations of pike-carrying foot soldiers pushed the battle forward. Everywhere, the size of armies increased dramatically. Most armies in the 1550s had fewer than 50,000 men, but Gustavus Adolphus had 100,000 men under arms in 1631; by the end of the seventeenth century, Louis XIV of France could count on 400,000 soldiers. The cost of larger armies and weapons such as cannon and warships strained the resources of every state. Maintaining discipline in these huge armies required harsher methods. Drill, combat training, and a clear chain of command became essential. Newly introduced "uniforms" created—as their name suggests—standardization, but uniforms soon lost their distinctiveness in the conditions of early modern warfare. An Englishman who fought for the Dutch army in 1633 described how he slept on the wet ground, got his boots full of water, and "at peep of day looked like a drowned ratt."

Although foreign mercenaries still predominated in many armies, rulers began to recruit more of their own subjects. Volunteers proved easiest to find in hard times, when the threat of starvation induced men to accept the bonus offered for signing up. A Venetian general explained the motives for enlisting: "To escape from being craftsmen [or] working in a shop; to avoid a criminal sentence; to see new things; to pursue honour (though these are very few) . . . all in the hope of having enough to live on and a bit over for shoes, or some other trifle."

The Peace of Westphalia, 1648

The comprehensive settlement provided by the Peace of Westphalia—named after the German province where negotiations took place—would serve as a model for resolving conflict among warring European states. For the first time, a diplomatic congress addressed international disputes, and the signatories to the treaties guaranteed the resulting settlement. A method still in use, the congress was the first to bring *all* parties together, rather than two or three at a time.

The Winners and Losers. France and Sweden gained most from the Peace of Westphalia. Although France and Spain continued fighting until 1659, France acquired parts of Alsace and replaced Spain as the prevailing power on the continent. Baltic conflicts would not be resolved until 1661, but Sweden took several northern territories from the Holy Roman Empire (Map 16.3).

The Habsburgs lost the most. The Spanish Habsburgs recognized Dutch independence after eighty years of war. The Swiss Confederation and the German princes demanded autonomy from the Austrian Habsburg rulers of the Holy Roman Empire. Each German prince gained the right to establish Lutheranism, Catholicism, or Calvinism in his state,

MAP 16.3 The Thirty Years' War and the Peace of Westphalia, 1648

The Thirty Years' War involved many of the major continental European powers. The arrows marking invasion routes show that most of the fighting took place in central Europe in the lands of the Holy Roman Empire. The German states and Bohemia sustained the greatest damage during the fighting. None of the combatants emerged unscathed because even ultimate winners such as Sweden and France depleted their resources of men and money.

a right denied to Calvinist rulers by the Peace of Augsburg in 1555. The independence ceded to German princes sustained political divisions that would remain until the nineteenth century and prepared the way for the emergence of a new power, the Hohenzollern Elector of Brandenburg, who increased his territories and developed a small but effective standing army. After losing considerable territory in the west, the Austrian Habsburgs turned eastward to concentrate on restoring Catholicism to Bohemia and wresting Hungary from the Turks.

The Peace of Westphalia permanently settled the distributions of the main religions in the Holy Roman Empire: Lutheranism would dominate in the north, Calvinism in the area of the Rhine River,

and Catholicism in the south. Most of the territorial changes in Europe remained intact until the nineteenth century. In the future, international warfare would be undertaken for reasons of national security, commercial ambition, or dynastic pride rather than to enforce religious uniformity. As the *politiques* of the late sixteenth century had hoped, state interests now outweighed motivations of faith in political affairs.

The Growth of State Authority. Warfare increased the reach of states: to field larger armies, governments needed more revenue and more officials to supervise the supply of troops, the collection of taxes, and the repression of resistance to higher taxes. In France the rate of land tax paid by peasants doubled in the eight years after France joined the war. In addition to raising taxes, governments frequently resorted to currency depreciation, which often resulted in inflation and soaring prices; the sale of new offices; forced loans to raise money in emergencies; and manipulation of the embryonic stock and bond markets. When all else failed, they declared bankruptcy; the Spanish government, for example, did so three times in the first half of the seventeenth century.

Poor peasants and city workers could hardly bear new demands for money, and the governments' creditors and high-ranking nobles resented monarchical intrusions. Opposition to royal taxation often set off uprisings. From Portugal to Muscovy, ordinary people resisted new impositions by forming makeshift armies and battling royal forces. With their colorful banners, unlikely leaders, strange names (the Nu-Pieds, or "Barefooted," in France, for instance), and crude weapons, the rebels usually proved no match for state armies, but they did keep officials worried and troops occupied.

As the demand for soldiers and for the money to supply them rose, the number of state employees multiplied, paperwork proliferated, and appointment to office began to depend on university education in the law. Monarchs relied on advisers who now took on the role of modern prime ministers. Axel Oxenstierna, for example, played a central part in Swedish governments between 1611 and 1654; continuity in Swedish affairs, especially after the death of Gustavus Adolphus, largely depended on him. As Louis XIII's chief minister, Richelieu arranged support for the Lutheran Gustavus even though Richelieu was a cardinal of the Catholic church. His priority was *raison d'état* ("reason of state"), that is, the state's interest above all else. He silenced Protestants within France because they had become too independent and crushed noble and popular resistance to Louis's policies. He set up *intendants*—delegates from the king's council dispatched to the provinces—to oversee police, army, and financial affairs.

To justify the growth of state authority and the expansion of government bureaucracies, rulers carefully cultivated their royal images. James I of England explicitly argued that he ruled by divine right and was accountable only to God: "The state of monarchy is the supremest thing on earth; for kings are not only God's lieutenant on earth, but even by God himself they are called gods." He

The Arts and State Power
Diego Velázquez painted King Philip IV of Spain and many members of his court. This painting of 1634–1635 shows Philip on horseback. In the seventeenth century, many rulers hired court painters to embellish the image of royal majesty. Philip IV commissioned this painting for his new palace called Buen Retiro.
All rights reserved. © Museo Nacional Del Prado – Madrid.

advised his son to maintain a manly appearance (his own well-known homosexual liaisons did not make him seem less manly to his subjects): "Eschew to be effeminate in your clothes, in perfuming, preening, or such like, and fail never in time of wars to be galliardest and bravest, both in clothes and countenance." Clothes counted for so much that most rulers regulated who could wear which kinds of cloth and decoration, reserving the richest and rarest such as ermine and gold for themselves.

Just as soldiers had to learn new drills for combat, courtiers had to learn to follow precise rituals at court. In Spain, court regulations set the wages, duties, and ceremonial functions of every official. Hundreds, even thousands, of people made up such a court. The court of Philip IV (r. 1621–1665), for example, numbered seventeen hundred. In the 1630s he built a new palace near Madrid. There the courtiers lived amid extensive parks and formal gardens, artificial ponds and grottoes, an iron aviary (which led some critics to call the whole thing a "chicken coop"), a wild animal cage, a courtyard for bullfights, and rooms filled with sculptures and paintings. State funerals, public festivities, and court display, like the acquisition of art and the building of sumptuous palaces, served to underline the power and glory of the ruler.

❖ Economic Crisis and Realignment

The devastation caused by the Thirty Years' War deepened an economic crisis that was already under way. After a century of rising prices, caused partly by massive transfers of gold and silver from the New World and partly by population growth, in the early 1600s prices began to level off and even to drop, and in most places population growth slowed. With fewer goods being produced, international trade fell into recession. Agricultural yields also declined. Just when states attempted to field ever-expanding standing armies, peasants and townspeople alike were less able to pay the escalating taxes needed to finance the wars. Famine and disease trailed grimly behind economic crisis and war, in some areas causing large-scale uprisings and revolts. Behind the scenes, the economic balance of power gradually shifted as northwestern Europe began to dominate international trade and broke the stranglehold of Spain and Portugal in the New World.

From Growth to Recession

Population grew and prices rose in the second half of the sixteenth century. Even though religious and political turbulence led to population decline in some cities, such as war-torn Antwerp, overall rates of growth remained impressive: in the sixteenth century, parts of Spain doubled in population and England's population grew by 70 percent. The supply of precious metals swelled too. Improvements in mining techniques in central Europe raised the output of silver and copper mines, and in the 1540s new silver mines had been discovered in Mexico and Peru. Spanish gold imports peaked in the 1550s, silver in the 1590s. (See "Taking Measure," below). This flood of precious metals combined with population

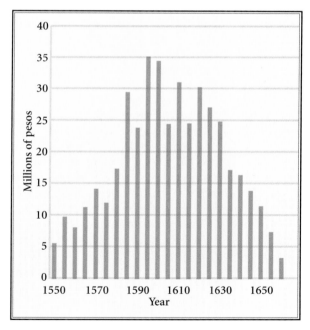

TAKING MEASURE **The Rise and Fall of Silver Imports to Spain, 1550–1660**

Gold and silver from the New World enabled the king of Spain to pursue aggressive policies in Europe and around the world. At what point did silver imports reach their highest level? Was the fall in silver imports precipitous or gradual? What can we conclude about the resources available to the Spanish king?

From Earl J. Hamilton, *American Revolution and the Price Revolution in Spain, 1501–1650* (Cambridge, Harvard University Press, 1934).

growth to fuel an astounding inflation in food prices in western Europe—400 percent in the sixteenth century—and a more moderate rise in the cost of manufactured goods. Wages rose much more slowly, at about half the rate of the increase in food prices. Governments always overspent revenues and by the end of the century most of Europe's rulers faced deep deficits.

Recession did not strike everywhere at the same time, but the warning signs were unmistakable. From the Baltic to the East Indies, foreign trade slumped as war and an uncertain money supply made business riskier. After 1625, silver imports to Spain declined, in part because so many of the native Americans who worked in Spanish colonial mines died from disease and in part because the ready supply of precious metals was progressively exhausted. Textile production fell in many countries and in some places nearly collapsed, largely because of decreased demand and a shrinking labor force. Even the relatively limited trade in African slaves stagnated, though its growth would resume after 1650 and skyrocket after 1700. African slaves were first transported to the new colony of Virginia in 1619, foreshadowing a major transformation of economic life in the New World colonies.

Demographic slowdown also signaled economic trouble. Overall, Europe's population may actually have declined, from 85 million in 1550 to 80 million in 1650. In the Mediterranean, growth apparently stopped in the 1570s. The most sudden reversal occurred in central Europe as a result of the Thirty Years' War: one-fourth of the inhabitants of the Holy Roman Empire perished in the 1630s and 1640s. The population continued to increase only in England and Wales, the Dutch Republic and the Spanish Netherlands, and Scandinavia.

Crop production eventually reflected these differences. Where the population stagnated or declined, agricultural prices dropped because of less demand, and farmers who produced for the market suffered. Many reacted by converting grain-growing land to pasture or vineyards (the prices of other foods fell less than the price of grain). Interest in improvement of the land diminished. In some places peasants abandoned their villages and left land to waste, as had happened during the plague epidemic of the late fourteenth century. The only country that emerged unscathed from this downturn was the Dutch Republic, principally because it had long excelled in agricultural innovation. Inhabiting Europe's most densely populated area, the Dutch developed systems of field drainage, crop rotation, and animal husbandry that provided high yields of grain for both people and animals. Their foreign trade, textile industry, crop production, and population all grew. After the Dutch, the English fared best; unlike the Spanish, the English never depended on New World gold and silver, and unlike most continental European countries, England escaped the direct impact of the Thirty Years' War.

Historians have long disagreed about the causes of the early-seventeenth-century recession. Some cite the inability of agriculture to support a growing population by the end of the sixteenth century; others blame the Thirty Years' War, the states' demands for more taxes, the irregularities in money supply resulting from rudimentary banking practices, or the waste caused by middle-class expenditures in the desire to emulate the nobility. To this list of causes, recent researchers have added climatic changes. (See "New Sources, New Perspectives," page 584.) Cold winters and wet summers meant bad harvests, and these natural disasters ushered in a host of social catastrophes. When the harvest was bad, prices shot back up and many could not afford to feed themselves.

Consequences for Daily Life

The recession of the early 1600s had both short-term and long-term effects. In the short term it aggravated the threat of food shortages and increased the outbreaks of famine and disease. In the long term it deepened the division between prosperous and poor peasants and fostered the development of a new pattern of late marriages and smaller families.

Famine and Disease. Outside of England and the Dutch Republic, grain had replaced meat as the essential staple of most Europeans' diets because meat had become too expensive. Most people consumed less butter, eggs, poultry, and wine and more grain products, ranging from bread to beer. The average adult European now ate more than four hundred pounds of grain per year. Peasants lived on bread, soup with a little fat or oil, peas or lentils, garden vegetables in season, and only occasionally a piece of meat or fish. In most places the poor existed on the verge of starvation; one contemporary observed that "the fourth part of the inhabitants of the parishes of England are miserable people and (harvest time excepted) without any subsistence."

The threat of food shortages haunted Europe whenever harsh weather destroyed crops. Local markets were vulnerable to problems of food distribution: customs barriers inhibited local trade, overland transport moved at a snail's pace, bandits disrupted traffic, and the state or private contractors commandeered available food for the perpetually warring armies. Usually the adverse years differed from place to place, but from 1594 to 1597 most of Europe suffered from shortages; the resulting famine triggered revolts from Ireland to Muscovy. To head off social disorder, the English government drew up a new Poor Law in 1597 that required each community to support its poor. Many other governments also increased relief efforts.

Most people, however, did not respond to their dismal circumstances by rebelling or mounting insurrections. They simply left their huts and hovels and took to the road in search of food and charity. Overwhelmed officials recorded pitiful tales of suffering. Women and children died while waiting in line for food at convents or churches. Husbands left their wives and families to search for better conditions in other parishes or even other countries. Those left behind might be reduced to eating chestnuts, roots, bark, and grass. In eastern France in 1637, a witness reported, "The roads were paved with people. . . . Finally it came to cannibalism." Eventually compassion gave way to fear as these hungry vagabonds, who sometimes banded together to beg for bread, became more aggressive, occasionally threatening to burn a barn if they were not given food.

Successive bad harvests led to malnutrition, which weakened people and made them more susceptible to such epidemic diseases as the plague, typhoid fever, typhus, dysentery, smallpox, and influenza. Disease did not spare the rich, although many epidemics hit the poor hardest. The plague was feared most: in one year it could cause the death of up to half of a town's or village's population, and it struck with no discernible pattern. Nearly 5 percent of France's entire population died just in the plague of 1628–1632.

The Changing Status of the Peasantry.   Other effects of economic crisis were less visible than famine and disease, but no less momentous. The most im-

The Life of the Poor
This mid-seventeenth-century painting by the Dutch artist Adriaen Pietersz van de Venne depicts the poor peasant weighed down by his wife and child. An empty food bowl signifies their hunger. In retrospect, this painting seems unfair to the wife of the family; she is shown in clothes that are not nearly as tattered as her husband's and is portrayed entirely as a burden, rather than as a help in getting by in hard times. In reality, many poor men abandoned their homes in search of work, leaving their wives behind to cope with hungry children and what remained of the family farm.
Allen Memorial Art Museum, Oberlin College, Oberlin, Ohio, Mrs. F. F. Prentiss Fund, 1960.

portant was the peasantry's changing status. Peasants faced many obligations, including rent and various fees for inheriting or selling land and tolls for using mills, wine presses, or ovens. States collected direct taxes on land and sales taxes on such consumer goods as salt, an essential preservative.

NEW SOURCES, NEW PERSPECTIVES

Tree Rings and the Little Ice Age

The economic crisis of the seventeenth century had many causes, and historians disagree about what they were and which were more important. One cause that has inspired intense debate is global cooling. Glaciers advanced, average temperatures fell, and winters were often exceptionally severe. Canals and rivers essential to markets froze over. Great storms disrupted ocean traffic (one storm changed the escape route of the Spanish Armada). Entire villages were demolished by glacier advance. Even in the valleys far from the mountains, cooler weather meant lower crop yields, which quickly translated into hunger and greater susceptibility to disease, leading in turn to population decline. Some historians of climate refer to the entire period 1600–1850 as the little ice age because glaciers advanced during this time and retreated only after 1850; others argue for the period 1550–1700 as the coldest, but either time frame includes the seventeenth century. Since systematic records of European temperatures were kept only from the 1700s onward, how do historians know that the weather was cooler? Given the current debates about global warming, how can we sift through the evidence to come up with a reliable interpretation?

Information about climate comes from various sources. The advance of glaciers can be seen in letters complaining to the authorities. In 1601, for example, panic-stricken villagers in Savoy (in the French Alps) wrote, "We are terrified of the glaciers . . . which are moving forward all the time and have just buried two of our villages." Yearly temperature fluctuations can be determined from the dates of wine harvests; growers harvested their grapes earliest when the weather was warmest and latest when it was coolest. Scientists study ice cores taken from Greenland to determine temperature variations; such studies seem to indicate that the coolest times were the periods 1160–1300; the 1600s; and 1820–1850. The period 1730–1800 appears to have been warmer. Recently, scientists have developed techniques for sampling corals in the tropics and sediments on oceanic shelves.

But most striking are data gathered from tree rings (the science is called *dendrochronology* or *dendroclimatology*). Timber samples have been taken from very old oak trees and also from ancient beams in buildings and archaeological digs and from logs left long undisturbed in northern bogs and riverbeds. In cold summers, trees lay down thinner growth rings; in warm ones, thicker rings.

Protestant and Catholic churches alike exacted a tithe (a tax equivalent to one-tenth of the parishioner's annual income); often the clergy took their tithe in the form of crops and collected it directly during the harvest. Any reversal of fortune could force peasants into the homeless world of vagrants and beggars, who numbered as much as 1 to 2 percent of the total population.

In the seventeenth century the mass of peasants in western Europe became more sharply divided into prosperous and poor. In England, the Dutch Republic, northern France, and northwestern Ger-

many, the peasantry was disappearing: improvements gave some peasants the means to become farmers who rented substantial holdings, produced for the market, and in good times enjoyed relative comfort and higher status. Those who could not afford to plant new crops such as maize (American corn) or buckwheat or to use techniques that ensured higher yields became simple laborers with little or no land of their own. The minimum plot of land needed to feed a family varied depending on the richness of the soil, available improvements in agriculture, and distance from markets. For example,

The Frozen Thames
This painting by Abraham Hondius of the frozen Thames River in London dates to 1677. In the 1670s and 1680s the Thames froze several times. Hondius himself depicted another such view in 1684. Diarists recorded that shopkeepers even set up their stalls on the ice. In other words, the expected routines of daily life changed during the cooling down of the seventeenth century. Contemporaries were shocked enough by the changes to record them for posterity.
Museum of London.

Information about tree rings confirms the conclusions drawn from wine harvest and ice core samples: the seventeenth century was relatively cold. Recent tree ring studies have shown that some of the coldest summers were caused by volcanic eruptions; according to a study of more than one hundred sites in North America and Europe, the five coldest summers in the past four hundred years were in 1601, 1641, 1669, 1699, and 1912 (four out of five in the seventeenth century), and all but the summer of 1699 came in years following recorded eruptions.

QUESTIONS FOR DEBATE

1. What were the historical consequences of global cooling in the seventeenth century?

2. Why would trees be especially valuable sources of information about climate?

FURTHER READING

H. H. Lamb, *Climate, History and the Modern World*, 2nd ed., 1995.

Patrick R. Galloway, "Long-Term Fluctuations in Climate and Population in the Preindustrial Era," *Population and Development Review* 12 (1986): 1–24.

only two acres could support a family in Flanders, as opposed to ten acres in Muscovy. One-half to four-fifths of the peasants did not have enough acreage to support a family. They descended deeper into debt during difficult times and often lost their land to wealthier farmers or to city officials intent on developing rural estates.

As the recession deepened, women lost some of their economic opportunities. Widows who had been able to take over their late husbands' trade now found themselves excluded by the urban guilds or limited to short tenures. Many women went into

domestic service until they married, some for their entire lives. When town governments began to fear the effects of increased mobility from country to town and town to town, they carefully regulated women's work as servants, requiring them to stay in their positions unless they could prove mistreatment by a master.

Effects on Marriage and Childbearing. Demographic historians have shown that European families reacted almost immediately to economic crisis. During bad harvests they postponed marriages and

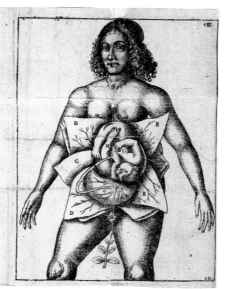

The Figure Explained:

Being a Diffection of the WOMB, with the ufual manner how the CHILD lies therein near the time of its Birth.

B B. The inner parts of the *Chorion* extended and branched out.

C. The *Amnios* extended.

D D. The Membrane of the Womb extended and branched.

E. The Fleshy fubftance call'd the *Cake* or *Placenta*, which nourifhes the Infant, it is full of Veffels.

F. The Veffels appointed for the Navel ftring.

G. The Navel ftring carrying nourifhment from the *Placenta* to the Navel.

H H H. The manner how the Infant lieth in the Womb near the time of its Birth.

I. The Navel ftring how it enters into the Navel.

The *Midwives Book* (1671)
The English woman Jane Sharp wrote the first book on midwifery by a woman. She endeavored to provide as much scientific information about the female body as was available at the time.
British Library.

had fewer children. When hard times passed, more people married and had more children. But even in the best of times, one-fifth to one-quarter of all children died in their first year, and half died before age twenty. In 1636, an Englishman described his grief when his twenty-one-month-old son died: "We both found the sorrow for the loss of this child, on whom we had bestowed so much care and affection . . . far to surpass our grief for the decease of his three elder brothers, who dying almost as soon as they were born, were not so endeared to us as this [one] was."

Childbirth still carried great risks for women, about 10 percent of whom died in the process. Even in the richest and most enlightened homes, childbirth often occasioned an atmosphere of panic. To allay their fears, women sometimes depended on magic stones and special pilgrimages and prayers. Midwives delivered most babies; physicians were scarce, and even if they did attend a birth they were generally less helpful. The Englishwoman Alice Thornton described in her diary how a doctor bled her to prevent a miscarriage after a fall; her son died anyway in a breech birth that almost killed her too.

It might be assumed that families would have more children to compensate for high death rates, but beginning in the early seventeenth century and continuing until the end of the eighteenth, families in all ranks of society started to limit the number of children. Because methods of contraception were not widely known, they did this for the most part by marrying later; the average age at marriage dur-

ing the seventeenth century rose from the early twenties to the late twenties. The average family had about four children. Poorer families seem to have had fewer children, wealthier ones more. Peasant couples, especially in eastern and southeastern Europe, had more children than urban couples because cultivation still required intensive manual labor.

The consequences of late marriage were profound. Young men and women were expected to put off marriage (*and* sexual intercourse) until their mid- to late twenties—if they were among the lucky 50 percent who lived that long and not among the 10 percent who never married. Because both the Reformation and Counter-Reformation had stressed sexual fidelity and abstinence before marriage, the number of births out of wedlock was relatively small (2–5 percent of births); premarital intercourse was generally tolerated only after a couple had announced their engagement.

The Economic Balance of Power

Just as the recession produced winners and losers among ordinary people, so too it created winners and losers among the competing states of Europe. The economies of southern Europe declined, whereas those of the northwest emerged stronger. Competition in the New World reflected and reinforced this shift as the English, Dutch, and French rushed to establish trading outposts and permanent settlements to compete with the Spanish and Portuguese.

Regional Differences. The crisis of the seventeenth century ended the dominance of Mediterranean economies, which had endured since the time of the Greeks and Romans, and ushered in the new powers of northwestern Europe with their growing Atlantic economies. With expanding populations and geographical positions that promoted Atlantic trade, England and the Dutch Republic vied with France to become the leading mercantile powers. Northern Italian industries were eclipsed; Spanish commerce with the New World dropped. Amsterdam replaced Seville, Venice, Genoa, and Antwerp as the center of European trade and commerce. The plague also had differing effects. Whereas central Europe and the Mediterranean countries took generations to recover from its ravages, northwestern Europe quickly replaced its lost population, no doubt because this area's people had suffered less from the effects of the Thirty Years' War and from the malnutrition related to the economic crisis.

East-west differences would soon overshadow those between northern and southern regions. Because labor shortages coincided with economic recovery, peasants in western Europe gained more independence and all but the remnants of serfdom disappeared. By contrast, from the Elbe River east to Muscovy, nobles reinforced their dominance over peasants, thanks to cooperation from rulers and lack of resistance from villagers, whose community traditions had always acknowledged nobles' rights of lordship.

The price rise of the sixteenth century prompted Polish and eastern German nobles to increase their holdings and step up their production of grain for western markets. To raise production, they demanded more rent and dues from their peasants, whom the government decreed must stay in their villages. Although noble landlords lost income in the economic downturn of the first half of the seventeenth century, their peasants gained nothing. Those who were already dependent became serfs—completely tied to the land. A local official might complain of "this barbaric and as it were Egyptian servitude," but he had no power to fight the nobles. In Muscovy the complete enserfment of the peasantry would eventually be recognized in the Code of Laws in 1649. Although enserfment produced short-term profits for landlords, in the long run it retarded economic development in eastern Europe and kept most of the population in a stranglehold of illiteracy and hardship.

Competition in the New World. Many European states, including Sweden and Denmark, rushed to join the colonial competition because they considered it a branch of mercantilist policy. According to the doctrine of mercantilism, governments should sponsor policies to increase national wealth. To this end, they chartered private joint-stock companies to enrich investors by importing fish, furs, tobacco, and precious metals, if they could be found, and to develop new markets for European

"Savages" of the New World
Europeans found the "savages" of the New World fascinating and terrifying. Both sides are captured in Paolo Farinati's 1595 painting America. *The half-dressed savage appears much like a noble Italian; he holds a crucifix in his right hand, signifying his conversion to Christianity. But to his right his comrades are roasting human flesh. Europeans were convinced that many native peoples were cannibals.*
Villa della Torre, Mezzane de Sotto, Verona.

products. Because Spain and Portugal had divided among themselves the rich spoils of South America, other prospective colonizers had to carve niches in seemingly less hospitable places, especially North America and the Caribbean (Map 16.4). Eventually the English, French, and Dutch would dominate commerce with these colonies.

English settlement policies had an unfortunate precedent in Ireland, where in the 1580s English armies drove the Irish clans from their strongholds and claimed the land for English and Scottish Protes-

tant colonists. When the Irish resisted with guerrilla warfare, English generals waged total war, destroying harvests and burning villages; one general lined the path to his headquarters with Irish heads. A few decades later, the English would use the same tactics against another group of "savages," this time in the New World.

Some colonists in North America justified their mission by promising to convert the native population to Christianity. As the English colonizer John Smith told his followers in Virginia, "The growing

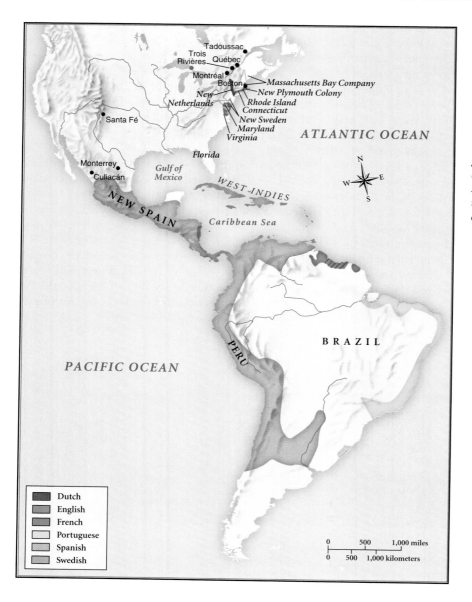

MAP 16.4 European Colonization of the Americas, c. 1640

Europeans established themselves first in coastal areas. The English, French, and Dutch set up most of their colonies in the Caribbean and North America because the Spanish and Portuguese had already colonized the easily accessible regions in South America. Vast inland areas still remained unexplored and uncolonized in 1640.

provinces addeth to the King's Crown; but the re-ducing heathen people to civility and true religion bringeth honour to the King of Heaven." Catholic France and Spain were more successful, however, than Protestant England in their efforts to convert American natives. Protestantism did not mesh well with native American cultures because it demanded an individual conversion experience based on a Christian notion of sin. Catholicism, in contrast, stressed shared rituals, which were more accessible to the native populations.

In establishing permanent colonies, the Euro-peans created whole new communities across the Atlantic. Careful plans often fell afoul of the hazards of transatlantic shipping, however. Originally, the warm climate of Virginia made it an attractive des-tination for the Pilgrims, a small English sect that, unlike the Puritans, attempted to separate from the Church of England. But the *Mayflower*, which had sailed for Virginia with Pilgrim emigrants, landed far to the north in Massachusetts, where in 1620 the settlers founded New Plymouth Colony. As the religious situation for English Puritans worsened, wealthier people became willing to emi-grate, and in 1629 a prominent group of Puritans incorporated themselves as the Massachusetts Bay Company. They founded a virtually self-governing colony headquartered in Boston.

Colonization gradually spread. Migrating set-tlers, including dissident Puritans, soon founded new settlements in Connecticut and Rhode Island. Catholic refugees from England established a much smaller colony in Maryland. By the 1640s, the British North American colonies had more than fifty thousand people—not including the Indians, whose numbers had been decimated in epidemics and wars—and the foundations of representative government in locally chosen colonial assemblies. By contrast, French Canada had only about three thousand European inhabitants by 1640. Because the French government refused to let Protestants emigrate from France and establish a foothold in the New World, it denied itself a ready population for the settling of permanent colonies abroad. Both England and France turned their attention to the Caribbean in the 1620s and 1630s when they occu-pied the islands of the West Indies after driving off the native Caribs. These islands would prove ideal for a plantation economy of tobacco and sugar cane.

❖ A Clash of Worldviews

The countries that moved ahead economically in this period—England, the Dutch Republic, and to some extent France—turned out to be the most re-ceptive to new secular worldviews. Although *secu-larization* did not entail a loss of religious faith, it did prompt a search for nonreligious explanations for political authority and natural phenomena. During the late sixteenth and early seventeenth cen-turies, art, political theory, and science all began to break some of their bonds with religion. The visual arts, for example, more frequently depicted secular subjects. Scientists and scholars sought laws in na-ture to explain politics as well as movements in the heavens and on earth. A "scientific revolution" was in the making. Yet traditional attitudes did not dis-appear. Belief in magic and witchcraft pervaded every level of society. People of all classes accepted supernatural explanations for natural phenomena, a view only gradually and partially undermined by new ideas.

The Arts in an Age of Religious Conflict

Two new forms of artistic expression—professional theater and opera—developed to express secular values in an age of conflict over religious beliefs. The greatest playwright of the English language, William Shakespeare, never referred to religious disputes in his plays, and he always set his most personal re-flections on political turmoil and uncertainty in far-away times or places. Religion played an important role in the new Mannerist and baroque styles of painting, however, even though many rulers com-missioned paintings on secular subjects for their own uses.

Theater in the Age of Shakespeare. Permanent professional theater companies appeared for the first time in Europe in the last quarter of the six-teenth century. In previous centuries, traveling companies made their living by playing at major religious festivals and by repeating their perfor-mances in small towns and villages along the way. In London, Seville, and Madrid, the first profes-sional acting companies performed before paying audiences in the 1570s. A huge outpouring of playwriting followed. The Spanish playwright Lope de Vega (1562–1635) alone wrote more than fifteen hundred plays. Between 1580 and 1640, three hundred English playwrights produced works for a hundred different acting companies. Theaters did a banner business despite Puritan opposition in England and Catholic objections in Spain. Shopkeepers, apprentices, lawyers, and court nobles crowded into open-air theaters to see everything from bawdy farces to profound tragedies.

The most enduring and influential playwright of the time was the Englishman William Shakespeare (1564–1616), son of a glovemaker, who wrote three dozen plays and acted in one of the chief troupes. Although Shakespeare's plays were not set in contemporary England, they reflected the concerns of his age: the nature of power and the crisis of authority. His greatest tragedies—*Hamlet* (1601), *King Lear* (1605), and *Macbeth* (1606)—show the uncertainty and even chaos that result when power is misappropriated or misused. In each play, family relationships are linked to questions about the legitimacy of government, just as they were for Elizabeth I herself. Hamlet's mother marries the man who murdered his royal father and usurped the crown; two of Lear's daughters betray him when he tries to divide his kingdom; Macbeth's wife persuades him to murder the king and seize the throne. Some of Shakespeare's female characters, like Lady Macbeth, are as driven, ambitious, powerful, and tortured as the male protagonists; others, like Queen Gertrude in *Hamlet*, reflect the ambiguity of women's role in public life—they were not expected to act with authority, and their lives were subject to men's control.

Shakespeare's stories of revenge, exile, political instability, broken families, betrayal, witchcraft, madness, suicide, and murder clearly mirror the anxieties of the period. One character in the final act describes the tragic story of Prince Hamlet as one "Of carnal, bloody, and unnatural acts; Of accidental judgments, casual slaughters; Of deaths put on by cunning and forced cause." Like many real-life people, Shakespeare's tragic characters found little peace in the turmoil of their times.

Mannerism and the Baroque in Art. New styles of painting reflected similar concerns less directly, but they too showed the desire for changed standards. In the late sixteenth century the artistic style

Mannerist Painting
With its distortion of perspective, crowding of figures, and mysterious allusions, El Greco's painting The Dream of Philip II *(1577) is a typical mannerist painting. Philip II can be seen in his usual black clothing with a lace ruffle as his only decoration.*
© National Gallery, London.

known as Mannerism emerged in the Italian states and soon spread across Europe. Mannerism was an almost theatrical style that allowed painters to distort perspective to convey a message or emphasize a theme. The most famous Mannerist painter, called El Greco because he was of Greek origin, trained in Venice and Rome before he moved to Spain in the

Baroque Painting
The Flemish baroque painter Peter Paul Rubens used monumental canvases to glorify the French queen Marie de Medici, wife of Henry IV and mother of Louis XIII. Between 1622 and 1625, Rubens painted twenty-four panels like this one to decorate Marie's residence in Paris. Their gigantic size (some were more than twenty feet wide), imposing figures captured in rich colors, and epic settings characterized the use of the baroque to exalt secular rulers. In this scene, Henry is shown handing over government to his wife on behalf of his young son (Henry was assassinated in 1610).
Giraudon/Art Resource, NY.

1570s. His paintings encapsulated the Mannerist style: he crowded figures or objects into every available space, used larger-than-life or elongated figures, and created new and often bizarre visual effects. This style departed abruptly from precise Renaissance perspective. The religious intensity of El Greco's pictures shows that faith still motivated many artists, as it did much political conflict.

The most important new style in seventeenth-century high art was the baroque, which, like Mannerism, originated in the Italian states. As is the case with many historical categories, *baroque* was not used as a label by people living at the time; in the eighteenth century, art critics coined the word to

mean shockingly bizarre, confused, and extravagant, and until the late nineteenth century, art historians and collectors largely disdained the baroque. Stylistically, the baroque rejected Renaissance classicism: in place of the classical emphasis on line, harmonious design, unity, and clarity, the baroque featured curves, exaggerated lighting, intense emotions, release from restraint, and even a kind of artistic sensationalism.

In church architecture and painting the baroque melodramatically reaffirmed the emotional depths of the Catholic faith and glorified both church and monarchy. The Catholic church encouraged the expression of religious feeling through art because its emotional impact helped strengthen the ties between the faithful and the Counter-Reform church (the label given the Catholic church in the aftermath of the Protestant Reformation, when it offered its own internal reforms). As an urban and spectacular style, the baroque was well suited to public festivities and display. Along with religious festivals, civic processions, and state funerals that served the interests of the church and state, baroque portraits, such as the many portraits of Philip IV by Diego Velázquez, celebrated authority.

Closely tied to the Counter-Reformation, the baroque style spread from Rome to other Italian states and then into central Europe. The Catholic Habsburg territories, including Spain and the Spanish Netherlands, embraced the style. The Spanish built baroque churches in their American colonies as part of their massive conversion campaign. Within Europe, Protestant countries largely resisted the baroque, as we can see by comparing Flemish painters from the Spanish Netherlands with Dutch artists. The first great baroque painter was an Italian-trained Fleming, Peter Paul Rubens (1577–1640). A devout Catholic, Rubens painted vivid, exuberant pictures on religious themes, packed with figures. His was an extension of the theatrical baroque style, conveying ideas through broad gestures and dramatic poses. The great Dutch Protestant painters of the next generation, such as Rembrandt van Rijn (1606–1669), sometimes used biblical subjects, but their pictures were more realistic and focused on everyday scenes. Many of them suggested the Protestant concern for an inner life and personal faith rather than the public expression of religiosity.

Church Music and Opera. As in the visual arts, differences in musical style during the late sixteenth and early seventeenth centuries reflected religious divisions. The new Protestant churches developed their own distinct music, which differentiated their worship from the Catholic Mass and also marked them as Lutheran or Calvinist. Lutheran composers developed a new form, the strophic hymn, or chorale, a religious text set to a tune that is then enriched through harmony. Calvinist congregations, in keeping with their emphasis on simplicity and austerity, avoided harmony and more often sang in unison, thereby encouraging participation.

A new secular musical form, the opera, grew up parallel to the baroque style in the visual arts. First influential in the Italian states, opera combined music, drama, dance, and scenery in a grand sensual display, often with themes chosen to please the ruler and the aristocracy. Operas could be based on typically baroque sacred subjects or on traditional stories. Like Shakespeare, opera composers often turned to familiar stories their audiences would recognize and readily follow. One of the most innovative composers of opera was Claudio Monteverdi (1567–1643), whose work contributed to the development of both opera and the orchestra. His earliest operatic production, *Orfeo* (1607), was the first to require an orchestra of about forty instruments and to include instrumental as well as vocal sections.

The Natural Laws of Politics

In reaction to the wars over religious beliefs, jurists and scholars not only began to defend the primacy of state interests over those of religious conformity but also insisted on secular explanations for politics. Machiavelli had pointed in this direction with his prescriptions for Renaissance princes in the early sixteenth century, but the intellectual movement gathered steam in the aftermath of the religious violence unleashed by the Reformation. Religious toleration could not take hold until government could be organized on some principle other than one king, one faith. The French *politiques* Michel de Montaigne and Jean Bodin started the search for those principles. During the Dutch revolt against Spain, the jurist Hugo Grotius gave new meaning to the notion of "natural law"—laws of nature that give legitimacy to government and stand above the actions of any particular ruler or religious group. His ideas would influence John Locke and the American revolutionaries of the eighteenth century.

Montaigne and Bodin. Michel de Montaigne (1533–1592) was a French magistrate who resigned his office in the midst of the wars of religion to write about the need for tolerance and open-mindedness. Although himself a Catholic, Montaigne painted on the beams of his study the words "All that is certain is that nothing is certain." To capture this need for personal reflection in a tumultuous age of religious discord, he invented the essay as a short and pithy form of expression. He revived the ancient doctrine of skepticism, which held that total certainty is never attainable—a doctrine, like toleration of religious differences, that was repugnant to Protestants and Catholics alike, both of whom were certain that their religion was the right one. He also questioned the common European habit of calling newly discovered peoples in the New World barbarous and savage: "Everyone gives the title of barbarism to everything that is not in use in his own country."

The French Catholic lawyer Jean Bodin (1530–1596) sought systematic secular answers to the problem of disorder in *The Six Books of the Republic* (1576). Comparing the different forms of government throughout history, he concluded that there were three basic types of sovereignty: monarchy, aristocracy, and democracy. Only strong monarchical power offered hope for maintaining order, he insisted. Bodin rejected any doctrine of the right to resist tyrannical authority: "I denied that it was the function of a good man or of a good citizen to offer violence to his prince for any reason, however great a tyrant he might be" (and, it might be added, whatever his ideas on religion). Bodin's ideas helped lay the foundation for absolutism, the idea that the monarch should be the sole and uncontested source of power. Nonetheless, the very discussion of types of governments in the abstract implied that they might be subject to choice rather than simply being God-given, as most rulers maintained.

Grotius and Natural Law. Hugo Grotius (1583–1645) argued that natural law stood beyond the reach of either secular or divine authority; it would be valid even if God did not exist. Natural law should govern politics, by this account, not Scripture, religious authority, or tradition. Not surprisingly, these ideas got Grotius into trouble. His work *The Laws of War and Peace* (1625) was condemned by the Catholic church. The Dutch Protestant government arrested him for his part in religious controversies; his wife helped him escape prison by hiding him in a chest of books. He fled to Paris, where he got a small pension from Louis XIII and served as his ambassador to Sweden. The Swedish king Gustavus Adolphus claimed that he kept Grotius's book under his pillow even while at battle. Grotius was one of the first to argue that international conventions should govern the treatment of prisoners of war and the making of peace treaties.

At the same time that Grotius expanded the principles of natural law, most jurists worked on codifying the huge amount of legislation and

jurisprudence devoted to legal forms of torture. Most states and the courts of the Catholic church used torture when the crime was very serious and the evidence seemed to point to a particular defendant but no definitive proof had been established. The judges ordered torture—hanging the accused by the hands with a rope thrown over a beam, pressing the legs in a leg screw, or just tying the hands very tightly—to extract a confession, which had to be given with a medical expert and notary present and had to be repeated without torture. Children, pregnant women, the elderly, aristocrats, kings, and even professors were exempt.

Grotius's conception of natural law directly challenged the use of torture. To be in accord with natural law, Grotius argued, governments had to defend natural rights, which he defined as life, body, freedom, and honor. Grotius did not encourage rebellion in the name of natural law or rights, but he did hope that someday all governments would adhere to these principles and stop killing their own and one another's subjects in the name of religion. Natural law and natural rights would play an important role in the founding of constitutional governments from the 1640s forward and in the establishment of various charters of human rights in our own time.

The Origins of the Scientific Revolution

Although the Catholic and Protestant churches encouraged the study of science and many prominent scientists were themselves clerics, the search for a secular, scientific method of determining the laws of nature eventually challenged the traditional accounts of natural phenomena. (See "Did You Know?" page 594.) Christian doctrine had incorporated the scientific teachings of ancient philosophers, especially Ptolemy and Aristotle; now these came into question. A revolution in astronomy challenged the Ptolemaic view, endorsed by the Catholic church, which held that the sun revolved around the earth. Startling breakthroughs took place in medicine, too, which laid the foundations for modern anatomy and pharmacology. By the early seventeenth century, a new scientific method had been established based on a combination of experimental observation and mathematical deduction. Conflicts between the new science and religion followed almost immediately.

The Gregorian Calendar: 1582

The Catholic church relied on the work of astronomers when it undertook a major reform of the calendar in 1582. Every culture has some kind of calendar by which it groups days to mark time, but the length of the day, the week, and the month have varied throughout much of human history. At different moments in the past, West Africans, for example, used four-day weeks, central Asians five-day weeks, and Egyptians ten-day weeks. These different systems became uniform when most of the world's countries adopted the Gregorian calendar. The spread of the use of the Gregorian calendar, which happened only very gradually after its introduction in 1582, marked the extension of Western influence in the world.

The Gregorian calendar got its name from Pope Gregory XIII, who ordered calendar reform to compute more accurately the exact date on which Easter—the Christian holiday commemorating the resurrection of Jesus—should fall. Easter was supposed to fall on the first Sunday after the first full moon after the vernal equinox. But over the years the dates had become confused because

no one had been able to calculate the exact length of a solar year (365.242199 days). As a result, the calendar had become increasingly out of phase with the seasons; by 1545, the vernal (spring) equinox had moved ten days from its proper date. In 1582, when the reform took effect, October 5 became October 15, thus omitting ten days and setting the vernal equinox straight—but causing any number of legal complications.

Although the Gregorian calendar was based on a truer calculation of the length of a year and thus required less adjustment than previous calendars, it was not immediately adopted, even in Christian Europe, in part because any change would have been difficult to enforce given the state of communications at the time. Because the pope had sponsored the reform, the Catholic countries embraced it first; Protestant countries used it only after 1700. England accepted it in 1752. Adoption followed in Japan in 1873, Egypt in 1875, Russia in 1918, and Greece in 1923. The Greek Orthodox church never accepted it, so Easter in that church is about one week later than elsewhere in Christianity.

Even though the Gregorian calendar is astronomically correct, it still has bothersome defects: the months are different in length, and holidays do not fall on the same day in each year. Two other calendars have been proposed. The International Fixed Calendar would divide the year into thirteen

The Revolution in Astronomy. The traditional account of the movement of the heavens derived from the second-century Greek astronomer Ptolemy, who put the earth at the center of the cosmos. Above the earth were fixed the moon, the stars, and the planets in concentric crystalline spheres; beyond these fixed spheres dwelt God and the angels. The planets revolved around the earth at the command of God. In this view, the sun revolved around the earth; the heavens were perfect and unchanging, and the earth was "corrupted." Ptolemy insisted that the

planets revolved in perfectly circular orbits (because circles were more "perfect" than other figures). To account for the actual elliptical paths that could be observed and calculated, he posited orbits within orbits, or epicycles.

In 1543, the Polish clergyman Nicolaus Copernicus (1473–1543) began the revolution in astronomy by publishing his treatise *On the Revolution of the Celestial Spheres.* Copernicus attacked the Ptolemaic account, arguing that the earth and planets revolved around the sun, a view known as *heliocentrism* (a

Calendar
This painting by Aldo Durazzi shows Gregory XIII presiding over the council of 1582 that reformed the calendar. The Catholic church sponsored the work of many astronomers and other scientists.
Archivio di Stato, Siena. Photo Lensini Fabrio.

months of twenty-eight days with an additional day at the end. The World Calendar would divide the year into four quarters of ninety-one days each with an additional day at the end of the year; the first month in each quarter would have thirty-one days and the second and third thirty days each. Neither has been adopted. Logic does not always win this kind of argument, for changing the length of the months seems almost equivalent to changing which side of the road you drive on; once a system is learned, no one really wants to give it up and start all over again. The same is true for the numbering of the years, which was set by the Council of Nicea in 325. The year 1 was designated as the year it was believed Jesus was born. Today scholars have determined that the date was wrong by several years, and many object in any case to the use of a calendar based on the birth of Jesus. But if that dating system were eliminated, what would replace it? Where should a common calendar begin?

sun-centered universe). He discovered that by placing the sun instead of the earth at the center of the system of spheres, he could eliminate many epicycles from the calculations. In other words, he claimed that the heliocentric view simplified the mathematics. Copernicus died soon after publishing his theories, but when the Italian monk Giordano Bruno (1548–1600) taught heliocentrism, perhaps with the aim of establishing a new religion, the Catholic Inquisition (set up to seek out heretics) arrested him and burned him at the stake.

For the most part, however, Copernicus's ideas attracted little sustained attention until the early seventeenth century, when astronomers systematically collected evidence that undermined the Ptolemaic view. A leader among them was the Danish astronomer Tycho Brahe (1546–1601), who was educated in Copenhagen and Leipzig. While at university he lost part of his nose in a duel and for the rest of his life he wore a metal insert to replace the missing part. Brahe designed and built new instruments for observing the heavens and trained a whole

The Trial of Galileo
In this anonymous painting of the trial held in 1633, Galileo appears seated on a chair in the center facing the church officials who accused him of heresy for insisting that the sun, not the earth, was the center of the universe (heliocentrism). Catholic officials forced him to recant or suffer the death penalty, but the trial did more damage in the long term to the Catholic church's reputation than it did to Galileo's.
Private collection, New York.
© Photograph by Erich Lessing/ Art Resource.

generation of astronomers. His observation of a new star in 1572 and a comet in 1577 called into question the Aristotelian view that the universe was unchanging. Brahe still rejected heliocentrism, but the assistant he employed when he moved to Prague in 1599, Johannes Kepler (1571–1630), was converted to the Copernican view. Kepler continued Brahe's collection of planetary observations and used the evidence to develop his three laws of planetary motion, published between 1609 and 1619. Kepler's laws provided mathematical backing for heliocentrism and directly challenged the claim long held, even by Copernicus, that planetary motion was circular. Kepler's first law stated that the orbits of the planets are ellipses, with the sun always at one focus of the ellipse.

The Italian Galileo Galilei (1564–1642) provided more evidence to support the heliocentric view and also challenged the doctrine that the heavens were perfect and unchanging. In 1609, he learned that two Dutch astronomers had built a telescope. He quickly invented a better one and observed the earth's moon, four satellites of Jupiter, the phases of Venus (a cycle of changing physical appearances), and sunspots. The moon, the planets, and the sun were no more perfect than the earth,

he insisted, and the shadows he could see on the moon could only be the product of hills and valleys like those on earth. Galileo portrayed the earth as a moving part of a larger system, only one of many planets revolving around the sun, not as the fixed center of a single, closed universe.

Because he recognized the utility of the new science for everyday projects, Galileo published his work in Italian, rather than Latin, to appeal to a lay audience of merchants and aristocrats. But he meant only to instruct an educated elite. The new science, he claimed, suited "the minds of the wise," not "the shallow minds of the common people." After all, his discoveries challenged the commonsensical view that it is the sun that rises and sets while the earth stands still. If the Bible were wrong about motion in the universe, as Galileo's position implied, the error came from the Bible's use of common language to appeal to the lower orders. The Catholic church was not mollified by this explanation. In 1616 the church forbade Galileo to teach that the earth moves and in 1633 accused him of not obeying the earlier order. Forced to appear before the Inquisition, he agreed to publicly recant his assertion that the earth moves to save himself from torture and death. Afterward he lived under house arrest and could publish his work only in the Dutch Republic, which had become a haven for iconoclastic scientists and thinkers.

Breakthroughs in Medicine. Until the mid-sixteenth century, medical knowledge in Europe had been based on the writings of the second-century Greek physician Galen, who was a contemporary of Ptolemy. Galen derived his knowledge of the anatomy of the human body from partial dissections. In the same year that Copernicus challenged the traditional account in astronomy (1543), the Flemish scientist Andreas Vesalius (1514–1564) did the same for anatomy. He published a new illustrated anatomical text, *On the Construction of the Human Body*, that revised Galen's work. Drawing on public dissections in the medical faculties of European universities, Vesalius at first hesitated to entirely reject Galen, but in his second edition of 1555 he explicitly refuted his predecessor. Theophrastus Bombastus von Hohenheim, better known as Paracelsus (1493–1541), went even further than Vesalius. He burned Galen's text at the University of Basel, where he was a professor of medicine. Paracelsus experimented with new drugs, performed operations (at the time most academic physicians taught medical theory, not practice), and pursued his interests in magic, alchemy, and astrology. He helped establish the modern science of pharmacology.

The Englishman William Harvey (1578–1657) also used dissection to examine the circulation of blood within the body, demonstrating how the heart worked as a pump. The heart and its valves were "a piece of machinery," Harvey insisted. They obeyed mechanical laws just as the planets and earth revolved around the sun in a mechanical universe. Nature could be understood by experiment and rational deduction, not by following traditional authorities.

Scientific Method: Bacon and Descartes. In the 1630s, the European intellectual elite began to accept the new scientific views. Ancient learning, the churches and their theologians, and even cherished popular beliefs seemed to be undermined by a new standard of truth—scientific method, which was based on systematic experiments and rational deduction. Two men were chiefly responsible for spreading the prestige of scientific method: the English politician Sir Francis Bacon (1561–1626) and the French mathematician and philosopher René

Descartes (1596–1650). They represented the two essential halves of scientific method: respectively, inductive reasoning through observation and experimental research and deductive reasoning from self-evident principles.

In *The Advancement of Learning* (1605), Bacon attacked reliance on ancient writers and optimistically predicted that scientific method would lead to social progress. The minds of the medieval scholars, he said, had been "shut up in the cells of a few authors (chiefly Aristotle, their dictator) as their persons were shut up in the cells of monasteries and colleges," and they could therefore produce only "cobwebs of learning" that were "of no substance or profit." Advancement would take place only through the collection, comparison, and analysis of information. Knowledge, in Bacon's view, must be empirically based (that is, gained by observation and experiment). Bacon ardently supported the scientific method over popular beliefs, which he rejected as "fables and popular errors." Claiming that God had called the Catholic church "to account for their degenerate manners and ceremonies," Bacon looked to the Protestant English state, which he served as lord chancellor, for leadership on the road to scientific advancement.

Although he agreed with Bacon's denunciation of traditional learning, Descartes saw that the attack on tradition might only replace the dogmatism of the churches with the skepticism of Montaigne—that nothing at all was certain. A Catholic who served in the Thirty Years' War, Descartes aimed to establish the new science on more secure philosophical foundations, those of mathematics and logic (Descartes invented analytic geometry). In his *Discourse on Method* (1637), he argued that mathematical and mechanical principles provided the key to understanding all of nature, including the actions of people and states. All prior assumptions must be repudiated in favor of one elementary principle: "I think, therefore I am." Everything else could—and should—be doubted, but even doubt showed the certain existence of someone thinking. Begin with the simple and go on to the complex, he asserted, and believe only those ideas that present themselves "clearly and distinctly." Descartes believed that rational individuals would see the necessity of strong state power and that only "meddling and restless spirits" would plot against it. He insisted that human reason could not only unravel the secrets of nature but also prove the existence of God. Although he hoped to secure the authority of both church and state, his reliance on human reason alone irritated authorities, and his books were banned in many places. He moved to the Dutch Republic to work in peace. Scientific research, like economic growth, became centered in the northern, Protestant countries, where it was less constrained by church control.

Magic and Witchcraft

Despite the new emphasis on clear reasoning, observation, and independence from past authorities, science had not yet become separate from magic. Many scholars, like Paracelsus, studied alchemy alongside other scientific pursuits. Elizabeth I maintained a court astrologer who was also a serious mathematician, and many writers distinguished between "natural magic," which was close to experi-

Persecution of Witches
This engraving from a pamphlet account of witch trials in England in 1589 shows three women hanged as accused witches. At their feet are frogs and toads, which were supposed to be the witches' "familiars," sent by the devil to help them ruin the lives of their neighbors by causing disease or untimely deaths among people and livestock. The ferret on the woman's lap was reported to be the devil himself in disguise.
Lambeth Palace Library.

mental science, and demonic "black magic." The astronomer Tycho Brahe defended his studies of alchemy and astrology as part of natural magic. For many of the greatest minds, magic and science were still closely linked.

In a world in which most people believed in astrology, magical healing, prophecy, and ghosts, it is hardly surprising that many of Europe's learned people also firmly believed in witchcraft, the exercise of magical powers gained by a pact with the devil. The same Jean Bodin who argued against religious fanaticism insisted on death for witches—and for those magistrates who would not prosecute them. In France alone, 345 books and pamphlets on witchcraft appeared between 1550 and 1650. Trials of witches peaked in Europe between 1560 and 1640, the very time of the celebrated breakthroughs of the new science. Montaigne was one of the few to speak out against executing accused witches: "It is taking one's conjectures rather seriously to roast someone alive for them," he wrote in 1580.

Belief in witches was not new in the sixteenth century. Witches had long been thought capable of almost anything: passing through walls, flying through the air, destroying crops, and causing personal catastrophes from miscarriage to demonic possession. What was new was the official persecution, justified by the notion that witches were agents of Satan whom the righteous must oppose. In a time of economic crisis, plague, warfare, and the clash of religious differences, witchcraft trials provided an outlet for social stress and anxiety, legitimated by state power. At the same time, the trials seem to have been part of the religious reform movement itself. Denunciation and persecution of witches coincided with the spread of reform, both Protestant and Catholic. The trials concentrated especially in the German lands of the Holy Roman Empire, the boiling cauldron of the Thirty Years' War.

The victims of the persecution were overwhelmingly female: women accounted for 80 percent of the accused witches in about 100,000 trials in Europe and North America during the sixteenth and seventeenth centuries. About one-third were sentenced to death. Before 1400, when witchcraft trials were rare, nearly half of those accused had been men. Explanations for this gender difference have raised many controversies. Some historians argue that the trials expressed a fundamental hatred of women that came to a head during conflicts over the Reformation. Official descriptions of witchcraft oozed lurid details of sexual orgies, incest, homosexuality, and cannibalism, in which women acted as the devil's sexual slaves. In this view, Catholic and Protestant reforming clergy attacked the presumably wild and undisciplined sexuality of women as the most obvious manifestation of popular unruliness and heretical tendencies. Lawyers and judges followed their lead.

Other historians see in the trials a social dimension that helps explain the prominence of women. Accusers were almost always better off than those they accused. The poorest and most socially marginal people in most communities were elderly spinsters and widows. Because they were thought likely to hanker after revenge on those more fortunate, they were singled out as witches. Another commonly accused woman was the midwife, who was a prime target for suspicion when a baby or mother died in childbirth. Although sometimes venerated for their special skill, midwives also numbered among the thousands of largely powerless women persecuted for their supposed consorting with the devil.

Witchcraft trials declined when scientific thinking about causes and effects raised questions about the evidence used in court: how could judges or jurors be certain that someone was a witch? The tide turned everywhere at about the same time, as physicians, lawyers, judges, and even clergy came to suspect that accusations were based on popular superstition and peasant untrustworthiness. As early as the 1640s, French courts ordered the arrest of witch-hunters and released suspected witches. In 1682, a French royal decree treated witchcraft as fraud and imposture, meaning that the law did not recognize anyone as a witch. In 1693, the jurors who had convicted twenty witches in Salem, Massachusetts, recanted, claiming: "We confess that we ourselves were not capable to understand. . . . We justly fear that we were sadly deluded and mistaken." The Salem jurors had not stopped believing in witches; they had simply lost confidence in their ability to identify them. This was a general pattern. Popular attitudes had not changed; what had changed was elites' attitudes. When physicians and judges had believed in witches and persecuted them officially, with torture, witches had gone to their deaths in record numbers. But when the same groups distanced themselves from popular beliefs, the trials and the executions stopped.

IMPORTANT DATES

1562	French Wars of Religion begin
1566	Revolt of Calvinists in the Netherlands against Spain begins
1569	Formation of commonwealth of Poland-Lithuania
1571	Battle of Lepanto marks victory of West over Ottomans at sea
1572	St. Bartholomew's Day Massacre of French Protestants
1588	Defeat of the Spanish Armada by England
1598	French Wars of Religion end with Edict of Nantes
1601	William Shakespeare, *Hamlet*
1618	Thirty Years' War begins
1625	Hugo Grotius publishes *The Laws of War and Peace*
1629	English Puritans set up the Massachusetts Bay Company and begin to colonize New England
1633	Galileo Galilei is forced to recant his support of heliocentrism
1635	French join the Thirty Years' War by declaring war on Spain
1648	Peace of Westphalia ends the Thirty Years' War

Conclusion

The witchcraft persecutions reflected the traumas of these times of religious war and economic decline. Marauding armies combined with economic depression, disease, and the threat of starvation to shatter the lives of many ordinary Europeans. Some people blamed the poor widow or upstart midwife for their problems; others joined desperate revolts; still others emigrated to the New World to seek a better life. Even rulers confronted frightening choices: forced abdication, death in battle, or assassination often accompanied their religious decisions, and economic shocks could threaten the stability of their governments.

Religious conflicts shaped the destinies of every European power in this period. These conflicts came to a head in 1618–1648 in the Thirty Years' War, which cut a path of destruction through central Europe and involved most of the European powers.

MAPPING THE WEST The Religious Divisions of Europe, c. 1648

The Peace of Westphalia recognized major religious divisions within Europe that have endured for the most part to the present day. Catholicism dominated in southern Europe, Lutheranism had its stronghold in northern Europe, and Calvinism flourished along the Rhine River. In southeastern Europe, the Islamic Ottoman Turks accommodated the Greek Orthodox Christians under their rule but bitterly fought the Catholic Austrian Habsburgs for control of Hungary.

Repulsed by the effects of religious violence on international relations, European rulers agreed to a peace that effectively removed disputes between Catholics and Protestants from the international arena. The growing separation of political motives from religious ones did not mean that violence or conflict had ended, however. Struggles for religious uniformity within states would continue, though on a smaller scale. Bigger armies required more state involvement, and almost everywhere rulers emerged from these decades of conflict with expanded powers. The growth of state power directly changed the lives

of ordinary people: more men went into the armies and most families paid higher taxes. The constant extension of state power is one of the defining themes of modern history; religious warfare gave it a jump start.

For all their power, rulers could not control economic, social, or intellectual trends, much as they often tried. The economic downturn of the seventeenth century produced unexpected consequences for European states even while it made life miserable for many ordinary people; economic power and vibrancy shifted from the Mediterranean world to the northwest because the countries of northwestern Europe—England, France, and the Dutch Republic especially—suffered less from the fighting of the Thirty Years' War and recovered more quickly from the loss of population and production during bad times.

In the face of violence and uncertainty, some began to look for secular alternatives in art, politics, and science. Although it would be foolish to claim that everyone's mental universe changed because of the clash between religious and secular worldviews, a truly monumental shift in attitudes had begun. Secularization combined a growing interest in non-religious forms of art, such as theater and opera, the search for nonreligious foundations of political authority, and the establishment of scientific method as the standard of truth. Proponents of these changes did not renounce their religious beliefs or even hold them less fervently, but they did insist that attention to state interests and scientific knowledge could serve as a brake on religious violence and popular superstitions.

Suggested References

Religious Conflicts and State Power, 1560–1618

The personalities of rulers such as Elizabeth I of England and Philip II of Spain remain central to the religious and political conflicts of this period. Recent scholarship also highlights more structural factors, especially in the French Wars of Religion and the rise of the Dutch Republic.

Cameron, Euan, ed. *Early Modern Europe: An Oxford History.* 1999.

Holt, Mack P. *The French Wars of Religion, 1562–1629.* 1995.

Israel, Jonathan. *The Dutch Republic: Its Rise, Greatness, and Fall, 1477–1806.* 1995.

Kamen, Henry. *Philip of Spain.* 1997.

Mattingly, Garrett. *The Defeat of the Spanish Armada.* 2nd ed. 1988.

Roberts, Penny. *A City in Conflict: Troyes during the French Wars of Religion.* 1996.

Strong, Roy. *The Cult of Elizabeth: Elizabethan Portraiture and Pageantry.* 1977.

The Thirty Years' War and the Balance of Power, 1618–1648

As ethnic conflicts erupt again in eastern Europe, historians have traced their roots back to the intertwined religious, ethnic, and dynastic struggles of the Thirty Years' War.

Asch, Ronald G. *The Thirty Years War: The Holy Roman Empire and Europe, 1618–48.* 1997.

Lee, Stephen J. *The Thirty Years War.* 1991.

Parker, Geoffrey. *The Military Revolution: Military Innovation and the Rise of the West, 1500–1800.* 1988.

———, ed. *The Thirty Years' War.* 2nd ed. 1997.

*Rabb, Theodore K. *The Thirty Years' War.* 2nd ed. 1972.

Economic Crisis and Realignment

Painstaking archival research has enabled historians to reconstruct the demographic, economic, and social history of this period. Recently, attention has focused more specifically on women, the family, and the early history of slavery.

Ashton, Trevor H., ed. *Crisis in Europe.* 1965.

Braudel, Fernand. *The Mediterranean and the Mediterranean World in the Age of Philip the Second.* 2 vols. Trans. Siân Reynolds. 1972–1973.

De Vries, Jan. *The Economy of Europe in an Age of Crisis, 1600–1750.* 1982.

Parry, J. H. *The Age of Reconnaissance.* 1981.

Pouncy, Carolyn Johnston, ed. and trans. *The "Domostroi": Rules for Russian Households in the Time of Ivan the Terrible.* 1994.

Spierenburg, Pieter. *The Broken Spell: A Cultural and Anthropological History of Preindustrial Europe.* 1991.

Wiesner, Merry E. *Women and Gender in Early Modern Europe.* 1993.

A Clash of Worldviews

The transformation of intellectual and cultural life has long fascinated scholars. Recent works have developed a new kind of study called "microhistory," focused on one person (like Ginzburg's Italian miller) or a series of individual stories (as in Roper's analysis of witchcraft in the German states).

Baroque architecture: http://www.lib.virginia.edu:80/dic/colls/arh102/index.html.

*Drake, Stillman, ed. *Discoveries and Opinions of Galileo.* 1957.

The Galileo Project: http://riceinfo.rice.edu/Galileo.

Ginzburg, Carlo. *The Cheese and the Worms: The Cosmos of a Sixteenth-Century Miller.* Trans. John and Anne Tedeschi. 1992.

Jacob, James. *The Scientific Revolution.* 1998.

Roper, Lyndal. *Oedipus and the Devil: Witchcraft, Sexuality, and Religion in Early Modern Europe.* 1994.

Skinner, Quentin. *The Foundations of Modern Political Thought.* Vol. 2, *The Age of Reformation.* 1978.

Thomas, Keith. *Religion and the Decline of Magic.* 1971.

Zagorin, Perez. *Francis Bacon.* 1998.

*Primary sources.

State Building and the Search for Order

1648–1690

IN ONE OF HER HUNDREDS OF LETTERS to her daughter, the French noblewoman Marie de Sévigné told a disturbing story about a well-known cook. The cook got upset when he did not have enough roast for several unexpected guests at a dinner for King Louis XIV. Early the next morning, when the fish he had ordered did not arrive on time, the cook felt personally dishonored. He rushed up to his room, put his sword against the door, and ran it through his heart on the third try. The fish arrived soon after. The king regretted the trouble his visit had caused, but others soon filled in for the chief cook. That evening, Sévigné wrote, there was "a very good dinner, light refreshments later, and then supper, a walk, cards, hunting, everything scented with daffodils, everything magical."

Reading this account now produces puzzlement and shock. It is difficult to comprehend how anyone could care that much about a shipment of fish. The story nonetheless reveals an important aspect of state building in the seventeenth century: to extend state authority, which had been challenged during the wars over religion and threatened by economic recession, many rulers created an aura of overwhelming power and brilliance around themselves. Louis XIV, like many rulers, believed that he reigned by divine right. He served as God's lieutenant on earth and even claimed certain godlike qualities. The great gap between the ruler and ordinary subjects accounts for the extreme reaction of Louis's cook, and even leading nobles such as Sévigné came to see the king and his court as somehow "magical."

Louis XIV in Roman Splendor
Images of Louis appear everywhere in his chateau at Versailles. This plaster relief by Antoine Coysevox in the Salon de la Guerre (War Hall) *represents Louis as Mars, the Roman god of war, riding roughshod over his enemies.* Giraudon/Art Resource, NY.

603

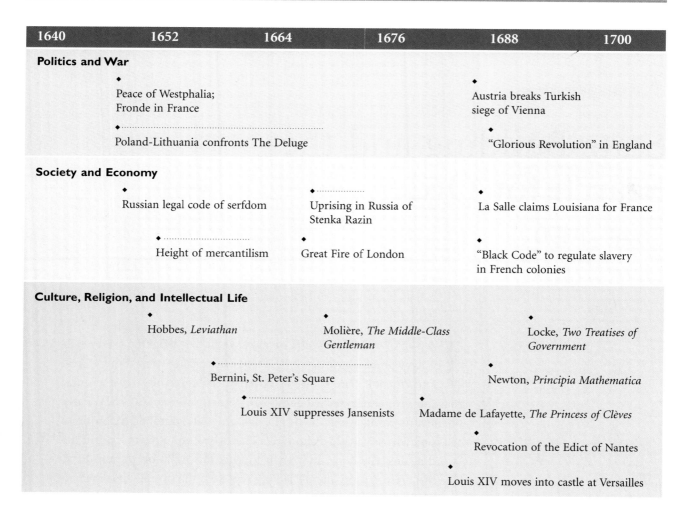

1640	1652	1664	1676	1688	1700

Politics and War

♦ Peace of Westphalia; Fronde in France

♦ Austria breaks Turkish siege of Vienna

♦ Poland-Lithuania confronts The Deluge

♦ "Glorious Revolution" in England

Society and Economy

♦ Russian legal code of serfdom

♦ Uprising in Russia of Stenka Razin

♦ La Salle claims Louisiana for France

♦ Height of mercantilism

♦ Great Fire of London

♦ "Black Code" to regulate slavery in French colonies

Culture, Religion, and Intellectual Life

♦ Hobbes, *Leviathan*

♦ Molière, *The Middle-Class Gentleman*

♦ Locke, *Two Treatises of Government*

♦ Bernini, St. Peter's Square

♦ Newton, *Principia Mathematica*

♦ Louis XIV suppresses Jansenists

♦ Madame de Lafayette, *The Princess of Clèves*

♦ Revocation of the Edict of Nantes

♦ Louis XIV moves into castle at Versailles

Louis XIV's model of state building was known as *absolutism,* a system of government in which the ruler claimed sole and uncontestable power. Although absolutism exerted great influence, especially in central and eastern Europe, it faced competition from *constitutionalism,* a system in which the ruler had to share power with parliaments made up of elected representatives. Constitutionalism led to weakness in Poland-Lithuania, but it provided a strong foundation for state power in England, the British North American colonies, and the Dutch Republic. Constitutionalism triumphed in England, however, only after one king had been executed as a traitor and another had been deposed.

Although the differences between absolutism and constitutionalism turned out to be very significant in the long run, these two methods of state building faced similar challenges in the mid-

seventeenth century. Competition in the international arena required resources, and all states raised taxes in this period, provoking popular protests and rebellions. The wars over religion that culminated in the Thirty Years' War left many economies in dire straits, and, even more significant, they created a need for new explanations of political authority. Monarchs still relied on religion to justify their divine right to rule, but they increasingly sought secular defenses of their powers too. Absolutism and constitutionalism were the two main responses to the threat of disorder and breakdown left as a legacy of the wars over religion.

The search for order took place not only at the level of states and rulers but also in intellectual, cultural, and social life. In science, the Englishman Isaac Newton explained the regular movement of the universe with the law of gravitation and thereby consolidated the scientific revolution. Artists sought means of glorifying power and expressing order and symmetry in new fashion. As states consolidated their power, elites endeavored to distinguish themselves more clearly from the lower orders. The upper classes emulated the manners developed at court and tried in every way to distance themselves from anything viewed as vulgar or lower class. Officials, clergy, and laypeople all worked to reform the poor, now seen as a major source of disorder. Whether absolutist or constitutionalist, seventeenth-century states all aimed to extend control over their subjects' lives.

❖ Louis XIV: Model of Absolutism

French king Louis XIV (r. 1643–1715) personified the absolutist ruler who shared his power with no one. Louis personally made all important state decisions and left no room for dissent. In 1651, he reputedly told the Paris high court of justice, "*L'état, c'est moi*" ("I am the state"), emphasizing that state authority rested in him personally. Louis cleverly manipulated the affections and ambitions of his courtiers, chose as his ministers middle-class men who owed everything to him, built up Europe's largest army, and snuffed out every hint of religious or political opposition. Yet the absoluteness of his power should not be exaggerated. Like all rulers of his time, Louis depended on the cooperation of many others: local officials who enforced his decrees, peasants and artisans who joined his armies and paid his taxes, creditors who loaned crucial funds, and nobles who might stay home and cause trouble rather than join court festivities organized to glorify the king.

The Fronde, 1648–1653

Absolutism was not made in a day. Louis XIV built on a long French tradition of increasing centralization of state authority, but before he could extend it he had to weather a series of revolts known as the *Fronde*. Derived from the French word for a child's slingshot, the term was used by critics to signify that the revolts were mere child's play. In fact, however, they posed an unprecedented threat to the French crown. Louis was only five when he came to the

throne in 1643 upon the death of his father, Louis XIII, who with his chief minister Cardinal Richelieu had steered France through increasing involvement in the Thirty Years' War, rapidly climbing taxes, and innumerable tax revolts. Louis XIV's mother, Anne of Austria, and her Italian-born adviser and rumored lover Cardinal Mazarin (1602–1661) ruled in the young monarch's name. French nobles and magistrates suspected the motives of the foreign-born Anne and Mazarin. Some of them hoped to use the crisis created by Louis XIII's death to move France toward a constitutional government.

To meet the financial pressure of fighting the Thirty Years' War, Mazarin sold new offices, raised taxes, and forced creditors to extend loans to the government. In 1648, a coalition of his opponents presented him with a charter of demands that, if granted, would have given the parlements (high courts) a form of constitutional power with the right to approve new taxes. Mazarin responded by arresting the leaders of parlements. He soon faced a series of revolts that at one time or another involved nearly every social group in France.

The Fronde posed an immediate menace to the young king. Fearing for his safety, his mother and

Anne of Austria
Wife of Louis XIII and mother of Louis XIV, Anne served as regent during her son's youth but delegated most authority to Cardinal Mazarin, her Italian-born adviser. She is shown here praying with Louis and his younger brother Philippe. The painting emphasizes her religious devotion.
Laurie Platt Winfrey, Inc.

members of his court took Louis and fled Paris. With civil war threatening, Mazarin and Anne agreed to compromise with the parlements. The nobles saw an opportunity to reassert their claims to power against the weakened monarchy and renewed their demands for greater local control, which they had lost when the religious wars ended in 1598. Leading noblewomen often played key roles in the opposition to Mazarin, carrying messages and forging alliances, especially when male family members were in prison. While the nobles sought to regain power and local influence, the middle and lower classes chafed at the constant tax increases. Conflicts erupted throughout the kingdom as nobles, parlements, and city councils all raised their own armies to fight either the crown or each other, and rampaging soldiers devastated rural areas and disrupted commerce. In places, such as the southwestern city of Bordeaux, the urban poor revolted as well.

The Fronde, 1648–1653

Despite the glaring weakness of central power, the monarchy survived. Neither the nobles nor the judges of the parlements really wanted to overthrow the king; they simply wanted a greater share in power. But Louis XIV never forgot the humiliation and uncertainty that marred his childhood. Years later he recalled an incident in which a band of Parisians invaded his bedchamber to determine whether he had fled the city, and he declared the event an affront not only to himself but also to the state. His own policies as ruler would be designed to prevent the repetition of any such revolts.

Court Culture as a Form of State Power

When Cardinal Mazarin died in 1661, Louis XIV decided to rule without a first minister. He described the dangers of his situation in memoirs he wrote later for his son's instruction: "Everywhere was disorder. My Court as a whole was still very far removed from the sentiments in which I trust you will find it." Louis listed many other problems in the

kingdom, but none occupied him more than his attempts to control France's leading nobles, some of whom came from families that had opposed him militarily during the Fronde.

Typically quarrelsome, the French nobles had long exercised local authority by maintaining their own fighting forces, meting out justice on their estates, arranging jobs for underlings, and resolving their own conflicts through dueling. Louis set out to domesticate the warrior nobles by replacing violence with court ritual. Using a systematic policy of bestowing pensions, offices, honors, gifts, and the threat of disfavor or punishment, he induced the nobles to cooperate with him and made himself the center of French power and culture. At Louis's court the great nobles vied for his favor, attended the ballets and theatricals he put on, and learned the rules of etiquette he supervised—in short, became his clients, dependent on him for advancement. Access to the king was the most valued commodity at court. Nobles competed for the honor of holding his shirt when he dressed; foreign ambassadors squabbled for places near him; and royal mistresses basked in the glow of his personal favor.

Participation at court required constant study. The preferred styles changed without notice, and the tiniest lapse in attention to etiquette could lead to ruin. Madame de Lafayette described the court in her novel *The Princess of Clèves* (1678): "The Court gravitated around ambition. Nobody was tranquil or indifferent—everybody was busily trying to better his or her position by pleasing, by helping, or by hindering somebody else." Occasionally the results were tragic, as in the suicide of the cook recounted by Marie de Sévigné. Elisabeth Charlotte, duchess of Orléans, the German-born sister-in-law of Louis, complained that "everything here is pure self-interest and deviousness," but she gloried in the special privileges of her closeness to the king, which included the right to a military honor guard and a special cloth to stand on during daily Mass.

Politics and the Arts.   Louis XIV appreciated the political uses of every form of art. Mock battles, extravaganzas, theatrical performances, even the king's dinner—Louis's daily life was a public performance designed to enhance his prestige. Calling himself the Sun King, Louis adorned his court with statues of Apollo, Greek god of the sun. He also emulated the style and methods of ancient Roman emperors. At a celebration for the birth of his first son in 1662, Louis dressed in Roman attire, and many engravings and paintings showed him as a Roman emperor. Sculpture and paintings adorned his palace; commissioned histories vaunted his achievements; and coins and medals spread his likeness throughout the realm.

The king's officials treated the arts as a branch of government. The king gave pensions to artists who worked for him and sometimes protected writers from clerical critics. The most famous of these was the playwright Molière, whose comedy *Tartuffe* (1664) made fun of religious hypocrites and was loudly condemned by church leaders. Louis forced Molière to delay public performances of the play but resisted calls for his dismissal. Louis's ministers set up royal academies of dance, painting, architecture, and music and took control of the Académie française (French Academy), which to this day decides on correct usage of the French language. A royal furniture workshop at the Gobelins tapestry works in Paris turned out the delicate and ornate pieces whose style bore the king's name. Louis's government also regulated the number and locations of theaters and closely censored all forms of publication.

Music and theater enjoyed special prominence. Louis commissioned operas to celebrate royal marriages, baptisms, and military victories. His favorite composer, Jean-Baptiste Lully, an Italian who began as a cook's assistant and rose to be virtual dictator of French musical taste, wrote sixteen operas for court performances as well as many ballets. Louis himself danced in the ballets if a role seemed especially important. Playwrights presented their new plays directly to the court. Pierre Corneille and Jean-Baptiste Racine wrote tragedies set in Greece or Rome that celebrated the new aristocratic virtues which Louis aimed to inculcate: a reverence for order and self-control. All the characters were regal or noble, all the language lofty, all the behavior aristocratic. The king's sister-in-law called the plays of Corneille "the best entertainment I have."

The Palace of Versailles. Louis glorified his image as well through massive public works projects. Military facilities, such as veterans' hospitals and new fortified towns on the frontiers, represented his military might. Urban improvements, such as the reconstruction of the Louvre palace in Paris, proved his wealth. But his most remarkable project was the construction of a new palace at Versailles, twelve miles from the turbulent capital.

Building began in the 1660s. By 1685, the frenzied effort engaged 36,000 workers, not including

Palace of Versailles
In this defining statement of his ambitions, Louis XIV emphasized his ability to impose his own personal will, even on nature itself. The sheer size and precise geometrical design of the palace underlined the presence of an all-powerful personality, that of the Sun King. The palace became a national historical monument in 1837 and was used for many momentous historical occasions, including the signing of the peace treaty after World War I.
Giraudon/Art Resource, NY.

Louis XIV Visits the Royal Tapestry Workshop
This tapestry was woven at the Gobelins tapestry workshop between 1673 and 1680. It shows Louis XIV (wearing a red hat) and his minister Colbert (dressed in black, holding his hat) visiting the workshop on the outskirts of Paris. The artisans of the workshop scurry around to show Louis all the luxury objects they manufacture. Louis bought the workshop in 1662 and made it a national enterprise for making tapestries and furniture.
Giraudon/Art Resource, NY.

the thousands of troops who diverted a local river to supply water for pools and fountains. Royal workshops produced tapestries, carpets, mirrors, and porcelains. Even the gardens designed by landscape architect André Le Nôtre reflected the spirit of Louis XIV's rule: their geometrical arrangements and clear lines showed that art and design could tame nature and that order and control defined the exercise of power. Le Nôtre's geometrical landscapes were imitated in Spain, the Italian states, Austria, the German states, and later as far away as St. Petersburg in Russia and Washington, D.C. Versailles symbolized Louis's success in reining in the nobility and dominating Europe, and other monarchs eagerly mimicked French fashion and often conducted their business in French.

Yet for all its apparent luxury and frivolity, life at Versailles was often cramped and cold. Fifteen thousand people crowded into the palace's apartments, including all the highest military officers, the ministers of state, and the separate households of each member of the royal family. Refuse collected in the corridors during the incessant building, and thieves and prostitutes overran the grounds.

By the time Louis actually moved from the Louvre to Versailles in 1682, he had reigned as monarch for thirty-nine years. After his wife's death in 1683, he secretly married his mistress, Françoise d'Aubigné, marquise de Maintenon, and conducted most state affairs from her apartments at the palace.

Her opponents at court complained that she controlled all the appointments, but her efforts focused on her own projects, including her favorite: the founding in 1686 of a royal school for girls from impoverished noble families. She also inspired Louis XIV to pursue his devotion to Catholicism.

Enforcing Religious Orthodoxy

Louis believed that as king he must defend the Catholic faith against Protestants and dissident Catholics; orthodox Catholicism was an essential pillar of his rule. One of his advisers, Bishop Jacques-Benigne Bossuet (1627–1704), explained the principle of divine right that justified the king's actions: "We have seen that kings take the place of God, who is the true father of the human species. We have also seen that the first idea of power which exists among men is that of the paternal power; and that kings are modeled on fathers." The king, like a father, should instruct his subjects in the true religion, or at least make sure that others did so. Some questioned Louis's understanding of the finer points of doctrine: according to his sister-in-law, Louis himself "has never read anything about religion, nor the Bible either, and just goes along believing whatever he is told."

Louis's campaign for religious conformity first focused on the Jansenists, Catholics whose doctrines and practices resembled some aspects of

Protestantism. Following the posthumous publication of the book *Augustinus* (1640) by the Flemish theologian Cornelius Jansen (1585–1638), the Jansenists stressed the need for God's grace in achieving salvation. They emphasized the importance of original sin; and, in their austere religious practice, resembled the English Puritans. Prominent among the Jansenists was Blaise Pascal (1623–1662), a mathematician of genius, who wrote his *Provincial Letters* (1656–1657) to defend Jansenism against charges of heresy. Many judges in the parlements likewise endorsed Jansenist doctrine.

Louis feared any doctrine that gave priority to considerations of individual conscience over the demands of the official church hierarchy. He preferred teachings that stressed obedience to authority. Therefore, in 1660 he began enforcing various papal bulls (decrees) against Jansenism and closed down Jansenist theological centers. Jansenists were forced underground for the rest of his reign.

After many years of escalating pressure on the Calvinist Huguenots, Louis revoked the Edict of Nantes in 1685 and eliminated all of the Calvinists' rights. Louis considered the Edict (1598), by which his grandfather Henry IV granted the Protestants religious freedom and civil rights, a temporary measure, and he fervently hoped to reconvert the Huguenots to Catholicism. He closed their churches and schools, banned all their public activities, and exiled those who refused to embrace the state religion. Thousands of Huguenots emigrated to England, Brandenburg-Prussia, or the Dutch Republic. Many now wrote for publications attacking Louis XIV's absolutism. Protestant European countries were shocked by this crackdown on religious dissent and would cite it when they went to war against Louis.

Extending State Authority at Home and Abroad

Louis XIV could not have enforced his religious policies without the services of a nationwide bureaucracy. *Bureaucracy*—a system of state officials carrying out orders according to a regular and routine line of authority—comes from the French word *bureau,* for "desk," which came to mean "office," both in the sense of a physical space and a position of authority. Louis personally supervised the activities of his bureaucrats and worked to ensure his

supremacy in all matters. The ultimate goal of developing absolute power at home was the pursuit of French glory abroad.

Bureaucracy and Mercantilism. Louis extended the bureaucratic forms his predecessors had developed, especially the use of intendants, officials who held their positions directly from the king rather than owning their offices, as crown officials had traditionally done. Louis handpicked them to represent his will against entrenched local interests such as the parlements, provincial estates, and noble governors. The intendants reduced local powers over finances and insisted on more efficient tax collection. Despite the doubling of taxes in Louis's reign, the local rebellions that had so beset the crown from the 1620s to the 1640s subsided in the face of these better-organized state forces.

Louis's success in consolidating his authority depended on hard work, an eye for detail, and an ear to the ground. In his memoirs he described how he operated:

> to learn each hour the news concerning every province and every nation, the secrets of every court, the mood and weaknesses of each Prince and of every foreign minister; to be well-informed on an infinite number of matters about which we are supposed to know nothing; to elicit from our subjects what they hide from us with the greatest care; to discover the most remote opinions of our courtiers and the most hidden interests of those who come to us with quite contrary professions [claims].

To gather all this information, Louis relied on a series of talented ministers, usually of modest origins, who gained fame, fortune, and even noble status from serving the king. Most important among them was Jean-Baptiste Colbert (1619–1683), the son of a wool merchant turned royal official. Colbert had managed Mazarin's personal finances and worked his way up under Louis XIV to become head of royal finances, public works, and the navy. Like many of Louis's other ministers, he founded a family dynasty that eventually produced five ministers of state, an archbishop, two bishops, and three generals.

Colbert used the bureaucracy to establish a mercantilist policy. According to the economic doctrine of *mercantilism*, governments must intervene to increase national wealth by whatever means

Wars of Louis XIV

1667–1668   War of Devolution
Enemies: Spain, Dutch Republic, England, Sweden
Ended by Treaty of Aix-la-Chapelle in 1668, with
France gaining towns in Spanish Netherlands
(Flanders)

1672–1678   Dutch War
Enemies: Dutch Republic, Spain, Holy Roman Empire
Ended by treaty of Nijmegen, 1678–1679, which gave
several towns in Spanish Netherlands and Franche-
Comté to France

1688–1697   War of the League of Augsburg
Enemies: Holy Roman Empire, Sweden, Spain, England
Ended by treaty of Rijswijk, 1697, with Louis returning
all his conquests made since 1678 except Strasbourg

possible. Such government intervention inevitably increased the role and eventually the number of bureaucrats needed. Under Colbert, the French government established overseas trading companies, granted manufacturing monopolies, and standardized production methods for textiles, paper, and soap. A government inspection system regulated the quality of finished goods and compelled all craftsmen to organize into guilds, in which masters could supervise the work of the journeymen and apprentices. To protect French production, Colbert rescinded many internal customs fees but enacted high foreign tariffs, which cut imports of competing goods. To compete more effectively with England and the Dutch Republic, Colbert also subsidized shipbuilding, a policy that dramatically expanded the number of seaworthy vessels. Such mercantilist measures aimed to ensure France's prominence in world markets and to provide the resources needed to fight wars against the increasingly long list of enemies. Although later economists questioned the value of this state intervention in the economy, virtually every government in Europe embraced mercantilism.

Colbert's mercantilist projects extended to Canada, where in 1663 he took control of the trading company that had founded New France. He transplanted several thousand peasants from western France to the present-day province of Quebec, which France had claimed since 1608. To guard his investment, Colbert sent fifteen hundred soldiers to join the settlers. Of particular concern to the French government were the Iroquois, who regularly interrupted French fur-trading convoys. Shows of French military force, including the burning of Indian villages and winter food supplies, forced the Iroquois to make peace with New France, and from 1666 to 1680, French traders moved westward with minimal interference. In 1672, fur trader Louis Jolliet and Jesuit missionary Jacques Marquette reached the upper Mississippi River and traveled downstream as far as Arkansas. In 1684, French explorer Sieur de La Salle went all the way down to the Gulf of Mexico, claiming a vast territory for Louis XIV and calling it Louisiana after him. Louis and Colbert encouraged colonial settlement as part of their rivalry with the English and the Dutch in the New World.

The Army and War.   Colonial settlement occupied only a small portion of Louis XIV's attention, however, for his main foreign policy goal was to extend French power in Europe. In pursuing this purpose, he inevitably came up against the Spanish and Austrian Habsburgs, whose lands encircled his. To expand French power Louis needed the biggest possible army. His powerful ministry of war centralized the organization of French troops. Barracks built in major towns received supplies from a central distribution system. The state began to provide uniforms for the soldiers and to offer veterans some hospital care. A militia draft instituted in 1688 supplemented the army in times of war and enrolled 100,000 men. Louis's wartime army could field a force as large as that of all his enemies combined.

Absolutist governments always tried to increase their territorial holdings, and as Louis extended his reach, he gained new enemies. In 1667–1668, in the first of his major wars after assuming personal control of French affairs, Louis defeated the Spanish armies but had to make peace when England, Sweden, and the Dutch Republic joined the war. In the Treaty of Aix-la-Chapelle in 1668, he gained control of towns on the border of the Spanish Netherlands. Pamphlets sponsored by the Habsburgs accused Louis of aiming for "universal monarchy," or domination of Europe. The chorus of denunciation would only grow over the years.

In 1672, Louis XIV opened hostilities against the Dutch because they stood in the way of his acquisition of more territory in the Spanish Netherlands. He declared war again on Spain in 1673. By now the Dutch had allied themselves with their former Spanish masters to hold off the French. Louis also marched his troops into territories of the Holy Roman Empire, provoking many of the German princes to join with the emperor, the Spanish, and the Dutch in an alliance against Louis, now denounced as a "Christian Turk" for his imperialist ambitions. But the French armies more than held their own. Faced with bloody but inconclusive results on the battlefield, the parties agreed to the Treaty of Nijmegen of 1678–1679, which ceded several Flemish towns and Franche-Comté to Louis, linking Alsace to the rest of France. These territorial additions were costly: French government deficits soared, and increases in taxes touched off the most serious antitax revolt of Louis's reign, in 1675.

Louis had no intention of standing still. Heartened by the Habsburgs' seeming weakness, he pushed eastward, seizing the city of Strasbourg in 1681 and invading the province of Lorraine in 1684. In 1688,

he attacked some of the small German cities of the Holy Roman Empire and was soon involved again in a long war against a Europe-wide coalition. As Louis's own mental powers diminished with age, he seems to have lost all sense of measure. His armies laid waste to German cities such as Mannheim; his government ordered the local military commander to "kill all those who would still wish to build houses there." Between 1689 and 1697, a coalition made up of England, Spain, Sweden, the Dutch Republic, the Austrian emperor, and various German princes fought Louis XIV to a stalemate. When hostilities ended in the Peace of Rijswijk in 1697, Louis returned many of his conquests made since 1678 with the exception of Strasbourg (Map 17.1). Louis never lost his taste for war, but his allies learned how to set limits on his ambitions.

Louis was the last French ruler before Napoleon to accompany his troops to the battlefield. In later generations, as the military became more professional, French rulers left the fighting to their generals. Although Louis had eliminated the private armies

MAP 17.1 Louis XIV's Acquisitions, 1668–1697
Every ruler in Europe hoped to extend his or her territorial control, and war was often the result. Louis XIV steadily encroached on the Spanish Netherlands to the north and the lands of the Holy Roman Empire to the east. Although coalitions of European powers reined in Louis's grander ambitions, he nonetheless incorporated many neighboring territories into the French crown.

of his noble courtiers, he constantly promoted his own military prowess in order to keep his noble officers under his sway. He had miniature battle scenes painted on his high heels and commissioned tapestries showing his military processions into cities, even those he did not take by force. He seized every occasion to assert his supremacy, insisting that other fleets salute his ships first.

War required money and men, which Louis obtained by expanding state control over finances, conscription, and military supply. Thus absolutism and warfare fed each other, as the bureaucracy created new ways to raise and maintain an army and the army's success in war justified further expansion of state power. But constant warfare also eroded the state's resources. Further administrative and legal reform, the elimination of the buying and selling of offices, and the lowering of taxes—all were made impossible by the need for more money.

The playwright Corneille wrote, no doubt optimistically, "The people are very happy when they die for their kings." What is certain is that the wars touched many peasant and urban families. The people who lived on the routes leading to the battlefields had to house and feed soldiers; only nobles were exempt from this requirement. Everyone, moreover, paid the higher taxes that were necessary to support the army. By the end of Louis's reign, one in six Frenchmen had served in the military.

❖ Absolutism in Central and Eastern Europe

Central and eastern European rulers saw in Louis XIV a powerful model of absolutist state building, yet they did not blindly emulate the Sun King, in part because they confronted conditions peculiar to their regions. The ruler of Brandenburg-Prussia had to rebuild lands ravaged by the Thirty Years' War and unite far-flung territories. The Austrian Habsburgs needed to govern a mosaic of ethnic and religious groups while fighting off the Ottoman Turks. The Russian tsars wanted to extend their power over an extensive but relatively impoverished empire. The great exception to absolutism in eastern Europe was Poland-Lithuania, where a long crisis virtually destroyed central authority and sucked much of eastern Europe into its turbulent wake.

Brandenburg-Prussia and Sweden: Militaristic Absolutism

Brandenburg-Prussia began as a puny, landlocked state on the Elbe River, but it had a remarkable future. In the nineteenth century, it would unify the disparate German states into modern-day Germany. The ruler of Brandenburg was an elector, one of the seven German princes entitled to select the Holy Roman Emperor. Since the sixteenth century the ruler of Brandenburg had also controlled the duchy of East Prussia; after 1618 the state was called Brandenburg-Prussia. Through marriages and alliances, including French support in the Thirty Years' War, Brandenburg-Prussia slowly added lands on the Rhine and the Baltic coast. Each territory had its own laws and representative institutions, called *estates*. Despite meager resources, Frederick William of Hohenzollern, the Great Elector of Brandenburg-Prussia (r. 1640–1688), succeeded in welding these scattered lands into an absolutist state.

Pressured first by the necessities of fighting the Thirty Years' War and then by the demands of reconstruction, Frederick William set four main tasks for himself: establishing his personal authority at the expense of the estates, founding a strong standing army, creating an efficient bureaucracy, and extending his territory. To force his territories' estates to grant him a dependable income, the Great Elector struck a deal with the Junkers (nobles) of each land: in exchange for allowing him to collect taxes, he gave them complete control over their enserfed peasants and exempted them from taxation. The tactic worked. By the end of his reign the estates met only on ceremonial occasions.

Supplied with a steady income, Frederick William could devote his attention to military and bureaucratic consolidation. Over forty years he expanded his army from eight thousand to thirty thousand men. (See "Taking Measure," page 613.) The army mirrored the rigid domination of nobles over peasants that characterized Brandenburg-Prussian society: peasants filled the ranks, and Junkers became officers. Each group learned discipline and obedience, with peasants serving the nobles and nobles serving the elector. Nobles also served the elector by taking positions as bureaucratic officials, but military needs always had priority. The elector named special war commissars to take charge not only of military affairs but also of tax collection. To

State	Soldiers	Population	Ratio of soldiers/ total population
France	300,000	20 million	1:66
Russia	220,000	14 million	1:64
Austria	100,000	8 million	1:80
Sweden	40,000	1 million	1:25
Brandenburg-Prussia	30,000	2 million	1:66
England	24,000	10 million	1:410

*Figures for the end of the seventeenth century, ranging from 1688 for Prussia to 1710 for France

TAKING MEASURE
The Seventeenth-Century Army
The figures in this chart are only approximate, but an important story. What conclusions can be drawn about the relative weight of the military in the different European states? Why would England have such a smaller army than the others? Is the absolute or the relative size of the military the most important indicator?
From André Corvisier. *Armées et sociétés en Europe de 1494 à 1789.* (Paris: Presses Universitaires de France, 1976), 126.

hasten military dispatches, he also established one of Europe's first state postal systems.

As a Calvinist ruler, Frederick William avoided the ostentation of the French court, even while following the absolutist model of centralizing state power. He boldly rebuffed Louis XIV by welcoming twenty thousand French Huguenot refugees after Louis's revocation of the Edict of Nantes. In pursuing foreign and domestic policies that promoted state power and prestige, Frederick William adroitly switched sides in Louis's wars and would stop at almost nothing to crush resistance at home. In 1701, his son Frederick I (r. 1688–1713) persuaded Holy Roman Emperor Leopold I to grant him the title "king in Prussia." Prussia had arrived as an important power.

Across the Baltic, Sweden also stood out as an example of absolutist consolidation. In the Thirty Years' War, King Gustavus Adolphus's superb generalship and highly trained army had made Sweden the supreme power of northern Europe. The huge but sparsely populated state included not only most of present-day Sweden but also Finland, Estonia, half of Latvia, and much of the Baltic coastline of modern Poland and Germany. The Baltic, in short, was a Swedish lake. After Gustavus Adolphus died, his daughter Queen Christina (r. 1632–1654) conceded much authority to the estates. Absorbed by religion and philosophy, Christina eventually abdicated and converted to Catholicism. Her successors temporarily made Sweden an absolute monarchy.

In Sweden (as in neighboring Denmark-Norway), absolutism meant simply the estates standing aside while the king led the army in lucrative foreign campaigns. The aristocracy went along because it staffed the bureaucracy and reaped war profits. Intrigued by French culture, Sweden also gleamed with national pride. In 1668, the nobility demanded the introduction of a distinctive national costume: should Swedes, they asked, "who are so glorious and renowned a nation . . . let ourselves be led by the nose by a parcel of French dancing-masters"? Sweden spent the forty years after 1654 continuously warring with its neighbors. By the 1690s, war expenses began to outrun the small Swedish population's ability to pay, threatening the continuation of absolutism.

An Uneasy Balance: Austrian Habsburgs and Ottoman Turks

Holy Roman Emperor Leopold I (r. 1658–1705) ruled over a variety of territories of different ethnicities, languages, and religions, yet in ways similar to his French and Prussian counterparts, he gradually consolidated his power. Like all the Holy Roman emperors since 1438, Leopold was an Austrian Habsburg. He was simultaneously duke of Upper and Lower Silesia, count of Tyrol, archduke of Upper and Lower Austria, king of Bohemia, king of Hungary and Croatia, and ruler of Styria and Moravia (Map 17.2). Some of these territories were provinces in the

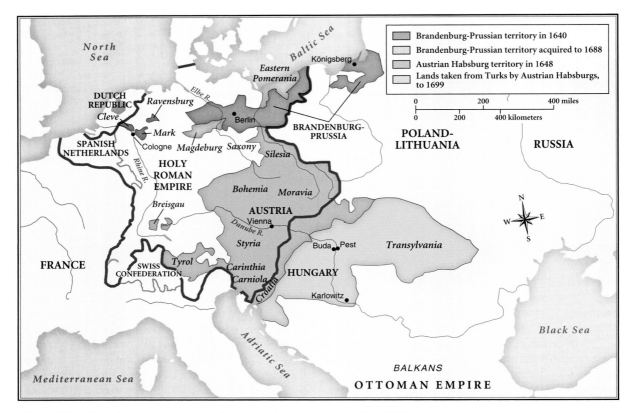

MAP 17.2 State Building in Central and Eastern Europe, 1648–1699
The Austrian Habsburgs had long contested the Ottoman Turks for dominance of eastern Europe, and by 1699, they had pushed the Turks out of Hungary. In central Europe, the Austrian Habsburgs confronted the growing power of Brandenburg-Prussia, which had emerged from relative obscurity after the Thirty Years' War to begin an aggressive program of expanding its military and its territorial base. As emperor of the Holy Roman Empire, the Austrian Habsburg ruler governed a huge expanse of territory, but the emperor's control was in fact only partial because of guarantees of local autonomy.

Holy Roman Empire; others were simply ruled from Vienna as Habsburg family holdings. Leopold needed to build up his armies and state authority in order to defend the Holy Roman Empire's international position, which had been weakened by the Thirty Years' War, and to push back the Ottoman Turks who steadily encroached from the southeast.

The Austrian Version of Absolutism. To forge a powerful central state, Leopold had to modernize his army and gain control over far-flung provinces that cherished their independent ways. The emperor and his closest officials took control over recruiting, provisioning, and strategic planning and worked to replace the mercenaries hired during the Thirty Years' War with a permanent standing army that promoted

professional discipline. When Leopold joined the coalition against Louis XIV in 1672, his new imperial troops fought well; and thanks to the emperor's astute diplomacy, the Austrians played a critical role in keeping Louis XIV's ambitions in check.

To pay for the army and staff his growing bureaucracy, Leopold had to gain the support of local aristocrats and chip away at provincial institutions' powers. As punishment for rebelling against Austrian rule, the Bohemians lost their right to elect a monarch; the Austrians named themselves hereditary rulers of Bohemia. To replace Bohemian nobles who had supported the 1618 revolt against Austrian authority, the Habsburgs promoted a new nobility made up of Czechs, Germans, Italians, Spaniards, and even Irish who used German as their common tongue, professed Catholicism, and loyally served the Austrian dynasty. Bohemia became a virtual Austrian colony. "You have utterly destroyed our home, our ancient kingdom, and have built us no new one in its place," lamented a Czech Jesuit in 1670, addressing Leopold. "Woe to you! . . . The nobles you have oppressed, great cities made small. Of smiling towns you have made straggling villages." Austrian censors prohibited publication of this protest for over a century.

Battle for Hungary. In addition to holding Louis XIV in check on his western frontiers, Leopold had to confront the ever-present challenge of the Ottoman Turks to his east. Hungary was the chief battle zone between Austria and the Turks for more than 150 years. In 1682, when war broke out again, Austria controlled the northwest section of Hungary; the Turks occupied the center; and in the east, the Turks demanded tribute from the Hungarian princes who ruled Transylvania. In 1683, the Turks pushed all the way to the gates of Vienna and laid siege to the Austrian capital; after reaching this high-water mark, however, Turkish power ebbed. With the help of Polish cavalry, the Austrians finally broke the siege and turned the tide in a major counter-offensive. By the Treaty of Karlowitz of 1699, the Ottoman Turks had to surrender almost all of Hungary to the Austrians.

Hungary's "liberation" from the Turks came at a high price. The fighting laid waste vast stretches of Hungary's central plain, and the population may have declined as much as 65 percent since 1600. To repopulate the land, the Austrians settled large communities of foreigners: Romanians, Croats, Serbs, and Germans. Magyar (Hungarian) speakers became a minority, and the seeds were sown for the poisonous nationality conflicts in nineteenth- and twentieth-century Hungary, Romania, and Yugoslavia.

Once the Turks had been beaten back, Austrian rule over Hungary tightened. In 1687, the Habsburg dynasty's hereditary right to the Hungarian crown was acknowledged by the Hungarian diet, a parliament revived by Leopold in 1681 to gain the support of Hungarian nobles. The diet was dominated by nobles who had amassed huge holdings in the liberated territories. They formed the core of a pro-Habsburg Hungarian aristocracy that would buttress the dynasty until it fell in 1918. As the

Turks retreated from Hungary, Leopold systematically rebuilt churches, monasteries, roadside shrines, and monuments in the flamboyant Austrian baroque style.

Ottoman State Authority. The Ottoman Turks also pursued state consolidation, but in a very different fashion from the Europeans. The Ottoman state centralized its authority through negotiation with and incorporation of bandit armies, which European rulers typically suppressed by armed force. In the seventeenth century, mutinous army officers often deposed the Ottoman ruler, or sultan, in a palace coup, but because the Ottoman state had learned to manage constant crises, the state itself survived and rarely faced peasant revolts. Rather than remaining in their villages and resisting state authorities, Ottoman peasants often left to become bandits who periodically worked for the state as

The Siege of Vienna, 1683
In this stylized rendition by Frans Geffels, the Ottoman Turks bombard the city, which had been surrounded for two months. The forces commanded by Polish king Jan Sobieski are arriving in the foreground to help lift the siege.
Museen der Stadt, Wien (detail).

mercenaries. Leaders of bandit gangs entered into negotiation with the Ottoman sultan, sometimes providing thousands of bandit mercenaries to the sultan's armies and even taking major official positions. Similarly, the Ottomans avoided revolt by the elites by playing them off against each other, absorbing some into the state bureaucracy and pitting one level of authority against another. This constantly shifting social and political system explains how the coup-ridden Ottoman state could appear "weak" in Western eyes and still pose a massive military threat on Europe's southeastern borders. In the end, the Ottoman state lasted longer than Louis XIV's absolute monarchy.

Russia: Foundations of Bureaucratic Absolutism

Superficially, seventeenth-century Russia seemed a world apart from the Europe of Louis XIV. Straddling Europe and Asia, it stretched across Siberia to the Pacific Ocean. Western visitors either sneered or shuddered at the "barbarism" of Russian life, and Russians reciprocated by nursing deep suspicions of everything foreign. But under the surface, Russia was evolving along paths much like the rest of absolutist Europe; the tsars wanted to claim unlimited autocratic power, but they had to surmount internal disorder and come to an accommodation with noble landlords.

Serfdom and the Code of 1649. When Tsar Alexei (r. 1645–1676) tried to extend state authority by imposing new administrative structures and taxes in 1648, Moscow and other cities erupted in bloody rioting. The government immediately doused the fire. In 1649, Alexei convoked the Assembly of the Land (consisting of noble delegates from the provinces) to consult on a sweeping law code to organize Russian society in a strict social hierarchy that would last for nearly two centuries. The code of 1649 assigned all subjects to a hereditary class according to their current occupation or state needs. Slaves and free peasants were merged into a serf class. As serfs they could not change occupations or move; they were tightly tied to the soil and to their noble masters. To prevent tax evasion, the code also forbade townspeople to move from the community where they resided. Nobles owed absolute obedience to the tsar and were required to serve in the army, but in return no other group could own estates worked by serfs. Serfs became the chattel of their lord, who could sell them like horses or land. Their conditions of life differed little from those of the slaves on the plantations in the Americas.

Some peasants resisted enserfment. In 1667, Stenka Razin, a Cossack from the Don region in southern Russia, led a rebellion that promised liberation from "the traitors and bloodsuckers of the peasant communes"—the great noble landowners, local governors, and Moscow courtiers. Captured

Stenka Razin in Captivity
After leading a revolt of thousands of serfs, peasants, and members of non-Russian tribes of the middle and lower Volga region, Razin was captured by Russian forces and led off to Moscow, as shown here, where he was executed in 1671. He has been the subject of songs, legends, and poems ever since.
Novosti Photo Library (London).

four years later by the tsar's army, Razin was dismembered, his head and limbs publicly displayed, and his body thrown to the dogs. Thousands of his followers also suffered grisly deaths, but his memory lived on in folk songs and legends. Landlords successfully petitioned for the abolition of the statute of limitations on runaway serfs, the use of state agents in searching for runaways, and harsh penalties against those who harbored runaways. The increase in Russian state authority went hand in hand with the enforcement of serfdom.

The Tsar's Absolute Powers. To extend his power and emulate his western rivals, Tsar Alexei wanted a bigger army, exclusive control over state policy, and a greater say in religious matters. The size of the army increased dramatically from 35,000 in the 1630s to 220,000 by the end of the century. The Assembly of the Land, once an important source of noble consultation, never met again after 1653. Alexei also imposed firm control over the Russian Orthodox church. In 1666, a church council reaffirmed the tsar's role as God's direct representative on earth. The state-dominated church took action against a religious group called the Old Believers, who rejected church efforts to bring Russian worship in line with Byzantine tradition. Old Believer leaders, including the noblewoman Fedosia Morozova, endured exile, prison, and torture; whole communities of Old Believers starved or burned themselves to death rather than submit. Religious schism opened a gulf between the Russian people and the crown.

Nevertheless, modernizing trends prevailed. As the state bureaucracy expanded, adding more officials and establishing regulations and routines, the government intervened more and more in daily life. Decrees regulated tobacco smoking, card playing, and alcohol consumption and even dictated how people should leash and fence their pet dogs. Western ideas began to seep into educated circles in Moscow. Nobles and ordinary citizens commissioned portraits of themselves instead of only buying religious icons. Tsar Alexei set up the first Western-style theater in the Kremlin, and his daughter Sophia translated French plays. The most adventurous nobles began to wear German-style clothing. Some even argued that service and not just birth should determine rank. A long struggle over Western influences had begun.

Poland-Lithuania Overwhelmed

Unlike the other eastern European powers, Poland-Lithuania did not follow the absolutist model. Decades of war weakened the monarchy and made the great nobles into virtually autonomous warlords. They used the parliament and demands for constitutionalism to stymie monarchical power. The result was a precipitous slide into political disarray and weakness.

In 1648, Ukrainian Cossack warriors revolted against the king of Poland-Lithuania, inaugurating two decades of tumult known as the Deluge. Cossack bands had formed from runaway peasants and poor nobles in the no man's land of southern Russia and Ukraine. The Polish nobles who claimed this potentially rich land scorned the Cossacks as troublemakers; but to the Ukrainian peasant population they were liberators. In 1654, the Cossacks offered Ukraine to Russian rule, provoking a

Poland-Lithuania in the Seventeenth Century

Russo-Polish war that ended in 1667 when the tsar annexed eastern Ukraine and Kiev. Neighboring powers tried to profit from the chaos in Poland-Lithuania; Sweden, Brandenburg-Prussia, and Transylvania sent armies to seize territory.

Many towns were destroyed in the fighting, and as much as a third of the Polish population perished. The once prosperous Jewish and Protestant minorities suffered greatly: some 56,000 Jews were killed either by the Cossacks, Polish peasants, or Russian troops, and thousands more had to flee or convert to Christianity. One rabbi wrote, "We were slaughtered each day, in a more agonizing way than cattle: they are butchered quickly, while we were being executed slowly." Surviving Jews moved from towns to *shtetls* (Jewish villages), where they took up petty trading, moneylending, tax gathering, and tavern leasing—activities that fanned peasant anti-Semitism. Desperate for protection amid the war, most Protestants backed the violently anti-Catholic Swedes, and the victorious Catholic majority branded them as traitors. Some Protestant refugees fled to the Dutch Republic and England. In Poland-Lithuania it came to be assumed that a good Pole was a Catholic. The commonwealth had ceased to be an outpost of toleration.

The commonwealth revived briefly when a man of ability and ambition, Jan Sobieski (r. 1674–1696), was elected king. He gained a reputation throughout Europe when he led 25,000 Polish cavalrymen into battle in the siege of Vienna in 1683. His cavalry helped rout the Turks and turned the tide against the Ottomans. Married to a politically shrewd French princess, Sobieski openly admired Louis XIV's France. Despite his efforts to rebuild the monarchy, he could not halt Poland-Lithuania's decline into powerlessness.

Elsewhere the ravages of war had created opportunities for kings to increase their power, but in Poland-Lithuania the great nobles gained all the advantage. They dominated the Sejm (parliament), and to maintain an equilibrium among themselves, they each wielded an absolute veto power. This "free veto" constitutional system soon deadlocked parliamentary government. The monarchy lost its room to maneuver, and with it much of its remaining power. An appalled Croat visitor in 1658 commented on the situation:

> Among the Poles there is no order in the state, and the subjects are not afraid either of the king or the judge. Everybody who is stronger thinks to have the right to oppress the weaker, just as the wolves and bears are free to capture and kill cattle. . . . Such abominable depravity is called by the Poles "aristocratic freedom."

The Polish version of constitutionalism fatally weakened the state and made it prey to neighboring powers.

❖ Constitutionalism in England

In the second half of the seventeenth century, western and eastern Europe began to move in different directions. The farther east one traveled, the more absolutist the style of government and the greater the gulf between landlord and peasant. In eastern Europe, nobles lorded over their serfs but owed almost slavish obedience in turn to their rulers. In western

Europe, even in absolutist France, serfdom had almost entirely disappeared and nobles and rulers alike faced greater challenges to their control. The greatest challenges of all would come in England.

This outcome might seem surprising, for the English monarchs enjoyed many advantages compared with their continental rivals: they needed less money for their armies because they had stayed out of the Thirty Years' War, and their island kingdom was in theory easier to rule because the population they governed was only one-fourth the size of France's and relatively homogeneous ethnically. Yet the English rulers failed in their efforts to install absolutist policies. The English revolutions of 1642–1660 and 1688–1689 overturned two kings, confirmed the constitutional powers of an elected parliament, and laid the foundation for the idea that government must guarantee certain rights under the law.

England Turned Upside Down, 1642–1660

Disputes about the right to levy taxes and the nature of authority in the Church of England had long troubled the relationship between the English crown and Parliament. For over a hundred years, wealthy English landowners had been accustomed to participating in government through Parliament and expected to be consulted on royal policy. Although England had no one constitutional document, a variety of laws, judicial decisions, charters and petitions granted by the king, and customary procedures all regulated relations between king and parliament. When Charles I tried to assert his authority over Parliament, a civil war broke out in 1642. It set in motion an unpredictable chain of events, which included an extraordinary ferment of religious and political ideas. Some historians view the English civil war of 1642–1646 as the last great war of religion because it pitted Puritans against those trying to push the Anglican church toward Catholicism; others see in it the first modern revolution because it gave birth to democratic political and religious movements.

Charles I versus Parliament. When Charles I (r. 1625–1649) succeeded his father, James I, he faced an increasingly aggressive Parliament that resisted new taxes and resented the king's efforts to extend his personal control. In 1628, Parliament

Artemisia Gentileschi, *Painting*
(an allegorical self-portrait)
Like all monarchs of his time, King Charles I of England spent lavishly on clothing, furniture, and art. Among the many paintings commissioned by him was this painting by the Italian woman artist Gentileschi (1630s), which shows the artist herself at work. Gentileschi lived at the English court and worked for Charles between 1638 and 1641. She painted as well for King Philip IV of Spain and for many Italian patrons. Coming from the hand of a woman, the painting must be seen as a kind of wry commentary on women's exclusion from most cultural endeavors. The figure supposedly represents an allegory of painting. Most allegories—symbolic figures standing for abstract concepts—relied on female figures, not because women did these things but because women could be imagined as symbols. The Italian word for painting, moreover, like many Romance-language words for abstractions, is gendered female (la pittura). But Gentileschi portrays herself, not an abstract female figure, as if to say that real women can paint too.
The Royal Collection. © 1998 Her Majesty Queen Elizabeth II.

forced Charles to agree to a Petition of Right by which he promised not to levy taxes without its consent. Charles hoped to avoid further interference with his plans by simply refusing to call Parliament into session between 1629 and 1640. Without it, the king's ministers had to find every loophole possible to raise revenues. They tried to turn "ship money," a levy on seaports in times of emergency, into an annual tax collected everywhere in the country. The crown won the ensuing court case, but many subjects still refused to pay what they considered to be an illegal tax.

Religious tensions brought conflicts over the king's authority to a head. The Puritans had long agitated for the removal of any vestiges of Catholicism, but Charles, married to a French Catholic, moved in the opposite direction. With Charles's encouragement, the archbishop of Canterbury, William Laud (1573–1645), imposed increasingly elaborate ceremonies on the Anglican church. Angered by these moves toward "popery," the Puritans poured forth vituperative pamphlets and sermons. In response Laud hauled them before the feared Court of Star Chamber, which the king personally controlled. The court ordered harsh sentences for Laud's Puritan critics; they were whipped, pilloried, branded, and even had their ears cut off and their noses split. When Laud tried to apply his policies to Scotland, however, they backfired completely: the stubborn Presbyterian Scots rioted against the imposition of the Anglican prayer book—the Book of Common Prayer—and in 1640 they invaded the north of England. To raise money to fight the war, Charles called Parliament into session and unwittingly opened the door to a constitutional and religious crisis.

The Parliament of 1640 did not intend revolution, but reformers in the House of Commons (the lower house of Parliament) wanted to undo what they saw as the royal tyranny of the 1630s. Parliament removed Laud from office, ordered the execution of an unpopular royal commander, abolished the Court of Star Chamber, repealed recently levied taxes, and provided for a parliamentary assembly at least once every three years, thus establishing a constitutional check on royal authority. Moderate reformers expected to stop there and resisted Puritan pressure to abolish bishops and eliminate the Anglican prayer book. But their hand was forced in January 1642, when Charles and his soldiers invaded

Parliament and tried unsuccessfully to arrest those leaders who had moved to curb his power. Faced with mounting opposition within London, Charles quickly withdrew from the city and organized an army. The stage was set for a civil war between king and parliament.

Civil War and the Challenge to All Authorities. The war lasted four years (1642–1646) and divided the country. The king's army of royalists, known as Cavaliers, enjoyed most support in northern and western England. The parliamentary forces, called Roundheads because they cut their hair short, had their stronghold in the southeast, including London. Although Puritans dominated on the parliamentary side, they were divided among themselves about the proper form of church government: the Presbyterians wanted a Calvinist church with some central authority, whereas the Independents favored entirely autonomous congregations free from other church government (hence the term *congregationalism*, often associated with the Independents). Putting aside their differences for the sake of military unity, the Puritans united under an obscure member of the House of Commons, the country gentleman Oliver Cromwell (1599–1658), who sympathized with the Independents. After Cromwell skillfully reorganized the parliamentary troops, his New Model Army defeated the Cavaliers at the battle of Naseby in 1645. Charles surrendered in 1646.

Although the civil war between king and Parliament had ended in victory for Parliament, divisions within the Puritan ranks now came to the fore: the Presbyterians dominated Parliament, but the Independents controlled the army. Both factions' leaders belonged to the social and political elite, but the Independents favored more far-reaching political and religious changes than the Presbyterians. Their disputes drew lower-class groups into the debate. (See "Contrasting Views," page 622.) The most

England during the Civil War

Area supporting Parliament in 1643

Area supporting Royalists in December 1643

✳ Battle

important were the Levellers, who emerged among disgruntled soldiers when Parliament tried to disband the New Model Army. In 1647, the Levellers honed their ideas about the nature of political authority in a series of debates between soldiers and officers at an army camp near London. They insisted that Parliament meet annually, that members be paid so as to allow common people to participate, and that all male heads of households be allowed to vote. Their proposed democracy excluded servants, the propertyless, and women but nonetheless "leveled" social differences (hence their name) by offering political access to artisans, shopkeepers, and modest farmers. Cromwell and other army leaders rejected the Levellers' demands as threatening to property owners. Cromwell insisted, "You have no other way to deal with these men but to break them in pieces. . . . If you do not break them they will break you."

Just as political differences between Presbyterians and Independents helped spark new democratic political movements, so too their conflicts over church organization fostered the emergence of new religious doctrines. The new sects had in common only their emphasis on the "inner light" of individual religious inspiration and a disdain for hierarchical authority. Their emphasis on equality before God and democracy within the church appealed to the middle and lower classes. The Baptists, for example, insisted on adult baptism because they believed that Christians should choose their own church and that every child should not automatically become a member of the Church of England. The Quakers demonstrated their beliefs in equality and the inner light by refusing to doff their hats to men in authority. Manifesting their religious experience by trembling, or "quaking," the Quakers believed that anyone—man or woman—inspired by a direct experience of God could preach.

Parliamentary leaders feared that the new sects would overturn the whole social hierarchy. Rumors abounded, for example, of naked Quakers running through the streets waiting "for a sign." Some sects did advocate sweeping change. The Diggers promoted rural communism—collective ownership of all property. Seekers and Ranters questioned just about everything. One notorious Ranter, John Robins, even claimed to be God. A few men advocated free love. These developments convinced the political elite that tolerating the new sects would lead to skepticism, anarchism, and debauchery.

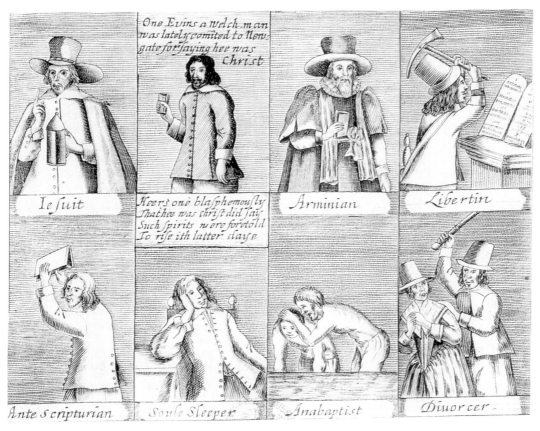

Heers one blasphemously
That hee was chrift did say
Such spirits were foretold
To rise ith latter dayse

Ie ſuit | Arminian | Libertin

Ante Scripturian | Soule Sleeper | Anabaptist | Diuorcer

One Evins a welch.man was lately comited to Newgate for saying hee was Christ

Religious Radicals

The Puritans in Parliament had opposed the Catholic leanings of the Church of England (shown as the Arminian here) and worried that Catholic missionary groups, such as the Jesuits (top left), might gain access to England. But they also detested the nonconformist Protestant sects that sprang up during the civil war: some individuals, called Ranters or Seekers, supposedly claimed they were Jesus come again; Arians rejected the doctrine of the Trinity; libertines attacked all sacramental objects of religion, anti-scripturians rejected the authority of the Bible; soul sleepers denied the afterlife; Anabaptists refused infant baptism; the family of love did not keep the sabbath; and some advocated easier divorce. It should be remembered that pamphlets such as this one represented the views of those who opposed these tendencies. It is questionable, for example, whether Arians believed in free love, libertines attacked religious objects, or those in favor of easier divorce beat their wives.
British Library.

In keeping with their notions of equality and individual inspiration, many of the new sects provided opportunities for women to become preachers and prophets. The Quakers thought women especially capable of prophecy. One prophet, Anna Trapnel, explained her vocation: "For in all that was said by me, I was nothing, the Lord put all in my mouth, and told me what I should say." Women presented petitions, participated prominently in street demonstrations, distributed tracts, and occasionally even dressed as men, wearing swords and joining armies. The duchess of Newcastle complained in 1650 that women were "affecting a Masculinacy . . . practicing the behaviour . . . of men." The outspoken women in new sects like the Quakers underscored the threat of a social order turning upside down.

Oliver Cromwell. At the heart of the continuing political struggle was the question of what to do with the king, who tried to negotiate with the Presbyterians in Parliament. In late 1648, Independents

The English Civil War

The civil war between Charles I and Parliament (1642–1646) excited furious debates about the proper forms of political authority, debates that influenced political thought for two centuries or more. The Levellers, who served in the parliamentary army, wanted Parliament to be more accountable to ordinary men like themselves (Document 1). When the king came to trial in January 1649, he laid out the royalist case for the supremacy of the king (Document 2). After the restoration of the monarchy in 1660, Lucy Hutchinson wrote a memoir in which she complained that *Puritan* had become a term of political slander. Her memoir shows how religious terms had been politicized by the upheaval (Document 3). Thomas Hobbes in his famous political treatise *Leviathan* (1651) develops the consequences of the civil war for political theory (Document 4).

1. The Levellers, "The Agreement of the People, as Presented to the Council of the Army" (October 28, 1647)

Note especially two things about this document: (1) it focuses on Parliament as the chief instrument of reform and demands proportional or democratic representation; and (2) it claims that government depends on the consent of the people.

. . . Since, therefore, our former oppressions and scarce-yet-ended troubles have been occasioned, either by want of frequent national meetings in Council [Parliament], or by rendering those meetings ineffectual, we are fully agreed and resolved to provide that hereafter our representatives be neither left to an uncertainty for the time nor made useless to the ends for which they are intended. In order whereunto we declare:—

That the people of England, being at this day very unequally distributed by Counties, Cities, and Borough for the election of their deputies in Parliament, ought to be more indifferently [equally] proportioned according to the number of the inhabitants. . . .

That the power of this, and all future Representatives of this Nation, is inferior only to theirs who choose them, and doth extend, without the consent or concurrence of any other person or persons [the king], to the enacting, altering, and repealing of laws, to the erecting and abolishing of offices and courts, to the appointing, removing, and calling to account magistrates and officers of all degrees, to the making war and peace, to the treating with foreign States [in other words, Parliament is the supreme power, not the king]. . . .

These things we declare to be our native rights, and therefore are agreed and resolved to maintain them with our utmost possibilities against all opposition whatsoever. . . .

Source: Samuel Rawson Gardiner, *The Constitutional Documents of the Puritan Revolution, 1625–1660* (1906), 333–35.

2. Charles I's Refusal of the Jurisdiction of the Court Appointed to Try Him (January 21, 1649)

Charles argued that his trial was illegal. He cast himself as the true defender of English liberties and accused Parliament of going against both the Bible and English law.

The duty I owe to God in the preservation of the true liberty of my people will not suffer me at this time to be silent: for, how can any free-born subject of England call life or anything he possesseth his own, if power without right daily make new, and abrogate the old fundamental laws of the land which I now take to be the present case? . . . Now I am most confident this day's proceeding cannot be warranted by God's laws; for, on the contrary, the authority of obedience unto Kings is clearly warranted, and strictly commanded in both the Old and New Testament. . . .

Then for the law of this land, I am no less confident, that no learned lawyer will affirm that an impeachment can lie against the King, they all going in his name: and one of the maxims is, that the King can do no wrong.

Thus you see that I speak not for my own right alone, as I am your King, but also for the true liberty of all my subjects, which consists not in the power of government, but in living under such laws, such a government, as may give themselves the best assurance of their lives, and property of their goods.

Source: Stuart E. Prall, ed., *The Puritan Revolution: A Documentary History* (Gloucester, Mass.: Peter Smith, 1973), 186–88.

3. *Lucy Hutchinson,* Memoirs of the Life of Colonel Hutchinson *(1664–1671)*

Lucy Hutchinson wrote her memoir to defend her Puritan husband, who had been imprisoned upon the restoration of the monarchy.

If any were grieved at the dishonour of the kingdom, or the griping of the poor, or the unjust oppressions of the subject by a thousand ways invented to maintain the riots of the courtiers and the swarms of needy Scots the king had brought in to devour like locusts the plenty of this land, he was a puritan; if any showed favour to any godly, honest person, kept them company, relieved them in want, or protected them against violent and unjust oppression, he was a puritan. . . . In short, all that crossed the views of the needy courtiers, the proud encroaching priests, the thievish projectors, the lewd nobility and gentry . . . all these were puritans; and if puritans, then enemies to the king and his government, seditious, factious hypocrites, ambitious disturbers of the public peace, and finally the pest of the kingdom.

Source: Christopher Hill and Edmund Dell, eds., *The Good Old Cause: The English Revolution of 1640–1660, Its Causes, Course and Consequences* (London: Lawrence and Wishart, 1949), 179–80.

4. *Thomas Hobbes,* Leviathan *(1651)*

In this excerpt, Hobbes depicts the anarchy of a society without a strong central authority, but he leaves open the question of whether that authority should be vested in "one Man" or "one Assembly of men," that is, a king or a parliament.

During the time men live without a common Power to keep them all in awe, they are in that condition which is called Warre; and such a warre, as is of every man, against every man. . . . In such condition, there is no place for Industry; because the fruit thereof is uncertain: and consequently no Culture of the Earth; no Navigation, nor use of the commodities that may be imported by Sea; no commodious Building; no Instrument of moving, and removing such things as require much force; no Knowledge of the face of the Earth; no account of Time; no Arts; no Letters; no Society; and which is worst of all, continuall feare, and danger of violent death; And the life of man, solitary, poore, nasty, brutish, and short.

The only way to erect such a Common Power, as may be able to defend them from the invasion of Forraigners, and the injuries of one another, and thereby to secure them in such sort, as that by their owne industrie, and by the Fruites of the Earth, they may nourish themselves and live contentedly; is, to conferre all their power and strength upon one Man, or upon one Assembly of men, that may reduce all their wills, by plurality of voices, unto one Will. . . . This is more than Consent, or Concord; it is a reall Unitie of them all, in one and the same Person, made by Covenant of every man with every man. . . . This done, the Multitude so united in one Person, is called a COMMON-WEALTH, in latine CIVITAS. This is the Generation of that great LEVIATHAN, or rather (to speake more reverently) of that *Mortall God,* to which wee owe under the *Imortall God,* our peace and defence.

Source: Thomas Hobbes, *Leviathan,* ed. Richard E. Flathman and David Johnston (New York: Norton, 1997), 70, 95.

QUESTIONS FOR DEBATE
1. Which of these views do you find most persuasive?
2. Why did Hobbes's arguments about political authority upset supporters of both monarchy and Parliament?

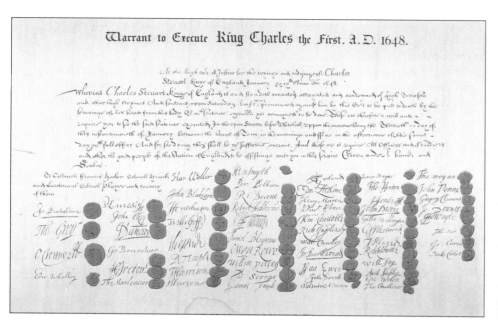

Death Warrant of Charles I
Parliament voted to try Charles I for treason, and the trial began in January 1649. A week later the court found Charles to be a "tyrant, traitor, murderer, and public enemy" and ordered his execution. When the monarchy was restored in 1660, everyone who signed Charles I's death warrant was hunted down and executed.
Mary Evans Picture Library.

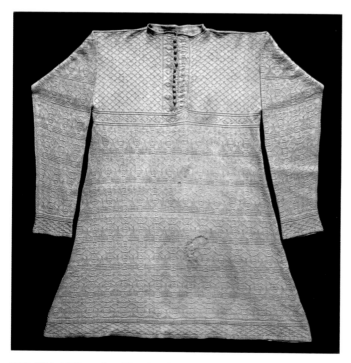

Silk Shirt Worn by Charles I at His Execution
The blood is still visible on the shirt worn by Charles I for his beheading. After his head was severed, many people rushed forward to dip their handkerchiefs in the blood, which some believed to have miraculous qualities. His wife and son fled to France.
Museum of London Photographic Library.

in the army purged the Presbyterians from Parliament, leaving a "rump" of about seventy members. This Rump Parliament then created a high court to try Charles I. The court found him guilty of attempting to establish "an unlimited and tyrannical power" and pronounced a death sentence. On January 30, 1649, Charles was beheaded before an enormous crowd, which reportedly groaned as one when the axe fell. Although many had objected to Charles's autocratic rule, few had wanted him killed. For royalists, Charles immediately became a martyr, and reports of miracles, such as the curing of blindness by the touch of a handkerchief soaked in his blood, soon circulated.

The Rump Parliament abolished the monarchy and the House of Lords (the upper house of Parliament) and set up a Puritan republic with Oliver Cromwell as chairman of the Council of State. Cromwell did not tolerate dissent from his policies. He saw the hand of God in events and himself as God's agent. Pamphleteers and songwriters ridiculed his red nose and accused him of wanting to be king, but few challenged his leadership. When his agents discovered plans for mutiny within the army, they executed the perpetrators; new decrees silenced the Levellers. Although Cromwell allowed the various Puritan sects to worship rather freely and permitted Jews with needed skills to return to England for the first time since the thirteenth century, Catholics could not worship publicly, nor could Anglicans use the Book of Common Prayer. The elites—many of them were still Anglican—were troubled by Cromwell's religious policies but pleased to see some social order reestablished.

The new regime aimed to extend state power just as Charles I had before. Cromwell laid the foundation for a Great Britain made up of England, Ireland, and Scotland by reconquering Scotland and subduing Ireland. Anti-English rebels in Ireland had seized the occasion of troubles between king and Parliament to revolt in 1641. When his position was secured in 1649, Cromwell went to Ireland with a large force and easily defeated the rebels, massacring whole garrisons and their priests. He encouraged expropriating the lands of the Irish "barbarous wretches," and Scottish immigrants resettled the northern county of Ulster. This seventeenth-century English conquest left a legacy of bitterness that

Oliver Cromwell
Shown here preparing for battle, Cromwell lived an austere life but believed fiercely in his own personal righteousness. As leader he tolerated no opposition. When he died, he was buried in Westminster Abbey, but in 1661 his body was exhumed and hanged in its shroud. His head was cut off and displayed outside Westminster Hall for nearly twenty years.
Courtesy of the National Portrait Gallery, London.

the Irish even today call "the curse of Cromwell." In 1651, Parliament turned its attention overseas, putting mercantilist ideas into practice in the first Navigation Act, which allowed imports only if they were carried on English ships or came directly from the producers of goods. The Navigation Act was aimed at the Dutch, who dominated world trade; Cromwell tried to carry the policy further by waging naval war on the Dutch from 1652 to 1654.

At home, however, Cromwell faced growing resistance. His wars required a budget twice the size of Charles I's, and his increases in property taxes and customs duties alienated landowners and merchants. The conflict reached a crisis in 1653: Parliament considered disbanding the army, whereupon Cromwell abolished the Rump Parliament in a military coup and made himself Lord Protector. He now silenced his critics by banning newspapers and using networks of spies and mail readers to keep tabs on his enemies. Although he assumed some trappings of royalty, he refused the crown. When he died in 1658, one opponent claimed, "There were none that cried but dogs." Cromwell intended that his son should succeed him, but his death only revived the prospect of civil war and political chaos. In 1660, a newly elected, staunchly Anglican Parliament invited Charles II, the son of the executed king, to return from exile.

The "Glorious Revolution" of 1688

Most English welcomed back the king in 1660. According to one royalist, throughout the realm "the ways were strewed with flowers, the bells ringing, the streets hung with tapestry, fountains running with wine." The restoration of royal authority in 1660 whisked away the more austere elements of Puritan culture and revived old traditions of celebration—drinking, merrymaking, and processions of young maidens in royalist colors. But the religious policies of Charles II and his successor, James II, ensured that conflicts between king and Parliament would erupt once again.

The Restored Monarchy.   In 1660, the traditional monarchical form of government was reinstated, restoring the king to full partnership with Parliament. Charles II (r. 1660–1685) promised "a liberty to tender consciences" in an attempt to extend religious toleration, especially to Catholics, with whom

Great Fire of London, 1666
This view of London shows the three-day fire at its height. The writer John Evelyn described the scene in his diary: "All the sky was of a fiery aspect, like the top of a burning oven, and the light seen above 40 miles round about for many nights. God grant mine eyes may never behold the like, who now saw above 10,000 houses all in one flame; the noise and cracking and thunder of people, the fall of towers, houses, and churches, was like an hideous storm." Everyone in London at the time felt overwhelmed by the catastrophe, and many attributed it to God's punishment for the upheavals of the 1640s and 1650s.
Museum of London Photographic Library.

he sympathized. Yet more than a thousand Puritan ministers lost their positions, and after 1664, attending a service other than one conforming with the Anglican prayer book was illegal.

Natural disasters marred the early years of Charles II's reign. The plague stalked London's rat-infested streets in May 1665 and claimed more than thirty thousand victims by September. Then in 1666, the Great Fire swept the city. Diarist Samuel Pepys described its terrifying progress: "It made me weep to see it. The churches, houses, and all on fire and flaming at once, and a horrid noise the flames made, and the cracking of houses at their ruine." The crown now had a city as well as a monarchy to rebuild.

The restoration of monarchy made some in Parliament fear that the English government would come to resemble French absolutism. This fear was not unfounded. In 1670, Charles II made a secret agreement, soon leaked, with Louis XIV in which he promised to announce his conversion to Catholicism in exchange for money for a war against the Dutch. Charles never proclaimed himself a Catholic, but in his Declaration of Indulgence (1673) he did suspend all laws against Catholics and Protestant dissenters. Parliament refused to continue funding the Dutch war unless Charles rescinded his Declaration of Indulgence. Asserting its authority further, Parliament passed the Test Act in 1673, requiring all government officials to profess allegiance to the Church of England and in effect disavow Catholic doctrine. Then in 1678, Parliament precipitated the so-called Exclusion Crisis by explicitly denying the throne to a Roman Catholic. This action was aimed at the king's brother and heir, James, an open convert to Catholicism. Charles refused to allow it to become law.

The dynastic crisis over the succession of a Catholic gave rise to two distinct factions in Parliament: the Tories, who supported a strong, hereditary monarchy and the restored ceremony of the Anglican church, and the Whigs, who advocated parliamentary supremacy and toleration for Protestant dissenters such as Presbyterians. Both labels were originally derogatory: *Tory* meant an Irish Catholic bandit; *Whig* was the Irish Catholic designation for a Presbyterian Scot. The Tories favored James's succession despite his Catholicism, whereas the Whigs opposed a Catholic monarch. The loose moral atmosphere of Charles's court also offended some Whigs, who complained tongue in cheek that Charles was father of his country in much too literal a fashion (he had fathered more than one child by his mistresses but produced no legitimate heir).

Parliament's Revolt against James II. Upon Charles's death, his brother, James, succeeded to the throne as James II (r. 1685–1688). James pursued pro-Catholic and absolutist policies even more aggressively than his brother. When a male heir—who would take precedence over James's two adult Protestant daughters and be reared a Catholic—was born, Tories and Whigs banded together. They invited the Dutch ruler William, prince of Orange and the husband of James's older daughter, Mary, to invade England. James fled to France and hardly any blood was shed. Parliament offered the throne jointly to William (r. 1689–1702) and Mary (r. 1689–1694) on the condition that they accept a bill of rights guaranteeing Parliament's full partnership in a constitutional government.

In the Bill of Rights, William and Mary agreed not to raise a standing army or to levy taxes without Parliament's consent. They also agreed to call meetings of Parliament at least every three years, to guarantee free elections to parliamentary seats, and to abide by Parliament's decisions and not suspend duly passed laws. The agreement gave England's constitutional government a written, legal basis by formally recognizing Parliament as a self-contained, independent body that shared power with the rulers. Victorious supporters of the coup declared it the "Glorious Revolution." Constitutionalism had triumphed over absolutism in England.

The propertied classes who controlled Parliament eagerly consolidated their power and prevented any resurgence of the popular turmoil of the 1640s. The Toleration Act of 1689 granted all Protestants freedom of worship, though non-Anglicans were still excluded from the universities; Catholics got no rights but were more often left alone to worship privately. In Ireland the Catholics rose to defend James II, but William and Mary's troops brutally suppressed them. With the Whigs in power and the Tories in opposition, wealthy landowners now controlled political life throughout the realm. The factions' differences, however, were minor; essentially, the Tories had less access to the king's patronage. A contemporary reported that King William had said "that if he had good places [honors and land] enough to bestow, he should soon unite the two parties."

❖ Constitutionalism in the Dutch Republic and the Overseas Colonies

When William and Mary came to the throne in England in 1689, the Dutch and the English put aside the rivalries that had brought them to war against each other in 1652–1654, 1665–1667, and 1672–1674. Under William, the Dutch and the English together led the coalition that blocked Louis XIV's efforts to dominate continental Europe. The English and Dutch had much in common: oriented toward commerce, especially overseas, they were the successful exceptions to absolutism in Europe. Also among the few outposts of constitutionalism in the seventeenth century were the British North American colonies, which developed representative government while the English were preoccupied with their revolutions at home. Constitutionalism was not the only factor shaping this Atlantic world; as constitutionalism developed in the colonies, so too did the enslavement of black Africans as a new labor force.

The Dutch Republic

When the Dutch Republic gained formal independence from Spain in 1648, it had already established a decentralized, constitutional state. The individual provinces granted power over foreign policy to the Estates General, an assembly made up of deputies from each province, but local authorities jealously guarded most of the power. Rich merchants called *regents* effectively controlled the internal affairs of each province and through the Estates General named the *stadholder*, the executive officer responsible for defense and for representing the state at all ceremonial occasions. They almost always chose one of the princes of the house of Orange, but the prince of Orange resembled a president more than a king. One foreign visitor observed that the Dutch "behave as if all men were created equal," but in fact real power remained in the hands of the regents, not the common people.

The decentralized state encouraged and protected trade, and the Dutch Republic soon became Europe's financial capital. The Bank of Amsterdam offered interest rates less than half those available in England and France. Praised for their industriousness, thrift, and cleanliness—and maligned as greedy, dull "butter-boxes"—the Dutch dominated overseas commerce with their shipping (Map 17.3). They imported products from all over the world: spices, tea,

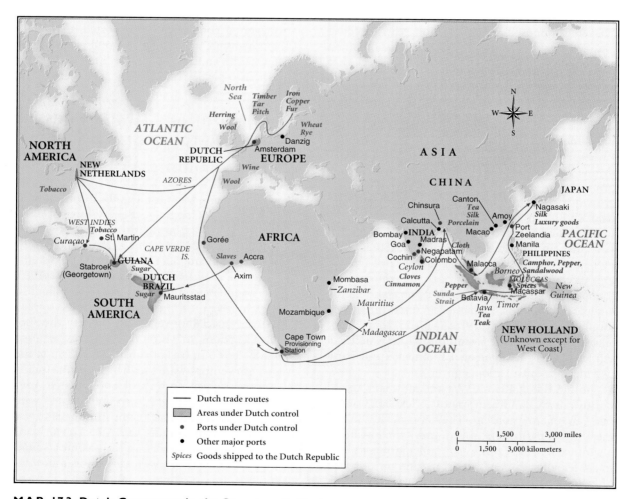

MAP 17.3 Dutch Commerce in the Seventeenth Century

Even before gaining formal independence from the Spanish in 1648, the Dutch had begun to compete with the Spanish and Portuguese all over the world. In 1602, a group of merchants established the Dutch East India Company, which soon offered investors an annual rate of return of 35 percent on the trade in spices with countries located on the Indian Ocean. Global commerce gave the Dutch the highest standard of living in Europe and soon attracted the envy of the French and the English.

and silk from Asia; sugar and tobacco from the Americas; wool from England and Spain; timber and furs from Scandinavia; grain from eastern Europe. (See "Did You Know?", page 630.) One English traveler in 1660 described the riches of Amsterdam as superior to those of Venice and called the Hague "the most pleasant place in the world." A widely reprinted history of Amsterdam that appeared in 1662 described the city as "risen through the hand of God to the peak of prosperity and greatness. . . . The whole world stands amazed at its riches and from east and west, north and south they come to behold it."

The Dutch rapidly became the most prosperous and best-educated people in Europe. Middle-class people supported the visual arts, especially painting, to an unprecedented degree. Artists and engravers produced thousands of works, and Dutch artists were among the first to sell to a mass market. Whereas in other countries kings, nobles, and churches bought art, Dutch buyers were merchants, artisans, and shopkeepers. Engravings, illustrated histories, and oil paintings, even those of the widely acclaimed Rembrandt van Rijn (1606–1669), were all relatively inexpensive. One foreigner commented that "pictures are very common here, there being scarce an ordinary tradesman whose house is not decorated with them." The pictures reflected the Dutch interest in familiar daily details: children at play, winter landscapes, and ships in port.

The family household, not the royal court, determined the moral character of this intensely commercial society. Dutch society fostered public enterprise in men and work in the home for women, who were expected to filter out the greed and materialism of commercial society by maintaining domestic harmony and virtue. Relative prosperity decreased the need for married women to work, so Dutch society developed the clear contrast between middle-class male and female roles that would become prevalent elsewhere in Europe and in America more than a century later. As one contemporary Dutch writer explained, "The husband must be on the street to practice his trade; the wife must stay at home to be in the kitchen."

Extraordinarily high levels of urbanization and literacy created a large reading public. Dutch presses printed books censored elsewhere (printers or authors censored in one province simply shifted operations to another), and the University of Leiden attracted students and professors from all over Eu-

A Typical Dutch Scene from Daily Life
Jan Steen painted The Baker Arent Oostward and His Wife *in 1658. Steen ran a brewery and tavern in addition to painting, and he was known for his interest in the details of daily life. Dutch artists popularized this kind of "genre" painting, which showed ordinary people at work and play.* Rijksmuseum, Amsterdam.

rope. Dutch tolerance extended to the works of Benedict Spinoza (1633–1677), a Jewish philosopher and biblical scholar who was expelled by his synagogue for alleged atheism but left alone by the Dutch authorities. Spinoza strove to reconcile religion with science and mathematics, but his work scandalized many Christians and Jews because he seemed to equate God and nature. Like nature, Spinoza's God followed unchangeable laws and could not be influenced by human actions, prayers, or faith.

Dutch learning, painting, and commerce all enjoyed wide renown in the seventeenth century, but this luster proved hard to maintain. The Dutch lived in a world of international rivalries in which strong central authority gave their enemies an advantage. Though inconclusive, the naval wars with England drained the state's revenues. Even more dangerous

Tobacco and the Invention of "Smoking"

In the early seventeenth century, a "new astonishing fashion," wrote a German ambassador, had come to the Dutch Republic from the New World. For a long time there was no word for what you did with tobacco; *smoking* came to be commonly used as a term only in the seventeenth century. Until then one spoke of "a fog-drinking bout," "drinking smoke," or "drinking tobacco." One Jesuit preacher called it "dry drunkenness." The analogy to inebriation is not entirely farfetched, for nicotine (named after the French ambassador to Portugal, Jean Nicot, who brought tobacco to France in the mid-sixteenth century) does have an effect more comparable to alcohol than to caffeine; nicotine is a nerve toxin that dulls the nervous system. It is not known exactly where in the Americas tobacco had its birthplace, but its use was widespread by the time the Europeans arrived. Mayans and Aztecs smoked ceremonial pipes, Incas used tobacco as a medicine, and Indians in Brazil took snuff.

Spain began exporting tobacco to other European countries in the sixteenth century. The Spanish did not exploit the possibilities of producing tobacco on plantations; tobacco growing began in earnest in the seventeenth century only with the spread of black slavery. Virginia and Maryland expanded their exports of tobacco sixfold between 1663 and 1699. Until 1700, Amsterdam dominated the curing process; half the tobacco factories in Amsterdam were owned by Jewish merchants of Spanish or Portuguese descent.

Smoking spread geographically from western to eastern Europe, socially from the upper classes downward, and from men to women. At first the Spanish preferred cigars, the British pipes, and the French snuff. In the eighteenth century, both upper- and middle-class women took snuff, which was considered an aristocratic taste. Before the end of the nineteenth century, women did not regularly take tobacco in any form other than snuff. A woman smoking a pipe or cigar was a favorite target of cartoonists in the eighteenth and nineteenth centuries. This changed with the Russian invention of the cigarette in the mid-nineteenth century. Women began to smoke cigarettes in the late 1800s as a sign of emancipation.

Source: Wolfgang Schivelbusch, *Tastes of Paradise: A Social History of Spices, Stimulants, and Intoxicants,* trans. David Jacobson, 1993.

The Vice of Tobacco
In this engraving of 1628, The Vice of Tobacco, *the Dutch artist Gillis van Scheyndel portrays smoking as similar to excessive drinking, a habit that makes people sick and leads them astray. Pipes often symbolized the folly and futility of a life given over to materialistic pleasures. The company of revelers is led on by a pipe-smoking ape who has features like a devil.*
Koninklijke Bibliotheek.

were the land wars with France, which continued into the eighteenth century. The Dutch survived these challenges but increasingly depended on alliances with other powers, such as England. At the end of the seventeenth century, the regent elite became more exclusive, more preoccupied with ostentation, less tolerant of deviations from strict Calvinism, and more concerned with imitating French styles. Dutch architecture, painting, and intellectual life eventually came under French influence.

Freedom and Slavery in the New World

The French and English also increasingly overshadowed the Dutch in the New World colonies. While the Dutch concentrated on shipping, including the slave trade, the seventeenth-century French and English established settler colonies that would eventually provide fabulous revenues to the home countries. Many European governments encouraged private companies to vie for their share of the slave trade, and slavery began to take clear institutional form in the New World in this period. Even while slavery offered only a degrading form of despotism to black Africans, whites found in the colonies greater political and religious freedom than in Europe.

The Rise of the Slave Trade. After the Spanish and Portuguese had shown that African slaves could be transported and forced to labor in South and Central America, the English and French endeavored to set up similar labor systems in their new Caribbean island colonies. White planters with large tracts of land bought African slaves to work fields of sugarcane, and as they gradually built up their holdings, the planters displaced most of the original white settlers, who moved to mainland colonies. After 1661, when Barbados instituted a slave code that stripped all Africans of rights under English law, slavery became codified as an inherited status that applied only to blacks. The result was a society of extremes: the very wealthy whites, about 7 percent of the population in Barbados; and the enslaved, powerless black majority. The English brought little of their religious or constitutional practices to the Caribbean. Other Caribbean colonies followed a similar pattern of development. Louis XIV promulgated a "black code" in 1685 to regulate the legal status of slaves in the French colonies. Although one

of his aims was to prevent non-Catholics from owning slaves in the French colonies, the code had much the same effect as the English codes on the slaves themselves: they had no legal rights.

The highest church and government authorities in Catholic and Protestant countries alike condoned the gradually expanding slave trade; the governments of England, France, Spain, Portugal, the Dutch Republic, and Denmark all encouraged private companies to traffic in black Africans. The Dutch West India Company was the most successful of them. In 1600, about 9,500 Africans were exported from Africa to the New World every year; by 1700, this had increased nearly fourfold to 36,000 annually. Historians advance several different factors for the increase in the slave trade: some claim that improvements in muskets made European slavers more formidable; others cite the rising price for slaves which made their sale more attractive for Africans; still others focus on factors internal to Africa such as the increasing size of African armies and their use of muskets in fighting and capturing other Africans for sale as slaves. Whatever the reason, the way had been prepared for the development of an Atlantic economy based on slavery.

Constitutional Freedoms in the English Colonies. Virtually left to themselves during the upheavals in England, the fledgling English colonies in North America developed representative government on their own. Almost every colony had a governor and a two-house legislature. The colonial legislatures constantly sought to increase their power and resisted the efforts of Charles II and James II to reaffirm royal control. William and Mary reluctantly allowed emerging colonial elites more control over local affairs. The social and political elite among the settlers hoped to impose an English social hierarchy dominated by rich landowners. Ordinary immigrants to the colonies, however, took advantage of plentiful land to carve out their own farms using white servants and, later, in some colonies, African slaves.

For native Americans, the expanding European presence meant something else altogether. They faced death through disease and warfare and the accelerating loss of their homelands. Unlike white settlers, native Americans believed that land was a divine gift provided for their collective use and not subject to individual ownership. As a result,

Europeans' claims that they owned exclusive land rights caused frequent skirmishes. In 1675–1676, for instance, three tribes allied under Metacomet (called King Philip by the English) threatened the survival of New England settlers, who savagely repulsed the attacks and sold their captives as slaves. Whites portrayed native Americans as conspiring villains and sneaky heathens, who were akin to Africans in their savagery.

❖ The Search for Order in Elite and Popular Culture

The early success of constitutionalism in England, the Dutch Republic, and the English North American colonies would help to shape a distinctive Atlantic world in the eighteenth century. Just how constitutionalism was linked to the growing commerce with the colonies remains open to dispute, however, since the constitutional governments, like the absolutist ones, avidly pursued profits in the burgeoning slave trade. Freedom did not mean liberty for everyone. One of the great debates of the time—and of much of the modern world that followed—concerned the meaning of freedom: for whom, under what conditions, with what justifiable limitations could freedom be claimed?

There was no freedom without order to sustain it, and most Europeans feared disorder above all else. In 1669, the English writer Margaret Cavendish, duchess of Newcastle, cataloged some of the sources of disorder in her time: "I wish Men were as Harmless as most Beasts are, then surely the World would be more Quiet and Happy than it is, for then there would not be such Pride, Vanity, Ambition, Covetousness, Faction, Treachery, and Treason, as is now." Cavendish wrote not long after the restoration of the monarchy in England, and her thoughts echoed the titanic struggles that had taken place over the nature of authority, not only in England but throughout Europe. Political theories, science, poetry, painting, and architecture all reflected in some measure the attempts to ground authority—to define the relation between freedom and order—in new ways. Authority concerned not just rulers and subjects but also the hierarchy of groups in society. As European states consolidated their powers,

elites worked to distinguish themselves from the lower classes. They developed new codes of correct behavior for themselves and tried to teach order and discipline to their social inferiors.

Social Contract Theory: Hobbes and Locke

The turmoil of the times prompted a major rethinking of the foundations of all authority. Two figures stood out prominently amid the cacophony of voices: Thomas Hobbes and John Locke. Their writings fundamentally shaped the modern subject of political science. Hobbes justified absolute authority; Locke provided the rationale for constitutionalism. Yet both argued that all authority came not from divine right but from a "social contract" between citizens.

Hobbes. Thomas Hobbes (1588–1679) was a royalist who sat out the English civil war of the 1640s in France, where he tutored the future king Charles II. Returning to England in 1651, he published his masterpiece, *Leviathan* (1651), in which he argued for unlimited authority in a ruler. Absolute authority could be vested in either a king or a parliament; it had to be absolute, he insisted, in order to overcome the defects of human nature. Believing that people are essentially self-centered and driven by the "right to self-preservation," Hobbes made his case by referring to science, not religion. To Hobbes, human life in a state of nature—that is, any situation without firm authority—was "solitary, poor, nasty, brutish, and short." He believed that the desire for power and natural greed would inevitably lead to unfettered competition. Only the assurance of social order could make people secure enough to act according to law; consequently, giving up personal liberty, he maintained, was the price of collective security. Rulers derived their power, he concluded, from a contract in which absolute authority protects people's rights.

Hobbes's notion of rule by an absolute authority left no room for political dissent or nonconformity, and it infuriated both royalists and supporters of Parliament. He enraged royalists by arguing that authority came not from divine right but from the social contract between citizens. Parliamentary supporters resisted Hobbes's claim that rulers must possess absolute authority to prevent the greater evil of anarchy; they believed that a constitution should guarantee shared power between king and parliament and protect individual rights under the law. Like Machiavelli before him, Hobbes became associated with a cynical, pessimistic view of human nature, and future political theorists often began their arguments by refuting Hobbes.

Locke. Rejecting both Hobbes and the more traditional royalist defenses of absolute authority, John Locke (1632–1704) used the notion of a social contract to provide a foundation for constitutionalism. Locke experienced political life firsthand as physician, secretary, and intellectual companion to the earl of Shaftesbury, a leading English Whig. In 1683, during the Exclusion Crisis, Locke fled with Shaftesbury to the Dutch Republic. There he continued work on his *Two Treatises of Government*, which, when published in 1690, served to justify the Glorious Revolution of 1688. Locke's position was thoroughly anti-absolutist. He denied the divine right of kings and ridiculed the common royalist idea that political power in the state mirrored the father's authority in the family. Like Hobbes, he posited a state of nature that applied to all people. Unlike Hobbes, however, he thought people were reasonable and the state of nature peaceful.

Locke insisted that government's only purpose was to protect life, liberty, and property, a notion that linked economic and political freedom. Ultimate authority rested in the will of a majority of men who owned property, and government should be limited to its basic purpose of protection. A ruler who failed to uphold his part of the social contract between the ruler and the populace could be justifiably resisted, an idea that would become crucial for the leaders of the American Revolution a century later. For England's landowners, however, Locke helped validate a revolution that consolidated their interests and ensured their privileges in the social hierarchy. Although he himself owned shares in the Royal African Company and justified slavery, Locke's writings were later used by abolitionists in their campaign against slavery.

Locke defended his optimistic view of human nature in the immensely influential *Essay Concerning Human Understanding* (1690). He denied the existence of any innate ideas and asserted instead that each human is born with a mind that is a tabula rasa

(blank slate). Everything humans know, he claimed, comes from sensory experience, not from anything inherent in human nature. Locke's views promoted the belief that "all men are created equal," a belief that challenged absolutist forms of rule and ultimately raised questions about women's roles as well. Not surprisingly, Locke devoted considerable energy to rethinking educational practices; he believed that education crucially shaped the human personality by channeling all sensory experience.

The Scientific Revolution Consolidated

New breakthroughs in science lent support to Locke's optimistic view of human potential. Building on the work of Copernicus, Kepler, and Galileo (see Chapter 16), the English scientist Isaac Newton finally synthesized astronomy and physics with his law of gravitation. His work further enhanced the prestige of science, but he sought no conflict with religious authorities. Indeed, many clergy applauded his refutation of atheism and his success in explaining the orderliness of God's creation. Some rulers supported scientific activity as another form of mercantilist intervention to enhance state power. Science also gained a broader audience among upper-class men and women.

Newton. A Cambridge University student at the time of Charles II's restoration, Isaac Newton (1642–1727) was a pious Anglican who aimed to reconcile faith and science. By proving that the physical universe followed rational principles, Newton argued, scientists could prove the existence of God and so liberate humans from doubt and the fear of chaos. Newton applied mathematical principles to formulate three physical laws: (1) in the absence of force, motion continues in a straight line; (2) the rate of change in the motion of an object is a result of the forces acting on it; and (3) the action and reaction between two objects are equal and opposite. The basis of Newtonian physics thus required understanding mass, inertia, force, velocity, and acceleration—all key concepts in modern science.

Extending these principles to the entire universe in his masterwork, *Principia Mathematica* (1687), Newton united celestial and terrestrial mechanics—astronomy and physics—with his law of gravitation. This law held that every body in the universe exerts over every other body an attractive force directly proportional to the product of their masses and inversely proportional to the square of the distance between them. The law of gravitation explained Kepler's elliptical planetary orbits just as it accounted for the motion of ordinary objects on earth. Once set in motion, the universe operated like clockwork, with no need for God's continuing intervention. Gravity, although a mysterious force, could be expressed mathematically. In Newton's words, "From the same principles [of motion] I now demonstrate the frame of the System of the World." The English poet Alexander Pope later captured the intellectual world's appreciation of Newton's accomplishment:

> Nature and Nature's laws lay hid in night
> God said, Let Newton be! and all was light.

Newton's science was not just mathematical and deductive; he experimented with light and helped establish the science of optics. Even while making these fundamental contributions to scientific method, Newton carried out alchemical experiments in his rooms at Cambridge University and spent long hours trying to calculate the date of the beginning of the world and of the second coming of Jesus. Not all scientists accepted Newton's theories immediately, especially on the continent, but within a couple of generations his work was preeminent, partly because of experimental verification. His "frame of the System of the World" remained the basis of all physics until the advent of relativity theory and quantum mechanics in the early twentieth century.

Public Interest in Science. Absolutist rulers saw science as a means for enhancing their prestige and glory. Frederick William, the Great Elector of Brandenburg-Prussia, for example, set up agricultural experiments in front of his Berlin palace, and various German princes supported the work of Gottfried Wilhelm Leibniz (1646–1716), one of the inventors of calculus. A lawyer, diplomat, and scholar who wrote about metaphysics, cosmology, and history, Leibniz helped establish scientific societies in the German states. Government involvement in science was greatest in France, where it became an arm of mercantilist policy; in 1666, Colbert founded the Royal Academy of Sci-

ences, which supplied fifteen scientists with government stipends.

Constitutional states supported science less directly but nonetheless provided an intellectual environment that encouraged its spread. The English Royal Society, the counterpart to the Royal Academy of Sciences in France, grew out of informal meetings of scientists at London and Oxford rather than direct government involvement. It received a royal charter in 1662 but maintained complete independence. The society's secretary described its business to be "in the first place, to scrutinize the whole of Nature and to investigate its activity and powers by means of observations and experiments; and then in course of time to hammer out a more solid philosophy and more ample amenities of civilization." Whether the state was directly involved or not, thinkers of the day now tied science explicitly to social progress.

Because of their exclusion from most universities, women only rarely participated in the new scientific discoveries. In 1667, nonetheless, the English Royal Society invited Margaret Cavendish, a writer of poems, essays, letters, and philosophical treatises, to attend a meeting to watch the exhibition of experiments. She attacked the use of telescopes and microscopes because she detected in the new experimentalism a mechanistic view of the world that exalted masculine prowess and challenged the Christian belief in freedom of the will. She also urged the formal education of women, complaining that "we are kept like birds in cages to hop up and down in our houses." "Many of our Sex may have as much wit, and be capable of Learning as well as men," she insisted, "but since they want Instructions, it is not possible they should attain to it."

Freedom and Order in the Arts

Even though Newtonian science depicted an orderly universe, most artists and intellectuals had experienced enough of the upheavals of the seventeenth century to fear the prospect of chaos and disintegration. The French mathematician Blaise Pascal vividly captured their worries in his *Pensées* ("Thoughts") of 1660: "I look on all sides, and I see only darkness everywhere. Nature presents to me nothing which is not a matter of doubt and concern. . . . It is incomprehensible that God should exist, and incomprehensible that He should not exist." Poets, painters, and architects all tried to make sense of the individual's place within what Pascal called "the eternal silence of these infinite spaces."

Milton. The English Puritan poet John Milton (1608–1674) gave priority to individual liberty. In 1643, in the midst of the civil war between king and Parliament, he published writings in favor of divorce. When Parliament enacted a censorship law aimed at such literature, Milton responded in 1644 with one of the first defenses of freedom of the press, *Areopagitica* ("Tribunal of Opinion"). Milton served as secretary to the Council of State during Cromwell's rule and earned the enmity of Charles II by writing a justification for the execution of his father, Charles I, based on biblical precedents.

In forced retirement and now totally blind, in 1667 Milton published his epic poem *Paradise Lost,* which some have read as a veiled commentary on English affairs. The poet used Adam and Eve's Fall to meditate on human freedom and the tragedies of rebellion. Although Milton wanted to "justify the ways of God to man," his Satan, the proud angel who challenges God, is so compelling as to be heroic. In the end, Adam and Eve learn to accept moral responsibility and face the world "all before them." Individuals learn the limits to their freedom, yet personal liberty remains essential to their definition as human.

The Varieties of Artistic Style. The dominant artistic styles of the time—the baroque and the classical—both submerged the individual in a grander design. The baroque style proved to be especially suitable for public displays of faith and power that overawed individual beholders. The combination of religious and political purposes in baroque art is best exemplified in the architecture and sculpture of Gian Lorenzo Bernini (1598–1680), the papacy's official artist. His architectural masterpiece was the gigantic square facing St. Peter's Basilica in Rome (1656–1671). His use of freestanding open colonnades and a huge open space is meant to impress the individual observer with the power of the popes and the Catholic religion. Bernini also sculpted tombs for the popes and a large statue of Constantine, the first Christian emperor of Rome—perfect examples of the marriage of power and religion.

Gian Lorenzo Bernini,
Ecstasy of St. Teresa of Ávila (c. 1650)
This ultimate statement of baroque sculpture captures all the drama and even sensationalism of a mystical religious faith. Bernini based his figures on a vision reported by St. Teresa in which she saw an angel: "In his hands I saw a great golden spear, and at the iron tip there appeared to be a point of fire. This he plunged into my heart several times so that it penetrated my entrails. When he pulled it out I felt that he took them with it, and left me utterly consumed by the great love of God." Scala/Art Resource, NY.

In 1665, Louis XIV hired Bernini to plan the rebuilding of the Louvre palace in Paris but then rejected his ideas as incompatible with French tastes. The one tangible result of his visit to Paris, a marble bust of Louis XIV, captured the king's strength and dynamism.

Although France was a Catholic country, French painters, sculptors, and architects, like their

French Classicism

In his 1638 painting Moses Saved from the Floods of the Nile, *the French painter Nicolas Poussin sets a biblical story in an antique Roman landscape, with a pyramid serving as the sole reference to Egypt. The austerity and statuesque poses of the figures convey the ideals of classicism rather than the exuberance of the baroque style.*
Giraudon/Art Resource, NY.

patron Louis XIV, preferred the standards of classicism to those of the baroque. French artists developed classicism to be a French national style, distinct from the baroque style that was closely associated with France's enemies, the Austrian and Spanish Habsburgs. As its name suggests, classicism reflected the ideals of the art of antiquity; geometric shapes, order, and harmony of lines took precedence over the sensuous, exuberant, and emotional forms of the baroque. Rather than being overshadowed by the sheer power of emotional display, in classicism the individual could be found at the intersection of converging, symmetrical, straight lines. These influences were apparent in the work of the leading French painters of the period,

Nicolas Poussin (1594–1665) and Claude Lorrain (1600–1682), both of whom worked in Rome and tried to re-create classical Roman values in their mythological scenes and Roman landscapes.

Dutch painters found the baroque and classical styles less suited to their private market, where buyers sought smaller-scale works with ordinary subjects. Dutch artists came from common stock themselves—Rembrandt's father was a miller, and the father of Jan Vermeer (1632–1675) was a silk worker. Their clients were people like themselves who purchased paintings much as they bought tables and chairs. Rembrandt occasionally worked on commission for the prince of Orange but even he painted ordinary people, suffusing his canvases with a radiant, otherworldly light that made the plainest people and objects appear deeply spiritual. Vermeer's best-known paintings show women working at home, and, like Rembrandt, he made ordinary activities seem precious and beautiful. In Dutch art, ordinary individuals had religious and political significance.

Art might also serve the interests of science. One of the most skilled illustrators of insects and flowers was Maria Sibylla Merian (1646–1717), a German-born painter-scholar whose engravings were widely celebrated for their brilliant realism and microscopic clarity. Merian eventually separated from her husband and joined a sect called the Labadists (after their French founder, Jean de Labadie), who did not believe in formal marriage ties and established a colony in the northern Dutch province of Friesland. After moving there with her daughters, Merian went with missionaries from the sect to the Dutch colony of Surinam in South America and painted watercolors of the exotic flowers, birds, and insects she found in the jungle around the cocoa and sugarcane plantations. In the seventeenth century, many women became known for their still-lifes and especially their paintings of flowers. Paintings by the Dutch artist Rachel Ruysch, for example, fetched higher prices than those received by Rembrandt.

Women and Manners

Poetry and painting imaginatively explored the place of the individual within a larger whole, but real-life individuals had to learn to navigate their own social worlds. Manners—the learning of individual self-discipline—were essential skills of social navigation, and women usually took the lead in teaching them. Women's importance in refining social relationships quickly became a subject of controversy.

The Cultivation of Manners. The court had long been a central arena for the development of individual self-discipline. Under the tutelage of their mothers and wives, nobles learned to hide all that was crass and to maintain a fine sense of social distinction. In some ways, aristocratic men were expected to act more like women; just as women had long been expected to please men, now aristocratic men had to please their monarch or patron by displaying proper manners and conversing with ele-

European Fascination with Products of the New World

In this painting of a banana plant, Maria Sybilla Merian offers a scientific study of one of the many exotic plants and animals found by Europeans who traveled to the colonies overseas. Merian was fifty-one when she traveled to the Dutch South American colony of Surinam with her daughter. Courtesy of Hunt Institute for Botanical Documentation, Carnegie Mellon University, Pittsburgh, PA.

gance and wit. Men as well as women had to master the art of pleasing—foreign languages (especially French), dance, a taste for fine music, and attention to dress.

As part of the evolution of new aristocratic ideals, nobles learned to disdain all that was lowly. The upper classes began to reject popular festivals and fairs in favor of private theaters, where seats were relatively expensive and behavior was formal. Clowns and buffoons now seemed vulgar; the last king of England to keep a court fool was Charles I.

Music and the Refinement of Manners
In Emanuel de Witte's Woman at the Clavecin, *the artist celebrates the importance of music in the Dutch home. The woman herself remains a mystery, but the sumptuous setting of heavy curtains, mirrors, and chandeliers signals that clavichord music was associated with refinement.*
The Netherlands Institut of Cultural Heritage, Rijswijk, the Netherlands; Museum Boijmans-Van Beuningen, Rotterdam.

Chivalric romances that had entranced the nobility down to the time of Cervantes's *Don Quixote* (1605) now passed into popular literature.

The greatest French playwright of the seventeenth century, Molière (the pen name of Jean-Baptiste Poquelin, 1622–1673), wrote sparkling comedies of manners that revealed much about the new aristocratic behavior. Son of a tradesman, Molière left law school to form a theater company, which eventually gained the support of Louis XIV. His play *The Middle-Class Gentleman* first performed at the royal court in 1670, revolves around the yearning of a rich, middle-class Frenchman, Monsieur Jourdain, to learn to act like a *gentilhomme* (meaning both "gentleman" and "nobleman" in French). Monsieur Jourdain buys fancy clothes, hires private instructors in dancing, music, fencing, and philosophy, and lends money to a debt-ridden noble in hopes of marrying his daughter to him. Only his sensible wife and his daughter's love for a worthier commoner stand in his way. The

women in the family, including the servant girl Nicole, are reasonable, sincere, and keenly aware of what behavior is appropriate to their social station, whereas Jourdain stands for social ambition gone wild. The message for the court seemed to be a reassuring one: Only true nobles by blood can hope to act like nobles. But the play also showed how the middle classes were learning to emulate the nobility; if one could learn to *act* nobly through self-discipline, could not anyone with some education and money pass himself off as noble?

As Molière's play demonstrated, new attention to manners trickled down from the court to the middle class. A French treatise on manners from 1672 explained:

If everyone is eating from the same dish, you should take care not to put your hand into it before those of higher rank have done so. . . . Formerly one was permitted . . . to dip one's bread into the sauce, provided only that one had not already bitten it.

Nowadays that would be a kind of rusticity. Formerly one was allowed to take from one's mouth what one could not eat and drop it on the floor, provided it was done skillfully. Now that would be very disgusting.

The key words *rusticity* and *disgusting* reveal the association of unacceptable social behavior with the peasantry, dirt, and repulsion. Similar rules now governed spitting and blowing one's nose in public. Ironically, however, once the elite had successfully distinguished itself from the lower classes through manners, scholars became more interested in studying popular expressions. They avidly collected proverbs, folktales, and songs—all of these now curiosities. In fact, many nobles at Louis XIV's court read fairy tales.

Debates about Women's Roles. Courtly manners often permeated the upper reaches of society by means of the *salon*, an informal gathering held regularly in private homes and presided over by a socially eminent woman. In 1661, one French author claimed to have identified 251 Parisian women as hostesses of salons. Although the French government occasionally worried that these gatherings might be seditious, the three main topics of conversation were love, literature, and philosophy. Hostesses often worked hard to encourage the careers of budding authors. Before publishing a manuscript, many authors would read their compositions to a salon gathering. Corneille, Racine, and even Bishop Bossuet sought female approval for their writings.

Some women went beyond encouraging male authors and began to write on their own, but they faced many obstacles. Marie-Madeleine de La Vergne, known as Madame de Lafayette, wrote several short novels that were published anonymously because it was considered inappropriate for aristocratic women to appear in print. Following the publication of *The Princess of Clèves* in 1678, she denied having written it. Hannah Wooley, the English author of many books on domestic conduct, published under the name of her first husband. Women were known for writing wonderful letters (Marie de Sévigné was a prime example), many of which circulated in handwritten form; hardly any appeared in print during their authors' lifetimes. In the 1650s, despite these limitations, French women began to turn out best-sellers in a new type of literature, the

novel. Their success prompted the philosopher Pierre Bayle to remark in 1697 that "our best French novels for a long time have been written by women."

The new importance of women in the world of manners and letters did not sit well with everyone. Although the French writer François Poulain de la Barre (1647–1723), in a series of works published in the 1670s, used the new science to assert the equality of women's minds, most men resisted the idea. Clergy, lawyers, scholars, and playwrights attacked women's growing public influence. Women, they complained, were corrupting forces and needed restraint. Only marriage, "this salutary yoke," could control their passions and weaknesses. Salons drew fire as promoting unrestrained social ambition; women were accused of raising "the banner of prostitution in the salons, in the promenades, and in the streets." Some feared the new manners would make men effeminate: "Thus, the entire nation, formerly full of courage, grows soft and becomes effeminate, and the love of pleasure and money succeeds that of virtue." Molière wrote plays denouncing women's pretension to judge literary merit. English playwrights derided learned women by creating characters with names such as Lady Knowall, Lady Meanwell, and Mrs. Lovewit. A real-life target of the English playwrights was Aphra Behn (1640–1689), one of the first professional woman authors, who supported herself by journalism and wrote plays and poetry. Her short novel *Oroonoko* (1688) told the story of an African prince wrongly sold into slavery. The story was so successful that it was adapted by playwrights and performed repeatedly in England and France for the next hundred years. Behn responded to her critics by demanding that "the privilege for my masculine part, the poet in me" be heard and by arguing that there was "no reason why women should not write as well as men."

Reforming Popular Culture

The illiterate peasants who made up most of Europe's population had little or no knowledge of the law of gravity, upper-class manners, or novels, no matter who authored them. Their culture had three main elements: the knowledge needed to work at farming or in a trade; popular forms of entertainment such as village fairs and dances; and their religion, which shaped every aspect of life and death. What changed most noticeably in the seventeenth century was the social elites' attitude toward lower-class culture. The division between elite and popular culture widened as elites insisted on their difference from the lower orders and tried to instill new forms of discipline in their social inferiors. Historians have learned much of what they know about popular culture from the attempts of elites to change it.

Popular Religion. In the seventeenth century, Protestant and Catholic churches alike pushed hard to change popular religious practices. Their campaigns against popular "paganism" began during the sixteenth-century Protestant Reformation and Catholic Counter-Reformation but reached much of rural Europe only in the seventeenth century. Puritans in England tried to root out maypole dances, Sunday village fairs, gambling, taverns, and bawdy ballads because they interfered with sober observance of the Sabbath. In Lutheran Norway, pastors denounced a widespread belief in the miracle-working powers of St. Olaf. *Superstition* previously meant "false religion" (Protestantism was a superstition for Catholics, Catholicism for Protestants). In the seventeenth century it took on its modern meaning of irrational fears, beliefs, and practices, which anyone educated or refined would avoid. *Superstition* became synonymous with popular or ignorant beliefs.

The Catholic campaign against superstitious practices found a ready ally in Louis XIV. While he reformed the nobles at court through etiquette and manners, Catholic bishops in the French provinces trained parish priests to reform their flocks by using catechisms in local dialects and insisting that parishioners attend Mass. The church faced a formidable challenge. One bishop in France complained in 1671, "Can you believe that there are in this diocese entire villages where no one has even heard of Jesus Christ?" In some places, believers sacrificed animals to the Virgin, prayed to the new moon, and worshiped at the sources of streams as in pre-Christian times.

Like its Protestant counterpart, the Catholic campaign against ignorance and superstition helped extend state power. Clergy, officials, and local police worked together to limit carnival celebrations, to regulate pilgrimages to shrines, and to replace "indecent" images of saints with more restrained and decorous ones. In Catholicism, the cult of the Virgin Mary and devotions closely connected with Jesus, such as the Holy Sacrament and the Sacred Heart, took precedence over the celebration of more popular saints who seemed to have pagan origins or were credited with unverified miracles. Reformers everywhere tried to limit the number of feast days on the grounds that they encouraged lewd behavior.

New Attitudes toward Poverty. The campaign for more disciplined religious practices helped generate a new attitude toward the poor. Poverty previously had been closely linked with charity and virtue in Christianity; it was a Christian duty to give alms to the poor, and Jesus and many of the saints had purposely chosen lives of poverty. In the sixteenth and seventeenth centuries, the upper classes, the church, and the state increasingly regarded the poor as dangerous, deceitful, and lacking in character. "Criminal laziness is the source of all their vices," wrote a Jesuit expert on the poor. The courts had previously expelled beggars from cities; now local leaders, both Catholic and Protestant, tried to reform their character. Municipal magistrates collected taxes for poor relief, and local notables organized charities; together they transformed hospitals into houses of confinement for beggars. In Catholic France, upper-class women's religious associations, known as *confraternities,* set up asylums that confined prostitutes (by arrest if necessary) and rehabilitated them. Confraternities also founded hospices where orphans learned order and respect. Such groups advocated harsh discipline as the cure for poverty.

Although hard times had increased the numbers of poor and the rates of violent crime as well, the most important changes were attitudinal. The elites wanted to separate the very poor from society either to change them or to keep them from contaminating others. Hospitals became holding pens for society's unwanted members, where the poor joined the disabled, the incurably diseased, and the insane. The founding of hospitals demonstrates the connection between these attitudes and state building. In 1676, Louis XIV ordered every French city to establish a hospital, and his government took charge of their finances. Other rulers soon followed the same path.

MAPPING THE WEST **Europe at the End of the Seventeenth Century**
A map can be deceiving. Although Poland-Lithuania looks like a large country on this map, it had been fatally weakened by internal conflicts. In the next century it would disappear entirely. The Ottoman Empire still controlled an extensive territory, but outside of Anatolia its rule depended on intermediaries. The Austrian Habsburgs had pushed the Turks out of Hungary and back into the Balkans. At the other end of the scale, the very small Dutch Republic had become very rich through international commerce. Size did not always prove to be an advantage.

Conclusion

The search for order took place on various levels, from the reform of the disorderly poor to the establishment of more regular bureaucratic routines in government. The biggest factor shaping the search for order was the growth of state power.

Whether absolutist or constitutionalist in form, seventeenth-century states all aimed to penetrate more deeply into the lives of their subjects. They wanted more men for their armed forces, higher taxes to support their projects, and more control over foreign trade, religious dissent, and society's unwanted.

IMPORTANT DATES

1642–1646   Civil war between King Charles I and Parliament in England

1648   Peace of Westphalia ends Thirty Years' War; the Fronde revolt challenges royal authority in France; Ukrainian Cossack warriors rebel against the king of Poland-Lithuania

1649   Execution of Charles I of England; new Russian legal code

1651   Thomas Hobbes publishes *Leviathan*

1660   Monarchy restored in England

1661   Slave code set up in Barbados

1667   Louis XIV begins first of many wars that continue throughout his reign

1670   Molière's play, *The Middle-Class Gentleman*

1678   Marie-Madeline de La Vergne (Madame de Lafayette) anonymously publishes her novel *The Princess of Clèves*

1683   Austrian Habsburgs break the Turkish siege of Vienna

1685   Louis XIV revokes toleration for French Protestants granted by the Edict of Nantes

1687   Isaac Newton publishes *Principia Mathematica*

1688   Parliament deposes James II and invites his daughter, Mary, and her husband, William of Orange, to take the throne

1690   John Locke's *Two Treatises of Government*, *Essay Concerning Human Understanding*

Some tearing had begun to appear, however, in the seamless fabric of state power. In England, the Dutch Republic, and the English North American colonies, property owners successfully demanded constitutional guarantees of their right to participate in government. In the eighteenth century, moreover, new levels of economic growth and the appearance of new social groups would exert pressures on the European state system. The success of seventeenth-century rulers created the political and economic conditions in which their critics would flourish.

Suggested References

Louis XIV: Model of Absolutism

Recent studies have examined Louis XIV's uses of art and imagery for political purposes and have also rightly insisted that absolutism could never be entirely absolute because the king depended on collaboration and cooperation to enforce his policies. Some of the best sources for Louis XIV's reign are the letters written by important noblewomen. The Web site of the Château of Versailles includes views of rooms in the castle.

Beik, William. *Absolutism and Society in Seventeenth-Century France: State Power and Provincial Aristocracy in Languedoc.* 1985.

Burke, Peter. *The Fabrication of Louis XIV.* 1992.

Collins, James B. *The State in Early Modern France.* 1995.

*Forster, Elborg, trans. *A Woman's Life in the Court of the Sun King: Elisabeth Charlotte, Duchesse d'Orléans.* 1984.

Ranum, Oreste. *The Fronde: A French Revolution, 1648–1652.* 1993.

*Sévigné, Madame de. *Selected Letters.* Trans. Leonard Tancock. 1982.

Versailles: http://www.chateauversailles.com.

Absolutism in Central and Eastern Europe

Too often central and eastern European forms of state development have been characterized as backward in comparison with those of western Europe. Now historians emphasize the patterns of ruler-elite cooperation shared with western Europe, but they also underscore the weight of serfdom in eastern economies and political systems.

Barkey, Karen. *The Ottoman Route to State Centralization.* 1994.

Davies, Norman. *God's Playground: A History of Poland.* Vol. 1, *The Origins to 1795.* 1981.

Dukes, Paul. *The Making of Russian Absolutism, 1613–1801.* 1990.

Kivelson, Valerie A. *Autocracy in the Provinces: The Muscovite Gentry and Political Culture in the Seventeenth Century.* 1996.

Vierhaus, Rudolf. *Germany in the Age of Absolutism.* Trans. Jonathan B. Knudsen. 1988.

Wilson, Peter H. *German Armies: War and German Politics, 1648–1806.* 1998.

Constitutionalism in England

Though recent interpretations of the English revolutions emphasize the limits on radical change, Hill's portrayal of the radical ferment of ideas remains fundamental.

Carlin, Norah. *The Causes of the English Civil War.* 1999.

Cust, Richard, and Ann Hughes, eds. *The English Civil War.* 1997.

*Primary sources.

*Graham, Elspeth, et al., eds. *Her Own Life: Autobiographical Writings by Seventeenth-Century English Women.* 1989.

*Haller, William, and Godfrey Davies, eds. *The Leveller Tracts, 1647–1653.* 1944.

Hill, Christopher. *The World Turned Upside Down: Radical Ideas during the English Revolution.* 1972.

Israel, Jonathan, ed. *The Anglo-Dutch Moment: Essays on the Glorious Revolution and Its World Impact.* 1991.

Mack, Phyllis. *Visionary Women: Ecstatic Prophecy in Seventeenth-Century England.* 1992.

Manning, Brian. *Aristocrats, Plebeians, and Revolution in England, 1640–1660.* 1996.

*Pincus, Steven Carl Anthony. *England's Glorious Revolution and the Origins of Liberalism: A Documentary History of Later Stuart England.* 1998.

Constitutionalism in the Dutch Republic and the Overseas Colonies

Studies of the Dutch Republic emphasize the importance of trade and consumerism. Recent work on the colonies has begun to explore the intersecting experiences of settlers, native Americans, and African slaves.

*Campbell, P. F. *Some Early Barbadian History.* 1993.

Delâge, Denys. *Bitter Feast: Amerindians and Europeans in Northeastern North America, 1600–64.* Trans. Jane Brierley. 1993.

*Foster, William C., ed. *The La Salle Expedition to Texas: The Journal of Henri Joutel, 1684–1687.* Trans. Johanna S. Warren. 1998.

Israel, Jonathan. *Dutch Primacy in World Trade, 1585–1740.* 1989.

Merrell, James Hart. *Into the American Woods: Negotiators on the Pennsylvania Frontier.* 1999.

Price, J. L. *The Dutch Republic in the Seventeenth Century.* 1998.

Schama, Simon. *The Embarrassment of Riches: An Interpretation of Dutch Culture in the Golden Age.* 1988.

Thornton, John. *Africa and Africans in the Making of the Atlantic World, 1400–1800.* 1992.

The Search for Order in Elite and Popular Culture

Historians do not always agree about the meaning of popular culture: was it something widely shared by all social classes or a set of activities increasingly identified with the lower classes, as Burke argues? The central Web site for Dutch museums allows the visitor to tour rooms and see paintings in scores of Dutch museums, many of which have important holdings of paintings by Rembrandt and Vermeer. The website on Isaac Newton links to many other sites on his scientific and mathematical discoveries.

Burke, Peter. *Popular Culture in Early Modern Europe.* 1978.

Davis, Natalie Zemon. *Women on the Margins: Three Seventeenth-Century Lives.* 1995.

DeJean, Joan E. *Tender Geographies: Women and the Origins of the Novel in France.* 1991.

Dobbs, Betty Jo Teeter and Margaret C. Jacob. *Newton and the Culture of Newtonianism.* 1994.

Dutch Museums: http://www.hollandmuseums.nl.

Elias, Norbert. *The Civilizing Process: The Development of Manners.* Trans. by Edmund Jephcott. 1978.

*Fitzmaurice, James, ed. *Margaret Cavendish: Sociable Letters.* 1997.

Isaac Newton: http://www.newtonia.freeserve.co.uk.

Todd, Janet M. *The Secret Life of Aphra Behn.* 1997.

CHAPTER

18

The Atlantic System and Its Consequences

1690–1740

J OHANN SEBASTIAN BACH (1685–1750), composer of mighty organ fugues and church cantatas, was not above amusing his Leipzig audiences, many of them university students. In 1732 he produced a cantata about a young woman in love—with coffee. Her old-fashioned father rages that he won't find her a husband unless she gives up the fad. She agrees, secretly vowing to admit no suitor who will not promise in the marriage contract to let her brew coffee whenever she wants. Bach offers this conclusion:

> *The cat won't give up its mouse,*
> *Girls stay faithful coffee-sisters*
> *Mother loves her coffee habit,*
> *Grandma sips it gladly too—*
> *Why then shout at the daughters?*

Bach's era might well be called the age of coffee. European travelers at the end of the sixteenth century had noticed Middle Eastern people drinking a "black drink," *kavah*. Few Europeans sampled it at first, and the Arab monopoly on its production kept prices high. This changed around 1700 when the Dutch East India Company introduced coffee plants to Java and other Indonesian islands. Coffee production then spread to the French Caribbean, where African slaves provided the plantation labor. In Europe, imported coffee spurred the development of a new kind of meeting place: the first coffeehouse opened in London in 1652, and the idea spread quickly to other European cities. The coffeehouses became

London Coffeehouse

This gouache (a variant on watercolor painting) from about 1725 depicts a scene from a London coffeehouse located in the courtyard of the Royal Exchange (merchants' bank). Middle-class men (wearing wigs) read newspapers, drink coffee, smoke pipes, and discuss the news of the day. The coffeehouse draws them out of their homes into a new public space.
British Museum, Bridgeman Art Library, NY.

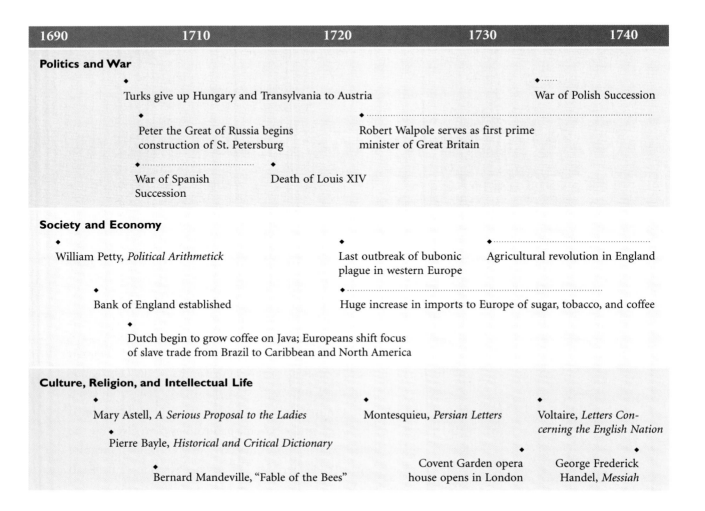

1690	1710	1720	1730	1740

Politics and War

◆ Turks give up Hungary and Transylvania to Austria

◆ War of Polish Succession

◆ Peter the Great of Russia begins construction of St. Petersburg

◆ Robert Walpole serves as first prime minister of Great Britain

◆ War of Spanish Succession

◆ Death of Louis XIV

Society and Economy

◆ William Petty, *Political Arithmetick*

◆ Last outbreak of bubonic plague in western Europe

◆ Agricultural revolution in England

◆ Bank of England established

◆ Huge increase in imports to Europe of sugar, tobacco, and coffee

◆ Dutch begin to grow coffee on Java; Europeans shift focus of slave trade from Brazil to Caribbean and North America

Culture, Religion, and Intellectual Life

◆ Mary Astell, *A Serious Proposal to the Ladies*

◆ Montesquieu, *Persian Letters*

◆ Voltaire, *Letters Concerning the English Nation*

◆ Pierre Bayle, *Historical and Critical Dictionary*

◆ Covent Garden opera house opens in London

◆ George Frederick Handel, *Messiah*

◆ Bernard Mandeville, "Fable of the Bees"

gathering places for men to drink, read newspapers, and talk politics. As a London newspaper commented in 1737, "There's scarce an Alley in City and Suburbs but has a Coffeehouse in it, which may be called the School of Public Spirit, where every Man over Daily and Weekly Journals, a Mug, or a Dram . . . devotes himself to that glorious one, his Country."

European consumption of coffee, tea, chocolate, and other novelties increased dramatically as European nations forged worldwide economic links. At the center of this new world economy was an "Atlantic system" that bound together western Europe, Africa, and the Americas. Europeans bought slaves in western Africa, transported and sold them in their colonies in North and South America and the Caribbean, bought the commodities such as

coffee and sugar that were produced by the new colonial plantations, and then sold the goods in European ports for refining and reshipment. This Atlantic system first took clear shape in the early eighteenth century; it was the hub of European expansion all over the world.

Coffee was one example among many of the new social and cultural patterns that took root between 1690 and 1740. Improvements in agricultural production at home reinforced the effects of trade overseas; Europeans now had more disposable income for "extras," and they spent their money not only in the new coffeehouses and cafés that sprang up all over Europe but also on newspapers, musical concerts, paintings, and novels. A new middle-class public began to make its presence felt in every domain of culture and social life.

Although the rise of the Atlantic system gave Europe new prominence in the global context, European rulers still focused most of their political, diplomatic, and military energies on their rivalries within Europe. A coalition of countries succeeded in containing French aggression, and a more balanced diplomatic system emerged. In eastern Europe, Prussia and Austria had to contend with the rising power of Russia under Peter the Great. In western Europe, both Spain and the Dutch Republic declined in influence but continued to vie with Britain and France for colonial spoils in the Atlantic. The more evenly matched competition among the great powers encouraged the development of diplomatic skills and drew attention to public health as a way of encouraging population growth.

In the aftermath of Louis XIV's revocation of the Edict of Nantes in 1685, a new intellectual movement known as the Enlightenment began to germinate. French Protestant refugees began to publish works critical of absolutism in politics and religion. Increased prosperity, the growth of a middle-class public, and the decline in warfare after Louis XIV's death in 1715 all fostered the development of this new critical spirit. Fed by the popularization of science and the growing interest in travel literature, the Enlightenment encouraged greater skepticism about religious and state authority. Eventually the movement would question almost every aspect of social and political life in Europe. The Enlightenment began in western Europe in those countries—Britain, France, and the Dutch Republic—most affected by the new Atlantic system. It too was a product of the age of coffee.

❖ The Atlantic System and the World Economy

Although their ships had been circling the globe since the early 1500s, Europeans did not draw most of the world into their economic orbit until the 1700s. Western European trading nations sent ships loaded with goods to buy slaves from local rulers on the western coast of Africa; then transported the slaves to the colonies in North and South America and the Caribbean and sold them to the owners of plantations producing coffee, sugar, cotton, and tobacco; and bought the raw commodities produced

in the colonies and shipped them back to Europe, where they were refined or processed and then sold to other parts of Europe and the world. The Atlantic system and the growth of international trade helped create a new consumer society.

Slavery and the Atlantic System

Spain and Portugal had dominated Atlantic trade in the sixteenth and seventeenth centuries, but in the eighteenth century European trade in the Atlantic rapidly expanded and became more systematically interconnected (Map 18.1, inset). By 1630, Portugal had already sent 60,000 African slaves to Brazil to work on the new plantations (large tracts of lands farmed by slave labor), which were producing some 15,000 tons of sugar a year. Realizing that plantations producing staples for Europeans could bring fabulous wealth, the European powers grew less interested in the dwindling trade in precious metals and more eager to colonize. Large-scale planters of sugar, tobacco, and coffee displaced small farmers who relied on one or two servants. Planters and their plantations won out because slave labor was cheap and therefore able to produce mass quantities of commodities at low prices.

State-chartered private companies from Portugal, France, Britain, the Dutch Republic, Prussia, and even Denmark exploited the 3,500-mile coastline of West Africa for slaves. Before 1675, most blacks taken from Africa had been sent to Brazil, but by 1700 half of the African slaves landed in the Caribbean (Figure 18.1). Thereafter, the plantation economy began to expand on the North American mainland. The numbers stagger the imagination. Before 1650, slave traders transported about 7,000 Africans each year across the Atlantic; this rate doubled between 1650 and 1675, nearly doubled again in the next twenty-five years, and kept going until the 1780s (Figure 18.2). In all, more than 11 million Africans, not counting those who died at sea or in Africa, were transported to the Americas before the slave trade began to wind down after 1850. Many traders gained spectacular wealth, but companies did not always make profits. The English Royal African Company, for example, delivered 100,000 slaves to the Caribbean, imported 30,000 tons of sugar to Britain, yet lost money after the few profitable years following its founding in 1672.

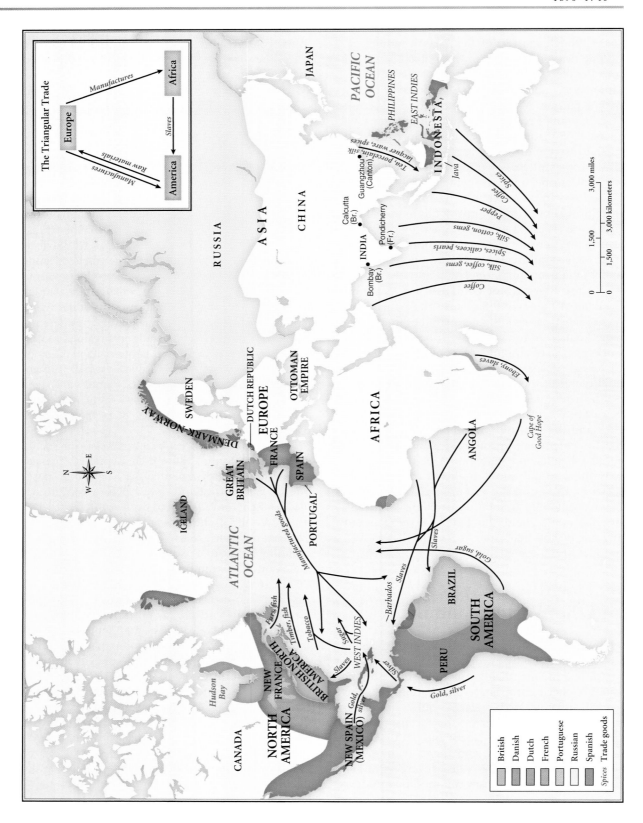

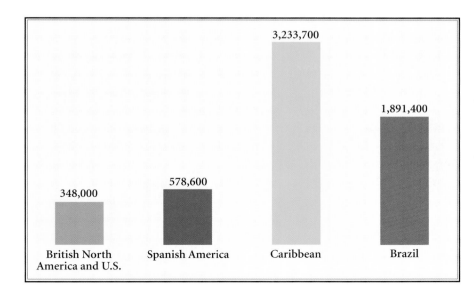

FIGURE 18.1 African Slaves Imported into American Territories, 1701–1810

During the eighteenth century, planters in the newly established Caribbean colonies imported millions of African slaves to work the new plantations that produced sugar, coffee, indigo, and cotton for the European market. The vast majority of African slaves transported to the Americas ended up in either the Caribbean or Brazil. Adapted from Philip D. Curtin, *The Atlantic Slave Trade: A Census* (Madison: University of Wisconsin Press, 1969).

The Life of the Slaves. The balance of white and black populations in the New World colonies was determined by the staples produced. New England merchants and farmers bought few slaves because they did not own plantations. Blacks—both slave and free—made up only 3 percent of the population in eighteenth-century New England, compared with 60 percent in South Carolina. On the whole, the British North American colonies contained a higher proportion of African Americans from 1730 to 1765 than at any other time in American history. The imbalance of whites and blacks was even more extreme in the Caribbean; in the early 1700s, the British sugar islands had a population of about 150,000 people, only 30,000 of them Europeans. The rest were African slaves, as most indigenous people died fighting Europeans or the diseases brought by them.

The slaves suffered terrible experiences. Most had been sold to European traders by Africans from the west coast who acquired them through warfare or kidnapping. The vast majority were between fourteen and thirty-five years old. Before being crammed onto the ships for the three-month trip, their heads were shaved, they were stripped naked, and some were branded with red-hot irons. The men and women were separated and the men shack-led with leg irons. Sailors and officers raped the women whenever they wished and beat those who refused their advances. In the cramped and appalling conditions of the voyage, as many as one-fourth of the slaves died in transit.

Once they landed, slaves were forced into degrading and oppressive conditions. As soon as masters bought slaves, they gave them new names, often only first names, and in some colonies branded them as personal property. Slaves had no social identities of their own; they were expected to learn their master's language and to do any job assigned. Slaves worked fifteen- to seventeen-hour days and were fed only enough to keep them on their feet. Brazilian slaves consumed more calories than the poorest Brazilians do today, but that hardly made them well fed. The manager of a plantation in Barbados insisted in 1711, "It is the greatest misfortune in this island that few planters give [the slaves] . . . a bellyful" of corn. The death rate among slaves was high, especially in Brazil, where quick shifts in the weather, lack of clothing, and squalid living conditions made them susceptible to a variety of deadly illnesses.

Not surprisingly, despite the threat of torture or death on recapture, slaves sometimes ran away. (See

◀ **MAP 18.1 European Trade Patterns, c. 1740**
By 1740, the European powers had colonized much of North and South America and incorporated their colonies there into a worldwide system of commerce centered on the slave trade and plantation production of staple crops. Europeans still sought spices and luxury goods in China and the East Indies, but outside of Java, few Europeans had settled permanently in these areas.

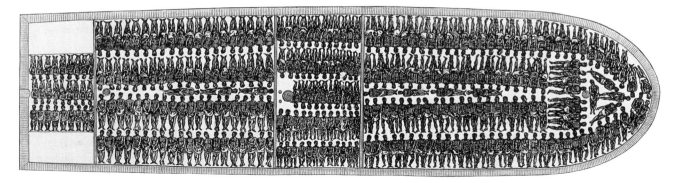

Conditions on Slave Ships

Although the viewer cannot tell if the slaves are lying down or standing, this engraving, inspired by the campaign to abolish slavery, has a clear message: the slaves had to endure crowded conditions on their long passage across the Atlantic. Most slaves (like crew members, who also died in large numbers) fell victim to dysentery, yellow fever, measles, or smallpox; a few committed suicide by jumping overboard. North Wind Picture Archive.

"New Sources, New Perspectives," page 652). In Brazil, runaways hid in *quilombos* (hideouts) in the forests or backcountry. When it was discovered and destroyed in 1695, the *quilombo* of Palmares had thirty thousand fugitives who had formed their own social organization complete with elected kings and councils of elders. Outright revolt was uncommon, especially before the nineteenth century, but other forms of resistance included stealing food, breaking tools, and feigning illness or stupidity. Slaveholders' fears about conspiracy and revolt lurked beneath the surface of every slave-based society. In 1710, the royal governor of Virginia reminded the colonial legislature of the need for unceasing vigilance: "We are not to Depend on Either Their Stupidity, or that Babel of Languages among 'em; freedom Wears a Cap which Can Without a Tongue, Call Togather all Those who Long to Shake off the fetters of Slavery." Masters defended whipping and other forms of physical punishment as essential to maintaining discipline. Laws called for the castration of a slave who struck a white person.

Effects on Europe. Plantation owners often left their colonial possessions in the care of agents and collected the revenue to live as wealthy landowners back home, where they built opulent mansions and gained influence in local and national politics. William Beckford, for example, had been sent from Jamaica to school in England as a young boy. When he inherited sugar plantations and shipping companies from his father and older brother, he moved the headquarters of the family business to London in the 1730s to be close to the government and financial markets. His holdings formed the single most powerful economic interest in Jamaica, but he preferred to live in England where he could collect art for his many luxurious homes, hold political office (he served as lord mayor of London and in Parliament), and even lend money to the government.

The slave trade permanently altered consumption patterns for ordinary people. Sugar had been prescribed as medicine before the end of the sixteenth century, but the development of plantations in Brazil and the Caribbean made it a standard food item. By 1700, the British sent home 50 million pounds of sugar a year, a figure that doubled by 1730. During the French Revolution of the 1790s, sugar shortages would become a cause for rioting in Paris. Equally pervasive was the spread of tobacco; by the 1720s, Britain imported two hundred shiploads of tobacco from Virginia and Maryland every year, and men of every country and class smoked pipes or took snuff.

The Origins of Racism. The traffic in slaves disturbed many Europeans. As a government memorandum to the Spanish king explained in 1610: "Modern theologians in published books commonly report on, and condemn as unjust, the acts of enslavement which take place in provinces of this Royal Empire." Between 1667 and 1671, the French Dominican monk Father Du Tertre published three volumes in which he denounced the mistreatment of slaves in the French colonies.

In the 1700s, however, slaveholders began to justify their actions by demeaning the mental and spiritual qualities of the enslaved Africans. White Europeans and colonists sometimes described black slaves as animal-like, akin to apes. A leading New England Puritan asserted about the slaves: "Indeed their *Stupidity* is a *Discouragement*. It may seem, unto as little purpose, to *Teach,* as to *wash an Aethiopian* [Ethiopian]." One of the great paradoxes of this time was that talk of liberty and self-evident rights, especially prevalent in Britain and its North American colonies, coexisted with the belief that some people were meant to be slaves. Although Christians believed in principle in a kind of spiritual equality between blacks and whites, the churches often defended or at least did not oppose the inequities of slavery.

World Trade and Settlement

The Atlantic system helped extend European trade relations across the globe. The textiles that Atlantic shippers exchanged for slaves on the west coast of Africa, for example, were manufactured in India and exported by the British and French East India Companies. As much as one-quarter of the British exports to Africa in the eighteenth century were actually re-exports from India. To expand its trade in the rest of the world, Europeans seized territories and tried to establish permanent settlements. The eighteenth-century extension of European power prepared the way for western global domination in the nineteenth and twentieth centuries.

The Americas. In contrast to the sparsely inhabited trading outposts in Asia and Africa, the colonies in the Americas bulged with settlers. The British North American colonies, for example, contained about 1.5 million nonnative (that is, white settler and black slave) residents by 1750. While the Spanish competed with the Portuguese for control of South America, the French competed with the British for control of North America. Spanish and

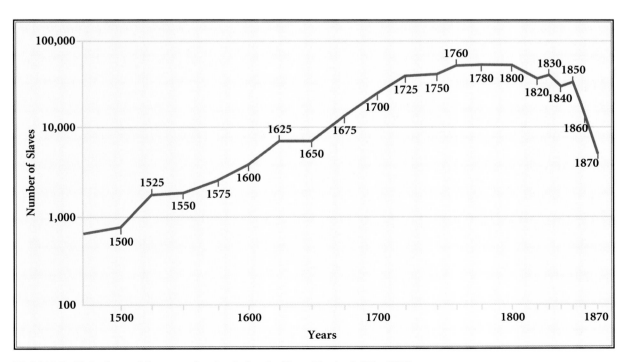

FIGURE 18.2 Annual Imports in the Atlantic Slave Trade, 1450–1870
The importation of slaves to the American territories reached its height in the second half of the eighteenth century and began to decline around 1800. Yet despite the abolition of the slave trade by the British in 1807, commerce in slaves did not seriously diminish until after the revolutions of 1848.
Adapted from Philip D. Curtin, *The Atlantic Slave Trade: A Census* (Madison: University of Wisconsin Press, 1969). Reprinted by permission of the University of Wisconsin Press.

Oral History and the Life of Slaves

Because slaves imported from Africa to the New World did not speak the language of their captors, historians have found it difficult to reconstruct slave life from the point of view of the slaves themselves. Ship records provide information about the number of slaves captured and transported, the deaths on the voyages across the Atlantic, and the prices paid for slaves when they finally arrived. This information comes from the point of view of slave traders, and it says very little about the realities of life on board ship or at the plantations. Scholars have attempted to fill in this blank by using a variety of overlapping sources. The most interesting and controversial of them are oral histories taken from descendants of slaves. In some former slave societies, descendants of slaves still tell stories about their ancestors' first days under slavery. The controversy comes from using twentieth-century memories to get at eighteenth-century lives.

One of the regions most intensively studied in this fashion is Dutch Surinam, on the northeast coast of South America between present-day Guyana and French Guiana. It is a good source of oral histories because 10 percent of the African slaves transported there between the 1680s and the 1750s escaped from the plantations and fled into the nearby rain forests. There they set up their own societies and developed their own language in which they carried on the oral traditions of the first runaway slaves. The twentieth-century descendants of the runaway slaves recount:

In slavery, there was hardly anything to eat. It was at the place called Providence Plantation. They

Slaves of Surinam in the 1770s
John Gabriel Stedman published an account of his participation in a five-year expedition against the runaway slaves of Surinam that took place in the 1770s. He provided drawings such as the one reproduced here, which shows Africans who have just come off a slave ship.
Schomburg Center for Research in Black Culture/New York Public Library.

whipped you there till your ass was burning. Then they would give you a bit of plain rice in a calabash [a bowl made from the tropical American tree known as calabash]. . . . And the gods told them that this is no way for human beings to live. They would help them. Let each person go where he could. So they ran.

British settlers came to blows over the boundary between the British colonies and Florida, which was Spanish.

Local economies shaped colonial social relations; men in French trapper communities in Canada, for example, had little in common with the men and women of the plantation societies in Barbados or Brazil. Racial attitudes also differed from place to place. The Spanish and Portuguese tolerated intermarriage with the native populations in both America and Asia. Sexual contact, both inside and outside marriage, fostered greater racial variety in the Span-

From other sources, historians have learned that there was a major slave rebellion at Providence Plantation in 1693.

By comparing such oral histories to written accounts of plantation owners, missionaries, and Dutch colonial officials, historians have been able to paint a more richly detailed picture not only of slavery but also of runaway slave societies, which were especially numerous in South America. At the end of the eighteenth century, a Portuguese-speaking Jew wrote his own history of plantation life based on records from the local Jewish community that are now lost. Because the Dutch, unlike most other Europeans, allowed Jews to own slaves, Portuguese-speaking Jews from Brazil owned about one-third of the plantations and slaves in Surinam. This eighteenth-century chronicler, David de Ishak Cohen Nassy, wrote his version of Surinam's first slave revolt:

> There was in the year 1690 a revolt on a plantation situated on the Cassewinica Creek, behind Jews Savannah, belonging to a Jew named Imanuël Machado, where, having killed their master, they fled, carrying away with them everything that was there. . . . The Jews . . . in an expedition which they undertook against the rebels, killed many of them and brought back several who were punished by death on the very spot.

The oral histories told about the revolt from the runaway slaves' perspective:

> There had been a great council meeting [of runaway slaves] in the forest. . . . They decided to burn a different one of his plantations from the place where he had whipped Lanu [one of the runaway slaves] because they would find more tools there. This was the Cassewinica Plantation, which had many slaves. They knew all about this plantation from slavery times. So, they attacked.

> It was at night. They killed the head of the plantation, a white man. They took all the things, everything they needed.

The runaway slaves saw the attack as part of their ongoing effort to build a life in the rain forest, away from the whites.

Over the next decades, the runaway slaves fought a constant series of battles with plantation owners and Dutch officials. Finally in 1762, the Dutch granted the runaway slaves their freedom in a peace agreement; offered them tools, gunpowder, and other necessities; and allowed them to trade in the main town of the colony in exchange for agreeing to return all future runaways. The runaways had not destroyed the slave system, but they had gained their own independence alongside it. From their oral histories it is possible to retrace their efforts to build new lives in a strange place, in which they combined African practices with New World experiences.

Source: Richard Price, *Alabi's World* (Baltimore: Johns Hopkins University Press, 1990), 17, 9.

QUESTIONS FOR DEBATE

1. What did runaway slaves aim to accomplish when they attacked plantations?
2. Why would runaway slaves make an agreement with the Dutch colonial officials to return future runaways?
3. Can oral histories recorded in the twentieth century be considered accurate versions of events that took place in the eighteenth century? How can they be tested?

FURTHER READING

Richard Price, *Alabi's World.* 1990.

John Gabriel Stedman, *Narrative of a Five Years' Expedition Against the Revolted Negroes of Surinam*, edited, and with an introduction and notes, by Richard Price and Sally Price. 1988.

ish and Portuguese colonies than in the French or the English territories (though mixed-race people could be found everywhere). By 1800, *mestizos*, children of Spanish men and Indian women, accounted for more than a quarter of the population in the Spanish colonies, and many of them aspired to join the local elite. Greater racial diversity seems not to have improved the treatment of slaves, however, which was probably harshest in Portuguese Brazil.

Where intermarriage between colonizers and natives was common, conversion to Christianity proved most successful. Although the Indians

India Cottons and Trade with the East
This brightly colored cotton cloth was painted and embroidered in Madras in southern India sometime in the late 1600s. The male figure with a mustache may be a European, but the female figures are clearly Asian. Europeans—especially the British—discovered that they could make big profits on the export of Indian cotton cloth to Europe. They also traded Indian cottons in Africa for slaves and sold large quantities in the colonies.
Victoria and Albert Museum, London.

maintained many of their native religious beliefs, many Indians in the Spanish colonies had come to consider themselves devout Catholics by 1700. Indian carpenters and artisans in the villages produced innumerable altars, retables (painted panels), and sculpted images to adorn their local churches, and individual families put up domestic shrines. Yet the clergy remained overwhelmingly Spanish: the church hierarchy concluded that the Indians' humility and innocence made them unsuitable for the priesthood.

In the early years of American colonization, many more men than women emigrated from Europe. Although the sex imbalance began to decline at the end of the seventeenth century, it remained substantial; two and one-half times as many men as women were among the immigrants leaving Liverpool, England, between 1697 and 1707, for example. Women who emigrated as indentured servants ran great risks: if they did not die of disease during the voyage, they might end up giving birth to illegitimate children (the fate of at least one in five servant women) or being virtually sold into marriage. Many upper-class women were kept in seclusion, especially in the Spanish and Portuguese colonies.

The uncertainties of life in the American colonies provided new opportunities for European women and men willing to live outside the law,

however. In the 1500s and 1600s, the English and Dutch governments had routinely authorized pirates to prey on the shipping of their rivals, the Spanish and Portuguese. Then, in the late 1600s, English, French, and Dutch bands made up of deserters and crews from wrecked vessels began to form their own associations of pirates, especially in the Caribbean. Called *buccaneers* from their custom of curing strips of beef, called *boucan* by the native Caribs of the islands, the pirates governed themselves and preyed on everyone's shipping without regard to national origin. In 1720, the trial of buccaneers associated with Calico Jack Rackham in Jamaica revealed that two women had dressed as men and joined the pirates in looting and plundering English ships. Mary Read and Anne Bonny escaped death by hanging only because they were pregnant. After 1700, the colonial governments tried to stamp out piracy. As one British judge argued in 1705, "A pirate is in perpetual war with every individual and every state. . . . They are worse than ravenous beasts."

Africa and Asia.   White settlements in Africa and Asia remained small and almost insignificant, except for their long-term potential. Europeans had little contact with East Africa and almost none with the continent's vast interior. A few Portuguese trading posts in Angola and Dutch farms on the Cape of Good Hope provided the only toeholds for future expansion. In China the emperors had welcomed Catholic missionaries at court in the seventeenth century, but the priests' credibility diminished as they squabbled among themselves and associated with European merchants, whom the Chinese considered pirates. "The barbarians [Europeans] are like wild beasts," one Chinese official concluded, "and are not to be ruled on the same principles as citizens." In 1720, only one thousand Europeans resided in Guangzhou (Canton), the sole place where foreigners could legally trade for spices, tea, and silk.

Europeans exercised more influence in Java in the East Indies and in India. Dutch coffee production in Java and nearby islands increased phenomenally in the early 1700s, and many Dutch settled there to oversee production and trade. In India, Dutch, English, French, Portuguese, and Danish companies competed for spices, cotton, and silk; by the 1740s the English and French had become the leading rivals in India, just as they were in North America. Both countries extended their power as India's Muslim rulers lost control to local Hindu princes, rebellious Sikhs, invading Persians, and their own provincial governors. A few thousand Europeans lived in India, though many thousand more soldiers were stationed there to protect them. The staple of trade with India in the early 1700s was calico—lightweight, brightly colored cotton cloth that caught on as a fashion in Europe.

Europeans who visited India were especially struck by what they viewed as exotic religious practices. In a book published in 1696 of his travels to western India, an Anglican minister described the fakirs (religious mendicants or beggars of alms), "some of whom show their devotion by a shameless appearance, walking naked, without the least rag of clothes to cover them." Such writings increased European interest in the outside world but also fed a European sense of superiority that helped excuse the more violent forms of colonial domination.

The Birth of Consumer Society

Worldwide colonization produced new supplies of goods, from coffee to calico, and population growth in Europe fueled demand for them. Beginning first in Britain, then in France and the Italian states,

and finally in eastern Europe, population surged, growing by about 20 percent between 1700 and 1750. The gap between a fast-growing northwest and a more stagnant south and central Europe now diminished, as regions that had lost population during the seventeenth-century downturn recovered. Cities, in particular, grew. Between 1600 and 1750, London's population more than tripled, and Paris's more than doubled.

Although contemporaries could not have realized it then, this was the start of the modern "population explosion." It appears that a decline in the death rate, rather than a rise in the birthrate, explains the turnaround. Three main factors contributed to this decline in the death rate: better

The Exotic as Consumer Item
In this painting by the Venetian woman Rosalba Carriera (1675–1757), Africa *(the title of the work) is represented by a young black girl wearing a turban. Carriera was known for her use of pastels. In 1720, she journeyed to Paris where she became an associate of Antoine Watteau and helped inaugurate the rococo style in painting.*
Staatliche Kunstsammlungen Dresden, Gemaldegalerie Alte Meister.

weather and hence more bountiful harvests, improved agricultural techniques, and the plague's disappearance after 1720.

By the early eighteenth century, the effects of economic expansion and population growth brought about a consumer revolution. The British East India Company began to import into Britain huge quantities of calicoes. British imports of tobacco doubled between 1672 and 1700; at Nantes, the center of the French sugar trade, imports quadrupled between 1698 and 1733. Tea, chocolate, and coffee became virtual necessities. In the 1670s, only a trickle of tea reached London, but by 1720 the East India Company sent 9 million pounds to England—a figure that rose to 37 million pounds by 1750. By 1700, England had two thousand coffeehouses; by 1740, every English country town had at least two. Paris got its first cafés at the end of the seventeenth century; Berlin opened its first coffeehouse in 1714; Bach's Leipzig boasted eight by 1725.

The birth of consumer society did not go unnoticed by eye witnesses. In the English economic literature of the 1690s, writers began to express a new view of humans as consuming animals with boundless appetites. Such opinions gained a wide audience with the appearance of Bernard Mandeville's poem "Fable of the Bees" (1705), which argued that private vices might have public benefits. In the poem a hive of bees abolishes evil in its society, only to discover that the society has also disappeared. Mandeville insisted that pride, self-interest, and the desire for material goods (all Christian vices) in fact promoted economic prosperity: "every part was full of Vice, Yet the whole mass a Paradise." Many authors attacked the new doctrine of consumerism, and the French government banned the poem's publication. But Mandeville had captured the essence of the emerging market for consumption.

❖ New Social and Cultural Patterns

The impact of the Atlantic system and world trade was most apparent in the cities, where people had more money for consumer goods. But rural changes also had significant long-term influence, as a revolution in agricultural techniques made it possible to feed more and more people with a smaller agricultural workforce. As population increased, more people moved to the cities, where they found themselves caught up in innovative urban customs such as attending musical concerts and reading novels. Along

Agricultural Revolution
This English painting of a manor in Gloucestershire from about 1730 demonstrates the concrete effects of the agricultural revolution. Fields are enclosed as far as the eye can see, and large groups of men and women work together to farm the consolidated plots of land owned by the wealthy local landlord. The individual peasant family working its own small plot of land has disappeared in favor of a new and more hierarchical labor structure.
Cheltenham Art Gallery & Museums, Gloucestershire. Bridgeman Art Library, NY.

with a general increase in literacy, these activities helped create a public that responded to new writers and artists. Social and cultural changes were not uniform across Europe, however; as usual, people's experiences varied depending on whether they lived in wealth or poverty, in urban or rural areas, or in eastern or western Europe.

Agricultural Revolution

Although Britain, France, and the Dutch Republic shared the enthusiasm for consumer goods, Britain's domestic market grew most quickly. In Britain, as agricultural output increased 43 percent over the course of the 1700s, the population increased by 70 percent. The British imported grain to feed the growing population, but they also benefited from the development of techniques that together constituted an agricultural revolution. No new machinery propelled this revolution—just more aggressive attitudes toward investment and management. The Dutch and the Flemish had pioneered many of these techniques in the 1600s, but the British took them further.

Four major changes occurred in British agriculture that eventually spread to other countries. First, farmers increased the amount of land under cultivation by draining wetlands and by growing crops on previously uncultivated common lands (acreage maintained by the community for grazing). Second, those farmers who could afford it consolidated smaller, scattered plots into larger, more efficient units. Third, livestock raising became more closely linked to crop growing, and the yields of each increased. (See "Taking Measure," opposite.) For centuries, most farmers had rotated their fields in and out of production to replenish the soil. Now farmers planted carefully chosen fodder crops such as clover and turnips that added nutrients to the soil, thereby eliminating the need to leave a field fallow (unplanted) every two or three years. With more fodder available, farmers could raise more livestock, which in turn produced more manure to fertilize grain fields. Fourth, selective breeding of animals combined with the increase in fodder to improve the quality and size of herds. New crops had only a slight impact; potatoes, for example, were introduced to Europe from South America in the 1500s, but because people feared they might cause leprosy, tuberculosis, or fevers, they were not grown in quantity until the late 1700s. By the 1730s and 1740s,

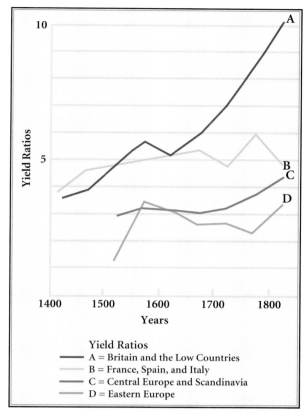

TAKING MEASURE Relationship of Crop Harvested to Seed Used, 1400–1800
The impact and even the timing of the agricultural revolution can be determined by this figure, based on yield ratios (the number of grains produced for each seed planted). Britain, the Dutch Republic, and the Austrian Netherlands all experienced huge increases in crop yields after 1700. Other European regions lagged behind right into the 1800s.
From Peter J. Hugill, *World Trade since 1431: Geography, Technology, and Capitalism* (Johns Hopkins University Press, 1995), p. 56. Reprinted by permission of Johns Hopkins University Press.

agricultural output had increased dramatically, and prices for food had fallen because of these interconnected innovations.

Changes in agricultural practices did not benefit all landowners equally. The biggest British landowners consolidated their holdings in the "enclosure movement." They put pressure on small farmers and villagers to sell their land or give up their common lands. The big landlords then fenced off ("enclosed") their property. Because enclosure eliminated community grazing rights, it frequently sparked a struggle between the big landlords and villagers, and in Britain it normally required an act of Parliament. Such acts became increasingly common in the second half of the eighteenth century, and by the century's end six million acres of common lands had been enclosed and developed. "Improvers" produced more food more efficiently and thus supported a growing population.

Contrary to the fears of contemporaries, small farmers and cottagers (those with little or no property) were not forced off the land all at once. But most villagers could not afford the litigation involved in resisting enclosure, and small landholders consequently had to sell out to landlords or farmers with larger plots. Landlords with large holdings leased their estates to tenant farmers at constantly increasing rents, and the tenant farmers in turn employed the cottagers as salaried agricultural workers. In this way the English peasantry largely disappeared, replaced by a more hierarchical society of big landlords, enterprising tenant farmers, and poor agricultural laborers.

The new agricultural techniques spread slowly from Britain and the Low Countries (the Dutch Republic and the Austrian Netherlands) to the rest of western Europe. Outside a few pockets in northern France and the western German states, however, subsistence agriculture (producing just enough to get by rather than surpluses for the market) continued to dominate farming in western Europe and Scandinavia. In southwestern Germany, for example, 80 percent of the peasants produced no surplus because their plots were too small. Unlike the populations of the highly urbanized Low Countries (where half the people lived in towns and cities), most Europeans, western and eastern, eked out their existence in the countryside.

In eastern Europe, the condition of peasants worsened in the areas where landlords tried hardest to improve their yields. To produce more for the Baltic grain market, aristocratic landholders in Prussia, Poland, and parts of Russia drained wetlands, cultivated moors, and built dikes. They also forced peasants off lands the peasants worked for themselves, increased compulsory labor services (the critical element in serfdom), and began to manage their estates directly. Some eastern landowners grew fabulously wealthy. The Potocki family in the Polish Ukraine, for example, owned three million

Treatment of Serfs in Russia

Visitors from western Europe often remarked on the cruel treatment of serfs in Russia. This drawing by one such visitor shows the punishment that could be inflicted by landowners. Serfs could be whipped for almost any reason, even for making a soup too salty or neglecting to bow when the lord's family passed by. Their condition actually deteriorated in the 1700s, as landowners began to sell serfs much like slaves. New decrees made it illegal for serfs to contract loans, enter into leases, or work for anyone other than their lord. Some landlords kept harems of serf girls. Although the Russian landlords' treatment of serfs was even more brutal than that in the German states and Poland, upper classes in every country regarded the serfs as dirty, deceitful, brutish, and superstitious.
New York Public Library Slavonic Division.

acres of land and had 130,000 serfs. The Eszterházy family of Hungary owned seven million acres; and the Lithuanian magnate Karol Radziwill controlled six hundred villages. In parts of Poland and Russia the serfs hardly differed from slaves in status, and their "masters" ran their huge estates much like American plantations.

Social Life in the Cities

Because of emigration from the countryside, cities grew in population and consequently exercised more influence on culture and social life. Between 1650 and 1750, cities with at least ten thousand inhabitants increased in population by 44 percent. From the eighteenth century onward, urban growth would be continuous. Along with the general growth of cities, an important south-to-north shift occurred in the pattern of urbanization. Around 1500, half of the people in cities of at least ten thousand residents could be found in the Italian states, Spain, or Portugal; by 1700, the urbanization of northwestern and southern Europe was roughly equal. Eastern Europe, despite the huge cities of Istanbul and Moscow, was still less urban than western Europe. London was by far the most populous European city, with 675,000 inhabitants in 1750; Berlin had 90,000 people, Warsaw only 23,000.

Urban Social Classes. Many landowners kept a residence in town, so the separation between rural and city life was not as extreme as might be imagined, at least not for the very rich. At the top of the ladder in the big cities were the landed nobles. Some of them filled their lives only with conspicuous consumption of fine food, extravagant clothing, coaches, books, and opera; others held key political, administrative, or judicial offices. However they spent their time, these rich families employed thousands of artisans, shopkeepers, and domestic servants. Many English peers (highest-ranking nobles) had thirty or forty servants at each of their homes.

The middle classes of officials, merchants, professionals, and landowners occupied the next rung down on the social ladder. London's population, for example, included about 20,000 middle-class families (constituting, at most, one-sixth of the city's population). In this period the middle classes began to develop distinctive ways of life that set them apart from both the rich noble landowners and the lower classes. Unlike the rich nobles, the middle classes lived primarily in the cities and towns, even if they owned small country estates. They ate more moderately than nobles but much better than peasants or laborers. For breakfast the British middle classes ate toast and rolls and, after 1700, drank tea. Dinner, served midday, consisted of roasted or boiled beef or mutton, poultry or pork, and vegetables. Supper was a light meal of bread and cheese with cake or pie. Beer was the main drink in London, and many families brewed their own. Even children drank beer because of the lack of fresh water.

In contrast to the gigantic and sprawling country seats of the richest English peers, middle-class houses in town had about seven rooms, including four or five bedrooms and one or two living rooms, still many more than the poor agricultural worker. New household items reflected society's increasing wealth and its exposure to colonial imports: by 1700, the middle classes of London typically had mirrors in every room, a coffeepot and coffee mill, numerous pictures and ornaments, a china collection, and several clocks. Life for the middle classes on the continent was quite similar, though wine replaced beer in France.

Below the middle classes came the artisans and shopkeepers (most of whom were organized in professional guilds), then the journeymen, apprentices, servants, and laborers. At the bottom of the social scale were the unemployed poor, who survived by intermittent work and charity. Women married to artisans and shopkeepers often kept the accounts, supervised employees, and ran the household as well. Every household from the middle classes to the upper classes employed servants; artisans and shopkeepers frequently hired them too. Women from poorer families usually worked as domestic servants until they married. Four out of five domestic servants in the city were female. In large cities such as London, the servant population grew faster than the population of the city as a whole.

Signs of Social Distinction. Social status in the cities was readily visible. Wide, spacious streets graced rich districts; the houses had gardens and the air was relatively fresh. In poor districts the streets were narrow, dirty, dark, humid, and smelly, and the houses were damp and crowded. The poorest people were homeless, sleeping under bridges or in abandoned homes. A Neapolitan prince described his homeless neighbors as "lying like filthy animals, with no distinction of age or sex." In some districts, rich and poor lived in the same buildings, with the poor having to clamber to the shabby, cramped apartments on the top floors.

Like shelter, clothing was a reliable social indicator. The poorest workingwomen in Paris wore woolen skirts and blouses of dark colors over petticoats, bodice, and corset. They also donned caps of various sorts, cotton stockings, and shoes (probably their only pair). Workingmen dressed even more drably. Many occupations could be recognized by their dress: no one could confuse lawyers in their dark robes with masons or butchers in their special

The Seedy Side of City Life

The English painter and engraver William Hogarth chronicled every aspect of social life in London. In Night (1738), he completes a cycle of engravings about greed and carelessness in city life. The Salisbury Flying Coach has overturned in Charing Cross Road, narrowly missing a bonfire. Despite the statue of King Charles I in the background, this is a sordid street filled with taverns, a quack pulling teeth, and urchins up to no good. About to be showered with the contents of a chamber pot is a drunken magistrate known for his anti-alcohol legislation. He is oblivious to the ills of the city that surround him, but Hogarth knew them well.
Carole Frohlich Archive.

aprons, for example. People higher on the social ladder were more likely to sport a variety of fabrics, colors, and unusual designs in their clothing and to own many different outfits. Social status was not an abstract idea; it permeated every detail of daily life.

The Growth of a Literate Public

The ability to read and write also reflected social differences. People in the upper classes were more literate than those in the lower classes; city people were more literate than peasants. Protestant countries appear to have been more successful at promoting education and literacy than Catholic

countries, perhaps because of the Protestant emphasis on Bible reading. Widespread popular literacy was first achieved in the Protestant areas of Switzerland and in Presbyterian Scotland, and rates were also very high in the New England colonies and the Scandinavian countries. In France, literacy doubled in the eighteenth century thanks to the spread of parish schools, but still only one in two men and one in four women could read and write. Despite the efforts of some Protestant German states to encourage primary education, primary schooling remained woefully inadequate almost everywhere in Europe: few schools existed, teachers received low wages, and no country had yet established a national system of control or supervision.

Despite the deficiencies of primary education, a new literate public arose especially among the middle classes of the cities. More books and periodicals were published than ever before. Britain and the Dutch Republic led the way in this powerful outpouring of printed words. The trend began in the 1690s and gradually accelerated. In 1695, the British government allowed the licensing system, through which it controlled publications, to lapse, and new newspapers and magazines appeared almost immediately. The first London daily newspaper came out in 1702, and in 1709 Joseph Addison and Richard Steele published the first literary magazine, *The Spectator*. They devoted their magazine to the cultural improvement of the increasingly influential middle class. By the 1720s, twenty-four provincial newspapers were published in England, and by the 1730s the new *Gentleman's Magazine*, a kind of *Reader's Digest* of news, literature, and humor, enjoyed a large national circulation. In the London coffeehouses, an edition of a single newspaper might reach ten thousand male readers. Women did their reading at home. Newspapers on the continent lagged behind and often consisted mainly of advertising with little critical commentary. France, for example, had no daily paper until 1777.

New Tastes in the Arts

The new literate public did not just read newspapers; its members now pursued an interest in painting, attended concerts, and besieged booksellers in search of popular novels. Because increased trade and prosperity put money into the hands of the growing middle classes, a new urban audience began to compete with the churches, rulers, and courtiers as chief patrons for new work. As the public for the arts expanded, printed commentary on them emerged, setting the stage for the appearance of political and social criticism. New artistic tastes thus had effects far beyond the realm of the arts.

Rococo Painting. Developments in painting reflected the tastes of the new public, as the rococo style challenged the hold of the baroque and classical schools, especially in France. Like the baroque, the rococo emphasized irregularity and asymmetry, movement and curvature, but it did so on a much smaller, subtler scale. Many rococo paintings depicted scenes of intimate sensuality rather than the monumental, emotional grandeur favored by classical and baroque painters. Personal portraits and pastoral paintings took the place of heroic landscapes and grand, ceremonial canvases. Rococo

paintings adorned homes as well as palaces and served as a form of interior decoration rather than as a statement of piety. Its decorative quality made rococo art an ideal complement to newly discovered materials such as stucco and porcelain, especially the porcelain vases now imported from China.

Rococo, like *baroque,* was an invented word (from the French word *rocaille,* meaning "shellwork") and originally a derogatory label, meaning "frivolous decoration." But the great French rococo painters, such as Antoine Watteau (1684–1721) and François Boucher (1703–1770), were much more than mere decorators. Although both emphasized the erotic in their depictions, Watteau captured the melancholy side of a passing aristocratic style of life, and Boucher painted middle-class people at home during their daily activities. Both painters thereby contributed to the emergence of new sensibilities in art that increasingly attracted a middle-class public.

Rococo Painting
Painted originally as a shop sign for an art merchant, Gersaint's Shopsign *(1721) by Antoine Watteau demonstrates the new rococo style. The colors are muted and the atmosphere is light and airy. The subject matter—the sale of art, gilded mirrors, and toiletries to the new urban aristocrats and middle classes—is entirely secular and even commercial. The canvas reflects the new urban market for art and slyly notes the passing of a era: a portrait of the recently deceased Louis XIV is being packed away on the left-hand side of the painting. Watteau painted the sign in eight days while suffering from the tuberculosis that would kill him just a few months later.*
Erich Lessing/Art Resource, NY.

Music for the Public.   The first public music concerts were performed in England in the 1670s, becoming much more regular and frequent in the 1690s. City concert halls typically seated about two hundred, but the relatively high price of tickets limited attendance to the better-off. Music clubs provided entertainment in smaller towns and villages. On the continent, Frankfurt organized the first regular public concerts in 1712; Hamburg and Paris began holding them within a few years. Opera continued to spread in the eighteenth century; Venice had sixteen public opera houses by 1700, and in 1732 Covent Garden opera house opened in London.

The growth of a public that appreciated and supported music had much the same effect as the extension of the reading public: like authors, composers could now begin to liberate themselves from court patronage and work for a paying audience. This development took time to solidify, however, and court or church patrons still commissioned much eighteenth-century music. Bach, a German Lutheran, wrote his *St. Matthew Passion* for Good Friday services in 1729 while he was organist and choirmaster for the leading church in Leipzig. He composed secular works (like the "Coffee Cantata") for the public and a variety of private patrons.

The composer George Frederick Handel (1685–1759) was among the first to grasp the new directions in music. He began his career playing second violin in the Hamburg opera orchestra and then moved to Britain in 1710. After distinguishing himself with operas and music composed for the British court, he turned to composing oratorios, a form he introduced in Britain. The oratorio combined the drama of opera with the majesty of religious and ceremonial music and featured the chorus over the soloists. Handel's most famous oratorio, *Messiah* (1741), reflected his personal, deeply felt piety but also his willingness to combine musical materials into a dramatic form that captured the enthusiasm of the new public. In 1740, a poem published in the *Gentleman's Magazine* exulted: "His art so modulates the sounds in all, / Our passions, as he pleases, rise and fall." Music had become an integral part of the new middle-class public's culture.

Novels.   Nothing captured the imagination of the new public more than the novel, the literary genre whose very name underscored the eighteenth-century taste for novelty. Over three hundred French novels appeared between 1700 and 1730. During this unprecedented explosion, the novel took on its modern form and became more concerned with individual psychology and social description than with the picaresque adventures popular earlier (such as Cervantes's *Don Quixote*). The novel's popularity was closely tied to the expansion of the reading public, and novels were available in serial form in periodicals or from the many booksellers who popped up to serve the new market.

Women figured prominently in novels as characters, and women writers abounded. The English novel *Love in Excess* (1719) quickly reached a sixth printing, and its author, Eliza Haywood (1693?–1756), earned her living turning out a stream of novels with titles such as *Persecuted Virtue*, *Constancy Rewarded*, and *The History of Betsy Thoughtless*—all showing a concern for the proper place of women as models of virtue in a changing world. Heywood had first worked as an actress when her husband deserted her and her two children, but she soon turned to writing plays and novels. In the 1740s, she began publishing a magazine, *The Female Spectator*, which argued in favor of higher education for women.

Haywood's male counterpart was Daniel Defoe (1660?–1731), a merchant's son who had a diverse and colorful career as a manufacturer, political spy, novelist, and social commentator. Defoe wrote about schemes for national improvement, the state of English trade, the economic condition of the countryside, the effects of the plague, and the history of pirates, as well as such novels as *Robinson Crusoe* (1719) and *Moll Flanders* (1722). The story of the adventures of a shipwrecked sailor, *Robinson Crusoe* portrayed the new values of the time: to survive, Crusoe had to meet every challenge with fearless entrepreneurial ingenuity. He had to be ready for the unexpected and be able to improvise in every situation. He was, in short, the model for the new man in an expanding economy. Crusoe's patronizing attitude toward the black man Friday now draws much critical attention, but his discovery of Friday shows how the fate of blacks and whites had become intertwined in the new colonial environment.

Religious Revivals

Despite the novel's growing popularity, religious books and pamphlets still sold in huge numbers, and most Europeans remained devout, even as their religions were changing. In this period a Protestant revival known as Pietism rocked the complacency of the established churches in the German Lutheran states, the Dutch Republic, and Scandinavia. Pietists believed in a mystical religion of the heart; they wanted a more deeply emotional, even ecstatic religion. They urged intense Bible study, which in turn promoted popular education and contributed to the increase in literacy. Many Pietists attended catechism instruction every day and also went to morning and evening prayer meetings in addition to regular Sunday services.

As a grassroots movement, Pietism appealed to both Lutherans and Calvinists, some of whom left their churches to form new sects. One of the most remarkable disciples of Pietism was the English woman Jane Leade (1623–1704), who founded the sect of Philadelphians (from the Greek for "brotherly love"), which soon spread to the Dutch Republic and the German states. Leade's visions and studies of mysticism led her to advocate a universal, nondogmatic church that would include all reborn Christians. Philadelphic societies maintained only loose ties to one another, however, and despite Leade's organizational aims they soon went off in different directions.

Catholicism also had its versions of religious revival, especially in France. A French woman, Jeanne Marie Guyon (1648–1717), attracted many noblewomen and a few leading clergymen to her own Catholic brand of Pietism, known as Quietism. Claiming miraculous visions and astounding prophecies, she urged a mystical union with God through prayer and simple devotion. Despite papal condemnation and intense controversy within Catholic circles in France, Guyon had followers all over Europe.

Even more influential were the Jansenists, who gained many new adherents to their austere form of Catholicism despite Louis XIV's harassment and repeated condemnation by the papacy. Under the pressure of religious and political persecution, Jansenism took a revivalist turn in the 1720s. At the funeral of a Jansenist priest in Paris in 1727, the crowd who flocked to the grave claimed to witness a series of miraculous healings. Within a few years a cult formed around the priest's tomb, and clandestine Jansenist presses reported new miracles to the reading public. When the French government tried to suppress the cult, one enraged wit placed a

sign at the tomb that read, "By order of the king, God is forbidden to work miracles here." Some believers fell into frenzied convulsions, claiming to be inspired by the Holy Spirit through the intercession of the dead priest. Although the Catholic church, the French state, and even some Jansenists ultimately repudiated the new cult, its remarkable emotional power showed that popular expressions of religion could not be easily contained. After midcentury, Jansenism became even more politically active as its adherents joined in opposition to crown policies on religion.

❖ Consolidation of the European State System

The spread of Pietism and Jansenism reflected the emergence of a middle-class public that now participated in every new development, including religion. The middle classes could pursue these interests because the European state system gradually stabilized. Warfare settled three main issues between 1690 and 1740: a coalition of powers held Louis XIV's France in check on the continent; Great Britain emerged from the wars against Louis as the preeminent maritime power; and Russia defeated Sweden in the contest for supremacy in the Baltic. After Louis XIV's death in 1715, Europe enjoyed the fruits of a more balanced diplomatic system, in which warfare became less frequent and less widespread. States could then spend their resources establishing and expanding control over their own populations, both at home and in their colonies.

The Limits of French Absolutism

When the seventy-six-year-old Louis XIV lay on his deathbed suffering from constipation and gangrene in 1715, he must have felt depressed by the unraveling of his accomplishments. Not only had his plans for territorial expansion been thwarted, but his incessant wars had exhausted the treasury, despite new taxes. In 1689, Louis's rival, William III, prince of Orange and king of England and Scotland (r. 1689–1702), had set out to forge a European alliance that eventually included Britain, the Dutch Republic, Sweden, Austria, and Spain. The allies fought Louis to a stalemate in the War of the League of Augsburg, sometimes called the Nine Years' War (1689–1697), but hostilities resumed four years later in the War of the Spanish Succession, which brought France's expansionist ambitions to a grinding halt.

The War of the Spanish Succession, 1701–1713. When the mentally and physically feeble Charles II (r. 1665–1700) of Spain died in 1700 without a direct heir, all of Europe poised for a fight over the spoils. The Spanish succession could not help but be a burning issue, given Spain's extensive territories in Italy and the Netherlands and colonies overseas. It seemed a plum ripe for picking. Spanish power had declined steadily since its golden age in the sixteenth century: the gold and silver of the New World had been exhausted, and the Spanish kings neglected manufactures, debased their coinage, and failed to adopt the new scientific ideas and commercial practices developed by the Dutch and the British. As a consequence, they lacked the resources for international competition.

Before Charles died, he named Louis XIV's second grandson, Philip, duke of Anjou, as his heir, but his bequest resolved nothing. Louis XIV and the Austrian emperor Leopold I had competing dynastic claims to the Spanish crown, and Leopold refused to accept Charles's deathbed will. The ensuing War of the Spanish Succession proved disastrous for the French because most of Europe once again allied against them, fearing the consequences of French control over Spanish territories. The French lost several major battles and had to accept disadvantageous terms in the Peace of Utrecht of 1713–1714 (Map 18.2). Although Philip was recognized as king of Spain, he had to renounce any future claim to the French crown, thus barring unification of the two kingdoms. Spain surrendered its territories in Italy and the Netherlands to the Austrians and Gibraltar to the British; France ceded possessions in North America (Newfoundland, the Hudson Bay area, and most of Nova Scotia) to Britain. France no longer threatened to dominate European power politics.

The Death of Louis XIV and the Regency. At home, Louis's policy of absolutism had fomented bitter hostility. Nobles fiercely resented his promotions of commoners to high office. The duke of Saint-Simon complained that "falseness, servility, admiring glances, combined with a dependent and cringing attitude, above all, an appearance of being nothing without him, were the only ways of pleasing him." Even some of the king's leading servants, such as Archbishop Fénelon, who tutored the king's grandson, began to call for monarchical reform. An admirer of Guyon's Quietism, Fénelon severely criticized the court's excesses: the "steady stream of extravagant adulation, which reaches the point of idolatry"; the constant, bloody wars; and the misery of the people.

On his deathbed, Louis XIV gave his blessing and some sound advice to his five-year-old great-grandson and successor, Louis XV (r. 1715–1774): "My child, you are about to become a great King. Do not imitate my love of building nor my liking for war." Squabbling over control of the crown began immediately. The duke of Orléans (1674–1723), nephew of the dead king, was named regent. He revived some of the parlements' powers and tried to give leading nobles a greater say in political affairs as a way to restore confidence and appease aristocratic critics. The regent also moved the court back to Paris, away from the atmosphere of moral rigidity and prudery that Louis had enforced in his last years at Versailles.

Financial problems plagued the Regency as they would beset all succeeding French regimes in the eighteenth century. In 1719, the regent appointed the Scottish adventurer and financier John Law to the top financial position of controller-general. Law founded a trading company for North America and a state bank that issued paper money and stock (without them trade depended on the available supply of gold and silver). The bank was supposed to offer lower interest rates to the state, thus cutting the cost of financing the government's debts. The value of the stock rose rapidly in a frenzy of speculation, only to crash a few months later. With it vanished any hope of establishing a state bank or issuing paper money for nearly a century.

France finally achieved a measure of financial stability under the leadership of Cardinal Hercule de Fleury (1653–1743), the most powerful member of the government after the death of the regent. Fleury aimed to avoid adventure abroad and keep social peace at home; he balanced the budget and carried out a large project for road and canal construction. Colonial trade boomed. Peace and the acceptance of limits on territorial expansion inaugurated a century of French prosperity.

MAP 18.2 Europe, c. 1715

Although Louis XIV succeeded in putting his grandson Philip on the Spanish throne, France emerged considerably weakened from the War of Spanish Succession. France ceded large territories in Canada to Britain, which also gained key Mediterranean outposts from Spain, as well as a monopoly on providing slaves to the Spanish colonies. Spanish losses were catastrophic. Philip had to renounce any future claim to the French crown and give up considerable territories in the Netherlands and Italy to the Austrians.

British Rise and Dutch Decline

The British and the Dutch had joined in a coalition against Louis XIV under their joint ruler William III, who was simultaneously stadholder of the Dutch Republic and, with his English wife, Mary (d. 1694), ruler of England, Wales, and Scotland. After William's death in 1702, the British and Dutch went their separate ways. Over the next decades, the English monarchy incorporated Scotland and subjugated Ireland, becoming "Great Britain." At the same time Dutch imperial power declined; even though Dutch merchants still controlled a substantial portion of world trade, by 1700 Great Britain dominated the seas and the Dutch, with their small population of less than two million, came to depend on alliances with bigger powers.

From England to Great Britain. English relations with Scotland and Ireland were complicated by the problem of succession: William and Mary had no children. To ensure a Protestant succession, Parliament ruled that Mary's sister, Anne, would succeed William and Mary and that the Protestant House of Hanover in Germany would succeed Anne if she had no surviving heirs. Catholics were excluded. When Queen Anne (r. 1702–1714) died leaving no children, the elector of Hanover, a Protestant great-grandson of James I, consequently became King George I (r. 1714–1727). The House of Hanover—it was renamed the House of Windsor during World War I—still occupies the British throne.

Support from the Scots and Irish for this solution did not come easily because many in Scotland and Ireland supported the claims to the throne of the deposed Catholic king, James II, and, after his death in 1701, his son James Edward. Out of fear of this "Jacobitism" (from the Latin *Jacobus* for "James"), Scottish Protestant leaders agreed to the Act of Union of 1707, which abolished the Scottish Parliament and affirmed the Scots' recognition of the Protestant Hanoverian succession. The Scots agreed to obey the Parliament of Great Britain, which would include Scottish members in the House of Commons and the House of Lords. A Jacobite rebellion in Scotland in 1715, aiming to restore the Stuart line, was suppressed. The threat of Jacobitism nonetheless continued into the 1740s.

The Irish—90 percent of whom were Catholic—proved even more difficult to subdue. When James

II had gone to Ireland in 1689 to raise a Catholic rebellion against the new monarchs of England, William III responded by taking command of the joint English and Dutch forces and defeating James's Irish supporters. James fled to France, and the Catholics in Ireland faced yet more confiscation and legal restrictions. By 1700, Irish Catholics, who in 1640 had owned 60 percent of the land in Ireland, owned just 14 percent. The Protestant-controlled Irish Parliament passed a series of laws limiting the rights of the Catholic majority: Catholics could not bear arms, send their children abroad for education, establish Catholic schools at home, or marry Protestants. Catholics could not sit in Parliament, nor could they vote for its members unless they took an oath renouncing Catholic doctrine. These and a host of other laws reduced Catholic Ireland to the status of a colony; one English official commented in 1745, "The poor people of Ireland are used worse than negroes." Most of the Irish were peasants who lived in primitive housing and subsisted on a meager diet that included no meat.

The Parliament of Great Britain was soon dominated by the Whigs. In Britain's constitutional system, the monarch ruled with Parliament. The crown chose the ministers, directed policy, and supervised administration, while Parliament raised revenue, passed laws, and represented the interests of the people to the crown. The powers of Parliament were reaffirmed by the Triennial Act in 1694, which provided that Parliaments meet at least once every three years (this was extended to seven years in 1716, after the Whigs had established their ascendancy). Only 200,000 propertied men could vote, out of a population of more than 5 million people, and, not surprisingly, most members of Parliament came from the landed gentry. In fact, a few hundred families controlled all the important political offices.

George I and George II (r. 1727–1760) relied on one man, Sir Robert Walpole (1676–1745), to help them manage their relations with Parliament. From his position as First Lord of the Treasury, Walpole made himself into first or "prime" minister, leading the House of Commons from 1721 to 1742. Although appointed initially by the king, Walpole established an enduring pattern of parliamentary government in which a prime minister from the leading party guided legislation through the House of Commons. Walpole also built a vast patronage machine that dispensed government jobs to win

Sir Robert Walpole at a Cabinet Meeting
Sir Robert Walpole and George II developed government by a cabinet, which consisted of Walpole as first lord of the treasury, the two secretaries of state, the lord chancellor, the chancellor of the exchequer, the lord privy seal, and the lord president of the council. Walpole's cabinet was the ancestor of modern cabinets in both Great Britain and the United States. Its similarities to modern forms should not be overstated, however. The entire staff of the two secretaries of state, who had charge of all foreign and domestic affairs other than taxation, numbered twenty-four in 1726.
The Fotomas Index, U.K.

support for the crown's policies. Some complained that his patronage system corrupted politics, but Walpole successfully used his political skills to convince the ruling class not to rock its own boat. Walpole's successors relied more and more on the patronage system and eventually alienated not only the Tories but also the middle classes in London and even the North American colonies.

The partisan division between the Whigs, who supported the Hanoverian succession and the rights of dissenting Protestants, and the Tories, who had backed the Stuart line and the Anglican church, did not hamper Great Britain's pursuit of economic, military, and colonial power. In this period, Great Britain became a great power on the world stage by virtue of its navy and its ability to finance major military involvement in the wars against Louis XIV. The founding in 1694 of the Bank of England—which, unlike the French bank, endured—enabled the government to raise money at low interest for foreign wars. The bank's success can be measured by the amount of money it lent in wartime: by the 1740s, the government could borrow more than four times what it could in the 1690s.

The Dutch Eclipse. When William of Orange (William III of England) died in 1702, he left no heirs, and for forty-five years the Dutch lived without a stadholder. The merchant ruling class of some two thousand families dominated the Dutch Republic more than ever, but they presided over a country that counted for less in international power politics. In some areas, Dutch decline was only relative: the Dutch population was not growing as fast as others, for example, and the Dutch share of the Baltic trade decreased from 50 percent in 1720 to less than 30 percent by the 1770s. After 1720, the Baltic countries—Prussia, Russia, Denmark, and Sweden—began to ban imports of manufactured goods to protect their own industries, and Dutch trade in particular suffered. The output of Leiden textiles dropped to one-third of its 1700 level by 1740. Shipbuilding, paper manufacturing, tobacco processing, salt refining, and pottery production all dwindled as well. The Dutch East India Company saw its political and military grip loosened in India, Ceylon, and Java.

The biggest exception to the downward trend was trade with the New World, which increased with escalating demands for sugar and tobacco. The Dutch shifted their interest away from great power rivalries toward those areas of international trade and finance where they could establish an enduring presence.

Russia's Emergence as a European Power

Dutch and British commerce and shipbuilding so impressed Russian tsar Peter I (r. 1689–1725) that he traveled incognito to their shipyards in 1697 to learn their methods firsthand. But the tsar intended to build a strong absolutist state in Russia, avoiding the weaknesses of decentralization that plagued the Dutch. As Britain gained dominance on the seas in the West, Peter aimed for dominance on land in the East. Known to history as Peter the Great, he dragged Russia kicking and screaming all the way to great power status. Although he came to the throne while still a minor (on the eve of his tenth birthday), grew up under the threat of a palace coup, and enjoyed little formal education, his accomplishments soon matched his seven-foot-tall stature. Peter transformed public life in Russia and established an absolutist state on the western model. His westernization efforts ignited an enduring controversy: did Peter set Russia on a course of inevitable westernization required to compete with the West, or did he forever and fatally disrupt Russia's natural evolution into a distinctive Slavic society?

Peter the Great's Brand of Absolutism. Peter reorganized government and finance on western models; he streamlined the ministries and assigned each a foreign adviser. Like other absolute rulers, he strengthened his army. With ruthless recruiting methods, which included branding a cross on every recruit's left hand to prevent desertion, he forged an army of 200,000 men and equipped it with modern weapons. He created schools for artillery, engineering, and military medicine and built the first navy in Russian history. Not surprisingly, taxes tripled.

The tsar allowed nothing to stand in his way. He did not hesitate to use torture and executed thousands. He allowed a special guards regiment unprecedented power to expedite cases against those suspected of rebellion, espionage, pretensions to the throne, or just "unseemly utterances" against him. Opposition to his policies reached into his own family: because his only son, Alexei, had allied himself with Peter's critics, he threw him into prison, where the young man mysteriously died.

To control the often restive nobility, Peter insisted that all noblemen engage in state service. A Table of Ranks (1722) classified them into military, administrative, and court categories, a codification of social and legal relationships in Russia that would last for nearly two centuries. All social and material advantages now depended on serving the crown. Because the nobles lacked a secure independent status, Peter could command them to a degree that was unimaginable in western Europe. State service was

Peter the Great Modernizes Russia
In this popular print, a barber forces a protesting noble to conform to Western fashions. (The barber is sometimes erroneously identified as Peter himself.) Peter ordered all nobles, merchants, and middle-class professionals to cut off their beards or pay a huge tax to keep them. An early biographer of Peter, the French writer Jean Rousset de Missy (1730), claimed that those who lost their beards saved them to put in their coffins, in fear that they would not enter heaven without them. Most western Europeans applauded these attempts to change Russian customs, but many Russians deeply resented the attack on traditional ways.
Carole Frohlich Archive.

not only compulsory but also permanent. Moreover, the male children of those in service had to be registered by the age of ten and begin serving at fifteen. To increase his authority over the Russian Orthodox church, Peter allowed the office of patriarch (supreme head) to remain vacant, and in 1721 he replaced it with the Holy Synod, a bureaucracy of laymen under his supervision. To many Russians, Peter was the Antichrist incarnate.

Westernization. With the goal of Westernizing Russian culture, Peter set up the first greenhouses, laboratories, and technical schools and founded the

Russian Academy of Sciences. He ordered translations of western classics and hired a German theater company to perform the French plays of Molière. He replaced the traditional Russian calendar with the western one,* introduced Arabic numerals, and brought out the first public newspaper. He ordered his officials and the nobles to shave their beards and dress in western fashion, and he even issued precise regulations about the suitable style of jacket, boots, and cap (generally French or German). He published a book on manners for young noblemen and experimented with dentistry on his courtiers.

Peter did not undertake these reforms alone. Elite men who were eager for social mobility and willing to adopt Western values cooperated with him. Peter encouraged foreigners to move to Russia to offer their advice and skills, especially for building the new capital city, St. Petersburg. The new capital, named after Peter, was meant to symbolize Russia's opening to the West. Construction began in 1703 in a Baltic province that had been recently conquered from Sweden. By the end of 1709, forty thousand recruits a year found themselves assigned to the work. Peter ordered skilled workers to move to the new city and commanded all landowners possessing more than forty serf households to build houses there. In the 1720s, a German minister described the city "as a wonder of the world, considering its magnificent palaces, . . . and the short time that was employed in the building of it." By 1710, the permanent population of St. Petersburg reached eight thousand. At Peter's death in 1725, it had forty thousand residents.

As a new city far from the Russian heartland around Moscow, St. Petersburg represented a decisive break with Russia's past. Peter widened that gap by every means possible. At his new capital he tried to improve the traditionally denigrated, secluded status of women by ordering them to dress in European styles and appear publicly at his dinners for diplomatic representatives. Imitating French manners, he decreed that women attend his new social salons of officials, officers, and merchants for con-

Russian Rococo
Peter the Great's insistence on incorporating western European influences extended even to tableware. This silver tureen might have been fashioned in Paris or any other western European center of decorative art. Its motifs and trim reveal rococo influences.
State Historical Museum, St. Petersburg.

versation and dancing. A foreigner headed every one of Peter's new technical and vocational schools, and for its first eight years the new Academy of Sciences included no Russians. Upper-class Russians learned French or German, which they often spoke even at home. Such changes affected only the very top of Russian society, however; the mass of the population had no contact with the new ideas and ended up paying for the innovations either in ruinous new taxation or by building St. Petersburg, a project that cost the lives of thousands of workers. Serfs remained tied to the land, completely dominated by their noble lords.

Despite all his achievements, Peter could not ensure his succession. In the thirty-seven years after his death in 1725, Russia endured six different rulers: three women, a boy of twelve, an infant, and an imbecile. Recurrent palace coups weakened the monarchy and enabled the nobility to loosen Peter's rigid code of state service. In the process the serfs' status only worsened. They ceased to be counted as legal subjects; the criminal code of 1754 listed them as property. They not only were bought and sold like cattle but also had become legally indistinguishable from them. Westernization had not yet touched the lives of the serfs.

The Balance of Power in the East

Peter the Great's success in building up state power changed the balance of power in eastern Europe. Overcoming initial military setbacks, Russia eventually defeated Sweden and took its place as the

---

*Peter introduced the Julian calendar, then still used in Protestant but not Catholic countries. Later in the eighteenth century, Protestant Europe abandoned the Julian for the Gregorian calendar. Not until 1918 was the Julian calendar abolished in Russia, at which point it had fallen thirteen days behind Europe's Gregorian calendar.

leading power in the Baltic region. Russia could then turn its attention to eastern Europe, where it competed with Austria and Prussia. Once mighty Poland-Lithuania became the playground for great power rivalries.

The Decline of Sweden. Sweden had dominated the Baltic region since the Thirty Years' War and did not easily give up its preeminence. When Peter the Great joined an anti-Swedish coalition in 1700 with Denmark, Saxony, and Poland, Sweden's Charles XII (r. 1697–1718) stood up to the test. Still in his teens at the beginning of the Great Northern War, Charles first defeated Denmark, then destroyed the new Russian army, and quickly marched into Poland and Saxony. After defeating the Poles and occupying Saxony, Charles invaded Russia. Here Peter's rebuilt army finally defeated him at the battle of Poltava (1709).

The Russian victory resounded everywhere. The Russian ambassador to Vienna reported, "It is commonly said that the tsar will be formidable to all Europe, that he will be a kind of northern Turk." Prussia and other German states joined the anti-Swedish alliance, and war resumed. Charles XII died in battle in 1718, and complex negotiations finally ended the Great Northern War. By the terms of the Treaty of Nystad (1721), Sweden ceded its eastern Baltic provinces—Livonia, Estonia, Ingria, and southern Karelia—to Russia. Sweden also lost territories on the north German coast to Prussia and the other allied German states (Map 18.3). An aristocratic reaction against Charles XII's incessant demands for war supplies swept away Sweden's absolutist regime, essentially removing Sweden from great power competition.

Prussian Militarization. Prussia had to make the most of every military opportunity, as it did in the Great Northern War, because it was much smaller in size and population than Russia, Austria, or France. King Frederick William I (r. 1713–1740) doubled the size of the Prussian army; though much smaller than those of his rivals, it was the best-trained and most up-to-date force in Europe. By 1740, Prussia had Europe's highest proportion of men at arms (1 of every 28 people, versus 1 in 157 in France and 1 in 64 in Russia) and the highest proportion of nobles in the military (1 in 7 noblemen, as compared with 1 in 33 in France and 1 in 50 in Russia).

The army so dominated life in Prussia that the country earned the label "a large army with a small state attached." So obsessed was he with his soldiers

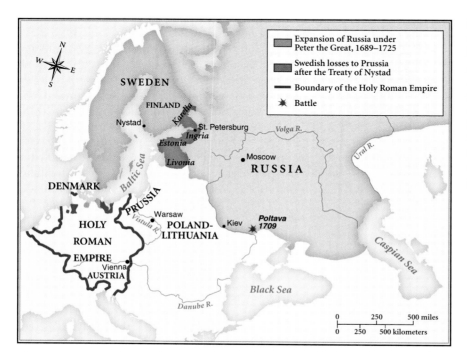

MAP 18.3 Russia and Sweden after the Great Northern War, 1721

After the Great Northern War, Russia supplanted Sweden as the major power in the north. Although Russia had a much larger population from which to draw its armies, Sweden made the most of its advantages and gave way only after a great military struggle.

that the five-foot-five-inch-tall Frederick William formed a regiment of "giants," the Grenadiers, composed exclusively of men over six feet tall. Royal agents scoured Europe trying to find such men and sometimes kidnapped them right off the street. Frederick William, the "Sergeant King," was one of the first rulers to wear a military uniform as his everyday dress. He subordinated the entire domestic administration to the army's needs. He also installed a system for recruiting soldiers by local district quotas. He financed the army's growth by subjecting all the provinces to an excise tax on food, drink, and manufactured goods and by increasing rents on crown lands. Prussia was now poised to become one of the major players on the continent.

The War of Polish Succession, 1733–1735. Prussia did not enter into military conflict foolishly. During the War of Polish Succession it stood on the sidelines, content to watch others fight. The war showed how the balance of power had changed since the heyday of Louis XIV: France had to maneuver within a complex great power system that now included Russia, and Poland-Lithuania no longer controlled its own destiny. When the king of Poland-Lithuania died in 1733, France, Spain, and Sardinia went to war against Austria and Russia, each side supporting rival claimants to the Polish throne.

After Russia drove the French candidate out of Poland-Lithuania, France agreed to accept the Austrian candidate; in exchange, Austria gave the province of Lorraine to the French candidate, the father-in-law of Louis XV, with the promise that the province would pass to France on his death. France and Britain went back to pursuing their colonial rivalries. Prussia and Russia concentrated on shoring up their influence within Poland-Lithuania.

Austrian Conquest of Hungary, 1657–1730

Austria did not want to become mired in a long struggle in Poland-Lithuania because its armies still faced the Turks on its southeastern border. Even though the Austrians had forced the Turks to recognize their rule over all of Hungary and Transylvania in 1699 and occupied Belgrade in 1717, the Turks did not stop fighting. In the 1730s, the Turks retook Belgrade, and Russia now claimed a role in the struggle against the Turks. Moreover, Hungary, though "liberated" from Turkish rule, proved less than enthusiastic about submitting to Austria. In 1703, the wealthiest Hungarian noble landlord, Ferenc Rákóczi (1676–1735), led a combined noble and peasant revolt against the Austrians. Rákóczi raised an army of seventy thousand men who pledged to fight for "God, Fatherland, and Liberty." Although the rebels did not win the ensuing war, which lasted until 1711, they forced the Austrians to recognize local Hungarian institutions, grant amnesty, and restore confiscated estates in exchange for confirming hereditary Austrian rule. Austria had more than sufficient reason to avoid committing itself to a long war against France.

The Power of Diplomacy

No single power emerged from the wars of the first half of the eighteenth century clearly superior to the others, and the idea of maintaining a balance of power guided both military and diplomatic maneuvering. The Peace of Utrecht had explicitly declared that such a balance was crucial to maintaining peace in Europe, and in 1720 a British pamphleteer wrote, "There is not, I believe, any doctrine in the law of nations, of more certain truth . . . than this of the balance of power." It was the law of gravity of European politics. This system of equilibrium often rested on military force, such as the leagues formed against Louis XIV or the coalition against Sweden. All states counted on diplomacy, however, to resolve issues even after fighting had begun.

To meet the new demands placed on it, the diplomatic service, like the military and financial bureaucracies before it, had to develop regular procedures. The French set a pattern of diplomatic service that the other European states soon imitated. By 1685, France had embassies in all the important capitals. Nobles of ancient families served as ambassadors to Rome, Madrid, Vienna, and London, whereas royal officials were chosen for Switzerland, the Dutch Republic, and Venice. Most held their appointments for at least three or four years, and all went off with elaborate written instructions that included explicit statements of policy as well as full accounts of the political conditions of the country to which they were posted. The ambassador selected and paid for his own staff. This practice could make the journey to a new post very cumbersome, because the staff might be as large as eighty people, and they brought along all their own furniture, pictures, silverware, and tapestries. It took one French ambassador ten weeks to get from Paris to Stockholm.

By the early 1700s, French writings on diplomatic methods were read everywhere. François de Callières's manual *On the Manner of Negotiating with Sovereigns* (1716) insisted that sound diplomacy was based on the creation of confidence, rather than deception: "The secret of negotiation is to harmonize the real interests of the parties concerned." Callières believed that the diplomatic service had to be professional—that young attachés should be chosen for their skills, not their family connections. These sensible views did not prevent the development of a dual system of diplomacy, in which rulers issued secret instructions that often negated the official ones sent by their own foreign offices. Secret diplomacy had some advantages because it allowed rulers to break with past alliances, but it also led to confusion and, sometimes, scandal, for the rulers often employed unreliable adventurers as their confidential agents. Still, the diplomatic system in the early eighteenth century proved successful enough to ensure a continuation of the principles of the Peace of Westphalia (1648); in the midst of every crisis and war, the great powers would convene and hammer out a written agreement detailing the requirements for peace.

The Power of Numbers

Successful diplomacy could smooth the road toward peace, but success in war still depended on sheer numbers—of men and muskets. Because each state's strength depended largely on the size of its army, the growth and health of the population increasingly entered into government calculations. The publication in 1690 of the Englishman William Petty's *Political Arithmetick* quickened the interest of government officials everywhere; Petty offered statistical estimates of human capital—that is, of population and wages—to determine Britain's national wealth. This "political arithmetic" inevitably drew attention to public health issues. Although hospitals were transformed in this period from public charities into medical institutions focused more narrowly on disease, health care remained precarious at best.

Political Arithmetic. A large, growing population could be as vital to a state's future as access to silver mines or overseas trade, so government officials devoted increased effort to the statistical estimation of total population and rates of births, deaths, marriages, and fertility. In 1727, Frederick William I of Prussia founded two university chairs to encourage population studies, and textbooks and handbooks advocated state intervention to improve the population's health and welfare.

Physicians used the new population statistics to explain the environmental causes of disease, another new preoccupation in this period. Petty devised a quantitative scale that distinguished healthy from unhealthy places largely on the basis of air quality, an early precursor of modern environmental studies. After investigating specific cities, German medical geographers urged government campaigns to improve public sanitation. Everywhere, environmentalists gathered and analyzed data on climate, disease, and population, searching for correlations to help direct policy. As a result of these efforts, local governments undertook such measures as draining low-lying areas, burying refuse, and cleaning wells, all of which eventually helped lower the death rates from epidemic diseases.

Public Hygiene and Health Care. Urban growth made public hygiene problems more acute. Cities were the unhealthiest places because excrement (animal and human) and garbage accumulated where people lived densely packed together. A traveler described the streets of Madrid in 1697 as "always very dirty because it is the custom to throw all the rubbish out of the window." Paris seemed to a visitor "so detestable that it is impossible to remain there" because of the smell; even the facade of the Louvre palace in Paris was soiled by the contents of night commodes that servants routinely dumped out of windows every morning. Only the wealthy could escape walking in mucky streets, by hiring men to carry them in sedan chairs or to drive them in coaches.

Founded originally as charities concerned foremost with the moral worthiness of the poor, hospitals gradually evolved into medical institutions that defined patients by their diseases. The process of diagnosis changed as physicians began to use specialized Latin terms for illnesses. The gap between medical experts and their patients increased, as physicians now also relied on postmortem dissections in the hospital to gain better knowledge, a practice most patients' families resented. Press reports of body snatching and grave robbing by surgeons and their apprentices outraged the public well into the 1800s.

Despite the change in hospitals, individual health care remained something of a free-for-all in which physicians competed with bloodletters, itinerant venereal-disease doctors, bonesetters, druggists, midwives, and "cunning women," who specialized in home remedies. Physicians often followed popular prescriptions for illnesses because they had nothing better to offer. Recipes for cures were part of most people's everyday conversation. The various "medical" opinions about childbirth highlight the confusion people faced. Midwives delivered most babies, though they sometimes encountered criticism, even from within their own ranks. One consulting midwife complained that ordinary midwives in Bristol, England, made women in labor drink a mixture of their husband's urine and leek juice. By the 1730s, female midwives faced competition from male midwives, who were known for using instruments such as forceps to pull the baby out of the birth canal. Women rarely sought a physician's help in giving birth, however; they preferred the advice and assistance of trusted local midwives. In any case, trained physicians were few in number and almost nonexistent outside cities.

Public and private hygiene improved only gradually. Patients were as likely to die of diseases caught in the hospital as to be cured there. Antiseptics were virtually unknown. The wealthy preferred treatment at home, sometimes by private physicians. The medical profession, with nationwide organizations and licensing, had not yet emerged, and no clear line separated trained physicians from quacks. For example, if a woman of the prosperous classes had breast cancer, she could have a doctor remove the breast tumors in a short, painful operation without anesthesia; but many opted instead to use folk remedies such as a plaster of mutton suet, beeswax, and flaxseed. Unfortunately, usually neither the surgery nor the concoctions proved effective.

Insanity was treated as a physical rather than an emotional ailment. Doctors believed most madness was caused by "melancolia," a condition they attributed to disorders in the system of bodily "humors." Their prescribed treatments included blood transfusions; ingestion of bitter substances such as coffee, quinine, and even soap; immersion in water; various forms of exercise; and burning or cauterizing the body to allow black vapors to escape.

Hardly any infectious diseases could be cured, though inoculation against smallpox spread from the Middle East to Europe in the early eighteenth century, thanks largely to the efforts of Lady Mary Wortley Montagu, who learned about the technique while living in Constantinople. (See "Did You Know?," page 674.) After 1750, physicians developed successful procedures for wide-scale vaccination, although even then many people resisted the idea of inoculating themselves with a disease. Other diseases spread quickly in the unsanitary conditions of urban life. Ordinary people washed or changed clothes rarely, lived in overcrowded housing with poor ventilation, and got their water from contaminated sources, such as refuse-filled rivers.

Until the mid-1700s, most people considered bathing dangerous. Public bathhouses had disappeared from cities in the sixteenth and seventeenth centuries because they seemed a source of disorderly behavior and epidemic illness. In the eighteenth century, even private bathing came into disfavor because people feared the effects of contact with water. Fewer than one in ten newly built private mansions in Paris had baths. Bathing was hazardous, physicians insisted, because it opened the body to disease. One manners manual of 1736 admonished, "It is correct to clean the face every morning by using a white cloth to cleanse it. It is less good to wash with water, because it renders the face susceptible to cold in winter and sun in summer." The upper classes associated cleanliness not with baths but with frequently changed linens, powdered hair, and perfume, which was thought to strengthen the body and refresh the brain by counteracting corrupt and foul air.

Lady Mary Wortley Montagu and Inoculation for Smallpox

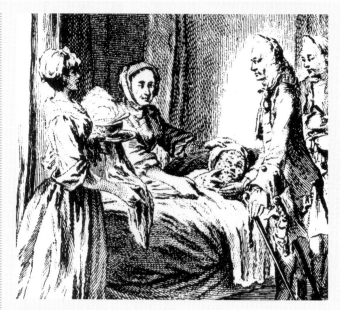

The Scourge of Smallpox
This engraving from a hospital report of 1750 shows a patient being tended in a smallpox hospital for the poor in London. The patient's face has been disfigured by the disease.
British Museum.

Daughter of a duke, wife of an ambassador, and mother-in-law of a prime minister, Lady Mary Wortley Montagu (1689–1762) might have confined herself to socializing in the highest circles and managing a large household. But her life changed as a result of two unexpected circumstances: in 1715 she caught smallpox, which left her disfigured by pitted skin and the loss of her eyelashes (her brother died of the dread disease); and in 1716 her husband was named the British ambassador to the Ottoman Empire. She undertook the long voyage with him and wrote letters filled with vivid descriptions of life in eastern Europe and the Ottoman Empire. She returned from Constantinople in 1718, determined to introduce a Turkish invention, inoculation against smallpox. Lady Mary studied inoculation in several Turkish towns and tried it on her son while still in the Ottoman Empire. In 1717, she wrote a friend describing how inoculation was carried out by old women who used needles to prick the skin with smallpox "venom." The children fell ill after eight days but recovered completely.

In 1721, when a new smallpox epidemic threatened England, Lady Mary called on her physician to inoculate her daughter with two additional physicians attending as witnesses. One of the observers immediately inoculated his own son: the newspapers picked up the story, and within a few weeks six convicted criminals had volunteered to serve as guinea pigs in front of a crowd of witnesses including scientists from the English Royal Society. All six survived, but when two new patients died after inoculation in the following months, clergymen and physicians attacked the practice. One physician denounced "an Experiment practiced only by a few *Ignorant Women*, amongst an illiterate and unthinking People." Montagu printed a stinging rejoinder under the anonymous signature "Turkey Merchant." Although she won this battle as inoculation spread in use, she never published anything under her own name in her lifetime.

Ridiculed by some male contemporaries for her meddling in public affairs, Montagu had the last word after her death when her letters about the Ottoman Empire were published, revealing her as a correspondent with a talent for description of foreign customs and a wide-ranging interest in philosophical and literary matters. Lady Mary incarnated the new perspective gained by travel, in which close study of another culture challenged preconceptions and might even suggest important innovations to bring back home.

❖ The Birth of the Enlightenment

Economic expansion, the emergence of a new consumer society, and the stabilization of the European state system all generated optimism about the future. The intellectual corollary was the *Enlightenment*, a term used later in the eighteenth century to describe the loosely knit group of writers and scholars who believed that human beings could apply a critical, reasoning spirit to every problem they encountered in this world. The new secular, scientific, and critical attitude first emerged in the 1690s, scrutinizing everything from the absolutism of Louis XIV to the traditional role of women in society. After 1740, criticism took a more systematic turn as writers provided new theories for the organization of society and politics, but even by the 1720s and 1730s, established authorities realized they faced a new set of challenges.

Popularization of Science and Challenges to Religion

The writers of the Enlightenment glorified the geniuses of the new science and championed scientific method as the solution for all social problems. (See "Terms of History," page 676.) One of the most influential popularizations was the French writer Bernard de Fontenelle's *Conversations on the Plurality of Worlds* (1686). Presented as a dialogue between an aristocratic woman and a man of the world, the book made the Copernican, sun-centered view of the universe available to the literate public. By 1700, mathematics and science had become fashionable pastimes in high society, and the public flocked to lectures explaining scientific discoveries. Journals complained that scientific learning had become the passport to female affection: "There were two young ladies in Paris whose heads had been so turned by this branch of learning that one of them declined to listen to a proposal of marriage unless the candidate for her hand undertook to learn how to make telescopes." Such writings poked fun at women with intellectual interests, but they also demonstrated that women now participated in discussions of science.

The New Skepticism. Interest in science spread in literate circles because it offered a model for all forms of knowledge. As the prestige of science increased, some developed a skeptical attitude toward attempts to enforce religious conformity. A French Huguenot refugee from Louis XIV's persecutions, Pierre Bayle (1647–1706), launched an internationally influential campaign against religious intolerance from his safe haven in the Dutch Republic. His *News from the Republic of Letters* (first published in

A Budding Scientist
In this engraving, Astrologia, *by the Dutch artist Jacob Gole (c. 1660–1723), an upper-class woman looks through a telescope to do her own astronomical investigations. Women with intellectual interests were often disparaged by men, yet some middle- and upper-class women managed to pursue serious interests in science. One of the best known of these was the Italian Laura Bassi (1711–1778), who was a professor of physics at the University of Bologna. Such a position was all but impossible to attain since women were not allowed to attend university classes in any European country. Yet because many astronomical observatories were set up in private homes rather than public buildings or universities, wives and daughters of scientists could make observations and even publish their own findings.*
Bibliothèque Nationale de France.

Progress

Believing as they did in the possibilities of improvement, many Enlightenment writers preached a new doctrine about the meaning of human history. They challenged the traditional Christian belief that the original sin of Adam and Eve condemned human beings to unhappiness in this world and offered instead an optimistic vision: human nature, they claimed, was inherently good, and progress would be continuous if education developed human capacities to the utmost. Science and reason could bring happiness in this world. The idea of novelty or newness itself now seemed positive rather than threatening. Europeans began to imagine that they could surpass all those who preceded them in history, and they began to think of themselves as more "advanced" than the "backward" cultures they encountered in other parts of the world.

More than an intellectual concept, the idea of progress included a new conception of historical time and of Europeans' place within world history. Europeans stopped looking back, whether to a lost Garden of Eden or to the writings of Greek and Roman antiquity. Growing prosperity, European dominance overseas, and the scientific revolution oriented them toward the future. Europeans began to call their epoch "modern" to distinguish it from the Middle Ages (a new term), and they considered their modern period superior in achievement. Consequently, Europeans took it as their mission to bring their modern, enlightened ways of progress to the areas they colonized.

The economic and ecological catastrophes, destructive wars, and genocides of the twentieth century cast much doubt on this rosy vision of continuing progress. As the philosopher George Santayana (1863–1952) complained, "The cry was for vacant freedom and indeterminate progress:

Vorwarts! Avanti! Onward! Full Speed Ahead!, without asking whether directly before you was a bottomless pit." In the movement toward *postmodernism*, which began in the 1970s, critics argued that we should no longer be satisfied with the modern; the modern brought us calamity and disaster, not reason and freedom. They wanted to go beyond the modern, hence "postmodernism." The most influential postmodern historian, the Frenchman Michel Foucault, argued in the 1970s and 1980s that history did not reveal a steady progress toward enlightenment, freedom, and humanitarianism but rather a descent into greater and greater social control, what he called a "carceral [prisonlike] society." He analyzed the replacement of torture with the prison, the birth of the medical clinic, and the movements for sexual liberation and declared that all simply ended up teaching people to watch themselves more closely and to cooperate in the state's efforts to control their lives.

Historians are now chastened in their claims about progress. They would no longer side with the German philosopher Georg W. F. Hegel who proclaimed in 1832, "The history of the world is none other than the progress of the consciousness of freedom." They worry about the nationalistic claims inherent, for example, in the English historian Thomas Babington Macaulay's insistence that "the history of England is emphatically the history of progress" (1843). But most would not go so far as Foucault in denouncing modern developments. As with many other historical questions, the final word is not yet in: is there a direction in human history? Or is history, as many in ancient times thought, a set of repeating cycles?

FURTHER READING

Bury, J. B. *The Idea of Progress: An Inquiry into Its Origin and Growth.* 1932.

Foucault, Michel. *Discipline and Punish: The Birth of the Prison.* Trans. Alan Sheridan. 1977.

1684) bitterly criticized the policies of Louis XIV and was quickly banned in Paris and condemned in Rome. After attacking Louis XIV's anti-Protestant policies, Bayle took a more general stand in favor of religious toleration. No state in Europe officially offered complete tolerance, though the Dutch Republic came closest with its tacit acceptance of Catholics, dissident Protestant groups, and open Jewish communities. In 1697, Bayle published the *Historical and Critical Dictionary*, which cited all the errors and delusions that he could find in past and present writers of all religions. Even religion must meet the test of reasonableness: "Any particular dogma, whatever it may be, whether it is advanced on the authority of the Scriptures, or whatever else may be its origins, is to be regarded as false if it clashes with the clear and definite conclusions of the natural understanding [reason]."

Although Bayle claimed to be a believer himself, his insistence on rational investigation seemed to challenge the authority of faith. As one critic complained, "It is notorious that the works of M. Bayle have unsettled a large number of readers, and cast doubt on some of the most widely accepted principles of morality and religion." Bayle asserted, for example, that atheists might possess moral codes as effective as those of the devout. Bayle's *Dictionary* became a model of critical thought in the West.

Other scholars challenged the authority of the Bible by subjecting it to historical criticism. Discoveries in geology in the early eighteenth century showed that marine fossils dated immensely farther back than the biblical flood. Investigations of miracles, comets, and oracles, like the growing literature against belief in witchcraft, urged the use of reason to combat superstition and prejudice. Comets, for example, should not be considered evil omens just because such a belief had been passed on from earlier generations. Defenders of church and state published books warning of the dangers of the new skepticism. The spokesman for Louis XIV's absolutism, Bishop Bossuet, warned that "reason is the guide of their choice, but reason only brings them face to face with vague conjectures and baffling perplexities." Human beings, the traditionalists held, were simply incapable of subjecting everything to reason, especially in the realm of religion.

State authorities found religious skepticism particularly unsettling because it threatened to undermine state power too. The extensive literature of criticism was not limited to France, but much of it was published in French, and the French government took the lead in suppressing the more outspoken works. Forbidden books were then often published in the Dutch Republic, Britain, or Switzerland and smuggled back across the border to a public whose appetite was only whetted by censorship.

The Young Voltaire Challenges Church and State. The most influential writer of the early Enlighten-

ment was a French man born into the upper middle classes, François Marie Arouet, known by his pen name, Voltaire (1694–1778). Voltaire took inspiration from Bayle: "He gives facts with such odious fidelity, he exposes the arguments for and against with such dastardly impartiality, he is so intolerably intelligible, that he leads people of only ordinary common sense to judge and even to doubt." In his early years Voltaire suffered arrest, imprisonment, and exile, but he eventually achieved wealth and acclaim. His tangles with church and state began in the early 1730s, when he published his *Letters Concerning the English Nation* (the English version appeared in 1733), in which he devoted several chapters to Newton and Locke and used the virtues of the British as a way to attack Catholic bigotry and government rigidity in France. Impressed by British toleration of religious dissent (at least among Protestants), Voltaire spent two years in exile in Britain when the French state responded to his book with yet another order for his arrest.

Voltaire also popularized Newton's scientific discoveries in his *Elements of the Philosophy of Newton* (1738). The French state and many European theologians considered Newtonianism threatening because it glorified the human mind and seemed to reduce God to an abstract, external, rationalistic force. So sensational was the success of Voltaire's book on Newton that a hostile Jesuit reported, "The great Newton, was, it is said, buried in the abyss, in the shop of the first publisher who dared to print him. . . . M. de Voltaire finally appeared, and at once Newton is understood or is in the process of being understood; all Paris resounds with Newton, all Paris stammers Newton, all Paris studies and learns Newton." The success was international too. Before long, Voltaire was elected a fellow of the Royal Society in London and in Edinburgh, as well as to twenty other scientific academies. Voltaire's fame continued to grow, reaching truly astounding proportions in the 1750s and 1760s (see Chapter 19).

Travel Literature and the Challenge to Custom and Tradition

Just as scientific method could be used to question religious and even state authority, a more general skepticism also emerged from the expanding knowledge about the world outside of Europe. During the seventeenth and eighteenth centuries, accounts of travel to exotic places dramatically increased as travel writers used the contrast between their home societies and other cultures to criticize the customs of European society.

Travel and Relativism in Morals. In their travels to the new colonies, visitors sought something resembling "the state of nature," that is, ways of life that preceded sophisticated social and political organization—although they often misinterpreted different forms of society and politics as having no organization at all. Travelers to the Americas found "noble savages" (native peoples) who appeared to live in conditions of great freedom and equality; they were "naturally good" and "happy" without taxes, lawsuits, or much organized government. In China, in contrast, travelers found a people who enjoyed prosperity and an ancient civilization. Christian missionaries made little headway in China, and visitors had to admit that China's religious systems had flourished for four or five thousand years with no input from Europe or from Christianity. The basic lesson of travel literature in the 1700s, then, was that customs varied: justice, freedom, property, good government, religion, and morality all were relative to the place. Europe—and Christianity— might be seen as just one of many options, as relatively and not absolutely true.

Europeans from all countries began to travel more, though most limited their itineraries to Europe. Philosophers and scientists traveled to exchange thoughts; even monarchs such as Peter the Great journeyed in search of new ideas. One critic complained that travel encouraged free thinking and the destruction of religion: "Some complete their demoralization by extensive travel, and lose whatever shreds of religion remained to them. Every day they see a new religion, new customs, new rites."

From Travel Account to Political Commentary. Travel literature turned explicitly political in Montesquieu's *Persian Letters* (1721). Charles-Louis de Secondat, baron of Montesquieu (1689–1755), the son of an eminent judicial family, was a high-ranking judge in a French court. He published *Persian Letters* anonymously in the Dutch Republic, and the book went into ten printings in just one year—a best-seller for the times. Montesquieu tells the story of two Persians, Rica and Usbek, who leave

their country "for love of knowledge" and travel to Europe. They visit France in the last years of Louis XIV's reign, writing of the king: "He has a minister who is only eighteen years old, and a mistress of eighty. . . . Although he avoids the bustle of towns, and is rarely seen in company, his one concern, from morning till night, is to get himself talked about." Other passages ridicule the pope. Beneath the satire, however, was a serious investigation into the foundation of good government and morality. Montesquieu chose Persians for his travelers because they came from what was widely considered the most despotic of all governments, in which rulers had life and death powers over their subjects. In the book, the Persians constantly compare France to Persia, suggesting that the French monarchy might verge on despotism itself.

The paradox of a judge publishing an anonymous work attacking the regime that employed him demonstrates the complications of the intellectual scene in this period. Montesquieu's anonymity did not last long, and soon Parisian society lionized him. In the late 1720s, he sold his judgeship and traveled extensively in Europe, including an eighteen-month stay in Britain. In 1748, he published a widely influential work on comparative government, *The Spirit of Laws*. The Vatican soon listed both *Persian Letters* and *The Spirit of Laws* in its index of forbidden books.

Raising the Woman Question

Many of the letters exchanged in *Persian Letters* focused on women, marriage, and the family because Montesquieu considered the position of women a sure indicator of the nature of government and morality. Although Montesquieu was not a feminist, his depiction of Roxana, the favorite wife in Usbek's harem, struck a chord with many women. Roxana revolts against the authority of Usbek's eunuchs and writes a final letter to her husband announcing her impending suicide: "I may have lived in servitude, but I have always been free, I have amended your laws according to the laws of nature, and my mind has always remained independent." Women writers used the same language of tyranny and freedom to argue for concrete changes in their status. Feminist ideas were not entirely new, but they were presented systematically for the first time and represented a fundamental challenge to the ways of traditional societies.

The most systematic of these women writers was the English author Mary Astell (1666–1731), the daughter of a businessman and herself a supporter of the Tory party and the Anglican religious establishment. In 1694, she published *A Serious Proposal to the Ladies,* in which she advocated founding a private women's college to remedy women's lack of education. Addressing women, she asked, "How can you be content to be in the World like Tulips in a Garden, to make a fine *shew* [show] and be good for nothing?" Astell argued for intellectual training based on Descartes' principles, in which reason, debate, and careful consideration of the issues took priority over custom or tradition. Her book was an immediate success: five printings appeared by 1701. In later works, Astell criticized the relationship between the sexes within marriage: "If absolute sovereignty be not necessary in a state, how comes it to be so in a family? . . . If all men are born free, how is it that all women are born slaves?" Her critics accused her of promoting subversive ideas and of contradicting the Scriptures.

Astell's work inspired other women to write in a similar vein. The anonymous *Essay in Defence of the Female Sex* (1696) attacked "the Usurpation of Men; and the Tyranny of Custom," which prevented women from getting an education. In 1709, Elizabeth Elstob published a detailed account of the prominent role women played in promoting Christianity in English history. She criticized men who "would declare openly they hated any Woman who knew more than themselves." Other women wrote poetry about the same themes. In the introduction to the work of one of the best-known poets, Elizabeth Singer Rowe, a friend of the author, complained of the "notorious Violations on the Liberties of Freeborn English Women" that came from "a plain and an open design to render us meer [mere] Slaves, perfect Turkish Wives."

Most male writers unequivocally stuck to the traditional view of women. Throughout the 1700s, male commentators complained about women's interest in reading novels, which they thought encouraged idleness and corruption. The French theologian Drouet de Maupertuis published an essay, *Dangerous Commerce between the Two Sexes* (1715), in which he harped once again on the traditional theme of women's self-centeredness: "Women love neither their husbands nor their children nor their lovers," he concluded. "They love themselves." Although the French writer François Poullain de la

---

IMPORTANT DATES

1690s Beginning of rapid development of plantations in Caribbean

1694 Bank of England established; Mary Astell's *A Serious Proposal to the Ladies* argues for the founding of a private women's college

1697 Pierre Bayle publishes *Historical and Critical Dictionary*, detailing errors of religious writers

1699 Turks forced to recognize Habsburg rule over Hungary and Transylvania

1703 Peter the Great of Russia begins construction of St. Petersburg, founds first Russian newspaper

1713–1714 Peace of Utrecht

1714 Elector of Hanover becomes King George I of England

1715 Death of Louis XIV

1719 Daniel Defoe publishes *Robinson Crusoe*

1720 Last outbreak of bubonic plague in western Europe

1721 Treaty of Nystad; Montesquieu publishes *Persian Letters* anonymously in the Dutch Republic

1733 War of the Polish Succession; Voltaire's *Letters Concerning the English Nation* attacks French intolerance and narrow-mindedness

1741 George Frederick Handel composes the *Messiah*

Barre (1647–1723) had asserted the equality of women's minds in a series of works published in the 1670s, most men resisted this idea. Bayle argued, for example, that women were more profoundly tied to their biological nature than were men; by nature less capable of discernment but for this very reason, more inclined to conform to God's wishes.

Such opinions about women often rested on biological suppositions. In the absence of precise scientific knowledge about reproduction, scientists of the time argued heatedly with one another about women's biological role. In the long-dominant Aristotelian view, only the male seed carried spirit and individuality. At the beginning of the eighteenth century, more physicians and surgeons began to champion the doctrine of *ovism*—that the female egg was essential in making new humans. During the decades that followed, male Enlightenment writers would continue to debate women's nature and appropriate social roles.

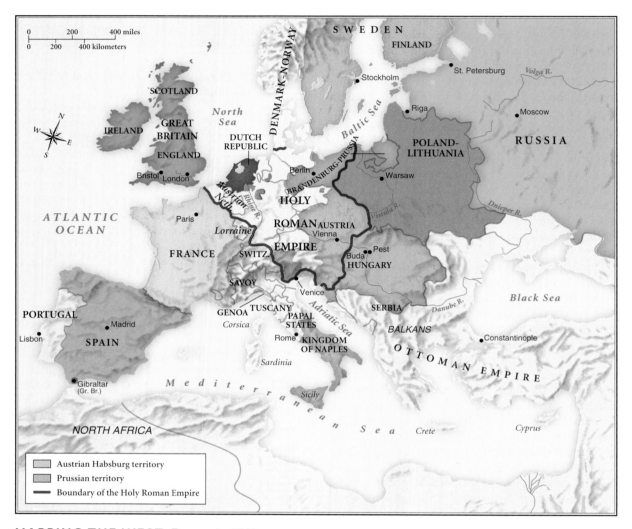

MAPPING THE WEST Europe in 1740

By 1740, Europe had achieved a kind of diplomatic equilibrium in which no one power predominated. But the relative balance should not deflect attention from important underlying changes: Spain, the Dutch Republic, Poland-Lithuania, and Sweden had all declined in power and influence while Great Britain, Russia, Prussia, and Austria had solidified their positions, each in a different way. France's ambitions had been thwarted, but its combination of a big army and rich overseas possessions made it a major player for a long time to come.

Conclusion

Europeans crossed a major threshold in the first half of the eighteenth century. They moved silently but nonetheless momentously from an economy governed by scarcity and the threat of famine to one of ever increasing growth and the prospect of continuing improvement. Expansion of colonies overseas and economic development at home created greater wealth, longer life spans, and higher expectations for the future. In these better times for many, a spirit of optimism prevailed. People could now spend money on newspapers, novels, and travel literature as well as on coffee, tea, and cotton cloth. The growing literate public avidly followed the latest trends in religious debates, art, and music. Everyone did not share equally in the benefits: slaves toiled in abjection in the Americas; serfs in eastern Europe found themselves ever more closely bound to their noble lords; and rural folk almost everywhere tasted fewer fruits of consumer society.

Politics changed too as population and production increased and cities grew. Experts urged government intervention to improve public health, and states found it in their interest to settle many international disputes by diplomacy, which itself became more regular and routine. The consolidation of the European state system allowed a tide of criticism and new thinking about society to swell in Great Britain and France and begin to spill throughout Europe. Ultimately, the combination of the Atlantic system and the Enlightenment would give rise to a series of Atlantic revolutions.

Suggested References

The Atlantic System and the World Economy

It is easier to find sources on individual parts of the system than on the workings of the interlocking trade as a whole, but work has been rapidly increasing in this area. The Dunn book nonetheless remains one of the classic studies of how the plantation system took root. Eze's reader should be used with caution, as it sometimes distorts the overall record with its selections.

Blackburn, Robin. *The Making of New World Slavery: From the Baroque to the Modern, 1492–1800.* 1997.

Dunn, Richard S. *Sugar and Slaves: The Rise of the Planter Class in the English West Indies, 1624–1713.* 1972.

*Eze, Emmanuel Chukwudi. *Race and the Enlightenment: A Reader.* 1997.

Jordan, Winthrop D. *The White Man's Burden: Historical Origins of Racism in the United States.* 1974.

Mintz, Sidney W. *Sweetness and Power: The Place of Sugar in Modern History.* 1985.

Morgan, Philip D. *Slave Counterpoint: Black Culture in the Eighteenth-Century Chesapeake and Low Country.* 1998.

Slave movement during the eighteenth and nineteenth centuries: http://dpls.dacc.wisc.edu/slavedata/.

Smith, Alan K. *Creating a World Economy: Merchant Capital, Colonialism, and World Trade, 1400–1825.* 1991.

New Social and Cultural Patterns

Many of the novels of the period provide fascinating insights into the development of new social attitudes and customs. In particular, see Daniel Defoe's *Robinson Crusoe* (1719) and *Moll Flanders* (1722); the many novels of Eliza Heywood; and Antoine François Prévost's *Manon Lescaut* (1731), a French psychological novel about a nobleman's fatal love for an unfaithful woman, which became the basis for an opera in the nineteenth century.

Artwork of Boucher, Chardin, and Watteau: http://mistral.culture.fr/lumiere/documents/peintres.html.

De Vries, Jan. *European Urbanization, 1500–1800.* 1984.

Earle, Peter. *The Making of the English Middle Class: Business, Society, and Family Life in London, 1660–1730.* 1989.

Handel's Messiah: The New Interactive Edition (CD-ROM). 1997.

Raynor, Henry. *A Social History of Music, from the Middle Ages to Beethoven.* 1972.

Roche, Daniel. *The People of Paris: An Essay in Popular Culture in the Eighteenth Century.* Trans. Marie Evans. 1987.

Consolidation of the European State System

Studies of rulers and states can be supplemented by work on "political arithmetic" and public health.

Aspromourgos, Tony. *On the Origins of Classical Economics: Distribution and Value from William Petty to Adam Smith.* 1996.

Black, Jeremy, ed. *Britain in the Age of Walpole.* 1984.

Brewer, John. *The Sinews of Power: War, Money, and the English State, 1688–1783.* 1990.

Brockliss, Laurence, and Colin Jones. *The Medical World of Early Modern France.* 1997.

Campbell, Peter R. *Power and Politics in Old Regime France, 1720–1745.* 1996.

Hughes, Lindsey. *Russia in the Age of Peter the Great.* 1998.

Frey, Linda, and Marsha Frey. *Societies in Upheaval: Insurrections in France, Hungary, and Spain in the Early Eighteenth Century.* 1987.

Lawrence, Susan C. *Charitable Knowledge: Hospital Pupils and Practitioners in Eighteenth-Century London.* 1996.

Raeff, Marc. *Understanding Imperial Russia: State and Society in the Old Regime.* Trans. Arthur Goldhammer. 1984.

The Birth of the Enlightenment

The definitive study of the early Enlightenment is the book by Hazard, but many others have contributed biographies of individual figures or, more recently, studies of women writers.

Besterman, Theodore. *Voltaire.* 1969.

Grendy, Isobel. *Lady Mary Wortley Montagu.* 1999.

Hazard, Paul. *The European Mind: The Critical Years, 1680–1715.* 1990.

*Hill, Bridget, ed. *The First English Feminist: Reflections upon Marriage and Other Writings by Mary Astell.* 1986.

*Jacob, Margaret C. *The Enlightenment: A Brief History with Selected Readings.* 2000.

Rothkrug, Lionel. *The Opposition to Louis XIV: The Political and Social Origins of the French Enlightenment.* 1966.

Smith, Hilda L. *Reason's Disciples: Seventeenth-Century English Feminists.* 1982.

---

*Primary sources.

The Promise of Enlightenment

1740–1789

I N THE SUMMER OF 1766, Empress Catherine II ("the Great") of Russia wrote to Voltaire, one of the leaders of the Enlightenment:

> *It is a way of immortalizing oneself to be the advocate of humanity, the defender of oppressed innocence. . . . You have entered into combat against the enemies of mankind: superstition, fanaticism, ignorance, quibbling, evil judges, and the powers that rest in their hands. Great virtues and qualities are needed to surmount these obstacles. You have shown that you have them: you have triumphed.*

Catherine the Great
At the time of this portrait by Johann Baptist Edler von Lampi of 1793, the Russian empress Catherine the Great had ruled for thirty-one years and was only three years from her death. Born Sophia Augusta Frederika of Anhalt-Zerbst in 1729, she was the daughter of a minor German prince. When she married the future tsar Peter III in 1745, she promptly learned Russian and adopted Russian Orthodoxy. Peter, physically and mentally frail, proved no match for her, and she took his place on his death in 1762. The painter of this portrait was a native of northern Italy who had worked at the Austrian court in Vienna before being summoned to St. Petersburg. He painted many portraits of the Russian court and royal family between 1792 and 1797.
Art Resource, NY.

Over a fifteen-year period Catherine corresponded regularly with Voltaire, a writer who, at home in France, found himself in constant conflict with authorities of church and state. Her admiring letter shows how influential Enlightenment ideals had become by the middle of the eighteenth century. Even an absolutist ruler such as Catherine endorsed many aspects of the Enlightenment call for reform; at this same time, Catherine set up a commission to write a new law code, and she introduced reforms in favor of education and religious toleration. She too wanted to be an "advocate of humanity."

Catherine's letter aptly summed up Enlightenment ideals: progress for humanity could be achieved only by rooting out the wrongs left by superstition, religious fanaticism, ignorance, and outmoded forms of justice. Enlightenment writers used every means at their disposal—from encyclopedias to novels to personal interaction with rulers—to argue for reform. Everything had to be examined in the cold light of reason,

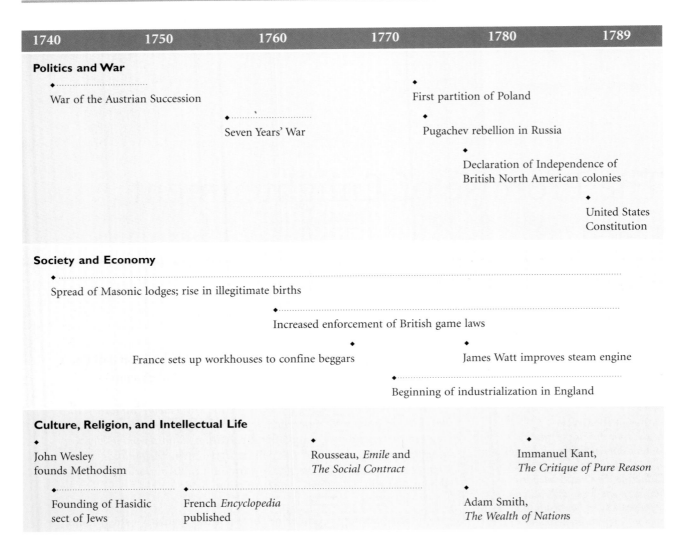

1740	1750	1760	1770	1780	1789

Politics and War

War of the Austrian Succession

Seven Years' War

First partition of Poland

Pugachev rebellion in Russia

Declaration of Independence of British North American colonies

United States Constitution

Society and Economy

Spread of Masonic lodges; rise in illegitimate births

Increased enforcement of British game laws

France sets up workhouses to confine beggars

James Watt improves steam engine

Beginning of industrialization in England

Culture, Religion, and Intellectual Life

John Wesley founds Methodism

Rousseau, *Emile* and *The Social Contract*

Immanuel Kant, *The Critique of Pure Reason*

Founding of Hasidic sect of Jews

French *Encyclopedia* published

Adam Smith, *The Wealth of Nations*

and if it did not promote the improvement of humanity, it should be jettisoned. As a result, Enlightenment writers attacked the legal use of torture to extract confessions and supported religious toleration. They favored the spread of education to eliminate ignorance and criticized censorship by state or church. These ideas spread far and wide through the book trade, some of it clandestine; coffeehouses; lending libraries; local academies; Masonic lodges (social clubs organized with the rituals of masons' guilds); and salons, sophisticated evening discussions organized by upper-class women.

Catherine's correspondence with Voltaire should not blind us to the limitations of Enlightenment. While a new elite of middle- and upper-class men and women embraced the Enlightenment, the lower classes had little contact with the new ideas. The continuing rise in population, the start of industrialization, and wars between the great powers shaped their lives more profoundly. States had to balance conflicting social pressures: on the one hand, rulers pursued those Enlightenment reforms that might enhance state power; and on the other hand, they feared changes that might unleash popular discontent. Catherine herself felt pulled in different directions. She had staged a coup against her husband Tsar Peter III; when he was killed, she succeeded him. German-born and educated, she aimed to bring Western ideas, culture, and reforms to Russia, but above all she intended to maintain and even extend her authority. When faced with a massive uprising of the serfs, she not only suppressed the revolt but also increased the powers of the nobles over their serfs. All reform-minded rulers faced similar potential challenges to their authority.

Even if the movement for reform had its limits, Catherine's letter should not be read as a cynical ploy. It reflected a very real shift in the basis of authority. Governments, almost all of them still ruled by hereditary monarchs, now had to respond to a new force known as "public opinion." The Russian educated public was minuscule, but Catherine nevertheless felt the need to justify her policies to her broader public, the intellectuals of western Europe. Other rulers confronted a much more aggressive, home-grown public that now read newspapers and closely followed political developments. Rulers had to portray themselves as modern, open to reform, and responsive to this public. By 1789, when revolution erupted in France, public opinion had begun to demand democracy—that is, government by, for, and of the people. Most Enlightenment writers did not embrace democracy, however; between the 1740s and the 1780s, they still looked to rulers to effect reform and addressed the educated classes as their audience. Writers such as Voltaire expressed little interest in the future of peasants or lower classes; they favored neither revolution nor political upheaval. Yet their ideas paved the way for something much more radical and unexpected. The American Declaration of Independence in 1776 showed how Enlightenment ideals could be translated into democratic political practice. After 1789, democracy would come to Europe as well.

❖ The Enlightenment at Its Height

The Enlightenment emerged as an intellectual movement before 1740 but reached its peak only in the second half of the eighteenth century. The writers of the Enlightenment called themselves *philosophes* (French for "philosophers"), but that term is somewhat misleading. Whereas philosophers concern themselves with abstract theories, the philosophes were public intellectuals dedicated to solving the real problems of the world. They wrote on subjects ranging from current affairs to art criticism, and they wrote in every conceivable format. The Swiss philosophe Jean-Jacques Rousseau,

for example, wrote a political tract, a treatise on education, a constitution for Poland, an analysis of the effects of the theater on public morals, a best-selling novel, an opera, and a notorious autobiography. The philosophes wrote for a broad educated public of readers who snatched up every Enlightenment book they could find at their local booksellers', even when rulers or churches tried to forbid their publication. Between 1740 and 1789, the Enlightenment acquired its name and, despite heated conflicts between the philosophes and state and religious authorities, gained support in the highest reaches of government. (See "Terms of History," page 687.)

The Men and Women of the Republic of Letters

Although *philosophe* is a French word, the Enlightenment was distinctly cosmopolitan; philosophes could be found from Philadelphia to Moscow and from Edinburgh to Naples. The philosophes considered themselves part of a grand "republic of letters" that transcended national political boundaries. They were not republicans in the usual sense, that is, people who supported representative government and opposed monarchy. Many, like Voltaire, warmly endorsed reform programs proposed by monarchs. What united them were the ideals of reason, reform, and freedom. The French editors of the *Encyclopedia* (published from 1751 to 1772) declared that they would "overturn the barriers that reason never erected" and "give back to the arts and sciences the liberty that is so precious to them." In 1784, the German philosopher Immanuel Kant summed up the program of the Enlightenment in two Latin words: *sapere aude*, "dare to know"—have the courage to think for yourself.

The philosophes used reason to attack superstition, bigotry, and religious fanaticism, which they considered the chief obstacles to free thought and social reform. Voltaire took religious fanaticism as his chief target: "Once fanaticism has corrupted a mind, the malady is almost incurable. . . . The only remedy for this epidemic malady is the philosophical spirit." Enlightenment writers did not necessarily oppose organized religion, but they strenuously objected to religious intolerance. They believed that the systematic application of reason could do what religious belief could not: improve the human

Bookbinding

In this plate from the Encyclopedia, *the various stages in bookbinding are laid out from left to right. Binding was not included in the sale of books; owners had to order leather bindings from a special shop. The man at (a) is pounding the pages to be bound on a marble block. The woman at (b) is stitching the pages with a special frame. The worker at (c) cuts the pages, and at (d) the volumes are pressed to prevent warping. This illustration is typical of the hundreds of plates in the* Encyclopedia *in its effort to represent precisely and thoroughly every stage in artisanal production.*

condition by pointing to needed reforms. Reason meant critical, informed, scientific thinking about social issues and problems. In the multivolume *Encyclopedia*, scores of collaborators gathered knowledge about every aspect of economic, social, and cultural life, from the secrets of manufacturing to theories of music. The chief editor of the *Encyclopedia*, Denis Diderot (1713–1784), explained their purpose: "All things must be examined, debated, investigated without exception and without regard for anyone's feelings."

The philosophes believed that the spread of knowledge would encourage reform in every aspect of life, from the grain trade to the penal system. Chief among their desired reforms was intellectual freedom, the freedom to use one's own reason and to publish the results. The philosophes wanted freedom of the press and freedom of religion, which they considered "natural rights" guaranteed by "natural law." In their view, progress depended on these

freedoms. As Voltaire asserted, "I quite understand that the fanatics of one sect slaughter the enthusiasts of another sect . . . [but] that Descartes should have been forced to flee to Holland to escape the fury of the ignorant . . . these things are a nation's eternal shame."

Most philosophes, like Voltaire, came from the upper classes, yet Rousseau's father was a modest watchmaker in Geneva, and Diderot was the son of a cutlery maker. Although it was a rare phenomenon, some women were philosophes, such as the French noblewoman Émilie du Châtelet (1706–1749), who wrote extensively about the mathematics and physics of Leibniz and Newton. (Her lover Voltaire learned much of his science from her.) Few of the leading writers held university positions, except those who were German or Scottish. Universities in France were so dominated by the clergy and unreceptive to Enlightenment ideals that they took the lead in banning Enlightenment books.

Enlightenment

In 1784, in an essay titled "What Is Enlightenment?," the German philosopher Immanuel Kant gave widespread currency to a term that had been in the making for several decades. The existence of an online database of French literature enables us to trace the actual appearance of the equivalent terms in French: *siècle de lumière(s)* or *siècle éclairé*—"century of light(s)" or "enlightened century." The term *enlightened century* became common beginning only in the 1760s. The even more common term *century of light(s)* first appeared in the inaugural volume of the *Encyclopedia* in 1751 and was soon taken up by all the major French Enlightenment writers. Closely related to Enlightenment was the French term *philosophe*, which was first used to mean "proponent of Enlightenment" in the 1740s. A clandestine tract of 1743 titled *Le Philosophe* explained that the philosophe was the man who saw through popular errors.

The Enlightenment gave itself its own name, and the name clearly had propaganda value. The philosophes associated Enlightenment with philosophy, reason, and humanity; religious tolerance; natural rights; and criticism of outmoded customs and prejudices. They tied Enlightenment to "progress" and to the "modern," and it came into question, just as these other terms did, when events cast doubt on the benefits of progress and the virtues of modernity. Although some opposed the Enlightenment from the very beginning as antireligious, undermining of authority, and even atheistic and immoral, the French Revolution of 1789 galvanized the critics of Enlightenment who blamed every excess of revolution on Enlightenment principles. Some critics believed that a conspiracy of Masonic lodges lay behind both the Enlightenment and the French Revolution.

For most of the nineteenth century, condemnation of the Enlightenment came from right-wing sources: those who opposed modernity, secularization, revolution, and sometimes any form of liberalization viewed the Enlightenment with distrust and even disdain. Some of the more extreme of these critics denounced a supposed "Jewish-Masonic conspiracy," believing that Jews and Freemasons benefited most from the spread of Enlightenment principles and worked secretly to jointly undermine Christianity and established monarchical authorities. Adolf Hitler and his followers shared these suspicions, and during World War II the Germans confiscated the records of Masonic lodges in every country they occupied. They sent the documents back to Berlin so that a special office could trace the links of this supposed conspiracy. They found nothing.

After the catastrophes of World War II, the Enlightenment came under attack for the first time from left-wing critics, those who had previously supported modernity, secularization, and even revolution. In a book published right after World War II, *Dialectic of Enlightenment*, Max Horkheimer and Theodor W. Adorno, two German Jewish refugees from Hitler's regime who had fled to the United States, denounced the Enlightenment as "self-destructive" and even "totalitarian" because its belief in reason led not to freedom but to greater bureaucratic control. They asked "why mankind, instead of entering into a truly human condition, is sinking into a new kind of barbarism," and they answered, because we have trusted too much in the Enlightenment and its belief in reason and science. Reason and science might have been tools of criticism of church and state in the eighteenth century, but in the twentieth century, Horkheimer and Adorno insisted, they resulted in concentration camps, ecological disasters, and a deadening mass culture incarnated by Hollywood films. Reason provided the technology to transport millions of Jews to their deaths in scientifically sound gas chambers. Reason invented the atomic bomb and gave us the factories that pollute the atmosphere. The masses did not rise up against these uses of reason because they were distracted by a mass culture that emphasized entertainment rather than reflection. These criticisms of the Enlightenment, however extreme and sometimes outlandish, show how central the Enlightenment remains to the very definition of modern history.

Sources: ARTFL (American Resource, Treasury of the French Language): http://humanities.uchicago.edu/ARTFL/ARTFL.html, Max Horkheimer and Theodor W. Adorno, *Dialectic of Enlightenment*, trans. John Cumming (New York: Continuum, 1993; first published 1947), xi, 6.

Enlightenment ideas developed instead through personal contacts; letters that were hand-copied, circulated, and sometimes published; salon readings of manuscripts; and letters to the editor and book reviews in periodicals. Commenting on the exchanges found in French and Italian newspapers, one writer exclaimed, "Never have new ideas had such rapid circulation at long distance." The salons gave intellectual life an anchor outside the royal court and the church-controlled universities. The best known was the Parisian salon of Madame Marie-Thérèse Geoffrin (1699–1777), a wealthy middle-class widow who had been raised by her grandmother and married off at fourteen to a much older man. Creating a salon was her way of educating herself and participating directly in the movement for reform. She brought together the most exciting thinkers and artists of the time; her social gatherings provided a forum for new ideas and an opportunity to establish new intellectual contacts. In the salon the philosophes could discuss ideas they might hesitate to put into print and thus test public opinion and even push it in new directions. Madame Geoffrin corresponded extensively with influential people across Europe, including Catherine the Great and King Stanislaw August Poniatowski of Poland-Lithuania. One Italian visitor commented, "There is no way to make Naples resemble Paris unless we find a woman to guide us, organize us, *Geoffrinize* us."

Women's role in creating salons provoked criticism from men who resented their power. (See "Contrasting Views," page 690.) Nevertheless, women's salons helped galvanize intellectual life and reform movements all over Europe. Wealthy Jewish women created nine of the fourteen salons in Berlin at the end of the eighteenth century, and in Warsaw, Princess Zofia Czartoryska gathered around her the reform leaders of Poland-Lithuania. Middle-class women in London used their salons to raise money to publish women's writings. Salons could be tied closely to the circles of power: in France, for example, Louis XV's mistress, Jeanne-Antoinette Poisson, first made her reputation as hostess of a salon frequented by Voltaire and Montesquieu. When she became Louis XV's mistress in 1745, she gained the title Marquise de Pompadour and turned her attention to influencing artistic styles by patronizing architects and painters.

Conflicts with Church and State

Madame Geoffrin did not approve of discussions that attacked the Catholic church, but elsewhere voices against organized religion could be heard.

Madame Geoffrin's Salon in 1755
This 1812 painting by Anicet Charles Lemonnier claims to depict the best-known Parisian salon of the 1750s. Lemonnier was only twelve years old in 1755 and so could not have based his rendition on firsthand knowledge. Madame Geoffrin is the figure in blue on the right facing the viewer. The bust is of Voltaire. Rousseau is the fifth person to the left of the bust (facing right) and behind him (facing left) is Raynal.
Giraudon/Art Resource, NY.

Criticisms of religion required daring because the church, whatever its denomination, wielded enormous power in society, and most influential people considered religion an essential foundation of good society and government. Defying such opinion, the Scottish philosopher David Hume (1711–1776) boldly argued in *The Natural History of Religion* (1755) that belief in God rested on superstition and fear rather than on reason. Hume soon met kindred spirits while visiting Paris; he attended a dinner party consisting of "fifteen atheists, and three who had not quite made up their minds."

Before the scientific revolution, virtually every European believed in God. After Newton, however, and despite Newton's own deep religiosity, people could conceive of the universe as an eternally existing, self-perpetuating machine, in which God's intervention was unnecessary. In short, such people could become either *atheists*, who did not believe in any kind of God, or *deists*, who believed in God but gave him no active role in earthly affairs. For the first time, writers claimed the label *atheist* and disputed the common view that atheism led inevitably to immorality.

Deists continued to believe in a benevolent, all-knowing God who had designed the universe and set it in motion. But deists usually rejected the idea that God directly intercedes in the functioning of the universe, and they often criticized the churches for their dogmatic intolerance of dissenters. Voltaire was a deist, and in his popular *Philosophical Dictionary* (1764) he attacked most of the claims of organized Christianity, both Catholic and Protestant. Christianity, he argued, had been the prime source of fanaticism and brutality among humans. Throughout his life, Voltaire's motto was *Ecrasez l'infâme*—"Crush the infamous thing" (the "thing" being bigotry and intolerance). The French authorities publicly burned his *Philosophical Dictionary*.

Criticism of religious intolerance involved more than simply attacking the churches. Critics also had to confront the states to which churches were closely tied. In 1761, a judicial case in Toulouse provoked an outcry throughout France that Voltaire soon joined. When the son of a local Calvinist was found hanged (he had probably committed suicide), authorities accused the father, Jean Calas, of murdering him to prevent his conversion to Catholicism. (Since Louis XIV's revocation of the Edict of Nantes in 1685, it had been illegal to practice Calvinism

Voltaire
In this marble bust by Jean-Antoine Houdon (1741–1828), Voltaire seems the same age as he does in the Lemonnier painting on page 688. However, Houdon began turning out a series of busts of eminent people only in 1771, so it seems likely that Lemonnier imported a later sculpture into his painting of Madame Geoffrin's salon in 1755. This bust shows Voltaire in his old age (he died in 1778).
Art Resource, NY.

publicly in France.) The all-Catholic parlement of Toulouse tried to extract a confession using torture—breaking all Calas's bones—and then executed him when he still refused to confess. Voltaire launched a successful crusade to rehabilitate Jean Calas's good name and to restore the family's properties, which had been confiscated after his death. Voltaire's efforts eventually helped bring about the extension of civil rights to French Protestants and encouraged campaigns to abolish the legal use of torture.

Critics also assailed state and church support for European colonization and slavery. One of the most popular books of the time was the *Philosophical and Political History of European Colonies and Commerce in the Two Indies*, published in 1770 by Abbé Guillaume Raynal (1713–1796), a French Catholic clergyman. Raynal and his collaborators described in excruciating detail the destruction of native populations by Europeans and denounced the inhumanity and irrationality of European ways.

Women and the Enlightenment

During the Enlightenment, women's roles in society became the subject of heated debates. Some men resented what they saw as the growing power of women, especially in the salons. Rousseau railed against their corrupting influence: "Every woman at Paris gathers in her apartment a harem of men more womanish than she." Male writers were divided in their attitudes. Many argued for greater education for women and for women's equality with men in marriage, but others still insisted on the natural weakness of women and their unsuitability for public affairs. Rousseau's *Emile* (Document 1) offered his own influential answer to the question of how women should be educated. The *Encyclopedia* ignored the contributions of salon women and praised women who stayed at home; in the words of one typical contributor, women "constitute the principal ornament of the world. . . . May they, through submissive discretion and through simple, adroit, artless cleverness, spur us [men] on to virtue." Many women objected to these characterizations. The editor of a prominent newspaper for women, Madame de Beaumer, wrote editorials blasting the masculine sense of superiority (Document 2). Many prominent women writers specifically targeted Rousseau's book because it proved to be the most influential educational treatise of the time (Document 3). Their ideas formed the core of nineteenth-century feminism.

1. Jean-Jacques Rousseau, Emile (1762)

Rousseau used the character of Emile's wife-to-be, Sophie, to discuss his ideas about women's education. "Woman is made to please and to be subjugated to man," he claimed. Sophie is educated for a domestic role as wife and mother, and she is taught to be obedient, always helpful to her husband and family, and removed from any participation in the public world. Despite his insistence on the differences between men's and women's roles, many women enthusiastically embraced Rousseau's ideas, for he placed great emphasis on maternalism, breastfeeding, and childrearing. Many women not only took to heart Rousseau's ideas about childrearing, some began to publish manuals for mothers. Rousseau's own children, however, suffered the contradictions that characterized his life. By his own admission, he abandoned to a foundling hospital all the children he had by his lower-class common-law wife because he did not think he could support them properly; if their fate was like that of most abandoned children of the day, they met an early death.

There is no parity between man and woman as to the importance of sex. The male is only a male at certain moments; the female all her life, or at least throughout her youth, is incessantly reminded of her sex and in order to carry out its functions she needs a corresponding constitution. She needs to be careful during pregnancy; she needs rest after childbirth; she needs a quiet and sedentary life while she nurses her children; she needs patience and gentleness in order to raise them; a zeal and affection that nothing can discourage. . . .

The relative duties of the two sexes are not and cannot be equally rigid. When woman complains about the unjust inequalities placed on her by man she is wrong; this inequality is by no means a human institution or at least it is not the work of prejudice but of reason. She to whom nature has entrusted the care of the children must hold herself accountable for them. . . .

On the good constitution of mothers depends primarily that of the children; on the care of women depends the early education of men; and on women, again, depend their morals, their passions, their tastes, their pleasures, and even their happiness. Thus the whole education of women ought to be relative to men. To please them, to be useful to them, to make themselves loved and honored by them, to educate them when young, to care for them when grown, to counsel them, to console them, and to make life agreeable and sweet to them—these are the duties of women at all times, and should be taught them from their infancy.

Source: Susan Groag Bell and Karen M. Offen, *Women, the Family, and Freedom: The Debate in Documents*, vol. 1, *1750–1880* (Stanford: Stanford University Press, 1983), 46–49.

2. Madame de Beaumer, editorial in Le Journal des Dames ("The Ladies' Journal"), 1762

Madame de Beaumer (d. 1766) was the first of three women editors of Le Journal des Dames. *She ran it for two years and published many editorials defending women against their male critics.*

The success of the *Journal des Dames* allows us to triumph over those frivolous persons who have regarded this periodical as a petty work containing only a few bagatelles suited to help them kill time. In truth, Gentlemen, you do us much honor to think that we could not provide things that unite the useful to the agreeable. To rid you of your error, we have made our Journal historical, with a view to putting before the eyes of youth striking images that will guide them toward virtue. . . . An historical *Journal des Dames*! these Gentlemen reasoners reply. How ridiculous! How out of character with the nature of this work, which calls only for little pieces to amuse [ladies] during their toilette. . . . Please, Gentlemen *beaux esprits* [wits], mind your own business and let us write in a manner worthy of our sex; I love this sex, I am jealous to uphold its honor and its rights. If we have not been raised up in the sciences as you have, it is you who are the guilty ones.

Source: Bell and Offen, 27–28.

3. Catharine Macaulay, Letters on Education (1787)

Catharine Sawbridge Macaulay-Graham (1731–1791) was one of the best-known English writers of the 1700s. She wrote immensely popular histories of England and also joined in the debate provoked by Rousseau's Emile.

There is another prejudice . . . which affects yet more deeply female happiness, and female importance; a prejudice, which ought ever to have been confined to the regions of the east, because [of the] state of slavery to which female nature in that part of the world has been ever subjected, and can only suit with the notion of a positive inferiority in the intellectual powers of the female mind. You will soon perceive, that the prejudice which I mean, is that degrading difference in the culture of the understanding, which has prevailed for several centuries in all European societies. . . . Be no longer niggards [misers], then O ye parents, in bestowing on your offspring, every blessing which nature and fortune renders them capable of enjoying! Confine not the education of your daughters to what is regarded as the ornamental parts of it, nor deny the graces to your sons. . . . Let your children be brought up together; let their sports and studies be the same. . . .

Among the most strenuous asserters of a sexual difference in character, Rousseau is the most conspicuous, both on account of that warmth of sentiment which distinguishes all his writing, and the eloquence of his compositions: but never did enthusiasm and the love of paradox, those enemies of philosophical disquisition, appear in more strong opposition to plain sense than in Rousseau's definition of this difference. He sets out with a supposition, that Nature intended the subjection of the one sex to the other; that consequently there must be an inferiority of intellect in the subjected party; but as man is a very imperfect being, and apt to play the capricious tyrant, Nature, to bring things nearer to an equality, bestowed on the woman such attractive graces, and such an insinuating address, as to turn the balance on the other scale. . . .

The situation and education of women . . . is precisely that which must necessarily tend to corrupt and debilitate both the powers of mind and body. From a false notion of beauty and delicacy, their system of nerves is depraved before they come out of the nursery; and this kind of depravity has more influence over the mind, and consequently over morals, than is commonly apprehended.

Source: Bell and Offen, 54–55.

QUESTIONS FOR DEBATE
1. Why would women in the eighteenth century read Rousseau with such interest and even enthusiasm?
2. Why does Madame de Beaumer address herself to male readers if the *Journal des Dames* is intended for women?
3. Why would Macaulay focus so much of her analysis on Rousseau? Why does she not just ignore him?
4. Was the Enlightenment intended only for men?

The book strongly opposed slavery and predicted the appearance of a black hero who would lead a rebellion of slaves "against the blind avarice of European and American colonists." Raynal was forced into exile as soon as the book appeared; like many other Enlightenment books, his work was banned by both the Catholic church and the French government.

The Enlightenment belief in natural rights led many to denounce slavery. An article in the *Encyclopedia* proclaimed, "There is not a single one of these hapless souls . . . who does not have the right to be declared free . . . since neither his ruler nor his father nor anyone else had the right to dispose of his freedom." Some Enlightenment thinkers, however, took a more ambiguous or even negative view. Montesquieu, for example, ridiculed arguments in favor of slavery yet argued that it was less irrational in hot climates because no one would work there without being compelled. Writing on national character, Hume judged blacks to be "naturally inferior to the whites," concluding, "There never was a civilized nation of any other complexion than white." Efforts to study the types of animals in nature led some scientists to rank humans according to their race, with European whites on top and African blacks at the bottom of the scale.

Enlightenment critics of church and state advocated reform, not revolution. Although he lived near the French-Swiss border in case he had to flee arrest, Voltaire, for example, made a fortune in financial speculations, wrote a glowing history called *The Age of Louis XIV* (1751), and lived to be celebrated in his last years as a national hero even by many former foes. Other philosophes also lived respectably, believing that published criticism, rather than violent action, would bring about necessary reforms. As Diderot said, "We will speak against senseless laws until they are reformed; and, while we wait, we will abide by them." Those few who lived long enough to see the French Revolution in 1789 resisted its radical turn, for the philosophes generally regarded the lower classes—"the people"—as ignorant, violent, and prone to superstition, hence in need of leadership from above. They pinned their hopes on educated elites and enlightened rulers.

Despite the philosophes' preference for reform, in the long run their books often had a revolutionary impact. For example, Montesquieu's widely reprinted *Spirit of the Laws* (1748) warned against the dangers of despotism, opposed the divine right of kings, and favored constitutional government. In his somewhat rosy view, Great Britain was "the one nation in the world which has political liberty as the direct object of its constitution." His analysis of British constitutionalism inspired French critics of absolutism and would greatly influence the American revolutionaries.

The Individual and Society

The controversy created by the most notorious conflicts between the philosophes and the various churches and states of Europe drew attention away from a subtle but profound transformation in worldviews. In previous centuries, questions of theological doctrine and church organization had been the main focus of intellectual and even political interest. The Enlightenment writers shifted attention away from religious questions toward the secular study of society and the individual's role in it. Religion did not drop out of sight, but the philosophes tended to make religion a private affair of individual conscience, even while rulers and churches still considered religion very much a public concern.

The Enlightenment interest in secular society produced two major results: it advanced the secularization of European political life that had begun after the Wars of Religion of the sixteenth and seventeenth centuries, and it laid the foundations for the social sciences of the modern era. Not surprisingly, then, many historians and philosophers consider the Enlightenment to be the origin of "modernity," which they define as the belief that human reason, rather than theological doctrine, should set the patterns of social and political life. This belief in reason as the sole foundation for secular authority has often been contested, but it has also proved to be a powerful force for change.

Although most of the philosophes believed that human reason could understand and even remake society and politics, they disagreed about what that reason revealed. Among the many different approaches were two that proved enduringly influential, those of the Scottish philosopher Adam Smith and the Swiss writer Jean-Jacques Rousseau. Smith provided a theory of modern capitalist society and devoted much of his energy to defending free markets as the best way to maximize individual efforts. The modern discipline of economics took shape around the questions raised by Smith. Rousseau set out the principles of a more communitarian philosophy, one that emphasized the needs of the community over those of the individual. His work led both toward democracy and toward communism and continues to inspire heated debate in political science and sociology.

Adam Smith. Adam Smith (1723–1790) optimistically believed that individual interests naturally harmonized with those of the whole society. He claimed, "The study of his own [the individual's] advantage necessarily leads him to prefer what is most advantageous to the society." To explain how this natural harmonization worked, he published *An Inquiry into the Nature and Causes of the Wealth of Nations* in 1776. Like Bernard Mandeville before him but much more systematically, Smith insisted that individual self-interest, even greed, was quite compatible with society's best interest: the laws of supply and demand served as an "invisible hand" ensuring that individual interests would be synchronized with those of the whole society. Market forces—"the propensity to truck, barter, and exchange one thing for another"—naturally brought individual and social interests in line.

Smith rejected the prevailing mercantilist views that the general welfare would be served by accumulating national wealth through agriculture or the hoarding of gold and silver. Instead, he argued that the division of labor in manufacturing increased productivity and generated more wealth for society and well-being for the individual. By performing a manufacturing task over and over again, a person functioned as a part in a well-running machine. In his much-cited example of the manufacture of pins, Smith showed that when the manufacturing process was broken down into separate operations—one man to draw out the wire, another to straighten it, a third to cut it, a fourth to point it, and so on—workers who could make only one pin a day on their own could make thousands working together.

To maximize the effects of market forces and the division of labor, Smith endorsed a concept called *laissez-faire* (that is, "to leave alone") to free the economy from government intervention and control. He insisted that governments eliminate all restrictions on the sale of land, remove restraints on the grain trade, and abandon duties on imports. He believed that free international trade would stimulate production everywhere and thus ensure

---

Major Works of the Enlightenment

1748 Charles-Louis de Secondat, baron of Montesquieu, *Spirit of Laws*

1751 Beginning of publication of the French *Encyclopedia*

1755 David Hume, *The Natural History of Religion*

1762 Jean-Jacques Rousseau, *The Social Contract* and *Emile*

1764 Voltaire, *Philosophical Dictionary*

1770 Abbé Guillaume Raynal, *Philosophical and Political History of European Colonies and Commerce in the Two Indies*

1776 Adam Smith, *An Inquiry into the Nature and Causes of the Wealth of Nations*

1781 Immanuel Kant, *The Critique of Pure Reason*

---

the growth of national wealth. He insisted: "The natural effort of every individual to better his own condition, when suffered to exert itself with freedom and security, is so powerful a principle, that it is alone, and without any assistance, not only capable of carrying the society to wealth and prosperity, but of surmounting a hundred impertinent obstructions with which the folly of human laws too often encumbers its operations." Governments should restrict themselves to providing "security," that is, national defense, internal order, and public works. Smith recognized that government had an important role in providing a secure framework for market activity, but he placed most emphasis on freeing individual endeavor from what he saw as excessive government interference.

Jean-Jacques Rousseau. Much more pessimistic about the relation between individual self-interest and the good of society was Jean-Jacques Rousseau (1712–1778). In Rousseau's view, society itself threatened natural rights or freedoms: "Man is born free, and everywhere he is in chains." Rousseau first gained fame by writing a prize-winning essay in 1749 in which he argued that the revival of science and the arts had corrupted social morals, not improved them. This startling conclusion seemed to oppose some of the Enlightenment's most cherished beliefs. Rather than improving society, he claimed, science and art raised artificial barriers between

Rousseau's Worries
Jean-Jacques Rousseau's novel
The New Heloise *(1761) sold
better than any other work in
French in the second half of
the eighteenth century. But
Rousseau himself was deeply
concerned about the effects of
novel reading, especially on
young women. The first of these
illustrations for the novel (on the
left) by Moreau the Younger, was
rejected by Rousseau because
the couple (Julie and Saint
Preux) are shown in direct physical contact. He accepted the engraving on the right, by Gravelot,
because it only hinted at passion.*
Bibliothèque Nationale.

people and their natural state. Rousseau's works ex-
tolled the simplicity of rural life over urban society.
Although he participated in the salons and contributed to the *Encyclopedia*, Rousseau always felt ill
at ease in high society, and he periodically withdrew
to live in solitude far from Paris. Paradoxically, his
"solitude" was often paid for by wealthy upper-class
patrons, who lodged him on their estates, even as
his writings decried the upper-class privilege that
made his efforts possible.

Rousseau explored the tension between the
individual and society in various ways. In his best-
selling novel *The New Heloise* (1761), he told the
story of Julie, who gives up her penniless lover Saint
Preux to marry someone else to please her father.
Rousseau completely transformed the medieval
story of Heloise and Abelard to focus on the conflict between social demands for virtue in marriage
and Julie's intensely personal feelings. Julie learns to
live a virtuous, domestic life with her husband and
sacrifices her feelings for Saint Preux; her death at
the end of the novel makes her into a saintly heroine, but it also raises questions about the cost to the
individual of social virtue. In his work on education, *Emile* (1762), Rousseau tried to find a less
tragic solution to the conflict between the individ-

ual and society. Without relying solely on books and
free from the supervision of the clergy, who controlled most schools, the boy Emile works alone
with his tutor to develop practical skills and independent ways of thinking. After developing his individuality, Emile joins society through marriage to
Sophie, who received the education Rousseau
thought appropriate for women. (See "Contrasting
Views," page 690.)

In *The Social Contract* (1762), Rousseau proposed a political solution to the tension between the
individual and society. Whereas earlier he had argued that society corrupted the individual by taking
him out of nature, in this work Rousseau insisted
that the right kind of political order could make
people truly moral and free. In other words, he
hoped to generalize the solution advanced in *Emile*
to all of society. Individual moral freedom could be
achieved only by learning to subject one's individual interests to "the general will," that is, the good
of the community. Individuals did this by entering
into a social contract not with their rulers, but with
one another. If everyone followed the general will,
then all would be equally free and equally moral because they lived under a law to which they had all
consented.

These arguments threatened the legitimacy of eighteenth-century governments. Rousseau derived his social contract from human nature, not from history, tradition, or the Bible. He implied that people would be most free and moral under a republican form of government with direct democracy, and his abstract model included no reference to differences in social status. He roundly condemned slavery: "To decide that the son of a slave is born a slave is to decide that he is not born a man." Not surprisingly, authorities in both Geneva and Paris banned *The Social Contract* for undermining political authority. Rousseau's works became a kind of political bible for the French revolutionaries of 1789, and his attacks on private property inspired the communists of the nineteenth century such as Karl Marx. Rousseau's rather mystical concept of the general will remains controversial. The "greatest

good of all," according to Rousseau, was liberty and equality, but he also insisted that the individual could be "forced to be free" by the terms of the social contract. He provided no legal protections for individual rights. Rousseau's particular version of democracy might not preserve the individual freedoms so important to Adam Smith.

Spreading the Enlightenment

The spread of the Enlightenment followed a distinct geographic and social pattern: it flourished in places where an educated middle class provided an eager audience for ideas of constitutionalism and reform. It therefore found its epicenter in the triangle formed by London, Amsterdam, and Paris and diffused outward to eastern and southern Europe and North America (Map 19.1). Where constitutionalism and

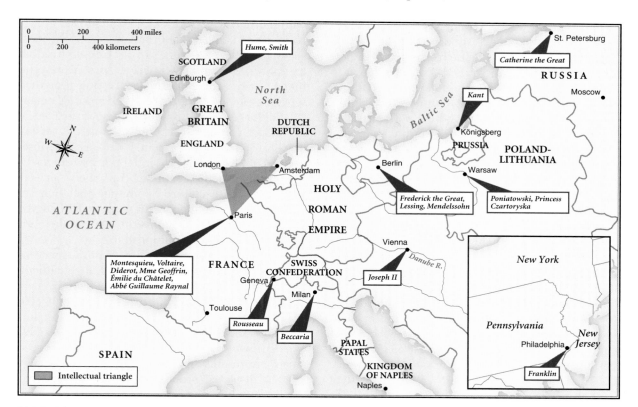

MAP 19.1 Centers of the Enlightenment
Paris was the heart of the Enlightenment because most philosophes, whatever their nationality, spoke and wrote French. Both Catherine the Great and Frederick the Great corresponded in French with their favorite French philosophes. Many French philosophes traveled to London where they met with their English and Scottish counterparts. Montesquieu and Voltaire wrote extensively about English customs. Dutch printers published books censored in France and made them available throughout Europe and the American colonies.

the guarantee of individual freedoms were most advanced, as in Great Britain and the Dutch Republic, the movement had less of an edge because there was, in a sense, less need for it. Scottish and English writers concentrated on economics, philosophy, and history rather than politics or social relations. Dutch printers made money publishing the books that were forbidden in France. In British North America, Enlightenment ideas helped stiffen growing colonial resistance to British rule after 1763. In places with small middle classes, such as Spain, the Italian states, and Russia, governments successfully suppressed writings they did not like. Italian philosophes, such as the Milanese penal reformer Cesare Beccaria (1738–1794), got moral support from their French counterparts in the face of stern censorship at home.

The French Enlightenment. The hot spot of the Enlightenment was France. French writers published the most daring critiques of church and state and suffered the most intense harassment and persecution. Voltaire, Diderot, and Rousseau all faced arrest, exile, or even imprisonment. The Catholic church and royal authorities routinely forbade the publication of their books, and the police arrested publishers who ignored their warnings. Yet the French monarchy was far from the most autocratic in Europe, and Voltaire, Diderot, and Rousseau all ended their lives as cultural heroes. France seems to have been curiously caught in the middle during the Enlightenment: with fewer constitutional guarantees of individual freedom than Great Britain, it still enjoyed much higher levels of prosperity and cultural development than most other European countries. In short, French elites had reason to complain, the means to make their complaints known, and a government torn between the desires to censor dissident ideas and to appear open to modernity and progress. The French government controlled publishing—all books had to get official permissions—but not as tightly as in Spain, where the Catholic Inquisition made up its own list of banned books, or in Russia, where Catherine the Great allowed no opposition.

By the 1760s, the French government regularly ignored the publication of many works once thought offensive or subversive. In addition, a growing flood of works printed abroad poured into France and circulated underground. In the Dutch Republic and Swiss cities, private companies made fortunes smuggling illegal books into France over mountain passes and back roads. Foreign printers provided secret catalogs of their offerings and sold their products through booksellers who were willing to market forbidden books for a high price. Among such books were not only the philosophical treatises of the Enlightenment but also pornographic books and pamphlets (some by Diderot) lampooning the Catholic clergy and leading members of the royal court. In the 1770s and 1780s, lurid descriptions of sexual promiscuity at the French court helped undermine the popularity of the throne.

The German Enlightenment. In the German states the Enlightenment followed a very different course. Whereas the French philosophes often took a violently anticlerical and combative tone, their German counterparts avoided direct political confrontations with authorities. Gotthold Lessing (1729–1781) complained in 1769 that Prussia was still "the most slavish society in Europe" in its lack of freedom to criticize government policies. As a playwright, literary critic, and philosopher, Lessing promoted religious toleration for the Jews and spiritual emancipation of Germans from foreign, especially French, models of culture, which still dominated. Lessing also introduced the German Jewish writer Moses Mendelssohn (1729–1786) into Berlin salon society. Mendelssohn labored to build bridges between German and Jewish culture by arguing that Judaism was a rational and undogmatic religion. He believed persecution and discrimination against the Jews would end as reason triumphed.

Reason was also the chief focus of the most influential German thinker of the Enlightenment, Immanuel Kant (1724–1804). Kant, a university professor who lectured on everything from economics to astronomy, wrote one of the most important works in the history of Western philosophy, *The Critique of Pure Reason* (1781). Kant admired Adam Smith and especially Rousseau, whose portrait he displayed proudly in his lodgings. Just as Smith founded modern economics and Rousseau modern political theory, Kant in *Critique of Pure Reason* set the foundations for modern philosophy. In this complex book, Kant established the doctrine of *idealism*, the belief that true understanding can come only from examining the ways in which ideas are formed in the mind. Ideas are shaped, Kant argued, not just by sensory information (a position central to *empiricism*, a philosophy based on John Locke's writings) but also by the operation on that information of mental categories such as space and time. In Kant's philosophy these "categories of understanding" were neither sensory nor supernatural; they were entirely ideal and abstract and located in the human mind. For Kant the supreme philosophical questions—Does God exist? Is personal immortality possible? Do humans have free will?—were unanswerable by reason alone. But like Rousseau, Kant insisted that true moral freedom could be achieved only by living in society and obeying its laws.

The Limits of Reason: Roots of Romanticism and Religious Revival

As Kant showed, reason had its limits: it could not answer all of life's pressing questions. In reaction to what some saw as the Enlightenment's excessive reliance on the authority of human reason, a new artistic movement called *romanticism* took root. Although it would not fully flower until the early nineteenth century, romanticism traced its emphasis on individual genius, deep emotion, and the joys of nature to thinkers like Rousseau who had scolded the philosophes for ignoring those aspects of life that escaped and even conflicted with the power of reason. Rousseau's autobiographical *Confessions*, published posthumously in 1782, caused an immediate sensation because it revealed so much about his inner emotional life, including his sexual longings and his almost paranoid distrust of other Enlightenment figures.

The appeal to feelings and emotions also increased interest in the occult. In the 1780s, a charismatic Austrian physician turned "experimenter," Franz Mesmer, awed crowds of aristocrats and middle-class admirers with his Paris demonstrations of "animal magnetism." He passed a weak electrical current through tubs filled with water or iron filings, around which groups of his disciples sat, holding hands; with this process of "mesmerism" he claimed to cure their ailments. (The word *mesmerize*, meaning "hypnotize" or "hold spellbound," is derived from Mesmer's name.)

A novel by the young German writer Johann Wolfgang von Goethe (1749–1832) captured the early romantic spirit with its glorification of emo-

tion. *The Sorrows of Young Werther* (1774) told of a young man who resembles Rousseau's Julie in many respects: he loves nature and rural life and is unhappy in love. When the woman he loves marries another, he falls into deep melancholy and eventually kills himself. Reason cannot save him. The book spurred a veritable Werther craze: there were Werther costumes, Werther engravings and embroidery, medallions, a perfume called Eau de Werther, and, unfortunately, a few imitations of Werther's suicide. The young Napoleon Bonaparte, who was to build an empire for France, claimed to have read Goethe's novel seven times.

Religious revivals underlined the limits of reason in a different way. Much of the Protestant world experienced an "awakening" in the 1740s. In the German states, Pietist groups founded new communities; and in the British North American colonies, revivalist Protestant preachers drew thousands of fervent believers in a movement called the Great Awakening. In North America bitter conflicts between revivalists and their opponents in the established churches prompted the leaders on

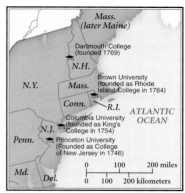

New Colleges in North America

both sides to set up new colleges to support their beliefs. These included Princeton, Columbia, Brown, and Dartmouth, all founded between 1746 and 1769.

Revivalism also stirred eastern European Jews at about the same time. Israel ben Eliezer (c. 1700–1760), later known as Ba'al Shem Tov (or the Besht, from the initials), laid the foundation for the Hasidic sect in the 1740s and 1750s. Teaching outside the synagogue system, Ba'al Shem Tov traveled the Polish countryside offering to cure men of their evil spirits. He invented a new form of popular prayer, in which the believer aimed to annihilate his own personality in order to let the supernatural speak through him. His followers, the *Hasidim* (Hebrew for "most pious" Jews), often prayed at the top of their lungs, joyfully swaying and clapping their hands. They scorned the formality of the regular synagogues in favor of their own prayer houses, where they gathered in rustic clothing and broad fur

A Hasid and His Wife
The followers of Ba'al Shem Tov were known as Hasidim ("most pious Jews"). They insisted on wearing Polish peasant-style clothing even if they themselves were not peasants. The Hasidim stressed devotion to the rebbe *("teacher and spiritual guide").*
Encyclopedia of Jewish History.

hats to emphasize their piety and simplicity. Their practices soon spread all over Poland-Lithuania.

Most of the waves of Protestant revivalism ebbed after the 1750s, but in Great Britain the movement known as *Methodism* continued to grow through the end of the century. John Wesley (1703–1791), the Oxford-educated son of an Anglican cleric, founded Methodism, a term evoked by Wesley's insistence on strict self-discipline and a methodical approach to religious study and observance. In 1738, Wesley had a mystical experience in which he felt the need to submit his life totally to Christ. Immediately afterward, he began to travel all over the British Isles, preaching a new brand of Protestantism that emphasized an intense personal experience of salvation and a life of thrift, abstinence, and hard work. In meadows and brickyards, in mine pits and copperworks, wherever ordinary people played or worked, Wesley would mount a table or a box to speak or begin a hymn. He slept in his followers' homes, ate their food, and treated their illnesses with various remedies, including small electric shocks for nervous diseases (Wesley eagerly followed Benjamin Franklin's experiments with electricity). In fifty years, Wesley preached forty thousand sermons, an average of fifteen a week. Not surprisingly, his preaching disturbed the Anglican authorities, who refused to let him preach in the churches. In response, Wesley began to ordain his

own clergy. Nevertheless, during Wesley's lifetime the Methodist leadership remained politically conservative; Wesley himself wrote many pamphlets urging order, loyalty, and submission to higher authorities. He denounced political agitation in the 1770s because he said it threatened to make Great Britain "a field of blood" ruled by "King Mob."

❖ Society and Culture in an Age of Enlightenment

Religious revivals and the first stirrings of romanticism show that all intellectual currents did not flow in the same channel. Similarly, some social and cultural developments manifested the influence of Enlightenment ideas but others did not. The traditional leaders of European societies—the nobles—responded to Enlightenment ideals in contradictory fashion: many simply reasserted their privileges and resisted the influence of the Enlightenment, but an important minority embraced change and actively participated in reform efforts. The expanding middle classes saw in the Enlightenment a chance to make their claim for joining society's governing elite. They bought Enlightenment books, joined Masonic lodges, and patronized new styles in art, music, and literature. The lower classes had much less contact with the Enlightenment. Economic growth affected them much more. Continuing population increase contributed to a rise in prices for basic goods, but the industrialization of textile manufacturing, which began in this period, made cotton clothing more accessible to those at the bottom of the social scale. Social change, however, was neither uniform nor painless. Most peasants remained tied to the land and their lords; those who moved to the cities in search of work did not always find their situations better.

The Nobility's Reassertion of Privilege

Nobles made up about 3 percent of the European population, but the proportion and their way of life varied greatly from country to country. At least 10 percent of the population in Poland was noble and 7 to 8 percent in Spain, in contrast to only 2 percent in Russia and between 1 and 2 percent in the rest of western Europe. Polish and Spanish nobles in particular often lived in poverty; titles did not guarantee wealth. The wealthiest European nobles luxuriated in almost unimaginable opulence. Many of the English peers, for example, owned more than ten thousand acres of land (the average western European peasant owned about five acres), invested widely in government bonds and trading companies, kept several country residences with scores of servants as well as houses in London, and occasionally even had their own private orchestras as well as libraries of expensive books, greenhouses for exotic plants, kennels of pedigree dogs, and collections of antiques, firearms, and scientific instruments.

In the face of the commercialization of agriculture and inflation of prices, European aristocrats converted their remaining legal rights (called *seigneurial dues*, from the French *seigneur*, for "lord") into money payments and used them to support an increasingly expensive lifestyle. Peasants felt the squeeze as a result. French peasants, for instance, paid a wide range of dues to their landlords, including payments to grind grain at the lord's mill, bake bread in his oven, press grapes at his winepress, and various inheritance taxes on the land. In addition, peasants had to work without compensation for a specified number of days every year on the public roads. They also paid taxes to the government on salt, an essential preservative, and on the value of their land; customs duties if they sold produce or wine in town; and the tithe on their grain (one-tenth of the crop) to the church.

In Britain, the landed gentry could not claim these same onerous dues from their tenants, but they tenaciously defended their exclusive right to hunt game. The game laws kept the poor from eating meat and helped protect the social status of the rich. The gentry enforced the game laws themselves by hiring gamekeepers who hunted down poachers and even set traps for them in the forests. According to the law, anyone who poached deer or rabbits while armed or disguised could be sentenced to death. After 1760, the number of arrests for breaking the game laws increased dramatically. In most other countries, too, hunting was the special right of the nobility and a cause of deep popular resentment.

Even though Enlightenment writers sharply criticized nobles' insistence on special privileges, most aristocrats maintained their marks of distinction. The male court nobility continued to sport swords, plumed hats, makeup, and powdered hair, while middle-class men wore simpler and more somber clothing. Aristocrats had their own seats in church and their own quarters in the universities. Frederick II ("the Great") of Prussia (r. 1740–1786) made sure that nobles dominated both the army officer corps and the civil bureaucracy. Catherine II of Russia (r. 1762–1796) granted the nobility vast tracts of land, the exclusive right to own serfs, and exemption from personal taxes and corporal punishment. Her Charter of the Nobility of 1785 codified these privileges in exchange for the nobles' political subservience to the state. In many countries, including Spain and France, the law prohibited aristocrats from engaging directly in retail trade. In Austria, Spain, the Italian states, Poland-Lithuania, and Russia, most nobles consequently cared little about Enlightenment ideas; they did not read the books of the philosophes and feared reforms that might challenge their dominance of rural society.

In France, Britain, and the western German states, however, the nobility proved more open to the new ideas. Among those who personally corresponded with Rousseau, for example, half were nobles, as were 20 percent of the 160 contributors to the *Encyclopedia*. It had not escaped their notice that Rousseau had denounced inequality. In his view, it was "manifestly contrary to the law of nature . . . that a handful of people should gorge themselves with superfluities while the hungry multitude goes in want of necessities."

The Middle Class and the Making of a New Elite

Enlightenment ideals helped break down the traditional barriers between the aristocracy and the middle class in western Europe and were in turn further energized by this development. The Enlightenment offered middle-class people an intellectual and cultural route to social improvement; it gave them the chance to join with nobles in a new mixed elite, united by common interests in reform and new cultural tastes. Intermarriage, the spread of businesslike attitudes among the nobility, and the middle-class emulation of noble ways encouraged this intermixing of the elite. Although middle-class people had many reasons to resent the nobles, they also aspired to be like them. The richest hoped to buy themselves a title and share all the special privileges accorded nobles.

The term *middle class* referred to the middle position on the social ladder; it comprised the families who did not have legal titles like the nobility above them but who did not work with their hands like the peasants, artisans, or workers below them. Most middle-class families lived in towns or cities and earned their living in some professional capacity—as doctors, lawyers, or lower-level officials or through investment in land, trade, or manufacturing. In the eighteenth century, the ranks of the middle class—also known as the *bourgeoisie* after *bourg*, the French word for "town," or *bourgeois*, the French word for "city dweller"—grew steadily in western Europe as a result of economic expansion. In France, for example, the overall population grew by about one-third in the 1700s, but the bourgeoisie nearly tripled in size.

Lodges and Learned Societies. Nobles and middle-class professionals mingled in Enlightenment salons and joined the new Masonic lodges and local learned societies. The Masonic lodges began as social clubs with elaborate secret rituals based on those of the masons' guilds. Their members were known as *freemasons* because that was the term given to apprentice masons when they were deemed "free" to practice as masters of their guild. Although not explicitly political in aim, the lodges encouraged equality among members, and both aristocrats and middle-class men could join. In France, women set up their own Masonic lodges. Members wrote constitutions for their lodges and elected their own officers, thus promoting a direct experience of constitutional government.

Freemasonry arose in Great Britain and spread eastward: the first French and Italian lodges opened in 1726; Frederick II of Prussia founded a lodge in 1740; and after 1750, freemasonry spread in Poland, Russia, and British North America. Despite the papacy's condemnation of freemasonry in 1738 as subversive of religious and civil authority, lodges continued to multiply throughout the eighteenth century because they offered a place for socializing outside of the traditional channels and a way of declaring one's interest in the Enlightenment and reform. In short, freemasonry offered a kind of secular religion. After 1789 and the outbreak of the French Revolution, conservatives would blame the lodges for every kind of political upheaval, but in the 1700s many high-ranking nobles became active members and saw no conflict with their privileged status.

Nobles and middle-class professionals also met in local learned societies, which greatly increased in number in this period. They gathered to discuss such practical issues as new scientific innovations

Neoclassical Style
In this Georgian interior of Syon House on the outskirts of London, various neoclassical motifs are readily apparent: Greek columns, Greek-style statuary on top of the columns, and Roman-style mosaics in the floor. The Scottish architect Robert Adams created this room for the duke of Northumberland in the 1760s. Adams had spent four years in Italy and returned in 1758 to London to decorate homes in the "Adams style," meaning the neoclassical manner.
Fotomas Index, UK.

or methods to eliminate poverty. The societies, or academies, brought the Enlightenment down from the realm of books and ideas to the level of concrete reforms. They sponsored essay contests, such as the one won by Rousseau in 1749, or the one set by the society in Metz in 1785 on the question "Are there means for making the Jews happier and more useful in France?" The Metz society approved essays that argued for granting the Jews civil rights.

New Cultural Styles.   Shared tastes in travel, architecture, and the arts helped solidify the intermingled elite of nobility and middle class. "Grand tours" of Europe often led upper-class youths to recently discovered Greek and Roman ruins at Pompeii, Herculaneum, and Paestum in Italy. These excavations aroused enthusiasm for the neoclassical style in architecture and painting, which began pushing aside the rococo and the long dominant baroque. Urban residences and new government buildings soon reflected the neoclassical emphasis on purity and clarity of forms. As one German writer noted, with considerable exaggeration, "Everything in Paris is in the Greek style." In the 1760s and 1770s in Britain, the upper classes began building magnificent houses in the neoclassical style called Georgian (after the reigning king, George III), and pottery, furniture, fabrics, cutlery, and even wall-paper incorporated classical themes and allowed middle-class people to emulate the richest aristocrats.

This period also supported artistic styles other than neoclassicism. Frederick II of Prussia built himself a palace in the earlier rococo style and gave it a French name, *Sans-souci* ("worry-free"), and filled it with the works of French masters of the rococo. The new emphasis on emotion and family life, represented in Rousseau's *The New Heloise*, was reflected in a growing taste for moralistic family scenes in painting. The paintings of Jean-Baptiste Greuze (1725–1805), much praised by Diderot, depicted ordinary families at moments of domestic crisis. Such subjects appealed in particular to the middle-class public, which now attended the official painting exhibitions in France that were held regularly every other year after 1737. Court painting nonetheless remained much in demand. Marie-Louise-Elizabeth Vigée-Lebrun (1755–1842), who painted portraits at the French court, reported that in the 1780s "it was difficult to get a place on my waiting list. . . . I was the fashion."

The English engraver and painter William Hogarth (1697–1764) ranged from noble portraits to popular moralistic print series. He sold his engravings to the middle class but he still hoped to have his work taken seriously as high art. The English potter Josiah Wedgwood (1730–1795) almost

Jean-Baptiste Greuze, *The Beloved Mother* (1765)
Greuze made his reputation as a painter of moralistic family scenes. In this one, a mother has just finished breast-feeding her infant, a practice urgently advocated at just this time by Rousseau. The contented mother is surrounded by adoring children and an admiring husband. Diderot praised Greuze's work as "morality in paint," but in later years Greuze began to depict much more ambiguous scenes, often with an erotic subtext.
Art Resource, NY.

single-handedly created a mass market for domestic crockery by appealing to middle-class desires to emulate the rich and royal. His designs of special tea sets for the British queen, for Catherine the Great of Russia, and for leading aristocrats allowed him to advertise his wares as fashionable. As he said, "Few ladies dare venture at anything out of the common stile 'till authorized by their betters." By 1767, he claimed that his Queensware pottery had "spread over the whole Globe," and indeed by then his pottery was being marketed in France, Russia, Venice, the Ottoman Empire, and British North America.

Although wealthy nobles still patronized Europe's leading musicians, music too began to reflect the broadening of the elite and the spread of Enlightenment ideals as classical forms replaced the baroque style. Complex polyphony gave way to melody, which made the music more accessible to ordinary listeners. The violin's tone became stronger and more resonant, and it overcame a reputation as fit only for village dances. Mass sections of string instruments became the backbone of professional orchestras, which now played to large audiences of well-to-do listeners in sizable concert halls. The public concert gradually displaced the private recital, and a new attitude toward "the classics" developed: for the first time in the 1770s and 1780s, concert groups began to play older music rather than simply playing the latest commissioned works.

This laid the foundation for what we still call *classical* music today, that is, a repertory of the greatest music of the eighteenth and early nineteenth centuries. Because composers now created works that would be performed over and over again as part of a classical repertory, rather than occasional pieces for the court or noble patrons, they deliberately attempted to write lasting works. As a result, the major composers began to produce fewer symphonies: the Austrian composer Franz Joseph Haydn (1732–1809) wrote more than one hundred symphonies, but his successor Ludwig van Beethoven (1770–1827) would create only nine.

The two supreme masters of the new musical style of the eighteenth century show that the transition from noble patronage to classical concerts was far from complete. The Austrians Haydn and Wolfgang Amadeus Mozart (1756–1791) both wrote for noble patrons, but by the early 1800s their compositions had been incorporated into the canon of concert classics all over Europe. Incredibly prolific, both excelled in combining lightness, clarity, and profound emotion. Both also wrote numerous Italian operas, a genre whose popularity continued to grow: in the 1780s, the Papal States alone boasted forty opera houses. Haydn spent most of his career working for a Hungarian noble family, the Eszterházys. Asked why he had written no string quintets (at which Mozart excelled), he responded simply: "No one has ordered any."

Reading Matters. The Enlightenment created a new public for reading that extended far beyond the narrow confines of standard secondary and higher education. In secondary school, whether lay- or church-run, boys studied Latin, Greek, philosophy, and logic but spent little time on mathematics, science, history, or modern languages. Girls learned domestic skills, some music, and one or two foreign languages, but they did not receive the classical education considered essential for government service or intellectual life. Boys and girls read Enlightenment books at home, not in school. The universities of many countries appeared rigid and behind the times. As an Austrian reformer complained about the universities in his country, "Critical history, natural sciences—which are supposed to make enlightenment general and combat prejudice—were neglected or wholly unknown."

Shaped by coffeehouses, Masonic lodges, and public concerts more than by formal schooling, the new reading public fed a frenzied increase in publication. By the end of the eighteenth century, six times as many books were being published in the German states, for instance, as at the beginning. One Parisian author commented that "people are certainly reading ten times as much in Paris as they did a hundred years ago." Although religious books still predominated, books on history, the arts, and the sciences proliferated. Provincial towns in Britain, France, the Dutch Republic, and the German states published their own newspapers; by 1780, thirty-seven English towns had local newspapers. Newspapers advertised arithmetic, dancing, and drawing lessons, and they did not always stick to high-minded subjects; they also advertised cures for venereal disease and abortifacients. Lending libraries multiplied, and, in England especially, even small villages housed secular book clubs. Women benefited as much as men from the spread of print. As one Englishman observed, "By far the greatest part of ladies now have a taste for books." Catherine Macaulay (1731–1791) published best-selling histories of Britain, and in France Stéphanie de Genlis (1746–1830) wrote children's books—a genre that was growing in importance as middle-class parents became more interested in education.

The novel had become a respectable and influential genre. Among the most widely read novels were those of the English printer and writer Samuel Richardson (1689–1761). In *Clarissa Harlowe* (1747–1748), a long novel in eight volumes, Richardson told the story of a young woman from a heartless upper-class family who is torn between her family's choice of a repulsive suitor and her attraction to Lovelace, an aristocratic rake. Although she runs off with Lovelace to escape her family, she resists his advances; after being drugged and raped by Lovelace—despite the frantic pleas of readers of the first volumes to spare her—Clarissa dies of what can only be called a broken heart. One woman complained to Richardson, "I verily believe I have shed a pint of tears, and my heart is still bursting." The French writer Diderot compared Richardson to Moses, Homer, Euripides, and Sophocles.

Novels aroused criticism, however, because they sympathetically portrayed characters from the lower classes. Even Richardson attacked his fellow English novelist Henry Fielding: "I found the characters and situations so wretchedly low and dirty, that I imagined I could not be interested for any one of them. . . . It is beyond my conception, that a man of family, and who had some learning, and who really is a writer, should descend so excessively low, in all his pieces. Who can care for any of his people?" Although Richardson wrote *Clarissa* as a kind of manual of virtuous female conduct, critics worried that novels undermined morals with their portrayals of low-life characters, the seductions of virtuous women, and other examples of immoral behavior.

Spotlight on Children. As the rates of child mortality gradually declined in the 1700s, children became the focus of much new attention. Rousseau's *Emile* attracted so many readers because it offered an educational approach for gently drawing the best out of children rather than repressing their natural curiosity and love of learning. The book helped change attitudes in the new elite toward children, who were no longer viewed only as little sinners in need of harsh discipline. Paintings now showed individual children playing at their favorite activities rather than formally posed with their families. Books about and for children became popular. *The Newtonian System of the Universe Digested for Young Minds*, by "Tom Telescope," was published in Britain in 1761 and reprinted many times. In 1730, no shops specialized in children's toys in Britain; by 1780, such shops could be found throughout the country. In 1762, John Spilsbury, a London engraver and mapmaker, invented the jigsaw puzzle when he mounted a map on a sheet of wood and cut around the borders of the countries using a fine-bladed saw. Babies' and children's clothing now differed in style from adult clothing: childhood was seen as a separate stage of life, and children were no longer considered miniature adults.

The Enlightenment's emphasis on reason, self-control, and childhood innocence made parents increasingly anxious about their children's sexuality. Moralists and physicians wrote books about the evils of masturbation, "proving" that it led to physical and mental degeneration and even madness. One English writer linked masturbation to debility of body and of mind; infertility; epilepsy; loss of memory, sight, and hearing; distortions of the eyes, mouth, and face; a pale, sallow, and bluish complexion; wasting of the limbs; idiotism; and death itself. The Enlightenment taught the middle and upper classes to value their children and to expect their improvement through education, but at the same time it encouraged excessive concern about children being left too much to their own devices.

Life on the Margins

The upper and middle classes worried most about the increasing numbers of poor people. Although booming foreign trade—French colonial trade increased tenfold in the 1700s—fueled a dramatic economic expansion, the results did not necessarily trickle all the way down the social scale. The population of Europe grew by nearly 30 percent, with especially striking gains in England, Ireland, Prussia, and Hungary. (See "Taking Measure," page 704.) Even though food production increased, shortages and crises still occurred periodically. Prices went up in many countries after the 1730s and continued to

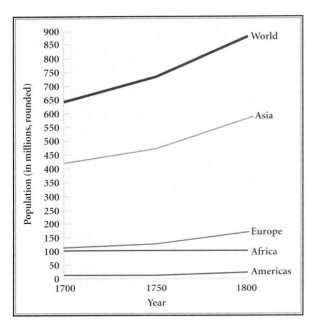

TAKING MEASURE World Population Growth, 1700–1800

Asia had many more people than Europe, and both Asia and Europe were growing much more rapidly in the 1700s than Africa or the Americas. The population stagnation in Africa has been the subject of much scholarly controversy. What are the advantages of a growing population? What are the disadvantages?

Adapted from Andre Gundar Frank, *Reorient: Global Economy in the Asian Age* (Berkeley: University of California Press), 1998.

rise gradually until the early nineteenth century; wages in many trades rose as well, but less quickly than prices. Peasants who produced surpluses to sell in local markets and shopkeepers and artisans who could increase their sales to meet growing demand prospered. But those at the bottom of the social ladder—day laborers in the cities and peasants with small holdings—lived on the edge of dire poverty, and when they lost their land or work, they either migrated to the cities or wandered the roads in search of food and work. In France alone, 200,000 workers left their homes every year in search of seasonal employment elsewhere. At least 10 percent of Europe's urban population depended on some form of charity.

The growing numbers of poor overwhelmed local governments. In some countries, beggars and vagabonds had been locked up in workhouses since the mid-1600s. The expenses for running these overcrowded institutions increased 60 percent in England between 1760 and 1785. After 1740, most German towns created workhouses that were part workshop, part hospital, and part prison. Such institutions also appeared for the first time in Boston, New York, and Philadelphia. To supplement the inadequate system of religious charity, offices for the poor, public workshops, and workhouse-hospitals, the French government created *dépôts de mendicité*, or beggar houses, in 1767. The government sent people to these new workhouses to labor in manufacturing, but most were too weak or sick to work, and 20 percent of them died within a few months of incarceration. The ballooning number of poor people created fears about rising crime. To officials, beggars seemed more aggressive than ever. The handful of police assigned to keep order in each town or district found themselves confronted with increasing incidents of rural banditry and crimes against property.

Persistence of Popular Culture. An increase in literacy, especially in the cities, allowed some lower-class people to participate in new tastes and ideas. One French observer insisted, "These days, you see a waiting-maid in her backroom, a lackey in an anteroom reading pamphlets. People can read in almost all classes of society." In France, however, only 50 percent of men and 27 percent of women could read and write in the 1780s (although that was twice the rate of a century earlier). Literacy rates were higher in England and the Dutch Republic, but much lower in eastern Europe. About one in four Parisians owned books, but the lower classes overwhelmingly read religious books, as they had in the past.

Whereas the new elite might attend salons, concerts, or art exhibitions, peasants enjoyed their traditional forms of popular entertainment, such as fairs and festivals, and the urban lower classes relaxed in cabarets and taverns. Sometimes pleasures were cruel. In Britain, bullbaiting, bearbaiting, dogfighting, and cockfighting were all common forms of entertainment that provided opportunities for organized gambling. Even "gentle" sports frequented by the upper classes had their violent side, showing that the upper classes had not become so different as they sometimes thought. Cricket matches, whose rules were first laid down in 1744, were often accompanied by brawls among fans (not unlike soccer matches today, though on a much smaller scale). Many Englishmen enjoyed what one observer called a "battle royal with sticks, pebbles and hog's dung."

Changes in Sexual Behavior. As population increased and villagers began to move to cities to better their prospects, sexual behavior changed too. The rates of births out of wedlock soared, from less than 5 percent of all births in the seventeenth century to nearly 20 percent at the end of the eighteenth. Historians have disagreed about the causes and meaning of this change. Some detect in this pattern a sign of sexual liberation and the beginnings of a modern sexual revolution: as women moved out of the control of their families, they began to seek their own sexual fulfillment. Others view this change more bleakly, as a story of seduction and betrayal: family and community pressure had once forced a man to marry a woman pregnant with his child, but now a man could abandon a pregnant lover, just by moving away.

Increased mobility brought freedom for some women, but it also aggravated the vulnerability of those newly arrived in cities from the countryside. For them, desperation, not reason, often ruled their choices. Women who came to the city as domestic servants had little recourse against masters or fellow servants who seduced or raped them. The result was a startling rise in abandoned babies. Most European cities established foundling hospitals in the 1700s, but infant and child mortality was 50 percent higher in such institutions than for children brought up at home. Some women tried herbs, laxatives, or crude surgical means of abortion; a few, usually servants who would lose their jobs if their employers discovered they had borne a child, resorted to infanticide.

European states had long tried to regulate sexual behavior but without much consistent success. Every country had laws against prostitution, adultery, fornication, sodomy, and infanticide. Despite official denunciations, sexual entertainment for men grew increasingly commercialized in this period of economic growth, and houses of prostitution became more specialized, developing into flagellation clubs and bagnios, which combined brothel and bathhouse. Reformers advocated lessening of punishments for fornication, which often included some form of public humiliation, and they criticized the

harshness of laws against infanticide, but they showed no mercy for "sodomites" (as male homosexuals were called), who in some places, in particular the Dutch Republic, were systematically persecuted and imprisoned or even executed. Male homosexuals attracted the attention of authorities because they had begun to develop networks and special meeting places. The stereotype of the effeminate, exclusively homosexual male seems to have appeared for the first time in the eighteenth century, perhaps as part of a growing emphasis on separate roles for men and women.

Roots of Industrialization

Although it was only starting to take hold, industrialization would eventually transform European society. The process began in England in the 1770s and 1780s and included four interlocking trends: (1) population increased dramatically, by more than 50 percent in England in the second half of the eighteenth century; (2) manufacturers introduced steam-driven machinery to increase output; (3) they established factories to concentrate the labor of their workers; and (4) the production of cotton goods, which were lighter and more versatile than woolens, increased tenfold. Together these factors sparked the Industrial Revolution, which would change the face of Europe—indeed, of the entire world—in the nineteenth century.

Innovations in the technology of cotton production permitted manufacturers to make use of the growing supply of raw cotton shipped from the plantations of North America and the Caribbean. In 1733, the Englishman John Kay patented the flying shuttle, which weavers operated by pulling a cord that drove the shuttle to either side, enabling them to "throw" yarn across the loom rather than draw it back and forth by hand. When the flying shuttle came into widespread use in the 1760s, weavers began producing cloth more quickly than spinners could produce the thread. The shortage of spun thread propelled the invention of machines to speed the process of spinning: the spinning jenny and the water frame, a power-driven spinning machine, were introduced in the 1760s. In the following decades, water frames replaced thousands of women spinners working at home by hand. In 1776, the Scottish engineer James Watt developed an improved steam engine, and, in the 1780s, Edmund

Handloom Weaving
This plate from the Encyclopedia *demonstrates handloom weaving of gold-threaded fabrics (tassels, trims, fringes, borders). Fancy threads could not be used on the early mechanical looms, which were suitable only for basic cotton thread. This kind of handloom weaving continued well into the 1800s.* Stock Montage, Inc.

Cartwright, an English clergyman and inventor, designed a mechanized loom, which when perfected could be run by a small boy and yield fifteen times the output of a skilled adult weaver working a handloom. By the end of the century, all the new power machinery was assembled in large factories that hired semiskilled men, women, and children to replace skilled weavers.

Historians have no single explanation for why England led the Industrial Revolution. Some have emphasized England's large internal market, increasing population, supply of private investment capital from overseas trade and commercial profits, or natural resources such as coal and iron. Others have cited England's greater opportunities for social mobility, its relative political stability in the eighteenth century, or the pragmatism of the English and Scottish inventors who designed the necessary machinery. These early industrialists hardly had a monopoly on ingenuity, but they did come out of a tradition of independent capitalist enterprise. They

also shared a culture of informal scientific education through learned societies and popular lectures (one of the prominent forms of the Enlightenment in Britain). For whatever reasons, the combination of improvements in agricultural production, growth in population and foreign trade, and willingness to invest in new machines and factories appeared first in this relatively small island.

Although the rest of Europe did not industrialize until the nineteenth century, textile manufacturing—long a linchpin in the European economy—expanded dramatically in the eighteenth century even without the introduction of new machines and factories. Textile production increased because of the spread of the "putting-out" or "domestic" system. Hundreds of thousands of families manufactured cloth in every country from Britain to Russia. Under the putting-out system, manufacturers supplied the families with raw materials, such as woolen or cotton fibers. Working at home in a dimly lit room, a whole family labored together. The mother and her children washed the fibers and carded and combed them. Then the mother and oldest daughters spun them into thread. The father, assisted by the children, wove the cloth. The cloth was then finished (bleached, dyed, smoothed, and so on) under the supervision of the manufacturer in a large workshop, located either in town or in the countryside. This system had existed in the textile industry for hundreds of years, but in the eighteenth century it expanded immensely, drawing in thousands of peasants in the countryside, and it included not only textiles but also the manufacture of such products as glassware, baskets, nails, and guns. The spread of the domestic system of manufacturing is sometimes called *proto-industrialization* to signify that the process helped pave the way for the full-scale Industrial Revolution.

All across Europe, thousands of people who worked in agriculture became part-time or full-time textile workers. Peasants turned to putting-out work because they did not have enough land to support their families. Men labored off-season and women often worked year-round to augment their meager incomes. At the same time, population growth and general economic improvement meant that demand for cloth increased because more people could afford it. Studies of wills left by working-class men and women in Paris at the end of the eighteenth century show that people owned more clothes of greater variety. Working-class men in Paris began to wear underclothes, something rare at the beginning of the century. Men and women now bought night-clothes; before, Europeans had slept naked except in cold weather. And white, red, blue, yellow, green, and even pastel shades of cotton now replaced the black, gray, or brown of traditional woolen dress.

❖ State Power in an Era of Reform

All rulers recognized that manufacturing created new sources of wealth, but the start of industrialization had not yet altered the standard forms of competition between states: commerce and war. The diffusion of Enlightenment ideas of reform had a more immediate impact on the ways European monarchs exercised power than did industrialization. Historians label many of the sovereigns of this time "enlightened despots" or "enlightened absolutists," for they aimed to combine Enlightenment reforms with absolutist powers. Catherine the Great's admiring relationship with Voltaire showed how even the most absolutist rulers championed reform when it suited their own goals. Voltaire considered the nobles and the established churches the real obstacles to reform, and, like many other Enlightenment writers, he looked to monarchs such as Catherine and Frederick the Great of Prussia to overcome their resistance.

Every European ruler tried to introduce reforms in this period, including improvements in the condition of the peasantry in Austria, freer markets in grain in France, extension of education in Prussia, and new law codes almost everywhere. Success or failure in the competition for trade and territory directly affected these reform efforts. French losses in the Seven Years' War, for example, prompted the French crown to introduce far-reaching reforms that provoked violent resistance and helped pave the way for the French Revolution of 1789. Reform proved to be a two-edged sword.

War and Diplomacy

Europeans no longer fought devastating wars over religion that killed hundreds of thousands of civilians; instead, professional armies and navies battled for control of overseas empires and for dominance on the European continent. Rulers continued to expand their armies: the Prussian army, for example, nearly tripled in size between 1740 and 1789. Widespread use of flintlock muskets required deployment in long lines, usually three men deep, with each line in turn loading and firing on command. Military strategy became cautious and calculating, but this did not prevent the outbreak of hostilities. The instability of the European balance of power resulted in two major wars, a diplomatic reversal of alliances, and the partition of Poland-Lithuania among Russia, Austria, and Prussia. By 1789, Prussia had confirmed its rise to great-power status, the British had eclipsed the French overseas, and once-great Poland-Lithuania had been reduced in size and importance.

War of the Austrian Succession, 1740–1748. The difficulties over the succession to the Austrian throne typified the dynastic complications that

Maria Theresa and Her Family
In this portrait by Martin van Meytens (1695–1770), Austrian empress Maria Theresa is shown with her husband, Francis I, and eleven of their sixteen children. Their eldest son eventually succeeded to the Austrian throne as Joseph II, and their youngest daughter, Maria Antonia, or Marie-Antoinette, became the queen of France.
Giraudon/Art Resource, NY.

repeatedly threatened the European balance of power. In 1740, Holy Roman Emperor Charles VI died without a male heir. Most European rulers recognized the emperor's chosen heiress, his daughter Maria Theresa, because Charles's Pragmatic Sanction of 1713 had given a woman the right to inherit the Habsburg crown lands. The new king of Prussia, Frederick II, who had just succeeded his father a few months earlier in 1740, saw his chance to grab territory and immediately invaded the rich Austrian province of Silesia. France joined Prussia in an attempt to further humiliate its traditional enemy Austria, and Great Britain allied with Austria to prevent the French from taking the Austrian Netherlands (Map 19.2). The War of the Austrian Succession (1740–1748) soon expanded to the overseas colonies of Great Britain and France as well. Maria Theresa (r. 1740–1780) survived only by conceding Silesia to Prussia in order to split the Prussians off from France. The Peace of Aix-la-Chapelle of 1748 recognized Maria Theresa as the heiress to the Austrian lands, and her husband, Francis I, became Holy

Roman Emperor, thus reasserting the integrity of the Austrian Empire.

The fighting between France and Great Britain quickly extended to India, where a series of naval battles left the British in control of the seas. The peace of 1748 failed to resolve the colonial conflicts, and British and French trading companies continued to fight unofficially for domination in India. French and British colonials in North America also fought each other all along their boundaries, enlisting native American auxiliaries. Britain tried but failed to isolate the French Caribbean colonies during the war, and hostilities and suspicions continued unabated.

Seven Years' War, 1756–1763.   In 1756, a major reversal of alliances—what historians call the "Diplomatic Revolution"—reshaped relations among the great powers. Prussia and Great Britain signed a defensive alliance, prompting Austria to overlook two centuries of hostility and ally with France. Russia and Sweden soon joined the Franco-Austrian

MAP 19.2 War of the Austrian Succession, 1740–1748

The accession of a twenty-three-year-old woman, Maria Theresa, to the Austrian throne gave the new king of Prussia, Frederick II, an opportunity to invade the province of Silesia. France joined on Prussia's side, Great Britain on Austria's. In 1745, the French defeated the British in the Austrian Netherlands and helped instigate a Jacobite uprising in Scotland. The rebellion failed and British attacks on French overseas shipping forced the French to negotiate. The peace treaties guaranteed Frederick's conquest of Silesia, which soon became the wealthiest province of Prussia. France came to terms with Great Britain to protect its overseas possessions; Austria had to accept the peace settlement after a formal public protest.

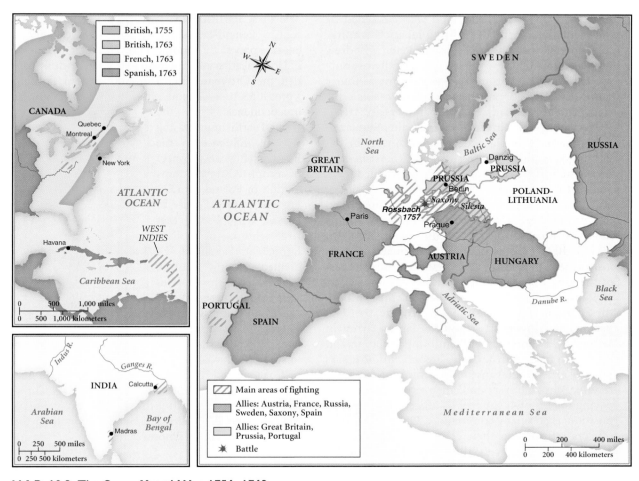

MAP 19.3 The Seven Years' War, 1756–1763

In what might justly be called the first worldwide war, the French and British fought each other on the European continent, in the West Indies, and in India. Their international struggle coincided with a realignment of forces within Europe caused by the desire of Austria, France, and Russia to check Prussian growth. Fearing, with reason, a joint Austrian-Russian attack, Frederick II of Prussia invaded Saxony in August 1756. Despite overwhelming odds, Frederick managed time and again to emerge victorious, until the Russians withdrew and the coalition against Prussia fell apart. The treaty between Austria and Prussia simply restored the status quo. The changes overseas were much more dramatic. Britain gained control over Canada and India but gave back to France the West Indian islands of Guadeloupe and Martinique. Britain was now the dominant power on the seas.

alliance. When Frederick II invaded Saxony, an ally of Austria, with his bigger and better-disciplined army, the long-simmering hostilities between Great Britain and France over colonial boundaries flared into a general war that became known as the Seven Years' War (1756–1763).

Fighting soon raged around the world (Map 19.3). The French and British battled on land and sea in North America (where the conflict was called the French and Indian War), the West Indies, and India. The two coalitions also fought each other in central Europe. At first, in 1757, Frederick the Great surprised Europe with a spectacular victory at Rossbach in Saxony over a much larger Franco-Austrian army. But in time, Russian and Austrian armies encircled his troops. Frederick despaired: "I believe all is lost. I will not survive the ruin of my country." A fluke of history saved him. Empress Elizabeth of

Russia (r. 1741–1762) died and was succeeded by the mentally unstable Peter III, a fanatical admirer of Frederick and things Prussian. Peter withdrew Russia from the war. (This was practically his only accomplishment as tsar. He was soon mysteriously murdered, probably at the instigation of his wife, Catherine the Great.) In a separate peace treaty Frederick kept all his territory, including Silesia.

Although Prussia suffered great losses in the fighting—some 160,000 Prussian soldiers died either in action or of disease—the army helped vault Prussia to the rank of leading powers. In 1733, Frederick II's father, Frederick William I, had instituted the "canton system," which enrolled peasant youths in each canton (or district) in the army, gave them two or three months of training annually, and allowed them to return to their family farms the rest of the year. They remained "cantonists" (reservists) as long as they were able-bodied. In this fashion, the Prussian military steadily grew in size; by 1740, Prussia had the third or fourth largest army in Europe even though it was tenth in population and thirteenth in land area. Under Frederick II, Prussia's military expenditures rose to two-thirds of the state's revenue. Virtually every nobleman served in the army, paying for his own support as officer and buying a position as company commander. Once retired, the officers returned to their estates, coordinated the canton system, and served as local officials. In this way, the military permeated every aspect of rural society, fusing army and agrarian organization. The army gave the state great power, but the militarization of Prussian society also had a profoundly conservative effect: it kept the peasants enserfed to their lords and blocked the middle classes from access to estates or high government positions.

The Anglo-French overseas conflicts ended more decisively than the continental land wars. British naval superiority, fully achieved only in the 1750s, enabled Great Britain to decisively defeat the French in their competition for colonial supremacy; the British routed the French in North America, India, and the West Indies. In the Treaty of Paris of 1763, France ceded Canada to Great Britain and agreed to remove its armies from India, in exchange for keeping its rich West Indian islands. Eagerness to avenge this defeat would motivate France to support the British North American colonists in their War of Independence just fifteen years later.

The First Partition of Poland, 1772. Eighteenth-century Poland-Lithuania was large but weak, and it became prey to the absolutist powers that surrounded it. Under Catherine the Great, Russia successfully battled the Ottoman Empire in intermittent fighting from 1768 to 1774 and promoted Greek efforts at independence from the Turks. Fearful of increasing Russian influence in the Balkans and the prospect of complete Russian domination of Poland, in 1772 Frederick the Great of Prussia proposed that large chunks of Polish-Lithuanian territory be divided among Austria, Prussia, and Russia. Despite the protests of the Austrian empress Maria Theresa that the partition would spread "a stain over my whole reign," she agreed to split one-third of Poland-Lithuania's territory and half of its people among the three powers. Conflicts between Catholics, Protestants, and Orthodox Christians were used to justify this cynical move. Russia took over most of Lithuania, effectively ending the Polish-Lithuanian commonwealth.

The First Partition of Poland, 1772

State-Sponsored Reform

In the aftermath of the Seven Years' War, all the belligerents faced pressing needs for more money to fund their growing armies, to organize navies to wage overseas conflicts, and to counter the impact of inflation. Rather than simply raise taxes as they had in the past, the enlightened absolutists—Frederick II in Prussia, Catherine II in Russia, Maria Theresa and Joseph II (r. 1780–1790) in Austria, Louis XV (r. 1715–1774) and Louis XVI (r. 1774–1792) in France—all proposed similar programs to increase economic and military power by modernizing society. In short, they tried to make tax increases more palatable by promising general social reforms. To harness Enlightenment ideals to their own ends, they appointed reform-minded ministers and gave them a mandate to inventory the country's resources in order to make taxes more equitable and standardize their collection, establish state independence from the church, make the legal system more predictable and accessible, and, in some instances, extend education and religious toleration. As one adviser to Joseph II put it, "A properly constituted state must be exactly analogous to a machine . . . and the ruler must be the foreman, the mainspring . . . which sets everything else in motion." Such reforms always threatened the interests of traditional groups, however, and the spread of Enlightenment ideas aroused sometimes unpredictable desires for more change.

Administrative and Legal Reforms.   The reforming monarchs did not invent government bureaucracy, but in Austria and Prussia especially they insisted on greater attention to merit, hard work, and professionalism, which made bureaucrats more like modern civil servants. As Joseph II of Austria explained, government must be organized according to "uniform principles," and it must unite "a single mass of people all subject to impartial guidance." In this view, the ruler should be a benevolent, enlightened administrator who worked for the general well-being of his or her people. Frederick II of Prussia, who drove himself as hard as he drove his officials, boasted, "I am the first servant of the state."

Legal reform, both of the judicial system and of the often disorganized and irregular law codes, was central to the work of many reform-minded monarchs. Although Frederick II favored all things French in culture—he insisted on speaking French in his court and prided himself on his personal friendship with Voltaire—he made Prussian justice the envy of Europe. His institution of a uniform civil justice system created the most consistently administered laws and efficient judiciary of the time. Joseph II also ordered the compilation of a unified law code, a project that required many years for completion. Catherine II of Russia began such an undertaking even more ambitiously. In 1767, she called together a legislative commission of 564 deputies and asked them to consider a long document called the *Instruction*, which represented her hopes for legal reform based on the ideas of Montesquieu and the Italian writer Cesare Beccaria. Montesquieu had insisted that punishment should fit the crime; he criticized the use of torture and brutal corporal punishment. In his influential book *On Crimes and Punishments* (1764), Beccaria argued

Dividing Poland, 1772
In this contemporary depiction, Catherine the Great, Joseph II, and Frederick II point on the map to the portion of Poland-Lithuania each plans to take. The artist makes it clear that Poland's fate rested in the hands of neighboring rulers, not its own people.
Mansell/Time, Inc.

that laws should be printed for everyone to read and administered in rational procedures, that torture should be abolished as inhumane, and that the accused should be presumed innocent until proven guilty. Despite much discussion and hundreds of petitions and documents about local problems, little came of Catherine's commission because the monarch herself—despite her regard for Voltaire and his fellow philosophes—was not very committed to reform.

The Church and Education.   Rulers everywhere wanted more control over church affairs, and they used Enlightenment criticisms of the organized churches to get their way. In Catholic countries, many government officials resented the influence of the Jesuits, the major Catholic teaching order. The

Jesuits trained the Catholic intellectual elite, ran a worldwide missionary network, enjoyed close ties to the papacy, and amassed great wealth. Critics mounted campaigns against the Jesuits in many countries, and by the early 1770s the Society of Jesus had been dissolved in Portugal, France, and Spain. In 1773, Pope Clement XIV (r. 1769–1774) agreed under pressure to disband the order, an edict that held until a reinvigorated papacy restored the society in 1814. Joseph II of Austria not only applauded the suppression of the Jesuits but also required Austrian bishops to swear fidelity and submission to him. Under Joseph, the Austrian state supervised seminaries, reorganized diocesan boundaries, abolished comtemplative monastic orders, and confiscated their property to pay for education and poor relief.

Enlightened absolutists tried to gain greater state authority over education, even while extending education to the lower classes. Joseph II launched the most ambitious educational reforms of the period. In 1774, once the Jesuits had been disbanded, a General School Ordinance in Austria ordered state subsidies for local schools, which the state would regulate. By 1789, one-quarter of the school-age children attended school. In Prussia the school code of 1763 required all children between the ages of five and thirteen to attend school. Although not enforced uniformly, the Prussian law demonstrated Frederick II's belief that modernization depended on education. Catherine II of Russia also tried to expand elementary education—and the education of women in particular—and founded engineering schools.

Religious Toleration. Many rulers favored religious toleration, but no one achieved more than Joseph II of Austria, who had become Holy Roman Emperor and co-regent with his mother, Maria Theresa, in 1765. Joseph was able to carry out his most radical policies only when he ruled alone after 1780, but then he acted swiftly and sometimes brutally. His own brother described him as "imbued with arbitrary, brutal principles and the most severe, brutal and violent despotism." These qualities nevertheless enabled Joseph to push through reforms that might otherwise have been resisted. In 1781, he granted freedom of religious worship to Protestants, Orthodox Christians, and Jews. For the first time

these groups were allowed to own property, build schools, enter the professions, and hold political and military offices.

The efforts of other rulers to extend religious toleration proved more limited. The French state regarded Protestants as heretics until 1787, when Louis XVI signed an edict of toleration restoring their civil rights—but still they could not hold political office. Great Britain continued to deny Catholics freedom of open worship and the right to sit in Parliament. Most European states limited the rights and opportunities available to Jews. In Russia, only wealthy Jews could hold municipal office, and the Polish and Lithuanian Jews in the territory incorporated into Russia were restricted to certain places of residence. In Prussia, Frederick the Great called the Jews "useless to the state" and imposed special taxes on them. Even in Austria, where Joseph encouraged toleration, the laws forced Jews to take German-sounding names, and in the Papal States, the pope encouraged forced baptism. The leading philosophes opposed persecution of the Jews in theory but often treated them with undisguised contempt. Diderot's comment was all too typical: the Jews, he said, bore "all the defects peculiar to an ignorant and superstitious nation."

Limits of Reform

When government leaders introduce reforms, they often run into resistance from groups who feel threatened by innovation. Such was the experience of the absolutist rulers, who on many occasions faced upsurges of reaction that forced a quick backpedal. The most contentious area of reform was agricultural policy. Whereas Frederick II and Catherine II reinforced the authority of nobles over their serfs, Joseph II tried to remove the burdens of serfdom in the Habsburg lands. In 1781, he abolished the personal aspects of serfdom: serfs could now move freely, enter trades, or marry without their lords' permission. Joseph abolished the tithe to the church, shifted more of the tax burden to the nobility, and converted peasants' labor services into cash payments.

The Austrian nobility furiously resisted these far-reaching reforms. When Joseph died in 1790, his brother Leopold II had to revoke most reforms to appease the nobles. On his deathbed, Joseph recognized the futility of many of his efforts; as his epitaph he suggested, "Here lies Joseph II, who was unfortunate in all his enterprises." Prussia's Frederick II, like Joseph, encouraged such agricultural innovations as planting potatoes and turnips (new crops that could help feed a growing population), experimenting with cattle breeding, draining swamplands, and clearing forests. But Prussia's noble landlords, the Junkers, continued to expand their estates at the expense of poorer peasants, and Frederick did nothing to ameliorate serfdom except on his own domains.

Reforming ministers also tried to stimulate agricultural improvement in France. Unlike most other western European countries, France still had about 100,000 serfs; though their burdens weighed less heavily than those in eastern Europe, serfdom did not entirely disappear until 1789. A group of economists called the *physiocrats* urged the French government to deregulate the grain trade and make the tax system more equitable to encourage agricultural productivity. In the interest of establishing a free market, they also insisted that urban guilds be abolished because they prevented free entry into the trades. Their proposed reforms applied the Enlightenment emphasis on individual liberties to the economy; Adam Smith took up many of the physiocrats' ideas in his writing in favor of free markets. The French government heeded some of this advice and gave up its system of price controls on grain in 1763, but it had to reverse this decision in 1770 when grain shortages caused a famine.

French reform efforts did not end there. To break the power of the parlements, the thirteen high courts of law that had led the way in opposing royal efforts to increase and equalize taxation, Louis XV appointed a reform-minded chancellor who replaced the parlements with courts in which the judges no longer owned their offices and thus could not sell them or pass them on as an inheritance. Justice would then be more impartial. Nevertheless, the judges of the displaced parlements aroused widespread opposition to what they portrayed as tyrannical royal policy. The furor calmed down only when Louis XV died in 1774 and his successor, Louis XVI, yielded to aristocratic demands and restored the old parlements. Louis XV died one of the most despised kings in French history, resented both for his highhanded reforms and his private vices. Underground pamphlets lampooned Louis, describing his final mistress, Madame Du Barry, as a prostitute who pandered to the elderly king's well-known taste

Russian Peasants

This engraving from the 1700s shows Russian peasants in their one-room hut. Two or more married brothers, their wives, children, and parents would share the space with poultry and livestock. Cooking took place in one corner, which was always diagonally across from the icon corner (left), where socializing took place. The fathers and younger men slept on benches, the rest of the family in the loft (right). In the winter, everyone slept near the oven.
Fotomas Index, UK.

for young girls. This often pornographic literature linked despotism to the supposedly excessive influence of women at court. Rousseau was not alone in attacking the feminizing influence of powerful women.

Louis XVI tried to carry out part of the program suggested by the physiocrats, and he chose one of their disciples, Jacques Turgot (1727–1781), as his chief minister. A contributor to the *Encyclopedia*, Turgot pushed through several edicts that again freed the grain trade, suppressed many guilds, converted the peasants' forced labor on roads into a money tax payable by all landowners, and reduced court expenses. He also began making plans to introduce a system of elected local assemblies, which would have made government much more representative. Faced with broad-based resistance led by the parlements and his own courtiers, as well as with riots against rising grain prices, Louis XVI dismissed Turgot, and one of the last possibilities to overhaul France's government collapsed.

The failure of reform in France paradoxically reflected the power of Enlightenment ideas; everyone now endorsed Enlightenment ideals but used them for different ends. The nobles in the parlements blocked the French monarchy's reform efforts using the very same Enlightenment language spoken by the crown's ministers. But unlike Austria, the other great power that faced persistent aristocratic resistance to reform, France had a large middle-class public that was increasingly frustrated by the failure to institute social change, a failure that ultimately helped undermine the monarchy itself. Where Frederick II, Catherine II, and even Joseph II used reform to bolster the efficiency of absolutist government, attempts at change in France backfired. French kings found that their ambitious programs for reform succeeded only in arousing unrealistic hopes.

❖ Rebellions against State Power

Although traditional forms of popular discontent had not disappeared, Enlightenment ideals and reforms changed the rules of the game in politics. Governments, especially in western Europe, now had to respond to public opinion; they had become accountable for their actions to a much wider range of people than ever before. In Britain and France, ordinary people rioted when they perceived government as failing to protect them against shortages created by free trade in grains. Monarchs justified their policies by appealing to the public, but they could not always control the consequences of the intensification of political interest. The growth of informed public opinion had its most dramatic consequences in the North American colonies, where a struggle over the British Parliament's right to tax turned into a full-scale war for independence. The American War of Independence showed that once put into practice, Enlightenment ideals could have revolutionary implications.

Food Riots and Peasant Uprisings

Population growth, inflation, and the extension of the market system put added pressure on the already beleaguered poorest classes of people. Seventeenth-century peasants and townspeople had rioted to protest new taxes. In the eighteenth century, they reacted violently when they feared that officials might fail to protect them from food shortages, either by freeing the grain market, which would benefit big farmers, or by requisitioning grain for the armies or the big cities. Other eighteenth-century forms of collective violence included riots against religious minorities, against militia recruiting, against turnpikes and tollgates, against attempts to arrest smugglers, and against enclosures of common fields. People sometimes rioted to express fear and anger in reaction to unexplained epidemics or to protest the execution of criminals who had captured the popular imagination.

In the last half of the eighteenth century, the food supply became the focus of political and social conflict. The poorer people in the villages and the towns believed it was the government's responsibility to ensure enough food for them, and in fact many governments did stockpile grain to make up for the occasional bad harvest. At the same time, in keeping with Adam Smith's and the French physiocrats' free market proposals, governments wanted to allow grain prices to rise with market demand, because higher profits would motivate producers to increase the overall supply of food.

But free trade in grain also meant selling to the highest bidder, even if that bidder was a foreign merchant. In the short run, in times of scarcity, big landowners and farmers could make huge profits by selling grain outside their hometowns or villages. This practice enraged poor farmers, agricultural workers, and city wageworkers, who could not afford the higher prices. Lacking the political means to affect policy, they could enforce their desire for old-fashioned price regulation only by rioting. Most did not pillage or steal grain but rather forced the sale of grain or flour at a "just" price and blocked the shipment of grain out of their villages to other markets. Women often led these "popular price fixings," as they were called in France, in desperate attempts to protect the food supply for their children.

Such food riots occurred regularly in Britain and France in the last half of the eighteenth century. One of the most turbulent was the so-called Flour War in France in 1775. Turgot's deregulation of the grain trade in 1774 caused prices to rise in several provincial cities. Rioting spread from there to the Paris region, where villagers attacked grain convoys heading to the capital city. Local officials often ordered merchants and bakers to sell at the price the rioters demanded, only to find themselves arrested by the central government for overriding free trade. The government brought in troops to restore order and introduced the death penalty for rioting.

Frustrations with serfdom and hopes for a miraculous transformation provoked the Pugachev rebellion in Russia begin-

The Pugachev Rebellion, 1773

ning in 1773. An army deserter from the southeast frontier region, Emelian Pugachev (1742–1775) claimed to be Tsar Peter III, the dead husband of Catherine II. Pugachev's appearance seemed to confirm peasant hopes for a "redeemer tsar" who would save the people from oppression. He rallied around him Cossacks like himself who resented the loss of their old tribal independence. Now increasingly enserfed or forced to pay taxes and endure army service, these nomadic bands joined with other serfs, rebellious mineworkers, and Muslim minorities. Catherine dispatched a large army to squelch the uprising, but

Pugachev eluded them and the fighting spread. Nearly three million people eventually participated, making this the largest single rebellion in the history of tsarist Russia. When Pugachev urged the peasants to attack the nobility and seize their estates, hundreds of noble families perished. Foreign newspapers called it "the revolution in southern Russia" and offered fantastic stories about Pugachev's life history. Finally, the army captured the rebel leader and brought him in an iron cage to Moscow, where he was tortured and executed. In the aftermath, Catherine tightened the nobles' control over their serfs and harshly punished those who dared to criticize serfdom.

Public Opinion and Political Opposition

Peasant uprisings might briefly shake even a powerful monarchy, but the rise of public opinion as a force independent of court society caused more enduring changes in European politics. Across much of Europe and in the North American colonies, demands for broader political participation reflected Enlightenment notions about individual rights. Aristocratic bodies such as the French parlements, which had no legislative role like that of the British Parliament, insisted that the monarch consult them on the nation's affairs, and the new educated elite wanted more influence too. Newspapers began to cover daily political affairs, and the public learned the basics of political life, despite the strict limits on political participation in most countries.

Monarchs turned to public opinion to seek support against aristocratic groups that opposed reform. Gustavus III of Sweden (r. 1771–1792) called himself "the first citizen of a free people" and promised to deliver the country from "insufferable aristocratic despotism." Shortly after coming to the throne, Gustavus proclaimed a new constitution that divided power between the king and the legislature, abolished the use of torture in the judicial process, and assured some freedom of the press.

In France both the parlements and the monarch appealed to the public through the printed word. The crown hired writers to make its case; the magistrates of the parlements wrote their own rejoinders. French-language newspapers published in the Dutch Republic provided many people in France with detailed accounts of political news and also gave voice to pro-parlement positions. One of the

IMPORTANT DATES

1740–1748 War of the Austrian Succession: France, Spain, and Prussia versus Austria and Great Britain

1751–1772 *Encyclopedia* published in France

1756–1763 Seven Years' War fought in Europe, India, and the American colonies

1762 Jean-Jacques Rousseau, *The Social Contract* and *Emile*

1764 Voltaire, *Philosophical Dictionary*

1770 Louis XV of France fails to break the power of the French law courts

1772 First partition of Poland

1773 Pugachev rebellion of Russian peasants

1776 American Declaration of Independence from Great Britain; James Watt improves the steam engine, making it suitable for new industrial projects; Adam Smith, *The Wealth of Nations*

1780 Joseph II of Austria undertakes a wide-reaching reform program

1781 Immanuel Kant, *The Critique of Pure Reason*

1785 Catherine the Great's Charter of the Nobility grants nobles exclusive control over their serfs in exchange for subservience to the state

1787 Delegates from the states draft a new United States Constitution

new French-language newspapers printed inside France, *Le Journal des Dames* ("The Ladies' Journal"), was published by women and mixed short stories and reviews of books and plays with demands for more women's rights.

The Wilkes affair in Great Britain showed that public opinion could be mobilized to challenge a government. In 1763, during the reign of George III (r. 1760–1820), John Wilkes, a member of Parliament, attacked the government in his newspaper, *North Briton*, and sued the crown when he was arrested. He won his release as well as damages. When he was reelected, Parliament denied him his seat, not once but three times.

The Wilkes episode soon escalated into a major campaign against the corruption and social exclusiveness of Parliament, complaints the Levellers had first raised during the English Revolution of the late 1640s. Newspapers, magazines, pamphlets, handbills, and cheap editions of Wilkes's collected works

all helped promote his cause. Those who could not vote demonstrated for Wilkes. In one incident eleven people died when soldiers broke up a huge gathering of his supporters. The slogan "Wilkes and Liberty" appeared on walls all over London. Middle-class voters formed a Society of Supporters of the Bill of Rights, which circulated petitions for Wilkes; they gained the support of about one-fourth of all the voters. The more determined Wilkesites proposed sweeping reforms of Parliament, including more frequent elections, more representation for the counties, elimination of "rotten boroughs" (election districts so small that they could be controlled by one big patron), and restrictions of pensions used by the crown to gain support. These demands would be at the heart of agitation for parliamentary reform in Britain for decades to come.

Popular demonstrations did not always support reforms. In 1780, the Gordon riots devastated London. They were named after the fanatical anti-Catholic crusader Lord George Gordon, who helped organize huge marches and petition campaigns against a bill the House of Commons passed to grant limited toleration to Catholics. The demonstrations culminated in a seven-day riot that left fifty buildings destroyed and three hundred people dead. Despite the continuing limitation on voting rights in Great Britain, British politicians were learning that public opinion could be ignored only at their peril.

Political opposition also took artistic forms, particularly in countries where governments restricted organized political activity. A striking example of a play with a political message was *The Marriage of Figaro* (1784) by Pierre-Augustin Caron de Beaumarchais (1732–1799), a watchmaker, a judge, a gunrunner in the American War of Independence, and a French spy in Britain. *The Marriage of Figaro* was first a hit at court, when Queen Marie-Antoinette had it read for her friends. But when her husband, Louis XVI, read it, he forbade its production on the grounds that "this man mocks at everything that should be respected in government." When finally performed publicly, the play caused a sensation. The chief character, Figaro, is a clever servant who gets the better of his noble employer. When speaking of the count, he cries, "What have you done to deserve so many rewards? You went to the trouble of being born, and nothing more." Two years later, Mozart based an equally famous but somewhat tamer opera on Beaumarchais's story.

Revolution in North America

Oppositional forms of public opinion came to a head in Great Britain's North American colonies, where the result was American independence and the establishment of a republican constitution that stood in stark contrast to most European regimes. The successful revolution was the only blow to Britain's increasing dominance in world affairs in the eighteenth century, and as such it was another aspect of the power rivalries existing at that time. Yet many Europeans saw the American War of Independence, or the American Revolution, as a triumph for Enlightenment ideas. As one German writer exclaimed in 1777, American victory would give "greater scope to the Enlightenment, new keenness to the thinking of peoples and new life to the spirit of liberty."

The American revolutionary leaders had been influenced by a common Atlantic civilization; they participated in the Enlightenment and shared political ideas with the opposition Whigs in Britain.

Supporters demonstrated for Wilkes in South Carolina and Boston, and the South Carolina legislature donated a substantial sum to the Society of Supporters of the Bill of Rights. In the 1760s and 1770s, both British and American opposition leaders became convinced that the British government was growing increasingly corrupt and despotic, and both were concerned with the lack of representation in Parliament. British radicals wanted to reform Parliament so the voices of a broader, more representative segment of the population would be heard. The colonies had no representatives in Parliament, and colonists claimed that "no taxation without representation" should be allowed. Indeed, they denied that Parliament had any jurisdiction over the colonies, insisting that the king govern them through colonial legislatures and recognize their traditional British liberties. The failure of the "Wilkes and Liberty" campaign to produce concrete results convinced many Americans that Parliament was hopelessly tainted and that they would have to stand up for their rights as British subjects.

Overthrowing British Authority
The uncompromising attitude of the British government went a long way toward dissolving long-standing loyalties to the home country. During the American War of Independence, residents of New York City pulled down the statue of the hated George III.
Lafayette College Art Collection, Easton, Pennsylvania.

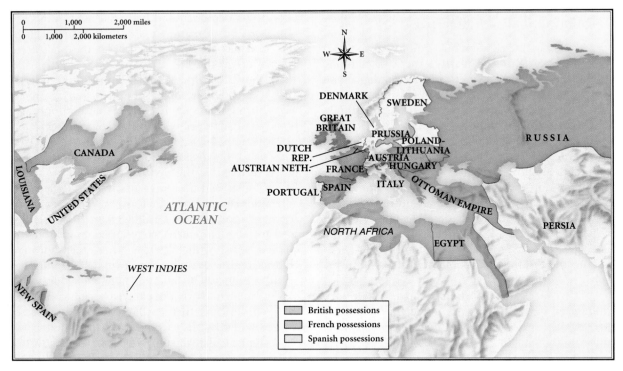

MAPPING THE WEST Europe and the World, c. 1780

Although Great Britain lost control over the British North American colonies, which became the new United States, European influence on the rest of the world grew dramatically in the eighteenth century. The slave trade linked European ports to African slave-trading outposts and to plantations in the Caribbean, South America, and North America. The European countries on the Atlantic Ocean benefited most from this trade. Yet almost all of Africa, China, Japan, and large parts of India still resisted European incursion, and the Ottoman Empire, with its massive territories, still towered over most European countries.

The British colonies remained loyal to the crown until Parliament's encroachment on their autonomy and the elimination of the French threat at the end of the Seven Years' War transformed colonial attitudes. Unconsciously, perhaps, the colonies had begun to form a separate nation; their economies generally flourished in the eighteenth century, and between 1750 and 1776 their population almost doubled. With the British clamoring for lower taxes and the colonists paying only a fraction of the tax rate paid by the Britons at home, Parliament passed new taxes, including the Stamp Act in 1765, which required a special tax stamp on all legal documents and publications. After violent rioting in the colonies, the new tax was repealed, but in 1773 a new Tea Act revived colonial resistance, which culminated in the so-called Boston Tea Party of 1773. Colonists dressed as Indians boarded

British ships and dumped the imported tea (by this time an enormously popular beverage) into Boston's harbor. The British government tried to clamp down on the unrest, but British troops in the colonies soon found themselves fighting locally organized militias.

Political opposition in the American colonies turned belligerent when Britain threatened to use force to maintain control. In 1774, the First Continental Congress convened, composed of delegates from all the colonies, and unsuccessfully petitioned the crown for redress. The next year the Second Continental Congress organized an army with George Washington in command. After actual fighting had begun, in 1776, the congress proclaimed the Declaration of Independence. An eloquent statement of the American cause written by Thomas Jefferson, the Declaration of Independence was couched in the language of universal human rights, which enlightened Europeans could be expected to understand. George III denounced the American "traitors and rebels," calling them "misled by dangerous and ill-designing men." But European newspapers enthusiastically reported on every American response to "the cruel acts of oppression they have been made to suffer." In the War of Independence (1775–1783), France boosted the American cause by entering on the colonists' side in 1778. Spain too saw an opportunity to check the growing power of Britain, though without actually endorsing American independence out of fear of the response of its Latin American colonies. Spain declared war on Britain in 1779; in 1780, Great Britain declared war on the Dutch Republic in retaliation for Dutch support of the rebels. The worldwide conflict that resulted was more than Britain could handle. The American colonies achieved their independence in the peace treaty of 1783.

The newly independent states still faced the challenge of republican self-government. The Articles of Confederation, drawn up in 1777 as a provisional constitution, proved weak because they gave the central government few powers. In 1787, a constitutional convention met in Philadelphia to draft a new constitution. It established a two-house legislature, an indirectly elected president, and an independent judiciary. The Constitution's preamble insisted explicitly, for the first time in history, that government derived its power solely from the people and did not depend on divine right or on the tradition of royalty or aristocracy. The new educated elite of the eighteenth century had now created government based on a "social contract" among male, property-owning, white citizens. It was by no means a complete democracy, and women and slaves were excluded from political participation. But the new government represented a radical departure from European models. In 1791, a Bill of Rights was appended to the Constitution outlining the essential rights (such as freedom of speech) that the government could never overturn. Although slavery continued in the American republic, the new emphasis on rights helped fuel a movement for its abolition in both Britain and the United States.

Interest in the new republic was greatest in France. The United States Constitution and various state constitutions were published in French with commentary by leading thinkers. Even more important in the long run were the effects of the American war. Dutch losses to Great Britain aroused a widespread movement for political reform in the Dutch Republic, and debts incurred by France in supporting the American colonies would soon force the French monarchy to the edge of bankruptcy and then to revolution. Ultimately, the entire European system of royal rule would be challenged.

Conclusion

The American Revolution was the most profound practical result of the general European movement known as the Enlightenment. When he looked back many years later on the Declaration of Independence, Thomas Jefferson said he hoped it would be "the signal of arousing men to burst the chains under which monkish ignorance and superstition had persuaded them to bind themselves." What began as a cosmopolitan movement of a few intellectuals in the first half of the eighteenth century reached a relatively wide audience among the educated elite of men and women. The spirit of reform swept from the salons and coffeehouses into the halls of government. Reasoned, scientific inquiry into the causes of social misery and laws defending individual rights and freedoms gained adherents everywhere.

For most Europeans, however, Enlightenment remained a promise rather than a reality. Rulers such as Catherine the Great had every intention of retaining their full, often unchecked, powers, even as they corresponded with leading philosophes, announced support for their causes, and entertained them at their courts. Moreover, would-be reformers often found themselves thwarted by the resistance of nobles, by the priorities rulers gave to waging wars, or by popular resistance to deregulation of trade that stripped away protection against the uncertainties of the market. Yet even the failure of reform contributed to the ferment in Europe after 1770. Peasant rebellions in eastern Europe, the "Wilkes and Liberty" campaign in Great Britain, the struggle over reform in France, and the revolution in America all occurred at about the same time, and their conjunction convinced many Europeans that the world was in fact changing. Just how much it had changed, and whether the change was for better or for worse, would become more evident in the next ten years.

Suggested References

The Enlightenment at Its Height

The interpretive study by Gay remains useful even though it is over thirty years old. Starobinski's intellectual biography of Rousseau shows the unities in the life and work of this enduringly controversial figure. Much more emphasis has been placed in recent studies on the role of women; on this point see Goodman and Landes. Equiano, an ex-slave, offers one of the earliest firsthand views of the experience of slavery. Voltaire's *Candide* is an accessible introduction to the thought of the philosophes.

*Equiano, Olaudah. *The Interesting Narrative and Other Writings*. Ed. Vincent Carretta. 1995.

Gay, Peter. *The Enlightenment: An Interpretation*. 2 vols. 1966, 1969.

Goodman, Dena. *The Republic of Letters: A Cultural History of the French Enlightenment*. 1994.

Griswold, Charles. *Adam Smith and the Virtues of Enlightenment*. 1999.

Jacob, Margaret C. *Living the Enlightenment: Freemasonry and Politics in Eighteenth-Century Europe*. 1991.

Landes, Joan B. *Women and the Public Sphere in the Age of the French Revolution*. 1988.

Starobinski, Jean. *Jean-Jacques Rousseau: Transparency and Obstruction*. Trans. Arthur Goldhammer. 1988.

*Voltaire. *Candide*. Ed. and trans. Daniel Gordon. 1999.

Voltaire Foundation: http://www.voltaire.ox.ac.uk.

Society and Culture in an Age of Enlightenment

Recent work has drawn attention to the lives of ordinary people. The personal journal of the French glassworker Ménétra is a rarity: it offers extensive documentation of the inner life of an ordinary person during the Enlightenment. Ménétra claimed to have met Rousseau. Even if not true, the claim shows that Rousseau's fame was not limited to the upper classes.

Darnton, Robert. *The Great Cat Massacre and Other Episodes in French Cultural History*. 1984.

Gullickson, Gay L. *Spinners and Weavers of Auffay: Rural Industry and the Sexual Division of Labor in a French Village, 1750–1850*. 1986.

Hull, Isabel V. *Sexuality, State, and Civil Society in Germany, 1700–1815*. 1996.

Jarrett, Derek. *England in the Age of Hogarth*. 1986.

McManners, John. *Death and the Enlightenment*. 1981.

*Ménétra, Jacques Louis. *Journal of My Life*. Trans. Arthur Goldhammer. Introd. Daniel Roche. 1986.

Mozart Project: http://www.frontiernet.net/~sboerner/mozart/biography/.

Stone, Lawrence. *The Family, Sex, and Marriage in England, 1500–1800*. Abridged ed. 1979.

Trumbach, Randolph. *Sex and the Gender Revolution*. 1998.

State Power in an Era of Reform

Biographies and general histories of this period tend to overemphasize the individual decisions of rulers. Although these are incontestably important, side-by-side reading of Büsch, Frederick II's writings on war, and Showalter's book on the wars themselves offers a broader view that puts Frederick II's policies into the context of military growth and its impact on society.

Blanning, T. C. W. *Joseph II and Enlightened Despotism*. 1970.

Büsch, Otto. *Military System and Social Life in Old Regime Prussia, 1713–1807: The Beginnings of the Social Militarization of Prusso-German Society*. Trans. John G. Gagliardo. 1997.

Crankshaw, Edward. *Maria Theresa*. 1996.

Cronin, Vincent. *Catherine, Empress of All the Russias*. 1996.

*Frederick II, King of Prussia. *Frederick the Great on the Art of War*. Ed. and trans. Jay Luvaas. 1999.

Showalter, Dennis E. *The Wars of Frederick the Great*. 1996.

Venturi, Franco. *The End of the Old Regime in Europe, 1768–1776: The First Crisis*. Trans. R. Burr Litchfield. 1989.

Rebellions against State Power

Exciting work has focused on specific instances of riot and rebellion. One of the most interesting studies is Thompson's work on the British repression of poaching and its significance for British social and political history. Palmer's overview remains valuable, especially for its comparative aspects.

Alexander, John T. *Autocratic Politics in a National Crisis: The Imperial Russian Government and Pugachev's Revolt, 1773–1775*. 1969.

Palmer, R. R. *The Age of Democratic Revolution: A Political History of Europe and America, 1760–1800*. Vol. 1, *The Challenge*. 1959.

*Rakove, Jack N. *Declaring Rights: A Brief History with Documents*. 1998.

Thomas, P. D. G. *John Wilkes: A Friend to Liberty*. 1996.

Thompson, E. P. *Whigs and Hunters: The Origin of the Black Act*. 1975.

Wood, Gordon S. *The Radicalism of the American Revolution*. 1992.

*Primary sources.

The Cataclysm of Revolution

1789–1800

Fall of the Bastille

The Bastille prison is shown here in all its imposing grandeur. The moment depicted is that of the surrender of the fortress's governor, Bernard René de Launay. Because so many of the besieging citizens had been killed (only one of the defenders died), popular anger ran high and de Launay was to be the sacrificial victim. As the hastily formed citizens' guard marched him off to city hall, huge crowds taunted and spat at him. When he lashed out at one of the men nearest him, he was immediately stabbed and shot. A pastry cook cut off the governor's head, which was promptly displayed as a trophy on a pike held high above the crowd. Royal authority had been successfully challenged and even humiliated.
Chateau de Versailles, France/
Bridgeman Art Library, NY.

O N OCTOBER 5, 1789, AN INCIDENT OCCURRED in France that reflected the trauma and unpredictability of revolutionary times. As tensions mounted over the rising price of bread and uncertainties about the future direction of the country, rumors spread that officers guarding the king at his palace at Versailles had stomped in drunken fury on the red, white, and blue cockades that adorned the hats of supporters of the emerging revolutionary movement. Outraged at this insult and determined to get the king's help in securing more grain for the hungry, a crowd of several thousand women marched in a drenching rain twelve miles from the center of Paris to Versailles. They sent delegates to talk with the king and demanded an audience with the deputies of the newly formed National Assembly, which met nearby. Before the evening was over, thousands of men had marched from Paris to reinforce the women. The atmosphere turned ominous as the crowd camped out all night near the palace.

Early the next morning, an angry mob forced its way into the palace grounds and broke into the royal family's private apartments. To prevent further bloodshed—two of the royal bodyguards had already been killed and their heads paraded on pikes—the king agreed to move his family and his government back to Paris. A dramatic procession guarded by thousands of ordinary men and women made its way back to Paris. The people's proud display of cannons and pikes underlined the fundamental transformation that was occurring. Ordinary people had forced the king of France to respond to their grievances. The French

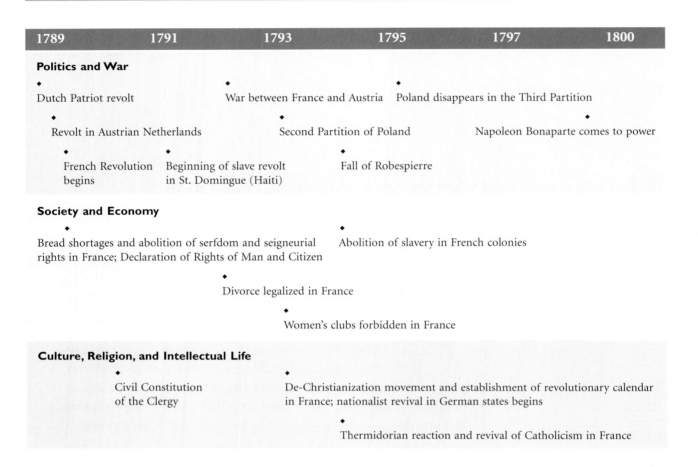

1789	1791	1793	1795	1797	1800

Politics and War

- Dutch Patriot revolt
- Revolt in Austrian Netherlands
- French Revolution begins
- Beginning of slave revolt in St. Domingue (Haiti)
- War between France and Austria
- Second Partition of Poland
- Fall of Robespierre
- Poland disappears in the Third Partition
- Napoleon Bonaparte comes to power

Society and Economy

- Bread shortages and abolition of serfdom and seigneurial rights in France; Declaration of Rights of Man and Citizen
- Divorce legalized in France
- Women's clubs forbidden in France
- Abolition of slavery in French colonies

Culture, Religion, and Intellectual Life

- Civil Constitution of the Clergy
- De-Christianization movement and establishment of revolutionary calendar in France; nationalist revival in German states begins
- Thermidorian reaction and revival of Catholicism in France

monarchy was now in danger, and if such a powerful and long-lasting institution could come under fire, then could any monarch of Europe rest easy?

Although entirely unpredicted when it erupted in 1789, the French Revolution followed a series of upheavals that began in the 1770s with the American fight for independence from Great Britain. In 1787 in the Dutch Republic and in 1788 in the Austrian Netherlands and Poland, protesters mounted campaigns for political reform that threatened the very existence of the governments in place. Unlike these protest movements, all of which failed in achieving their aims, the French Revolution exceeded everyone's expectations. It had its immediate origins in a constitutional crisis provoked by a growing government deficit, traceable to French involvement in the American War of Independence. The constitutional crisis came to a head on July 14, 1789, when armed Parisians captured the Bastille, a royal fortress and symbol of monarchical authority in the center of the capital. In the march to Versailles

of October 1789—soon known as "the October days"—the common people of Paris showed once again their determination to shape unfolding events.

In its early days, the French Revolution grabbed the attention of the entire world because it seemed to promise universal human rights, constitutional government, and broad-based political participation. In the words of its most famous slogan, it pledged "liberty, equality, and fraternity." Many Europeans greeted 1789 as the dawn of a new era. Wrote an enthusiastic German, "One of the greatest nations in the world, the greatest in general culture, has at last thrown off the yoke of tyranny." Others expressed horror at the violence that accompanied the dramatic events. In 1790, the British politician Edmund Burke denounced the "vilest of women" and the "cruel ruffians and assassins" who participated in the march to Versailles. He saw anarchy and terror where others saw liberation.

As events unfolded with astonishing rapidity after 1789, the French Revolution became *the* model

Women's March to Versailles, October 5, 1789
This anonymous engraving shows a crowd of armed women marching to Versailles to confront the king. The sight of armed women frightened many observers and demonstrated that the Revolution was not only men's affair. Note the middle-class woman in a hat at the far left. She is obviously reluctant to join in but is being pulled along by the market women in their simple caps.
Musée de la Ville de Paris/Musée Carnavalet, Paris/Giraudon/Art Resource, NY.

of modern revolution and in the process set the enduring patterns of all modern politics. Republicanism, democracy, terrorism, nationalism, and military dictatorship all took their modern forms during the French Revolution. The revolutionaries used a blueprint based on the Enlightenment idea of reason to remake all of society and politics: they executed the king and queen, established a republic for the first time in French history, abolished nobility, and inaugurated bold programs for political reeducation that included reforming the calendar, introducing the metric system, and celebrating festivals of reason to replace Christianity. When they encountered resistance to their programs, they set up a government of terror to compel obedience. As a result, the Revolution became linked in some minds with violence and intimidation, and some see in it the origins of modern *totalitarianism*—that is, governments that try to control every aspect of life, including daily activities, while limiting all forms of political dissent.

The Revolution might have remained a strictly French affair if war had not involved the rest of Europe. After 1792, huge French republican armies, fueled by patriotic nationalism, marched across Europe, promising liberation from traditional monarchies but often delivering old-fashioned conquest and annexation. French victories spread revolutionary ideas far and wide, from the colonies in the Caribbean, where the first successful slave revolt established the republic of Haiti, to Poland and Egypt. The army's success ultimately undermined the republic and made possible the rise of Napoleon Bonaparte, a remarkable young general who brought France more wars, more conquests, and a form of military dictatorship.

The breathtaking succession of regimes in France between 1789 and 1799 and the failure of the republican experiment after ten years of upheaval raised disturbing questions about the relationship between rapid political change and violence. Do all revolutions inevitably degenerate into terror or wars of conquest? Is a regime democratic if it does not allow poor men, women, or blacks to vote? The French Revolution raised these questions and many more. The questions resonated in many countries because the French Revolution seemed to be only the most extreme example of a much broader political and social movement at the end of the eighteenth century.

❖ The Revolutionary Wave, 1787–1789

From Philadelphia to Warsaw, the new public steeped in Enlightenment ideas now demanded to be heard. In 1787, at the same time the recently independent United States of America was preparing a new constitution, a broad-based Dutch Patriot movement challenged the powers of the ruling Dutch stadholder. In the Austrian Netherlands (present-day Belgium and Luxembourg), the upper classes resisted, in the name of constitutional liberties, the reforms of Emperor Joseph II of Austria. In Warsaw, patriotic reformers hoped to lead Poland out of the quagmire of humiliating political impotence, dependence on Russia, and large territorial losses in the partition of 1772. All these movements included calls for more representative government, but only the French revolt developed into a full-fledged revolution.

Europe on the Eve of Revolution

In the early spring of 1787, few felt the tremors forewarning a cataclysm. Many Europeans enthusiastically greeted the American experiment in republican government, but most did not consider the changes taking place far away in a former colony a likely model for their much older, more populous, and traditional states. The Enlightenment had spread into most of the circles of high society in western Europe without affecting the social prominence of aristocrats or the political control of kings and queens. In fact, the European monarchies seemed more securely established than ever, and the French monarchy appeared as sturdy as any. Montesquieu and Rousseau, the leading political theorists of the Enlightenment, taught that republics suited only small countries, not big ones like France or Austria.

After suffering humiliation at the hands of the British in the Seven Years' War (1756–1763), the French had regained international prestige by supporting the victorious Americans, and the monarchy had shown its eagerness to promote reforms. In 1787, for example, the French crown granted civil rights to Protestants.

Europeans in general were wealthier, healthier, more numerous, and better educated than they had ever been before. They had more newspapers and books to read, more concerts to attend, and more coffeehouses to enjoy, all subtle signs of economic growth and development. Ironically, political agitation would be most dramatic in some of the wealthiest and best-educated societies within Europe, such as the Low Countries. The eighteenth-century revolutions were a product of long-term prosperity and high expectations; the short-term downturn and depression after 1786 seemed all the more disappointing after the preceding decades of robust growth.

Historians have sometimes referred to the revolts of the 1780s as the *Atlantic revolutions* because so many protest movements arose in countries on both shores of the North Atlantic in the late 1700s. Most scholars agree now, however, that the French Revolution differed greatly from the others: not only was France the richest, most powerful, and most populous state in western Europe, but its revolution was also more violent, more long-lasting, and more influential in its effects. (See "Terms of History," page 728.)

Interpretation of the Revolutionary Outbreak

Many different explanations for the French Revolution have been offered. The Marxist interpretation, presented by the nineteenth-century revolutionary philosopher Karl Marx and his modern followers, was one of the most influential. Marx saw the French Revolution as the classic example of a *bourgeois*, that is, middle-class, revolution. According to the Marxist interpretation, the *bourgeoisie* (middle class) overthrew the monarchy because of its association with the remnants of feudalism. French revolutionaries used the term *feudalism* to refer to everything that seemed outdated in their nation's economic and social systems, particularly the legal privileges long held by the aristocracy and the seigneurial rights of landowners, such as the many dues landlords levied on their tenants—payments for the use of the lord's baking oven or winepress, for example. Marxists believed the remains of the feudal order needed to be swept away to facilitate the development of capitalism.

Recent historians have successfully challenged many aspects of the Marxist interpretation, especially the link between revolution and capitalism. They argue that the French Revolution did not foster the development of capitalism and that a capitalist middle class composed of merchants and manufacturers did not lead the revolt. A kind of middle class did play an important role in the protest movements of the 1780s across Europe, but this middle class comprised lawyers, journalists, intellectuals, and lower-ranking officials rather than capitalist manufacturers. Moreover, the middle classes did not start most protest movements, which began only when aristocratic elites themselves challenged their rulers' powers. Once the uprisings began, the participation of men and women from the urban lower classes propelled the movements, just as it had during the English Revolution of the mid-seventeenth century. The volatility of this combination of upper, middle, and lower classes ultimately defeated each revolution. The appeal to "the people" as the source of legitimacy pitted one group against another and opened the way to new and sometimes dangerous forms of political mobilization. According to this interpretation, concerns about politics and power completely overshadowed interests in economic change.

Protesters in the Low Countries and Poland

If the eighteenth-century revolutions began in the British North American colonies with the War of American Independence, they took their next step on the other side of the Atlantic. Political protests in the Dutch Republic attracted European attention because Dutch banks still controlled a hefty portion of the world's capital at the end of the eighteenth century, even though the Dutch Republic's role in international politics had diminished. Revolts also broke out in the neighboring Austrian Netherlands and Poland. Although none of these movements ultimately succeeded, they showed how quickly political discontent could boil over in this era of rising economic and political expectations.

The Dutch Patriot Revolt, 1787. The Dutch Patriots, as they chose to call themselves, wanted to follow the American example and reduce the powers of the kinglike stadholder, the prince of Orange, who favored close ties with Great Britain. Government-sponsored Dutch banks owned 40 percent of the British national debt, and by 1796 they held the entire foreign debt of the United States. Relations with the British deteriorated during the American War of Independence, however, and by the middle of the 1780s, agitation in favor of the Americans had boiled over into an attack on the stadholder.

The Patriots began their protest in the relatively restricted circles of middle-class bankers, merchants, and writers who supported the American cause. They soon gained a more popular audience by demanding political reforms in a petition campaign and forming armed citizen militias of men, called Free Corps. Parading under banners that read "Liberty or Death," they forced local officials to set up new elections to replace councils that had been packed with Orangist supporters through patronage or family connections. The future American president John Adams happened to be visiting Utrecht when such a revolt occurred. He wrote admiringly to Thomas Jefferson that "in no instance, of ancient or modern History, have the People ever asserted more unequivocally their own inherent and unalienable Sovereignty."

In 1787, the protest movement coalesced when a national assembly of the Free Corps joined with a group of Patriot Regents (the upper-class officials who ran the cities) to demand "the true republican form of government in our commonwealth," that is, the reduction of stadholder powers. The Free Corps fought the prince's troops and soon got the upper hand. In response, Frederick William II of Prussia, whose sister had married the stadholder, intervened with tacit British support. Thousands of Prussian troops soon occupied Utrecht and Amsterdam, and the House of Orange regained its former position.

The Low Countries in 1787

Revolution

Many of our most important political labels and concepts—*left* and *right, terrorist,* and even *revolution* itself—come from the French Revolution. *Left* and *right* correlated spatial locations in the hall of the National Assembly with political positions. Those deputies who favored extensive change sat in the seats on the speaker's left hand; the Jacobins became the most prominent group on the left. On the right were the deputies who preferred a more cautious and conservative stance; royalists were most consistently on the right. A *terrorist* was someone who supported the revolutionary regime of the Terror (1793–1794), but it came to mean anyone who used terror to achieve his or her political ends.

Revolution provided the context for all these changes in meaning. It had previously meant cyclical change that brought life back to a starting point, as a planet makes a revolution around the sun. Revolutions could come and go, by this definition, and change nothing fundamental in the structure of society. After 1789, *revolution* came to mean a self-conscious attempt to leap into the future by reshaping society and politics and even the human personality. A revolutionary official analyzed the meaning of the word in 1793: "A revolution is never made by halves; it must either be total or it will abort. . . . *Revolutionary* means outside of all forms and all rules; *revolutionary* means that which affirms, consolidates the revolution, that which removes all the obstacles which impede its progress." In short, *revolution* soon had an all-or-nothing meaning; you were either for the revolution or against it. There could be no in between.

Revolution still has the same meaning given it by the French revolutionaries, but it is now an even more contested term because of its association with communist theory. In the nineteenth century, Karl Marx incorporated the French Revolution into his new doctrine of communism. In his view, the middle-class French revolutionaries had overthrown the monarchy and the "feudal" aristocracy to pave the way for capitalist development. In the future, the proletariat (industrial workers) would overthrow the capitalist middle class to install a communist government that would abolish private property. Since Marxists claimed the French Revolution as the forerunner of the communist revolution in the nineteenth and twentieth centuries, it was perhaps inevitable that those who opposed communism would also criticize the French Revolution.

The Patriots fell to the fatal combination of outside intervention and their own internal social divisions. Many of the Patriot Regents from the richest merchant families resisted the growing power of the Free Corps. The Free Corps wanted a more democratic form of government and encouraged the publication of pamphlets and cartoons attacking the prince and his wife, the rapid spread of clubs and societies made up of common people, and crowd-pleasing public ceremonies, such as parades and bonfires, that sometimes turned into riots. As divisiveness within the Patriot ranks increased, the prince of Orange was able to muster his own popular support. In the aftermath of the Prussian invasion in September 1787, the Orangists got their revenge: lower-class mobs pillaged the houses of prosperous Patriot leaders, forcing many to flee to the United States, France, or the Austrian Netherlands. Those Patriots who remained nursed their grievances until the French republican armies invaded in 1795.

The Belgian Independence Movement. If Austrian emperor Joseph II had not tried to introduce reforms, the Belgians of the ten provinces of the Austrian Netherlands might have remained tranquil. Yet Joseph, inspired by Enlightenment ideals, made changes that both extended civil rights and enhanced his own power. He abolished torture, decreed toleration for Jews and Protestants (in this resolutely Catholic area), and suppressed monasteries. His 1787 reorganization of the administrative and judicial systems eliminated many offices that belonged to nobles and lawyers. The upper classes felt their power was being usurped.

Belgian resistance to Austrian reforms consequently began as a reactionary movement, which was intended to defend historic local liberties against an

The most influential example of this view is that of the French scholar François Furet. An ex-communist, Furet argues that the French Revolution can be seen as the origin of totalitarianism: "Today the Gulag [the Soviet system of prison camps for dissidents] is leading to a rethinking of the Terror precisely because the two undertakings are seen as identical." The Soviet Gulag and the Terror were identical systems for repressing all avenues of dissent. The French Revolution ended up in totalitarianism during the Terror because it incarnated what Furet calls "the illusion of politics," that is, the belief that people can transform social and economic relationships through political revolution. The French revolutionaries became totalitarian, in Furet's view, however, because they wanted to establish a kind of political and social utopia (a perfect society), in which reason alone determined the shape of political and social life. Because this dream was impossible given human resistance to rapid change, the revolutionaries had to use force to achieve their goals. In other words, revolution itself was a problematic idea, according to Furet.

Controversy about the relationship between the French Revolution and totalitarianism continues. Critics of Furet argue that he focuses too narrowly on the Terror, which, after all, lasted only about one year, from mid-1793 to mid-1794. The French Revolution included many different political experiments: constitutional monarchy (1789–1792), a democratic republic (which preceded and succeeded the period of the Terror), and, later, a more authoritarian republic and then an empire under Napoleon Bonaparte. Is the central meaning of the French Revolution to be found in any single one of these periods or in the very fact of the succession of different phases? France went on in the nineteenth and twentieth centuries to have another constitutional monarchy, one more empire, and four more republics—and never another period of terror. Which kind of experiment was more significant in its lasting effects? Since the French government today is a democratic republic, might it not be argued that this tradition—democratic republicanism—was the most lasting outcome of the French Revolution? In short, *revolution* as a term remains as contested as the events that gave rise to it.

FURTHER READING

Furet, François. *Interpreting the French Revolution.* Trans. Elborg Forster. 1981.

Hunt, Lynn. *Politics, Culture, and Class in the French Revolution.* 1984.

---

overbearing reform-minded government. The upper classes initiated the resistance. The countess of Yves, for example, wrote pamphlets against Joseph's reforms and provided meeting places for the rebels. The movement nonetheless soon attracted democrats, who wanted a more representative government and organized clubs to give voice to their demands. At the end of 1788, a secret society formed armed companies to prepare an uprising. By late 1789, each province had separately declared its independence, and the Austrian administration had collapsed. Delegates from the various provinces declared themselves the United States of Belgium, a clear reference to the American precedent.

Once again, however, internal squabbling doomed the rebels. The democrats denounced aristocratic authority. "The nobles have no acquired right over the people," one writer proclaimed. In the face of increasing democratic ferment, aristocratic leaders drew to their side the Catholic clergy and peasants, who had little sympathy for the democrats of the cities. Every Sunday in May and June 1790, thousands of peasant men and women, led by their priests, streamed into Brussels carrying crucifixes, nooses, and pitchforks to intimidate the democrats and defend the church. Faced with the choice between the Austrian emperor and "our current tyrants," the democrats chose to support the return of the Austrians under Emperor Leopold II (r. 1790–1792), who had succeeded his brother.

Polish Patriots. A reform party calling itself the Patriots also emerged in Poland, which had been shocked by the loss of a third of its territory in the First Partition of 1772. The Patriots sought to overhaul the weak commonwealth along modern western European lines. Reformers included a few leading aristocrats; middle-class professionals and clergy who espoused Enlightenment ideas; and King Stanislaw August Poniatowski (r. 1764–1795). A nobleman who owed his crown solely to the dubious honor of being Catherine the Great's discarded lover but who was also a favorite correspondent of the Parisian salon hostess Madame Geoffrin, Poniatowski saw in moderate reform the only chance for his country to escape the consequences of a century's misgovernment and cultural decline. Ranged against the Patriots stood most of the aristocrats and the formidable Catherine the Great, determined to uphold imperial Russian influence.

Watchful but not displeased to see Russian influence waning in Poland, Austria and Prussia allowed the reform movement to proceed. In 1788, the Patriots got their golden chance. Bogged down in war with the Ottoman Turks, Catherine could not block the summoning of a reform-minded parliament, which with King Stanislaw's aid outmaneuvered the antireform aristocrats. Amid much oratory denouncing Russian overlordship, the parliament enacted the constitution of May 3, 1791, which established a hereditary monarchy with somewhat strengthened authority, at last freed the two-house legislature from the individual veto power of every aristocrat, granted townspeople limited political rights, and vaguely promised future Jewish emancipation. Abolishing serfdom was hardly mentioned. Modest though they were, the Polish reforms did not endure. Catherine II could not countenance the spread of revolution into eastern Europe and within a year engineered the downfall of the Patriots and further weakened the Polish state.

The Beginning of the French Revolution, 1787–1789

The French Revolution began with a fiscal crisis caused by a mounting deficit. After trying every available avenue to raise needed funds, Louis XVI (r. 1774–1792) was forced to call a meeting of the Estates General, a body which had not met since 1614. After the Estates General opened in May 1789, a constitutional stalemate soon pitted deputies of the commons against deputies of the nobility. Fear of a noble-led conspiracy inspired the people of Paris to revolt and attack the Bastille prison on July 14, 1789. Unlike the revolts elsewhere in Europe, the fall of the Bastille would open the way to a rev-

olutionary movement that lasted ten years and reshaped modern European, even world, politics.

Fiscal Crisis.   France's fiscal problems stemmed from its support of the Americans against the British in the American War of Independence. About half of the French national budget went to paying interest on the debt that had accumulated. In contrast to Great Britain, which had a national bank to help raise loans for the government, the French government lived off relatively short-term, high-interest loans from private sources including Swiss banks,

Marie-Antoinette

In this gouache of 1775 by T. Gautier d'Agoti, Marie-Antoinette Playing the Harp, *the queen is shown playing music and surrounded by figures of the court. At the time she was only twenty years old, having married the future Louis XVI at age fifteen in 1770. Her mother, Maria Theresa, frequently wrote to advise her on her behavior at court and expressed disapproval because Marie-Antoinette had a reputation for being frivolous and flirtatious.*
Photo Bulloz.

government annuities, and advances from tax collectors.

For years the French government had been trying unsuccessfully to modernize the tax system to raise more revenue and respond to widespread criticism that the system was unfair. The peasants bore the greatest burden of taxes, whereas the nobles and clergy were largely exempt. Tax collection was also far from systematic: private contractors collected many taxes and pocketed a large share of the proceeds. The failure of the crown's various reform efforts left it at the mercy of its creditors at the end of the American War of Independence. With the growing support of public opinion, the bond and annuity holders from the middle and upper classes now demanded a clearer system of fiscal accountability. Declaring bankruptcy, as many rulers had in the past, was no longer an option.

In a monarchy the ruler's character is always crucial. Louis XVI was the model of a virtuous husband and father, but he took a limited view of his responsibilities in this time of crisis. Many complained that he showed more interest in hunting or in his hobby of making locks than in the problems of government. His wife, Marie-Antoinette, was blond, beautiful, and much criticized for her ex-travagant taste in clothes, elaborate hairdos, and supposed indifference to popular misery. "The Austrian bitch," as underground writers called her, had been the target of an increasingly nasty pamphlet campaign in the 1780s. By 1789, the queen had become an object of popular hatred; when confronted by the inability of the poor to buy bread, she was mistakenly reported to have replied, "Let them eat cake." The king's ineffectiveness and the queen's growing unpopularity helped undermine the monarchy as an institution.

Faced with a mounting deficit, in 1787 Louis called an Assembly of Notables, a group of hand-picked nobles, clergymen, and officials that had last met in 1626. After considering royal proposals for a more uniform land tax, the abolition of internal tariffs, and the establishment of a state bank, the assembly refused to cooperate. Next the king tried his old rival the parlement of Paris. When it too refused to agree to his proposals, he ordered the parlement judges into exile in the provinces. Overnight, the judges (members of the nobility because of the offices they held) became popular heroes for resisting the king's "tyranny"; in reality, however, the judges, like the notables, wanted reform only on their own terms. Nobles in the parlement and in the Assembly

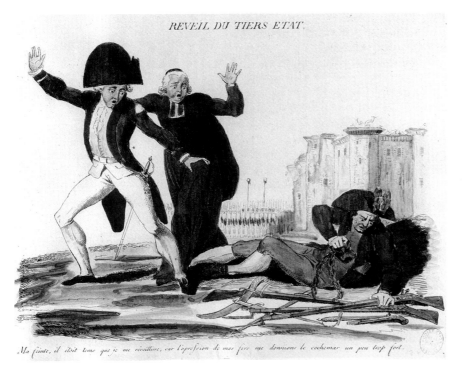

REVEIL DU TIERS ETAT.

Ma feinte, il étoit tems que je me réveillasse, car l'oppression de mes fers me donnoient le cochemar un peu trop fort.

The Third Estate Awakens
This print, produced after the fall of the Bastille (note the heads on pikes outside the prison), shows a clergyman (First Estate) and a noble (Second Estate) alarmed by the awakening of the commoners (Third Estate). The Third Estate breaks the chains of oppression and arms itself to battle for its rights. The message is that social conflicts lay behind the political struggles in the Estates General.
Musée Carnavale/Photo Bulloz.

of Notables saw an opportunity to make themselves partners in running France. Louis finally gave in to their demands that he call a meeting of the Estates General, which had last met 175 years before.

The Estates General.   The calling of the Estates General galvanized public opinion. Who would determine the fate of the nation? There were three estates, or orders, in the Estates General. The deputies in the First Estate represented some 100,000 clergy of the Catholic church, which owned about 10 percent of the land and collected its own taxes (the tithe) on peasants. The deputies of the Second Estate represented the nobility, about 400,000 men and women who owned about 25 percent of the land, enjoyed many tax exemptions, and collected seigneurial dues and rents from their peasant tenants. The deputies of the Third Estate represented everyone else, at least 95 percent of the nation. In 1614, at the last meeting of the Estates General, each order had voted separately, and either the clergy or the nobility could therefore veto any decision of the Third Estate. Before the elections to the Estates General in 1789, the king agreed to double the number of deputies for the Third Estate (making them equal in number to the other two combined), but he left it to the Estates General to decide whether the estates would continue to vote separately by order rather than by individual head. Voting by order would conserve the traditional powers of the clergy and nobility; voting by head would give the Third Estate an advantage since many clergymen and even some nobles sympathized with the Third Estate.

As the state's censorship apparatus broke down, pamphleteers by the hundreds denounced the traditional privileges of the nobility and clergy and called for voting by head rather than order. Critics charged that the interests of the Third Estate clashed with those of the nobility; the clergy were caught in between because most ordinary clergy were not nobles but many bishops and archbishops were. The middle class, made more self-confident by the boom in trade and its participation in the Enlightenment, would no longer settle for crumbs from the political table. In the most vitriolic of all the pamphlets, *What Is the Third Estate?*, the middle-class clergyman Abbé Emmanuel-Joseph Sieyès charged that the nobility contributed nothing at all to the nation's well-being; they were "a malignant disease which preys upon and tortures the body of a sick man."

In the winter and spring of 1789, thousands of men (and a few women by proxy) held meetings to elect deputies and write down their grievances. The effect was electric. Although educated men dominated the meetings at the regional level, the humblest peasants also voted in their villages and burst forth with complaints, especially about taxes. As one villager lamented, "The last crust of bread has been taken from us." The long series of meetings raised expectations that the Estates General would help the king to solve all the nation's ills.

These new hopes soared just at the moment France experienced an increasingly rare but always dangerous food shortage. (See "Taking Measure," below.) Bad weather damaged the harvest of 1788, causing bread prices to rise in many places in the spring and summer of 1789 and threatening starvation for the poorest people. A serious slump in textile production had been causing massive unemployment since 1786, when France signed a free-trade treaty with Great Britain, opening the door to the more rapidly industrializing—and therefore cheaper—British suppliers. In the biggest French

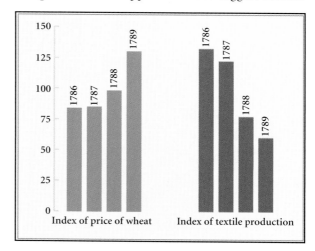

TAKING MEASURE   Wheat Prices and Textile Production in France, 1786–1789
This chart, comparing yearly averages against an index set at 100 (based on the average of all four years), shows the dramatic change over time in wheat prices and textile production. The price of wheat steadily increased in the years just prior to the French Revolution, while the production of textiles dramatically declined. What would be the consequences of this movement in opposite directions? Which groups in the French population would be especially at risk? From Ernest Labrousse et al., *Historie économique et sociale de la France* (Paris: Presses Universitaries de France, 1970), 553.

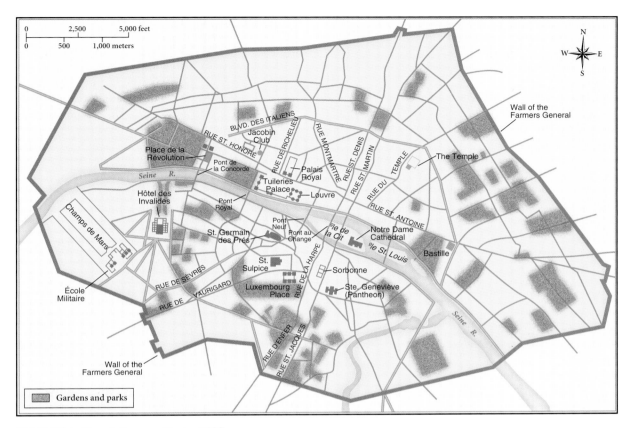

MAP 20.1 Revolutionary Paris, 1789
The French Revolution began with the fall of the Bastille prison on July 14, 1789. The huge fortified prison was located on the eastern side of the city in a neighborhood of working people. Before attacking the Bastille, crowds had torn down many of the customs booths located in the wall of the Farmers General (the private company in charge of tax collection), and taken the arms stored in the Hôtel des Invalides, a veterans hospital on the western side of the city where the upper classes lived. In other words, the crowds had roamed throughout the city.

cities, thousands of textile workers were out of work and hungry, adding another volatile element to an already tense situation.

In May 1789, some 1,200 deputies journeyed to the king's palace of Versailles for the opening of the Estates General. Many readers avidly followed the developments in newspapers that sprouted overnight. Although most nobles insisted on voting by order, the deputies of the Third Estate refused to proceed on that basis. After six weeks of stalemate, on June 17, 1789, the deputies of the Third Estate took unilateral action and declared themselves and whoever would join them the "National Assembly," in which each deputy would vote as an individual. Two days later the clergy voted by a narrow margin to join them. A constitutional revolution was under

way, for now the elected deputies of "the nation" displaced the old estates in which nobles and clergy dominated. As one new newspaper asserted, "The day of the seventeenth will be forever memorable." Barred from their meeting hall on June 20, the deputies met on a nearby tennis court and swore an oath not to disband until they had given France a constitution that reflected their newly declared authority. This "tennis court oath" expressed the determination of the Third Estate to carry through a constitutional revolution.

July 14, 1789: The Fall of the Bastille. At first Louis appeared to agree to the new representative assembly, but he also ordered thousands of soldiers to march to Paris (Map 20.1). The deputies who supported the new National Assembly feared a plot by the king and high-ranking nobles to arrest them and disperse the assembly. "Everyone is convinced that the approach of the troops covers some violent design," one deputy wrote home. Their fears were confirmed when on July 11 the king fired Jacques Necker, the Swiss Protestant finance minister and the one high official regarded as sympathetic to the deputies' cause.

The popular reaction in Paris to Necker's dismissal and the threat of military force changed the course of the French Revolution. When the news spread, the common people in Paris began to arm themselves and attack places where either grain or arms were thought to be stored. A deputy in Versailles reported home: "Today all of the evils overwhelm France, and we are between despotism, carnage, and famine." On July 14, 1789, an armed crowd marched on the Bastille, a fortified prison that symbolized royal authority. After a chaotic battle in which one hundred armed citizens died, the prison officials surrendered. The angry crowd hacked to death the governor of the prison and flaunted his head on a pike.

The fall of the Bastille (an event now commemorated as the French national holiday) set an important precedent. The common people showed themselves willing to intervene violently at a crucial political moment. All over France, food riots turned into local revolts. The officials in one city wrote of their plight: "Yesterday afternoon [July 19] more than seven or eight thousand people, men and women, assembled in front of the two gates to the city hall. . . . We were forced to negotiate with them and to promise to give them wheat . . . and to reduce the price of bread." Local governments were forced out of power and replaced by committees of "patriots" loyal to the revolutionary cause. The patriots relied on newly formed National Guard units composed of civilians. One of their first du-

The Great Fear, 1789

ties was to calm the peasants in the countryside, who feared that the beggars and vagrants crowding the roads might be part of an aristocratic plot to starve the people by burning crops or barns. In some places, the Great Fear (the term used by historians to describe this rural panic) turned into peasant attacks on aristocrats or on seigneurial records of peasants' dues kept in the lord's château. The king's government began to crumble. One of Louis XVI's brothers and many other leading aristocrats fled into exile. In Paris, the marquis de Lafayette, a hero of the American War of Independence and a noble deputy in the National Assembly, became commander of the new National Guard. The Revolution thus had its first heroes, its first victims, and its first enemies.

❖ From Monarchy to Republic, 1789–1793

Until July 1789, the French Revolution followed a course much like that of the protest movements in the Low Countries. Unlike the Dutch and Belgian uprisings, however, the French Revolution did not come to a quick end. The French revolutionaries first tried to establish a constitutional monarchy based on the Enlightenment principles of human rights and rational government. The constitutional monarchy failed, however, when the king tried to raise a counter-revolutionary army. When war broke out in 1792, new tensions culminated in a second revolution that deposed the king and established a republic in which all power rested in an elected legislature.

The Revolution of Rights and Reason

For two years after July 1789, the deputies of the National Assembly strove to establish an enlightened, constitutional monarchy. The National Assembly included the lawyers and officials who had represented the Third Estate in 1789 as well as most of the deputies from the clergy and a substantial number of nobles. Their first goal was to write a constitution, but they faced more immediate problems. In the countryside, peasants refused to pay seigneurial dues to their landlords, and the persistence of peasant violence raised alarms about the potential for a general peasant insurrection.

Major Events of the French Revolution

1789
May 5   The Estates General opens at Versailles
June 17   The Third Estate decides to call itself the National Assembly
June 20   "Tennis court oath" shows determination of deputies to carry out a constitutional revolution
July 14   Fall of the Bastille
August 4   Night session of the National Assembly abolishes "feudalism"
August 26   National Assembly passes Declaration of the Rights of Man and Citizen
October 5–6   Women march to Versailles and join with men in bringing the royal family back to Paris

1790
July 12   Civil Constitution of the Clergy

1791
June 20   Louis and Marie-Antoinette attempt to flee in disguise and are captured at Varennes

1792
April 20   Declaration of war on Austria
August 10   Insurrection in Paris and attack on Tuileries palace lead to suspension of the king
September 2–6   Murder of prisoners in "September massacres" in Paris
September 22   Establishment of the republic

1793
January 21   Execution of Louis XVI
March 11   Beginning of uprising in the Vendée
May 31–June 2   Insurrection leading to arrest of the Girondins
July 27   Robespierre named to the Committee of Public Safety
September 29   Convention establishes General Maximum on prices and wages
October 16   Execution of Marie-Antoinette

1794
February 4   Slavery abolished in the French colonies
March 13–24   Arrest, trial, and executions of so-called ultrarevolutionaries
March 30–April 5   Arrest, trial, and executions of Danton and his followers
July 27   "The Ninth of Thermidor" arrest of Robespierre and his supporters (executed July 28–29)

1795
October 26   Directory government takes office
April 1796–October 1797   Succession of Italian victories by Bonaparte
May 1798–October 1799   Bonaparte in Egypt and Middle East

1799
November 9   Bonaparte's coup of 18 Brumaire

The Night of August 4, 1789.   In response to peasant unrest, the National Assembly decided to make sweeping changes. On the night of August 4, 1789, noble deputies announced their willingness to give up their tax exemptions and seigneurial dues, thereby freeing the peasants from some of their most pressing burdens. By the end of the night, amid wild enthusiasm, dozens of deputies had come to the podium to relinquish the tax exemptions of their own professional groups, towns, or provinces. The National Assembly decreed the abolition of what it called "the feudal regime"—that is, it freed the few remaining serfs and eliminated all special privileges in matters of taxation, including all seigneurial dues on the land (a few days later the deputies insisted on financial compensation for some of these dues, but most peasants refused to pay). Peasants had

achieved their goals, and most now turned conservative. The Assembly also mandated equality of opportunity in access to official posts. Talent, rather than birth, was to be the key to success. Enlightenment principles were beginning to become law.

The Declaration of the Rights of Man and Citizen.
Passed three weeks later, the Declaration of the Rights of Man and Citizen, was the National Assembly's most stirring statement of Enlightenment principles. In words reminiscent of the American Declaration of Independence, whose author Thomas Jefferson was in Paris at the time, it proclaimed, "Men are born and remain free and equal in rights." The Declaration granted freedom of religion, freedom of the press, equality of taxation, and equality before the law. It established the principle of

national sovereignty: since "all sovereignty rests essentially in the nation," the king derived his authority henceforth from the nation rather than from tradition or divine right. By pronouncing all "men" free and equal, the Declaration immediately created new dilemmas. Did women have equal rights with men? What about free blacks in the colonies? How could slavery be justified if all men were born free? Did religious toleration of Protestants and Jews include equal political rights? Women never received the right to vote during the French Revolution, though Protestant and Jewish men did. Women were theoretically citizens under civil law but without the right to full political participation.

Some women did not accept their exclusion, viewing it as a betrayal of the promised new order.

In addition to joining demonstrations, such as the march to Versailles in October 1789, women wrote petitions, published tracts, and organized political clubs to demand more participation. In her Declaration of the Rights of Women of 1791, Olympe de Gouges (1748–1793) played on the language of the official Declaration to make the point that women should also be included. In Article I, she announced, "Woman is born free and lives equal to man in her rights." She also insisted that since "woman has the right to mount the scaffold," she must "equally have the right to mount the rostrum." De Gouges linked her complaints to a program of social reform in which women would have equal rights to property and public office and equal responsibilities in taxes and criminal punishment.

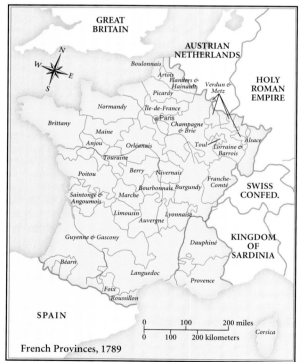 

MAP 20.2 Redrawing the Map of France, 1789–1791

Before 1789, France had been divided into provinces, each with its own administration. Some provinces had their own law codes. As it began its deliberations, the new National Assembly determined to install uniform administrations and laws for the entire country. Discussion of the administrative reforms began in October 1789 and was completed on February 15, 1790, when the Assembly voted to divide the provinces into eighty-three departments, with names based on their geographical characteristics: Basses-Pyrenees for the Pyrenees mountains, Haute-Marne for the Marne River, and so on. By eliminating the old names of provinces, with their historical associations, and supplanting them with geographical ones, the Assembly aimed to show that reason would now govern all French affairs.

Anticlerical Sentiments
This satirical anti-Catholic engraving celebrates the National Assembly's decree of February 16, 1790, which abolished all religious orders. Nuns and monks are depicted as overjoyed at being released from their religious vows and encouraged to marry. In fact, many resisted the destruction of their way of life. Actions taken against the Catholic church alienated a considerable number of French people from the Revolution.
Snark/Art Resource, NY.

The Constitution and the Church. Unresponsive to calls for women's equality, the National Assembly turned to preparing France's first written constitution. The deputies gave voting rights only to white men who passed a test of wealth. The Constitution defined them as the "active citizens"; all others were "passive." Despite this limitation, the Constitution produced fundamental changes in French government. France became a constitutional monarchy in which the king was simply the leading state functionary. A one-house legislature was responsible for making laws. The king could hold up enactment of laws but could not veto them absolutely. The deputies abolished all the old administrative divisions of the provinces and replaced them with a national system of eighty-three departments (*départements*) with identical administrative and legal structures (Map 20.2). All officials were elected; no offices could be bought and sold. The deputies also abolished the old taxes and re-

placed them with new ones that were supposed to be uniformly levied. The new government had difficulty collecting taxes, however, because many people had expected a substantial cut in the tax rate. The new administrative system survived, nonetheless, and the departments are still the basic units of the French state today.

When the deputies turned to reforming the Catholic church, they created conflicts that would erupt again and again over the next ten years. Following a long tradition of state involvement in church affairs but with the new aim of countering aristocratic domination of high church offices, the National Assembly passed a Civil Constitution of the Clergy in July 1790. The constitution set pay scales for the clergy and provided that the voters elect their own parish priests and bishops just as they elected other officials. Motivated partly by the ongoing financial crisis, the National Assembly confiscated all the church's property and promised to pay clerical salaries in return. The impounded property served as a guarantee for the new paper money, called *assignats*, issued by the government. The *assignats* soon became subject to inflation because the government began to sell the church lands to the highest bidders in state auctions. The sales increased the landholdings of wealthy city dwellers and prosperous peasants but cut the ground out from under the *assignats*.

The government's offensive on the church did not stop at confiscation of church lands. Convinced that monastic life encouraged idleness and a decline in the nation's population, the deputies outlawed any future monastic vows and encouraged monks and nuns to return to private life on state pensions. Many monks took the opportunity, but few nuns did; for nuns, the convent was all they knew. As the Carmelite nuns of Paris responded, "If there is true happiness on earth, we enjoy it in the shelter of the sanctuary."

In November 1790, the National Assembly required all clergy to swear an oath of loyalty to the Civil Constitution of the Clergy. Pope Pius VI in Rome condemned the constitution, and half of the French clergy refused to take the oath. The oath of allegiance permanently divided the Catholic population, which had to choose between loyalty to the old church and commitment to the Revolution with its "constitutional" church. The revolutionary government lost many supporters by passing laws against the clergy who refused the oath and by forcing them into exile, deporting them forcibly, or executing them as traitors. Riots and demonstrations led by women greeted many of the oath-taking priests who showed up to replace those who refused.

The End of Monarchy

Louis XVI was reluctant to recognize the new limits on his powers, and the reorganization of the Catholic church particularly offended him. On June 20, 1791, the royal family escaped in disguise from the Tuileries palace in Paris and fled to the eastern border of France, where they hoped to gather support to overturn the Revolution from Austria, whose emperor, Leopold II, was the brother of Marie-Antoinette. The plans went awry when a postmaster recognized the king from his portrait on the new French money, and the royal family was arrested at Varennes, forty miles from the Austrian border. The National Assembly tried to depict this incident as a kidnapping, but the "flight to Varennes" touched off demonstrations in Paris against the royal family, whom some now regarded as traitors. Cartoons circulated depicting the royal family as animals being returned "to the stable."

War with Austria and Prussia. The Constitution that Louis finally endorsed in 1791 provided for the immediate election of a new Legislative Assembly. In a rare act of self-denial, the deputies of the National Assembly declared themselves ineligible for the new Assembly. Those who had experienced the Revolution firsthand now departed from the scene, opening the door to men with little previous experience in national politics. The status of the king might have remained uncertain if war had not intervened, but by early 1792 everyone seemed intent on war with Austria. Louis and Marie-Antoinette hoped that war would lead to the definitive defeat of the Revolution, whereas the deputies who favored a republic hoped that war would reveal the king's treachery and lead to his downfall. On April 21, 1792, Louis declared war on Leopold. Prussia immediately entered on the Austrian side. Thousands of French aristocrats, including two-thirds of the army officer corps, had already emigrated, including both the king's brothers, and they were gathering along France's eastern border in expectation of joining Leopold's counterrevolutionary army.

When fighting broke out in 1792, all the powers expected a brief and relatively contained war. Instead, it would continue despite brief interruptions for the next twenty-three years. In 1792, the French were woefully unprepared, and in the first battles the Austrians promptly routed the French armies, joking that the new French motto was "Conquer or Run."

The Second Revolution of August 10, 1792. As the French frantically reorganized their armies to replace the thousands of aristocratic officers who had emigrated, the authority of the Legislative Assembly came under fire. In June 1792, an angry crowd invaded the hall of the Assembly in Paris and threatened the royal family. In response, Lafayette left his command on the eastern front and came to Paris to insist on punishing the demonstrators. His appearance only fueled distrust of the army commanders, which increased to a fever pitch when the Prussians crossed the border and advanced on Paris. The Prussian commander, the duke of Brunswick, issued

The Guillotine

Before 1789 only nobles were decapitated if condemned to death; commoners were usually hanged. Equalization of the death penalty was first proposed by J. I. Guillotin, a professor of anatomy and a deputy for the Third Estate in the National Assembly. He also suggested that a mechanical device be constructed for decapitation, leading to the instrument's association with his name. The Assembly decreed decapitation as the death penalty in June 1791 and another physician, A. Louis, actually invented the guillotine. Its use began in April 1792 and did not end until 1981, when the French government abolished the death penalty. Although it was invented to make death equal and painless, the guillotine disturbed many observers; its mechanical operation and efficiency — the executioner only pulled up the blade by a cord and then released it — seemed somehow inhuman. Nonetheless, the guillotine fascinated much as it repelled. Reproduced in miniature, painted onto snuffboxes and china, worn as jewelry, and even serving as a toy, the guillotine became a part of popular culture, celebrated as the people's avenger by supporters of the Revolution and vilified as the preeminent symbol of the Terror by opponents. Musée Carnavalet/Photo Bulloz.

wives and daughters, had followed every twist and turn in revolutionary fortunes. Political clubs had multiplied since the founding in 1789 of the first and most influential of them, the Jacobin Club (named after the former monastery in Paris where the first club met). Newspapers, pamphlets, posters, and cartoons proliferated. Every local district in Paris had its club, where men and women listened to the news of the day and discussed their options.

Faced with the threat of military retaliation and frustrated with the inaction of the Legislative Assembly, on August 10, 1792, leaders of the local district governments of Paris (called *sections*) organized an insurrection and attacked the Tuileries palace, where the king resided. The king and his family had to escape into the meeting room of the Legislative Assembly, where the frightened deputies ordered new elections—this time by universal male suffrage (no wealth qualifications as in the Constitution of 1791)—for a National Convention that would write yet another constitution. When it met, the Convention abolished the monarchy and on September 22, 1792, established the first republic in French history. The republic would answer only to the people, not to any royal authority. Lafayette and other liberal aristocrats who had supported the constitutional monarchy fled into exile.

Violence soon exploded again. Early in September 1792, as the Prussians approached Paris, hastily gathered mobs stormed the overflowing prisons to seek out traitors who might help the enemy. In an atmosphere of near hysteria, eleven hundred inmates were killed, including many ordinary and completely innocent people. The princess of Lamballe, one of the queen's favorites, was hacked to pieces and her mutilated body displayed beneath the windows where the royal family was kept under guard. These "September massacres" showed the dark side of popular revolution, in which the common people demanded instant revenge on supposed enemies and conspirators.

Republican Rivals and the Execution of the King.

The National Convention faced a dire situation. It needed to write a new constitution for the republic while fighting a war with external enemies and confronting increasing resistance at home. The Revolution had divided the population: for some it had not gone far enough toward providing food, land, and retribution against enemies; for others it had

a manifesto—the Brunswick Manifesto—announcing that Paris would be totally destroyed if the royal family suffered any violence.

The ordinary people of Paris did not passively await their fate. Known as *sans-culottes* ("without breeches")—because men who worked with their hands wore long trousers rather than the knee breeches of the upper classes—tailors, shoemakers, cabinetmakers, and shopkeepers, along with their gone too far by dismantling the church and the monarchy. The French people had never known any government other than monarchy. Only half the population could read and write at even a basic level. In this situation, symbolic actions became very important. Any public sign of monarchy was at risk, and revolutionaries soon pulled down statues of kings and burned reminders of the former regime.

The fate of Louis XVI and the future direction of the republic divided the deputies elected to the National Convention. The deputies came from very similar social backgrounds and shared many political beliefs; most of them were middle-class lawyers and professionals who had developed their ardent republican beliefs in the national network of Jacobin Clubs. After the fall of the monarchy in August 1792, however, the Jacobins divided into two factions. The Girondins (named after a department in southwestern France, the Gironde, which provided some of its leading orators) met regularly at the salon of Jeanne Roland, the wife of a minister. They resented the growing power of Parisian militants and tried to appeal to the departments outside of Paris. The Mountain (so called because its deputies sat in the highest seats of the Convention), in contrast, was closely allied with the Paris militants.

The first showdown between the Girondins and the Mountain occurred during the trial of the king in December 1792. Although the Girondins agreed that the king was guilty of treason, many of them argued for clemency, exile, or a popular referendum on his fate. After a long and difficult debate, the Convention supported the Mountain and voted by a very narrow majority to execute the king. Louis XVI went to the guillotine on January 21, 1793, sharing the fate of Charles I of England in 1649. "We have just convinced ourselves that a king is only a man," wrote one newspaper, "and that no man is above the law."

❖ The Terror and the Republic of Virtue

The execution of the king did not end the new regime's problems. The continuing war required even more men and money, and the introduction of a national draft provoked massive resistance in some parts of France. In response to growing pressures,

the National Convention set up a highly centralized government designed to provide food, direct the war effort, and punish counterrevolutionaries. Thus began "the Terror," in which the guillotine became the most frightening instrument of a government that suppressed almost every form of dissent. The leader of this government, Maximilien Robespierre, aimed to create a "Republic of Virtue," in which the government would teach, or force, citizens to become virtuous republicans through a massive program of political reeducation. These policies only increased divisions, which ultimately led to Robespierre's fall from power and to a dismantling of government by terror.

Robespierre and the Committee of Public Safety

The conflict between the Girondins and the Mountain did not end with the execution of Louis XVI. Militants in Paris agitated for the removal of the deputies who had proposed a referendum on the king, and in retaliation the Girondins tried to single out Parisian leaders for punishment. First the Girondins engineered the arrest of Jean-Paul Marat, a deputy who styled himself in his newspaper "the friend of the people" and urged violent measures against enemies of the republic. Marat was acquitted. Then the Girondins devised a special commission to investigate the situation in Paris, ordering the arrest of various local leaders. In response, Parisian militants organized an armed demonstration and invaded the National Convention on June 2, 1793, forcing the deputies to decree the arrest of their twenty-nine Girondin colleagues. The Convention agreed to the establishment of paramilitary bands called "revolutionary armies" to enforce the distribution of grain and hunt down hoarders and political suspects and to the increased use of revolutionary courts to try political suspects and execute the guilty. In a series of decrees over the next few months, the Convention also tried to stabilize prices; on September 29, 1793, it established a General Maximum on the prices of thirty-nine essential commodities and on wages.

Setting the course for government and the war increasingly fell to the Committee of Public Safety, set up by the Convention on April 6, 1793. Composed of twelve deputies elected by the Convention, the committee gradually established its paramount

An Anti-Jacobin Satire
In The Purifying Pot of the
Jacobins *(1793), the anonymous
artist makes fun of the Jacobin
Club's penchant for constantly
examining the political correct-
ness of its members. Those who
failed the test suffered harsh,
sometimes fatal consequences.*
Art Resource, NY.

authority. When Maximilien Robespierre (1758–1794) was named to the committee on July 27, 1793, he became in effect its guiding spirit and the chief spokesman of the Revolution. A lawyer from northern France known as "the incorruptible" for his stern honesty and fierce dedication to democratic ideals, Robespierre remains one of the most controversial figures in world history because of his association with the Terror. In September 1793, again in response to popular pressure, the deputies of the Convention voted to "put Terror on the agenda." Robespierre took the lead in implementing this decision. Although he originally opposed the death penalty and the war, he was convinced that the emergency situation of 1793 required severe measures, including death for those, such as the Girondins, who opposed the committee's policies.

Robespierre was the theorist of the Terror and the chief architect of the Republic of Virtue. Like many other educated eighteenth-century men, he had read all the classics of republicanism from Tacitus and Plutarch to Montesquieu and Rousseau. But he took them a step further. He spoke eloquently about "the theory of revolutionary government" as "the war of liberty against its enemies." He defended the people's right to democratic government, while in practice he supported many emergency measures

that restricted their liberties. He personally favored a free market economy, as did almost all middle-class deputies, but in this time of crisis he was willing to enact price controls and requisitioning. Like Rousseau, he believed the republic would have to reform its citizens by establishing a new civic religion. In a famous speech to the Convention, he insisted: "The first maxim of your policies must be to lead the people by reason and the people's enemies by terror . . . without virtue, terror is deadly; without terror, virtue is impotent." *Terror* was not an idle term; it seemed to imply that the goal of democracy justified what we now call totalitarian means, that is, the suppression of all dissent.

Through a series of desperate measures, the Committee of Public Safety set the machinery of the Terror in motion. It sent deputies out "on mission" to purge unreliable officials, work with local leaders of the Jacobin Clubs and other popular societies to uncover dissidents, and organize the war effort. In the first universal draft of men in history, every unmarried man and childless widower between the ages of eighteen and twenty-five was declared eligible for conscription into the army. Revolutionary tribunals set up in Paris and provincial centers tried political suspects. In October 1793, the Revolutionary Tribunal in Paris convicted Marie-Antoinette of

The Revolutionary Tricolor

This painting by an anonymous artist probably shows a deputy in the uniform prescribed for those sent to supervise military operations. His dress prominently displays the revolutionary tricolor — red, white, and blue — both on his official sash and on the trim of his hat. Plumes had once been reserved to nobles; now nonnobles could wear them on their hats, but they still signaled dignity and importance. Dress became a contested issue during the Revolution, and successive governments considered prescribing some kind of uniform, at least for the deputies in the legislature.
Louvre/Reunion des Musées Nationaux.

one. Its basis was reason and republican principles. Year I dated from the beginning of the republic on September 22, 1792. Twelve months of exactly thirty days each received new names derived from nature: Pluviôse (roughly equivalent to February), for example, recalled the rain of late winter (*la pluie* is French for "rain"). Instead of seven-day weeks, ten-day *décades* provided only one day of rest every ten days and pointedly eliminated the Sunday of the Christian calendar. The five days left at the end of the calendar year were devoted to special festivals called *sans-culottides*. The calendar remained in force for twelve years despite continuing resistance to it. More enduring was the new metric system based on units of ten that was invented to replace the hundreds of local variations in weights and measures. Other countries in Europe and throughout the world eventually adopted the metric system.

Successive revolutionary legislatures had also changed the rules of family life. The state took responsibility for all family matters away from the Catholic church: birth, death, and marriage registration now happened at city hall, not the parish church. Marriage became a civil contract and as such could be broken. The new divorce law of September 1792 was the most far-reaching in the West: a couple could divorce by mutual consent or for reasons such as insanity, abandonment, battering, or criminal conviction. Thousands of men and women took advantage of the law to dissolve unhappy marriages, even though the pope had condemned the measure. (In 1816, the government revoked the right to divorce, and not until the 1970s did French divorce laws return to the principles of the 1792 legislation.) The revolutionary government also limited fathers' rights over their children; they could not imprison them without cause or control their lives after the age of twenty-one. In one of its most influential actions, the National Convention passed a series of laws that created equal inheritance among all children in the family, including girls. The father's right to favor one child, especially the oldest male, was considered aristocratic and hence antirepublican.

Resisting the Revolution

By intruding into religion, culture, and daily life, the republic inevitably provoked resistance. Shouting curses against the republic, uprooting liberty trees, carrying statues of the Virgin Mary in procession,

Roman republic (Brutus, Gracchus, Cornelia), revolutionary heroes, or flowers and plants. Such changes symbolized adherence to the republic and to Enlightenment ideals rather than to Catholicism.

Even the measures of time and space were revolutionized. In October 1793, the Convention introduced a new calendar to replace the Christian

Charlotte Corday

In this anonymous painting, Charlotte Corday has just stabbed Marat to death in his bath. Her gaily decorated hat seems incongruous in the gruesome setting. Corday stabbed Marat when she gained admission to his bathroom, where he spent hours every day writing and even receiving visitors. The twenty-five-year-old Corday was tried the next day and amazed even her opponents by remaining absolutely calm and convinced of the rightness of her act.
Musée Carnavalet/Laurie Platt Winfrey, Inc.

hiding a priest who would not take the oath, singing a royalist song—all these expressed dissent with the new symbols, rituals, and policies. Resistance also took more violent forms, from riots over food shortages or religious policies to assassination and full-scale civil war.

Women's Resistance.   Many women, in particular, suffered from the hard conditions of life that persisted in this time of war, and they had their own ways of voicing discontent. The long bread lines in the cities exhausted the patience of women already overwhelmed by the demands of housekeeping, childrearing, and working as shop assistants, fishwives, laundresses, and textile workers. Police spies reported their constant grumbling, which occasionally turned into spontaneous demonstrations or riots over high prices or food shortages.

Other forms of resistance were more individual. One young woman, Charlotte Corday, assassinated Jean-Paul Marat in July 1793. Corday fervently supported the Girondins, and she considered it her patriotic duty to kill the deputy who, in the columns of his paper *The Friend of the People,* had constantly demanded more heads and more blood. Marat was immediately eulogized as a great martyr: Corday went to the guillotine vilified as a monster but confident that she had "avenged many innocent victims."

Rebellion and Civil War.   Violent resistance broke out for various reasons in many parts of France. In the early years of the Revolution, Catholics rioted in places with large Protestant or Jewish populations, which tended to support the Revolution and the religious toleration and civil rights it promised. The arrest of the Girondin deputies in June 1793 sparked insurrections in several departments. After the government retook the city of Lyon, one of the centers of the revolt, the deputy on mission ordered sixteen hundred houses demolished. Special courts sentenced almost two thousand people to death. The name of the city was changed to Ville Affranchie (Liberated Town).

Nowhere was resistance to the republic more persistent and violent than in the Vendée region of western France. Between March and December 1793, peasants, artisans, and weavers joined under noble leadership to form a "Catholic and Royal Army." One rebel group explained its motives: "They [the republicans] have killed our king, chased away our priests, sold the goods of our church, eaten everything we have and now they want to take our bodies [in the draft]." The uprising took two different forms: in the Vendée itself, a counterrevolutionary army organized to fight the republic; in nearby Brittany, resistance took the form of guerrilla bands, which united to attack a target and then quickly melted into the countryside. Great Britain provided money and underground contacts for these attacks, which were almost always aimed at towns. Town officials sold church lands, enforced measures against the clergy, and supervised conscription. In many ways this was a civil war between town and country, for the townspeople were the ones who supported the Revolution and bought church lands for themselves. The peasants had gained most of what they wanted in 1789 with the abolition of seigneurial dues, and they resented the government's demands for money and manpower and actions taken against their local clergy.

For several months in 1793, the Vendée rebels stormed the largest towns in the region. Both sides committed horrible atrocities. At the small town of Machecoul, for example, the rebels massacred five hundred republicans, including administrators and National Guard members; many were tied together, shoved into freshly dug graves, and shot. By the fall, however, republican soldiers had turned back the rebels. A republican general wrote to the Committee of Public Safety claiming, "There is no more Vendée, citizens, it has perished under our free sword along with its women and children. . . . Following the orders that you gave me I have crushed children under the feet of horses, massacred women who at least . . . will engender no more brigands." "Infernal columns" of republican troops marched through the region to restore control, military courts ordered thousands executed, and republican soldiers massacred thousands of others. In one especially gruesome incident, the deputy Jean-Baptiste Carrier supervised the drowning of some two thousand Vendée rebels, including a number of priests. Barges loaded with prisoners were floated into the Loire River near Nantes and then sunk. Controversy still rages about the rebellion's death toll. Estimates of rebel deaths alone range from about 20,000 to 250,000 and higher. Many thousands of republican soldiers and civilians also lost their lives. Even the low estimates reveal the carnage of this catastrophic confrontation between the republic and its opponents.

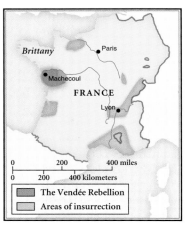

The Vendée Rebellion, 1793

The Fall of Robespierre and the End of the Terror, 1794–1799

In an atmosphere of fear of conspiracy that was fueled by overt resistance in places like the Vendée, Robespierre tried simultaneously to exert the Convention's control over popular political activities and to weed out opposition among the deputies. As a result, the Terror intensified until July 1794, when a group of deputies joined within the Convention to order the arrest and execution of Robespierre and his followers. The Convention then ordered elections and drew up a new republican constitution that gave executive power to five directors. This Directory government maintained power during four years of seesaw battles between royalists and former Jacobins. Ultimately it gave way to Napoleon Bonaparte.

The Revolution Devours Its Own. In the fall of 1793, the Convention cracked down on popular clubs and societies. First to be suppressed were women's political clubs. Founded in early 1793, the Society of Revolutionary Republican Women played a very active part in *sans-culottes* politics. The society agitated for harsher measures against the republic's enemies and insisted that women have a voice in politics even if they did not have the vote. Women set up their own clubs in many provincial towns and also attended the meetings of local men's organizations. The closing of women's clubs marked an important turning point in the Revolution. From then on the *sans-culottes* and their political organizations came increasingly under the thumb of the Jacobin deputies in the National Convention.

The Convention severely limited women's participation in the public sphere because the deputies associated women's groups with political disorder and social upheaval. As one deputy stated, women's clubs consisted of "adventuresses, knights-errant, emancipated women, amazons." Another deputy continued, "Women are ill suited for elevated thoughts and serious meditations." In subsequent years physicians, priests, and philosophers amplified such opinions by formulating explanations for women's "natural" differences from men to justify their inferior status.

In the spring of 1794, the Committee of Public Safety moved against its critics among leaders in Paris and deputies in the Convention itself. First a handful of men labeled "ultrarevolutionaries"—in fact a

A Women's Club
In this gouache by the Lesueur brothers, The Patriotic Women's Club, *the club president urges the members to contribute funds for poor patriot families. Women's clubs focused on philanthropic work but also discussed revolutionary legislation and the debates in the National Assemblies. The colorful but sober dress indicates that the women are middle class.*
Musée de la Ville de Paris/Musée Carnavalet, Paris/Giraudon/Art Resource, NY.

motley collection of local Parisian politicians—were arrested and executed. Next came the other side, the "indulgents," so called because they favored a moderation of the Terror. Included among them was the deputy Danton, himself once a member of the Committee of Public Safety and a friend of Robespierre, despite the striking contrast in their personalities. Danton was the Revolution's most flamboyant orator and, unlike Robespierre, a high-living, high-spending, excitable politician. At every critical turning point in national politics, his booming voice had swayed opinion in the National Convention. Now, under government pressure, the Revolutionary Tribunal convicted him and his friends of treason and sentenced them to death.

With the arrest and execution of these leaders in Paris, the prophecies of doom for the Revolution seemed about to be realized. "The Revolution," as one of the Girondin victims of 1793 had remarked, "was devouring its own children." The middle-class leaders were killing each other. Even after the major threats to the committee's power had been eliminated, the Terror continued and even worsened. A law passed in June 1794 denied the accused the right of legal counsel, reduced the number of jurors necessary for conviction, and allowed only two judgments: acquittal or death. The category of political crimes expanded to include "slandering patriotism" and "seeking to inspire discouragement." Ordinary

people risked the guillotine if they expressed any discontent. (Ironically, the guillotine had been introduced just a few months before the king's execution as a way of making capital punishment more humane and uniform.) The rate of executions in Paris rose from five a day in the spring of 1794 to twenty-six a day in the summer. The political atmosphere darkened even though the military situation improved. At the end of June, the French armies decisively defeated the main Austrian army and advanced through the Austrian Netherlands to Brussels and Antwerp. The emergency measures for fighting the war were working, yet Robespierre and his inner circle had made so many enemies that they could not afford to loosen the grip of the Terror.

The Terror hardly touched many parts of France. But overall the experience was undeniably traumatic. Across the country the official Terror cost the lives of at least 40,000 French people, most of them living in the regions of major insurrections or near the borders with foreign enemies, where suspicion of collaboration ran high. As many as 300,000 people went to prison as suspects between March 1793 and August 1794 (that is, one out of every fifty French). The toll for the aristocracy and the clergy was especially high. Many leading nobles perished under the guillotine, and thousands emigrated. Thirty thousand to forty thousand clergy who refused the oath emigrated, at least two thousand (including many nuns) were executed, and thousands were imprisoned. The clergy were singled out in particular in the civil war zones: 135 priests were massacred at Lyon in November 1793 and 83 shot in one day during the Vendée revolt. Yet many victims of the Terror were peasants or ordinary working people.

The final crisis of the Terror came in July 1794. Conflicts within the Committee of Public Safety and the National Convention left Robespierre isolated. On July 27, 1794 (the ninth of Thermidor, Year II, according to the revolutionary calendar), Robespierre appeared before the Convention with yet another list of deputies to be arrested. Many feared they would be named, and they shouted him down and ordered him arrested along with his followers on the committee, the president of the Revolutionary Tribunal in Paris, and the commander of the Parisian National Guard. An armed uprising led by the Paris city government failed to save Robespierre when most of the Parisian *sections* and two-thirds of the National Guard took the side of the Convention. Robespierre tried to kill himself with a pistol but only broke his jaw. The next day he and scores of followers went to the guillotine.

The Thermidorian Reaction and the Directory, 1794–1799. The men who led the attack on Robespierre in Thermidor (July 1794) did not intend to reverse all his policies, but that happened nonetheless. Newspapers attacked the Robespierrists as "tigers thirsting for human blood." The new government released hundreds of suspects and arranged a temporary truce in the Vendée. It purged Jacobins from local bodies and replaced them with their opponents. It arrested some of the most notorious "terrorists" in the National Convention, such as Carrier, and put them to death. Within the year the new leaders abolished the Revolutionary Tribunal and closed the Jacobin Club in Paris. Popular demonstrations met severe repression. In southeastern France, in particular, a "White Terror" replaced the Jacobins' "Red Terror." Former officials and local Jacobin leaders were harassed, beaten, and often murdered by paramilitary bands who had tacit support from the new authorities. Those who remained in the National Convention prepared yet another constitution in 1795, setting up a two-house legislature and an executive body—the Directory, headed by five directors.

The Directory regime tenuously held on to power for four years, all the while trying to fend off challenges from the remaining Jacobins and the resurgent royalists. The puritanical atmosphere of the Terror gave way to the pursuit of pleasure—low-cut dresses of transparent materials, the reappearance of prostitutes in the streets, fancy dinner parties, and "victims balls" where guests wore red ribbons around their necks as reminders of the guillotine. Bands of young men dressed in knee breeches and rich fabrics picked fights with known Jacobins and disrupted theater performances with loud antirevolutionary songs. All over France people banded together and petitioned to reopen churches closed during the Terror. If necessary they broke into a church to hold services with a priest who had been in hiding or a lay schoolteacher who was willing to say Mass.

Although the Terror had ended, the revolution had not. In 1794, the most democratic and most repressive phases of the Revolution ended both at once. Between 1795 and 1799, the republic endured in France, but it directed a war effort abroad that would ultimately bring to power the man who would dismantle the republic itself.

❖ Revolution on the March

Beginning in 1792, war raged almost constantly until 1815. At one time or another, and sometimes all at once, France faced every principal power in Europe. The French republic—and later the French Empire under its supreme commander, Emperor Napoleon Bonaparte—proved an even more formidable opponent than the France of Louis XIV. New means of mobilizing and organizing soldiers enabled the French to dominate Europe for a generation. The influence of the Revolution as a political model and the threat of French military conquest combined to challenge the traditional order in Europe.

Arms and Conquests

The allied powers had a chance to defeat France in 1793, when the French armies verged on chaos because of the emigration of noble army officers and the problems of integrating new draftees. At that moment, however, Prussia, Russia, and Austria were preoccupied with clamping down on Poland. For France, this diversion meant a reprieve.

Because of the new national draft, the French had a huge and powerful fighting force of 700,000 men by the end of 1793. But the army faced many problems in the field. As many as a third of the recent draftees deserted before or during battle. Uniforms fashioned out of rough cloth constricted movements, tore easily, and retained the damp of muddy battlefields, exposing the soldiers to the elements and the spread of disease. At times the soldiers were fed only moldy bread, and if their pay was late, they sometimes resorted to pillaging and looting. Generals might pay with their lives if they lost a key battle and their loyalty to the Revolution came under suspicion. France nevertheless had one overwhelming advantage: its soldiers, drawn largely from the peasantry and the lower classes of the cities, fought for a revolution that they and their brothers and sisters had helped make. The republic was their government, and the army was in large measure theirs too; many officers had risen through the ranks by skill and talent rather than by inheriting or purchasing their positions. One young peasant boy wrote to his parents, "Either you will see me return bathed in glory, or you will have a son who is a worthy citizen of France who knows how to die for the defense of his country."

When the French armies invaded the Austrian Netherlands and crossed the Rhine in the summer of 1794, they proclaimed a war of liberation. But as they annexed more and more territory, "liberated" people in many places began to view them as an army of occupation (Map 20.3). Those just across the northern and eastern borders of France reacted most positively to the French invasion. In the

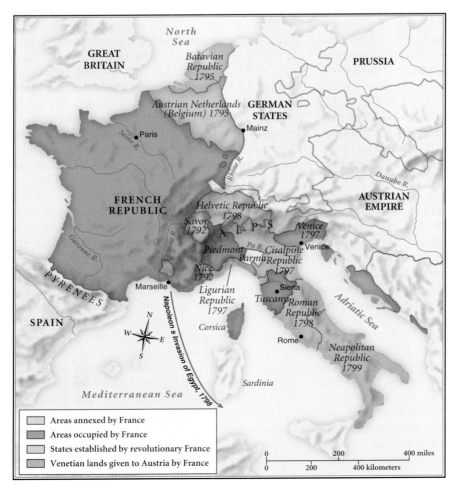

MAP 20.3 French Expansion, 1791–1799
The influence of the French Revolution on neighboring territories is dramatically evident in this map. The French directly annexed the papal territories in southern France in 1791, Nice and Savoy in 1792, and the Austrian Netherlands in 1795. They set up a series of sister republics in the former Dutch Republic and in various Italian states. Local people did not always welcome these changes. For example, the French made the Dutch pay a huge war indemnity, support a French occupying army of 25,000 soldiers, and give up some southern territories. One of the generals who invaded the Dutch Republic wrote, "Holland has done nothing to avoid being classed among the general order of our conquests. . . . It follows from this that there can be no reason to treat her any differently from a conquered country." The sister republics faced a future of subordination to French national interests.

Austrian Netherlands, Mainz, Savoy, and Nice, French officers organized Jacobin Clubs that attracted middle-class locals. The clubs petitioned for annexation to France, and French legislation was then introduced, including the abolition of seigneurial dues. Despite resistance, especially in the Austrian Netherlands, these areas remained part of France until 1815, and the legal changes were permanent. Like Louis XIV a century before, most deputies in the National Convention considered the annexed territories within France's "natural frontiers"—the Rhine, the Alps, and the Pyrenees.

The Directory government that came to power in 1795 was torn between defending the new frontiers and launching a more aggressive policy of creating semi-independent "sister" republics wherever the armies succeeded. When Prussia declared neutrality in 1795, the French armies swarmed into the Dutch Republic, abolished the stadholderate, and, with the revolutionary penchant for renaming, created the new Batavian Republic, a satellite of France. The brilliant young general Napoleon Bonaparte defeated the Austrian armies in northern Italy in 1797 and created the Cisalpine Republic. Next he overwhelmed Venice and then handed it over to the Austrians in exchange for a peace agreement that lasted less than two years. After the French attacked the Swiss cantons in 1798, they set up the Helvetic Republic and curtailed many of the Catholic church's privileges. They conquered the Papal States in 1798 and installed a Roman Republic; the pope fled to Siena.

The same year, 1798, Bonaparte took a great army, originally raised to invade England, across the Mediterranean Sea to Egypt. The Directory government hoped that an occupation of Egypt would strike a blow at British trade by cutting the route to India and thus compensate France for its losses there years before. Once the army disembarked, however, the British admiral Horatio Nelson destroyed the French fleet while it was anchored in Aboukir Bay. In the face of determined resistance and an outbreak of the bubonic plague, Bonaparte's armies retreated from a further expedition in Syria. But the French occupation of Egypt lasted long enough for that largely Muslim country to experience the same kinds of Enlightenment-inspired legal reforms that had been introduced in Europe: the French abolished torture, introduced equality before the law, eliminated religious taxes, and proclaimed religious toleration.

The revolutionary wars had an immediate impact on European life at all levels of society. Thousands of men died in every country involved, with perhaps as many as 200,000 casualties in the French armies alone in 1794 and 1795. No accurate statistics documenting casualties in these wars exist, but we do know that more soldiers died in hospitals as a result of their wounds than on the battlefields. Constant warfare hampered world commerce and especially disrupted French overseas shipping. (The abolition of slavery in the French colonies in 1794 also cut off one lucrative market for the French port cities.) In contrast to the prosperous times that preceded the French Revolution, times were now hard almost everywhere, because the dislocations of internal and external commerce provoked constant shortages.

European Reactions to Revolutionary Change

The French Revolution profoundly transformed European politics and social relations. (See "Contrasting Views," page 752.) In 1789, an English supporter, the Unitarian minister Richard Price, wrote enthusiastically about the Revolution's prospects: "Behold, the light . . . after setting AMERICA free, reflected to FRANCE, and there kindled into a blaze that lays despotism in ashes, and warms and illuminates EUROPE." The governing elites of Europe became alarmed, however, when the revolutionaries abolished monarchy and nobility and encouraged popular participation in politics. Democrats and reformers from many countries flooded to Paris to witness events firsthand. Supporters of the French Revolution in Great Britain, like the earlier reformers of the 1760s and 1770s, joined constitutional and reform societies that sprang up in many cities. The most important of these societies, the London Corresponding Society, founded in 1792, corresponded with the Paris Jacobin Club and served as a center for reform agitation in England. The British government quickly suppressed the societies and harassed their leaders, charging that their ideas and their contacts with the French were seditious.

Pro-French feeling ran even stronger in Ireland. Catholics and Presbyterians, both excluded from the vote, came together in 1791 in the Society of United Irishmen, which eventually pressed for secession from England. In 1798, the society timed a rebellion

FRENCH LIBERTY.   BRITISH SLAVERY.

The English Rebuttal
In this caricature, James Gillray satirizes the French version of liberty. Gillray, a supporter of the Tories in Britain, produced thousands of political caricatures. British Museum.

to coincide with a French invasion, but the French sent too few soldiers and the British mercilessly repressed the revolt. Thirty thousand people were killed. Twice as many regular British troops (seventy thousand) as fought in any of the major continental battles were required to put down the rebellion.

Those countries near France with a substantial middle class and access to newspapers and other publications generally sympathized the most with French ideas. Yet even countries close to France sometimes fiercely resisted French occupation, often in the form of banditry. In the German Rhineland, for example, gangs of bandits preyed on the French and on Jews. One German traveler reported, "It is characteristic of the region in which the bandits are based that these two nations [the French and the Jews] are hated. So crimes against them are motivated not just by a wish to rob them but also by a variety of fanaticism which is partly political and partly religious." Because the French offered the Jews religious toleration and civil and political rights wherever they conquered, anti-French groups sometimes attacked Jews.

Many leading intellectuals in the German states, including the philosopher Immanuel Kant, initially supported the revolutionary cause, but after 1793 most of them turned against the popular violence and military aggressiveness of the Revolution. One of the greatest writers of the age, Friedrich Schiller

(1759–1805), typified the turn in sentiment against revolutionary politics:

Freedom is only in the realm of dreams
And the beautiful blooms only in song.

The German states, still run by many separate rulers, experienced a profound artistic and intellectual revival, which eventually connected with anti-French nationalism. This renaissance included a resurgence of intellectual life in the universities, a thriving press (1,225 journals were launched in the 1780s alone), and the multiplication of Masonic lodges and literary clubs.

Not surprisingly, the areas farthest from France—Russia, the Ottoman Empire, the Balkans, Austria, Hungary, and the Scandinavian states—were generally least affected by the French Revolution. One exception was the United States, where opinion fiercely divided on the virtues of the French Revolution. Sweden was a second exception. Gustavus III (r. 1771–1792) was assassinated in Stockholm by a nobleman who claimed that "the king has violated his oath . . . and declared himself an enemy of the realm." The king's murder changed little in Sweden's power structure, however; his son Gustavus IV (r. 1792–1809) was convinced that the French Jacobins had sanctioned his father's assassination, and he insisted on avoiding "licentious liberty." Although just across the border from France, Spain's royal

Consequences of the French Revolution

Contemporaries instantly grasped the cataclysmic significance of the French Revolution and began to argue about its lessons for their own countries. A member of the British Parliament, Edmund Burke, ignited a firestorm of controversy with his *Reflections on the Revolution in France* (Document 1). He condemned the French revolutionaries for attempting to build a government on abstract reasoning rather than taking historical traditions and customs into account; his book provided a foundation for the doctrine known as *conservatism*, which argued for "conserving" the traditional foundations of society and avoiding the pitfalls of radical or revolutionary change. Burke's views provoked a strong response from the English political agitator Thomas Paine. Paine's pamphlet *Common Sense* (1776) helped inspire the British North American colonies to demand independence from Great Britain. In *The Rights of Man* (Document 2), written fifteen years later, Paine attacked the traditional order as fundamentally unjust and defended the idea of a revolution to uphold rights. Joseph de Maistre, an aristocratic opponent of both the Enlightenment and the French Revolution, put the conservative attack on the French Revolution into a deeply religious and absolutist framework (Document 3). In contrast, Anne-Louise-Germaine de Staël, an opponent of Napoleon and one of the most influential intellectuals of the early nineteenth century, took the view that the violence of the Revolution had been the product of generations of superstition and arbitrary rule, that is, rule by an absolutist Catholic church and monarchical government (Document 4).

1. Edmund Burke, Reflections on the Revolution in France *(1790)*

Born in Ireland and a supporter of the American colonists in their opposition to the British Parliament, Edmund Burke (1729–1797) opposed the French Revolution, warning his countrymen against the dangerous abstractions of the French. He argued the case for tradition, continuity, and gradual reform based on practical experience— what he called "a sure principle of conservation."

Can I now congratulate the same nation [France] upon its freedom? Is it because liberty in the abstract may be classed amongst the blessings of mankind, that I am seriously to felicitate a madman, who has escaped from the protecting restraint and wholesome darkness of his cell, on his restoration to the enjoyment of light and liberty? Am I to congratulate an highwayman and murderer, who has broke prison, upon the recovery of his natural rights? . . .

Government is not made in virtue of natural rights, which may and do exist in total independence of it; and exist in much greater clearness, and in a much greater degree of abstract perfection: but their abstract perfection is their practical defect. By having a right to every thing they want every thing. Government is a contrivance of human wisdom to provide for human *wants*. . . .

The science of constructing a commonwealth, or renovating it, or reforming it, is, like every other experimental science, not to be taught *a priori* [based on theory rather than on experience]. Nor is it a short experience that can instruct us in that practical science; because the real effects of moral causes are not always immediate; but that which in the first instance is prejudicial may be excellent in its remoter operation; and its excellence may arise even from the ill effects it produces in the beginning. . . .

All the pleasing illusions, which made power gentle, and obedience liberal, which harmonized the different shades of life, and which, by a bland assimilation, incorporated into politics the sentiments which beautify and soften private society, are to be dissolved by this new conquering empire of light and reason. All the decent drapery of life is to be rudely torn off. All the super-added ideas, furnished from the wardrobe of a moral imagination, which the heart owns, and the understanding ratifies, as necessary to cover the defects of our naked shivering nature, and to raise it to dignity in our own estimation, are to be exploded as a ridiculous, absurd, and antiquated fashion.

On this scheme of things, a king is but a man; a queen is but a woman; a woman is but an animal; and an animal not of the highest order. All homage paid to the sex in general as such, and without distinct views, is to be regarded as romance and folly. Regicide, and parricide, and sacrilege, are but fictions of superstition. . . .

In the groves of *their* academy, at the end of every visto [vista], you see nothing but the gallows. Nothing is left which engages the affections on the part of the commonwealth. . . . To make us love our country, our country ought to be lovely.

Source: *Two Classics of the French Revolution: Reflections on the Revolution in France (Edmund Burke) and The Rights of Man (Thomas Paine)* (New York: Doubleday Anchor Books, 1973), 19, 71–74, 90–91.

2. *Thomas Paine,* The Rights of Man *(1791)*

In his reply to Burke, The Rights of Man, *which sold 200,000 copies in two years, Thomas Paine (1737–1809) defended the idea of reform based on reason, advocated a concept of universal human rights, and attacked the excesses of privilege and tradition in Great Britain. Elected as a deputy to the French National Convention in 1793 in recognition of his writings in favor of the French Revolution, Paine narrowly escaped condemnation as an associate of the Girondins.*

Before anything can be reasoned upon to a conclusion, certain facts, principles, or data, to reason from, must be established, admitted, or denied. Mr. Burke, with his usual outrage, abuses the *Declaration of the Rights of Man*, published by the National Assembly of France, as the basis on which the Constitution of France is built. This he calls "paltry and blurred sheets of paper about the rights of man."

Does Mr. Burke mean to deny that *man* has any rights? If he does, then he must mean that there are no such things as rights any where, and that he has none himself; for who is there in the world but man? . . .

Hitherto we have spoken only (and that but in part) of the natural rights of man. We have now to consider the civil rights of man, and to show how the one originates from the other. Man did not enter into society to become *worse* than he was before, nor to have fewer rights than he had before, but to have those rights better secured. His natural rights are the foundation of all his civil rights. . . .

Every civil right has for its foundation some natural right pre-existing in the individual, but to the enjoyment of which his individual power is not, in all cases, sufficiently competent. Of this kind are all those which relate to security and protection. . . .

A constitution is not a thing in name only, but in fact. It has not an ideal, but a real existence; and wherever it cannot be produced in a visible form, there is none. A constitution is a thing *antecedent* to a government, and a government is only the creature of a constitution. The constitution of a country is not the act of its government, but of the people constituting a government. . . .

Can then Mr. Burke produce the English Constitution? If he cannot, we may fairly conclude, that though it has been so much talked about, no such thing as a constitution exists, or ever did exist, and consequently that the people have yet a constitution to form.

Source: *Two Classics of the French Revolution: Reflections on the Revolution in France (Edmund Burke) and The Rights of Man (Thomas Paine)* (New York: Doubleday Anchor Books, 1973), 302, 305–306, 309.

3. *Joseph de Maistre,* Considerations on France *(1797)*

An aristocrat born in Savoy, Joseph de Maistre (1753–1821) believed in reform but he passionately opposed both the Enlightenment and the French Revolution as destructive to good order. He believed that Protestants, Jews, lawyers, journalists, and scientists all threatened the social order because they questioned the need for absolute obedience to authority in matters both religious and political. De Maistre set the foundations for reactionary conservatism, a conservatism that defended throne and altar.

In a word, if there is no moral revolution in Europe, if the religious spirit is not reinforced in this part of the world, the social bond will dissolve. Nothing can be predicted, and anything must be expected, but if there is to be improvement in this matter, either France is called upon to produce it, or there is no more analogy, no more induction, no more art of prediction.

This consideration especially makes me think that the French Revolution is a great epoch and that its consequences, in all kinds of ways, will be felt far beyond the time of its explosion and the limits of its birthplace. . . .

There is a satanic quality to the French Revolution that distinguishes it from everything we have ever seen or anything we are ever likely to see in the future. Recall the great assemblies, Robespierre's speech against the priesthood, the solemn apostasy [renunciation of vows] of the clergy, the desecration of objects of worship, the installation of the goddess of reason, and that multitude of extraordinary actions by which the provinces sought to outdo Paris. All this goes beyond the ordinary circle of crime and seems to belong to another world.

Source: Joseph de Maistre, *Considerations on France*, trans. Richard A. Lebrun (Cambridge: Cambridge University Press, 1994), 21, 41.

4. Anne-Louise-Germaine de Staël, Considerations on the Main Events of the French Revolution *(1818)*

De Staël published her views long after the Revolution was over, but she had lived through the events herself. She was the daughter of Jacques Necker, Louis XVI's Swiss Protestant finance minister. Necker's dismissal in July 1789 had sparked the attack on the Bastille. De Staël published novels, literary tracts, and memoirs and became one of

the best-known writers of the nineteenth century. In her writings she defended the Enlightenment; though she opposed the violence unleashed by the Revolution, she traced it back to the excesses of monarchical government.

Once the people were freed from their harness there is no doubt that they were in a position to commit any kind of crime. But how can we explain their depravity? The government we are now supposed to miss so sorely [the former monarchy] had had plenty of time to form this guilty nation. The priests whose teaching, example, and wealth were supposed to be so good for us had supervised the childhood of the generation that broke out against them. The class that revolted in 1789 must have been accustomed to the privileges of feudal nobility which, as we are also assured, are so peculiarly agreeable to those on whom they weigh [the peasants]. How does it happen, then, that the seed of so many vices was sown under the ancient institutions? . . . What can we conclude from this, then?—That no people had been as unhappy for the preceding century as the French. If the Negroes of Saint-Domingue have committed even greater atrocities, it is because they had been even more greatly oppressed.

Source: Vivian Folkenflik, ed. *An Extraordinary Woman: Selected Writings of Germaine de Staël* (New York: Columbia University Press, 1987), 365–66.

Questions for Debate
1. Which aspect of the French Revolution most disturbed these commentators?
2. How would you align each of these writers on a spectrum running from extreme right to extreme left in politics?
3. How would each of these writers judge the Enlightenment that preceded the French Revolution?

government suppressed all news from France, fearing that it might ignite the spirit of revolt. This fear was not misplaced because even in Russia, for instance, 278 outbreaks of peasant unrest occurred between 1796 and 1798. One Russian landlord complained, "This is the self-same . . . spirit of insubordination and independence, which has spread through all Europe."

Poland Extinguished, 1793–1795

The spirit of independence made the Poles and Lithuanians especially discontent, for they had already suffered a significant loss of territory and population. "I shall fight Jacobinism, and defeat it in Poland," vowed Catherine the Great in 1792. Frightened by reports of a few friends of the

French Revolution cropping up throughout eastern Europe—even in St. Petersburg—Catherine determined to smite the moderate reformers in Warsaw. Prussia joined her, fearing a regenerated, pro-French Poland. While Prussian and Austrian troops battled the French in the west, a Russian army easily crushed Polish resistance. In effect for barely a year, Poland's constitution of May 3, 1791, was abolished, and Prussia and Russia helped themselves to generous new slices of Polish territory in the Second Partition of 1793 (Map 20.4).

Poland's reform movement became even more pro-French. Some leaders fled abroad, including Tadeusz Kościuszko (1746–1817), an officer who had been a foreign volunteer in the War of American Independence and who now escaped to Paris. In the spring of 1794, Kościuszko returned from

MAP 20.4 The Second and Third Partitions of Poland, 1793 and 1795

In 1793, after Russian armies invaded Poland, Russia and Prussia agreed to another partition of Polish territories. Prussia took over territory that included 1.1 million Poles while Russia gained 3 million new inhabitants. Austria gave up any claims to Poland in exchange for help from Russia and Prussia in acquiring Bavaria. When Kościuszko's nationalist uprising failed in 1794, Russia, Prussia, and Austria agreed to a final division. Prussia absorbed an additional 900,000 Polish subjects, including those in Warsaw; Austria incorporated 1 million Poles and the city of Cracow; Russia gained another 2 million Poles. The three powers determined never to use the term "Kingdom of Poland" again.

France as "dictator," empowered by his fellow conspirators to lead a national revolt. He incited an uprising at Cracow, which then spread to Warsaw and the old Lithuanian capital, Vilnius. Kościuszko faced an immediate, insoluble dilemma. He could win only if the peasants joined the struggle—highly unlikely unless villagers could be convinced that serfdom would end. But such a drastic step risked alienating the nobles who had started the revolt. So Kościuszko compromised. In his proclamation of May 7, 1794, he summoned the peasantry to the national cause and promised a reduction of their obligations as serfs, but not freedom itself. He received an equally equivocal response. Armed with scythes, a few peasant bands joined the insurrection, but most let their lords fight it out alone. Urban workers displayed more enthusiasm; at Warsaw, for example, a mob hanged several Russian collaborators, including an archbishop in his full regalia.

The uprising failed. Kościuszko led his troops to a few victories over the surprised Russians, but when Catherine's forces regrouped, they routed the Poles and Lithuanians. Kościuszko and other Patriot leaders languished for years in Russian and Austrian prisons. Taking no further chances, Russia, Prussia, and Austria wiped Poland completely from the map in the Third Partition of 1795. "The Polish question" would plague international relations for more than a century as Polish rebels flocked to any international upheaval that might undo the partitions. Beyond all this maneuvering lay the unsolved problem of Polish serfdom, which isolated the nation's gentry and townspeople from the rural masses.

Revolution in the Colonies

The Caribbean colonies lay far from France, but inevitably they felt the effects of revolution. From the beginning, political leaders in Paris feared the potential for conflict in the colonies, as aspirations for broader political rights might threaten French authority. The Caribbean colonies were crucial to the French economy. Twice the size in land area of the neighboring British colonies, they also produced nearly twice as much revenue in exports. The slave population had doubled in the French colonies in the twenty years before 1789. St. Domingue (present-day Haiti) was the most important French colony, with its approximately 465,000 slaves, 30,000 whites, and 28,000 free people of color, who were employed primarily to apprehend runaway slaves and assure plantation security.

Despite the efforts of a Paris club called the Friends of Blacks, most French revolutionaries did

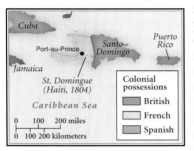

St. Domingue on the Eve of the Revolt, 1791

not consider slavery a pressing problem. As one deputy explained, "This regime [in the colonies] is oppressive, but it gives a livelihood to several million Frenchmen. This regime is barbarous but a still greater barbarity will result if you interfere with it without the necessary knowledge."

In August 1791, however, the slaves in northern St. Domingue organized a large-scale revolt with the slogan "Listen to the voice of Liberty which speaks in the hearts of all." To restore authority over the slaves, the Legislative Assembly in Paris granted civil and political rights to the free blacks—an action that alienated the white planters and merchants, who in 1793 signed an agreement with Great Britain, now France's enemy in war, declaring British sovereignty over the island. To complicate matters further, Spain, which controlled the rest of the island and had entered on Great Britain's side in the war, offered freedom to individual slave rebels who joined the Spanish armies as long as they agreed to maintain the slave regime for the other blacks.

The few thousand French republican troops on the island were outnumbered, and to prevent complete military disaster the French commissioner freed all the slaves in his jurisdiction in August 1793 without permission from the government at home. In February 1794, the National Convention formally abolished slavery and granted full rights to all black men in the colonies. These actions had the desired effect. One of the ablest black generals allied with the Spanish, the ex-slave François Dominique Toussaint L'Ouverture (1743–1803), changed sides and committed his troops to the French. The French eventually appointed Toussaint governor of St. Domingue as a reward for his efforts. The vicious fighting and flight of whites left the island's economy in ruins; in 1800, the plantations produced one-fifth of what they had in 1789. In the zones Toussaint controlled, army officers or officials took over the great estates and kept all those working in

Toussaint L'Ouverture
The leader of the St. Domingue slave uprising appears in his general's uniform, sword in hand. This portrait appeared in one of the earliest histories of the revolt, Marcus Rainsford's Historical Account of the Black Empire of Hayti *(London, 1805). Toussaint, a former slave who educated himself, fascinated many of his contemporaries in Europe as well as the New World by turning a chaotic slave rebellion into an organized and ultimately successful independence movement.* North Wind Picture Archives.

agriculture under military discipline. The former slaves were bound to their estates like serfs and forced to work the plantations in exchange for an autonomous family life and the right to maintain personal garden plots.

Toussaint remained in charge until 1802, when Napoleon sent French armies to regain control of the island. They arrested Toussaint and transported him to France, where he died in prison. The arrest prompted the English poet William Wordsworth to write of him:

There's not a breathing of the common wind
That will forget thee; thou hast great allies;
Thy friends are exultations, agonies,
And love, and man's unconquerable mind.

Toussaint became a hero to abolitionists everywhere, a potent symbol of black struggles to win freedom. Napoleon attempted to restore slavery, sending Polish volunteers to do much of the grueling work, but the remaining black generals defeated his armies and in 1804 proclaimed the Republic of Haiti.

The Rise of Napoleon Bonaparte

Toussaint had followed with interest Napoleon's rise to power in France; he once wrote to Bonaparte, "From the First of the Blacks to the First of the Whites." He was not alone in his fascination, for the story of the rise of Napoleon Bonaparte (1769–1821) is one of the most remarkable in Western history. It would have seemed astonishing in 1795 that the twenty-six-year-old son of a noble family from the island of Corsica off the Italian coast would within four years become the supreme ruler of France and one of the greatest military leaders in world history. In 1795, he was a penniless artillery officer, only recently released from prison as a presumed Robespierrist. Thanks to some early military successes and links to Parisian politicians, he was named commander of the French army in Italy in 1796.

Bonaparte's astounding success in the Italian campaigns of 1796–1797 launched his meteoric career. With an army of fewer than fifty thousand men, he defeated the Piedmontese and the Austrians. In quick order he established client republics dependent on his own authority; he negotiated with the Austrians himself; and he molded the army into his

Bonaparte in Egypt
This engraving, based on Antoine Jean Gros's painting Napoleon Visiting the Victims of the Plague at Jaffa *(1804), is meant to glorify Bonaparte's courage: he is not afraid to touch the victims of the plague. Yet it also signals a terrible problem in Bonaparte's campaign for domination in the western Mediterranean. He has won many battles at this moment in 1799, but he is losing the war through attrition, disease, and mounting resistance.*
National Library of Medicine, Bethesda/Visual Image Presentations.

IMPORTANT DATES

1787   Dutch Patriot revolt is stifled by Prussian invasion

1788   Beginning of resistance of Austrian Netherlands against reforms of Joseph II; opening of reform parliament in Poland

1789   French Revolution begins

1790   Internal divisions lead to collapse of resistance in Austrian Netherlands

1791   Beginning of slave revolt in St. Domingue (Haiti)

1792   Beginning of war between France and the rest of Europe; second revolution of August 10 overthrows monarchy

1793   Second Partition of Poland by Austria and Russia; Louis XVI of France executed for treason

1794   France annexes the Austrian Netherlands; abolition of slavery in French colonies; Robespierre's government by terror falls

1795   Third (final) Partition of Poland

1797–1798   Creation of "sister" republics in Italian states and Switzerland

1799   Napoleon Bonaparte comes to power in a coup that effectively ends the French Revolution

personal force by paying the soldiers in cash taken as tribute from the newly conquered territories. He mollified the Directory government by sending home wagonloads of great Italian masterpieces of art, which were added to Parisian museum collections after being paraded in victory festivals. (Most are still there.) Even the failures of the Egyptian campaign did not dull his luster. Bonaparte had taken France's leading scientists with him on the expedition, and his soldiers had discovered a slab of black basalt dating from 196 B.C. written in both hieroglyphic and Greek. Called the *Rosetta stone* after a nearby town, it enabled scholars to finally decipher the hieroglyphs used by the ancient Egyptians. When his army was pinned down after its initial successes, Napoleon slipped out of Egypt and made his way secretly across the Mediterranean to southern France.

In October 1799, Bonaparte arrived home at just the right moment. The war in Europe was going badly; the departments of the former Austrian Netherlands had revolted against new conscription laws; deserters swelled the ranks of the rebels in

western France; a royalist army had tried to take the city of Toulouse in the southwest; and many government leaders wanted to revise the Constitution of 1795. Amidst increasing political instability, generals in the field had become virtually independent, and the troops felt more loyal to their units and generals than to the republic. As one army captain wrote, "In a conquering people the military spirit must prevail over other social conditions." Its victories had made the army a parallel and rival force to the state.

Disillusioned members of the government saw in Bonaparte's return an occasion to overturn the Constitution of 1795. On November 9, 1799 (18 Brumaire, Year VIII by the revolutionary calendar), the conspirators persuaded the legislature to move out of Paris to avoid an imaginary Jacobin plot. But when Bonaparte marched into the meeting hall the next day and demanded changes in the Constitution, he was greeted by cries of "Down with the dictator." His quick-thinking brother Lucien, president of the Council of Five Hundred (the lower house), saved Bonaparte's coup by summoning troops guarding the hall and claiming that the deputies had tried to assassinate the popular general. The soldiers ejected the deputies, and a hastily assembled rump legislature voted to abolish the Directory and establish a new three-man executive called the consulate. Bonaparte became First Consul, a title revived from the ancient Roman republic.

Shortly after the coup, a new constitution was submitted to the voters. Millions abstained from voting, and the government falsified the results to give an appearance of even greater support to the new regime. Altogether it was an unpromising beginning; yet within five years Bonaparte would crown himself Napoleon I, emperor of the French. A new order would rise from the ashes of the republic, and the French armies would recover from their reverses of 1799 to push the frontiers of French influence even farther eastward.

Conclusion

In 1799, no one knew what course Napoleon Bonaparte would follow. Inside France, political apathy had overtaken the original enthusiasm for revolutionary ideals. Yet the political landscape had been permanently altered by the revolutionary cataclysm.

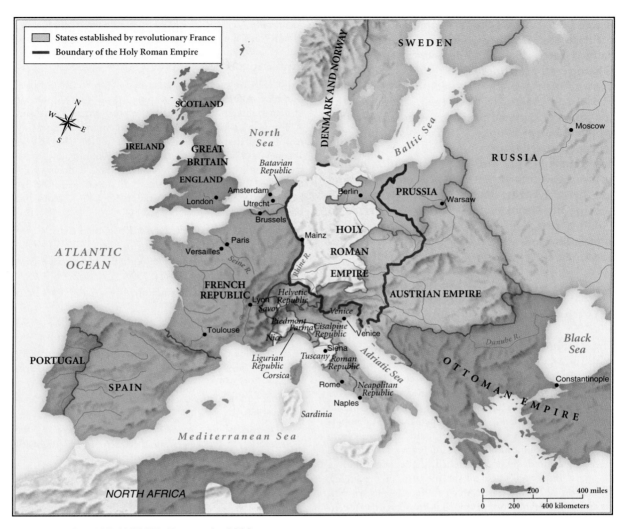

MAPPING THE WEST Europe in 1800

France's expansion during the revolutionary wars threatened to upset the balance of power in Europe. A century earlier the English and Dutch had allied and formed a Europe-wide coalition to check the territorial ambitions of Louis XIV. Thwarting French ambitions after 1800 would prove to be even more of a challenge to the other European powers. The Dutch had been reduced to satellite status, as had most of the Italian states. After 1800, even Austria and Prussia would suffer devastating losses to the French on the battlefield. Only a new coalition of European powers could stop France in the future.

Between 1789 and 1799, monarchy as a form of government had given way to a republic whose leaders were elected. Aristocracy based on rank and birth had been undermined in favor of civil equality and the promotion of merit. The people who marched in demonstrations, met in clubs, and, in the case of men, voted in national elections for the first time had insisted that government respond to them. Thousands of men had held elective office.

A revolutionary government had tried to teach new values with a refashioned calendar, state festivals, and a civic religion. Its example would inspire future revolutionaries.

But the French Revolution also had its darker side. The divisions created by the Revolution within France endured in many cases until after World War II. Even now, French public-opinion surveys ask if it was right to execute the king in 1793 (most believe Louis XVI was guilty of treason but should not have been executed). The revolutionaries proclaimed human rights and democratic government as a universal goal, but they also explicitly excluded women, even though they admitted Protestant, Jewish, and eventually black men. They used the new spirit of national pride to inspire armies that conquered other peoples. Their ideals of universal education, religious toleration, and democratic participation could not prevent the institution of new forms of government terror to persecute, imprison, and kill dissidents. These paradoxes created an opening for Napoleon Bonaparte, who rushed in with his remarkable military and political skills to push France—and with it all of Europe—in new directions.

Suggested References

The Revolutionary Wave, 1787–1789

In the 1950s and 1960s, historians debated vehemently about whether the French Revolution should be considered part of a more general phenomenon of Atlantic revolutions, as R. R. Palmer argues. Recent work on the Dutch Republic and the Austrian Netherlands has developed nuanced comparisons that show both similarities with and differences from the French Revolution. Historians of France have focused more single-mindedly on the French origins of revolution. The most influential book on the meaning of the French Revolution is still the classic study of Tocqueville, who insisted that the Revolution continued the process of state centralization undertaken by the monarchy.

*Baker, Keith Michael, ed. *The Old Regime and the French Revolution.* University of Chicago Readings in Western Civilization, vol. 7. 1987.

Chartier, Roger. *The Cultural Origins of the French Revolution.* Trans. Lydia G. Cochrane. 1991.

Lefebvre, Georges. *The Coming of the French Revolution.* Trans. with a new preface, R. R. Palmer. 1989.

Palmer, R. R. *The Age of the Democratic Revolution: A Political History of Europe and America, 1760–1800.* Vol. 2, *The Struggle.* 1964.

Polasky, Janet L. *Revolution in Brussels, 1787–1793.* 1987.

Te Brake, Wayne. *Regents and Rebels: The Revolutionary World of an Eighteenth-Century Dutch City.* 1989.

Tocqueville, Alexis de. *The Old Regime and the French Revolution.* Trans. Stuart Gilbert. 1955. Originally published 1856.

From Monarchy to Republic, 1789–1793

From 1789 onward, commentators on the French Revolution have differed over its meaning: was it a revolution for human rights and democracy (the positions of Paine and Wollstonecraft) or a dangerous experiment in implementing reason and destroying religion and tradition (Burke and Tocqueville)? The collections edited by Blanning and Kates sample some of the newer versions of these enduring controversies. Among the most important additions to the debate have been new works on women, Jews, Protestants, and slaves.

Blanning, T. C. W., ed. *The French Revolution: Class War or Culture Clash?* 2nd ed. 1998.

*Hunt, Lynn, ed. *The French Revolution and Human Rights: A Brief Documentary History.* 1996.

Images of the French Revolution: http://chnm.gmu.edu/revolution.

Kates, Gary, ed. *The French Revolution: Recent Debates and New Controversies.* 1998.

*Levy, Darline Gay, Harriet Branson Applewhite, and Mary Durham Johnson, eds. *Women in Revolutionary Paris, 1789–1795.* 1979.

Schama, Simon. *Citizens: A Chronicle of the French Revolution.* 1989.

Two Classics of the French Revolution: Reflections on the Revolution in France (*Edmund Burke*) and The Rights of Man (*Thomas Paine*). 1973.

*Wollstonecraft, Mary. *A Vindication of the Rights of Woman.* Ed. Miriam Brody. 1992.

The Terror and the Republic of Virtue

The most controversial episode in the French Revolution has not surprisingly provoked conflicting interpretations. Soboul offers the Marxist interpretation, which Furet specifically opposes. Very recently interest has shifted from these broader interpretive issues back to the principal actors themselves: Robespierre, the Jacobins, and women's clubs have all attracted scholarly attention.

Desan, Suzanne. *Reclaiming the Sacred: Lay Religion and Popular Politics in Revolutionary France.* 1990.

Furet, François. *Interpreting the French Revolution.* Trans. Elborg Forster. 1981.

Godineau, Dominique. *The Women of Paris and Their French Revolution.* Trans. Katherine Streip. 1998.

Haydon, Colin, and William Doyle, eds. *Robespierre.* 1999.

Higonnet, Patrice L. R. *Goodness beyond Virtue: Jacobins during the French Revolution.* 1998.

---

*Primary sources.

Hunt, Lynn. *Politics, Culture, and Class in the French Revolution*. 1984.

Palmer, R. R. *Twelve Who Ruled: The Year of the Terror in the French Revolution*. 1989.

Soboul, Albert. *The Sans-Culottes: The Popular Movement and Revolutionary Government, 1793–1794*. Trans. Remy Inglis Hall. 1980.

Sutherland, D. M. G. *France, 1789–1815: Revolution and Counterrevolution*. 1986.

Revolution on the March

In the past, controversy about the Revolution in France raged while its influence on other places was relatively neglected. This imbalance is now being redressed in studies of the colonies and the impact of the revolutionary wars on areas from Egypt to Ireland. Recent work pays close attention to the social background of soldiers as well as their experiences in warfare.

Beaucour, Fernand Emile, Yves Laissus, and Chantal Orgogozo. *The Discovery of Egypt*. Trans. Bambi Ballard. 1990.

Blackburn, Robin. *The Overthrow of Colonial Slavery, 1776–1848*. 1988.

Blanning, T. C. W. *The French Revolutionary Wars, 1787–1802*. 1996.

Elliot, Marianne. *Partners in Revolution: The United Irishmen and France*. 1982.

Forrest, Alan I. *The Soldiers of the French Revolution*. 1990.

James, C. L. R. *Black Jacobins: Toussaint L'Ouverture and the San Domingo Revolution*, 2nd ed. 1989.

BONAPARTE

DAVID L'AN IX

CHAPTER
21

Napoleon and the Revolutionary Legacy

1800–1830

Napoleon as Military Hero
In this painting from 1800–1801, Napoleon Crossing the Alps at St. Bernard, Jacques-Louis David reminds the French of Napoleon's heroic military exploits. Napoleon is a picture of calm and composure while his horse shows the fright and energy of the moment. David painted this propagandistic image shortly after one of his former students went to the guillotine on a trumped-up charge of plotting to assassinate the new French leader. The former organizer of republican festivals during the Terror had became a kind of court painter for the new regime.
© Photo RMN/Herve Lewandowski.

I N HER NOVEL *FRANKENSTEIN* (1818), the prototype for modern thrillers, Mary Shelley tells the story of a Swiss technological genius who creates a humanlike monster in his pursuit of scientific knowledge. The monster, "so scaring and unearthly in his ugliness," terrifies all who encounter him and ends by destroying Dr. Frankenstein's own loved ones. Despite desperate chases across deserts and frozen landscapes, Frankenstein never manages to trap the monster, who is last seen hunched over his creator's deathbed.

Frankenstein's monster can be taken as a particularly horrifying incarnation of the fears of the postrevolutionary era, but just what did Shelley intend? Did the monster represent the French Revolution, which had devoured its own children in the Terror? Shelley was the daughter of Mary Wollstonecraft, an English feminist who had defended the French Revolution and died in childbirth when Mary was born. Did the monster stand for the dangerous possibilities that might be unleashed by science and industry in the new age of industrial growth? She was also the wife of the romantic poet Percy Bysshe Shelley, who often wrote against the ugliness of contemporary life and celebrated nature and the "beautiful idealisms of moral excellence." Whatever the meaning—and Mary Shelley may well have intended more than one—the novel makes the forceful point that humans cannot always control their own creations. The Enlightenment and the French Revolution had celebrated the virtues of human creativity, but Shelley shows that innovation often has a dark and uncontrollable side.

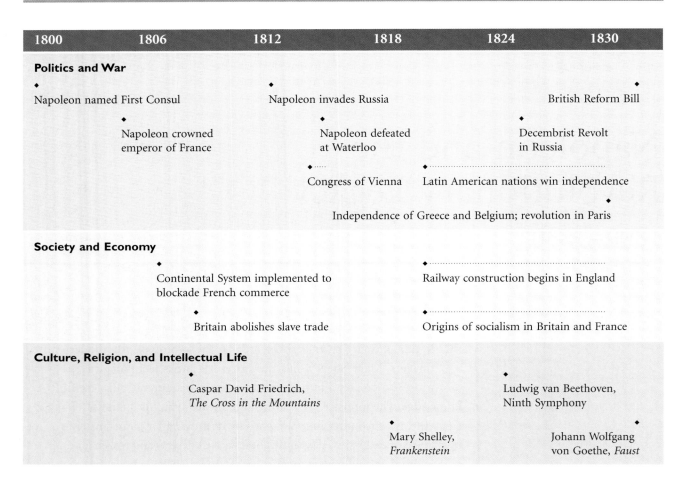

1800	1806	1812	1818	1824	1830

Politics and War

Napoleon named First Consul

Napoleon crowned emperor of France

Napoleon invades Russia

Napoleon defeated at Waterloo

Congress of Vienna

Latin American nations win independence

British Reform Bill

Decembrist Revolt in Russia

Independence of Greece and Belgium; revolution in Paris

Society and Economy

Continental System implemented to blockade French commerce

Britain abolishes slave trade

Railway construction begins in England

Origins of socialism in Britain and France

Culture, Religion, and Intellectual Life

Caspar David Friedrich, *The Cross in the Mountains*

Mary Shelley, *Frankenstein*

Ludwig van Beethoven, Ninth Symphony

Johann Wolfgang von Goethe, *Faust*

Those who witnessed Napoleon Bonaparte's stunning rise to European dominance after 1800 might have cast him as either Frankenstein or his monster. Though short and physically unimpressive, like the scientist Frankenstein, Bonaparte created something dramatically new: the French Empire with himself as emperor. Like the former kings of France, he ruled under his first name. This Corsican artillery officer who spoke French with an Italian accent ended the French Revolution even while maintaining some of its most important innovations. Bonaparte transformed France from a democratically elected republic to an empire with a new aristocracy based on military service. But he kept the revolutionary administration and most of its laws that ensured equal treatment to all citizens. Although he tolerated no opposition at home, he prided himself on bringing French-style changes to peoples elsewhere.

Bonaparte continued the revolutionary policy of conquest and annexation until it reached grotesque dimensions. His foreign policies made many see him as a monster hungry for dominion; he turned the sister republics of the revolutionary era into kingdoms personally ruled by his relatives, and he exacted tribute from subject peoples wherever he triumphed. Eventually resistance to the French armies and the ever-mounting costs of military glory toppled Napoleon. The powers allied against him met and agreed to restore the monarchical governments that had been overthrown by the French, shrink France back to its prerevolutionary boundaries, and maintain this settlement against future demands for change.

Although the people of Europe longed for peace and stability in the aftermath of the Napoleonic whirlwind, they lived in a world that was deeply unsettled by two parallel revolutions: the Industrial

Revolution and the French Revolution. The Industrial Revolution spread from Great Britain to the continent in the early 1800s in the form of factories and railroads. Even those who resisted the impact of the French Revolution with its Napoleonic sequel had to confront the underlying changes in social and economic structures that resulted from industrialization. These changes inevitably reinforced the legacy of the French Revolution, which included equality before the law, religious toleration, and, eventually, nationalism. Profoundly affected by French military occupation, many peoples organized to demand ethnic and cultural autonomy, first from Napoleon and then from the restored governments after 1815. Alongside nationalism, other new ideologies such as liberalism and socialism emerged under the impact of the Industrial and French Revolutions. These offered their adherents a doctrine that explained social change and advocated political transformation. In 1830, the development of liberalism, socialism, and nationalism shocked Europe with a new round of revolutions in France, Belgium, Poland, and some of the Italian states. By then the spread of industry, the growing awareness of social problems, and aspirations for national self-determination had reinvigorated the force of the revolutionary legacy.

❖ From Consulate to Empire: The Napoleonic State

When Napoleon Bonaparte came to power in 1799, his coup d'état appeared to be just the latest in a long line of upheavals in revolutionary France. Within the year, however, he had effectively ended the French Revolution and set France on a new course toward an authoritarian state. As emperor after 1804, he dreamed of European integration in the tradition of Augustus and Charlemagne, but he also mastered the details of practical administration. To achieve his goals, he compromised with the Catholic church and with exiled aristocrats willing to return to France. His most enduring accomplishment, the new Civil Code, tempered the principles of the Enlightenment and the Revolution with an insistence on the powers of fathers over children, husbands over wives, and employers over workers.

His influence spread into many spheres as he personally patronized scientific inquiry and encouraged artistic styles in line with his vision of imperial greatness.

The End of the French Republic

Napoleon had no long-range plans to establish himself as emperor and conquer most of Europe. Yet by seizing every opportunity, he first gained control over the new French government and then eliminated the republic and put an empire in its place. The deputies of the legislature who engineered the coup d'état of November 1799 picked him as one of three provisional consuls (the title drew on the ancient Roman precedent) only because he was a

Francisco de Goya, *The Colossus* (1808–1812)
The Spanish painter Goya might be imagined as capturing Frankenstein's monster or Napoleon himself as the new giant overwhelming much of Europe. Goya painted for the Spanish court before Napoleon invaded and occupied the country; after an illness left him deaf, he turned toward darkly imaginative works such as this one.
Museo del Prado, Madrid.

Napoleon's Coronation as Emperor
In The Coronation of Napoleon and Josephine (*1805–1807*), *Jacques-Louis David shows Napoleon crowning his wife at the ceremony of 1804. Napoleon orchestrated the entire event and took the only active role in it: Pope Pius VII gave his blessing to the ceremony, but Napoleon crowned himself.*
Scala/Art Resource, NY.

famous general. Napoleon immediately asserted his leadership over the other two consuls in the process of drafting another constitution—the fourth since 1789 and the third for the republic established in 1792.

Toward Empire. The constitution of 1799 made Napoleon the First Consul with the right to pick the Council of State, which drew up all laws. He quickly exerted control by choosing men loyal to him. Government was no longer representative in any real sense: the new constitution eliminated direct elections for deputies and granted no independent powers to the three houses of the legislature. Napoleon and his advisers chose the legislature's members out of a small pool of "notables." Almost all men over twenty-one could vote in the plebiscite (referendum) to approve the constitution, but their only option was to choose Yes or No.

Napoleon's most urgent task was to reconcile to his regime Catholics who had been alienated by revolutionary policies. Although nominally Catholic, Napoleon held no deep religious convictions. "How can there be order in the state without religion?" he asked cynically. "When a man is dying of hunger beside another who is stuffing himself, he cannot accept this difference if there is not an authority who tells him: 'God wishes it so.'" In 1801, a concordat with Pope Pius VII (r. 1800–1823) ended a decade of church-state conflict. The pope validated all sales of church lands, and the government agreed to pay the salaries of bishops and priests who would swear loyalty to the state. Catholicism was officially recognized as the religion of "the great majority of French citizens." (The state also paid Protestant pastors' salaries.) The pope thus brought the huge French Catholic population back into the fold and Napoleon gained the pope's support for his regime.

Napoleon continued the centralization of state power that had begun under the absolutist monarchy of Louis XIV and resumed under the Terror. As First Consul he appointed prefects who directly supervised local affairs in every *département*, or region. He created the Bank of France to facilitate government borrowing and relied on gold and silver coinage rather than paper money. He made good use of budgets and improved tax collection, but he also frequently made ends meet by exacting tribute from the territories he conquered. The government directly managed every aspect of education: at the new *lycées*, the state-run secondary schools for boys from better-off families, students wore military uniforms, and drumrolls signaled the beginning and end of classes. (Without the military trappings, the lycées are now coeducational and still the heart of the French educational system.) Napoleon took little interest in girls' education, believing that they should spend most of their time at home learning religion, manners, and such "female occupations" as sewing and music.

Napoleon promised order and an end to the upheavals of ten years of revolutionary turmoil, but his regime severely limited political expression. He never relied on mass executions to achieve control, but he refused to allow those who opposed him to meet in clubs, influence elections, or publish newspapers. A decree reduced the number of newspapers in Paris from seventy-three to thirteen (and then finally to four), and the newspapers that remained became government organs. Government censors had to approve all operas and plays, and they banned "offensive" artistic works even more frequently than their royal predecessors. The minister of police, Joseph Fouché, once a leading figure in the Terror of 1793–1794, could impose house arrest, arbitrary imprisonment, and surveillance of political dissidents. Political contest and debate shriveled to almost nothing. When a bomb attack on Napoleon's carriage failed in 1800, Fouché suppressed the evidence of a royalist plot and instead arrested hundreds of former Jacobins. More than one hundred of them were deported and seven hundred imprisoned.

Napoleon feared the influence of fervent supporters of the republic more than that of supporters of the monarchy. In 1802, his intentions became clear: he planned to eliminate the republic. He named himself First Consul for life, and in 1804,

Empire Style
Philibert-Louis Debucourt made a reputation with paintings and engravings of everyday life such as this one, Frascati Café. *Napoleon admired neoclassicism, and its influence can be seen in the Greek columns and archways of the room as well as in the high empire waists of the women's dresses. Note that some men now wear pantaloons—the forebears of modern trousers—rather than the knee breeches of the Old Regime aristocracy.*
The Metropolitan Museum of Art, Harris Brisbane Dick Fund, 1935. (35.100.31)

with the pope's blessing, he crowned himself emperor. Once again, plebiscites approved his decisions, but no alternatives were offered.

The Civil Code. This was government from the top down, yet it was government based on law. The revolutionary governments had tried to unify and standardize France's multiple legal codes, but only Napoleon successfully established a new one, partly because he personally presided over the commission that drafted the new Civil Code, completed in 1804. Called the Napoleonic Code as a way of further exalting his image, it defined and assured property rights, guaranteed religious liberty, and established a uniform system of law that provided equal treatment for all adult males and affirmed the right of men to choose their professions.

The code sharply curtailed women's rights in almost every aspect of public and private life. Napoleon wanted to restrict women to the private sphere of the home. One of his leading jurists remarked, "There have been many discussions on the equality and superiority of the sexes. Nothing is more useless than such disputes. . . . Women need protection because they are weaker; men are free because they are stronger." The law obligated a husband to support his wife, but he alone controlled any property held in common; a wife could not sue in court, sell or mortgage her own property, or contract a debt without her husband's consent.

The Civil Code modified even those few revolutionary laws that had been favorable to women and in some instances denied women rights they had had under the monarchy. Divorce was still possible but severely restricted, especially for women. Adultery was an acceptable grounds for divorce, but the law considered a wife's infidelity more reprehensible than a husband's. A wife could petition for divorce only if her husband brought his mistress to live in the family home. In contrast, a wife convicted of adultery could be imprisoned for up to two years. The code's framers saw these discrepancies as a way to reinforce the family and make women responsible for private virtue, while leaving public decisions to men. The French code was imitated in many European and Latin American countries and the French colony of Louisiana, where it had a similar negative effect on women's rights. Not until 1965 did French wives gain legal status equal to that of their husbands.

Imperial Rule

Napoleon's charismatic personality dominated the new regime. He worked hard at establishing his reputation as an efficient administrator with broad intellectual interests: he met frequently with scientists, jurists, and artists, and stories abounded of his unflagging energy. He set an example by rising at 2:00 A.M., after only four or five hours' sleep, and working for three hours before going back to bed from 5:00 to 7:00 A.M. When not on military campaigns, he worked on state affairs, usually until 10:00 P.M., taking only a few minutes for each meal. "Authority," declared his adviser Sieyès, "must come from above and confidence from below."

As emperor, Napoleon cultivated personal symbolism to enhance his image as a hero. His face and name adorned coins, engravings, histories, paintings, and public monuments. His favorite painters embellished his legend by depicting him as a warrior-hero of mythic proportions. In his imperial court, Napoleon staged his entrances carefully to maximize his personal presence: his wife and courtiers were dressed in regal finery, and he was announced with great pomp—but he usually arrived dressed in a simple military uniform with no medals.

Believing that "what is big is always beautiful," Napoleon embarked on ostentatious building projects that would outshine even those of Louis XIV. Government-commissioned architects built the Arc de Triomphe, the Stock Exchange, fountains, and even slaughterhouses. Most of his new construction reflected his neoclassical taste for monumental buildings set in vast empty spaces. Old, winding streets with their cramped houses were demolished to make way for Napoleon's grand designs.

Despite appearances, Napoleon did not rule alone. Among his most trusted officials were men who had served with him in Italy and Egypt. His chief of staff Alexandre Berthier, for example, became minister of war, and the chemist Claude Berthollet, who had organized the scientific part of the expedition to Egypt, became vice president of the Senate in 1804. Napoleon's bureaucracy was based on a patron-client relationship, with Napoleon as the ultimate patron. Some of Napoleon's closest associates married into his family.

Napoleon reinstituted a social hierarchy in France by rewarding merit and talent, regardless of social origins. He used the Senate to dispense his patronage and personally chose as senators the nation's most illustrious generals, ministers, prefects, scientists, rich men, and former nobles. Intending to replace both the old nobility of birth and the republic's strict emphasis on equality, in 1802 he took the first step toward creating a new nobility by founding a Legion of Honor. (Members of the legion received lifetime pensions along with their titles.) Napoleon usually equated honor with military success. By 1814, the legion had 32,000 members, only 5 percent of them civilians.

In 1808, Napoleon introduced a complete hierarchy of noble titles, ranging from princes down to barons and chevaliers. All Napoleonic nobles had served the state. Titles could be inherited but had to be supported by wealth—a man could not be a duke without a fortune of 200,000 francs, or a chevalier without 3,000 francs. To go along with their new titles, Napoleon gave his favorite generals huge fortunes, often in the form of estates in the conquered territories.

Napoleon's own family reaped the greatest benefits. He made his older brother, Joseph, ruler of the newly established kingdom of Naples in 1806, the same year he installed his younger brother Louis as king of Holland. He proclaimed his twenty-three-year-old stepson Eugène de Beauharnais viceroy of Italy in 1805 and established his sister Caroline and brother-in-law General Murat as king and queen of Naples in 1808 when he moved Joseph to the throne of Spain. Napoleon wanted to establish an imperial

succession, but he lacked an heir. In thirteen years of marriage, his wife Josephine had borne no children, so in 1809 he divorced her and in 1810 married the eighteen-year-old Princess Marie-Louise of Austria. The next year she gave birth to a son to whom Napoleon immediately gave the title king of Rome.

The New Paternalism

Since Napoleon shared the rewards of rule with his own family, it is perhaps not surprising that he brought a familial model of power to his empire, instilling his personal version of paternalism. The Civil Code not only reasserted the Old Regime's patriarchal system of male domination over women but also insisted on a father's control over his children, which revolutionary legislation had limited. For example, if children under age sixteen refused to follow their fathers' commands, they could be sent to prison for up to a month with no hearing of any sort. At the same time, the code required fathers to provide for their children's welfare. Napoleon himself encouraged the foundation of private charities to help indigent mothers, and one of his decrees made it easier for women to abandon their children anonymously to a government foundling hospital. Napoleon hoped such measures would discourage abortion and infanticide, especially among the poorest classes in the fast-growing urban areas.

In periods of economic crisis the government opened soup kitchens, but in time-honored fashion it also arrested beggars and sent them to newly established workhouses. The state also intervened in prostitutes' lives. Migration from the countryside and wartime upheavals had caused a surge of prostitution in French cities. The authorities arrested prostitutes who worked on their own, but they tolerated brothels, which could be supervised by the police, and required the women in them to have monthly medical examinations for venereal disease.

The new paternalism extended to relations between employers and employees. The state required all workers to carry a work card attesting to their good conduct, and it prohibited all workers' organizations. The police considered workers without cards as vagrants or criminals and could send them to workhouses or prison. After 1806, arbitration boards settled labor disputes, but they took

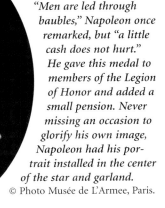

Medal of the Legion of Honor
"Men are led through baubles," Napoleon once remarked, but "a little cash does not hurt." He gave this medal to members of the Legion of Honor and added a small pension. Never missing an occasion to glorify his own image, Napoleon had his portrait installed in the center of the star and garland.
© Photo Musée de L'Armee, Paris.

employers at their word while treating workers as minors, demanding that foremen and shop superintendents represent them. Occasionally strikes broke out, led by secret, illegal journeymen's associations, yet many employers laid off employees when times were hard, deducted fines from their wages, and dismissed them without appeal for being absent or making errors. These limitations on workers' rights won Napoleon the support of French business.

Patronage of Science and Intellectual Life

Napoleon did everything possible to promote French scientific inquiry, especially that which could serve practical ends. (See "Did You Know?," page 771.) He closely monitored the research institutes established during the Revolution, sometimes intervening personally to achieve political conformity. An impressive outpouring of new theoretical and practical scientific work rewarded the state's efforts. Experiments with balloons led to the discovery of laws about the expansion of gases, and research on fossil shells prepared the way for new theories of evolutionary change later in the nineteenth century. The surgeon Dominique-Jean Larrey developed new techniques of battlefield amputation and medical care during Napoleon's wars, winning an appointment as an officer in the Legion of Honor and becoming a baron with a pension.

Napoleon had his own forward-looking vision for modernizing French society through science and central administration, but to maintain his control he stifled dissent. Napoleon considered most writers useless or dangerous, "good for nothing under any government." Some of the most talented French writers of the time had to live in exile. The best-known expatriate was Germaine de Staël (1766–1817), known as Madame de Staël, the daughter of Louis XVI's chief minister Jacques Necker. When explaining his desire to banish her, Napoleon exclaimed, "She is a machine in motion who stirs up the salons." While exiled in the German states, Madame de Staël wrote a novel, *Corinne* (1807), whose heroine is a brilliant woman thwarted by a patriarchal system, and *On Germany* (1810), an account of the important new literary currents east of the Rhine. Her books were banned in France.

Although Napoleon restored the strong authority of state and religion in France, many royalists and

Germaine de Staël
One of the most fascinating intellectuals of her time, Anne-Louise Germaine de Staël seemed to irritate Napoleon more than any other person did. Daughter of Louis XVI's Swiss Protestant finance minister, Jacques Necker, and wife of a Swedish diplomat, Madame de Staël frequently criticized Napoleon's regime. She published best-selling novels and influential literary criticism and whenever allowed to reside in Paris she encouraged the intellectual and political dissidents from Napoleon's regime.
Photographie Bulloz.

Catholics still criticized him as an impious usurper. (See "Contrasting Views," page 778.) François-René de Chateaubriand (1768–1848) admired Napoleon as "the strong man who has saved us from the abyss," but he preferred monarchy. In his view, Napoleon had not properly understood the need to defend Christian values against the Enlightenment's excessive reliance on reason. Chateaubriand wrote his *Genius of Christianity* (1802) to draw attention to the power and mystery of faith. He warned, "It is to the vanity of knowledge that we owe almost all our misfortunes. . . . The learned ages have always been followed by ages of destruction."

How the Orient Became Oriental

As a result of Napoleon's expedition to conquer Egypt in 1798, Europeans began to study systematically what they named "the Orient" (from *oriēns*, Latin for "rising sun"), meaning the lands east of Europe. Napoleon took with him 151 French scientific experts in everything from architecture to mineralogy. Their mission was to discover and record the natural and human history of Egypt. While some set up the Institute of Egypt in Cairo to conduct scientific experiments, others traveled with army units, collecting information and data on Egypt.

Of course, Europeans had visited the Middle East before, but they had never so rigorously studied its cultures. Although Napoleon's occupation of Egypt eventually failed, enthusiasm for "Orientalism" spread far and wide; scholarly societies set up professorships and periodicals dedicated to Oriental studies, and before long romantic poets, novelists, and painters flocked to North Africa and the Middle East in search of new themes for their work.

Europeans viewed the Orient as exotic but also backward. In the introduction to the twenty-three-volume *Description of Egypt* published by French scholars of the Institute of Egypt between 1809 and 1828, Jean-Baptiste Fourier wrote, "Napoleon wanted to offer a useful European example to the Orient, and finally also to make the inhabitants' lives more pleasant, as well as to procure for them all the advantages of a perfect civilization." According to Fourier, "This country [Egypt], which has transmitted its knowledge to so many nations, today is plunged into barbarism." Civilization vs. barbarism; advancement vs. backwardness, science vs. superstition: before long Europeans had set up a series of mutually reinforcing categories to distinguish their culture from that of the Orient. It is probably fair to say that Orientalism led to much new knowledge but also to many unpleasant stereotypes of non-Western peoples and cultures.

It is important to remember, moreover, that *West* and *East* are relative terms; they can be defined only in relation to each other. Americans sometimes call Japan, for instance, the "Far East," following European usage, but it is closest to the western, not the eastern, half of the United States. For Japan, in fact, the United States is the "Far East."

Source: Edward W. Said, *Orientalism* (New York: Pantheon Books, 1978), quote from page 85.

Eugène Delacroix, *The Death of Sardanapalus* (1826–1827)
All of the exoticism, violence, and erotic imagery of the East are on view in this romantic painting that aims to recapture a moment in ancient history when the Assyrian king Sardanapalus first killed his harem before killing himself. Delacroix was presumably influenced by a play by Byron on the subject, though Delacroix's rendition is much less favorable to the king than Byron's.
© Photo RMN/Herve Lewandowski.

❖ "Europe Was at My Feet": Napoleon's Conquests

Napoleon left an indelible stamp on French institutions and political life, yet his fame and much of his power rested on his military conquests. Building on innovations introduced by the republican governments before him, Napoleon revolutionized the art of war with tactics and strategy based on a highly mobile army. By 1812, he ruled an empire more extensive than any since the time of ancient Rome (Map. 21.1). Yet that empire had already begun to crumble, and with it went Napoleon's power at home. Napoleon's empire failed because it was based on a contradiction: Napoleon tried to reduce virtually all of Europe to the status of colonial dependents when Europe had long consisted of independent states. The result, inevitably, was a great upsurge in nationalist feeling that has dominated European politics to the present.

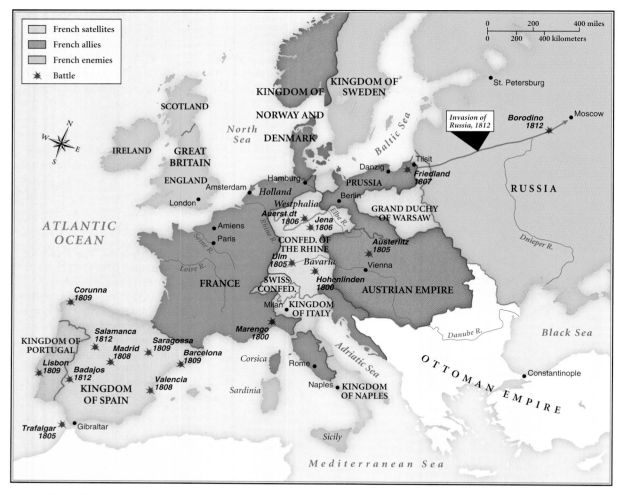

MAP 21.1 Napoleon's Empire at Its Height, 1812

In 1812, Napoleon had at least nominal control of almost all of western Europe. Even before he made his fatal mistake of invading Russia, however, his authority had been undermined in Spain and seriously weakened in the Italian and German states. His efforts to extend French power sparked resistance almost everywhere: as Napoleon insisted on French domination, local people began to think of themselves as Italian, German, or Dutch. Thus Napoleon inadvertently laid the foundations for the nineteenth-century spread of nationalism.

Following the Wars
Louis-Léopold Boilly's Reading of the XIth and XIIth Bulletins of the Grand Army *shows ordinary people on the home front eagerly reading Napoleon's own bulletins of the army's progress.*
Collection Privée/Photo Bulloz.

The Grand Army and Its Victories, 1800–1807

Napoleon attributed his military success "three-quarters to morale" and the rest to leadership and superiority of numbers at the point of attack. Conscription provided the large numbers: 1.3 million men age twenty to twenty-four were drafted between 1800 and 1812, another million in 1813–1814. So many willingly served because the republic had taught them to identify the army with the nation. Military service was both a patriotic duty and a means of social mobility. The men who rose through the ranks to become officers were young, ambitious, and accustomed to the new ways of war. Consequently, the French army had higher morale than the armies of other powers, most of which rejected conscription as too democratic and continued to restrict their officer corps to the nobility. Only in 1813–1814 did French morale plummet, as the military tide turned against Napoleon.

When Napoleon came to power in 1799, France had been at war for almost seven years, and its military position was precarious. Desertion was rampant, and the generals competed with one another for predominance. Napoleon ended this squabbling

by uniting all the armies into one Grand Army under his personal command. By 1812, he commanded 700,000 troops; while 250,000 soldiers fought in Spain, others remained garrisoned in France. In any given battle, between 70,000 and 180,000 men, not all of them French, fought for France. Life on campaign was no picnic—ordinary soldiers slept in the rain, mud, and snow and often had to forage for food—but Napoleon nonetheless inspired almost fanatical loyalty. A brilliant strategist who carefully studied the demands of war, he outmaneuvered virtually all his opponents. He fought alongside his soldiers in some sixty battles and had nineteen horses shot from under him. One opponent said that Napoleon's presence alone was worth 50,000 men.

Napoleon had a pragmatic and direct approach to strategy: he went for the main body of the opposing army and tried to crush it in a lightning campaign. He gathered the largest possible army for one great and decisive battle and then followed with a relentless pursuit to break enemy morale altogether. His military command, like his domestic role, was personal and highly centralized. He essentially served as his own operations officer: "I alone know what I have to do," he insisted. This style worked as long as Napoleon could be on the battlefield, but he failed to train independent subordinates to take over in his absence. He also faced constant difficulties in supplying a rapidly moving army, which could not always live off the land.

One of Napoleon's greatest advantages was the lack of coordination among his enemies. Britain dominated the seas but did not want to field huge land armies. On the continent, the French republic had already set up satellites in the Netherlands and Italy, which served as a buffer against the big powers to the east, Austria, Prussia, and Russia. By maneuvering diplomatically and militarily, Napoleon could usually take these on one by one. After reorganizing the French armies in 1799, for example, Napoleon won striking victories against the Austrians at Marengo and Hohenlinden in 1800, forcing them to agree to peace terms. Once the Austrians had withdrawn, Britain agreed to the Treaty of Amiens in 1802, effectively ending hostilities on the continent. Napoleon considered the peace with Great Britain merely a truce, however, and it lasted only until 1803.

Napoleon used the breathing space not only to consolidate his position before taking up arms again but also to send an expeditionary force to St. Domingue to regain control of the island. Continuing resistance among the black population and an epidemic of yellow fever forced Napoleon to withdraw his troops from St. Domingue and abandon his plans to extend his empire to the Western Hemisphere. As part of his retreat, he sold the Louisiana Territory to the United States in 1803.

France's Retreat from America

When war resumed in Europe, the British navy once more proved its superiority by blocking an attempted French invasion and by defeating the French and their Spanish allies in a huge naval battle at Trafalgar in 1805. France lost many ships; the British lost no vessels, but their renowned admiral Lord Horatio Nelson died in the battle. On land, Napoleon remained invincible. In 1805, Austria took up arms again when Napoleon demanded that it declare neutrality in the conflict with Britain. Napoleon promptly captured 25,000 Austrian soldiers at Ulm in Bavaria in 1805. After marching on to Vienna, he again trounced the Austrians, who had been joined by their new ally, Russia. The battle of Austerlitz, often considered Napoleon's greatest victory, was fought on December 2, 1805, the first anniversary of his coronation.

After maintaining neutrality for a decade, Prussia now declared war on France. In 1806, the French promptly destroyed the Prussian army at Jena and Auerstadt. In 1807, Napoleon defeated the Russians at Friedland. Personal negotiations between Napoleon and the young tsar Alexander I (r. 1801–1825) resulted in a humiliating settlement imposed on Prussia, which paid the price for temporary reconciliation between France and Russia; the Treaties of Tilsit turned Prussian lands west of the Elbe River into the kingdom of Westphalia under Napoleon's brother Jerome, and Prussia's Polish provinces became the duchy of Warsaw. Alexander recognized Napoleon's conquests in central and western Europe and promised to help him against the British in exchange for Napoleon's support against the Turks. Neither party kept the bargain. Napoleon once again had turned the divisions among his enemies in his favor.

The Impact of French Victories

Wherever the Grand Army conquered, Napoleon's influence soon followed. By annexing some territories and setting up others as satellite kingdoms with much reduced autonomy, Napoleon attempted to colonize large parts of Europe (see Map 21.1). But even where he did not rule directly or through his relatives, his startling string of victories forced the other powers to reconsider their own methods of rule.

Rule in the Colonized Territories. Napoleon brought the disparate German and Italian states together to rule them more effectively and to exploit their resources for his own ends. In 1803, he consolidated the tiny German states by abolishing some of them and attaching them to larger units. In July 1806, he established the Confederation of the Rhine, which soon included almost all the German states except Austria and Prussia. The Holy Roman Emperor gave up his title, held since the thirteenth century, and became simply the emperor of Austria. Napoleon established three units in Italy: the territories directly annexed to France and the satellite kingdoms of Italy and Naples. Italy had not been so unified since the Roman Empire.

Napoleon forced French-style reforms on both the annexed territories, which were ruled directly from France, and the satellite kingdoms, which were usually ruled by one or another of Napoleon's relatives but with a certain autonomy. French reforms included abolishing serfdom, eliminating seigneurial dues, introducing the Napoleonic Code, suppressing monasteries, and subordinating church to state, as well as extending civil rights to Jews and other religious minorities. The experience in the kingdom of Westphalia was typical of a French satellite. When Jerome Bonaparte and his wife Catherine arrived as king and queen in 1807, they relied on French experts who worked with a hand-picked committee of Germans to write a constitution and install legal reforms. The Westphalian army had the first Jewish officers in the German states, and the army, administration, and judiciary were all opened to the middle classes. As time passed, however, the German subjects began to chafe under French rule. German officials enforced French decrees only halfheartedly, and the French army had to forbid its soldiers to frequent local taverns and shops because their presence often started fights.

Consolidation of German and Italian States, 1812

As the example of Westphalia shows, reactions to Napoleonic innovations were mixed. Napoleon's chosen rulers often made real improvements in roads, public works, law codes, and education. The removal of internal tariffs fostered economic growth by opening up the domestic market for goods, especially textiles. By 1814, Bologna had five hundred factories and Modena four hundred. Yet almost everyone had some cause for complaint. Republicans regretted Napoleon's conversion of the sister republics into kingdoms after his coronation. Tax increases and ever-rising conscription quotas

also fomented discontent. The annexed territories and satellite kingdoms paid half the French war expenses.

Almost everywhere, conflicts arose between Napoleon's desire for standardized, central government and local insistence on maintaining customs and traditions. Sometimes his own relatives sided with the countries they ruled. Napoleon's brother Louis, for instance, would not allow conscription in the Netherlands because the Dutch had never had compulsory military service. When Napoleon tried to introduce an economic policy banning trade with Great Britain, Louis's lax enforcement prompted the frustrated emperor to complain that "Holland [the leading province in the Netherlands] is an English province." In 1810, Napoleon annexed the satellite kingdom because his brother had become too sympathetic to Dutch interests.

Pressure for Reform in Prussia and Russia. Napoleon's victories forced defeated rulers to rethink their political and cultural assumptions. After the crushing defeat of Prussia in 1806 left his country much reduced in territory, Frederick William III (r. 1797–1840) appointed a reform commission, and on its recommendation he abolished serfdom and allowed nonnobles to buy and enclose land. Peasants gained their personal independence from their noble landlords, who could no longer sell them to pay gambling debts, for example, or refuse them permission to marry. Yet the lives of the former serfs remained bleak; they were left without land and their landlords no longer had to care for them in hard times. The king's advisers also overhauled the army to make the high command more efficient and to open the way to the appointment of middle-class officers. Prussia instituted these reforms to try to compete with the French, not to promote democracy. As one reformer wrote to Frederick William, "We must do from above what the French have done from below."

Reform received lip service in Russia. Tsar Alexander I had gained his throne after an aristocratic coup deposed and killed his autocratic and capricious father, Paul (r. 1796–1801), and in the early years of his reign the remorseful young ruler created Western-style ministries, lifted restrictions on importing foreign books, and founded six new universities; reform commissions studied abuses; nobles were encouraged voluntarily to free their serfs (a few actually did so); and there was even talk of drafting a constitution. But none of these efforts reached beneath the surface of Russian life, and by the second decade of his reign Alexander began to reject the Enlightenment spirit that his grandmother Catherine the Great had instilled in him.

The Continental System. The one power always standing between Napoleon and total dominance of Europe was Great Britain. The British ruled the seas and financed anyone who would oppose Napoleon. In an effort to bankrupt this "nation of shopkeepers" by choking its trade, Napoleon inaugurated the Continental System in 1806. It prohibited all commerce between Great Britain and France, as well as between Great Britain and France's dependent states and allies. At first the system worked: British exports dropped 20 percent in 1807–1808, and industrial production declined 10 percent; unemployment and a strike of 60,000 workers in northern England resulted. The British retaliated by confiscating merchandise on ships, even those of powers neutral in the wars, that sailed to or from ports from which the British were excluded by the Continental System.

In the midst of continuing wars, moreover, the system proved impossible to enforce, and widespread smuggling brought British goods into the European market. British industrial growth continued, despite some setbacks; calico-printing works, for example, quadrupled their production, and imports of raw cotton increased 40 percent. At the same time, French and other continental industries benefited from the temporary protection from British competition.

Resistance to French Rule, 1807–1812. Smuggling British goods was only one way of opposing the French. Almost everywhere in Europe, resistance began as local opposition to French demands for money or draftees, but it eventually prompted that patriotic defense of the nation known as nationalism (see page 791). In southern Italy, gangs of bandits harassed the French army and local officials; 33,000 Italian bandits were arrested in 1809 alone. But resistance continued via a network of secret societies, called the *carbonari* ("charcoal-burners"), which got its name from the practice of marking each new member's forehead with a charcoal mark. Throughout the nineteenth century the *carbonari* played a leading role in Italian nationalism. In the

German states, intellectuals wrote passionate defenses of the virtues of the German nation and of the superiority of German literature.

No nations bucked Napoleon's reins more than Spain and Portugal. In 1807, Napoleon sent 100,000 troops through Spain to invade Portugal, Great Britain's ally. The royal family fled to the Portuguese colony of Brazil, but fighting continued, aided by a British army. When Napoleon got his brother Joseph named king of Spain in place of the senile Charles IV (r. 1788–1808), the Spanish clergy and nobles raised bands of peasants to fight the French occupiers. Even Napoleon's taking personal command of the French forces failed to quell the Spanish, who for six years fought a war of national independence that pinned down thousands of French soldiers. Germaine de Staël commented that Napoleon "never understood that a war might be a crusade. . . . He never reckoned with the one power that no arms could overcome— the enthusiasm of a whole people."

The Spanish War for Independence, 1807–1813

More than a new feeling of nationalism was aroused in Spain. Peasants hated French requisitioning of their food supplies and sought to defend their priests against French anticlericalism. Spanish nobles feared revolutionary reforms and were willing to defend the old monarchy in the person of the young Ferdinand VII, heir to Charles IV, even while Ferdinand himself was congratulating Napoleon on his victories. The Spanish Catholic church spread anti-French propaganda that equated Napoleon with heresy. As the former archbishop of Seville wrote to the archbishop of Granada in 1808, "You realize that we must not recognize as king a free-mason, heretic, Lutheran, as are all the Bonapartes and the French nation." In this tense atmosphere, the Spanish peasant rebels, assisted by the British, countered every French massacre with atrocities of their own. They tortured their French prisoners (boiling one general alive) and lynched collaborators.

Napoleon's Mamelukes Massacre the Spanish
In one of the paintings he produced to criticize Napoleon's occupation of Spain, Second of May 1808
*at the Puerta del Sol (1814), Goya depicts the brutal suppression of the Spanish revolt in Madrid
against Napoleon. Napoleon used Mamelukes, Egyptian soldiers descended from freed Turkish slaves.
For the Spanish Christians—and for European viewers of the painting—use of these mercenaries
made the event even more horrifying. Europeans considered Muslims, and Turks in particular, as
menacing because the Europeans had been fighting them for centuries.*
Museo del Prado, Madrid.

From Russian Winter to Final Defeat, 1812–1815

Despite opposition, Napoleon ruled over an extensive empire by 1812. He controlled more territory than any European ruler had since Roman times. Only two major European states remained fully independent—Great Britain and Russia—but once allied they would successfully challenge his dominion and draw many other states to their side. Britain sent aid to the Portuguese and Spanish rebels, while Russia once again prepared for war. Tsar Alexander I made peace with Turkey and allied himself with Great Britain and Sweden. In 1812, Napoleon invaded Russia with 250,000 horses and 600,000 men, including contingents of Italians, Poles, Swiss, Dutch, and Germans. This daring move proved to be his undoing.

Invasion of Russia, 1812.   Napoleon followed his usual strategy of trying to strike quickly, but the Russian generals avoided confrontation and retreated eastward, destroying anything that might be useful to the invaders. In September, on the road to Moscow, Napoleon finally engaged the main Russian force in the gigantic battle of Borodino (see Map 21.1). French casualties were 30,000 men, including 47 generals; the Russians lost 45,000. The French soldiers had nothing to celebrate around their campfires: as one soldier wrote, "Everyone . . . wept for some dead friend." Once again the Russians retreated, leaving Moscow undefended. Napoleon entered the deserted city, but the victory turned hollow because the departing Russians had set the wooden city on fire. Within a week, three-fourths of it had burned to the ground. Still Alexander refused to negotiate, and French morale plunged with

Napoleon: For and Against

Napoleon and Hitler are the two most controversial figures in all of modern Western history, and they are often compared with each other. What they shared was a desire to dominate Europe by military force, and they both came very close to achieving that goal. But they differed entirely in ideas: to take just the most important example, Napoleon offered emancipation to the Jews wherever he ruled, whereas Hitler tried to eliminate them as a group, ultimately by murdering as many as he could.

Napoleon enthralled Europe. The Prussian philosopher Georg W. F. Hegel dubbed him "world history on horseback." After his final exile, Napoleon presented himself as a martyr to the cause of liberty whose goal was to create a European "federation of free people." Few were convinced by this "gospel according to St. Helena" (Document 1). Followers such as Emmanuel de Las Cases burnished the Napoleonic legend (Document 2), but detractors such as Benjamin Constant viewed him as a tyrant (Document 3). For all his defects, Napoleon fascinated even those who were too young to understand his rise and fall. The French romantic poet Victor Hugo celebrated both the glory and the tragedy of Napoleonic ambitions (Document 4).

1. Napoleon's Own View from Exile

As might be expected, Napoleon put the most positive possible construction on his plans for France. In exile he wrote letters and talked at length to Emmanuel de Las Cases (1766–1842), an aristocratic officer in the royal navy who rallied to Napoleon in 1802, served in the Council of State, and later accompanied him to St. Helena. Much of what we know about Napoleon's views comes from a book published by Las Cases in 1821.

March 3, 1817:
In spite of all the libels, I have no fear whatever about my fame. Posterity will do me justice. The truth will be known; and the good I have done will be compared with the faults I have committed. I am not uneasy as to the result. Had I succeeded, I would have died with the reputation of the greatest man that ever existed. As it is, although I have failed, I shall be considered as an extraordinary man: my elevation was unparalleled, because unaccompanied by crime. I have fought fifty pitched battles, almost all of which I have won. I have framed and carried into effect a code of laws that will bear my name to the most distant posterity. I raised myself from nothing to be the most powerful monarch in the world. Europe was at my feet. I have always been of the opinion that the sovereignty lay in the people. In fact, the imperial government was a kind of republic. Called to the head of it by the voice of the nation, my maxim was, *la carrière est ouverte aux talents* ["careers open to talent"] without distinction of birth or fortune, and this system of equality is the reason that your oligarchy hates me so much.

Source: R. M. Johnston, *The Corsican: A Diary of Napoleon's Life in His Own Words* (Boston: Houghton Mifflin, 1921), 492.

2. Napoleon's Own History of France

Las Cases included in his book parts of a history of France that Napoleon himself had undertaken to write. Napoleon here argues that his ascent to the throne was legitimate, though he did not come from the Bourbon family of kings, and that he reconciled the old nobles to the new regime by creating a new standard of nobility in the Legion of Honor. In short, he offered something for everyone.

No prince mounted the throne with more legitimate rights than Napoleon. The throne was tendered to Hugh Capet by some bishops and some nobles; the imperial throne was given to Napoleon by the will of all the citizens, verified three times in a solemn manner. Pope Pius VII, chief of the Roman, Catholic, and Apostolic religion, the religion of the majority of Frenchmen, crossed the Alps to anoint the Emperor with his own hands, surrounded by all the bishops of France, by all the cardinals of the Roman Church, and by the deputies of all the cantons of the Empire. . . .

The Emperor bound up the wounds of the Revolution; all the émigrés returned and that list of proscribed persons was destroyed. The prince performed the most kindly glorious act, that of recalling to their country, and thus reestablishing, more than twenty thousand families. Their unsold property was returned to them; and wiping clean the slate of the past, he welcomed equally to all employments individuals of all the classes, whatever their conduct had been. . . . All titles were forgotten; there were no longer aristocrats or Jacobins, and the establishment of the Legion of Honor, which was the reward for military, civil, and judicial service, united side by side the soldier, the scholar, the artist, the prelate, and the magistrate; it was a symbol of reunion of all the estates, of all the parties.

Source: Emmanuel de Las Cases, *Le Mémorial de Sainte-Hélène* (Paris: Garnier Frères, n.d.) 3:430–34, translated and excerpted by David H. Pinkney, *Napoleon, Historical Enigma* (Lexington: D. C. Heath, 1969), 1–2.

3. Benjamin Constant, Spokesman for the Liberal Opposition to Napoleon

Benjamin Constant (1767–1830) came from an old French Calvinist family that had fled to Switzerland to escape persecution. Constant spent the early years of the French Revolution in a minor post at a minor German court. He moved to Paris in 1795 and became active in French politics during the Directory. Under Napoleon he went into exile, where he published a romantic novel (Adolphe, 1806) and pamphlets like this one attacking Napoleon. He reconciled to Napoleon during the Hundred Days and then opposed the restored Bourbon monarchy. In this selection, written during his exile, he expresses his hostility to Napoleon as a usurper dependent on war to maintain himself in power.

Surely, Bonaparte is a thousand times more guilty than those barbarous conquerors who, ruling over barbarians, were by no means at odds with their age. Unlike them, he has chosen barbarism; he has preferred it. In the midst of enlightenment, he has sought to bring back the night. He has chosen to transform into greedy and bloodthirsty nomads a mild and polite people: his crime lies in this premeditated intention, in his obstinate effort to rob us of the heritage of all the enlightened generations who have preceded us on this earth. But why have we given him the right to conceive such a project?

When he first arrived here, alone, out of poverty and obscurity, and until he was twenty-four, his greedy gaze wandering over the country around him, why did we show him a country in which any religious idea was the object of irony? [Constant refers here to de-Christianization during the French Revolution.] When he listened to what was professed in our circles, why did serious thinkers tell him that man had no other motivation than his own interest? . . .

[Napoleon] judged France by her own words, and the world by France as he imagined her to be. Because immediate usurpation was easy, he believed it could be durable, and once he became a usurper, he did all that usurpation condemns a usurper to do in our century.

It was necessary to stifle inside the country all intellectual life: he banished discussion and proscribed the freedom of the press.

The nation might have been stunned by that silence: he provided, extorted or paid for acclamation which sounded like the national voice. . . . War flung onto distant shores that part of the French nation that still had some real energy. It prompted the police harassment of the timid, whom it could not force abroad. It struck terror into men's hearts, and left there a certain hope that chance would take responsibility for their deliverance: a hope agreeable to fear and convenient to inertia. How many times have I heard men who were pressed to resist tyranny postponing this, during wartime till the coming of peace, and in peacetime until war commences!

I am right therefore in claiming that a usurper's sole resource is uninterrupted war. Some object:

what if Bonaparte had been pacific? Had he been pacific, he would never have lasted for twelve years. Peace would have re-established communication among the different countries of Europe. These communications would have restored to thought its means of expression. Works published abroad would have been smuggled into the country. The French would have seen that they did not enjoy the approval of the majority of Europe.

Source: Benjamin Constant, "Further Reflections on Usurpation," in *Political Writings*, trans. Biancamaria Fontana (Cambridge: Cambridge University Press, 1988), 161–63.

4. Victor Hugo, "The Two Islands," 1825

Victor Hugo (1802–1885) was France's greatest romantic poet and novelist, author of The Hunchback of Notre Dame *and* Les Misérables. *His father was a Napoleonic general, but his mother was an equally ardent royalist. In this early poem, Hugo compares Napoleon to one of Napoleon's favorite icons, the eagle, symbol of empire. The two islands of the title are Corsica, Napoleon's birthplace, and St. Helena, his place of final exile and death.*

> These Isles, where Ocean's shattered spray
>   Upon the ruthless rocks is cast,
> Seem like two treacherous ships of prey,
>   Made by eternal anchors fast.
> The hand that settled bleak and black
> Those shores on their unpeopled rack,
> And clad in fear and mystery,
>   Perchance thus made them tempest-torn,

> That Bonaparte might there be born,
> And that Napoleon there might die.
> . . . .
> He his imperial nest hath built so far and high,
> He seems to us to dwell within that tranquil sky,
> Where you shall never see the angry tempest break.
>   'Tis but beneath his feet the growling storms
>   are sped,
>   And thunders to assault his head
> Must to their highest source go back.
> The bolt flew upwards: from his eyrie [nest] riven,
> Blazing he falls beneath the stroke of heaven;
>   Then kings their tyrant foe reward—
> They chain him, living, on that lonely shore;
> And earth captive giant handed o'er
>   To ocean's more resistless guard.
> . . . .
> Shame, hate, misfortune, vengeance, curses sore,
> On him let heaven and earth together pour:
>   Now, see we dashed the vast Colossus low.
>   May he forever rue, alive and dead,
>   All tears he caused mankind to shed,
>   And all the blood he caused to flow.

Source: Henry Carrington, *Translations from the Poems of Victor Hugo* (London: Walter Scott, 1885), 34–41.

QUESTIONS FOR DEBATE
1. Which of these views of Napoleon has the most lasting value as opposed to immediate dramatic effect?
2. Based on these selections, what was Napoleon's greatest accomplishment? His greatest failure?
3. Victor Hugo called Napoleon "the vast Colossus." Why did he pick this larger-than-life metaphor even when writing lines critical of Napoleon's legacy of tears and bloodshed?

---

worsening problems of supply. Weeks of constant marching in the dirt and heat had worn down the foot soldiers, who were dying of disease or deserting in large numbers.

In October Napoleon began his retreat; in November came the cold. Napoleon himself reported that on November 14 the temperature fell to −4 degrees Fahrenheit. A German soldier in the Grand Army described trying to cook fistfuls of raw bran with snow to make something like bread. For him the retreat was "the indescribable horror of all possible plagues." Within a week the Grand Army lost 30,000 horses and had to abandon most of its artillery and food supplies. Russian forces harassed the retreating army, now more pathetic than grand. By December only 100,000 troops remained, one-sixth the original number, and the retreat had turned into a rout: the Russians had captured 200,000 soldiers, including 48 generals and 3,000 other officers.

Napoleon had made a classic military mistake that would be repeated by Adolf Hitler in World War II: fighting a war on two distant fronts simultaneously. The Spanish war tied down 250,000 French troops and forced Napoleon to bully Prussia and Austria into supplying soldiers of dubious loyalty for the Moscow campaign. They deserted at the first opportunity. The fighting in Spain and Portugal also exacerbated the already substantial logistical and communications problems involved in marching to Moscow.

The End of Napoleon's Empire.   Napoleon's humiliation might have been temporary if the British and Russians had not successfully organized a coalition to complete the job. Napoleon still had resources at his command; by the spring of 1813 he had replenished his army with another 250,000 men. With British financial support, Russian, Austrian, Prussian, and Swedish armies met the French outside Leipzig in October 1813 and defeated Napoleon in the Battle of the Nations. One by one, Napoleon's German allies deserted him to join the German nationalist "war of liberation." The Confederation of the Rhine dissolved, and the Dutch revolted and restored the prince of Orange. Joseph Bonaparte fled Spain, and a combined Spanish-Portuguese army under British command invaded France. In only a few months the allied powers crossed the Rhine and marched toward Paris. In March 1814, the French Senate deposed Napoleon, who abdicated when his remaining generals refused to fight. Napoleon went into exile on the island of Elba off the Italian coast. His wife Marie-Louise refused to accompany him. The allies restored to the throne Louis XVIII (r. 1814–1824), the brother of Louis XVI (whose son was known as Louis XVII even though he died in prison in 1795 without ever ruling).

Napoleon had one last chance to regain power because Louis XVIII lacked a solid base of support. The new king tried to steer a middle course through a charter that established a British-style monarchy with a two-house legislature and guaranteed civil rights. But he was caught between returning emigré nobles who demanded a complete restoration of their lands and powers and those who had supported either the republic or Napoleon during the previous twenty-five years. Sensing an opportunity, Napoleon escaped from Elba in early 1815 and, landing in southern France, made swift and unimpeded progress to Paris. Although he had left in ignominy, now crowds cheered him and former

soldiers volunteered to serve him. The period known as the "Hundred Days" (the length of time between his escape and his final defeat) had begun. Louis XVIII fled across the border, waiting for help from France's enemies.

Napoleon quickly moved his reconstituted army into present-day Belgium. At first it seemed that he might succeed in separately fighting the two armies arrayed against him—a Prussian army and a joint force of Belgian, Dutch, German, and British troops led by Sir Arthur Wellesley (1769–1852), duke of Wellington. But the Prussians evaded him and joined with Wellington at Waterloo. Completely routed, Napoleon had no choice but to abdicate again. This time the victorious allies banished him permanently to the remote island of St. Helena, far off the coast of West Africa, where he died in 1821 at the age of fifty-two.

The cost of Napoleon's rule was high: 750,000 French soldiers and 400,000 others from annexed and satellite states died between 1800 and 1815. Yet no other military figure since Alexander the Great had made such an impact on world history. (See "Contrasting Views," page 778.) His plans for a united Europe, his insistence on spreading the legal reforms of the French Revolution, his social welfare programs, and even his inadvertent awakening of national sentiment set the agenda for European history in the modern era.

❖ The "Restoration" of Europe

Even while Napoleon was making his last desperate bid for power, his enemies were meeting in the Congress of Vienna (1814–1815) to decide the fate of postrevolutionary Europe. Although interrupted by the Hundred Days, the Congress of Vienna settled the boundaries of European states, determined who would rule each nation, and established a new framework for international relations based on periodic meetings, or congresses, between the major powers. This congress system, or "concert of Europe," helped prevent another major war until the 1850s, and no conflict comparable to the Napoleonic wars would occur again until 1914.

Many of Europe's rulers hoped to nullify revolutionary and Napoleonic reforms and thus

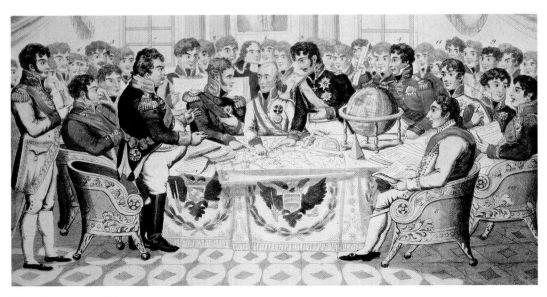

The Congress of Vienna
An unknown French engraver caricatured the efforts of the diplomats at the Congress of Vienna,
complaining that they used the occasion to divide the spoils of European territory. At the far left
is Metternich preparing to take Venice and Lombardy (northern Italy).
Historisches Museum der Stadt Wien.

"restore" their old regimes. Some of the returning rulers so detested French innovations that they tore French plants out of their gardens and threw French furniture out of their palaces. The most successful rulers compromised between old traditions and new ideas. Total negation of the revolutionary legacy might work for a time, but in the long run, accommodation was unavoidable.

The Congress of Vienna, 1814–1815

The Vienna settlement established a new equilibrium that relied on cooperation among the major powers while guaranteeing the status of smaller states. The revolutionary and Napoleonic wars had produced a host of potentially divisive issues. In addition to determining the boundaries of France, the congress had to decide the fate of Napoleon's duchy of Warsaw, the German province of Saxony, the Netherlands, the states once part of the confederation of the Rhine, and various Italian territories. All had either changed hands or been created during the wars. These issues were resolved by face-to-face negotiations among representatives of the five major powers: Austria, Russia, Prussia, Britain, and France. With its aim to establish a long-lasting,

negotiated peace endorsed by all parties, both winners and losers, the Congress of Vienna provided a model for the twentieth-century League of Nations and United Nations.

Austria's chief negotiator, Prince Klemens von Metternich (1773–1859), took the lead in devising the settlement. A well-educated nobleman who spoke five languages, Metternich served as a minister in the Austrian cabinet from 1809 to 1848. More than anyone else, he shaped the post-Napoleonic order. Although his penchant for womanizing made him a security risk in the eyes of the British Foreign Office (he even had an affair with Napoleon's younger sister), he worked with the British prime minister Robert Castlereagh (1769–1822) to ensure a moderate agreement that would check French aggression and yet maintain its great-power status. Metternich and Castlereagh believed that French aggression must be contained because it had threatened the European peace since the days of Louis XIV, but that France must remain a major player precisely so that no one European power might dominate the others. In this way France could help Austria and Britain counter the ambitions of Prussia and Russia. Castlereagh hoped to make Britain the arbiter of European affairs, but he knew this could be accomplished only through adroit diplomacy because the British constitutional monarchy had little in common with most of its more absolutist continental counterparts.

The task of ensuring France's status at the congress fell to Prince Charles Maurice de Talleyrand (1754–1838), an aristocrat and former bishop who had embraced the French Revolution, served as Napoleon's foreign minister, and ended as foreign minister to Louis XVIII after helping to arrange the emperor's overthrow. Informed of Talleyrand's betrayal, Napoleon called him "excrement in silk stockings." When the French army failed to oppose Napoleon's return to power in the Hundred Days, the allies took away all territory conquered since 1790 and required France to pay an indemnity and support an army of occupation until it had paid. Talleyrand nonetheless successfully argued that the restored French monarchy could succeed only if it retained its great-power status and fully participated in the negotiations.

The goal of the congress was to achieve postwar stability by establishing secure states with guaranteed borders (Map 21.2). Where possible, the

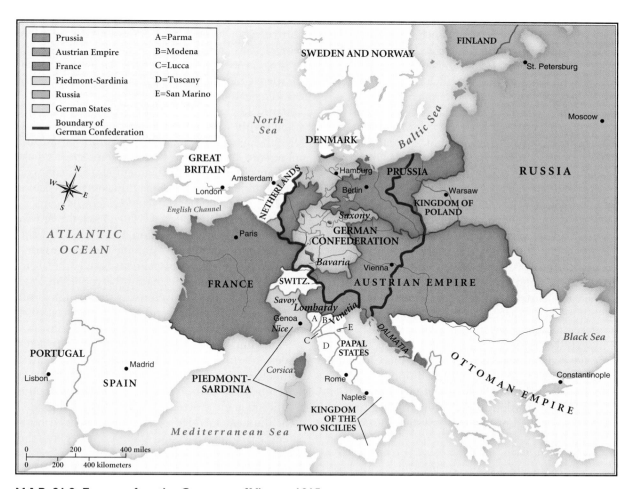

MAP 21.2 Europe after the Congress of Vienna, 1815
The diplomats meeting at the Congress of Vienna could not simply "restore" Europe to its prerevolutionary borders. Too much had changed since 1789. France was forced to return to its 1789 borders and Spain and Portugal regained their former rulers. The Austrian Netherlands and the Dutch Republic were united in a new kingdom of the Netherlands, the German states were joined in a Germanic Confederation that built upon Napoleon's Confederation of the Rhine, and Napoleon's Grand Duchy of Warsaw became the kingdom of Poland with the tsar of Russia as king.

congress simply restored traditional rulers, as in Spain and the Italian states. Where restoration was impossible, it rearranged territory to balance the competing interests of the great powers. Thus the congress turned the duchy of Warsaw into a new Polish kingdom but made the tsar of Russia its king. (Poland would not regain its independence until 1918.) The former Dutch Republic and the Austrian Netherlands, both annexed to France, now united as the new kingdom of the Netherlands under the restored stadholder. Prussia gained territory in Saxony and on the left bank of the Rhine to compensate for its losses in Poland. To make up for its losses in Poland and Saxony, Austria reclaimed the Italian provinces of Lombardy and Venetia and the Dalmatian coast. Austria now presided over the German Confederation, which replaced the defunct Holy Roman Empire and also included Prussia. The lesser powers were not forgotten. The kingdom of Piedmont-Sardinia took Genoa, Nice, and part of Savoy. Sweden obtained Norway from Denmark but had to accept Russia's conquest of Finland. Finally, various international trade issues were also resolved. At the urging of Great Britain, the congress agreed to condemn in principle the slave trade, abolished by Great Britain in 1807. In reality, however, the slave trade continued in many places until the 1840s.

To impart spiritual substance to this very calculated settlement of political affairs, Tsar Alexander proposed a Holy Alliance that would ensure divine assistance in upholding religion, peace, and justice. Prussia and Austria signed the agreement, but Great Britain refused to accede to what Castlereagh called "a piece of sublime mysticism and nonsense." Pope Pius VII also refused on the grounds that the papacy needed no help in interpreting the Christian truth. Despite the reassertion of traditional religious principle, the congress had in fact given birth to a new diplomatic order: in the future, the legitimacy of states depended on the treaty system, not on divine right.

The Emergence of Conservatism

The French Revolution and Napoleonic domination of Europe had shown contemporaries that government could be changed overnight, that the old hierarchies could be overthrown in the name of reason, and that even Christianity could be written off or at least profoundly altered with the stroke of a pen. The potential for rapid change raised many questions about the proper sources of authority. Kings and churches could be restored and former revolutionaries locked up or silenced, but the old order no longer commanded automatic obedience. The old order was now merely *old*, no longer "natural" and "timeless." It had been ousted once and therefore might fall again. People insisted on having reasons to believe in their "restored" governments. The political doctrine that justified the restoration was *conservatism*.

Conservatives benefited from the disillusionment that permeated Europe after 1815. In the eyes of most Europeans, Napoleon had become a tyrant who ruled in his own interests. Conservatives believed it was crucial to analyze the roots of such tyranny so established authorities could use their knowledge of history to prevent its recurrence. They saw a logical progression in recent history: the Enlightenment based on reason led to the French Revolution, with its bloody guillotine and horrifying Terror, which in turn spawned the authoritarian and militaristic Napoleon. Conservative intellectuals therefore either rejected Enlightenment principles or at least subjected them to scrutiny and skepticism.

The most influential spokesman of conservatism was Edmund Burke (1729–1799), the British critic of the French Revolution. He argued that the revolutionaries erred in thinking they could construct an entirely new government based on reason. Government, Burke said, had to be rooted in long experience, which evolved over generations. All change must be gradual and must respect national and historical traditions.

Like Burke, later conservatives believed that religious and other major traditions were an essential foundation for any society. Conservatives blamed the French Revolution's attack on religion on the skepticism and anticlericalism of such Enlightenment thinkers as Voltaire, and they defended both hereditary monarchy and the authority of the church, whether Catholic or Protestant. The "rights of man," according to conservatives, could not stand alone as doctrine based simply on nature and reason. The community too had its rights, more important than those of any individual, and established institutions best represented those rights. The church, the state, and the patriarchal family would provide an enduring social order for everyone. Faith, sentiment, history, and tradition must fill the vacuum left by the failures of reason and excessive belief in individual rights. Across Europe these views were taken up and elaborated by government advisers, professors, and writers. Not surprisingly, they had their strongest appeal in ruling circles and guided the politics of men such as Metternich in Austria and Alexander I in Russia.

The restored monarchy in France provided a major test for conservatism because the returning Bourbons had to confront the legacy of twenty-five years of upheaval. Louis XVIII tried to ensure a measure of continuity by maintaining Napoleon's Civil Code. He also guaranteed the rights of ownership to church lands sold during the revolutionary period and created a parliament composed of a Chamber of Peers nominated by the king and a Chamber of Deputies elected by very restricted suffrage (fewer than 100,000 voters in a population of 30 million, or about 3 percent). In making these concessions, the king tried to follow a moderate course of compromise, but the Ultras (ultraroyalists) pushed for complete repudiation of the revolutionary past. When Louis returned to power after Napoleon's final defeat, armed royalist bands attacked and murdered hundreds of Bonapartists and former revolutionaries. In 1816, the Ultras insisted on abolishing divorce and set up special courts to punish opponents of the regime. More extreme measures were to come.

The Revival of Religion

The experience of revolutionary upheaval and nearly constant warfare prompted many to renew their religious faith once peace returned. In France, the Catholic church sent missionaries to hold open-air "ceremonies of reparation" to express repentance for the outrages of revolution. In Rome, the papacy reestablished the Jesuit order, which had been disbanded during the Enlightenment. In the Italian states and Spain, governments used religious societies of laypeople to combat the influence of reformers and nationalists such as the Italian *carbonari*.

Revivalist movements, especially in Protestant countries, could on occasion challenge the status quo, not support it. In parts of Protestant Germany and Britain, religious revival had begun in the eighteenth century with the rise of Pietism and Methodism, movements that stressed individual religious experience rather than reason as the true path to moral and social reform. The English Methodists followed John Wesley (1703–1791), who preached an emotional, morally austere, and very personal "method" of gaining salvation. The Methodists, or Wesleyans, gradually separated from the Church of England and in the early decades of the nineteenth century attracted thousands of members in huge revival meetings that lasted for days.

Shopkeepers, artisans, agricultural laborers, miners, and workers in cottage industry, both male and female, flocked to the new denomination, even though at first Methodism seemed to emphasize conservative political views: Methodist statutes of 1792 had insisted that "none of us shall either in writing or in conversation speak lightly or irreverently of the government." In their hostility to rigid doctrine and elaborate ritual and their encouragement of popular preaching, however, the Methodists fostered a sense of democratic community and even a rudimentary sexual equality. From the beginning, women preachers traveled on horseback to preach in barns, town halls, and textile dye houses. The Methodist Sunday schools that taught thousands of poor children to read and write eventually helped create greater demands for working-class political participation.

The religious revival was not limited to Europe. In the United States, the second "Great Awakening" began around 1790 with huge camp meetings that brought together thousands of worshippers and scores of evangelical preachers, many of them Methodist. (The original Great Awakening took place in the 1730s and 1740s, sparked by the preaching of George Whitefield, a young English evangelist and follower of John Wesley.) Men and women danced to exhaustion, fell into trances, and spoke in "tongues." During this period, Protestant sects began systematic missionary activity in other parts of the world, with British and American missionary societies taking the lead in the 1790s and early 1800s. In the British colony of India, for example, Protestant missionaries argued for the reform of Hindu customs. *Sati*—the burning of widows on the funeral pyres of their husbands—was abolished by the British administration of India in 1829. Missionary activity by Protestants and Catholics would become one of the arms of European imperialism and cultural influence in the nineteenth century.

❖ Forces for Social and Cultural Change

Conservatives hoped to clamp a lid on European affairs, but the lid kept threatening to fly off. In France in 1820, an assassin killed Louis XVIII's nephew, inspiring a like-minded group to try, unsuccessfully, to blow up Britain's Tory cabinet. Rapid urban growth and the spread of industry created new social tensions and inspired new political doctrines to explain the meaning of economic and social changes. These doctrines soon galvanized opponents of the conservative Vienna settlement. Cutting across and drawing on the turmoil in society and politics was romanticism, a new international movement in the arts and literature that originated in reaction to the Enlightenment in the eighteenth century and dominated artistic expression in the first half of the nineteenth.

Industrial and Urban Growth in Britain

Historians today use the term *Industrial Revolution* to describe the set of changes that brought steam-driven machinery, large factories, and a new working class first to Britain, then to the rest of Europe, and eventually to the rest of the world. French and English writers of the 1820s introduced the term to capture the drama of contemporary change and to draw a parallel with the French Revolution. But we should not take the comparison too literally. Unlike the French upheaval, the Industrial Revolution was not over in a decade. From Great Britain in the second half of the eighteenth century it spread slowly; even by the 1830s it had little effect on the continent outside of northern France, Belgium, and the Rhineland. Most Europeans were still peasants working in the old ways.

Factories and Workers.   Steam-driven machines first brought workers together in factories in the textile industry. By 1830, more than one million people in Britain depended on the cotton industry for employment, and cotton cloth constituted 50 percent of the country's exports. Factories quickly sprang up in urban areas, where the growing population provided a ready source of labor. The rapid expansion of the British textile industry had as its colonial corollary the destruction of the hand manu-

facture of textiles in India. The British put high import duties on Indian cloth entering Britain and kept such duties very low for British cloth entering India. The figures are dramatic: in 1813, the Indian city of Calcutta exported to England £2,000,000 of cotton cloth; by 1830, Calcutta was importing from England £2,000,000 of cotton cloth. When Britain abolished slavery in its Caribbean colonies in 1833, British manufacturers began to buy raw cotton in the southern United States, where slavery still flourished. (See "Taking Measure," page 787.)

Factories drew workers from the urban population surge, which had begun in the eighteenth century and now accelerated. The reasons for urban growth are not entirely clear. The population of such new industrial cities as Manchester and Leeds increased 40 percent in the 1820s alone. Historians long thought that factory workers came from the countryside, pushed off the land by the field enclosures of the 1700s. But recent studies have shown that the number of agricultural laborers actually increased during industrialization in Britain, suggesting that a growing birthrate created a larger population and fed workers into the new factory system.

The new workers came from several sources: families of farmers who could not provide land for all their children, soldiers demobilized after the Napoleonic wars, artisans displaced by the new machinery, and children of the earliest workers who had moved to the factory towns. A system of employment that resembled family labor on farms or in cottage industry also developed in the new factories. Entire families came to toil for a single wage, although family members performed different tasks. Workdays of twelve to seventeen hours were typical, even for children, and the work was grueling. Community ties remained important as workers migrated from rural to urban areas to join friends and family from their original villages.

As urban factories grew, their workers gradually came to constitute a new socioeconomic class with a distinctive culture and traditions. Like *middle class*, the term *working class* came into use for the first time in the early nineteenth century. It referred to the laborers in the new factories. In the past, workers had labored in isolated trades: water and wood carrying, gardening, laundry, and building. In contrast, factories brought working people together with machines, under close supervision by their employers. They soon developed a sense of

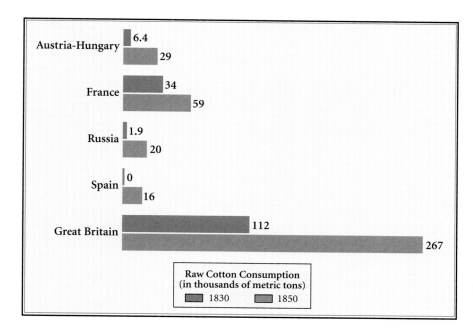

TAKING MEASURE
Raw Cotton Consumption,
1830–1850
The consumption of raw cotton correlates with the level of industrialization in the textile industry. Great Britain already imported more raw cotton in 1830 than any other country in Europe, and it widened the gap in the next generation. But the rate of increase was even greater in Austria-Hungary, Russia, and Spain (but not France). Can you calculate the rate of increase between 1830 and 1850?
From B. R. Mitchell, *European Historical Statistics 1750–1970* (New York: Columbia University Press, 1975), FD13.

common interests and organized societies for mutual help and political reform. From these would come the first labor unions.

The new factories and new technology threatened some people's very existence, especially in hard times. To protect livelihoods at risk from the introduction of new technology, bands of handloom weavers, fearing their displacement by machines, wrecked factory machinery and burned mills in the Midlands, Yorkshire, and Lancashire. To restore order and protect industry, the government sent in an army of twelve thousand regular soldiers and made machine wrecking punishable by death. The rioters were called *Luddites* after the fictitious figure Ned Ludd, whose signature appeared on their manifestos. (The term is still used to describe those who resist new technology.)

Other workers focused their organizing efforts on reforming Parliament, whose members were chosen in elections dominated by the landowning elite. One reformer complained that the members of the House of Commons were nothing but "toad-eaters, gamblers, public plunderers, and hirelings." Reform clubs held large open-air meetings, and ordinary people eagerly bought cheap newspapers that clamored for change. In August 1819, sixty thousand people attended an illegal meeting held in St. Peter's Fields in Manchester. When the local authorities sent the cavalry to arrest the speaker,

panic resulted; eleven people were killed and many hundreds injured. Punsters called it the Battle of Peterloo or the Peterloo Massacre. An alarmed government passed the Six Acts, which forbade large political meetings and restricted press criticism, suppressing the reform movement for a decade.

The Rise of the Railroad. Steam-driven engines were not limited to factory production. They appeared in the 1820s in a dramatic new form when the English engineer George Stephenson perfected an engine to pull wagons along rail tracks. Suddenly, railroad building became a new industry. (See "Taking Measure," page 788.) The idea of a railroad was not new: iron tracks had been used since the seventeenth century to haul coal from mines in wagons pulled by horses. A railroad system as a mode of transport, however, developed only after Stephenson's invention of a steam-powered locomotive.

New companies soon manufactured rails and laid track, with Parliament's permission. In 1830, the Liverpool and Manchester Railway line opened to the cheers of crowds and the congratulations of government officials, including the duke of Wellington, the hero of Waterloo and now prime minister. In the excitement, some of the dignitaries gathered on a parallel track. Another engine, George Stephenson's famous Rocket, approached at high speed. Most of the gentlemen scattered to safety, but

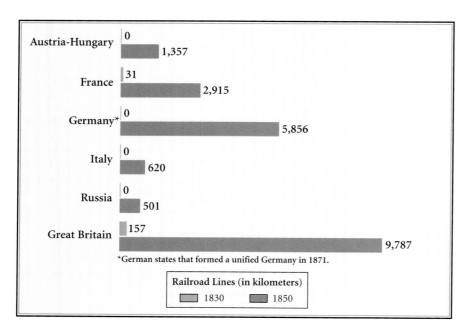

TAKING MEASURE
Railroad Lines, 1830–1850
Great Britain quickly extended its lead in the building of railroads. The extension of commerce and, before long, the ability to wage war would depend on the development of effective railroad networks. These statistics might be taken as predicting a realignment of power within Europe after 1850. What do the numbers say about the relative position of Germany (the German states, including Prussia but excluding Austria) and Austria-Hungary and Germany and France?
From B. R. Mitchell, *European Historical Statistics* 1750–1970 (New York: Columbia University Press, 1975), F1.

former cabinet minister William Huskisson fell and was hit. In a few hours he died, the first official casualty of the newfangled railroad. Despite the tragedy, the line was an immediate success, carrying up to 110 passengers and freight in each direction. One of the many commentators described it as "a kind of miracle exhibited before my astonished eyes."

Railroads were dramatic and expensive—the most striking symbol of the new industrial age. Placed on the new tracks, steam-driven carriages could transport people and goods to the cities and link coal and iron deposits to the new factories. They gave industrialization a big push forward as every European country soon tried to set up its own railroad system.

The New Ideologies

Although traditional ways of life still prevailed in much of Europe, new modes of thinking about the changes in the social and political order arose in direct response to what some have called the "dual revolution" of the French Revolution and the Industrial Revolution. The 1820s and 1830s were an era of "isms"—conservatism, liberalism, nationalism, romanticism, and, newest on the scene, socialism. The French Revolution had caused people to

ask questions about the best possible form of government, and its effects had made clear that people acting together could change their political system. The events of the 1790s and the following decades, however, also produced enormous differences of opinion over what constituted the ideal government. Similarly, the Industrial Revolution, first in Britain and then in western Europe, posed fundamental questions about changes in society and social relations: How did the new social order differ from the earlier one, which was less urban and less driven by commercial concerns? Who should control this new order? Should governments try to moderate or accelerate the pace of change? Answers to these questions about the social and political order were called *ideologies*, a word coined during the French Revolution. An *ideology* is a coherent set of beliefs about the way a society's social and political order should be organized. In the 1830s and 1840s, new political and social movements organized around these ideologies.

Liberalism. As an ideology, liberalism traced its origins to the writings of John Locke in the seventeenth century and the Enlightenment philosophy of the eighteenth. The adherents of *liberalism* defined themselves in opposition to conservatives on one end of the political spectrum and revolutionaries on the other. Unlike conservatives, liberals supported the Enlightenment ideals of constitutional guarantees of personal liberty and free trade in economics, believing that greater liberty in politics and economic matters would promote social improvement and economic growth. For that reason, they also generally applauded the social and economic changes produced by the Industrial Revolution, while opposing the violence and excessive state power promoted by the French Revolution. The leaders of the rapidly expanding middle class composed of manufacturers, merchants, and professionals favored liberalism.

Liberals' demands varied from country to country. In divided countries like Italy, liberals allied with movements for national unification. In France and Britain, liberals agitated largely for parliamentary reforms, including more middle-class representation, but also wanted economic changes, notably free trade, because they believed lifting tariffs would

lower prices, increase consumption, and consequently stimulate economic activity. Economic liberalism was much less important in countries such as Spain, where commercial and industrial change had not yet affected much of society. Nowhere did liberals favor democracy, however, because they feared that extending the vote to all men (let alone women) would lead to anarchy and disorder.

The foremost exponent of early-nineteenth-century liberalism was the English philosopher and jurist Jeremy Bentham (1748–1832). He called his brand of liberalism *utilitarianism* because he held that the best policy is the one that produces "the greatest good for the greatest number" and is thus the most useful, or utilitarian. Liberalism and utilitarianism were closely identified in England. Such views clearly challenged aristocratic dominance, which relied on policies that defended the privileges of a small minority. Bentham's criticisms spared no institution; he railed against the injustices of the British parliamentary process, the abuses of the prisons and the penal code, and the educational system. In his zeal for social engineering, he proposed elaborate schemes for managing the poor and model prisons that would emphasize rehabilitation through close supervision rather than corporal punishment. British liberals like Bentham wanted government involvement, including deregulation of trade, but they shied away from any association with revolutionary violence.

Bentham and many other liberals joined the abolitionist, antislavery movement that intensified between the 1790s and 1820s. One English abolitionist put the matter in these terms: "[God] has given to us an unexampled portion of civil liberty; and we in return drag his rational creatures into a most severe and perpetual bondage." The contradiction between calling for more liberty at home and maintaining slavery in the West Indies seemed intolerable to British liberals and to many religious groups, especially the Quakers, who since the 1780s had taken the lead in forming antislavery societies in both the United States and Great Britain. Agitation by such groups as the London Society for Effecting the Abolition of the Slave Trade succeeded in gaining a first victory in 1807 when the British House of Lords voted to abolish the slave trade. Throughout the 1820s, antislavery activism expanded in the United States, Great Britain, and France because the slave trade still continued in

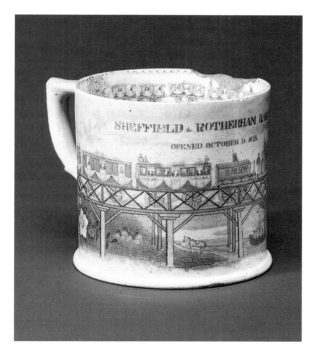

Railroads in Britain
A commemorative mug shows an early railway carriage. The mug was manufactured to celebrate the opening of the Sheffield and Rotherham line on October 31, 1838. Items such as this spread awareness of railroads to people who lived far from the places first linked together.
Fitzwilliam Museum, University of Cambridge.

some countries and because slavery itself had not been abolished. As one disappointed British abolitionist explained in 1830:

> We supposed that when by the abolition of the slave trade the planters could get no more slaves, they would not only treat better those whom they then had in their power, but that they would gradually find it to their advantage to emancipate them. . . . We did not sufficiently take into account the effect of unlimited power.

The abolitionists' efforts would bear fruit in 1833 when Britain abolished slavery in all its colonies.

Socialism. The newest ideology of the 1820s, *socialism*, took up where liberalism left off: socialists believed that the liberties advocated by liberals benefited only the middle class, the owners of factories and businesses, not the workers. They sought to reorganize society totally rather than to reform it piecemeal through political measures. Many were *utopians* who believed that ideal communities are based on cooperation rather than competition. Like Thomas More, whose book *Utopia* (1516) gave the movement its name, the utopian socialists believed that society would benefit all its members only if private property did not exist.

Socialists criticized the new industrial order for dividing society into two classes: the new middle class, or *capitalists*, who owned the wealth; and the working class, their downtrodden and impoverished employees. Such divisions tore the social fabric, and, as their name suggests, the socialists aimed to restore harmony and cooperation through social reorganization. Robert Owen (1771–1858), a successful Welsh-born manufacturer, founded British socialism. In 1800, he bought a cotton mill in New Lanark, Scotland, and began to set up a model factory town, where workers labored only ten hours a day (instead of seventeen, as was common) and children between the ages of five and ten attended school rather than working in the factory. Owen moved to the United States in the 1820s to put his principles once more into action in the community in Indiana he named New Harmony. The experiment collapsed after three years, a victim of internal squabbling. But out of Owen's experiments and writings, such as *The Book of the New Moral World*

(1820), would come the movement for producer cooperatives (businesses owned and controlled by their workers), consumers' cooperatives (stores in which consumers owned shares), and a national trade union.

Owen's utopian counterparts in France were Claude Henri de Saint-Simon (1760–1825) and Charles Fourier (1772–1837). Saint-Simon was a noble who had served as an officer in the War of American Independence and lost a fortune speculating in national property during the French Revolution. Fourier traveled as a salesman for a Lyon cloth merchant. Both shared Owen's alarm about the effects of industrialization on social relations. Saint-Simon—who coined the terms *industrialism* and *industrialist* to define the new economic order and its chief animators—believed that work was the central element in the new society and that it should be controlled not by politicians but by scientists, engineers, artists, and industrialists themselves. To correct the abuses of the new industrial order, Fourier urged the establishment of utopian communities that were part garden city and part agricultural commune; all jobs would be rotated to maximize happiness. Fourier hoped that a network of small, decentralized communities would replace the state. The emancipation of women was essential to Fourier's vision of a harmonious community: "The extension of the privileges of women is the fundamental cause of all social progress." Fourier's projects sometimes included outlandish predictions; he envisioned a world in which the oceans would turn into lemonade and the population would include 37 million poets equal to Homer, 37 million mathematicians equal to Newton, and 37 million dramatists equal to Molière.

After Saint-Simon's death in 1825, some of his followers established a quasi-religious cult with elaborate rituals and a "he-pope" and "she-pope," or ruling father and mother. Saint-Simonians lived and worked together in cooperative arrangements and scandalized some by advocating free love. They set up branches in the United States and Egypt. In 1832, Saint-Simonian women founded a feminist newspaper, *The Free Woman*, asserting that "with the emancipation of woman will come the emancipation of the worker." These early utopian socialists were lonely voices. Their emphasis on community and cooperation gained more adherents after 1830.

Nationalism. Nationalists could be liberals, socialists, or even conservatives. Their ability to cross political lines helped nationalism to influence the course of modern world history more than any other ideology. *Nationalism* holds that all peoples derive their identities from their nations, which are defined by common language, shared cultural traditions, and sometimes religion. When such "nations" do not coincide with state boundaries, as they often did not in the nineteenth and twentieth centuries, nationalism can produce violence and warfare as different national groups compete for control over territory.

The French showed the power of national feeling in their revolutionary and Napoleonic wars, but they also provoked nationalism in the people they conquered. Once Napoleon and his satellite rulers departed, nationalist sentiment turned against other outside rulers—the Ottoman Turks in the Balkans, the Russians in Poland, and the Austrians in Italy. Intellectuals took the lead in demanding unity and freedom for their peoples. They collected folktales, poems, and histories and prepared grammars and dictionaries of their native languages. Students, middle-class professionals, and army officers formed secret societies to promote national independence and constitutional reform.

Nationalist aspirations were especially explosive for the Austrian Empire, which included a variety of peoples united only by their enforced allegiance to the Habsburg emperor. The empire included three main national groups: the Germans, who made up one-fourth of the population; the Magyars of Hungary (which included Transylvania and Croatia); and the Slavs, who together formed the largest group in the population but were divided into different nationalities such as Poles, Czechs, Croats, and Serbs. The empire also included Italians in Lombardy and Venetia and Romanians in Transylvania. Efforts to govern such diverse peoples preoccupied Metternich, chief minister to the weak Habsburg emperor Francis I (r. 1792–1835). Metternich's domestic policy aimed to restrain nationalist impulses, and it largely succeeded until the 1840s.

As a conservative, Metternich believed that the experience of the French Revolution proved the superiority of monarchy and aristocracy as forms of government and society. But he did not hesitate to use new methods of governing when necessary.

Consequently, he set up a secret police on the Napoleonic model. The secret police opened letters of even the highest officials, reported any "suspicious" conversations, and followed travelers. Censorship in the Italian provinces was so strict that even the works of Dante were expurgated, and Metternich announced that "the Lombards must forget that they are Italians."

In reaction, novelists, playwrights, and poets used their pens to arouse nationalist sentiment. Membership grew in secret societies such as the *carbonari*; before the fall of Napoleon, many had been anti-French, but now the societies turned anti-Austrian and supported political rights and national self-determination. The societies had no common program across Italy and no central organization, but they attracted tens of thousands of members, including physicians, lawyers, officers, and students.

The new Germanic Confederation had a federal assembly, but it largely functioned as a tool of Metternich's policies. The only sign of resistance came from university students, who formed nationalist student societies, or *Burschenschaften*. In 1817, they held a mass rally at which they burned books they did not like, including Napoleon's Civil Code. One of their leaders, Friedrich Ludwig Jahn, spouted such xenophobic (antiforeign) slogans as "If you let your daughter learn French, you might just as well train her to become a whore." Metternich was convinced that the *Burschenschaften* in the German states and the *carbonari* in Italy were linked in an international conspiracy; in 1820, when a student assassinated the playwright August Kotzebue because he ridiculed the student movement, Metternich convinced the leaders of the biggest German states to pass the Karlsbad Decrees dissolving the student societies and more strictly censoring the press. No evidence for a conspiracy was found.

Tsar Alexander faced similar problems in Poland, his "congress kingdom" (so called because the Congress of Vienna had created it), which in 1815 was one of Europe's most liberal states. The tsar reigned in Poland as a limited monarch, having bestowed a constitution that provided for an elected parliament, a national army, and guarantees of free speech and a free press. But by 1818, Alexander had begun retracting his concessions. Polish students and military officers responded by forming secret nationalist societies to plot for change by illegal means. The government then cracked down, arresting student leaders and dismissing professors who promoted reforms. By the 1820s, Polish nationalists and the Russian imperial government were on a collision course.

Romanticism

More of an artistic movement than a true ideology, *romanticism* glorified nature, emotion, genius, and imagination. It proclaimed these as antidotes to the Enlightenment and to classicism in the arts, challenging the reliance on reason, symmetry, and cool geometric spaces. Classicism idealized models from Roman history; romanticism turned to folklore and medieval legends. Classicism celebrated orderly, crisp lines; romantics sought out all that was wild, fevered, and disorderly. Chief among the arts of romanticism were poetry, music, and painting, which captured the deep-seated emotion characteristic of romantic expression. Romantics might take any political position, but they exerted the most political influence when they expressed nationalist feelings.

Romantic Poetry. Romantic poetry celebrated overwhelming emotion and creative imagination. George Gordon, Lord Byron (1788–1824) explained his aims in writing poetry:

> For what is Poesy but to create
> From overfeeling, Good and Ill, and aim
> At an external life beyond our fate,
> And be the new Prometheus of new man.

Prometheus was the mythological figure who brought fire from the Greek gods to human beings. Byron did not seek the new Prometheus among the men of industry; he sought him within his own "overfeeling," his own intense emotions. Byron became a romantic hero himself when he rushed off to act on his emotions by fighting and dying in the Greek war for independence from the Turks. An English aristocrat, Byron nonetheless claimed, "I have simplified my politics into a detestation of all existing governments."

Romantic poetry elevated the wonders of nature almost to the supernatural. In a poem that became one of the most beloved exemplars of romanticism, "Tintern Abbey" (1798), the English poet William Wordsworth (1770–1850) compared

Lord Byron
George Gordon, Lord Byron (1788–1824), lived a short, tumultuous life, wrote enduring romantic poetry, loved both women and young men, and died a heroic death fighting for Greek independence. In the midst of the Napoleonic wars, he left Britain in 1809 for a two-year trip through Spain and Portugal, Greece, Turkey, and Turkish-controlled Albania. He visited the Turkish rulers in Greece and Albania and collected souvenir costumes, such as that worn in this portrait by Thomas Philips (1813). As a result of this trip, he became passionately involved in things Greek; when the Greek rebellion broke out, he promptly joined the British Committee that gathered aid for the Greeks. He died of a fever in Greece where he had gone to distribute funds. National Portrait Gallery, London.

himself to a deer even while making nature seem filled with human emotions:

> I came among these hills; when like a roe
> I bounded o'er the mountains, by the sides
> Of the deep rivers, and the lonely streams,
> Wherever nature led.

Nature, wrote Wordsworth, "to me was all in all." It allowed him to sing "the still, sad music of humanity" and was "a presence that disturbs me with the joy of elevated thoughts; a sense sublime." Like many poets of his time, Wordsworth greeted the French Revolution with joy; in his poem "French Revolution" (1809), he remembered his early enthusiasm: "Bliss was it in that dawn to be alive." But gradually he became disenchanted with the revolutionary experiment and celebrated British nationalism instead; in 1816, he published a poem to commemorate the "intrepid sons of Albion [England]" who died at the battle of Waterloo.

Their emphasis on authentic self-expression at times drew romantics to exotic, mystical, or even reckless experiences. Such transports drove one leading German poet to the madhouse and another to suicide. Some romantics depicted the artist as possessed by demons and obsessed with hallucinations. This more nightmarish side was captured, and perhaps criticized, by Mary Shelley in *Frankenstein*. The aged German poet Johann Wolfgang von Goethe (1749–1832) likewise denounced the extremes of romanticism, calling it "everything that is sick." In his epic poem *Faust* (1832), he seemed to warn of the same dangers Shelley portrayed in her novel. In Goethe's retelling of a sixteenth-century legend, Faust offers his soul to the devil in return for a chance to taste all human experience—from passionate love to the heights of power—in his effort to reshape nature for humanity's benefit. Faust's striving, like Frankenstein's, leaves a wake of suffering and destruction. Goethe did not make the target of his warning explicit, but the French revolutionary legacy and industrialization both seemed to be releasing "faustian" energies that could turn destructive.

Romantic Painting and Music. Romanticism in painting also idealized nature and often expressed anxiety about the coming industrial order. These concerns came together in an emphasis on natural landscape. The German romantic painter Caspar David Friedrich (1774–1840) depicted scenes—often in the mountains, far from any factory—that captured the romantic fascination with the sublime power of nature. His melancholy individual figures looked lost in the vastness of an overpowering nature. Friedrich hated the new modern world and considered industrialization a disaster. His landscapes often had religious meaning as well, as in his controversial painting *The Cross in the Mountains* (1808), which showed a Christian cross standing alone in a mountain scene. It symbolized the steadfastness of faith but seemed to separate religion from the churches and attach it to mystical experience.

Many other artists developed similar themes. The English painter Joseph M. W. Turner (1775–1851) depicted his vision of nature in mysterious, misty seascapes, anticipating later artists by blurring

William Blake, *The Circle of the Lustful* (1824)
An English romantic poet, painter, engraver, and printmaker, Blake always sought his own way. Self-taught, he began writing poetry at age twelve and apprenticed to an engraver at fourteen. His works incorporate many otherworldly attributes; they are quite literally visionary—imagining other worlds. In this engraving of hell, the figures twist and turn and are caught up in a kind of spiritual ether. Blake, "Circle of the Lustful"/ Birmingham Museums and Art Gallery.

Caspar David Friedrich, *Wanderer above the Sea of Fog* (1818)
Friedrich, a German romantic painter, captured many of the themes most dear to romanticism: melancholy, isolation, and individual communion with nature. He painted trees reaching for the sky and mountains stretching into the distance. Nature to him seemed awesome, powerful, and overshadowing of human perspectives. The French sculptor David d'Angers said of Friedrich, "Here is a man who has discovered the tragedy of landscape."
Co Elke Walford, Hamburg/Hamburger Kunsthalle.

the outlines of objects. The French painter Eugène Delacroix (1798–1863) chose contemporary as well as medieval scenes of great turbulence to emphasize light and color and break away from what he saw as "the servile copies repeated *ad nauseum* in academies of art." Critics denounced the new techniques as "painting with a drunken broom." To broaden his experience of light and color, Delacroix traveled in the 1830s to North Africa and painted many exotic scenes in Morocco and Algeria.

The towering presence of the German composer Ludwig van Beethoven (1770–1827) in early nineteenth-century music helped establish the direction for musical romanticism. His music, ac-

cording to one leading German romantic, "sets in motion the lever of fear, of awe, of horror, of suffering, and awakens just that infinite longing which is the essence of Romanticism." Beethoven transformed the symphony into a connected work with recurring and evolving musical themes. Romantic symphonies conveyed the impression of growth, a metaphor for the organic process with an emphasis on the natural that was dear to the romantics. For example, Beethoven's Sixth Symphony, the *Pastoral* (1808), used a variety of instruments to represent sounds heard in the country. Beethoven's work showed remarkable diversity ranging from religious works to symphonies, sonatas, and concertos. Some of his work was explicitly political; his Ninth Symphony (1824) employed a chorus to sing the German poet Friedrich Schiller's verses in praise of universal human solidarity.

Romantic Nationalism. If romantics had any common political thread, it was the support of nationalist aspirations, especially through the search for the historical origins of national identity. In the German states, the Austrian Empire, Russia and other Slavic lands, and Scandinavia, romantic poets and writers collected old legends and folktales that expressed a shared cultural and linguistic heritage stretching back to the Middle Ages. These collections showed that Germany, for example, had always existed even if it did not currently take the form of a single unified state. Romantic nationalism permeated the enormously popular historical novels of Sir Walter Scott (1771–1832) and *The Betrothed* (1825–1827), a novel by Alessandro Manzoni (1785–1873) that constituted a kind of bible for Italian nationalists.

Scott's career incorporates many of the strands of romanticism. He translated Goethe and published Scottish ballads that he heard as a child. After achieving immediate success with his poetry, he switched to historical novels, but he also wrote a nine-volume life of Napoleon and edited historical memoirs. His novels are almost all renditions of historical events, from *Rob Roy* (1817), with its account of Scottish resistance to the English in the early eighteenth century, to *Ivanhoe* (1819), with its tales of medieval England. The influence of Scott's historical novels was immense. One historian claimed that *Ivanhoe* was more historically true than any scholarly work: "There is more history in the novels of Walter Scott than in half of the historians."

❖ Political Challenges to the Conservative Order

As the spread of romanticism shows, the challenges to the conservative order ran deep but not always in the same political direction. Yet in many places, discontent with the conservative Vienna settlement threatened to rise over its banks as liberals, nationalists, and socialists expressed their exasperation. The revolutionary legacy kept coming to the surface to challenge Europe's rulers. Isolated revolts threatened the hold of some conservative governments in the 1820s, but most of them were quickly bottled up. Then in 1830, successive uprisings briefly overwhelmed the established order. Across Europe, angry protesters sought constitutional guarantees of individual liberties and national unity and autonomy.

Political Revolts in the 1820s

Combinations of liberalism and nationalism fueled political upheavals in the 1820s in Spain and Italy, Russia, Greece (Map 21.3), and across the Atlantic in the Spanish and Portuguese colonies of Latin Amer-ica. Most revolts failed, but those in Greece and Latin America succeeded, largely because they did not threaten the conservative order in Europe.

Uprisings in Spain and Italy.   The restoration of regimes after Napoleon's fall disappointed those who dreamed of constitutional freedoms. When Ferdinand VII regained the Spanish crown in 1814, he quickly restored the prerevolutionary nobility, church, and monarchy. He had foreign books and newspapers confiscated at the frontier and allowed the publication of only two newspapers. Not surprisingly, such repressive policies disturbed the middle class, especially the army officers who had encountered French ideas. Many responded by joining secret societies. In 1820, disgruntled soldiers demanded that Ferdinand proclaim his adherence to the Constitution of 1812, which he had abolished in 1814. When the revolt spread, Ferdinand convened the *cortes* (parliament), which could agree on virtually nothing. Ferdinand bided his time, and in 1823 a French army invaded and restored him to absolute power. The French acted with the consent of the other great powers, who had met to discuss the Spanish situation and agree on a course of

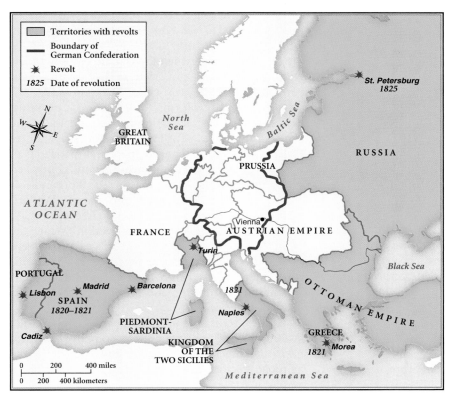

MAP 21.3 Revolutionary Movements of the 1820s
The revolts of the 1820s took place on the periphery of Europe, in Spain, Italy, Greece, Russia, and in the Spanish and Portuguese colonies of Latin America. Rebels in Spain and Russia wanted national independence. Although the Italian revolts failed, as did the uprisings in Spain and Russia, the Greek and Latin American independence movements succeeded.

action. The restored Spanish government tortured and executed hundreds of rebels; thousands were imprisoned or forced into exile.

The uprising in Spain proved contagious. Hearing of the Spanish struggles, rebellious soldiers in the kingdom of Naples joined forces with the *carbonari* and demanded a constitution. When a new parliament met, it too broke down over internal disagreements. The promise of reform sparked rebellion in the northern Italian kingdom of Piedmont-Sardinia, where rebels urged Charles Albert, the young heir to the Piedmont throne, to fight the Austrians for Italian unification. He vacillated; but in 1821, after the rulers of Austria, Prussia, and Russia met and agreed on intervention, the Austrians defeated the rebels in Naples and Piedmont. Liberals were arrested in many Italian states, and the pope condemned the secret societies as "at heart only devouring wolves." Despite the opposition of Great Britain, which condemned the "indiscriminate" suppression of revolutionary movements, Metternich convinced the other powers to agree to his muffling of the Italian opposition to Austrian rule.

The Decembrist Revolt in Russia. Aspirations for constitutional government surfaced in Russia when Alexander I died suddenly in 1825. On the December day that the troops assembled in St. Petersburg to take an oath of loyalty to Alexander's brother Nicholas as the new tsar, rebel officers insisted that the crown belonged to another brother, Constantine, whom they hoped would be more favorable to constitutional reform. Constantine, though next in the line of succession after Alexander, had refused the crown. The soldiers nonetheless raised the cry "Long live Constantine, long live the Constitution." (Some troops apparently thought that "the Constitution" was Constantine's wife.) Soldiers loyal to Nicholas easily suppressed the Decembrists (so called after the month of their uprising), who were so outnumbered that they had no realistic chance to succeed. The subsequent trial, however, made the rebels into legendary heroes. Of their imprisonment at hard labor, the Russian poet Alexander Pushkin (1799–1837) wrote:

> *The heavy-hanging chains will fall,*
> *The walls will crumble at a word,*
> *And Freedom greet you in the light,*
> *And brothers give you back the sword.*

Pushkin would not live to see this freedom. For the next thirty years, Nicholas I (r. 1825–1855) used a new political police, the Third Section, to spy on potential opponents and stamp out rebelliousness.

Greek Independence from the Turks. The Greek movement for independence eventually succeeded, largely because it was a nationalist movement against the Ottoman Turks, who enjoyed little support in Christian Europe and whose authority had been declining steadily. As the French ambassador explained to Chateaubriand when the writer visited Istanbul in 1807, "To make an alliance with Turkey is the same as putting your arms around a corpse to make it stand up!" Serbs revolted against Turkish rule in the Balkans and won virtual independence by 1817. A Greek general in the Russian army, Prince Alexander Ypsilanti, tried to lead a revolt against the Turks in 1820, but he failed when the tsar, urged on by Metternich, disavowed him. Metternich feared rebellion even by Christians against their Turkish rulers.

Nationalistic Movements in the Balkans, 1815–1830

A second revolt, this time by Greek peasants, sparked a wave of atrocities in 1821 and 1822. The Greeks killed every Turk who did not escape; in retaliation the Turks hanged the Greek patriarch of Constantinople, and in the areas they still controlled they pillaged churches, massacred thousands of men, and sold the women into slavery. Western opinion turned against the Turks; Greece, after all, was the home of Western civilization. While the great powers negotiated, Greeks and pro-Greece committees around the world sent food and military supplies; like the English poet Byron, a few enthusiastic European and American volunteers joined the Greeks.

The Greeks held on until the great powers were willing to intervene. In 1827, a combined force of British, French, and Russian ships destroyed the Turkish fleet at Navarino Bay; and in 1828, Russia

Greek Independence
From 1836 to 1839 the Greek painter Panagiotis Zographos worked with his two sons on a series of scenes from the Greek struggle for independence from the Turks. Response was so favorable that one Greek general ordered lithographic reproductions for popular distribution. Nationalistic feeling could be thus encouraged even among those who were not directly touched by the struggle. Here Turkish sultan Mehmet the Conqueror, exulting over the fall of Constantinople in 1453, views a row of Greeks under the yoke, a sign of submission. Collection, Visual Connection.

declared war on Turkey and advanced close to Istanbul. The Treaty of Adrianople of 1829 gave Russia a protectorate over the Danubian principalities in the Balkans and provided for a conference among representatives of Britain, Russia, and France, all of whom had broken with Austria in support of the Greeks. In 1830, Greece was declared an independent kingdom under the guarantee of the three powers; in 1833, the son of King Ludwig of Bavaria became Otto I of Greece. Nationalism, with the support of European public opinion, had made its first breach in Metternich's system.

Wars of Independence in Latin America. Across the Atlantic, national revolts also succeeded after a series of bloody wars of independence. Taking advantage of the upheavals in Spain and Portugal that began under Napoleon, restive colonists from Mexico to Argentina rebelled. Their leader was Simon Bolívar, son of a slave owner, who was educated in Europe on the works of Voltaire and Rousseau. Although Bolívar fancied himself a Latin American Napoleon, he had to acquiesce to the formation of a series of independent republics between 1821 and 1823, even in Bolivia, which is named after him. At the same time, Brazil (then still a monarchy) separated from Portugal (Map 21.4). The United States recognized the new states, and in 1823 President James Monroe announced his Monroe Doctrine, closing the Americas to European intervention—a

prohibition that depended on British naval power and British willingness to declare neutrality. Great Britain dominated the Latin American economies, which had suffered great losses during the wars for independence. The new Latin American states would be politically unstable for years to come.

Revolution and Reform, 1830–1832

In 1830 a new wave of liberal and nationalist revolts broke against the bulwark of conservatism. The revolts of the 1820s served as warning shots, but the earlier uprisings had been largely confined to the peripheries of Europe. Now revolution once again threatened the established order in western Europe.

The French Revolution of 1830. Louis XVIII's younger brother and successor, Charles X (r. 1824–1830), brought about his own downfall by steering the monarchy in an increasingly repressive direction. In 1825, a Law of Indemnity compensated nobles who had emigrated during the Revolution for the loss of their estates, and a Law of Sacrilege in the same year imposed the death penalty for such offenses as stealing religious objects from churches. Charles enraged liberals when he dissolved the legislature, removed many wealthy and powerful voters from the rolls, and imposed strict censorship. Spontaneous demonstrations in Paris led to fighting on July 26, 1830. After three days of street battles in

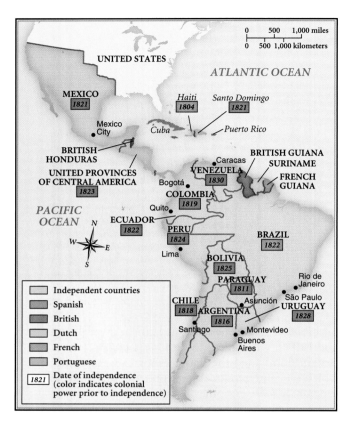

MAP 21.4 Latin American Independence, 1804–1830

The French lost their most important remaining American colony in 1804 when St. Domingue declared its independence as Haiti. But the impact of the French Revolution did not end there. Napoleon's occupation of Spain and Portugal seriously weakened those countries' hold on their Latin American colonies. Despite the restoration of the Spanish and Portuguese rulers in 1814, most of their colonies successfully broke away in a wave of rebellions between 1811 and 1830. Meanwhile a revolt in Spain in 1820–1823 led to a constitutional regime. For example, the Spanish general sent to suppress the revolt in Mexico ended up joining the rebels' cause and helping them establish independence in 1821.

which 500 citizens and 150 soldiers died, a group of moderate liberal leaders, fearing the reestablishment of a republic, agreed to give the crown to Charles X's cousin Louis-Philippe, duke of Orléans.

Charles X went into exile in England, and the new king extended political liberties and voting rights. Although the number of voting men nearly doubled, it remained minuscule—approximately 170,000 in a country of 30 million, between 5 and 6 percent. Such reforms did little for the poor and

working classes, who had manned the barricades in July. Dissatisfaction with the 1830 settlement boiled over in Lyon in 1831, when a silk-workers' strike over wages turned into a rebellion that died down only when the army arrived. Revolution had broken the hold of those who wanted to restore the pre-1789 monarchy and nobility, but it had gone no further this time than installing a more liberal, constitutional monarchy.

Belgian Independence from the Dutch. The success of the July Revolution in Paris ignited the Belgians, whose country had been annexed to the kingdom of the Netherlands in 1815. Differences in traditions, language, and religion separated the largely Catholic Belgians from the Dutch. An opera about a seventeenth-century insurrection in Naples provided the spark, and students in Brussels rioted, shouting "Down with the Dutch."

The riot turned into revolt. King William of the Netherlands appealed to the great powers to intervene; after all, the Congress of Vienna had established his kingdom. But Great Britain and France opposed intervention and invited Russia, Austria, and Prussia to a conference that guaranteed Belgium independence in exchange for its neutrality in international affairs. Belgian neutrality would remain a cornerstone of European diplomacy for a century. After much maneuvering, the crown of the new kingdom of Belgium was offered to a German prince, Leopold of Saxe-Coburg, in 1831. Belgium, like France and Britain, now had a constitutional monarchy.

Revolts in Italy and Poland. The Russian tsar and the Austrian emperor would have supported intervention in Belgium had they not been preoccupied with their own revolts. Anti-Austrian uprisings erupted in a handful of Italian states, but they fizzled without the hoped-for French aid. The Polish revolt was more serious. Once again, in response to news of revolution in France, students raised the banner of rebellion, this time in Warsaw in November 1830. Polish aristocrats soon formed a provisional government. Despite some victories on the battlefield, the provisional government got no support from Britain or France and was defeated. In reprisal, Nicholas abolished the Polish constitution that Alexander had granted and ordered thousands of Poles executed or banished.

IMPORTANT DATES

1799   Coup against Directory government in France; Napoleon Bonaparte named First Consul
1801   Napoleon signs a concordat with the pope
1804   Napoleon crowned as emperor of France; issues new Civil Code
1805   British naval forces defeat the French at the battle of Trafalgar; Napoleon wins his greatest victory at the battle of Austerlitz
1812   Napoleon invades Russia
1814–1815   Congress of Vienna
1815   Napoleon defeated at Waterloo and exiled to island of St. Helena, where he dies in 1821
1818   Mary Shelley, *Frankenstein*
1820   Robert Owen, *The Book of the New Moral World*; revolt of liberal army officers against the Spanish crown; the Karlsbad Decrees abolish German student societies and tighten press censorship
1824   Ludwig van Beethoven, Ninth Symphony
1825   Russian army officers demand constitutional reform in the Decembrist Revolt
1830   The Manchester and Liverpool Railway opens in England; Greece gains its independence from Ottoman Turks; rebels overthrow Charles X of France and install Louis-Philippe
1832   English Parliament passes Reform Bill; Johann Wolfgang von Goethe, *Faust*

The British Reform Bill of 1832. The British had long been preoccupied with two subjects: the royal family and elections for control of Parliament. In 1820, the domestic quarrels between the new king George IV (r. 1820–1830) and his German wife Caroline seemed to threaten the future of the monarchy. When George IV came to the throne, he tried to divorce Caroline, and he refused to have her crowned queen. He hoped to use rumors of her love affairs on the continent to win his case, but the divorce trial provoked massive demonstrations in support of Caroline. Women's groups gathered thousands of signatures on petitions supporting her, and popular songs and satires portrayed George as a fat, drunken libertine. Caroline's death a few months after George's coronation ended the Queen Caroline Affair. The monarchy survived but with a tarnished reputation.

The 1820s had brought into British government new men who were open to change. Sir Robert Peel (1788–1850), the secretary for home affairs, revised the criminal code to reduce the number of crimes punishable by death and introduced a municipal police force in London, called the *Bobbies* after him. In 1824, the laws prohibiting labor unions were repealed, and though restrictions on strikes remained, workers could now organize themselves legally to confront their employers collectively. In 1828, the appointment of the duke of Wellington, the hero of Waterloo, as prime minister kept the Tories in power, and his government pushed through a bill in 1829 allowing Catholics to sit in Parliament and hold most public offices.

When in 1830, and again in 1831, the Whigs in Parliament proposed an extension of the right to vote, Tory diehards, principally in the House of Lords, dug in their heels and predicted that even the most modest proposals would doom civilization itself. Even though the proposed law would not grant universal male suffrage, mass demonstrations in favor of it took place in many cities. One supporter of reform described the scene: "Meetings of almost every description of persons were held in cities, towns, and parishes; by journeymen tradesmen in their clubs, and by common workmen who had no trade clubs or associations of any kind." In this "state of diseased and feverish excitement" (according to its opponents), the Reform Bill of 1832 passed, after the king threatened to create enough new peers to obtain its passage in the House of Lords.

Although the Reform Bill altered Britain's political structure in significant ways, the gains were not revolutionary. One of the bill's foremost backers, historian and member of Parliament Thomas Macaulay, explained, "I am opposed to Universal Suffrage, because I think that it would produce a destructive revolution. I support this plan, because I am sure that it is our best security against a revolution." Although the number of male voters increased by about 50 percent, only one in five Britons could now vote, and voting still depended on holding property. Nevertheless, the bill gave representation to new cities in the industrial north for the first time and set a precedent for further widening suffrage. Exclusive aristocratic politics now gave way to a mixed middle-class and aristocratic structure that would prove more responsive to the problems of a

MAPPING THE WEST Europe in 1830

By 1830, the fragilities of the Congress of Vienna settlement had become apparent. Rebellion in Poland failed, but Belgium won its independence from the kingdom of the Netherlands, and a French revolution chased out the Bourbon ruler and installed Louis-Philippe, who promised constitutional reform. Most European rulers held on to their positions in this period of ferment, but they had to accommodate to some extent the new demands created by industrialization, desires for constitutional guarantees of rights, and growing nationalist sentiment.

fast-growing industrial society. Those disappointed with the outcome would organize with renewed vigor in the 1830s and 1840s.

Conclusion

The agitations and uprisings of the 1820s and early 1830s showed that the revolutionary legacy still smoldered and might erupt into flames again at any moment. The efforts of the great powers to maintain the European peace by shoring up established governments and damping down aspirations for constitutional freedoms and national

autonomy sometimes failed. Belgium separated from the Netherlands, Greece achieved independence from the Turks, Latin American countries shook off the rule of Spain and Portugal, and the French installed a more liberal monarchy than the one envisioned by the Congress of Vienna. Yet Metternich's vision of a conservative Europe still held: Russia clamped down on Poland, Austria stifled any sign of Italian nationalism, and the elites of Britain and France managed to maintain their hold by compromising at the right moment.

In her novel *Frankenstein*, Mary Shelley had captured some of the deepest worries of the age; human creativity might have an unpredictably destructive side in spite of every good intention. Although she did not intend her novel as a brief in support of political conservatism—she hated what Metternich stood for—she did tap into European fears about the changes taking place. The French and Industrial Revolutions promised to transform European life, for better or worse. Napoleon Bonaparte had used the French revolutionary legacy to propel his attempted colonization of much of Europe. Others used the revolutionary legacy to argue for new ideologies that would become even more important in the future. The machines of industrialization seemed to some Europeans just as horrible as Frankenstein's monster; others welcomed them as promising a brighter future. In the years to come industrialization would proceed even faster, and revolution would return to shatter the order so carefully nurtured by Metternich and his colleagues.

Suggested References

From Consulate to Empire: The Napoleonic State

Much has been written about Napoleon as a military leader, but only recently has his regime within France attracted interest. Historians now emphasize the mixed quality of Napoleon's rule. He carried forward some revolutionary innovations and halted others.

*Arnold, Eric A., Jr., ed. *A Documentary Survey of Napoleonic France.* 1994.

Crook, Malcolm. *Napoleon Comes to Power: Democracy and Dictatorship in Revolutionary France, 1795–1804.* 1998.

Ellis, Geoffrey James. *Napoleon.* 1996.

Kafker, Frank A., and James M. Laux. *Napoleon and His Times: Selected Interpretations.* 1989.

Lyons, Martyn. *Napoleon Bonaparte and the Legacy of the French Revolution.* 1994.

Napoleon Foundation: http://www.napoleon.org.

Wilson-Smith, Timothy. *Napoleon and His Artists.* 1996.

"Europe Was at My Feet": Napoleon's Conquest

Recent work shows how powerfully Napoleon's armies affected every European state. Whether annexed, allied, or simply defeated, every nation had to come to terms with this dynamo of activity.

*Brunn, Geoffrey. *Napoleon and His Empire.* 1972.

Connelly, Owen. *Napoleon's Satellite Kingdoms.* 1965.

Dallas, Gregor. *The Final Act: The Roads to Waterloo.* 1997.

Gates, David. *The Napoleonic Wars, 1803–1815.* 1997.

Simms, Brendan. *The Impact of Napoleon: Prussian High Politics, Foreign Policy, and the Crisis of the Executive, 1797–1806.* 1997.

The "Restoration" of Europe

New visions of diplomacy are emerging in recent scholarship, but internal affairs are relatively understudied. As a consequence, Artz's book is still a good introduction.

Artz, Frederick B. *Reaction and Revolution, 1814–1832.* 1934.

Johnson, Paul. *The Birth of the Modern: World Society, 1815–1830.* 1991.

Schroeder, Paul W. *The Transformation of European Politics, 1763–1848.* 1994.

Seward, Desmond. *Metternich: The First European.* 1991.

Forces for Social and Cultural Change

The new ideologies have been the subject of a steady stream of excellent work, ranging from individual figures such as Fourier to the antislavery movement and the origins of working-class activism. The Web site Romantic Chronology provides access to a wealth of information about every aspect of romanticism.

Beecher, Jonathan. *Charles Fourier: The Visionary and His World.* 1986.

Berlin, Sir Isaiah. *The Roots of Romanticism.* 1999.

Davis, David Brion. *The Problem of Slavery in the Age of Revolution, 1770–1823.* 1975.

*Hugo, Howard E., ed. *The Romantic Reader.* 1957.

Romantic Chronology: http://english.ucsb.edu:591/rchrono/.

Thompson, E. P. *The Making of the English Working Class.* 1964.

Wright, Beth S. *Painting and History during the French Restoration: Abandoned by the Past.* 1997.

Political Challenges to the Conservative Order

Recent work in British history has been particularly impressive, but in general this is an understudied period of European history. Unsuccessful revolts attract less attention than successful ones, but even the Greek, Latin American, and Belgian independence movements need to be better integrated into European history.

Clark, Anna. "Queen Caroline and the Sexual Politics of Popular Culture in London, 1820," *Representations* 31 (1990): 47–68.

Colley, Linda. *Britons: Forging the Nation, 1707–1837.* 1992.

Di Scala, Spencer. *Italy: From Revolution to Republic, 1700 to the Present.* 2nd ed. 1998.

Spitzer, Alan B. *The French Generation of 1820.* 1987.

*Primary sources.

Useful Facts and Figures

PROMINENT ROMAN EMPERORS

Julio-Claudians

27 B.C.–14 A.D.	Augustus
14–37	Tiberius
37–41	Gaius (Caligula)
41–54	Claudius
54–68	Nero

Flavian Dynasty

69–79	Vespasian
79–81	Titus
81–96	Domitian

Golden Age Emperors

96–98	Nerva
98–117	Trajan
117–138	Hadrian
138–161	Antonius Pius
161–180	Marcus Aurelius

Severan Emperors

193–211	Septimius Severus
211–217	Antoninus (Caracalla)
217–218	Macrinus
222–235	Severus Alexander

Period of Instability

235–238	Maximinus Thrax
238–244	Gordian III
244–249	Philip the Arab
249–251	Decius
251–253	Trebonianus Gallus
253–260	Valerian
270–275	Aurelian
275–276	Tacitus
276–282	Probus
283–285	Carinus

Dominate

284–305	Diocletian
306	Constantius
306–337	Constantine I
337–340	Constantine II
337–350	Constans I
337–361	Constantius II

(Continued)

361–363	Julian
363–364	Jovian
364–375	Valentinian I
364–378	Valens
367–383	Gratian
375–392	Valentinian II
378–395	Theodosius I (the Great)

The Western Empire

| 395–423 | Honorius |
| 406–407 | Marcus |

407–411	Constantine III
409–411	Maximus
411–413	Jovinus
412–413	Sebastianus
423–425	Johannes
425–455	Valentinian III
455–456	Avitus
457–461	Majorian
461–465	Libius Severus
467–472	Anthemius
473–474	Glycerius
474–475	Julius Nepos
475–476	Romulus Augustulus

PROMINENT BYZANTINE EMPERORS

Dynasty of Theodosius

395–408	Arcadius
408–450	Theodosius II
450–457	Marcian

Dynasty of Leo

457–474	Leo I
474	Leo II
474–491	Zeno
475–476	Basiliscus
484–488	Leontius
491–518	Anastasius

Dynasty of Justinian

518–527	Justin
527–565	Justinian I
565–578	Justin II
578–582	Tiberius II
578–582	Tiberius II (I) Constantine
582–602	Maurice
602–610	Phocas

Dynasty of Heraclius

610–641	Heraclius
641	Heraclonas
641	Constantine III
641–668	Constans II
646–647	Gregory
649–653	Olympius
669	Mezezius

668–685	Constantine IV
685–695	Justinian II (banished)
695–698	Leontius
698–705	Tiberius III (II)
705–711	Justinian II (restored)
711–713	Bardanes
713–716	Anastasius II
716–717	Theodosius III

Isaurian Dynasty

717–741	Leo III
741–775	Constantine V Copronymus
775–780	Leo IV
780–797	Constantine VI
797–802	Irene
802–811	Nicephorus I
811	Strauracius
811–813	Michael I
813–820	Leo V

Phrygian Dynasty

820–829	Michael II
821–823	Thomas
829–842	Theophilus
842–867	Michael III

Macedonian Dynasty

| 867–886 | Basil I |
| 869–879 | Constantine |

887–912	Leo VI
912–913	Alexander
913–959	Constantine VII Porphygenitus
920–944	Romanus I Lecapenus
921–931	Christopher
924–945	Stephen
959–963	Romanus II
963–969	Nicephorus II Phocas
976–1025	Basil II
1025–1028	Constantine VIII (IX) alone
1028–1034	Romanus III Argyrus
1034–1041	Michael IV the Paphlagonian
1041–1042	Michael V Calaphates
1042	Zoe and Theodora
1042–1055	Constantine IX Monomchus
1055–1066	Theodora alone
1056–1057	Michael VI Stratioticus

Prelude to the Comnenian Dynasty

1057–1059	Isaac I Comnenos
1059–1067	Constantine X (IX) Ducas
1068–1071	Romanus IV Diogenes
1071–1078	Michael VII Ducas
1078–1081	Nicephorus III Botaniates
1080–1081	Nicephorus Melissenus

Comnenian Dynasty

1081–1118	Alexius I
1118–1143	John II
1143–1180	Manuel I
1180–1183	Alexius II

1183–1185	Andronieus I
1183–1191	Isaac, Emperor of Cyprus

Dynasty of the Angeli

1185–1195	Isaac II
1195–1203	Alexius III
1203–1204	Isaac II (restored) with Alexius IV
1204	Alexius V Ducas Murtzuphlus

Lascarid Dynasty in Nicaea

1204–1222	Theodore I Lascaris
1222–1254	John III Ducas Vatatzes
1254–1258	Theodore II Lascaris
1258–1261	John IV Lascaris

Dynasty of the Paleologi

1259–1289	Michael VIII Paleologus
1282–1328	Andronicus II
1328–1341	Andronicus III
1341–1391	John V
1347–1354	John VI Cantancuzenus
1376–1379	Andronicus IV
1379–1391	John V (restored)
1390	John VII
1391–1425	Manuel II
1425–1448	John VIII
1449–1453	Constantine XI (XIII) Dragases

PROMINENT POPES

314–335	Sylvester
440–461	Leo I
590–604	Gregory I (the Great)
687–701	Sergius I
741–752	Zachary
858–867	Nicholas I
1049–1054	Leo IX
1059–1061	Nicholas II
1073–1085	Gregory VII
1088–1099	Urban II
1099–1118	Paschal II
1159–1181	Alexander III
1198–1216	Innocent III
1227–1241	Gregory IX

1243–1254	Innocent IV
1294–1303	Boniface VIII
1316–1334	John XXII
1447–1455	Nicholas V
1458–1464	Pius II
1492–1503	Alexander VI
1503–1513	Julius II
1513–1521	Leo X
1534–1549	Paul III
1555–1559	Paul IV
1585–1590	Sixtus V
1623–1644	Urban VIII
1831–1846	Gregory XVI

(Continued)

1846–1878	Pius IX
1878–1903	Leo XIII
1903–1914	Pius X
1914–1922	Benedict XV
1922–1939	Pius XI

1939–1958	Pius XII
1958–1963	John XXIII
1963–1978	Paul VI
1978	John Paul I
1978–	John Paul II

THE CAROLINGIAN DYNASTY

687–714	Pepin of Heristal, Mayor of the Palace
715–741	Charles Martel, Mayor of the Palace
741–751	Pepin III, Mayor of the Palace
751–768	Pepin III, King
768–814	Charlemagne, King
800–814	Charlemagne, Emperor
814–840	Louis the Pious

West Francia

840–877	Charles the Bald, King
875–877	Charles the Bald, Emperor
877–879	Louis II, King

879–882	Louis III, King
879–884	Carloman, King

Middle Kingdoms

840–855	Lothair, Emperor
855–875	Louis (Italy), Emperor
855–863	Charles (Provence), King
855–869	Lothair II (Lorraine), King

East Francia

840–876	Ludwig, King
876–880	Carloman, King
876–882	Ludwig, King
876–887	Charles the Fat, Emperor

GERMAN KINGS CROWNED EMPEROR

Saxon Dynasty

962–973	Otto I
973–983	Otto II
983–1002	Otto III
1002–1024	Henry II

Franconian Dynasty

1024–1039	Conrad II
1039–1056	Henry III
1056–1106	Henry IV
1106–1125	Henry V
1125–1137	Lothair II (Saxony)

Hohenstaufen Dynasty

1138–1152	Conrad III
1152–1190	Frederick I (Barbarossa)

1190–1197	Henry VI
1198–1208	Philip of Swabia
1198–1215	Otto IV (Welf)
1220–1250	Frederick II
1250–1254	Conrad IV

Interregnum, 1254–1273: Emperors from Various Dynasties

1273–1291	Rudolf I (Habsburg)
1292–1298	Adolf (Nassau)
1298–1308	Albert I (Habsburg)
1308–1313	Henry VII (Luxemburg)
1314–1347	Ludwig IV (Wittelsbach)
1347–1378	Charles IV (Luxemburg)
1378–1400	Wenceslas (Luxemburg)
1400–1410	Rupert (Wittelsbach)
1410–1437	Sigismund (Luxemburg)

Habsburg Dynasty

1438–1439	Albert II
1440–1493	Frederick III
1493–1519	Maximilian I
1519–1556	Charles V
1556–1564	Ferdinand I
1564–1576	Maximilian II
1576–1612	Rudolf II
1612–1619	Matthias
1619–1637	Ferdinand II
1637–1657	Ferdinand III
1658–1705	Leopold I
1705–1711	Joseph I
1711–1740	Charles VI
1742–1745	Charles VII (not a Habsburg)
1745–1765	Francis I
1765–1790	Joseph II
1790–1792	Leopold II
1792–1806	Francis II

RULERS OF FRANCE

Capetian Dynasty

987–996	Hugh Capet
996–1031	Robert II
1031–1060	Henry I
1060–1108	Philip I
1108–1137	Louis VI
1137–1180	Louis VII
1180–1223	Philip II (Augustus)
1223–1226	Louis VIII
1226–1270	Louis IX (St. Louis)
1270–1285	Philip III
1285–1314	Philip IV
1314–1316	Louis X
1316–1322	Philip V
1322–1328	Charles IV

Valois Dynasty

1328–1350	Philip VI
1350–1364	John
1364–1380	Charles V
1380–1422	Charles VI
1422–1461	Charles VII
1461–1483	Louis XI
1483–1498	Charles VIII
1498–1515	Louis XII
1515–1547	Francis I

1547–1559	Henry II
1559–1560	Francis II
1560–1574	Charles IX
1574–1589	Henry III

Bourbon Dynasty

1589–1610	Henry IV
1610–1643	Louis XIII
1643–1715	Louis XIV
1715–1774	Louis XV
1774–1792	Louis XVI

After 1792

1792–1799	First Republic, 1792–1799
1799–1804	Napoleon Bonaparte, First Consul
1804–1814	Napoleon I, Emperor
1814–1824	Louis XVIII (Bourbon Dynasty)
1824–1830	Charles X (Bourbon Dynasty)
1830–1848	Louis Philippe
1848–1852	Second Republic
1852–1870	Napoleon III, Emperor
1870–1940	Third Republic
1940–1944	Vichy government, Pétain regime
1944–1946	Provisional government
1946–1958	Fourth Republic
1958–	Fifth Republic

MONARCHS OF ENGLAND AND GREAT BRITAIN

Anglo-Saxon Monarchs

829–839	Egbert
839–858	Ethelwulf
858–860	Ethelbald
860–866	Ethelbert
866–871	Ethelred I
871–899	Alfred the Great
899–924	Edward the Elder
924–939	Ethelstan
939–946	Edmund I
946–955	Edred
955–959	Edwy
959–975	Edgar
975–978	Edward the Martyr
978–1016	Ethelred the Unready
1016–1035	Canute (Danish nationality)
1035–1040	Harold I
1040–1042	Hardicanute
1042–1066	Edward the Confessor
1066	Harold II

Norman Monarchs

1066–1087	William I (the Conqueror)
1087–1100	William II
1100–1135	Henry I

House of Blois

1135–1154	Stephen

House of Plantagenet

1154–1189	Henry II
1189–1199	Richard I
1199–1216	John
1216–1272	Henry III
1272–1307	Edward I
1307–1327	Edward II
1327–1377	Edward III
1377–1399	Richard II

House of Lancaster

1399–1413	Henry IV
1413–1422	Henry V
1422–1461	Henry VI

House of York

1461–1483	Edward IV
1483	Edward V
1483–1485	Richard III

House of Tudor

1485–1509	Henry VII
1509–1547	Henry VIII
1547–1553	Edward VI
1553–1558	Mary
1558–1603	Elizabeth I

House of Stuart

1603–1625	James I
1625–1649	Charles I

Commonwealth and Protectorate (1649–1660)

1653–1658	Oliver Cromwell
1658–1659	Richard Cromwell

House of Stuart (Restored)

1660–1685	Charles II
1685–1688	James II
1689–1694	William III and Mary II
1694–1702	William III (alone)
1702–1714	Anne

House of Hanover

1714–1727	George I
1727–1760	George II
1760–1820	George III
1820–1830	George IV
1830–1837	William IV
1837–1901	Victoria

House of Saxe-Coburg-Gotha

1901–1910	Edward VII

House of Windsor

1910–1936	George V
1936	Edward VIII
1936–1952	George VI
1952–	Elizabeth II

PRIME MINISTERS OF GREAT BRITAIN

Term	Prime Minister	Government
1721–1742	Sir Robert Walpole	Whig
1742–1743	Spencer Compton, Earl of Wilmington	Whig
1743–1754	Henry Pelham	Whig
1754–1756	Thomas Pelham-Holles, Duke of Newcastle	Whig
1756–1757	William Cavendish, Duke of Devonshire	Whig
1757–1761	William Pitt (the Elder), Earl of Chatham	Whig
1761–1762	Thomas Pelham-Holles, Duke of Newcastle	Whig
1762–1763	John Stuart, Earl of Bute	Tory
1763–1765	George Grenville	Whig
1765–1766	Charles Watson-Wentworth, Marquess of Rockingham	Whig
1766–1768	William Pitt, Earl of Chatham (the Elder)	Whig
1768–1770	Augustus Henry Fitzroy, Duke of Grafton	Whig
1770–1782	Frederick North (Lord North)	Tory
1782	Charles Watson-Wentworth, Marquess of Rockingham	Whig
1782–1783	William Petty FitzMaurice, Earl of Shelburn	Whig
1783	William Henry Cavendish Bentinck, Duke of Portland	Whig
1783–1801	William Pitt, the Younger	Tory
1801–1804	Henry Addington	Tory
1804–1806	William Pitt (the Younger)	Tory
1806–1807	William Wyndham Grenville (Baron Grenville)	Whig
1807–1809	William Henry Cavendish Bentinck, Duke of Portland	Tory
1809–1812	Spencer Perceval	Tory
1812–1827	Robert Banks Jenkinson, Earl of Liverpool	Tory
1827	George Canning	Tory
1827–1828	Frederick John Robinson (Viscount Goderich)	Tory
1828–1830	Arthur Wellesley, Duke of Wellington	Tory
1830–1834	Charles Grey (Earl Grey)	Whig
1834	William Lamb, Viscount Melbourne	Whig
1834–1835	Sir Robert Peel	Tory
1835–1841	William Lamb, Viscount Melbourne	Whig
1841–1846	Sir Robert Peel	Tory
1846–1852	John Russell (Lord)	Whig
1852	Edward Geoffrey–Smith Stanley Derby, Earl of Derby	Whig
1852–1855	George Hamilton Gordon Aberdeen, Earl of Aberdeen	Peelite
1855–1858	Henry John Temple Palmerston, Viscount Palmerston	Tory
1858–1859	Edward Geoffrey–Smith Stanley Derby, Earl of Derby	Whig
1859–1865	Henry John Temple Palmerston, Viscount Palmerston	Tory
1865–1866	John Russell (Earl)	Liberal
1866–1868	Edward Geoffrey–Smith Stanley Derby, Earl of Derby	Tory
1868	Benjamin Disraeli, Earl of Beaconfield	Conservative
1868–1874	William Ewart Gladstone	Liberal
1874–1880	Benjamin Disraeli, Earl of Beaconfield	Conservative
1880–1885	William Ewart Gladstone	Liberal
1885–1886	Robert Arthur Talbot, Marquess of Salisbury	Conservative
1886	William Ewart Gladstone	Liberal
1886–1892	Robert Arthur Talbot, Marquess of Salisbury	Conservative
1892–1894	William Ewart Gladstone	Liberal
1894–1895	Archibald Philip–Primrose Rosebery, Earl of Rosebery	Liberal

(Continued)

Term	Prime Minister	Government
1895–1902	Robert Arthur Talbot, Marquess of Salisbury	Conservative
1902–1905	Arthur James Balfour, Earl of Balfour	Conservative
1905–1908	Sir Henry Campbell-Bannerman	Liberal
1908–1915	Herbert Henry Asquith	Liberal
1915–1916	Herbert Henry Asquith	Coalition
1916–1922	David Lloyd George, Earl Lloyd-George of Dwyfor	Coalition
1922–1923	Andrew Bonar Law	Conservative
1923–1924	Stanley Baldwin, Earl Baldwin of Bewdley	Conservative
1924	James Ramsay MacDonald	Labour
1924–1929	Stanley Baldwin, Earl Baldwin of Bewdley	Conservative
1929–1931	James Ramsay MacDonald	Labour
1931–1935	James Ramsay MacDonald	Coalition
1935–1937	Stanley Baldwin, Earl Baldwin of Bewdley	Coalition
1937–1940	Neville Chamberlain	Coalition
1940–1945	Winston Churchill	Coalition
1945	Winston Churchill	Conservative
1945–1951	Clement Attlee, Earl Attlee	Labour
1951–1955	Sir Winston Churchill	Conservative
1955–1957	Sir Anthony Eden, Earl of Avon	Conservative
1957–1963	Harold Macmillan, Earl of Stockton	Conservative
1963–1964	Sir Alec Frederick Douglas-Home, Lord Home of the Hirsel	Conservative
1964–1970	Harold Wilson, Lord Wilson of Rievaulx	Labour
1970–1974	Edward Heath	Conservative
1974–1976	Harold Wilson, Lord Wilson of Rievaulx	Labour
1976–1979	James Callaghan, Lord Callaghan of Cardiff	Labour
1979–1990	Margaret Thatcher (Baroness)	Conservative
1990–1997	John Major	Conservative
1997–	Tony Blair	Labour

RULERS OF PRUSSIA AND GERMANY

1701–1713	*Frederick I
1713–1740	*Frederick William I
1740–1786	*Frederick II (the Great)
1786–1797	*Frederick William II
1797–1840	*Frederick William III
1840–1861	*Frederick William IV
1861–1888	*William I (German emperor after 1871)
1888	Frederick III
1888–1918	*William II
1918–1933	Weimar Republic
1933–1945	Third Reich (Nazi dictatorship under Adolf Hitler)
1945–1952	Allied occupation
1949–1990	Division of Federal Republic of Germany in west and German Democratic Republic in east
1990–	Federal Republic of Germany (united)

*King of Prussia

RULERS OF AUSTRIA AND AUSTRIA-HUNGARY

1493–1519	*Maximillian I (Archduke)
1519–1556	*Charles V
1556–1564	*Ferdinand I
1564–1576	*Maximillian II
1576–1612	*Rudolf II
1612–1619	*Matthias
1619–1637	*Ferdinand II
1637–1657	*Ferdinand III
1658–1705	*Leopold I
1705–1711	*Joseph I
1711–1740	*Charles VI
1740–1780	Maria Theresa
1780–1790	*Joseph II
1790–1792	*Leopold II
1792–1835	*Francis II (emperor of Austria as Francis I after 1804)
1835–1848	Ferdinand I
1848–1916	Francis Joseph (after 1867 emperor of Austria and king of Hungary)
1916–1918	Charles I (emperor of Austria and king of Hungary)
1918–1938	Republic of Austria (dictatorship after 1934)
1945–1956	Republic restored, under Allied occupation
1956–	Free Republic

*Also bore title of Holy Roman Emperor

LEADERS OF POST–WORLD WAR II GERMANY

West Germany (Federal Republic of Germany), 1949–1990

Years	Chancellor	Party
1949–1963	Konrad Adenauer	Christian Democratic Union (CDU)
1963–1966	Ludwig Erhard	Christian Democratic Union (CDU)
1966–1969	Kurt Georg Kiesinger	Christian Democratic Union (CDU)
1969–1974	Willy Brandt	Social Democratic Party (SPD)
1974–1982	Helmut Schmidt	Social Democratic Party (SPD)
1982–1990	Helmut Kohl	Christian Democratic Union (CDU)

East Germany (German Democratic Republic), 1949–1990

Years	Communist Party Leader
1946–1971	Walter Ulbricht
1971–1989	Erich Honecker
1989–1990	Egon Krenz

Federal Republic of Germany (reunited), 1990–

1990–1998	Helmut Kohl	Christian Democratic Union (CDU)
1998–	Gerhard Schroeder	Social Democratic Party (SPD)

RULERS OF RUSSIA, THE USSR, AND THE RUSSIAN FEDERATION

c. 980–1015	Vladimir
1019–1054	Yaroslav the Wise
1176–1212	Vsevolod III
1462–1505	Ivan III
1505–1553	Vasily III
1553–1584	Ivan IV
1584–1598	Theodore I
1598–1605	Boris Godunov
1605	Theodore II
1606–1610	Vasily IV
1613–1645	Michael
1645–1676	Alexius
1676–1682	Theodore III
1682–1689	Ivan V and Peter I
1689–1725	Peter I (the Great)
1725–1727	Catherine I
1727–1730	Peter II
1730–1740	Anna
1740–1741	Ivan VI
1741–1762	Elizabeth
1762	Peter III
1762–1796	Catherine II (the Great)
1796–1801	Paul
1801–1825	Alexander I
1825–1855	Nicholas I
1855–1881	Alexander II
1881–1894	Alexander III
1894–1917	Nicholas II

Union of Soviet Socialist Republics (USSR)*

1917–1924	Vladimir Ilyich Lenin
1924–1953	Joseph Stalin
1953–1964	Nikita Khrushchev
1964–1982	Leonid Brezhnev
1982–1984	Yuri Andropov
1984–1985	Konstantin Chernenko
1985–1991	Mikhail Gorbachev

Russian Federation

1991–1999	Boris Yeltsin
1999–	Vladimir Putin

*USSR established in 1922

RULERS OF SPAIN

1479–1504	Ferdinand and Isabella
1504–1506	Ferdinand and Philip I
1506–1516	Ferdinand and Charles I
1516–1556	Charles I (Holy Roman Emperor Charles V)
1556–1598	Philip II
1598–1621	Philip III
1621–1665	Philip IV
1665–1700	Charles II
1700–1746	Philip V
1746–1759	Ferdinand VI
1759–1788	Charles III
1788–1808	Charles IV
1808	Ferdinand VII
1808–1813	Joseph Bonaparte
1814–1833	Ferdinand VII (restored)
1833–1868	Isabella II
1868–1870	Republic
1870–1873	Amadeo
1873–1874	Republic
1874–1885	Alfonso XII
1886–1931	Alfonso XIII
1931–1939	Republic
1939–1975	Fascist dictatorship under Francisco Franco
1975–	Juan Carlos I

RULERS OF ITALY

1861–1878	Victor Emmanuel II
1878–1900	Humbert I
1900–1946	Victor Emmanuel III
1922–1943	Fascist dictatorship under Benito Mussolini (maintained in northern Italy until 1945)
1946 (May 9–June 13)	Humbert II
1946–	Republic

SECRETARIES-GENERAL OF THE UNITED NATIONS

		Nationality
1946–1952	Trygve Lie	Norway
1953–1961	Dag Hammarskjold	Sweden
1961–1971	U Thant	Myanmar
1972–1981	Kurt Waldheim	Austria
1982–1991	Javier Pérez de Cuéllar	Peru
1992–1996	Boutros Boutros-Ghali	Egypt
1997–	Kofi A. Annan	Ghana

UNITED STATES PRESIDENTIAL ADMINISTRATIONS

Term(s)	President	Political Party
1789–1797	George Washington	No party designation
1797–1801	John Adams	Federalist
1801–1809	Thomas Jefferson	Democratic-Republican
1809–1817	James Madison	Democratic-Republican
1817–1825	James Monroe	Democratic-Republican
1825–1829	John Quincy Adams	Democratic-Republican
1829–1837	Andrew Jackson	Democratic
1837–1841	Martin Van Buren	Democratic
1841	William H. Harrison	Whig
1841–1845	John Tyler	Whig
1845–1849	James K. Polk	Democratic
1849–1850	Zachary Taylor	Whig
1850–1853	Millard Filmore	Whig
1853–1857	Franklin Pierce	Democratic
1857–1861	James Buchanan	Democratic
1861–1865	Abraham Lincoln	Republican
1865–1869	Andrew Johnson	Republican
1869–1877	Ulysses S. Grant	Republican
1877–1881	Rutherford B. Hayes	Republican
1881	James A. Garfield	Republican
1881–1885	Chester A. Arthur	Republican
1885–1889	Grover Cleveland	Democratic
1889–1893	Benjamin Harrison	Republican
1893–1897	Grover Cleveland	Democratic
1897–1901	William McKinley	Republican
1901–1909	Theodore Roosevelt	Republican
1909–1913	William H. Taft	Republican
1913–1921	Woodrow Wilson	Democratic
1921–1923	Warren G. Harding	Republican
1923–1929	Calvin Coolidge	Republican
1929–1933	Herbert C. Hoover	Republican
1933–1945	Franklin D. Roosevelt	Democratic
1945–1953	Harry S. Truman	Democratic
1953–1961	Dwight D. Eisenhower	Republican
1961–1963	John F. Kennedy	Democratic
1963–1969	Lyndon B. Johnson	Democratic
1969–1974	Richard M. Nixon	Republican
1974–1977	Gerald R. Ford	Republican
1977–1981	Jimmy Carter	Democratic
1981–1989	Ronald W. Reagan	Republican
1989–1993	George H. W. Bush	Republican
1993–	William J. Clinton	Democratic

MAJOR WARS OF THE MODERN ERA

1546–1555	German Wars of Religion
1526–1571	Ottoman wars
1562–1598	French Wars of Religion
1566–1609, 1621–1648	Revolt of the Netherlands
1618–1648	Thirty Years' War
1642–1648	English Civil War
1652–1678	Anglo-Dutch Wars
1667–1697	Wars of Louis XIV
1683–1697	Ottoman wars
1689–1697	War of the League of Augsburg
1702–1714	War of Spanish Succession
1702–1721	Great Northern War
1714–1718	Ottoman wars
1740–1748	War of Austrian Succession
1756–1763	Seven Years' War
1775–1781	American Revolution
1796–1815	Napoleonic wars
1846–1848	Mexican-American War
1853–1856	Crimean War
1861–1865	United States Civil War
1870–1871	Franco-Prussian War
1894–1895	Sino-Japanese War
1898	Spanish-American War
1904–1905	Russo-Japanese War
1914–1918	World War I
1939–1945	World War II
1946–1975	Vietnam wars
1950–1953	Korean War
1990–1991	Persian Gulf War
1991–1997	Civil War in the former Yugoslavia

POPULATION OF MAJOR CITIES, 1750–1990

City	1750	1800	1850	1900	1950	1990
Amsterdam	210,000	217,000	224,000	511,000	804,000	713,000
Athens	10,000	12,000	31,000	111,000	565,000	772,000
Berlin	90,000	172,000	419,000	1,889,000	3,337,000	3,438,000
Brussels	60,000	66,000	251,000	599,000	956,000	954,000
Budapest	xxxxxxxx[1]	54,000	178,000	732,000	1,571,000	2,017,000
Dublin	90,000	165,000	272,000	373,000	522,000	920,000
Geneva	22,000	22,000	31,000	59,000	145,000	167,000
St. Petersburg	150,000	336,000	485,000	1,267,000	xxxxxxxx	4,437,000
Lisbon	148,000	180,000	240,000	356,000	790,000	678,000
London	675,000	1,117,000	2,685,000	6,586,000	8,348,000	6,803,000
Madrid	109,000	160,000	281,000	540,000	1,618,000	2,991,000
Moscow	130,000	250,000	365,000	989,000	xxxxxxxx	8,747,000
Paris	576,000	581,000	1,053,000	2,714,000	2,850,000	2,152,000
Prague	59,000	75,000	118,000	202,000	922,000	1,212,000
Rome	156,000	163,000	175,000	463,000	1,652,000	2,828,000
Stockholm	60,000	76,000	93,000	301,000	744,000	679,000
Warsaw	23,000	100,000	160,000	638,000	601,000	1,654,000
Zurich	11,000	12,000	17,000	151,000	390,000	342,000
New York	22,000	60,000	696,000	3,437,000	7,892,000	7,322,000
Montreal	6,000	xxxxxxxx	58,000	268,000	1,022,000	1,017,000
Mexico City	xxxxxxxx	137,000	170,000	345,000	2,234,000	8,235,000
Buenos Aires	11,000	40,000	99,000	664,000	2,981,000	2,960,000
Cairo	xxxxxxxx	211,000	267,000	570,000	2,091,000	6,452,000
Alexandria	xxxxxxxx	15,000	60,000	320,000	919,000	3,413,000
Istanbul	xxxxxxxx	600,000	xxxxxxxx	1,125,000	983,000	6,220,000
Damascus	xxxxxxxx	130,000	150,000	140,000	335,000	1,451,000
Jerusalem	xxxxxxxx	xxxxxxxx	xxxxxxxx	42,000	83,000	524,000
Tokyo	xxxxxxxx	xxxxxxxx	xxxxxxxx	1,819,000	6,778,000	8,163,000
Delhi	xxxxxxxx	xxxxxxxx	xxxxxxxx	209,000	914,000	8,419,000

[1] xxxxxxxx = population statistics unavailable
Source: B. R. Mitchell, ed. *International Historical Statistics* (1998).

Index

A note about the index:

Names of individuals appear in boldface; biographical dates are included for major historical figures.

Letters in parentheses following pages refer to:
(i)   illustrations, including photographs and artifacts
(f)   figures, including charts and graphs
(m)   maps
(b)   boxed features (such as "Contrasting Views")